D1571813

SOUTH CAROLINA

A SHORT HISTORY

SOUTH CAROLINA

A Short History

1520-1948

BY DAVID DUNCAN WALLACE

UNIVERSITY OF SOUTH CAROLINA PRESS • COLUMBIA

First published by
the University of South Carolina Press, Columbia, S.C., 1961
Second Printing, 1966
Third Printing, 1969
Standard Book Number: 87249–079–3
Library of Congress Catalog Card Number: 61–15974
Manufactured in the United States of America

To

MR. JOHN WILKINS NORWOOD

March 18, 1865—July 10, 1945

A PROMOTER OF INTELLECTUAL AND MORAL BETTERMENT
THROUGH THE DISSEMINATION AND SUPPORT OF BOOKS AND LIBRARIES
AND A CITIZEN OF THE HIGHEST IDEALS OF PUBLIC CHARACTER AND SERVICE
THIS WORK IS DEDICATED

PREFACE

THE PRESENT VOLUME represents a reduction of my three-volume *History of South Carolina* published in 1934. The numerous citations of sources in the original edition are here generally omitted, as anyone can readily find the authority for most points by reference to the larger work. All dates within the period during which English speaking people sometimes used "old style" or "new style," frequently to the confusion of later generations, are here given "new style" as to the year, but with the day of the month as originally written.

May we not hope that the time has arrived when the distance from ancient passionate crises and the maturity of our intellectual life make it possible for South Carolinians to study their past with intellectual frankness? And may not outsiders be sufficiently free from the bitterness of former conflicts to wish to know more truly the character and contribution of this one of the original thirteen States to American history?

It would be idle for me to deny a predilection for the State of my birth; but when I record her history I am not primarily the patriot, but the investigator and, I trust, the unflinching recorder, of truth. An impartial friend of truth cannot be a constant upholder of any group or interest, either the colonists against the King, the up country against the low country, the South against the North, the common people against the aristocrats. All prove themselves to be too thoroughly human to play consistently the part of angel against the other's devil. In the face of certain powerful climatic and geological conditions, the people of South Carolina have sought to realize certain economic, political, and social ideals. It is our task to study the successes and failures of this human element operating in conjunction with these natural forces.

My obligations to the friends who assisted me in my three-volume history extend to them in this one-volume edition. Mr. Howard B. Carlisle has afforded valuable help by the use of his law library and his extensive knowledge of legal history. The wide knowledge and critical ability of Mr. A. S. Salley and the consultations and loans of rare material by the late Dr. Yates Snowden have been of inestimable value. Valuable also as lenders of rare material or facilities for work or as translators of foreign languages were the services of the former Presidents of the University of South Carolina D. M. Douglas and L. T. Baker; the

Librarian of the University Mr. R. M. Kennedy; the Librarian of the Charleston Library Society Miss Ellen FitzSimons; the former Secretary of the South Carolina Historical Society Miss Mabel L. Webber; Dr. J. F. Jameson of the Library of Congress, Mrs. Helen Kohn Hennig, Dr. R. L. Meriwether, Mr. William Elliott, Mr. Jesse Cleveland, Mr. J. W. Earhart, Doctor A. M. DuPre, Professor J. L. Salmon, Mrs. Charles A. Pettis, and Professor Adolph Vermont. In preparing this one-volume edition I am indebted to the help of my wife, Mrs. Maud Orr Wallace, and for reading the proofs to Dr. J. H. Easterby and my son, Dr. Robert M. Wallace. I thank the American Historical Company, the publishers of my three-volume *History of South Carolina,* for permission to use any part of that work, and the Denoyer-Geppert Company for permission to reproduce any maps in my South Carolina series published by them. I have used several of these large maps in much reduced and simplified form.

D. D. Wallace

Wofford College, Spartanburg, S. C.
March 30, 1951

A Note by Robert M. Wallace

David Duncan Wallace, the author of this history, died April 29, 1951, about four months before production of the book was completed. He had worked on this and the history of his alma mater, Wofford College, till the day before his last. For *South Carolina, a Short History* he finished reading galley proof and made characteristically full and careful additions and corrections even at that late stage. It remained for me to complete the largely routine task of reading page proofs in the light of his latest express wishes and the prompt, generous, and now perhaps unmatchable advice of Dr. J. H. Easterby, Director of the Historical Commission of South Carolina. To clarify the limits of Dr. Easterby's responsibility, I must report that I followed my father nearly always where variations from Dr. Easterby's suggestions seemed to me permissible.

The index, modeled on my father's own index to his three-volume *History of South Carolina,* was prepared by staff members of the University of North Carolina Press.

R. M. W.

CONTENTS

APPENDICES

MAPS AND CHARTS

SOUTH CAROLINA

A SHORT HISTORY

CHAPTER I

THE GEOGRAPHICAL BASIS

South Carolina lies on the southeastern Atlantic seaboard approximately between 32 degrees and 35 degrees 14 minutes north latitude. Of its 31,055 square miles 599 are water. Although appearing on the map roughly as an equilateral triangle poised upon its southern point, the State can more accurately be viewed as a triangle with its 190-mile base resting upon the Atlantic Ocean and its apex 235 miles to the northwest resting on the crest of the Blue Ridge; for this recognizes the fact that the broad belts both of its geological formation and of its historical development run parallel with the sea.

The State is divided geologically into two great regions by the "fall line" running from North Augusta northeastward through Columbia and on to the North Carolina line near Cheraw. Above this line is the crystalline region, or up country, the surface of which has been formed by the decomposition of some of earth's oldest rocks, whose vast Archaean masses everywhere underlie the surface and frequently protrude in great masses or produce low falls and rapids in the streams. Throughout the whole region are scattered a great variety of minerals, among them gold, tin, and iron, but rarely in profitable quantities. From the Haile mine in the southern part of Lancaster County, the most notable gold mine east of the Mississippi, about $2,500,000 worth of the precious metal has been taken since 1829, but almost all of it since the beginning of systematic operations in 1880; even this, the richest of the many gold deposits in the State, cannot be profitably worked under the depreciated value of gold in recent years. The limestone beds of York and Cherokee and the iron deposits of these counties and Spartanburg have likewise long been abandoned.

The greatest elevation in the State is Sassafras Mountain, a point in the Blue Ridge 3,548 feet above sea level on the line between Pickens County and North Carolina. In the northern parts of Oconee, Pickens, and Greenville counties spurs of the Blue Ridge jut southward to produce imposing precipices and rock mountains or wooded ridges, from which descend narrow, steep-sided valleys of great beauty.

So abundant is the rainfall in the mountains that their principal waterways leave them as already bold rivers. The Piedmont plateau, with its long rolling hills from 700 to 900 feet above sea level separating the deeply cut valleys of the rivers, begins rather abruptly at the foot of the Blue Ridge and slopes gradually to the fall line. The ancient rocks of the crystalline region there pass beneath the overlying cretaceous formations of the upper edge of the coastal plain at levels varying from 119 feet above the sea in the deeper valleys to 680 feet on the plateau between the Savannah and the Congaree and 597 feet between the Wateree and the Great Peedee.

There is a great gap in geological age between the rocks of the Archaean, or most ancient, era and the cretaceous formations of later ages which they meet at the fall line. There is a corresponding lack of the geological formations of the intervening period, a hiatus of profound significance. Says Mr. Earle Sloan in his report of 1907 as State Geologist: "Here logically belong the Upper Silurian, with its vast fossiliferous iron ore beds, and the Carboniferous, with its coal measures, which characterize the Birmingham and other districts west of the line of the Blue Ridge Mountains, east of which line the conditions appear to have been unfavorable; or, if they obtained, the associate formations were subsequently effaced or submerged beyond the depths hitherto explored by borings, and therefore beyond economic consideration."

Thus South Carolina was predestined not to possess the resources of coal and iron which confer concentrated wealth and power. Until she learned to use her waterfalls to manufacture the products of her fields and forests, she was to have the virtues and shortcomings of a predominantly agricultural region.

With gentle elevations at places the coastal plain, or low country, descends to a broad belt skirting the coast that rises only a few feet above sea level. The rivers, navigable for small vessels, flow sluggishly between low banks, beyond which in flood they spread over a million and three-quarter acres of thickly wooded swamps. The difficulty of bridging these has until recent years caused contiguous counties to be in effect widely separated. Kaolin and other fine clays are abundant, and there are small scattered deposits of valuable minerals. Beneath the lower two-thirds of the coastal plain and frequently exposed on the rivers' banks lie enormous beds of marl suitable for use as a fertilizer and for the manufacture of lime, cement, and high-grade brick. Extensive deposits of phosphate rocks are found beneath the beds of the Ashley, Cooper, and Coosaw rivers and extend out under the sea and at places back under the land for twenty-five miles at varying depths. The fair productivity of a large part of the coastal plain invited the early colonists to the cultivation of staple crops by means of slave labor, while the timber and deer and other animals afforded additional sources of wealth.

So gently does the coastal plain rise that the bottom of the rapids at the fall line 120 miles inland is 133 feet above sea level at Augusta and

Camden and 135 at Columbia. North of Georgetown the smooth, hard beach is cut by a few small inlets; but from Georgetown southward the coast is more and more intersected by a bewildering maze of arms of the sea dividing into "rivers" and "creeks" that reach around the numerous "sea islands" thus formed. These waterways were among the principal early means of travel and strongly influenced the location of settlements.

Such are the two main divisions of the State; but also important are the differences of their seven subordinate belts paralleling the coast. The first four are in the low country; the fifth covers the fall line, and the sixth and seventh unequally divide the up country. These seven belts are as follows:

I. The coastal region consists of the sea islands, the salt marshes, and the shore north of Georgetown.

II. The lower pine belt, about fifty miles wide, comprises the rice

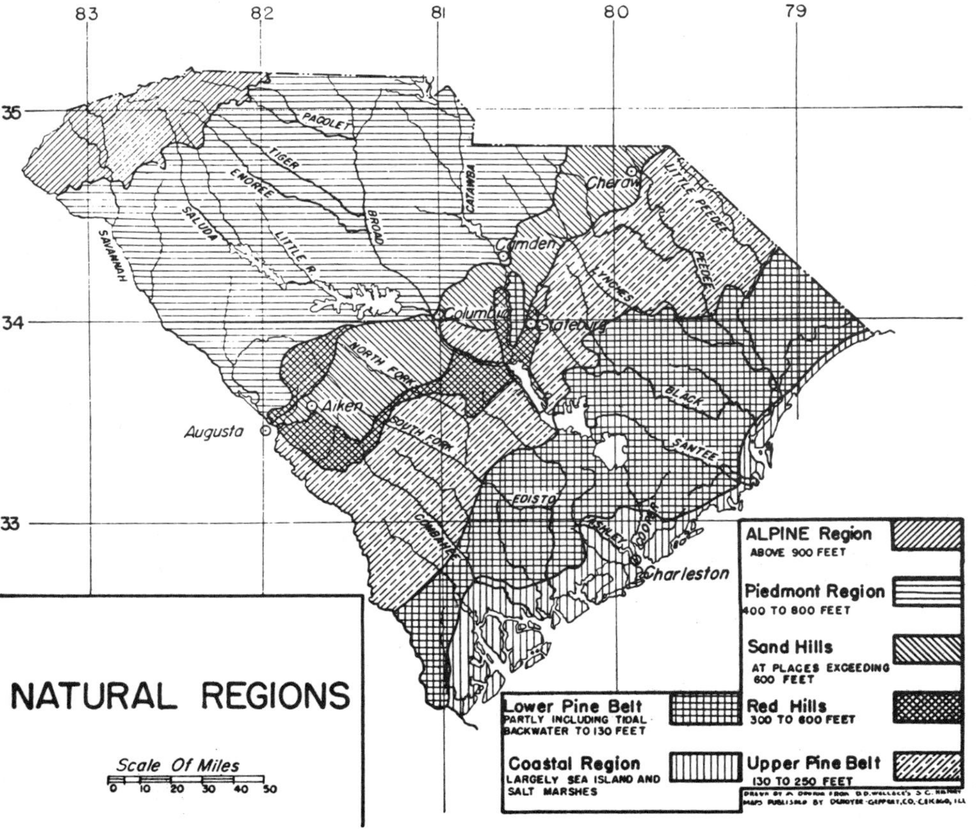

region where the land is low enough to be flooded by the rivers at high tide. Its higher levels, rising to 130 feet above the sea, abound in magnificent long-leaf pines.

III. The upper pine belt, 130 to 250 feet above sea level, abounds in long-leaf pine interspersed with oak and hickory. These 5,500 square miles embrace some fair, loose land and considerable rich bottom land.

IV. The red hill region, elevated from 250 to 600 feet above sea level, comprises the hill country from Aiken through Edgefield, Calhoun and upper Orangeburg counties, and Sumter, at about the northern end of which it terminates. The High Hills of Santee paralleling the Wateree River on its east attain an almost mountainous appearance. The region contains much good land.

V. The sand hills, lying on both sides of the fall line though mostly below it and rising from 600 to 700 feet above sea level, roll their white domes, often covered with scrubby trees, entirely across the State and far beyond in both directions. Though generally so infertile as to have fostered an underprivileged population, under modern skilled fruit culture, landscape gardening, manufacturing, and winter resort development many parts of the region have become progressive and prosperous.

VI. The Piedmont region of from 400 to 800 feet elevation comprises the great body of the up country and contains a growing majority of the white population. Its lands vary widely, and because the irregular surface necessitates careful cultivation to avoid erosion, they range from utterly ruined fields once bearing a rich surface to level or rolling lands of great fertility. Its water powers have in modern times profoundly affected its history.

VII. The Alpine region consists of the northern parts of Oconee, Pickens, and Greenville counties, with an elevation from 900 to 3,500 feet, and bears the general characteristics of the great mountain region of North Carolina.

After population had spread over the entire State, the fundamental physical fact influencing its internal history was the existence of the two geological and topographical regions dividing it into up country and low country, as already described. Conventionally it is said that these sections are divided by the fall line; but the sand hills, thrust between the two distinctly up and low country sections, make it difficult to say exactly where the social and economic dividing line lies; for this middle belt, thirty miles wide in places, but generally much narrower, does not fully partake of the characteristics of either section. As natural conditions have been conquered, the economic, social, and political contrasts and conflicts that marked earlier periods have diminished. Nevertheless, their influence has been so profound that it is impossible to understand the history of the State without a knowledge of them.

CHAPTER II

THE INDIANS OF SOUTH CAROLINA

ON THE BASIS of language, ethnologists divide the American Indians living north of Mexico into about sixty stocks which are subdivided into about a hundred and sixty-five tribes. The stocks represented among the Indians that formerly inhabited South Carolina are the Iroquoian, the Siouan, the Muskhogean, the Yuchian, and the Algonkian. All but a few small or briefly resident tribes are assigned to the first three of these stocks, which thus comprise almost all the Indians who formerly lived within the present South Carolina. These three, extending far beyond Carolina, are the richest of all the stocks north of Mexico in literary and historical records and are also the largest and strongest.

Northeast of the Catawba-Santee waterway were the numerous tribes of the Siouan stock, the southern portion of the great mass of Siouan tribes extending in a long narrowing triangle to the Potomac above Washington. South of the Congaree-Santee were a number of little Muskhogean tribes, a stock extending beyond the Mississippi. The northwest third of the State was occupied by the Cherokees, of Iroquoian stock, the most powerful of the tribes occupying her borders in historic times, though barely able to hold their own with the shrewd and warlike Creeks, the great Muskhogean confederation extending across Georgia and Alabama and meeting the Chickasaws of northern Mississippi and western Tennessee and the formidable Choctaws (both fellow Muskhogeans) in the south of the present Mississippi. The Cherokees were mountaineers, inhabiting very scatteringly an area of about 40,000 square miles in the extreme northwestern corner of South Carolina, northern Georgia, western North Carolina, and eastern Tennessee; but in addition to the territory over which their villages were scattered, they generally made good their claim to vast hunting grounds of about ten times this extent spreading into eight modern states.

The tribes of the low country were numerous and small; those of the up country, few and generally large. Any exact location of many of them is impossible, for the ranges of the smaller ones were vague. An idea of the general location of many tribes may be derived from the streams bearing their names. But caution is necessary here, for tribes frequently extended along only part of a river and sometimes shifted their residence to an entirely different region. Our information regarding all within our present bounds except the Cherokees and the Catawbas is very slight. War, pestilence, whiskey, and systematic slave hunts, says James Mooney, nearly exterminated them before anybody had thought them of sufficient importance to inquire about their habits or beliefs. Of all Indians the least known are those of Virginia and the Carolinas.

Siouan Tribes.—Beginning at the point where the Catawba River enters the State and extending south and southeastward to the coast, covering the region between the North Carolina line and the Santee River, lived fourteen or more of the South Carolina Siouan tribes. Ethnologists agree that the ancient home of the Siouans was in the Virginia-Carolina region, from which they spread to the northwest. Siouans occupied all North Carolina east of the mountain-dwelling Cherokees except the portion lying to the east of the seventy-seventh meridian and a long wedge from Cape Lookout to Raleigh held by the Tuscaroras of the Iroquoian stock.

Most important of the South Carolina Siouans were the Catawbas, living mainly to the south of the line dividing the Carolinas along the Catawba River. They maintained a standing enmity with the Cherokees, next to whom they were long the most powerful body within South Carolina. Catawba was not only the name of a tribe but was a group name also including the Waterees lower down the river, the Congarees below them, the Santees along the stream named for them, the Waxhaws near the Catawbas, the Seewees extending perhaps for thirty miles along the coast around Bull's and Seewee Bays and inland to about Monck's Corner, and the Enos, to the north. The name Zantee is today borne by a Siouan tribe in the Dakotas.

Smallpox and whiskey contributed more than all their wars to destroy the Catawbas. They were said in 1700 to have 1,500 warriors, in 1750 only 400, and in 1787 only 150, at which date they remained the only organized tribe in South Carolina, except that the Cherokees still held a tiny strip in the extreme northwest. With the single exception of the Yemassee War in 1715 the Catawbas were always friendly with the whites. In 1763 they were confirmed in the possession of an area fifteen miles square, one corner of which, just east of the Catawba River, still appears as a sharp angle jutting into North Carolina. By 1826 this reservation of 225 square miles had been leased to whites. In 1841 the Catawbas sold to South Carolina their equity, but in 1842 the State gave them a small part of it for residence. All but a few of those who then went in dissatisfaction to the Cherokees in North Carolina soon returned. Their few score descendants, largely of mixed blood, numbered in 1942 forty-five families living on a reservation of 652 acres in the southeastern corner of York County, partly by their own labor and partly on State aid, and eighteen families, almost all working in cotton mills, in Rock Hill. In 1944 they were made citizens and placed on enlarged lands under Federal supervision.

The Cheraws, who during the late seventeenth and early eighteenth centuries lived to the eastward of the Catawbas on both sides of the line dividing the Carolinas, were also of the Siouan stock. Formerly much more numerous, they had extended north of the Catawbas to the Cherokees on the headwaters of the Broad in North Carolina, where De Soto in 1540 found them. The mountain-dwelling Cherokees called the trail leading up a certain river valley and on eastward over the Blue Ridge the Suwali-nana, i.e., the Cheraw path, which on the tongue of the white man became the Swannanoa. The Cheraws seem to have been driven from their home on the Dan in Virginia by their hereditary enemies, the Iroquois of New York. By the time of the American Revolution they appear to have been absorbed into the wasted body of the Catawbas.

Also as Siouan are classed the tribes of the Peedees, the Waccamaws and the Winyaws (or Weenees). All these petty tribes were worn down under their feudish little wars, drunkenness, and general bad habits or were desolated by the greatest terror, the smallpox, which before 1700 had already, says Lawson, destroyed many thousands.

The Siouan classification of the obscure tribes between the Santee and the North Carolina line by James Mooney is confessedly "open to question at many points." Of them we know less than of any others.

Tribes of Muskhogean and Other Stocks.—Crossing the Santee River and moving along the coast toward Savannah, we find the same condition of small, weak, disunited groups. West and southwest of Charleston were more than twenty of these little tribes referred to collectively as the Cusabees or Cusabos or Cusaboys. Among these were the Wandos, the Etiwans (sometimes called Eutaws), the Kiawahs on the Ashley, and the Edistos on the large sea island bearing their name. More powerful than their neighbors were the Coosas, living around the upper waters of the Coosawhatchie, Combahee, Ashepoo, and Ashley, and around the mid-Edisto. And so on, almost every river, creek, and sea island in that region preserves the name of the Indians who presumably at some time lived upon it. All these tribes of southeastern South Carolina, except a few interlopers presently to be noticed, are classed by Dr. John R. Swanton as members of the Cusabo group, of Muskhogean stock.

In the southwestern part of South Carolina along the Savannah we come upon the Westos, the most warlike of the early tribes near Charleston, at whose very footsteps their neighbors trembled. In the opinion of

Dr. Swanton they are of the Yuchian, one of the smallest stocks. Another tribe, called Yuchi, or Uchee, or perhaps a division of the Westos, thrust itself a little way into South Carolina in two branches, one at Silver Bluff in Aiken County and one nearer the sea. The little group of Hogolees along the Savannah are considered to belong to these Yuchis. Verner W. Crane, from a passage in the South Carolina Council Journal of January 13, 1693, identifies the Westos with the mysterious Rickohockans, early expelled from Virginia; but the mystery remains unsolved as to whether the Rickohockans were Cherokee wanderers, as some early writers guess. The Westos were driven out of the present bounds of South Carolina in 1681 by the aid of the Shawanos, now called Shawnees, rovers who remained long enough to give their name, transmuted to Savanno and Savannah, to the river upon whose midcourse they settled.*

The Yemassees along the Georgia coast were Spanish subjects until, terrified by attacks of French and English freebooters, they scattered into the Georgia interior and the southern corner of South Carolina, arriving in the latter in 1684. They settled with the permission of the Carolina government in the present Beaufort, Jasper, and Hampton counties. Their massacre of the Spanish mission on St. Catherine's Island was instigated by the Port Royal Scotch. After the failure of the Yemassee War of 1715-16, the most dangerous Indian attack ever made upon the province, the remnants who fled to Florida were ultimately merged with their kinsmen of the heterogeneous refugees called Seminoles.

According to the best information that we have (a notation of George Hunter's manuscript map of 1730), the Saludas settled in South Carolina in 1695 and moved to Pennsylvania in 1712 from their homes along the lower reaches of the river that bears their name, where Saluda Old Town preserves the memory of their chief settlement. Their antecedents and stock are a complete mystery. In 1730 they were living at Conestoga, Pennsylvania, with the Shawnees.

After the numerous little tribes of the low country, united under the leadership of the Yemassees to destroy the whites, were crushed in that crucial time of 1715-16, they lived by sufferance in little groups among the settlements or merged in some stronger tribe. By 1755 this was the condition in the coastal plain, while the powerful tribes of the interior were becoming deeply alarmed at the nearer approach of the farms that destroyed their hunting grounds. The coast Indians considered themselves the remnants of once stronger tribes whom their enemies had "driven to the salt water." The weakness and the consequent friendliness on the part of the divided natives were fortunate for the whites.

* See Bibliography for complete names of authors and titles referred to.

Until irritated by mistreatment, they were most amiable to Spaniards, Frenchmen, and English. The presence on the coast of powerful and warlike nations like the Creeks or Cherokees might have drowned the infant colony in blood.

When in 1566 Juan Pardo marched from Port Royal to the foot of the Appalachians, he found in possession along this route a Muskhogean people—the Creeks, says Woodbury Lowery, if we may judge by the names preserved in the *Spanish Relations*. Early in the eighteenth century they agreed to claim no territory east of the Savannah, and the government of South Carolina agreed to permit no settlements to its west.

The Cherokees, Iroquoian Stock.—This brings us to the Cherokees, the most important of all the Indians of the southeastern portion of the United States. The Cherokee nation, says C. C. Royce, has probably occupied a more prominent place in the history of this country than any other except possibly their warlike kinsmen the Iroquois, or Six Nations, of New York. They are one of the few Indian peoples, according to J. W. Powell, who have been able to pass through the ordeal of more than two centuries of wars, councils, and litigation with the white man into present prosperity.

The Cherokees were a mountain people when De Soto found them in 1540 near where the Eastern Band still dwell among the Great Smokies. Their language indicates that they had long been separated from other Iroquoians. The lands which they claimed were bounded thus: leaving a point on the Santee River near Eutawville in the southeastern part of Orangeburg County, go west to the junction of the North and South Edisto; up the South Edisto to its source and westward to the line dividing Alabama and Mississippi thirty miles south of Tennessee; thence north to and along the Tennessee River to the point at which it receives the Duck River halfway across the State of Tennessee; thence to the Ohio along the watershed that divides the Tennessee and the Cumberland; up the Ohio to the Great Kanawha; up the Great Kanawha and the New River to Chiswell's Mine on the northern slope of the Iron Mountains; thence east along the Iron Mountains thirty-five miles to the Blue Ridge just southeast of Floyd, Virginia; southwest along the crest of the Blue Ridge to the source of Linnville River, North Carolina, and down that stream, the Catawba, and the Santee to the point from which we started.

The Cherokees, though claiming this great empire, were essentially a mountain people. Their lower towns (east of the Blue Ridge) studded the northern parts of Oconee and Pickens counties, and, until abandoned on account of Creek hostility, northeastern Georgia east of the Blue

Ridge; their valley towns, the upper waters of the Hiwassee and the vales of its tributary the Valley River southeast of the Unaka Mountains (the southern extension of the Great Smokies); their middle towns, the valleys of the Little Tennessee and its tributaries southeast of the Great Smokies; and their overhill towns, southeast of the valleys of the Tennessee and its tributaries west of the Great Smokies. In this vast area they gathered the hundreds of thousands of deerskins and much smaller quantities of other pelts which for sixty years formed one of the principal exports of Charleston. But these hunting preserves had to be held at the cost of frequent wars. The distinctive home of the nation comprised about fifty villages in the heart of the Appalachians 400 miles long, extending from the northeastern corner of the present Tennessee to the northeastern corner of Alabama and spreading eastward to 200 miles in width toward its southern part, embracing 40,000 square miles. There were also mere hunting settlements or temporary outposts, and villages in north Georgia abandoned because of Creek hostility.

About 1735 the Cherokees were said to number 6,000 warriors. About 1765 they could muster only 2,300.

Indian Civilization.—That women were honored among the coast tribes is shown by the fact that a deed to the whites in 1675 is signed by "women captains" as well as by men. De Soto met an Indian "queen" of territory along the east bank of the Savannah. The roles assigned to women in religion, war, or social functions indicate an honorable standing. If the woman bore the burden, it was in part at least that the man might meet a sudden attack. If she tilled the fields, he endured the hardships of the hunt and the battle. Polygamy was practiced by those who could afford it, but the Indians' sex morality, barring few and doubtful exceptions, compares favorably with that of any people of a similar degree of civilization. Rapes of white women who were completely in their power were uncommon.

Great distances were traversed for war or trade. A path led from Charleston to the Mississippi. A tribe might migrate in a few years upward of a thousand miles. The Iroquois of New York were familiar and dreaded visitants in their hereditary war against their Siouan enemies as far south as the boundary between the Carolinas, and as late as 1751 they appeared near Charleston.

Indian government was essentially democratic. Generally speaking, the chiefs were leaders rather than rulers, and, after the oldest and wisest had given their advice, every warrior had his part in determining whether there should be peace or war. The lashing of passions by the war dance shows how well the party bent on action understood mass psychology. This freedom of action without adequate means of enforcing any definite authority was frequently responsible for the forays upon other tribes or upon the whites.

The religion of American Indians was generally based on a belief in powers residing in animals or other objects. A great variety of animals were worshiped, differing as widely as the rattlesnake and the rabbit. Nor was it always the powerful or beautiful beast which evoked worship. Some of the nobler tribes, such as the Cherokees, seemed on the verge of a sort of pantheism which might have developed into belief in a single divine spirit inhabiting all things. The conception of "the Great Spirit" was apparently derived from contact with Christianity.

The two or three thousand of the Eastern Band of the Cherokees, many with blood mixed with white and some with Negro, who live on the Qualla Reservation in western North Carolina, set off for them in 1848, remind us of the powerful nation that once spread for hundreds of miles in the southeastern United States. They live the life of simple farmers. The body of the nation long ago moved to the Indian Territory (now Oklahoma), where they stand with the most advanced Indians in civilization. Many of their leaders of partly white blood have manifested high intellectual ability. Such was Sequoyah, in honor of whom the giant trees of California were named. With little knowledge of English, after years of labor he completed in 1821 an alphabet of eighty-five characters representing practically every separate syllable sound in the Cherokee language. Man or child, by merely learning this alphabet, can at once read anything in the language. The invention was a powerful implement for Cherokee civilization and sent them forward with almost revolutionary rapidity. After a life of manifold service to his people Sequoyah died at about the age of eighty-three as he was searching in Mexico for "the lost Cherokees."

White marriages, Mooney believes, account for much of the advance in civilization made by the Cherokees. He says, speaking of the period since the removal to the West: "The families that have made Cherokee history were nearly all of this mixed descent," and, moreover, "most of this white blood was of good stock, very different from the 'squaw man' element among the Western tribes."

The Indians can hardly be said to have checked the advance of white settlement in South Carolina, for the only very strong tribe after the Yemassee War was the distant Cherokees, whom the colonists were able, with the help of a force of British regulars, summarily to crush as soon as it really stood in their way. But to deny that the Indians have influenced our history would be untrue. The constant readiness for war which their presence necessitated and the mental state of determined self-reliance which they helped to produce in the colonists were impor-

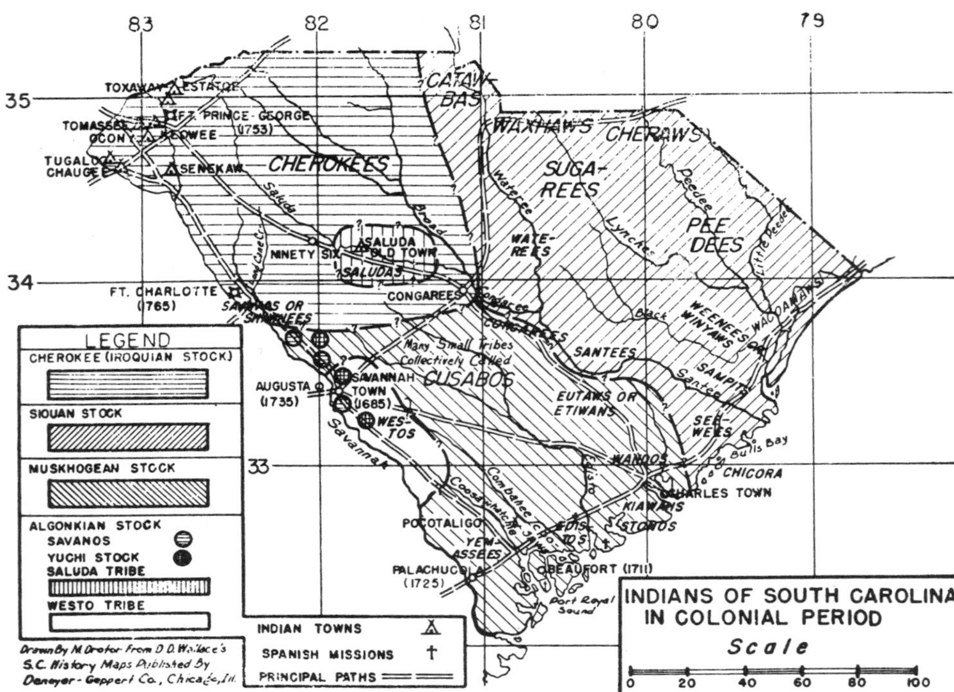

tant parts of the latter's training for the struggle in which they were to defend their rights against the mother country. The vegetables and other products that the Indians already raised made an important contribution to the white man's comfort and wealth, and their tobacco became the economic foundation of a notable civilization. The memory of the red man is inscribed on every part of the State in many of the most beautiful and appropriate of our geographical names. The Indian has supplied a great body of material for our literature and has given us some expressions compact of his own sententious speech. Despite his manifest faults and the bitter enmity between white and red, the dignity, the romance, the tragedy of the Indian have their part in the background of our history.

Indian Stocks and Tribes at Various Times in South Carolina

Iroquoian Stock (northwestern section):

Cherokees—Many villages, which are sometimes erroneously spoken of as tribes. The Elasses (Elatse, Elatseyi, Ellijay) were really a group of settlements, e.g., of the Cherokees, some of which at one time were in South Carolina.

Siouan Stock (northern, northeastern, and eastern sections):

Catawbas—Largest and most important of this stock. Many names, including almost every conceivable way of imitating the sound (Kaddapaw, e.g., to such as Atakwa, Cattoways, Esaws, and Usheree).

Waxhaws.

Cheraws.

Chicoras (called also Chickorees, Chichanees, and perhaps Waterees).

Waterees.

Sampits (Sampas)—Most probably Siouan.

Sutarees—(east of Catawbas).

Sugarees (Sugaus, Sagarees).

Hooks, Back Hooks, Black Hooks, or Pohocs—Probably Siouan.

Congarees—(south of the river by Popple's map, 1733).

Keyauwee—From North Carolina along the Peedee. No connection with Keowee or Kiawah.

Santees—(spelled also Seretees, Sattees, etc.).

Peedees.

Seewees—Elasie named among Siouan tribes (*Shaftesbury Papers*, 334), but see under Cherokees.

Enos—(came to upper Peedee from North Carolina before 1730; perhaps before 1715; perhaps with Keyauwees).

Waccamaws (Waggamaws).

Winyaws—(also called Weenees).

Muskhogean Stock:

Apalachees—(Allendale of Hampton County apparently, near the Savannah River, 1704-16. Seem the same as tribe called in South Carolina Palachuckola. Merged with Creeks after Yemassee War).

Yemassees—(Yoas apparently a subdivision).

The Salchichees are surmised by J. T. Lanning in his *Spanish Missions in Georgia* to have been connected with the Yemassees.

Creeks—(on middle or upper Savannah, apparently 1566. Original name Apalachees).

Chickasaws—(small number of refugees from west on the Savannah opposite Augusta until Revolution).

Notchees—(small band of Natchez expelled from Mississippi).

Cusabos—(also called Cussabees, Corsaboys, etc.). Most, if not all, of the following little tribes were of the Cusabo group:

Escamacus (Uscamus)—Of or near St. Helena Island.

Ashepoos (Ishpows).

Bohickotts (Bohicketts).

Coosaws.

Cotachicach—(Chatuache, Satuache, near Ashepoo mouth).

Cusso—(also called Casors, Cusaboys; by Ribault's men, apparently Couexi).

Combahees.

Edistos—(French Audusta, Spanish Orista).

Etiwans—(also called Itawans, Eutaws).

Isaws.

Kiawahs.

Salchichees (in South Carolina or Georgia? Connected with Saltketchers?).

Stonos.

Wandos.

Wappoos.

Witcheaus.

Wimbees (Wimbehee).

Yuchi (Uchee) Stock:

Westos—(Yuchis in the contested opinion of Dr. Swanton).

Yuchis—Along middle Savannah River.

Hogologis—Above the Yuchis along the Savannah, perhaps the same tribe.

Algonkian Stock:

Shawano—(Shawnee; Savano; Savannah).

Unclassified:

Saludas.

CHAPTER III

SPANISH AND FRENCH SETTLEMENTS AND EXPLORATIONS, 1521-1586

South Carolina has been an outpost, first of Spain, then of France, again of Spain, and finally of England, in their fateful contest for empire. The first Europeans to set foot upon her soil were Spaniards.

Ayllon's Settlement.—Lucas Vasquez de Ayllon, of Toledo, was one of the better type of officials who had come to seek wealth and fame in Santo Domingo, or, as they called it, Hispaniola. Late in 1520, having associated with himself another official, he dispatched a ship to explore the Atlantic coast of North America. After sailing far to the north, Ayllon's ship on its return voyage met among the Bahamas a vessel that had been sent out from Santo Domingo by another official but on a less creditable mission—the capture of Indians as slaves to supplement the waning supply in Santo Domingo, half of whose population had perished in a few years under the Spaniards' inhuman treatment. Ayllon, though the owner of hundreds of Santo Domingan natives, had charged his captain against enslaving the people of any coasts that he might discover, but the result of a conference with Quexos, the captain of the other vessel, was that the two set sail for the mainland with this very purpose. On June 24, 1521, they came upon the coast at latitude 33 degrees 30 minutes at the mouth of a considerable river, to which, since it was St. John Baptist's Day, they gave his name. The mouth of Winyaw Bay, which narrows down to the size of a bold river through which the united waters of the Peedee, the Black, the Sampit, and the Waccamaw enter the sea, seems to be the River Saint John Baptist. It lies only 17½ minutes south of 33 degrees 30 minutes, the latitude which Quexos gives, and, moreover, reference to crossing the bay adds to the probability that this was the entrance into which the explorers sailed.

The natives, who called the region Chicora, fled in terror, but the Spaniards overtook a man and a woman and brought them on board. After treating them with flattering kindness and clothing their nakedness with European dress, they sent them ashore. The captains took formal possession of the country in the name of their king and of their respective employers. They explored inland and were treated by the natives with hospitality. This friendliness was made by the Spaniards the means of crowding their ships with Indians under the pretext of an entertainment, during which they suddenly put to sea with a hundred and fifty of their guests as slaves. One of the little vessels sank, and numbers of the enslaved Indians, carried to Santo Domingo by the other, starved themselves to death.

After heartbreaking delays Ayllon, in the middle of July, 1526, finally got away from Santo Domingo with eighty-nine horses and five hundred men and women, including a number of Negro slaves. Among the three Dominican friars carried for converting the natives was Antonio Montesino, the first man to preach against the enslavement of the natives of Santo Domingo.

Ayllon himself now saw the mainland for the first time. The fleet entered a river said to be at 33 degrees 40 minutes, which Ayllon named the Jordan, almost certainly the Cape Fear. Scouting parties convinced Ayllon that the marshy region of the Jordan was inferior to a location to the southwest, and so he sent the sick and the women and children by water and the strong men by land "to a great river (forty or forty-five leagues from there, a little more or less), which is called Gualdape, and there they pitched their camp." The latitude they calculated as 33 degrees. Here rose Ayllon's San Miguel, the earliest European settlement in South Carolina and the earliest settlement of Europeans north of Mexico. Peer as we may across the four intervening centuries, we cannot distinguish the spot, but the probabilities are strongly in favor of Winyaw Bay.

The settlement was probably made about the middle of August. It dwindled under fever and starvation, and Ayllon himself died on October 18. Mutiny against his successor, a fire set by slaves, and a general state of misery and discontent led to the decision in the midst of a terrible winter to abandon the settlement. Only one hundred and fifty remained out of the original five hundred.

De Soto and Villafañe.—The next approach of Europeans was on the west. De Soto in 1540 marched northward from the Gulf of Mexico through Georgia. He was told of a great province of Cofitachiqui, and toward the end of April, 1540, came upon the capital bearing the same name, situated probably upon Silver Bluff in Aiken County overlooking the Savannah thirteen miles below the present Augusta. The Queen (for the ruler was a woman) loaded her guests with presents and was forced to guide them northward to the supposed gold-bearing mountains. In May, De Soto pushed on apparently through what are now the South Carolina counties lying near the Savannah and entered North Carolina by or near the valley of the Keowee. Passing through this corner of the Cherokee country, he passed eastward near the headwaters of the Broad. Turning west, he passed through the mountains into northeastern Georgia on his long march to the Mississippi.

For some years the exploitation of Mexico, the exploration of the Gulf coast, and a series of disasters at sea so engaged Spanish energies that the Atlantic coast was neglected; but in 1558, Philip II ordered a great move to be made upon the "Florida" coast at Santa Elena, as the Spaniards called Port Royal harbor. An expedition was at last got off from Vera Cruz under Villafañe.

He reached Port Royal Sound on May 27, 1561. Finding no place that suited his fancy after ascending the river four or five leagues, he took possession of the country and sailed northward as far as Cape Hatteras, from which point he was driven in distress to Santo Domingo.

The motives for Spain's repeated efforts to settle the coast of Florida or South Carolina were the hope of finding riches and the fear that unless actual possession were established the French might snatch these regions. After the failure of Villafañe, Spanish officials in the New World and the King himself concluded that there was at present no such danger. Within less than a year events were to prove how ill-grounded was this confidence.

Ribaut at Parris Island, 1562.—Ayllon's short-lived colony was a move in Spain's war for empire. The second attempt to settle on the South Carolina coast, made a generation later by Huguenots, was a part of the hundred years' conflict between France and Spain. Although at Cateau-Cambresis in 1559 they had made peace and promised to root out heresy, to many in France Spain was still their country's foe. The bold seamen of Brittany and Normandy, among whom were many Protestants, continued after the peace as before to serve God and line their own pockets by pillaging the Spanish merchantmen and treasure ships. One of these French soldier-seamen was Jean Ribaut of the Norman port of Dieppe. Ribaut, born about 1515 or 1520, now in the prime of life, was a devout Huguenot, a skilled seaman, an experienced soldier, a courageous leader and a successful diplomat. He was a captain in the French navy as was also his son. Coligny, Admiral of France and leader of the Huguenots, who had already in 1555 sent an unsuccessful Protestant colony to Brazil, now chose Ribaut to lead a second expedition to found in the New World an asylum for his fellow-religionists and an outpost for France.

Although Ribaut's expedition planned in 1562 for "Florida" was composed almost entirely of Huguenots, it was even more distinctly French. The national character of the enterprise was exemplified by the fact that the Catholic Queen Regent Catherine de' Medici and great nobles of both religious factions were among the backers. Spain had long been harassed by French and English preying upon her commerce, and feared that France was planning the still more serious encroachment of a colony in Florida, which in addition to being a trespass upon her territory, would menace the route of her treasure fleet. Philip's agents in France kept him informed of every suspicious move in a French port. The Queen Regent and Coligny denied all knowledge of the affair, and, despite Philip's protests, Ribaut sailed from Dieppe on February 16, 1562. Most of his company of 150 men were Huguenots, including a Calvinist preacher. On April 30 he sighted the coast of Florida near the point at which St. Augustine was founded three years later as the immediate result of these French encroachments. The next day he entered the mouth of the St. John's River and set up beside the river a stone column bearing the arms of France, and as he sailed northward he gave names to nine rivers or inlets. The only one of these that has stuck is that at which he decided to plant his colony, Port Royal.

For the settlement he selected a small island, lying between the two rivers, which we know as Parris Island from the name of its owner long later. On this little pear-shaped island, five miles long with its point toward the sea, he built Charlesfort, a structure of about ninety-six by seventy-eight feet consisting of "a blockhouse of logs and clay, thatched with straw, with a ditch around it, with four bastions, and two bronze falconets and six iron culverins therein." The evidence points with all but certainty to the spot on the northern bank of Ballast Creek (formerly called Pilot Creek), near the first turn as one ascends the stream. This is the only location which meets all the details that we know and which contradicts none. March 27, 1926, there was unveiled on Parris Island a beautiful column almost an exact copy of Ribaut's column as depicted by LeMoyne, but about twice as large, bearing the inscription: "Erected 1925 by the Government of the United States of America to mark the first stronghold of France on this continent." Unfortunately the spot selected, despite the availability of correct information, was the site of the later Spanish fort San Marcos.

Ribaut addressed his men in a speech full of the democratic ideals which were common among the Huguenots. "I think there is none of you," he said, "that are ignorant of how great consequence this our enterprise is." Here was the opportunity, he assured them, for men who could never gain position under the conditions of the old world to grasp the wealth and distinction which their daring and fidelity might deserve. The greater part of the company were unenthusiastic about remaining. Leaving "XXX in all, gentilmen, souldiers, and merryners," says Ribaut, he sailed away to explore the coast to the north, promising to return in six months with reinforcements. But the dangers of the coast, bad weather, and other hardships moved him to abandon this and sail for France.

Ribaut found France plunged in the welter of the religious wars that had broken out a few days after he had sailed for America and were to rage for thirty-four years. Coligny, the soul of the colonization, was engrossed with the struggle, and Ribaut himself took an active part. The promised reinforcements for the twenty-eight or thirty men at Charlesfort must wait. Going to England, Ribaut published an account of his voyage and obtained an audience with Queen Elizabeth, who was ready to make a profit by fishing in troubled French or Spanish waters. Although seeking to guard herself, "so that if Philip should complain she would be able to swear that nothing had been done by her order," she was anxious to take over Ribaut's colony. She offered him half the profits, reminding him that, even if the country proved not to be so good as he thought, it afforded an excellent station from which to plunder the Spanish ships bearing the treasures of Mexico and Peru, and urged upon him a house and a pension of 300 ducats if he would undertake the enterprise—a bribe to betray France which Ribaut denied that he ever accepted.

An English fleet of five vessels was prepared, one of which was contributed by Ribaut and one by the Queen herself. There were three French pilots who had accompanied Ribaut on his former voyage. Misunderstandings arose. Ribaut was thrown into prison with the threat of hanging, and the pilots were chained on board to guide the expedition that never sailed. Elizabeth's part in the story may be concluded with Woodbury Lowery's statement that "the incident establishes beyond doubt . . . her serious design to occupy Florida, and that the rumor of such an intention was not a mere blind given out to conceal an ulterior object of preying upon the Spanish fleets, as some have supposed."

Meanwhile the twenty-eight or thirty Frenchmen at Charlesfort were impatiently awaiting reinforcements and supplies. While laboring to complete their fort, they coaxed into camp and treated kindly a young Indian grandiloquently described as "a vassel of King Audusta," which in plain language means a member of the tribe of the Edistos. This led to the French's visiting "Audusta" and four other Indian chiefs, an excursion extending upward of forty miles from their fort. They were royally entertained everywhere, although they gave offense by laughing at a religious dance and one of their number spied on certain sacred ceremonies. So kindly were the Indians that they gave the needy colonists so much of their food that they were themselves reduced to eating acorns.

The improvident soldiers subsisted on food gotten from the Indians.

Hardships, monotony, the unrewarded longing for Ribaut's return, and the merciless discipline of their commander ended in their killing him. While it was still mild weather they built a little vessel and sailed for France. In their eagerness to depart they took too little food and were forced to eat one of their own number. When at last land appeared the men were bereft of reason by the sight and had to be taken in by a passing ship. Thus tragedy, as with Ayllon thirty-six years before, ended the second attempt of Europeans to colonize South Carolina.

Menéndez and Ribaut.—Coligny was not deterred by the failure of his effort at Port Royal. His purpose was not so much to maintain a colony at some particular spot as to strike at the enemy of France and of Protestantism, if not in one place, then in another. Since Ribaut was still in an English prison, Coligny placed in command Laudonnière, an officer of the previous expedition to whom we are indebted for the story of these events. As this second attempt to plant a French colony on our South Atlantic shores touches the history of South Carolina only incidentally, we must pass rapidly to its conclusion. Laudonnière sailed to the mouth of the St. John's River in the present State of Florida, and in the summer of 1564 erected his frail Fort Caroline on the southern bank five miles from the mouth.

At this point we meet one of those brilliant and ruthless conquerors who added such an enormous extent of the New World to Spain. Pedro Menéndez de Avilés united in the highest degree the unquenchable courage, the devoted loyalty, and the settled bigotry that drove the typical Spaniard of that day like a consecrated demon against the enemies of his country and his church. To these men even the barbarous manner of war of the sixteenth century was too mild a course toward heretics; they were simply to be exterminated as a duty to God.

Menéndez, yearning to convert the barbarous subjects of Satan in Florida, to make Spain's sovereignty real, and to raise by such worthy means his own fortune and fame, obtained a commission to these effects from Philip II. While he was preparing a large expedition at his own expense news came of the settlement of Laudonnière's Protestants and of the assembling of a relief expedition by the now liberated Ribaut. Menéndez arrived at the mouth of the St. John's River seven days after Ribaut. Obliged to retire before ships superior in strength to his own, Menéndez sailed thirty-five miles down the coast and in August, 1565, founded St. Augustine, which thus remains a monument to the activity to which Coligny's and Ribaut's efforts stirred Spain.

In the midst of a hurricane that destroyed Ribaut's ships Menéndez massacred the garrison in the French fort. The men of Ribaut's fleet, who had surrendered to avoid starvation, were killed in cold blood, "by divine inspiration," thus saving his people from being corrupted, wrote a Spanish historian. The wealthy gentlemen among them offered Menéndez 100,000 ducats if he would save the lives of the company; but the conscientious bigot could not be corrupted into sparing heretics.

Catherine de Medici, using these Protestants for building a French empire, had to swallow her anger, as faction-torn France could not incur a war with Spain. Revenge was undertaken by an outraged French Catholic patriot, Dominique de Gourgues, in 1568. Skillfully capturing almost the entire garrison, he killed as few as possible in action, in order that there might be a large number to endure a humiliating death by hanging. He completed his revenge by drowning the crews of several Spanish vessels that he captured. Like Menéndez before him, he gave thanks to heaven for its aid and rejoiced that he had been able to serve his king. "Thus Spaniards and Frenchmen alike," says Parkman, "laid their reeking swords on God's altar."

The Spanish at Port Royal.—The immediate effect of Ribaut's proving to Philip II how mistaken he had been in supposing that there was no danger of French aggression near Port Royal was the establishment of a chain of Spanish forts, with some efforts at colonization outside their walls, on the coasts of South Carolina, Georgia, and Florida.

After exterminating the French in Florida, Menéndez proceeded to establish his garrisons along the coast as far as the abandoned French post at Port Royal. In April, 1566, he built on Parris Island his Fort San Felipe, beside Means's Creek, at almost the southeastern point of the island almost two miles below the old French fort. Menéndez left a garrison of 110 men and placed a soldier with each chief to teach the Catholic religion.

Exploring the Interior.—Misery and intermittent mutiny figured conspicuously in the history of San Felipe. November 1, 1566, Pardo was sent "to discover and conquer the interior country from there to Mexico." Marching up the country east of the Savannah and touching at De Soto's stopping place of Cofitachiqui, he built a blockhouse at the foot of the mountains. He was at Guatari (Wateree) when orders reached him to return to San Felipe. Leaving a priest and four soldiers, he returned to the coast after having spent more than a month in the region, not including the march there and back.

Marching again into the interior on September 1, 1567, Pardo pressed into the present Alabama and returned to Port Royal after leaving garrisons (soon destroyed by the Indians) along his route.[1]

[1] In June, 1935, a bogged, skidding tractor drawing a binder exposed in wet ground on the farm of Mr. W. Bryson Hammett twelve miles northwest of Spartanburg, S. C., a stone 17½ inches long, 12 inches broad, and 4 or 5 inches thick. When throwing aside the stone some days later, Mr. Hammett noticed carvings of a parallelogram, an arrow,

In June or August, 1569, the Jesuit Father Rogel and Brother Juan Carrera arrived at San Felipe. The Spanish farmers and their families suffered as miserably under hunger and tyranny as the soldiers. In July, 1576, an Indian rising drove the Spaniards to St. Augustine and destroyed their fort. But the next year they rebuilt on a better site near by and named their new fort San Marcos. There now began a series of unofficial French inroads and intrigues and Indian uprisings aimed at expelling Spain from the region. When Sir Francis Drake burned St. Augustine in 1586 Spain withdrew permanently from Port Royal. Thus was struck a blow by a new aggressor whose descendants were ultimately to push Spain beyond the Rio Grande.

The friars continued their work, undeterred even by the bloody Indian massacre of 1597, in which only one friar north of the present Florida escaped. There was no mission at San Felipe in 1617, but that and another station at the mouth of the South Edisto (the latter established in or just before 1633) appear in a list of 1655. One existed for a while on the Ashepoo, but it had disappeared before 1663. The zeal and extent of the labors of the friars were extraordinary, dotting the whole southeast with missions. The mission at St. Catherine's Island did not disappear before English and Indian attack until 1680.

a rising (or setting) sun, two parallel lines, the figures 15(?)7, and several scratches, perhaps by plows. The third digit was almost certainly 6, though its top is gouged by the tongue of the binder which was laid upon it so as to suggest the possibility of its having been some other digit whose lower half resembles a 6. An east-west Indian trail ran near here, and Pardo's journal records that he passed in 1567 through this region. The idea of fraud perpetrated by some farm hand, which skeptics have suggested, is rendered impossible by the fact that the existence of Pardo or anything else of sixteenth-century events in this region was unknown to any one in the vicinity. For full account and photograph of stone, see D. D. Wallace, *Hispanic American Historical Review,* XVI (August, 1936), 447.

CHAPTER IV

THE COMING OF THE ENGLISH

Heath's Charter, 1629.—The terrible warning given by Spain at Fort Caroline served to keep intruders away long after her power had declined. Philip's ambassador warned a company of Englishmen that if they settled in Florida Spain would cut off their heads as she had done with the followers of Ribaut. Charles I nevertheless showed his intention to assert England's claims, based upon the discoveries of Cabot, to the region as far south as the present State of Florida by granting in 1629, to his attorney-general, Sir Robert Heath, a charter to all America from sea to sea between north latitudes 36 and 31 under the name Carolana. This is the first application of the name which it was afterward to bear (with the change of an a to an i) to the territory of the two Carolinas.[1] The English themselves usually called it Florida until their king, Charles II, renamed it, with the change of one letter, Carolina.

The Heath charter was prompted by efforts of French Huguenot refugees in England to found a new home in South Carolina. In 1630 the *Mayflower* sailed from England with a company of Huguenots for Carolina, but for some reason landed them in Virginia. Only "few and feeble attempts" were made to effect any settlement under the Heath charter, and the King declared it forfeited when granting the charter of 1663. For this violation of their rights Heath's legal successors were in 1768 given 100,000 acres in the interior of New York.

Charles II chose the easy method of granting enormous tracts in America to friends to whom he was financially or politically indebted. Carolina he granted March 24, 1662-63,[2] to eight of his most faithful

[1] Mr. A. S. Salley has shown that the misconception of the name's having been derived from that of the French monarch originated over a century later from a misunderstanding of an engraving of Fort Caroline on the St. John's and was popularized by Oldmixon and Hewat.

[2] That is, old style 1662 or new style 1663. Dates between January 1 and March 24 inclusive for the period 1582 to 1752 are often written by the English double, as 1662-3, meaning that by old style it was still 1662, while by new style it was already 1663. Catholic Europe followed Gregory XIII in 1582 in correcting the Julian calendar by dropping the ten days that had erroneously accumulated and changing New Year's from March 25 to January 1. Protestant England continued the old style until 1752, when she set herself right by dropping eleven days (as the error grew to be with February 29, 1700) and also adopted January 1 as New Year's. Hence there is a difference of ten or eleven days in English and continental numbering of the days from 1582 to 1752. To

supporters in his days of war and exile. These lords and gentlemen were the Earl of Clarendon, the Duke of Albemarle, Lord Craven, Lord Berkeley, Lord Ashley, Sir George Carteret, Sir William Berkeley, and Sir John Colleton. Several were among the most daring men in England, who thought to enrich themselves by what to them was a commercial enterprise. Edward Hyde, Earl of Clarendon; George Monck, Duke of Albemarle; Anthony Ashley-Cooper, Lord Ashley (the later Earl of Shaftesbury) were men of high ability. The first was Charles II's leading minister; the second was the chief person to restore him to his throne; and the third was to win immortality by writing the habeas corpus act and wrecking the attempt to re-establish Stuart despotism. Under these heterogeneous guides Carolina began her career.

The Charter granted the Proprietors the ownership of the vast territory between 31 and 36 degrees north latitude and the two oceans in return for a payment to the King annually of twenty marks and one-fourth of all gold and silver that might be found. All laws were to be made "of and with the advice, assent and approbation of the freemen of the said province, or the greater part of them, or of their delegates or deputies." The Proprietors could make such temporary laws as necessary when the people could not be consulted provided these did not change or take away anyone's possessions. They could with popular consent establish the Anglican as the State Church. To attract Dissenters the proprietors were authorized to grant liberty of worship. Such was the Charter, which by the standards of the governing class in England at that time seemed generous. Under the requirement that the laws must receive popular approval the little society in Carolina was largely self-governing from the start.

Since the Heath charter had not been annulled after the granting of the Charter of 1663, the Lords Proprietors secured a second charter on June 30, 1665. The chief difference was an extension of the boundaries to 36 degrees 30 minutes on the north and 29 degrees on the south, that is, from Virginia to a point sixty-five miles south of St. Augustine. The latter was a trespass upon territory which had been settled by Spain for a century and naturally increased the hostility which Spain would have felt toward any near-by settlement.

Carolina at once attracted the attention of various dissatisfied English settlers in Barbados. The Dissenters desired a freer religious system; the Royalists sulked at the grudging recognition of their loyalty; the large plantation system was crowding out the poor and causing the rich

avoid confusion in the matter of the year, it was sometimes best to give the double figure, as 1669-70, for days before March 25. All year dates in this book are new style unless stated as old style, but days of the month, for convenience in reference, are as in the original.

to look to the mainland for new areas of expansion, and a series of destructive hurricanes inclined many to desert the West Indies.

On August 10, 1663, Captain William Hilton sailed from Barbados to find a location in Carolina for settlement by a group of wealthy Barbadians. The publication of his laudatory account of the country helped the Proprietors in securing settlers. Hilton's Head preserves his name. His voyage produced no settlement, as the Lords Proprietors declined to accept the proposals of his employers.

From 1664 to 1667 a colony of Barbadians existed near the western lip of the Cape Fear. In 1666 Robert Sandford, an official of that colony, sailed along the coast from that point to Port Royal and explored a short distance inland in the latter neighborhood.

The Fundamental Constitutions.—After several ineffectual spurts at colonization, leadership was assumed in 1669 by the brilliant Lord Ashley (Earl of Shaftesbury from 1672). As the traditional account goes, he had his secretary, John Locke, draw up the Fundamental Constitutions for Carolina, which proposed a government of many liberal features, but was in other respects reactionary even for the England of that day. Mr. H. F. Russell Smith, in his *Harrington and His Oceana,* questions Locke's authorship, on, to my mind, quite insufficient grounds; but aside from this we must agree with his conclusion that the Constitutions were largely drawn from Harrington's work, published in 1656, sketching a model republican government, and that Penn and other thinkers on colonies were also largely influenced by Harrington.[3]

The people of South Carolina, protected by the Charter from having laws forced upon them, never accepted the Constitutions, which the Proprietors virtually abandoned in 1693. Their declared purpose, "that we may avoid erecting a numerous democracy," was not inconsistent with Shaftesbury's and Locke's defense of parliamentary government against Stuart tyranny; for both men believed in government mainly by a landed class, as the Constitutions provided in extreme form. Shaftesbury warned the young South Carolina that she needed men of substance, "for it is as bad as a state of war for men that are in want to make laws over men that have estates."

The Constitutions decreed that two-fifths of the land was to belong to the Proprietors personally and the landgraves and cassiques, and three-fifths to the people. The feudal estates were to be inhabited by "leetmen" bound to the land and controlled by the lord's leet court. "All children of leetmen shall be leetmen, and so to all generations." Holders of land were to pay the Proprietors after 1689, an annual quit-rent of a penny an acre.

[3] Smith, pp. 159-61, *passim.* I thank Mr. Arthur Ravenel, Jr., for calling Mr. Smith's work to my attention.

The Grand Council, to consist of the Lords Proprietors and a host of dignitaries that were never created, was to have the power to propose laws, and the Parliament, dominated by the nobility, only the right to accept or reject. Juries in courts for freemen were to find all verdicts by majority vote. No persons might plead a case for pay or write any commentary upon the laws. A complete system of vital and marriage statistics was enjoined. There was to be self-government for towns.

The religious sections contrast most favorably with the intolerance then almost universal. Even heathen and slaves were to be unmolested, Christian example alone being used to reclaim them; but the theory that Christians could not be held in slavery by Christians was specifically denied.

Outfitting the Expedition.—The Proprietors during the six years following their grant developed no effective program; but even so their various offers, advertisements, and negotiations had served to adumbrate a sort of policy fairly liberal for the period. In 1669 Lord Ashley assumed leadership. Quarrels with squatters, the drain of expenses, and the unavoidable remission of quitrents to necessitous settlers who had for some years been filtering from Virginia into what was later North Carolina determined the Proprietors to launch a better-planned colony at Port Royal, South Carolina.

The commission of July 26, 1669, set the Governor over all Carolina southwest of Cape Romain.[4] Temporarily, five men to be elected by the freemen together with the five Proprietors' deputies were to constitute the Council, by whose advice and consent the Governor was to administer the government. The freemen were to elect also twenty members of Parliament. Acts of the two bodies when signed by the Governor and three of the Proprietors' deputies were to be law.

Every freeman above sixteen years of age should have fifty acres of land and a like amount for every servant, slave, or member of his family. This allotment remained the same throughout colonial history.[5] Indentured servants at the end of their terms were to receive land at the same rate.

Joseph West, one of the most useful men in early South Carolina, was appointed governor and commander-in-chief of the fleet, but was to surrender his authority to whomever Sir John Yeamans in Barbados should appoint. Eighteen months' provisions were sent, a large portion of which was lost at sea. The King gave twelve cannon and twelve rounds of ammunition for each. Goods for the Indian trade completed the equipment.

[4] Cape Romain here, as with the Spaniards, probably meant Cape Fear. Early statutes frequently describe South Carolina as that part of Carolina south and west of Cape Fear.

[5] For a short time at first the allotments were larger.

These prosaic details in large measure account for the success of the colony and its freedom from the heart-rending privations that so commonly attend such enterprises. But there were other favoring circumstances. The colony was in constant touch with the prosperous and well-established colony of Barbados, some of whose leading merchants and planters were in active co-operation with the new planting. The colonists themselves, composed in part of shrewd men of business and of "servants," were ready to hew out a better destiny for themselves in a new country.

The Voyage to Carolina.—A list of the ninety-three passengers aboard the largest vessel, the *Carolina,* contains names that were to become distinguished in South Carolina history. With the exception of a few Scotch and Irish, all were thoroughly English. Of the two French-looking names, one is evidently plain English misspelled and the other is apparently the name of an Englishman of French ancestry. Sixty-two were servants, seventeen were masters (including the wife of a master), and thirteen were unbound persons without servants. Sixteen were women. Several appear as "servants," however, who were much above the servant class and were really near relatives of their "masters," who adopted this means of increasing their allotments of land. Later the "servants" would also be entitled to their allotments. How many were in reality indentured servants cannot be known, but such were expected from the first and soon began to be imported.

Among the varying social levels there was a small group of pushing, active men of affairs on whom the development of the colony must largely depend. Some, we know, were from families of wealth and standing. Numerous letters prove some to have been of good education, and several aptly nailed a point with a Latin phrase. But many were so poor as to be obliged to go out under the assistance of those styled masters. Joseph West complained in September, 1670, that there were not enough freemen in the colony to constitute a parliament.

The three vessels arrived at Barbados late in October, where a storm wrecked the *Albemarle* and injured the others. A sloop, the *Three Brothers,* was obtained to replace the *Albemarle.* About the middle of November or later they sailed for Port Royal. After touching at Nevis they were separated by a storm. The *Port Royal* was wrecked in the Bahamas after experiencing the horrors of thirst from the exhaustion of drinking water during six weeks of wandering. Although the crew of eight and the thirty-six passengers got to shore, many died before the captain built a new vessel. At New Providence he hired a shallop that took most of the survivors to Bermudas, where the *Carolina* had already taken refuge. Of the third vessel they had no news for months.

At last the storm-tossed emigrants were ready for their fourth, and with some their sixth, start for Carolina. But their unintended stop at Bermudas had important results, for it determined the selection of their first governor. Sir John Yeamans, who accompanied them from Barbados to Bermudas, at the latter place, in accord with his instructions, inserted in the blank commission the name of Colonel William Sayle of Bermudas as governor, whom he described as "a man of no great sufficiency, yet the best I could get."

Sayle was then about seventy-nine or eighty years of age, an experienced colonial administrator as governor and in other offices, a steady man of character, and according to Yeamans a dissenting "zealot"; but he offended the New England Puritans by seeking to found a colony in the Bahamas with complete liberty of conscience and separation of church and state. Both his age and his religion caused grave dissatisfaction among the colonists.

Under the command of Governor Sayle the ship *Carolina* and the vessel obtained in Bermudas sailed for Port Royal, and on March 15, 1669-70, sighted the South Carolina coast at Bull's Bay. The Indians hailed them as English, their broken Spanish showing how far north the influence of St. Augustine still extended.

Proceeding to Port Royal Sound and thence into St. Helena Sound or one of its branches, the Governor had the freemen elect five Council members to be associated with the five deputies of the Proprietors. The lowness of the ground and the proximity of the Spaniards raised serious doubts as to the advisability of settling at Port Royal, doubts which were actively fostered by "this very ingenious Indian," the cacique of Kiawah, who urged the charms of the banks of the Ashley. A scouting party reported it a better location, and, since the Governor leaned that way, the voices of the Council and the people were generally for Kiawah.

The colonists entered Charleston harbor early in April. On May 23 the Barbados sloop the *Three Brothers,* which had been driven by the storm to Nansemond River, Virginia, came straggling in. She had been as far south as St. Catherine's Island, Georgia, where on May 15 she put in for water and provisions. Eleven or twelve persons venturing ashore were seized by the Indians and eight of them were murdered. Sayle sent to demand the release of his people, but two of his messengers, in disregard of their flag of truce, were detained by the Spanish on the pretext that they were "pirates" without proper credentials. The real reason was probably that the Spaniards did not dare let them carry away an account of the weakness of St. Augustine.

Thus three vessels had landed their passengers at Ashley River; but it is indicative of the trials of the voyage that only the *Carolina* among the three that left England escaped destruction by storms. Yet the survivors of the two wrecked vessels, in spite of peril, suffering, and the death of their companions, had pressed on to their original purpose. The little settlement numbered about one hundred and forty-eight souls.

The nine-acre site chosen for the town was on the western bank of the Ashley just above Town Creek, a short distance above where the Seaboard Air Line Railroad now crosses the Ashley and nearly opposite the Citadel. The fertile land, elevated some six or eight feet above high tide, is protected by the steep bank of Town Creek on the lower side, where the boat landing was, and on the side next to the river by an "inaccessible marsh" flooded at high tide, while the approach from inland could be closed by a short palisade. The situation is invisible to vessels coming in from sea until they round the bend of the river at the foot of the present Charleston several miles downstream. The need for safety from the Spaniards and, until they had made sure of their attachment, also from the Indians forced the settlers to keep together. As late as September, 1670, West writes, they had taken up only ten acres near town and would not scatter until more people came. The settlers called their town Albemarle Point, in honor of the eldest of the Lords Proprietors, who was called the Palatine. But the Proprietors complimented the King by changing the name to Charles Town.

Their measures for defense were soon justified. The Spaniards at St. Augustine came in August with a body of Indians to cut off the ships and destroy the settlement. The invaluable services of Dr. Henry Woodward now bore fruit. He had been left at Port Royal by Sandford four years before to learn the Indians' language and, after having been a prisoner at St. Augustine until he was rescued by Searle, had joined the Carolina adventurers at Nevis. He had recently returned from an exploration to the delightful fertile rolling country around Chufytachyqui (as he spells it) at or near Silver Bluff on the Savannah, with whose "emperor" and with the intervening petty caciques he had formed a league. The little South Carolina coast tribes welcomed the English as possible defenders against the Spaniards and the terrible Westos. It was Woodward's Indian friends around Port Royal Sound who now gave warning that the Spaniards and their Indian allies were approaching. The Spaniards withdrew without venturing an attack—a fiasco that proved how Spain had declined since Menéndez annihilated the French under Ribaut.

"Settled in the very chaps of the Spaniards," the little group was forced to live as much as soldiers as farmers. But the tyranny of the Spaniards rendered their Indians almost as much a danger to them as a help against the English. Spain drew in her outposts but strengthened her central station. The coming of the English, says Professor Bolton, began the stone age at St. Augustine. By 1687 the castle was "completed in the main" of stone instead of wood as before.

A Wise Governor and Factional Politics.—The smallness of the discontents common amid the hardships of a new colony attest the general good sense and character of the settlers, and this is the more creditable in view of the lack of a vigorous and inspiring leader. "Our Governor . . . is very aged, and hath much lost himself in his government. . . . I doubt he will not be so advantageous to a new colony as we did expect," wrote West in September, 1670. And yet we may easily overlook Sayle's merits. He showed sound judgment in refusing to settle at Port Royal, where the peril of destruction by Spaniards would have been much greater, and he selected a strong natural position at Albemarle Point, which the Spaniards and Indians did not venture to attack in 1670. And he discerned that the tongue of land between the Ashley and the Cooper was a much better permanent site for a town than the one temporarily chosen and ordered 600 acres reserved there for that purpose. Not least among the proofs of his sound judgment is his having on his deathbed selected for his successor the most valuable man in our early history, Joseph West. Sayle died March 4, 1671. The Council unanimously confirmed his nomination of Joseph West as his successor until the will of the Proprietors should be known.

The Barbadians—Economic Beginnings.—Despite the glowing letters and advertisements, hardships were prolonged and growth was slow. Governor West writes of being personally in need. On February 8, 1671, there arrived from Barbados the first considerable reinforcement of about forty-two settlers, and eight days later sixty-four more from the same island. The Barbadians thus early came to be almost half the population, and since they soon included many of the strongest and most experienced personalities, self-confident from their success in an older colony, they for a while so dominated the province as to make it seem at times a sort of Barbadian outpost.

It was hard to feed the new mouths. West wrote that he had cleared thirty acres and built houses and palisades fit to hold against a thousand Indians. This was apparently on the Proprietors' plantation, the first land settled on the southern unprotected side of Old Town Creek. There appeared thus early the conflict between the interests of the colonists and the Proprietors.

The settlers, like the Proprietors, expected to find the climate more nearly tropical than it was. The oranges, lemons, limes, pomecitrons, pomegranates, figs, and plantains "flourish very bravely"; but ice an inch thick the first winter ended experiments with many West Indian products. Slavery was coeval with the settlement. Governor Sayle, we know, brought in three Negroes in the first fleet and a fourth in September, 1670. Captain Henry Brayne of the *Carolina* owned "a lusty negro man" in South Carolina in November, 1670. Three slaves arrived in February, 1671, and from 1671 to 1674 Lady Margaret Yeamans imported eight. The same allotment of land was allowed as for white settlers.

With the spring of 1671 the colony faced its second year with reasonably encouraging prospects. The friendship of the Indians had been gained over a wide area. Profitable lumbering had quickly become the basis of a wholesome commerce. Planting of food crops had been unduly but not wholly neglected, but ample land had been taken up and some cleared for the coming year. The system of government was generally approved, despite protests of agitators. The temporary basis of wealth that was ultimately to prove a lasting curse, Negro slavery, had perfectly naturally begun with the landing of the first colonists. Accretions by immigration had already set in, and the Barbadian element that was to exercise such a powerful influence for many years constituted a helpful bond with the prosperous English colonies in the West Indies. Destiny was being shaped by the acts of this little company of pioneers. By the energy and foresight of the active members among the Lords Proprietors, the business enterprise of a group of pushing Barbados planters, and the hopes of a band of misused Dissenters seeking a freer atmosphere for their religion, a new English community had risen, and England had thrust her outposts far down upon Spain in the contest for empire.

CHAPTER V

CONFLICTS AND PROBLEMS—WEST'S FIRST ADMINISTRATION, 1671-1674

The Profit-Seeking Proprietors.—Although a final verdict upon the Proprietary government must await the remaining account of that experiment, it can hardly be denied that under the existing conditions such a plan secured the earlier establishment and the necessary help through infancy of an English outpost in the South. To say that the government should have undertaken these duties instead of squandering a vast belt of the national domain on court favorites is merely to call attention to one of the particulars in which the government was asleep to its opportunities and duties.

The Proprietors' dominant motive was to make money. From the complaint in one of their earliest letters that their ship took timber to Barbados for the settlers' account but none for the Proprietors', to the end of the chapter, their correspondence is full of injunctions to reserve for them the best lands and the richest Indian trade and to keep strict account of the debts of the settlers, with interest at eight or ten per cent, for advances of food, clothing, and tools, and if the debts were paid in labor, the agent was to take care that the wages be "moderate." As months rolled into years with large outlay and small returns, even Shaftesbury fell into threats to cut off further help to those he testily described as "idlers living at our expense."

Fortunately there was among the Proprietors one man of strong and liberal mind, and among the colonists one so "moderate, just, pious and valiant" as to command general confidence. Shaftesbury in England and West here may almost be called the creators of South Carolina. Joseph West, who on the death of Sayle was unanimously elected by the Council temporary governor, was to receive that mark of confidence three times and to be commissioned twice by the Proprietors in thirteen years.

Governor Yeamans.—"We have always had some differences in this colony," West wrote, September 1, 1671. The arrival of Sir John Yeamans about July 1, 1671, with almost fifty of his fellow-Barbadians, again raised "broils and heats." He made now no claim to the governorship, but felt out opinion. Finding the people hostile, he retired in disgust to his plantation. The opportunity to make trouble soon arose. Governor West, in view of the increase in population, ordered the election of twenty men as a parliament. Of this parliament, the first entirely popular house in the colony, erected July 11, 1671, Yeamans was chosen speaker. He now sought the governorship by the indirect means of inducing West to resign, rather than the direct plan of having himself, on account of being the Palatine's deputy and the sole landgrave in the colony, recognized as automatically superseding West. West refused to resign and Yeamans, having now organized his Barbadians, induced Parliament to declare itself dissolved. West promptly summoned the people for a new election and, despite Sir John's "preaching this doctrine . . . to choose such as will stand at the greatest distance from the Governor," soon had both a parliament and a council fully supporting his leadership. Here the matter rested until December 14, when Yeamans in Council openly demanded the governorship on the strength of the Fundamental Constitutions. The Council refused to displace the colony's most trusted servant by a man whose conduct had always been a source of disturbance. But a commission to Yeamans arrived, and he was, April 19, 1672, proclaimed governor. This ill-advised appointment was made in slavish compliance with the Fundamental Constitutions against the Proprietors' own judgment. West was complimented in the highest degree, but was told that "the nature of our government . . . required that a Landgrave should be preferred to any Commoner."

The System of Government.—The Grand Council for the early years was much the most important part of the government. A quorum consisted of the Governor and six members, three being Proprietors' deputies and three elected by the people's Parliament. The Governor and Council, instead of the Governor, were in effect the executive. Lord Ashley warned Yeamans, on June 20, 1672: "The distinction of the Governor from the rest of our deputies is a thing rather of order than of overruling power, and he hath no more freedom thereby than any one of the council to swerve from these rules." Turning to the Council, he warned them against "making themselves but cyphers and submitting too much to the will of any Governor whatsoever." The Governor in fact seems merely to have voted as a member of the Council.

The power of this compact body extended to every branch of government, legislative, executive, and judicial. Except for a few statutes by the provincial Parliament, which, moreover, had first to be formulated by the Council, the Council for some years exercised large semi-legislative functions in its unlimited duties of administration. It issued pretty much such orders as it saw fit regulating in large and small matters the conduct of individuals and classes; but it did not meddle with fundamental matters of law.

The Council administered all branches of law and equity, civil, criminal, and admiralty. It provided viewers to settle disputes as to quality or size of pipe staves used in "payments or exchange between party and party in the province of Carolina." This and other instances showed that staves were used as a standard of value at a certain fixed rate in sterling. No case was too trivial, as witness that of "Thomas Sceman, gentleman," whipped for stealing a turkey, and none too serious, as those of traitors sentenced to be hanged for treason. More serious cases were tried before jury, with the Governor and Council presiding; but the jurors were impatient of the possible losses through pillaging by Indians and "vermine" while they were listening to trials.

Passing now to the Parliament, a popularly elected body of twenty representatives, we find that temporary laws issued by the Proprietors directed the Governor to call a Parliament the first Monday in November every two years and oftener if necessary. These same regulations seem to indicate that the Parliament was to include the Proprietors' deputies; but, if they were ever allowed to sit with the Parliament, it was without voting power. The Parliament members elected as councillors did not thereby lose their membership in the lower house. Laws had to be framed by the Council and submitted for adoption or rejection to the Parliament, which was forbidden to discuss any other subject.

Clashes with Indians.—Clashes were hard to avoid, although the Proprietors forbade molesting the Indians, exploring for mines in the interior, or grasping at Spanish possessions. Lord Ashley insisted on paying for the Indians' lands, by a deed of March 10, 1675, by which the Kassoes ceded "the great and the lesser Cassoe" between the Ashley, the Stono, and the Edisto for certain cloths, hatchets, beads, etc. In February, 1684, in a series of treaties, the various coast tribes from the Ashley to the Savannah ceded to the Proprietors their lands back to the mountains (an absurd extension, as they owned only the coastal strip), preparatory to the Scotch settlement at Port Royal.

One of the most valuable members of the colony was Dr. Henry Woodward. As interpreter and negotiator he was so valuable that the Proprietors sent him £100—equal to the Governor's salary for a year—besides £20 from Lord Ashley personally, and refused to allow him to come to England, as he wished, to communicate his discoveries. Woodward was the chief pioneer in making South Carolina the most important factor in the southern Indian trade and establishing her, through her relations extending as far as the Mississippi, as England's main bulwark in this region against the influences of France and Spain. But all Indian relations were not so happy. Prowlers were invading plantations at night, stealing corn and threatening lives and boasting that with the Spanish they would cut off the colony. The Council on September 23, 1671, ordered open war, captives to be sold abroad as slaves, unless redeemed, and the proceeds to be distributed among the soldiers.

Against the very fierce Westos along the lower Savannah, the Council, on September 3, 1673, ordered war. The Westo trouble was hardly over before the Council had to send against the Stono Casseca who was trying to form a confederation to attack the colony, and to order a force to destroy the Kussoes, who were reported to have killed three Englishmen and to be wandering without fixed abode. These energetic measures of defense taught the Indians better conduct.

Slaves and Indentured Servants.—Added to the troubles with Indians was continued scarcity. In 1671 the people were reported weak from lack of food, and large importations were necessary. Right wisely did they determine, with the spring of 1671, "to plant what plantations we can this year, it being the hope of a new settlement in the first place to provide for the belly and make some experiment in what the land will produce." Cotton and indigo were planted the first year. The latter at once proved a success. The easier building of fortunes through rice culture, lumber, and other qui kly profitable forest industries, and through the Indian trade caused the neglect of an early successful indigo experiment. So much tobacco was being raised by 1675 that viewers were appointed. The early failure with cotton delayed its cultivation much longer. At first the major portion of the population were white servants who were subjected to strict discipline, including scourging at the public whipping post, to enforce labor and discipline until their term of servitude, sometimes running to seven years, expired and they received their allotments of land, tools, and clothes. This indentured labor was supplemented at once by that of Negro slaves from the West Indies. Sir John Yeamans immediately upon his arrival proceeded to bring a hundred cattle from Virginia, and by 1673 there were many horses.

Growth of Population and Agriculture.—The growth of population was slow. Secretary Dalton wrote on January 20, 1672, that 337 men, 71 women, and 62 children had come since the first settlement. Forty-three men, two women, and three children were dead, and sixteen men absent, leaving 278 men able to bear arms, 69 women, and 59 persons under sixteen years old, making a remaining population of 406. The enormous death rate of men is expressive of their exposure to climate and danger. Perhaps the few Negro slaves then present were included, as Dalton was giving "the total number of persons who have arrived." The Proprietors as a corporation took up plantations, cultivated by agents, and one or two had separate plantations and cultivated them individually.

Between August 3 and 13, 1674, Governor Sir John Yeamans died in South Carolina, and not, as is sometimes stated, in Barbados. There thus passed one of the most able and energetic, but by no means most admirable, characters in our early history, a type of the shrewd, pushing, selfish, and not overly scrupulous man of business who was assuming prominence in expanding England's empire. He had bought up provisions in the hungry settlement and shipped them to Barbados, where they would bring a better price than the miserable Carolinians were able to pay. As governor he showed no more regard for the interests of the Proprietors.

The removal of Yeamans and the beginning of the long administration of Governor West from 1674 to 1682, together with other important incidents, close the early period of painful and precarious struggle for mere existence and open another which, though by no means free from difficulty and danger, saw the little settlement expand into a growing and important colony.

CHAPTER VI

COMMERCE AND EMPIRE EXPANDING WESTWARD, 1674-1682

The Difficult Ten Years 1670-80.—Joseph West had already been commissioned as governor, but the letter censuring the old governor and commending the new did not arrive until after the Council had already unanimously filled the vacancy by the election of West. West served during his three terms longer than anyone else in the Proprietary period. He was now created landgrave to afford the requisite dignity for the office, as was every governor until 1712 except, of course, those who were Proprietors.

The situation indeed demanded energetic action. The colony had repeatedly been obliged to send for food. Disturbances led by Surveyor General Culpepper, Captain Gray, and others had necessitated their flight or banishment. Nothing could save the settlement, West wrote, except the Proprietors' assistance with provisions, tools, and supplies. Shaftesbury fully realized the necessity for prompt and vigorous action. His program, adopted in the spring of 1674, comprised five moves: first, the appointment of West as governor; second, a scheme for the better payment of debts due the Proprietors; third, a settlement at Shaftesbury's expense on the Ashley River; fourth, the expansion of the back country Indian trade as a proprietary monopoly; and fifth, the contribution of £700 a year for seven years by each of the Proprietors. By 1679 the Proprietors had spent £18,000 (probably $800,000 in modern value) for nothing but "vexation and poverty."

Rapid Growth from 1680.—With 1680 there opened a new era. That spring the town was moved to its present site, though it was confined for some years to a small plot on the Cooper between Broad and Water streets. In 1680 forty-five French Protestants arrived from England, soon to be followed by larger numbers. Although the French failed to develop the wines, silks, and oils which were hoped from them, they were soon giving the English an example of thrift, neatness, and efficiency in agriculture and trade.

A large part of the rapid growth of the 1680's consisted of Dissenters fleeing from persecution in England. In the movement, led by Benjamin Blake (brother of the Admiral), came his son, Joseph, who was to be one of the strongest of the proprietary governors and next to West the one of longest tenure, Daniel Axtell, Joseph Morton (another future governor), and others of force and substance. So active were Axtell and Morton in bringing in their fellow-religionists that five hundred arrived through their influence in less than a month. Both were rewarded with the title of landgrave and the accompanying lands. Thomas Colleton sent in large numbers of a different class from Barbados and was also later made a landgrave. In two years 1680 to 1682, the population doubled from about 1,100 to about 2,200. The Dissenting element was particularly strengthened both in numbers and character by this movement. These and the new Huguenot element and the work now begun by ministers of the Anglican and other churches distinctly improved the moral tone.

Indian Slave Trade—Morton Supersedes West.—Friction between the Proprietors and the people arose from the efforts of the former to secure the acceptance of the Fundamental Constitutions in one amended form after another, the insistence on quitrents, the restraint upon the people's retaliation against hostile Indians, and the Proprietors' engrossing for their own profit the richest portion of the Indian trade. Governor West alone seemed able to soften the hand of distant authority, irritated at its unremunerative expenditures, or to calm Carolina resentment and check the tendency to factionalism. There were problems just ahead for which West's talents were needed. But he had offended, says Oldmixon, in dealing in Indian slaves and in opposing the Proprietary party. More likely the real motive for superseding West by Morton in 1682 was the desire to foster the latter's influence in bringing over more of the Dissenter immigrants.[1] West was himself a Dissenter, but he had no such influence with the faction in England as did Morton.

Realizing that slave raids on the Indians would ultimately destroy legitimate commerce with them or incur disastrous wars, the Proprietors, on December 16, 1671, forbade the enslavement of Indians and later threw safeguards around the exportation of captives, which had been adopted as a means of paying the volunteer soldiers when war was unavoidable. Enslaving Indians on any pretext inevitably led to gross abuses. Neighboring Indians were ensnared or were encouraged to make war on tribes outside the colony's allies with the purpose of selling their captives to the colonial merchants, who sold them to New England or the West Indies. Some were placed on Carolina plantations, but the planters soon learned to prefer the more docile blacks. South Carolina achieved leadership in this dark form of Indian trade as well as in the legitimate exchange of European goods for the skins and furs offered by the natives.

[1] Rivers, McCrady and Salley all hold this opinion.

West's degree of guilt in this traffic it is impossible to determine. At all events, on May 18, 1682, Joseph Morton was commissioned governor to succeed him. Although West was later to serve a brief term, his public career was now virtually closed. In July, 1685, after having again been elected by the Council and also appointed by the Proprietors, he retired to look after his private interests in New York, where he died in May or June, 1691. In 1686 died the only other man who can be classed near him as the province's most useful citizen during its first fifteen years, Dr. Henry Woodward, the founder and expander of Indian trade and relations. Rivers' eulogy of West errs only in calling him a plebeian, for he was a gentleman with a coat of arms.[2]

International Rivalries for the Indian Trade.—Indian relations and Indian trade profoundly influenced the colony's history. Intertwined with this rapidly expanding commerce were the imperialistic policies of three nations in a desperate game in which the stakes represented some of the most valuable possessions of the modern world. The trade connections of the Charles Town merchants were soon pushed so far westward as to become points of conflict both with the declining Spanish power and with the vigorous French aggression led by La Salle and Iberville. The expansion of the South Carolina Indian trade therefore takes its place as one of the most important moves in the long war for empire among England, France, and Spain. South Carolina, says Professor Crane, was until Georgia was established more favorably situated for exploring the interior of the continent than any other colony with the possible exception of New York. These colonies were free from the barrier of the Appalachians. The South Carolinians enjoyed a further advantage in that no powerful Indians interposed as did the Iroquois confederacy in New York, who insisted on serving as middlemen between the Albany traders and the West. The Charles Town traders were free to press as far into the West as profits invited.

But the Carolinians were at a disadvantage compared with the Spanish in Florida and the French in Louisiana. The latter could use the broad rivers deeply penetrating the interior, whereas the Charlestonians had to carry out their goods across hills and valleys and conquer as additional barriers the very water courses that afforded natural highways to their competitors. But the superiority of English goods overcame all this and drew the trade of the Indians from beneath the very walls of the Spaniards at Pensacola and the French at Mobile.

The English colonists cannot be regarded purely as peace-loving homemakers periodically massacred by the ruthless Spaniards swooping from the dark fortress of St. Augustine. The Spanish side of the story

[2] Helen Kohn Hennig, *Great South Carolinians* (1940), p. 15.

reveals that there was an unofficial aspect of Carolinian doings which sometimes expressed more truly the aims of those in power and was of more importance than the instructions to governors or the recorded votes of Councils and Assemblies. The Spaniards had as much reason to fear what the Carolinians might do to them as the Carolinians had to fear the Spaniards.

Spain's Indian system in Florida, says Professor Crane, was based on agriculture and missions guarded by soldiers. It was passive and unprogressive, but generally speaking easy-going and kindly. There were no mines or vast estates to lead to the ruthless exploitation of the natives as laborers as in the West Indies, Mexico, and South America. The English system, on the other hand, was based on trade frequently marked by commercial abuses, and in its ultimate results was destructive of Indian civilization and existence. The cheating and licentiousness too common among the traders were unchecked by the religious influence which among the French and Spanish was exercised by the priests and friars. Moreover, the English system was the forerunner of a numerous white migration which dispossessed instead of using and mingling with the Indians. Unprogressive Spain oppressed the natives; the progressive Anglo-Americans destroyed or expelled them.

The Scotch at Port Royal.—Under these circumstances a bloody clash between Spaniards and English might come at any time. The treaty of North America, July, 1670, by which the rivals acknowledged the right of each other to their settlements, was taken by the Spaniards to legalize English occupancy as far south as Charles Town harbor; by the British as warranting much more considerable progress toward St. Augustine. Mutual aggressions showed that neither side proposed to respect the rights of the other.

In 1680 there began a series of raids by Indians under South Carolina influence against the Spanish Indians and missions along the Georgia coast, where a considerable degree of peace and civilization had been maintained, and this soon drove the Indians inland and the missions far to the southward. The attempt of the Spanish to remove their Indians to a safer location (as they said) aroused misunderstandings and fears and caused the migration into South Carolina of the warlike Yemassees, the first installment of whom settled near Port Royal in 1684, henceforth to be bitter enemies of their old friends the Spaniards.

Into this maelstrom of intrigue and violence was thrust the plan of a great Scottish migration to South Carolina, which, however, reached only small proportions. In 1682 negotiations were begun for bringing 10,000 Scots to Carolina. Henry Erskine, third Baron Cardross, a leader of the persecuted Covenanters, was commissioned governor of his colony at Port Royal with authority independent of the Governor at Charles Town.

On July 21, 1684, 148 westland Covenanters sailed from Gourock Bay on the Clyde. They landed at Charles Town October 2. Many of them had been released from imprisonment for their religion to be banished to America with this expedition. Sickness swept away many soon after landing, and many deserted, leaving only fifty-one willing to proceed to Port Royal. The men among these, led by Lord Cardross and William Dunlop, settled in early November at Stuart's Town, a mile and a half south of the present Beaufort, and on the same side of the river.

The natural view that Charles Town would have welcomed the Scots as a buffer against the Spaniards overlooks two facts. First, the Carolinians had come to have small regard for the Spaniards, and second, they saw in the Scots rivals for the same rich Indian trade to the farther back country, the Proprietors' monopoly of which had been recently ended. The Scots showed themselves grasping and exclusive. Traders from Charles Town were forbidden to pass through their territory, and even Woodward was arrested on his exploring expedition to the Creeks. The Scots were equally aggressive toward the Spanish. They annexed Georgia coast islands, armed the Indians against the mission settlement, and even contemplated seizing the Spanish mines of New Mexico. In February, 1685, "led by Chief Altamaha and encouraged and outfitted by Lord Cardross, the Yamassees now made a raid clear across Guale to the Timucua mission west of San Agustin. . . . When they returned the raiders were met at the Savannah by Lord Cardross and his men, eager to buy their plunder."[3]

In August, 1686, the Spaniards took their revenge. They rushed the settlers, numbering not over twenty-five men in health, who fled to the woods so quickly as to lose only three as prisoners. Destroying at leisure, 150 Spaniards, Indians, and mulattoes moved toward Charles Town. Before the rapidly assembled militia and a frightful storm they withdrew about August 29.

The Charles Town government raged for revenge; but their punitive expedition was checked at the point of departure by the arrival of James Colleton as governor, who sternly forbade one blow to be struck, since England and Spain were at peace. The Spanish and Carolina governors patched up affairs with mutual disavowals of hostile intentions, and the Carolinians had to swallow their wrath and for the time being shift the conflict to the backwoods along the Chattahoochee.

Indian Traders as Empire Builders.—Despite his arrest by Cardross, Woodward, by the summer of 1685, had accomplished his mission and

[3] H. E. Bolton, ed., *Arredondo's Historical Proof of Spain's Title to Georgia,* p. 40.

"with a half dozen hardy followers" was among the lower Creeks on the middle course of the Chattahoochee. This, the farthest west that any Carolinian had yet pushed, presented a crisis in the contest for trade and territory. The Spanish commander at Apalachee on the Gulf was soon marching with 250 Spaniards and "Christian" Indians to save Spanish prestige and trade. Woodward withdrew, but he led back to Charles Town from this, his last far western trip, a train of 150 Indians loaded with skins. The Indians preferred the English goods and in resentment against Spain moved from the Chattahoochee to the Ocmulgee in middle Georgia to enjoy uninterrupted trade with the English. "Ocheese Creek Indians," or, for short, "Creek Indians," they were thenceforth called.

Thus Spain found herself deprived in the interior of another broad belt and from now on had to defend Florida itself from the incursions of the Creeks, inspired, they charged, by the South Carolina traders. Protests to the South Carolina government brought from even the Quaker Governor Archdale in 1696 an unyielding assertion of English rights in the disputed territory and a warning of meeting force by force.

The rich Creek trade grew in ten years to large dimensions and remained the chief branch of Indian commerce until the Yemassee War of 1715 destroyed the Carolina-Creek alliance and forced a complete readjustment of Indian relations. The arrival of the traders turned Charles Town into a scene of business and hilarity, in which the shrewd laid the foundation of family fortunes and the thriftless spent their wages on coarse pleasures. The large profits went to the Charles Town merchants with capital sufficient to hire numerous traders and stock numbers of storehouses in the Indian villages. Though men of education, enterprise, and high intelligence were sometimes found among the actual traders, these counterparts of the *coureurs de bois* were of a strain inferior to the merchants. The laxity of morals and general unscrupulousness of the traders and their oppressive dealings, often at the instigation of their employers, despite the regulations that the government early began to attempt, were among the most fruitful causes of Indian discontent.

Great as was the significance of this commerce in the development of the colony, its influence on the Indians was far more profound. It revolutionized the Indians' desires and habits. They began to expend a large part of their energies to get skins or slaves, by hunting or by intertribal wars, with which to obtain the commodities to satisfy a wide range of new desires. The Englishman's pace was too fast for the red man. Under the unprogressive Spaniard he had maintained his old life with a little veneer of mission Christianity, but the more aggressive

English tended to destroy the old Indian life and put nothing in its place.

The French were meanwhile striving to confine the English to the east of the mountains in "a half century of conflict" during which they erected forts from the St. Lawrence to New Orleans and Mobile. It was the activities of the South Carolina Indian traders, backed by the bold and far-sighted merchants who sent them out, that so largely nullified the daring and sacrifices of La Salle, Iberville, Bienville, and Tonti. England, it has been said, created a colonial empire in a fit of absent-mindedness. London officials were absent-minded enough; but the colonists, confronted by the representatives of a government that earlier understood its interests, had their wits about them. It was these far-seeing colonists, as Professor Crane points out, who finally brought the English government to realize the crisis presented by France's policy of "encirclement."

When the French established Mobile in 1702 and New Orleans in 1718, they found that the English from Charles Town had ten years previously forestalled them by establishing a commercial league with the Chickasaws between the Tennessee and Mississippi. As the South Carolina alliance with the Creeks broke the Spanish power in Georgia and eastern Alabama, so that with the Chickasaws restricted the French advance inland from Mobile and New Orleans.

In 1698 Thomas Welch marched from Charles Town through the Creek and Chickasaw countries to the Mississippi and crossed it near the mouth of the Arkansas. In 1700 Governor Blake engaged a *coureur de bois* who, having deserted Tonti, had made his way to Charles Town, to lead a party of traders back over his route, down the Tennessee, Ohio, and Mississippi rivers, "to claim the great river for Britain and divert its trade to Carolina."

The years from 1682 to 1706 were full of domestic turmoil in the settlement around Charles Town. But the small knot of enterprising merchants and politicians had not neglected to attach, so far as commerce and Indian allies could do so, the vast western area which by the Charter was a part of Carolina. Besides the trade alliances described above, they had by 1690 begun the Cherokee trade, which later assumed large proportions. It was trade that carried English sovereignty into the distant interior and confined the French and the Spaniards to a narrow strip along the Gulf or finally pushed them beyond the Mississippi—trade, constantly at its task, unremittingly boring deeper and deeper into the vast region bounded by the Ohio, the Mississippi, and the Gulf long before statesmen realized the significance of the forces that were shaping the destinies of three empires. These alert, active men had done more in twenty years to make good a claim to the interior than Spain had in a century, because she had failed to make the natives dependent on her for goods.

It was the already established position of the South Carolinians, supported and organized by scores of shrewd and daring traders scattered over the whole region westward to the present Mississippi-Alabama line, that enabled England so seriously to break the power of Spain and check that of France in Queen Anne's War, 1702-13. Great bodies of Indians led by small numbers of white men were generally the fighting forces of both sides. James Moore at the head of fifty South Carolinians and many Indians spread desolation among the towns and missions of the Spanish Indians in the area of the Tallahassee of today. Across the formerly prosperous and populous region that lined the road from there to St. Augustine an official Spanish map bears the words, "Wholly laid waste, being destroyed by the Carolinians, 1706." The combined French and Spanish attack on Charles Town in the same year was such a complete failure that a large part of the invading force remained as prisoners, and France trembled for Mobile and sent aid to help save Pensacola. In 1707 a few English at the head of several hundred Indians burned the town of Pensacola. In the same year the South Carolina Assembly voted that it was an "absolute necessity" that the French at Mobile "should be removed." It was with a feeling of disappointment that the South Carolinians saw the war close before they had been able to execute this design.

In 1708 Thomas Nairne, elected South Carolina's first regular Indian agent under the law of 1707 regulating the trade and relations with the savages, far more foresighted than the British ministry, formulated a plan for fortifying the Tennessee River route to the Mississippi. This was ten years before Governor Spotswood's celebrated proposal of a fort on Lake Erie. In 1713 Price Hughes, one of the most brilliant of the early South Carolina explorers, definitely planned a great colony of Welshmen on the Mississippi—the first trans-Appalachian settlement definitely planned, says Professor Crane, by any British subject. But in this he appears to overlook the expedition sent out in 1698 by Coxe, the claimant under the Carolina Charter of 1629, to settle on the Mississippi. The ship, carrying Englishmen and Huguenots, some said to be from the Carolinas, abandoned the Mississippi when falsely told by Bienville that they were on some other river. The murder of Hughes by Indians near the mouth of the Alabama River in 1715 removed an enemy whom the French greatly feared.

CHAPTER VII

POLITICAL TURMOIL—ECONOMIC PROGRESS, 1683-1700

Royal Government Unfriendly to Proprietors.—The thirteen years from the removal of Governor West to the arrival of Governor Archdale in 1695 were filled with turmoil. The friction inseparable from a form of government in which the people habitually suspected their overlords of seeking their private advantage gave rise to heated contests whose tendency was logically toward superseding the Proprietors by a sovereign whose power existed for serving the public good.

The three counties ordered by the Proprietors in 1682, but not yet laid out, were given the following bounds by the directions of 1685: Craven was to extend north along the coast from Seewee River (Awendaw Creek, a tributary of Bull's Bay); Berkeley was to extend from Craven County to Stono River, and Colleton from the Stono to the Combahee. Granville (established a little later) extended from the Combahee to the Savannah. The counties thus laid out were to be used as election districts. Craven, being as yet unsettled, was neglected, or as it acquired inhabitants was supposed to be represented along with Berkeley. Berkeley (containing by far the greatest number of inhabitants) and Colleton were each to elect ten members. But the order for each to elect its own representatives on the same day was disregarded, and all were chosen in Charles Town, where the Indian slave traders, the Proprietors were informed, boasted that they could carry the election and later the Parliament itself with a bowl of punch. They then, the complaint goes on, had laws passed hindering the trade of other persons with the Indians and broke these laws themselves. Elections were by ballot. There is every reason to believe that from the first election held by the immigrants in 1670 there has never been election in South Carolina except by ballot, a method not accorded the people of England until 1872.

The popular party was verging more and more toward opposition to the Proprietors, while a minority of placemen and seekers of special privilege tended to form a Proprietary party, the two being compared by contemporary observers to the country party and the King's party in England. The popular party tended to look beyond the Proprietors to the Royal Charter; for this, although granted to the Proprietors and not to the people, contained passages protecting the people against arbitrary proprietary action.

The Proprietors continually complained that the South Carolinians harbored pirates—a charge often made then against other colonies also. General McCrady explains the unreasonableness of expecting a weak settlement to punish great bands of armed men whom even the royal navy had failed to suppress. The sweeping generalization of Hewat (and of Ramsay following him) is unreliable. Ramsay's improvements of Hewat's description of the debasement of the Charles Town bar, whose leaders the pirates reputedly bought, overlooks, as McCrady shows, that there was not then a practicing lawyer in South Carolina. The practice of licensing privateers during the wars of the period had fostered a sort of legalized piracy. During the brief periods of peace these desperate sea-rovers merely continued to live by the same business. Some of them were honored by the King, and many colonial merchants welcomed their free spending and were glad of their depredations on the Spanish to the southward.

The Proprietors met these charges by an investigation showing that one pirate captain and several of the most guilty of his crew had been hanged in chains at the Charles Town entrance in about 1684, but that barring an Englishman with a French privateer's commission, not then known in Carolina to be illegal, no other pirate seemed to have visited the colony. The colonial Parliament in 1685 and again in 1687 enacted drastic statutes against privateers and pirates. The insistence of the Proprietors upon such a law was stimulated by their desire to allay the royal government's growing hostility to proprietary charters. In 1688 pirates were in Charles Town jail. In her new energy against sea robbers England in 1688 sent Admiral Sir Robert Holmes against those in the West Indies.

Along with James II's determination to force the buccaneers to recognize the authority of the King went his plan to assert the royal authority over the colonies. The Proprietary governments were an offense in excluding the King's direct authority from an important part of his dominions. Pressure on the Proprietaries continued under William III, under whom several were sequestered; but the Lords of Carolina for the time being escaped.

A further aim in James's colonial policy was the enforcement of the acts of navigation and trade. The restored royal government had adopted and extended the legislation of Cromwell's Parliament controlling colonial commerce for the benefit of the mother country. In 1685 arrived in Charles Town the first direct representative of the royal authority, George Muschamp, collector of customs, charged with the duty of collecting all duties due the royal treasury and enforcing the law by seizure and sale of offending goods and ships. Obsequious as were the Proprietors in acknowledging the fullness of the law's authority, quite the contrary were the people and even the Carolina officials. When Muschamp seized a vessel because it was manned by Scots instead of, as the law required, by Englishmen, the Carolina court released the vessel; but Muschamp wrote that, although the evidence was not very clear, "in effect it was declared that, if it had been ever so clear, they would have pleaded the benefit of their charter, pretending that it gives them power to trade with Scotland and Ireland, and likewise that the natives have liberty to transport their own products in ships navigated with Scotchmen; which I am sure is against the law, *which the people believe to be of no force against their charter, which was granted after the act was passed.*"

Before the issue had been pressed to a conclusion, James II had been superseded by William and Mary, and the question, so full of danger to the Charter, was dropped for the time.

Banishing a Governor.—Into the colony's seething discontent the Proprietors now injected two new grievances: changing the terms of land tenure, and appointing a tyrannical governor. In the future, instead of the requirement that lands were to pay as quitrents a penny an acre "or the value thereof," the requirement was to be a penny an acre in money only, with forfeiture for nonpayment. In the face of universal protest they soon abandoned this violation of their promise with the assurance that they had never intended to refuse to accept payment in a fair equivalent of the products of the colony when money was not obtainable.

The new Governor, James Colleton, who arrived in November, 1686, had nothing to recommend him except being the brother of a Proprietor. He disbanded the force about to move against St. Augustine to avenge the destruction of Stuart's Town, intimating that its leaders might have been hanged for their contemplated crime and outraging the colonists' patriotism by apologies for the Spaniards. One act of tyranny after another followed, such as imposing an enormous fine on a minister for a displeasing sermon, until the crowning act of proclaiming martial law. The Governor and the Parliament had almost immediately fallen into a three years' deadlock, in which the latter finally took the position that the Council should no longer have the exclusive right of initiating legislation and that the government was henceforth to be conducted according to the Royal Charter alone. The arrival in 1690 of Seth Sothell, one of the Proprietors, afforded a legal rallying-point which prevented conflicting parties from seeking control by arms.

Sothell had bought Lord Clarendon's share and, from 1683 to 1689, as governor of North Carolina had capped the climax of almost twenty years of confusion worse than that which afflicted South Carolina for a much briefer period. Driven from North Carolina, he arrived in South Carolina at the psychological moment. Backed by his own ambition, his indubitable legal right as a Proprietor, and the urgency of the opponents of Colleton, he claimed the governorship. Colleton refused to yield, and Sothell, at the petition of four or five hundred of the best inhabitants, summoned a Parliament, which banished Colleton and proclaimed Sothell governor.

Among the grievances enumerated by Sothell's Parliament was the continual changing of the Fundamental Constitutions and attempting to force them upon the colony. As a matter of fact, the Fundamental Constitutions never acquired any legal force. A committee of the Council reported on May 7, 1745, that the Proprietors at various times had made five different drafts, none of which was ever passed into law by the consent of the people. The Proprietors might observe or violate them as they pleased in their relations with each other, but of legal force, which by the express provision of the Charter could come only from the consent of the people or their legally elected representatives, they never possessed the slightest semblance.

Perhaps Sothell's banishment from North Carolina had taught him discretion. The wisdom and justice of the legislation passed with his approval illustrate the benefits which a bad man with a statesman's mind can bestow when he is on his good behavior. He set a much-needed example of just treatment of those disliked foreigners the Huguenots by constituting them free subjects; forbade supplying Indians with liquor and firearms; elaborately regulated the Indian trade; required licenses from all retailers of liquor; provided for organization of the militia and the town watch; provided a store of powder; provided for the trying of small cases by justices of the peace; provided for roads and waterways; set rules and rates for pilots; granted a patent for an improved rice-husking machine; guarded against trading with slaves and servants and other commercial abuses; enacted a slave code based on that of Barbados, but more humane.

On November 8, 1691, the Proprietors commissioned Philip Ludwell governor of Carolina, before whom Sothell by their order retired. Sothell is said to have died a few years later in North Carolina.

Introduction of Rice Culture.—It was during this confusion that an industry of enormous future influence was developing—rice culture. All that is known regarding its introduction is that it probably took place in or shortly before 1685. Rice was being raised in such quantities by

1696 that it was named by the legislature as a commodity in which quit-rents might be paid. The first seven months of 1700 saw three hundred tons sent to England and thirty to the West Indies. Increase now became rapid.

Two varieties were raised, the red and the white, so-called from the color of the husk, for the grain of both was white. This supports the tradition that the province had derived seed from Madagascar and from India. Captain John Thurber, a New England sea captain, apparently gave some Madagascar rice before 1685 to Dr. Henry Woodward, for which in response to his petition when apparently he had become a needy old man the captain was rewarded by the South Carolina Assembly. In 1696 the treasurer of the East India Company sent "a money bag full of East India rice" to South Carolina.

Anglicans, Dissenters, and Huguenots.—Although Sothell had given a brief period of peaceful co-operation, the colony was soon again afflicted with "broils and heats." When the Proprietors at one stroke annulled all legislation of Sothell's Parliaments some excellent laws died, for the re-enactment of some of which the province was to wait long. Philip Ludwell, who had followed Sothell as governor in North Carolina, arrived in 1692 to supersede him in South Carolina. Ludwell's commission, however, made him governor of all Carolina, forming thus an incident in the repeated tentative proposal of the Proprietors to fuse their entire domain into one government. But if their directions for one legislature and one governor for the whole should prove impracticable, Ludwell was to appoint a deputy governor for the region north of Cape Fear. None of the proposals for one government materialized, although several of the governors who resided at Charles Town held commissions over all Carolina and appointed deputy governors for Albemarle.

The name South Carolina occurs in a grant in 1685, says Mr. S. C. Hughson, and the name North Carolina, he says, occurs in the Virginia Council proceedings in 1689. The Proprietors used the name South Carolina, e.g., on November 30, 1693. The first use of the name in our laws is in 1696. But for several years after 1700 the Assembly speaks, sometimes in the same act, of legislation for South Carolina or for "the southwest portion of this province." Until the revolution in 1719 the regular form of legal enactment was for the southwest part of the province of Carolina, even after legal forms had been legislatively prescribed using the name South Carolina. The names North and South Carolina had doubtless become common long before they were legally adopted.

The white population was already divided into three elements, whose potential antagonism was increased by the fact that they to a considerable extent occupied distinct localities. Berkeley County (the Charles Town region) was mainly Anglican, while Colleton (southwest of the Stono) was the Dissenters' stronghold. The sparsely settled Craven County (north of Bull's Bay) contained a large proportion of that small, and as yet uninfluential and little assimilated group, the French. The Barbadian-Church of England element was the most aggressive, both in asserting rights against the Proprietors and in seeking privileges or position for itself. Its wealth, though probably not exceeding that of the Dissenters (who comprised many of the richest men of the province, as Axtell and Governors Morton and Smith and Blake), its social and political antecedents, and the colonial experience of its Barbadian element as veteran planters from an aristocratic and successful older colony, all contributed to its aggressive leadership.

The banishment of Governor Colleton forced the Proprietors to recognize that they must conciliate as well as assert their authority. Ludwell was instructed to call a new Assembly with seven members for Berkeley, seven for Colleton, and six for Craven. This offended the two more populous counties, and particularly Berkeley, which contained in 1692 three-fourths of the population and was already resentful that less populous Colleton had been given equality of representation in 1683. "Shall the Frenchmen, who cannot speak our language, make our laws?" asked those who petitioned the Governor to forbid the six Frenchmen from Craven seats in the Assembly (but they were nevertheless allowed to hold their positions).

Grievances Against the Proprietors.—After losing most of the advantage of the general indemnity for acts during the late disturbances by granting it ungraciously under compulsion, the Proprietors were served by the Assembly in 1693 with a long statement of the grievances which were eating away the ground on which popular loyalty must stand. The following protests are significant in the development of American constitutional ideas: against the Proprietors' deputies who assumed the authority to put in force such laws of England as they saw fit, which "we conceive either are in effect by their own force or can be made of force only by the act of the Assembly"; against the inferior courts which took it upon themselves to declare invalid acts of the Assembly or to judge the powers or other matters done by it; against the setting up of martial law, which except in cases of rebellion, tumult, sedition, or invasion, "we conceive is not warranted by the King's charter."

The protest against the courts' annulling colonial laws affords one of the earliest suggestions of the practice of judicial refusal to permit an inferior legislature to contravene the will of the sovereign. The development led, through the acknowledged superior force of charters or the King's instructions to the Governor as the constitution of the colony, to the American theory of the duty of the courts to maintain the State or Federal constitution as supreme, and thus to annul, by refusing to enforce, acts of legislatures or executives which violate that expression of the people's sovereign will. We discuss this and other early South Carolina cases of judicial annulment of statutes in Chapter XLII.

Concessions to Popular Rights.—The Assembly proceeded also to appoint a committee to report a frame of government based on the Charter. "We take notice that there is a committee appointed to draw up what they would have for a system of government for the future . . . ," wrote the Proprietors on April 12, 1693. "Since they have so disrespectfully refused that excellent system we offered in our Constitutions, we have thought it best both for ourselves and them to govern by all the powers granted to us by our letters patent from the Crown." Therefore, they proclaimed on May 11, "the rule and limitations appointed by the said Constitutions for the government are now ceased."

Contrasted with the people's grievances are their steady gains in controlling their affairs. The banishment of Governor Colleton was proof that they would not tolerate extreme abuse of power. Governor Ludwell found it impossible to bring even the most extreme agitators to account. The Proprietors felt obliged to remove all restraint on free trading with the Indians.

Despite the prevalence of "broils and heats," the Governor, Council, and Assembly got together on a number of important laws. One enacted the habeas corpus act for South Carolina, another provided for drawing juries, and another gave the ballot to all men worth ten pounds without any requirement as to length of residence. At the habeas corpus act the Proprietors grumbled. It was, they held, already of effect by its own force, as were the laws of England in general. Lord Mansfield years later ruled that laws passed after the settlement of a colony were not of force there unless the act so indicated, thus endorsing the colonists' position. The law for qualifying voters the Proprietors annulled as it made no requirement as to residence, and so would allow any pirate crew to vote. The jury law they vetoed because it allowed the sheriff to make up jury lists of twelve each, on all of which might be "notorious harborers of *pyrates,*" thus preventing their punishment. Each name must be drawn on a separate slip, they instructed the Governor, as prescribed, with admirable safeguards, in the Fundamental Constitutions. In this the Proprietors, as in their insistence on equality of religious rights, conferred benefits upon South Carolina; for, as we shall see, their insistence on a fair jury law eliminated the abuse of packed juries, which they said, had been practiced in South Carolina.[1]

[1] For terms of the jury law of 1695 see p. 115 below.

Ludwell, unable to secure the co-operation of either the Council or the Commons or to satisfy the Proprietors, resigned and was succeeded in May, 1693, by Landgrave Thomas Smith, chosen by the Council.

The excellent Thomas Smith, a loyal supporter of the Proprietors, was gladly accepted by them and commissioned governor of both Carolinas, with directions to appoint a deputy over the northern colony. He began his administration with the conciliatory announcement that the Proprietors had consented to the Commons' originating laws. He died in office November 16, 1694, after having bequeathed his title of landgrave to Joseph Blake in order to qualify as his successor the man whom he considered best suited for the position. The Council chose Blake until the Proprietors should act. Blake was generally beloved and, as his second administration from 1696 to 1700 was to prove, was of a strong but even temper that served well the situation. His supercession by Archdale was not a reflection, for there was strong reason for the Proprietors' agreeing with Governor Smith's opinion that only a Proprietor could quiet the people.

The chronic state of controversy between Proprietors and people is easily understood when we consider the condition to which the Proprietors had come. By 1694, as General McCrady points out, the shares of the seven deceased Proprietors had with one exception passed by inheritance or sale into the hands of minors or persons of no distinction and generally of no statesmanlike qualities. When Governor Smith urged them to send out one of their own number as the only hope of settling the colony's difficulties only four of them could even be got to a meeting. The experience was typical. This corporation owning an empire of 284,000 square miles never had even an office and of late years had even seen its affairs transacted through the secretary, who carried papers from one to another for signature. The handful of Proprietors who could be got together induced John Archdale to go as governor, "being in the nature of Proprietor" as the guardian of his son, for whom he had bought a share. The Quaker Archdale was a man of character and ability. Shortly after his 1681 purchase he was commissioned to collect rents in North Carolina, where he remained for several years. In South Carolina he accomplished the pacification for which he was selected. The chief criticism to which he appears liable is that he too soon laid down his task; but the fact that he accomplished so much in a year is itself a tribute to his statesmanship, and he must be credited with appointing as his successor Joseph Blake, who for four years, until his death, proved one of the best of the Proprietary governors.

Settling the Land Question.—Archdale's unusual powers included the right to sell lands at half the former prices and to make generous remission of arrears of quitrents. He assumed the government August 17, 1695, and at once conciliated factions. He constructed a Council in which the High Church party, whom he regarded as assertive mischief-makers, were overborne two to one by "Moderate Churchmen," with the moderate Dissenter element represented by Joseph Blake. The fact that he thus balanced parties proves that religious factionalism in politics was already troublesome. Moderation, respect for the rights of all parties, including the misused Huguenots, firmness, and the allaying of prejudices by the gentleness of steady toleration—such was the spirit of his administration.

Considering the majority "obstinate," Archdale dissolved Parliament and ordered a new election. The new Assembly and the Governor produced a series of important and beneficent laws. Let us first dispose of the land question, for that, involving the security of titles and the payment of quitrents, was the key to the situation. The Proprietors had not required the payment of quitrents before 1690, and since they had become due people had fallen into arrears until the total had become burdensome. Archdale's act fixed the quitrent on free grants at one penny an acre. The price of lands sold by the Proprietors was limited to £20 a thousand acres, and quitrents on them to 12 pence per hundred acres. Quitrent on granted land was fixed at a penny an acre. Rents were made payable in indigo, cotton, silk, rice, beef, pork, or peas as appraised by commissioners appointed equally by the Proprietors and the Assembly.

The other act, dealing with rent arrears, reveals that quantities of land were held without any title other than occupancy. Squatters were allowed to abandon these holdings without charge, and if they obtained title to them four years' arrears of rent were remitted. Three years' arrears were remitted to such as held by grant. Holders of baronies were not allowed the above benefits, but all arrears of rent on lands of all descriptions obtained by purchase from the Proprietors before the arrival of Governor Archdale were remitted.

These acts were declared not subject to repeal (i.e., veto) without the consent of the Assembly. Moreover, the last section of the first act sought to correct a general grievance by enacting that no act to which the Proprietors' deputies had assented should be annulled without the Assembly's consent, unless it touched the dignity of prerogatives of the King or concerned the lands, rents, revenues, or charter rights of the Proprietors. Laws on these sacred subjects should continue of force only until the next biennial Assembly unless signed by the Proprietors.

Archdale's Other Legislation.—Archdale's Act, as the land tenure act was called, constituted a sort of Magna Charta for the province. The colonists from that time contended that the Proprietors had no right to veto any act agreed to by their deputies. As a matter of fact the Proprietors never did so veto until their wholesale action of 1718 and 1719 which led directly to their overthrow; but neither did they ever ratify Archdale's law. They merely allowed it to stand.

Sixteen other acts followed. One regulating the slaughtering of unmarked cattle indicates how numerous had become the beeves raised at large for the export of hides and meat. Another shows that the Saint Helena, Coosa, Wimbee, Combahee, Edisto, Stono, Kiawah, Etiwan, Seewee, Santee, and Cusso Indians had become so weak that, in consideration of having supplied and defended them at great expense, the Assembly required every bowman to deliver annually one skin of wolf, tiger (as the South Carolinians called the panther), or bear, or two skins of wildcats, on penalty of a public whipping on the bare back. Severe fines were imposed for supplying these Indians with liquor; and commissioners were empowered to try causes, civil or criminal, short of life or limb, between Indians or Indians and whites. Clearly the tribal organization, though still existing, had lost its vigor for the tribes in immediate contact with the whites.

For preventing "all such vices as are the usual production of drunkenness," all persons were forbidden to sell any liquor in smaller quantities than one gallon without a license. All English laws, statute and common, for regulating taverns and eating and drinking houses were declared of force in the colony.

Another piece of social legislation began South Carolina's public relief of the poor, while others forbade trading with servants and slaves, regulated the latter, and ordered the registration of marriages, births, and burials. Navigation was improved by cutting waterways, and the militia law was improved. Although he ended the petty spites with St. Augustine by forcing his Indians to return captives taken for slaves, and thus secured a generous response in the form of the release of shipwrecked English subjects, Archdale, Quaker though he was, warned the Spanish that meddling with Carolina traders or Indians between the Savannah and the Mississippi would be at the risk of war.

Having, as he considered, "settled the country," Archdale hurried away after a brief healing administration of about a year. He named Landgrave Joseph Blake his successor and left South Carolina shortly before December, 1696, having proved, like Penn, that Christian virtues united with manly firmness are no less beneficent in public than in private life.

With a period of ten years of conflict frequently bordering upon anarchy and involving the very fundamentals of property and government thus happily ended, the Commons thanked Governor Archdale for composing differences and providing for the "peace, welfare, tranquility, plenty, prosperity, and safety of this colony, and the people therein . . . all which we do and forever shall be obliged most heartily and gratefully to acknowledge as the production of the wisdom, discretion, patience and labor of the Honorable John Archdale, Esq."[2]

Governor Blake's administration was liberal internally and aggressive in western expansion. He signed no more creditable law than the Act of 1697 giving "all aliens . . . of what nation soever" the civil rights of native-born Englishmen, and liberty of conscience to all Christians except Papists. Catholics and Jews were unmolested, though not legally tolerated. Not until 1790 was absolute religious equality established. The purpose of the act of 1697 was primarily justice to the Huguenots, for its benefits (except liberty of conscience) were confined to the persons signing the petition for the law and such others as should within three months apply. But these and all others alien born had to wait until 1704 for the right to vote and until 1784 to hold office—the latter a right denied in England until 1844.

An act of 1698 sought to counterbalance the alarming number of Negro slaves by encouraging the immigration of white servants. For three years the colonial government would pay masters of vessels or other non-residents at the rate of £13 for every white male servant from sixteen to forty years of age imported and £12 for boys between twelve and sixteen. The term of indenture which those above sixteen years old should serve must be not less than four years, and for those under sixteen not less than seven years. The law fixed five years as the term for those over sixteen who arrived without a term fixed by contract; which meant that a youth stolen in London could be sold into virtual slavery for not over five years. Constables were required to hand in lists of all planters owning six or more Negro men. One card was to be made out for each planter for each six slaves he owned. Every planter whose name was drawn by lot was required to receive one white servant, paying the public official the sum that he had paid for such servant; but no planter could have additional servants forced on him until all other planters had been drawn for their proper proportion. White servants already held by a planter met his obligation. The same fear of Roman Catholics exhibited in withholding from them religious freedom appears in the clause of this act excluding Irish servants from the benefits of the bounty. This feeble effort to counterbalance the mounting blacks ended in 1701.

[2] *House Journal,* March, 1695-96. The *Statutes at Large,* II, 102, erroneously date the land tenure act March 16, 1694-95, instead of 1695-96. The ridiculous charge of Edward Randolph, notoriously irresponsible sensationalist, March 24, 1701, that Archdale harbored pirates is mentioned merely to show that it is not overlooked.—*Public Records,* 5, 5.

The King Demands Observance of Navigation Laws—Afflictions.— The arrival in 1699 of the King's collector of customs, Edward Randolph, emphasized the fact that the royal government was tightening its grasp on the colonies and was looking toward the extinguishing of the Proprietaries. Randolph poured into the ears of the Lords of Trade sweeping charges of illicit trade and special complaints against the Proprietaries, which, he charged, sought to establish a sort of independence of the King. The Carolinians traded with the Dutch through Curaçoa, welcomed pirates as free spenders, and "have no regard to the acts of trade."

The Proprietors of the various colonies denied the charges, but had to submit to the introduction of royal Admiralty Courts. So unpopular were these measures that the South Carolina Commons in 1700 and 1701 attempted to impose laws intimidating the customs officers, and popular displeasure dogged their lives. Fearing to lose their Charter, the Proprietors exerted themselves to improve their government. In 1698, they commissioned Nicholas Trott as attorney-general[3] and Edmund Bohun chief justice. Quite vexatious proved dual government under officers some of whom were responsible to the Proprietors and some to the King, mutually jealous and accusatory.

Collector of Customs Randolph wrote March 16, 1699, that the people of South Carolina were "greatly alarmed" at the reported intention of the French to settle along the Mississippi lest they attack the province from the rear. But the attitude of Governor Blake was not that of fear. To an emissary from St. Augustine in 1698 he pointed out Pensacola Bay on a large map. "When Romo exclaimed that it was within the Spanish jurisdiction, Blake replied that he expected to occupy it next year for England!" Blake was one of the leading Indian traders and so realized the value of the West commercially and was one of the earliest Americans to appreciate the vital necessity of England's meeting the French and Spaniards with English expansion. His death on September 7, 1700, prevented his participation in the South Carolina push to the west and southwest during Queen Anne's war; but he was succeeded by James Moore, a leader who fully shared these views and was ready to guide South Carolina in her role as England's southwestern frontier.

From 1697 to 1699, smallpox raged with fearful mortality. On February 24, 1698, fire destroyed about a third of Charles Town. A plague swept away many cattle, and an earthquake added its terror. In August, 1699, the province suffered its first visitation of yellow fever. By Novem-

[3]General McCrady, I, 436, 297, 387, etc., confuses Nicholas Trott of South Carolina with Nicholas Trott, his cousin, governor of the Bahamas, whose reputation as a pirate harborer, etc., was very evil, and thus unjustly magnifies the faults of the by no means faultless South Carolina Trott.

ber 1 it had killed at least one hundred and sixty people in town; but the ten or eleven who died after having gone into the country did not spread it there, which seems to prove that the fever-bearing mosquito had not spread from the port. In the fall of 1699 a hurricane, driving the sea into the town, forced the people to flee to the upper stories. Though few were drowned on shore, the calamity added to the gloom of a tragedy near the harbor. A vessel bearing refugees from the ill-fated Scotch colony at Darien was destroyed near the bar with the loss of almost every person on board. This was one of the seven ships bearing away the inhabitants of the abandoned colony, only one of which ever reached Scotland. The day before, the Congregational Church had requested Rev. Archibald Stobo to preach in town. He with his wife and several others thus escaped the destruction which overtook their companions and gave the province one of its earliest and strongest Presbyterian ministers.

The few thousand people founding a state faced this accumulation of losses, as their letters show, with the dumb heroism of our common humanity. They stuck to the field that they had chosen.

CHAPTER VIII

BEGINNINGS OF THE CHURCHES AND THE COMING OF THE HUGUENOTS, 1682-1697

ALTHOUGH BOTH the King and the Proprietors planned that the Anglican should be the established church in the province without denying full freedom in the exercise of all other forms of Protestantism, no church was built for some years. The common interests of the settlers and remoteness from English religious antagonisms suspended sectarianism among the struggling wilderness dwellers. Governor Sayle, a Dissenter, requested the sending of an Episcopal clergyman whose ministrations in Bermuda had been medicine to his soul. The Dissenter wife of the Dissenter Governor Blake contributed liberally almost twenty years later to the Episcopal Church in Charles Town; and during the first thirty years of the colony the governors for eighteen years were Dissenters. None of these circumstances would have been possible without a far friendlier feeling between Churchmen and Dissenters than existed in England. The renewed attack on the Dissenters in England about 1700 roused sleeping religious animosities in the South Carolinians. The peace established in England by the Toleration Act of 1689 was threatened by the deliberate campaign in which Lord Granville was a leader to destroy Dissent in one generation; and Lord Granville was Palatine of Carolina. The heat of the renewed conflict was soon reflected in the colony. The able and aggressive leaders of the Episcopal party, backed by powerful influence in England, put an end to the early golden age of Dissent in South Carolina through a combination of good works and evil.

The fact that Thomas Ash, who came out in 1680 "and returned this present year, 1682," says that "they have reserved places for building a church," fixes its erection at least as late as 1682. St. Philip's Church was in all probability the oldest organized church in the province and the first to erect a building. It stood on the site now occupied by St. Michael's and was built of black cypress on a brick foundation. A law of March 1, 1711, directed the building of a brick church on the site of the present St. Philip's. Not until 1751 was the city divided into two parishes, St. Philip's lying north and St. Michael's south of Broad Street. An early Episcopal house of worship outside of Charles Town was

Pompion Hill Chapel, built on the Cooper in 1703. Rev. William Corbin worked in the most wealthy and populous neighborhood outside of Charles Town, i.e., Goose Creek, for about three years (1700-03) and left a few communicants to his successor, Rev. Samuel Thomas, who arrived at Christmas, 1702, and served the community for about a year. Thomas was the third missionary, and their first to South Carolina, to be sent out by the Society for the Propagation of the Gospel in Foreign Parts, an organization of earnest Churchmen who ultimately covered the empire with their labors and made South Carolina one of their special fields until they deemed, in 1766, that its wealth precluded the propriety of missionaries. The first Anglican Church at Goose Creek, begun before 1704, was succeeded by the present brick structure dedicated in 1719, the oldest church building in the State.

Although the Anglican Church was not until 1704 formally established by law (and more formally organized in 1706), it was in 1698 marked as virtually the official church by an Act of Assembly reciting the King's and the Proprietors' forbidding the public support of any church except that established by law in England, and naming Samuel Marshall as pastor of St. Philip's for life, fixing on him and his successors forever an annual salary of £150. When Mr. Marshall died the next year the Governor and Council asked the Society for the Propagation of the Gospel to send out a successor, as they never did on vacancies in any of the dissenting pulpits. This law was passed while Blake, a Dissenter, was governor and the Dissenters were apparently a majority of the inhabitants.

The Presbyterians, the other largely represented denomination in the early decades, seem to have organized a little later than the Anglicans. The first minister of their faith in the province was apparently William Dunlop in 1684, who later became principal of the University of Glasgow. The Presbyterian Rev. Thomas Barrett was in South Carolina briefly about the same time. The circumstances of Rev. Archibald Stobo's becoming minister to the Charles Town Presbyterians in 1699 have been related. He long remained a tower of strength to his denomination.

It is unreasonable to suppose that the numerous and earnest Presbyterians delayed unnecessarily their organization, which their historians hold was between 1680 and 1690; but the loss of records in the 1713 storm renders it impossible to fix the date.

This first Dissenter church, later known from its shape as the Circular Church, was at first for all non-Anglican Protestants. Its members consisted of Independents, Congregationalists, Presbyterians, and a few Huguenots. Its popular names were almost as numerous as its constituencies. From its being called "the New England meeting," "the white meeting," as well as the Independent, the Congregational, the Presbyterian, or the Independent Congregational, came the name of Meeting Street, on which the present building still stands. Its present corporate name, the Independent, or Congregational, Church of Charleston, was given after the Revolution. It became a mother of churches as its various elements separated to their more distinctive organizations, as did the Presbyterians in 1732.

A noteworthy incident was the founding of the Congregational Church at Dorchester, South Carolina, in 1696 by a group from Dorchester, Massachusetts. The ruins of their brick building still remain, though the congregation, finding the region sickly, migrated in 1754 to Midway, Georgia.

Traditions originating long after the event of the founding of the first Baptist Church in South Carolina in the middle or early 1680's are untenable. There were Baptists of wealth and prominence in the province earlier, such as Lady Blake and Lady Axtell and the Elliotts; but the organization of the Charles Town congregation seems to have resulted in 1697 or 1698 from the arrival of Rev. William Screven. Screven was a strong personality who had suffered imprisonment in Maine for denouncing infant baptism as an ordinance of the devil. Records in Maine show Screven there until January, 1696, and the first record of him in South Carolina is in December, 1696. Screven and his New England followers first founded a church at "Somerton" somewhere on Cooper River. He founded the town of Georgetown in 1729.

Quakers were evidently in South Carolina as early as 1675. The seventeenth century in Carolina, says Weeks, was to the Quakers a golden age, free from molestation and restraint. The date of their first organization is not known, but shortly after 1713 the meeting house was closed.

A notable characteristic of all the early South Carolina churches was their strongly congregational tendency. Even the Episcopalians insisted on virtual congregational self-government, extending in practice to the choice of a minister. When the Methodists came later they experienced in Charleston a spasm of the same spirit of congregational independence, and even the Roman Catholics of that city were at one time so self-assertive as violently to oppose their bishop. This intense ecclesiastical individualism was undoubtedly due in large measure to the strong Presbyterian and Baptist influences operating under frontier conditions favorable to individualism.

Having only briefly noticed in chronological order the first coming of the Huguenots, we may now trace their history, which falls naturally here on account of its strong element of religion. By faith and system of church government they were Presbyterians, and numbers of them joined that denomination in South Carolina. The Anglicans, wrote a South Carolinian, apparently Thomas Nairne, in 1710, were four and a quarter in ten of the population; the Presbyterians, including those French who retained their separate organization, four and a half in ten; the Baptists one in ten, and the Quakers one-fourth in ten. In this estimate the Congregationalists and Independents are counted Presbyterians. But it must also be noted that the bulk of the Huguenots had by 1710 joined the Church of England; and hence it appears that about 1700 the Dissenters must have comprised an appreciable majority of the population, as several contemporary authorities among both elements state. The Anglican clergyman, Marston, represented them in 1706 as over two-thirds of the population; but circumstances forbid us to believe that they were such a large majority.

At the time of the act of 1706 organizing the Anglican as the state church, there were, therefore, in the province two Episcopal houses of worship besides the work being conducted at Goose Creek, five Huguenot churches, one mixed Presbyterian and Independent, one Congregational (Dorchester), one Baptist, and one Quaker meeting house.

The Huguenots, to Their Enfranchisement, 1680-97.—Like the Dissenters from England and the Baptists from Maine, the Huguenots were attracted to South Carolina by her policy of religious freedom. The cruelty of the Established Church in the years following the Restoration disfigured English history with a degree of religious persecution not equalled there since the days of the Tudors. The Stuart restoration brought upon the Dissenters far severer sufferings than they, under the Commonwealth, had inflicted upon the Anglicans. In Scotland the jails were crowded with Presbyterians, and numbers were put to death. John Bunyan's lying in jail for twelve years for being a Baptist preacher was typical of the treatment of nonconformists in England. Various motives combined for these persecutions. The execution of the King and of Archbishop Laud, though on political charges, horrified the Anglicans and inflamed their desire for revenge for the expulsion of their clergy. Since the Commonwealthians were almost all Separatists (or, as they were later called, Dissenters), dissent was looked upon as synonymous with disloyalty.

But in France the zeal of Roman Catholic orthodoxy went much further. Children were snatched from parents, property was confiscated, tens of thousands were driven into exile, and hundreds were put to death. These cruelties began some years before the revocation in 1685 of the Edict of Nantes, in violation of its guarantee of religious freedom and equality in civil and political rights; but with the revocation Catholic intolerance, private vengeance, and public and personal greed for the wealth of the Huguenots loosed a perfect storm of persecution. To be caught in flight from France was to incur the penalty of death. Confiscation and execution continued even to the middle of the eighteenth century. The Huguenots thus occupy a position of distinction in South Carolina history as the group who had endured the most for their faith.

The first forty-five Huguenots arrived from England early in 1680. The immigration naturally increased under the severer persecution following 1685; but our information as to dates and numbers is slight. A considerable portion of a fleeing group of six hundred, says Professor Hirsch, came to South Carolina in 1687. These were chiefly artisans and laborers to whom even their tools were given in England.

The total Huguenot migration to South Carolina was small. Peter Girard wrote on March 14, 1699, that there were then one hundred and ninety-five French Protestants of their church in Charles Town, thirty-one of their church at Goose Creek, one hundred and one on the Eastern Branch of Cooper River, and one hundred and eleven of their Santee River church, making a total of four hundred and thirty-eight. Small groups continued to drift in, but no more considerable body came until those participating in the founding of Purrysburg in 1732, and no other large company arrived after that until the party founding New Bordeaux in 1764. Two small additions to this settlement in 1767 and 1772 were the last French immigrants to South Carolina before the Revolution. In addition to the main stream from England, some came, generally after 1700, from New York, Pennsylvania, and Virginia, which colonies (as also New Jersey) received considerable numbers of Huguenots. A report of 1713 estimates them as one-sixth of the population, and a petition of one hundred and twenty-three Charlestonians in 1723 estimates them as one-fifth of the population of the town. As other migration increased the proportion of the Huguenots greatly declined.

The motives of the King and the Proprietors in encouraging Huguenot migration were largely mercenary. They pictured the wealth to be expected from the development of silk, wine, and olive oil in Carolina, for all of which England was anxious to be free from dependence upon France. These expectations were disappointed. Although silk was raised sporadically for almost a century, and olive trees and the grape flourished, other crops returned profits so much larger that these remained trivial in amount and generally the diversion of wealthy fanciers.

The Huguenots have exercised an influence beyond their proportional numbers, and thus their numerical strength has been overestimated.

Their influence has been due to their moral and intellectual fibre. Although they were thus an exceptional strain of the French nation and an exceptionally valuable addition to ours, the idea that they were all of the upper classes is groundless. Several who settled in South Carolina were of the lower nobility, but generally their aristocracy was that of worth rather than blood. A list of sixty-three persons, all Huguenots except four Jews, signing a petition in 1697 contains twelve planters, twelve weavers, eleven merchants, four shipwrights, three coopers, three smiths, two goldsmiths, two gunsmiths, two joiners, two shammy dressers, one apothecary, one blockmaker, one brazier, one doctor, one gardener, one saddler, one sailmaker, one silk throwster, one watch maker, one wheelwright—a significant predominance of skilled craftsmen. A Huguenot name is almost unknown among the recipients of public charity, despite the desperate poverty in which many arrived. This was in part due to their warm-heartedness in relieving distress among their own numbers. Lawson described them as bound together as one great family. Some, however, circumvented the French penalty of confiscation of estates for heresy and succeeded in bringing away money or other valuables which enabled them to set up at once as considerable land and slave owners in their new home.

Even the utterly ruined, who were forced to live while in England on charity, were soon self-sustaining in South Carolina. But their trials were sometimes agonizing. Wives toiled beside their husbands, wielding hoe and ax and whipsaw, reducing forest and field to the uses of civilization and laying the foundation of future fortune or independence. Judith, the mother of Gabriel Manigault, one of the wealthiest of colonial South Carolina merchants, relates the perils and trials in flight from France and a nine months' broken voyage from England to South Carolina, and the suffering here: "I have been for six months together without tasting bread, working the ground like a slave; and I have even passed three and four years without always having it when I wanted it."

Some of the Huguenots remained in Charles Town or obtained lands in the already settled parts of the province. Grants to Huguenots on Goose Creek, one of the choice sections, occur quite early. Others settled the almost uninhabited region between the Cooper and the Wando, part of which long retained the name of the French Quarter, or Orange Quarter, or pressed as far north as the Santee River forty miles from Charles Town.

The settlement along the southern bank of the Santee contained the largest number of French outside of Charles Town. Settled as early as 1685, it contained in 1706 one hundred French families and sixty English families.

The Huguenots established six churches in South Carolina. The oldest, that in Charles Town, the only one still existing, accepts 1687 as the date of its origin; but the loss of its records renders certainty impossible. The French at Purrysburg joined the Episcopal establishment at once without organizing a Huguenot church.

After a few decades the Huguenots generally fully assimilated by intermarriage, business relations, etc., with the English; but some obscurity surrounds the question of their early readiness to become a normal part of the community. Their love for France impelled many for years to long to return when persecution should cease or to settle in some French colony. Aliens intending to enjoy the advantages of a country only to depart later for a better-loved land are everywhere disliked. When to this was added the existing animosity of Englishmen for Frenchmen, the harshness of the Carolinians to the newcomers is easily understood. And yet as early as 1691 Sothell's Parliament enfranchised the French, an act which was annulled by the Proprietors along with all his laws.

The Presbyterians, who constituted almost the whole body of Dissenters then in South Carolina, naturally expected these French Presbyterians to join them or at least to throw their influence to the Dissenter element. But there were shrewd Anglican politicians and proselyters who saw that these French had inherited no hostility toward the Anglican establishment. The French realized the advantage of joining the official church of the country that had given them land and freedom and could not overlook the advantage of freedom from the double burden of supporting their own clergy and also contributing through the taxes to the support of the Anglicans. All their six churches joined the establishment except one, which still exists. The Anglicans' absorption of the great body of the Huguenots rendered secure their supremacy in the province.[1]

[1] Dr. Hirsch, in his *Huguenots of Colonial South Carolina,* represents that from the first the hostility to the Huguenots was on the part of the Dissenters. He seems to transfer to this early period of natural friendship among all Dissenters the undoubted hostility which the Dissenters a decade later felt in their disappointment in failing to annex the Huguenots. Dr. Hirsch's confusion at places is hopeless. He speaks (p. 117) utterly without authority of the Dissenters driving Governor Smith to resign, whereas Smith was the leading Dissenter of the province and died in office in 1694. Again Dr. Hirsch charges the Dissenters in the Council in 1695 with aiming a petition against the Huguenots, whereas Moore, the head and front of the aggressive anti-Dissenter party, not to speak of others, signed the paper. He even charges that "The sacredness and validity of their marriages, the sufficiency of their ministry, and the legitimacy of their children were all challenged by the Dissenter party, because the Huguenots were not naturalized" (p. 117). Apart from the fact that his citation is incorrect, and that the challenge of these things was because their ministers were not ordained by bishops, and therefore could not legally perform the marriage service (Rivers, 438, and not, as he cites, an entirely different topic, 455), let us consider the ludicrousness of French Presbyterian marriages being challenged as illegitimate by English Presbyterians and Baptists, who were then bitterly

The naturalization act of March, 1697, was an important measure of peace and justice and facilitated the tendency of the great body of the French to assimilate themselves with the general population. A few families to this day remain predominantly French, and occasionally an individual is found of perfect French type.

The Huguenot took his place in every department of the province's life, though until well into the eighteenth century he was not conspicuous in politics. By the skill of his agriculture, the deftness of his hand, his reverence for family solidarity, the large success of his business, the soundness of his public views, the integrity of his character as the sifted grain of our immigration, he added one of the most beneficent elements of our life. Though occasionally reminded during the first generation of being merely a tolerated Frenchman, he conquered narrowness and prejudice by native worth, discretion, and forbearance.

---

opposing all bishops as contrary to Scripture. But the Anglican Dr. Le Jau of St. James, Goose Creek, was actually in 1715 and 1716 marrying persons over again who had been married by dissenting ministers on the ground that these were no marriages. It might also be remembered that, in the 1690's when Dr. Hirsch represents the English Presbyterians as persecuting their fellow French Presbyterians, the latter enjoyed representation in the Assembly until their county of Craven was united with the Episcopalian-dominated Berkeley, by which their representation at once almost totally ceased. Until the Huguenots finally decided about 1700 to throw in their lot with the Anglicans, I perceive no hostility to them by any Dissenter party. Dr. Hirsch inserts the word Dissenter without a shred of evidence in the account of English hostility to the French, as, e.g., p. 117. Dr. Hirsch's emphasis on the conflicts of Dissenter and anti-Dissenter parties before 1700 is itself misleading, as this became prominent later.

CHAPTER IX

CHURCHMEN VERSUS DISSENTERS, 1692-1706

Antecedents of Religious Strife.—It is hard to avoid reading into earlier events a phase of religious controversy because of our knowledge of contemporaneous animosities in England, and of what they became in South Carolina early in the eighteenth century. At one extreme is Dr. Hirsch saying that "the undertone of that struggle [between Dissenters and Churchmen] is heard in nearly every important political issue for twenty years" before 1700. At the other is Professor Rivers, who says that "the tranquil administration of Blake (1696-1700) had been succeeded by a period of disturbance and by the domination of a faction, the first that rose to power in the province that truly deserves the name"; and, further, "I find no evidence that religious differences had yet [in 1700] entered into the politics of the colony." General McCrady speaks of the religious factionalism of England existing in the colony from the first, but offers little proof of it before the conflict following 1700.

It seems to me that the religious antagonisms brought from England were obscured and mollified in the first thirty years of the colony by common difficulties and by common grievances against the Proprietors. The fact that for over ten years there was no organized congregation submerged religious issues. We find the Dissenter Governor Sayle requesting that an Episcopal minister by whose preaching he had been edified in Bermuda be sent to Carolina, and other early leaders urging the need of ministers without denominational discrimination. If religious factionalism had been running strongly before 1700, it is hardly conceivable that the Proprietors would have allowed Dissenters to act as governors for eighteen out of thirty years, or that a jealous Anglican faction in the colony would have failed to fill their correspondence with sectarian complaints, as both factions did so plentifully from 1703. If there had been decided sectarian politics before 1700, the Dissenters would not have been found in 1698 joining in voting a salary to the generally beloved Episcopal minister of St. Philip's; nor Dissenter Lady Blake contributing liberally to decorate the building; nor the various Dissenter governors, and especially Blake from 1696 to 1700, treating the Anglican church and people with such liberality. Governor Archdale testified that "religious differences did not yet peculiarly distinguish the parties" until the bigoted High Churchman Governor Nathaniel Johnson (1703-9) by his "chimical wit" turned the political quarrel into a religious one.

And yet there is evidence of religious factionalism as early as 1692, when certain English were persecuting the Huguenots with the bugaboo of having their children considered illegitimate and their land forfeited because they had not been married by ministers with Episcopal ordination—a mean deception, for English law specifically validated such marriages. Further, Archdale himself indicated the existence of religious factionalism before his own coming in 1695 when he later boasted that he "did not wholly exclude the High-Church party but mixed two Moderate Churchmen to one High Churchman in the Council, whereby the balance of government was preserved peaceable and quiet." With these he also "mixed" Blake, "in some measure a Dissenter." Nor did he, while laying the principal blame on the High Churchmen, acquit the Dissenters of "many unjustifiable words and actions."

A series of events beginning in 1700 greatly inflamed factional spirit. On the death of Governor Blake, September 7, 1700, the Council (by three to two, Morton not voting) elected as governor from among the landgraves present Joseph Morton, son of the deceased Governor and a moderate Dissenter. James Moore (not then a landgrave, but eligible if no landgrave was available), an ambitious and aggressive High Churchman, objected on the ground that Morton's royal commission as admiralty judge was a breach of trust to the Proprietors. He had his way and was himself elected on September 11. But if the Council had known, says Rivers, of Moore's double-dealing in attempting to secure from the Crown to the Proprietors' disadvantage the profits of supposed silver mines, they would have paid small attention to his objection to Morton as having broken faith by accepting a commission from the King, whom all were obligated to serve. Though refusing to confirm Moore, they allowed him to hold office temporarily.

The supercession of Morton by Moore was the preface, though not to the extent represented by Oldmixon the cause, of the bitter fight that soon followed between the Anglicans and the Dissenters. The immediate issue, aside from Moore's desire for office and its perquisites, seems to have been popular opposition to the enforcement of the acts on navigation and trade; for Morton's own bitter resentment of his displacement makes no allusion to religion, but emphasizes the desire to evade the trade laws by preventing the election of a governor who would block such lawlessness.

Mixing Religion and Politics.—Two days after his election Governor Moore and Council dissolved the Commons, but their successors proved equally tenacious of rights by which they could force conciliar surrender.

Governor Moore censured their lack of zeal for the public defense in view of the approaching war with Spain, and also their failure to agree with the Council on regulations for the Indian trade. His enemies on the other hand accused him of seeking to mend his desperate fortunes by engrossing the profits of that trade through his official position and keeping up the trade in Indian slaves after every other colony had abandoned it. That Moore was an Indian slave trader is true; but apparently his critics exaggerated his opposition to general regulation. The fact that he died, in 1706, indebted to the Proprietors for the revenue collected as their receiver-general, points to his bad finances.

Religious antagonism entered the 1701 election to an extent exceeding anything previous, partly as a reflection of renewed persecution in England, where mobs raged and bills were introduced to exclude Dissenters from office. Every circumstance united to irritate and alarm the Dissenters: Moore the High Churchman pushing the leading Dissenter Morton out of his election for governor on the pretext of his holding a royal commission, and reluctance to see the office, which had for seven years been held by Dissenters, pass into hands from which their faction feared that they could not expect the generous treatment that the Anglicans had received from them. Fair dealing toward the Churchmen was a necessity for the Dissenters, but no such necessity imposed tolerance on the Churchmen.

General McCrady points out that at this time a number of new leaders of ability and aggressiveness, all High Churchmen, came into public life. We shall see that the Dissenters at the same time failed to produce new leaders of the wisdom, strength, and public spirit of the men who, like West, Blake, and Landgrave Smith, had given them distinction in the past. Captain James Moore, Colonel Sir Nathaniel Johnson, Colonel Robert Daniel, Captain William Rhett, and Chief Justice Nicholas Trott just now turning his great abilities to the High Church party, were more notable for their political High Churchmanship than for their piety; but they were bold, strong leaders, and several of them unscrupulous as to means.

The Dissenters charged that in the November, 1701, election in Charles Town strangers, indentured servants, paupers, and free Negroes voted, besides "very many unqualified aliens," by whom they meant among others those Huguenots who had neglected to register in three months as required for enfranchisement under the act of 1697, a negligence remedied under the law of 1704. The Commons in 1702 voted that Catholics if registered could vote, a ruling which I have not found reversed during the colonial period. The persons summoned for illegal voting were by no means all French. Forty-six out of eighty-three summoned May 14, 1702, had British or Irish names, and one Dutch.

Attack on St. Augustine.—Since the Queen had declared war against France and Spain, Governor Moore urged the taking of St. Augustine and the expulsion of the French from the Gulf Coast. War already virtually existed. The South Carolina traders, dominating the Indians in the present Tennessee, Georgia, and Alabama, had raided the Spanish Indians with Creeks around the later Tallahassee and in May, 1702, desolated the Santa Fe mission sixty miles west of St. Augustine. Spain's attempted revenge in the summer of 1702 (not yet known in Carolina) led to a terrible defeat on the lower Flint at the hands of the Creeks led by the South Carolina traders. Governor Moore's offense in repeating Colonel Robert Daniel's threat of martial law was forgotten in an enthusiastic request that he lead the army instead of Daniel, whose removal from the Council they urged for having induced the Governor to profane "that sacred word law" by joining it with "martial." Were not the fate of Charles I and James II, they asked, sufficient warning against "presuming to be so absolute"? But Daniel's known efficiency led them to ask for him as second in command.

Moore sailed in September for St. Augustine while Daniel ascended the St. John's to attack the town from the rear. When two Spanish men-of-war appeared, Moore burned the town, the churches and his ships, and left his ammunition and supplies to the enemy. Despite the failure to take the fort, the English were gainers; for, as Professor Bolton says, "the Spanish frontier fell back another step" from the St. Mary's to the St. John's. The debt incurred by the expedition led in 1703 to South Carolina's first issue of paper money, beginning a derangement of the currency that lasted for eighty years.

Factional Quarrels and Alien Rights.—In February, 1703, the Dissenter John Ash introduced in the Commons a bill regulating elections and "granting as much freedom to the French and other aliens as could be granted by the Assembly, or the French reasonably expect." The Commons, holding that the exceptions which the Council desired would leave the privileges of the aliens too uncertain, asked for a conference, which the Council refused; but it could not have been because the Dissenter's measure sought to exclude the French from the Assembly as some writers have surmised, for the act of November, 1704, passed with the Anglicans in full control, while granting aliens of three months' residence and the regular property qualifications the right to vote, excluded all aliens born from being elected. Governor Sir Nathaniel Johnson, having discovered private letters of Landgrave Smith criticizing his faction, and having secured an act excluding Dissenters from the Assembly, submitted the letters to the Commons, who, following his suggestion, put the writer under arrest, as the Governor said, "to deter all other persons for the future."

A few days later began four or five days of rioting in which (not to specify violence to lesser persons) the Dissenter leaders John Ash, Landgrave Thomas Smith, Justice Landgrave Edmund Bellinger, and Joseph Boone were beaten or threatened, while Governor Moore looked on approvingly. Officials would take no notice of the demands for prosecuting the rioters, and, as Professor Rivers remarks, "no doubt enjoyed the joke, when the Attorney-General would not prosecute himself, and the Chief Justice said it was none of his business, . . . and the new Governor declared that 'it happened before his time.' "

Representing, as some modern writers do, the Churchmen as a class favoring war and the Dissenters as a class opposing it, so simplifies as to misrepresent a complicated situation. Colleton County, the Dissenter stronghold, may have been less hot for war because it remembered from 1686 how open it was to Spanish attack. Thomas Nairne, settled on St. Helena Island as early as 1698, and an eminent Dissenter leader, demanded, as long as he lived, the expulsion of the Spanish and French from the West and Southwest, while his friend and neighbor, John Barnwell, was devoted to the same policies, and, though a Churchman, so firmly defended the rights of the Dissenters in 1704 as to incur expulsion from office.

The election of 1703 again witnessed violence and alleged illegal voting. The newly elected Assembly, like its predecessor, was closely balanced between parties, and like it persisted in the determination to conquer Florida; but ere Governor Moore could arrange a second attack he was superseded by Sir Nathaniel Johnson, well qualified by his military training for meeting his war-time duties and by his aggressive personality and ardent High-Churchmanship for pushing, in South Carolina, the attack upon the Dissenters that had recently been renewed in England.[1]

Attacking Florida from the Rear.—The judgment of Governor Johnson as an experienced soldier prompted him to insist on improving the Charles Town defenses instead of raiding against St. Augustine. But Colonel Moore, burning to redeem his failure of 1702, was allowed to strike a blow in the rear of St. Augustine, the expense to be borne by himself in hope of reimbursement through Indian slaves and plunder. Marching west to the colony's Creek allies on the Ocmulgee, he gathered fifty white men and a thousand savages, with whom he swept south-

[1] My account of these factional quarrels, quite similar to that of Professor Rivers, differs widely from the accounts by General McCrady (*South Carolina under the Proprietary Government*, 386 *passim*) and by Mr. A. S. Salley (*Narratives of Early Carolina*, 272 n.). For my discussion, see my *History of South Carolina*, I, 166-7.

ward upon the Apalachees, allies of Spain living around Apalachee Bay and northward beyond Tallahassee of today, in January, 1704. The region, dotted with Spanish missions, was utterly ruined at the cost to the Carolinians of but three white lives. Moore carried away, besides Indians as slaves, 1,390 Apalachees, whom he settled on the Savannah below Augusta, where they remained until they took revenge in 1715.

Spain's hold on the whole Southeast had received a staggering blow, and her hope of retaining the interior of Georgia and Alabama vanished. Even Pensacola was in danger. Some of the feeble remnants of the natives abandoned their cultivated fields for safety around San Marcos on the Gulf, while most of the remaining Apalachees deserted a power that could not protect them and sought shelter with the French at Mobile, although some later returned to Florida. English supremacy from the Atlantic to the Mississippi was for eleven years unquestioned.

Dissenters Excluded from Legislature.—With the governorship and the Council now in the control of the "somewhat bigoted Johnson," ably seconded by the "astute" and "unprincipled" Chief Justice Trott, as General McCrady too softly describes the former and rather too harshly the latter, a plan was secretly formed for expelling from the legislature all persons not members of the Anglican Church and establishing it by law as the state religion supported at public expense.

As the Dissenters were either a majority of the population, as was constantly asserted at the time on both sides, or at all events almost a majority, and the Anglicans comprised a large proportion of fair-minded men who would defend the rights of their fellow-subjects, it was impossible to overcome the Dissenters without such tactics as the recent rioting or the parliamentary trickery presently to be described. The Assembly due to meet May 10, 1704, was summoned by the Governor for April 26. On May 4 a bill to exclude from future Assemblies all but persons communing in the Church of England was rushed through. Twelve voted for the act, eleven against, among the latter being a number of Anglicans. The presence of twenty-three out of thirty members, extraordinary so early in a session unless for some special reason, favors Professor Rivers' supposition that word had been secretly passed to those who could be relied on to support the conspiracy. A clause was added for the benefit of irreligious Anglicans permitting such to sit if they merely swore that they had not in a year communed with Dissenters. Many of the Assembly passing the act were constant absentees from church, and eleven of them had not taken communion in Rev. Marston's five years at St. Philip's. The law further provided that after all Dissenters voted for had been eliminated, the Anglican receiving the most votes (which might be a single ballot) should be declared elected.

Foremost among those denouncing the exclusion act was Rev. Edward Marston of St. Philip's. The Assembly's demand for his notes was met by assertions Sunday after Sunday of his independence of any authority but the Bishop of London. After an unseemly dispute carried on by sermons, Assembly resolutions, etc., he was deprived of his salary and escaped arrest at the hands of the tyrannical legislators only out of respect for his profession.

The act excluding Dissenters from the Assembly was both better and worse than it appears upon its face if we are to believe Governor Johnson's later statement as sober truth and not merely justification by way of afterthought, for the Governor, as we shall see, was not above lying for a good end. There was no intention, he stated, permanently to exclude the Dissenters from the government, but only to get rid of them until an Assembly had firmly established the Anglican Church. Trott, however, writing on September 15, 1707, said: "The reason why we passed the Act to exclude them from being chosen of the Assembly [was] because they never did any good there nor never will do any." When the Assembly met in the fall it proceeded to adopt an elaborate act for the establishment and support of the Church of England. This law was soon superseded by that of 1706.

The Dissenters sent Joseph Boone to England, on whose representation the Whig House of Lords and the attorney-general condemned the exclusion act and the church act. The attorney-general and the solicitor-general reported that such an abuse of power had forfeited the charter. The Queen ordered the Proprietors to declare both acts void. Legal difficulties caused the move for annulling the Charter to be dropped.

The Church Act of 1706.—Meanwhile, in 1706, the only election ever held under the act excluding Dissenters occurred. The Assembly, after threatening to disqualify for life their critic Landgrave Smith, and having arrested Dr. Charles Burnham, a Low-Church member, for asking the Commons whether they were a legal house, repealed the laws of 1704 and passed a more carefully drawn church act. This divided the colony into ten parishes. Funds were appropriated for churches, etc. The rector of St. Philip's was to receive £150 a year and the others £50 for three years, and afterward £100. Fees in some instances doubled this, not to speak of the use of the glebe.

The members of the Church of England who were freeholders or taxpayers in each parish were to choose the minister, vestrymen, and wardens. Lay officers were henceforth forbidden to perform the marriage ceremony. A register was to be kept of the marriages, births, christenings, and burials of all white persons within the parish. Repairs and parochial charges were to be assessed on all inhabitants of the parish.

The Bishop of London, whose jurisdiction included the colonies, sent his first South Carolina commissary in 1708. The parishes, with others later constituted, continued until 1865 to be the civil subdivisions of the low country for public purposes, not including judicial, for which when circuit courts were later organized they were too small. In 1716 they were made the basis of representation in the Commons House of Assembly. This provision was vetoed in 1718, but was re-enacted in 1721.

Anglican violence in securing the exclusion and church acts of 1704 was answered by Dissenter defiance, accentuated by a bitter contest for the appointment of the public receiver (i.e., the colonial treasurer), in which the Dissenter party now in control of the Commons won the important and lasting victory for their house of choosing that officer. Riots and political clubs sought the removal of Chief Justice Trott as "an unfit man for any public office." Trott's reputation, in my opinion, has suffered unjustly from historians' narrating these proceedings without sufficiently emphasizing their partisan character. We know that Trott was grossly partisan, unscrupulous in controversy, and self-seeking; but there is no evidence that he was corrupt. Governor Johnson's replies to the attacks on Trott, completely out-arguing the Commons, bear the marks of that skilled lawyer arguing his own case and not the slightest resemblance to the known compositions of the Governor.

To the riots and the club of 170 enemies of Trott were added two wonders—a woman's political club and a witch. Says Dr. Francis Le Jau, July 3, 1707: "I must observe that the last sedition was begun while the Judge was examining evidences relating to the accused witch that is still in our prison. It don't belong to me to judge, but she said she will come off and that she had many friends here. It is a dismal sight to perceive how powerful the spirit of the Devil contrary to that of Christ is here."

Dr. Le Jau's letter explains what has heretofore been a mystery—Judge Trott's charge to the grand jury on witchcraft, March 20, 1706. Evidently Trott's elaborate charge was aimed at this woman who apparently remained in jail over fifteen months. Trott was not singular in his views, for many eminent men all over Europe still approved persecuting and sometimes killing peculiar old women. The New England fanatics who hanged a score of men and women in 1691-92 were merely carrying on the holy work then largely practiced in the Old World. South Carolina in 1712 enacted for herself the English laws punishing witches with death, though there is no reason to suppose she ever came nearer to trying a witch than the attempt by Trott. In 1792 witches were supposed to abound in Fairfield, and in 1813 or 1814 a South Carolina judge silenced a girl who was testifying to an old woman's coming through her keyhole, riding her from town to town, etc. Astonishing evidences of belief in witchcraft exist in a manuscript from York County, e.g., in about 1790.

The church act of 1706 is one of the most important in the history of the province. Leaving aside the question of the benefit and harm in the long run from an established church, the Episcopal element, constituting practically half of the population, at once received a degree and quality of spiritual ministration which it would otherwise for a long time not have experienced. They were less earnest religiously than the Presbyterians, Huguenots, and Baptists, many of whom had come to the colony because of the stern determination to maintain their religion. The public funds and the assistance from the Society for the Propagation of the Gospel in Foreign Parts stirred them from the lethargy which had permitted them to remain with far fewer churches than their rivals. And as to the evils inseparable from a union of church and state, it must be remembered that the Anglicans merely did what the Independents of New England had done and the Presbyterians of South Carolina, following the example of the Presbyterians in Scotland, would doubtless have done if they had had the power.

There were at this time only three Episcopal churches in the province —St. Philip's in Charles Town, Pompion Hill Chapel, and Goose Creek. The eight or nine Dissenting churches were now put upon their mettle to meet the competition of a growing number of active and educated Episcopal clergy. To the good fortune of the colony, the Society for the Propagation of the Gospel, organized in 1701 by an element in the English Church notably humane and deeply religious, took South Carolina under its special care, by means of which some of the evils of a politically supported church were minimized.

CHAPTER X

POLITICS AND INDIAN AFFAIRS DURING QUEEN ANNE'S WAR, 1702-1713

THE PART PLAYED by South Carolina in Queen Anne's War has already been described down to the year 1706. The boldness of Moore's thrust into the heart of Spain's possessions around Apalachee Bay in January, 1704, alarmed the French for Mobile and convinced both Latin powers that it was time to execute Bienville's plan of 1702 for crushing Carolina. An expedition of five French privateers, reinforced by Spanish troops from Havana and St. Augustine, appeared before Charles Town on August 24, 1706. In the absence of Governor Johnson at his plantation, Silk Hope on the Cooper, Colonel William Rhett skillfully posted the militia.

The fact that Charles Town was suffering from yellow fever encouraged the French commander to think that the country militia would be afraid to come to the defense of the town, but in this he was mistaken. When the invaders observed the recently strengthened fortifications, they lay by and sent in a demand for surrender in one hour, to which Governor Johnson replied he did not need one minute to refuse. Colonel William Rhett with a fire ship and six small vessels drove the enemy from the harbor on the thirty-first. Meanwhile landing parties of the invaders had been defeated with severe losses north and south of Charles Town. A few days later two hundred Frenchmen entered Seewee Bay and were all killed or captured. The Carolinians, with the loss of one man, had inflicted heavy fatalities upon the invaders and were embarrassed with the care of some two hundred and thirty prisoners.

Echoes of Religious Factionalism.—On the appearance of the enemy, Public Receiver George Logan, the Governor's political enemy, advanced £468 *7s. 1d.*, of his personal funds on the personal pledge of Governor Johnson for its repayment, a pledge the Assembly promptly redeemed. The doughty old soldier, after briefly narrating to the Commons controlled by his political opponents his account of repelling the invaders as merely a part of the day's work and lecturing them on leaving his hands tied financially, continued: "Having given this account of our public enemies, I suppose I need not tell you of our domestic foes who are still busy with their false and malicious complaints against us by their agent Mr. Boone in England." He then launched into a discourse on the church act, the Dissenters, and their defender Rev. Marston (the minister of St. Philip's) far outbulking anything else in his speech; for "our" domestic foes (as though the Dissenters were not a part of the community) were very much on his heart. So dangerous did he consider them to religion and morals that he was moved in the election of 1707 to do a little evil that good might come. Having dissolved the Assembly, he ordered Peter Mailhett, a French political climber, to write to several of his fellow-Huguenots urging them to vote, "for the Governor was obliged to dissolve the last Assembly because they were going to take away our privileges not only of voting but also in inheriting, and the gentlemen Presbyterians would bring a tyranny upon us as Pharaoh did upon the Children of Israel, and that you may come to my house and find the true list of those you should vote for, and in so doing you will not only oblige me, but also the Governor and the rest of the French." To Bonneau he wrote that the Presbyterians would "put you slaves," and urged that his letter be read in church, as what could be more fitting, since the Governor's efforts were for the preservation of religion against those by whose influence otherwise "we should turn heathens ourselves."

Despite these efforts to save the state from "our domestic enemies" the Governor was forced to face as the undisputed leaders of the Assembly the same old foes of his conception of the public good, including George Logan, who had advanced his own money to repel the French and Spaniards, and Landgrave Thomas Smith himself, whom he had had the Commons of 1704 arrest for a private letter more than a year old criticizing a bill, and Thomas Nairne, for personal vengeance on whom he a little later sacrificed the public interest atrociously.

But making the best of it he opened the Assembly with the words, "Notwithstanding former discouragements, and though I see several of the same faces here, I am yet willing to hope for a sincere and hearty concurrence with me in . . . adjusting our common interest, laying aside particular piques or private grudges, very unreasonable to be remembered at this juncture." The Commons replied that such things were improper not only at this, but at all times, between Christians, who are under the highest obligation to promote peace and union. They followed the Governor's ideal by declining to molest Rev. Marston, as he requested in the next breath, for an insulting letter to him, but they spent a little time establishing, through the testimony of some good Huguenots and Thomas Lynch, that Mailhett had sent them such letters as quoted above, and through the testimony of the poor worm himself that he had done it by the order of Governor Johnson. The Governor, following his recommendation to let bygones be bygones, neglected to prosecute Mailhett as requested by the Commons, whose unanimous declaration of the falsity of the letter he silently accepted, which merely showed that a good soldier can take defeat as calmly as victory. But he could strike, through keeping silence. John Barnwell, the friend and fellow-expansionist with Nairne against French and Spanish encirclement and a defender of the Dissenter rights, though himself an Anglican, was ejected from his office of messenger for the Council.

To Remove France from the Gulf.—The Assembly's passes with the Governor in no wise lessened the attention of these "our domestic foes" to defense against "our public enemies." The Commons voted the men to expel the French from Mobile as an "absolute necessity," and elected Captain Nairne as commander. The Indian allies were organized under white officers. Bienville's warning to Pensacola did not prevent a party of Talapoosas led by a few English in August, 1707, from burning the town and actually entering the fort before they were driven off, and in December they again beseiged it.

Nairne, possessed of the boldest imagination of any of the group leading South Carolina's westward expansion, proposed to fall upon the French with a force of 1,500 Indians, to destroy or force into alliance with South Carolina all the French tribes, to dominate the entire country along the Mississippi up to latitude 36, and to divert to Charles Town by the Tennessee the whole trade that had been going down the Mississippi. He even included a settlement west of the Mississippi, with visions of striking ultimately at the Spanish mines in Mexico.

In the spring of 1708 Nairne established peace with the Choctaws—old friends of the French—in west middle Mississippi (as we now call it), while Thomas Welch organized the tribes along the lower Mississippi. Bienville might have been overwhelmed; but rumors of a second naval attack being planned against Charles Town checked for the time the plans against Mobile. Immediately there followed a miscarriage growing out of the factional politics of the colony. Nairne was hated by Governor Johnson as one of the most active leaders against the church act and as favoring measures taking from the Governor and Council any part in appointing the receiver of public dues or any part in controlling the Indian trade. He was hated by Colonel Broughton, the Governor's son-in-law, for having as Indian agent interfered with his enslaving of friendly Indians. In 1706 the Assembly set free a body of unlawfully enslaved Indians and requested the Governor to prosecute the responsible offender, who in offering them for sale was said to have represented half of them as being on the Governor's account; but the governor did not disturb the transaction. Nairne was charged with telling the Indians that they should look to him now as agent of South Carolina, and that the Governor was a foolish old man; and he was blamed for sending his map of the West to the Queen's secretary of state without showing it to the provincial government. Though that bore small resemblance to treason, he was thrown into prison June 23, 1708, by Governor Johnson on a charge of seeking to dethrone Queen Anne in favor of the Pretender. As bail was not allowed in charges of high treason, Nairne lay in jail for five months. He was of course never tried, but it is not improbable, as Professor Crane surmises, that his complaints to the Proprietors, dispatched from his prison along with his glowing plans for conquering the West, may have helped to remove the Governor.

Regulating the Indian Trade.—Everyone recognized that the ambitious plans against Pensacola and Mobile could be realized only through holding the loyalty of the western Indians. The regulation of the Indian traders was therefore a pressing necessity. The men who came into actual contact with the savages were often of low character. Some married squaws and obtained a strong, permanent influence in the tribe, but others debauched the women, cheated the men, and intrigued them into burdensome debt.

But who should control the trade, and to whom should go its perquisites? The chiefs and "beloved men" not only received presents, through which largely their loyalty was held, but they made presents in return, customarily of half the value. These had gone to the Governor and amounted to more than his salary. Even the Assembly of the Governor's friends elected under the law of 1704 insisted on his surrendering these presents despite his pleas that his services in the late invasion were "sufficient to excite their gratitude and liberality." The "penurious" £200 that they offered in place of the presents he spurned. Defying the law by which he and they had so recently prolonged the life of the existing Assembly to prevent any reaction against the church act, Governor Johnson, determined to preserve his profits, dissolved the Assembly—an ungracious act of displeasure. For the Assembly, after having reluctantly declined to excuse him from paying his delinquent taxes, at last yielded to his begging and ordered that he be excused for all arrears.

The Governor's position in thus clinging to an ancient abuse was in his case particularly indefensible. His son-in-law was an Indian merchant interested in the official influence which liberal presents might secure. Aside from the reports that the Governor was privately interested in the profits of his son-in-law's business and that his refusal to punish grave abuses was due to similar motives, he should not have been in a situation to afford countenance to such suspicions. How generally his course was condemned is attested by the election of an Assembly overwhelmingly against him.

When the new Assembly insisted on the same plans as their predecessors, the Governor yielded, though gaining a concession for his financial benefit. The act of 1707 substituted for the Governor's perquisites in presents, which in future were to go to the public, a flat gift of £400 and an annual stipend of £100. As his own removal was only a year away, the Governor's refusal to accept the former offer of £200 a year netted him £300 to the permanent cost of his successors. "That a free province should be forced to purchase their deliverance from abuses" the Assembly denounced to the Proprietors as "a corruption almost beyond example." Johnson had the additional mortification of seeing his political and personal enemy, Thomas Nairne, elected Indian agent.

The Supremacy of the Commons.—Several acts of the new Assembly besides its settlement of the Indian trade illustrate the dominant position it was coming to occupy in the government. Important among these was the Commons' determination to make good their claim to dictating the choice of the public receiver (i.e., treasurer of the province) on the ground of their right to control everything relating to their taxes.[1] The contest ended with the Commons winning the right to elect not only the treasurer, but also every other official to whom they paid a fixed salary. When the Governor signified his approval of their man, they replied they were not concerned whether he approved or not, and proceeded to appoint his three archenemies, Nairne, Smith, and Logan to draw up their grievances for the Queen—one more blow in undermining the authority of the Proprietors by appealing beyond them to a power that was seeking a pretext for their abolition.

The Governor was thus beaten at almost every point and was about to experience in addition removal from office. His course in excluding the Dissenters from the Assembly, his securing church establishment by a trick, and his denominating half the population as "internal enemies" had caused them to attack him in England. Joseph Boone, who with Berresford had been sent to England to present the grievances of the Dissenters, had not only succeeded in defeating the discriminatory laws, but was also clearly largely responsible for the removal of the Governor.

The old Governor, weary and weak of body, stubborn, courageous, grasping, bigoted, and equally ready to meet "our public enemies" or our "domestic foes" with open blow or underhanded trick, was saved from ending his administration in a snuff when the new election re-

[1] General McCrady, I, 456 ff., confuses the office of public receiver and that of receiver general, the latter being an appointee of the Proprietors for collecting their revenues. When merely the word "receiver" was used (perfectly clear then), the context generally made clear which was meant.

turned an Assembly controlled by his friends. Boone, as a Proprietor's deputy, refused to obey the Commons' summons to sustain his charges. The house thereupon presented the Governor an affectionate testimonial of his paternal care, brave defense, and faithful administration of the province, and particularly of "your earnest desire to settle the Church of England as now by law established," thus revealing in their ardor the crucial point of the whole matter.

The Tuscarora War.—Governor Johnson's successor, Colonel Edward Tynte, died after a seven months' administration, and the three Proprietors' deputies in the colony proceeded to choose a governor. At the morning session Robert Gibbes and Thomas Broughton each voted for himself. Turbeville voted for Broughton, but in the afternoon changed his vote to Gibbes, who was thus declared elected. But when Turbeville was found to have been bribed by Gibbes, a battle between the town militia and Broughton's armed supporters was barely averted by persuading Broughton to recognize Gibbes and await the decision of the Proprietors. The latter declared Gibbes's election illegal because of bribery. He was allowed to continue in office for practically a year and made an excellent governor.

Under Gibbes occurred the first campaign against the Tuscaroras, who, offended by prospecting for a proposed Swiss settlement around the later Newbern, massacred over two hundred persons on September 22, 1711. South Carolina instantly responded to the appeal with money and men. Colonel John Barnwell was dispatched with a small body of white men and four hundred and ninety-five Indians, many of whom deserted before the battle.

Though defeated by Barnwell, the Tuscaroras soon renewed the war. A second and larger South Carolina expedition was led by Colonel James Moore, son of the now deceased Governor. In March, 1713, the Tuscaroras were so severely crushed that they fled and finally joined their Iroquoian kinsmen in New York, thus converting the confederacy of the Five Nations into the Six Nations. A few remained South.

South Carolina had never given up the purpose of expelling the French from Mobile. She was sadly disappointed when the Peace of Utrecht in 1713 ended the war before she could strike, and was still more disappointed that her urging the exclusion of France from the lower Mississippi region went unheeded. Well might John Barnwell congratulate Governor Craven on the "honor and glory of virtuous South Carolina, whose armies are the same winter gathering laurels from Cape Florida and from the Bay of Spirita Sancta, even to the borders of Virginia."

CHAPTER XI

ASPECTS OF CULTURE AND LAW, 1698-1736

SOUTH CAROLINA entered after Queen Anne's War the most prosperous years of the Proprietary period. Governor Charles Craven, who assumed office early in 1712, was a natural leader of noble and generous character. Commanding respect without arrogance, he was firm without harshness, devout without sanctimony or intolerance, and brave without violence. His influence went far to close the long era of religious contention and political factionalism that had vexed the relations of Governor and Assembly since 1700. The Commons maintained the position of importance they had won, but they now carried their privileges with a respecful moderation that constituted an acknowledgment of Governor Craven's dignity and strength.

Governor Craven was distinctly a man of business. Instead of the long controversial messages between the two houses, we have communications brief and to the point, sometimes consisting of a single sentence. The first year of his administration is one of the most fruitful of important legislation in our history. In this his talent for facilitating business played a large part.

Schools and Libraries.—Private tutors are found as early as 1694. Before 1696 Richard Morgan left part of his estate in trust for a free school. The Rev. Mr. Thomas opened a school at Goose Creek in 1704. Boone brought two Dissenting ministers and a Scotch Presbyterian schoolmaster from Britain in 1703. The law of 1712 promised for each parish £12 to help build a school and £10 a year for any master opening a school, provided he was approved by the vestry.

The "free school" act of 1710 was ignored by the more elaborate act of 1712. The purpose was in part to provide care for educational legacies already made. The term "free school" meant that the master should teach at public expense a few pupils while collecting fees from others. The master had to be able to teach Latin and Greek and be of the Church of England. In 1712, apparently only in St. James Goose Creek was there a school of the approved religion outside of Charles Town.

Irrespective of the number of schools in the early period, there was a high degree of educated intelligence in the province, as public and private papers prove, both by their excellent composition and sound sense, and frequently by their beautiful hands. The Court of Ordinary (i.e., probate) records in Charles Town from 1672 to 1692 are said to show only nine per cent of the signers making their marks, which is the more remarkable as the existing custom of deferring wills until near death necessitated some men's making marks of whose handwriting examples exist. The Commons clerk in 1703 or '04 amused himself by scribbling Latin on blank pages. The excessive illiteracy found at a later day was due to population's pressing into remote or isolated regions away from the cultural agencies brought from England.

Benjamin Dennis, Schoolmaster for Goose Creek, in 1712, was teaching twenty-seven whites, two Indians, and one Negro. The Anglican Dr. Francis Le Jau and his wife tried unsuccessfully to run a boarding school there. That this rich parish depended on ministers or occasional teachers is proved by Rev. Richard Ludlam's reporting in 1727, after being there four years, that it contained no school foundation. The children were taught at home or in private schools. Dennis's one Negro and Morritt's "ten charity scholars, two of which are malatas," reveals an easy-going association of the races that experience later modified.

The will of James Childs probated in 1720 gives land in the projected "town" of Childsbury for a school of writing and accounting, to which persons who helped build the ferry and causeway might send their children free. The £500 sterling value in 1739 was mainly additions by others to the original bequest.

In 1715 Richard Berresford left the whole of his large estate for founding a free school in St. Thomas parish under vestry supervision in case his son should not reach maturity, and a considerable sum in that event. His bequest nevertheless, despite the vicissitudes of time, still yields a small income. Numbers of small legacies and a few of one or two thousand pounds currency are found, while that of the pious and learned Anglican clergyman, Rev. Richard Ludham (1728), was officially reported in 1759 as then equaling £2,076 sterling. In 1723 the Rev. Mr. Morritt was teaching the free school in Charles Town with an advertised curriculum similar to that of an English classical school. His strongest competitor was a master in the country, with fifteen boarding pupils that had been intended for him, who had neither license from the Bishop of London nor toleration from the Governor, who had not kept his promise to silence him. Morritt had forty-five boys next year and was expecting to reach sixty by Christmas. He complains of a few pretending pedagogues scattered about the country and finds it difficult to compete with the utilitarian courses of some newcomers in town.

Libraries.—In 1697 Dr. Thomas Bray began in Maryland his founding of Anglican parochial libraries, which grew to thirty-nine in North America and about eighty in England and Wales. His foundation in

Charles Town followed in 1698. The Assembly at once enlarged this "public library," and the Proprietors made a generous contribution. This appropriation by the Assembly is the earliest known instance in the present United States of a governmental contribution for such a purpose.[1]

In 1701 and '02 Dr. Bray sent additional books for the parochial library, and also another collection for a layman's library. The collection must have been considerable, for the balance due in 1698 on the part purchased by the Assembly would approximate $900 today. By 1724 the library appears to have virtually disappeared through "embezzlement" or mere carelessness, as every inhabitant had the right to borrow the books. There are references in the same document to "the provincial library" and the "laymen's library," referring, I surmise, to the two parts of one public collection.

Libraries were given to several parishes by the Society for the Propagation of the Gospel and by Governor Francis Nicholson. An example of private libraries was that of Rev. Richard Ludlam, who left at his death in 1728 about two hundred and fifty volumes, in which some history and general literature was mixed with English and Latin theological works.

Industrial Interests and an Agent.—In December, 1712, the Assembly created an office which continued to be one of importance during the colonial period, namely that of agent in London to solicit the interests of the province with Parliament, Proprietors, or ministers. The immediate purpose was to help the trade in naval stores and rice. The agent was directed first to do all he could to obtain a continuation of the bounty on pitch, tar, turpentine, and other naval stores sent from the colonies to Great Britain, and then if possible to secure the removal of rice from the list of "enumerated" articles that could be shipped only to Great Britain. The modification in 1724 of the bounty on pitch and tar, dating from January 1, 1706, greatly injured the province. It was not until 1730 that the ministry persuaded Parliament to grant the privilege of sending rice direct to any port south of Cape Finisterre. The leading exports for the year ending June 6, 1713, were 73,790 deerskins, 75 Indian slaves, 12,677 barrels of rice, 4,580 barrels of pitch, 2,037 barrels of tar, 661 barrels of turpentine, 1,965 sides of leather, and 1,963 barrels of beef.

English Laws Made of Force, 1712.—The year 1712 saw the most notable legislation in our legal history, that stating the English laws which should be of force in South Carolina. The code thus enacted consists of 167 acts of Parliament or parts of acts selected from English statutes from 1225 to 1700. Besides the above, which the act contains in

[1] There is no evidence that the library in the Boston Town House as early as 1675 received public aid.—Mr. Austin B. Keep, quoting Mr. Charles Knowles Bolton.

full, it declares in force also (1) the acts of Parliament from 1710 to December 12, 1712; (2) all acts for allegiance to the British Crown, and those for the protection of the liberty of the subject; (3) all laws on the King's customs and trade and navigation; and (4) the English common law except as modified by English or South Carolina statutes. All other English statutes "are hereby declared impracticable in this province." For a complete statement of English law in force in South Carolina from that day to the present we have only to add: (1) Acts of Parliament specifically mentioning the colonies; (2) a few British acts subsequently adopted by the colonial Assembly; and (3) a number of English statutes which the highest court in South Carolina, after the Revolution, in construing the intention of the Act of 1712, declared to be of force in South Carolina.

The act of 1712 assumed a high degree of autonomy for the province. The right of Parliament to legislate for the colonies in any case whatever was not questioned. The rule finally adopted by the English courts was that laws existing when a colony was settled became of force so far as applicable, but later statutes only if they mentioned the colonies.

Trott was probably the editor and also largely the inspirer and maker of the code, possessed as he was of the highest legal learning and ability in the province and delighting in scholarly work. He had already systematized the statutes of the province for his own use. To add to that a compilation of English statutes applicable here would lay a double pedestal for him as the South Carolina Justinian.

Trott's Compilation of the Provincial Statutes, 1736.—Up to this time the South Carolina statutes had not been printed. The laws had been kept carefully guarded in duplicate books, one set for the use of each house. The right of anyone to make copies was guaranteed. Judges and justices of the peace were supplied with copies of special statutes. Trott's systematic, annotated, indexed compilation, comprising the statutes of the colonial Assembly from the foundation of the province, was also adopted, on December 12, 1712. This was declared the official statement of the law and was ordered to be sent away for printing. The fifteen years of confusion that soon descended upon the province postponed printing until 1736, when the work was done in Charles Town by Peter Timothy with an excellence worthy of a London publisher. This, the "First Part," containing the permanent laws through May, 1734, was ready December, 1736. The "Second Part," containing the temporary laws, was apparently finished in 1737, and certainly by 1738. It covers the years 1694 to 1723 inclusive. From at least 1734 after each Assembly or sometimes every few years Timothy's shop in Charles Town printed booklets of the laws currently passed. When the American Revolution disarranged the channels of life, the province had recently ordered the long-needed service of providing a systematic collection and perhaps codification of the laws to date. The achievement of both tasks, postponed until after the Revolution, will be traced in due course.

Trott's great legal works by no means fully measure his contributions to culture. In 1719 he issued at Oxford *Clavis Linguae Sanctae* in fifty-one pages, and in 1721 *The Laws of the British Plantations in America, Relating the Church and the Clergy, Religion and Learning.* On February 17, 1703, he wrote the Archbishop of Canterbury of a work he was preparing on the Hebrew text of the Bible. In 1728 he was still working on this, which he would rather do than anything else in the world, but he could not afford to come to England merely on the willingness of several bishops to do what they could toward its publication. January 28, 1723, he wrote regarding "my specimen on the Hebrew text of the Bible" which an author at the University of Franeker had desired to insert in a work he was preparing.

CHAPTER XII

THE YEMASSEE WAR, 1715-1717

THE HAPPY period of Governor Craven's administration was succeeded by one of tragedy followed by prolonged depression; but the Governor met the crisis of war as splendidly as he had led in the constructive work of peace.

The Indians (as far west as the Mississippi) supposed to owe allegiance to South Carolina in 1715 numbered 26,731, of whom 9,004 (plus the probable 18 or 20 among the 57 Seewees) were men.[1] The Yemassees were a Muskhogean tribe who in the 1680's moved from the Georgia coast to South Carolina and finally located on Coosawhatchie Island and the mainland between the Combahee and Savannah rivers.

The cause of the Yemassee War may be summarily stated as Indian resentment of long-standing abuses by traders, followed by settlers' taking up Yemassee lands. The Carolinians were fully aware for years before this of the danger of wars of revenge on account of traders' abuses. The submission of the Indians to wrong, such as cheating, beatings, seduction of their women, burden bearing, etc., when they felt helpless was as marked as their "insolence" when they felt in a position to be feared. An abuse against which there were frequent warnings, and sometimes prohibitions, was the persuading or permitting of Indians to run in debt to the traders. Heavy debts either made the Indians indifferent, drove them to flight, or inflamed them to wiping out their debts in blood. Estimates of the burdens that the Indians in 1715 planned thus to throw off are wild: £10,000 sterling; £50,000 sterling; 100,000 deerskins. A weighty cause with the Yemassees, though hardly with the more distant tribes, was encroachments on their lands.

The common assertion of South Carolina historians that the St. Augustine Spaniards instigated the rising has never been proved. That the Spanish were delighted and that the Governor of St. Augustine extended the Indians aid for years after the war is certain. Neither have we proof of instigation by the French. The Creeks were accused by some of being the originators of the conspiracy, but the following from trader Samuel Sleigh's journal disproves this, which was in itself improbable: At a great council of the chiefs and head warriors of the

[1] See accompanying table, from a contemporary chart; original spelling.

INDIANS OWING ALLEGIANCE TO SOUTH CAROLINA IN 1715

Distance from Charles Town in Miles	Name of Tribe	No. of Villages	Men	Women	Boys	Girls	Total No. of Souls
90 S.W.	1—Yamasees	10	413	345	234	228	1,220
130 S.W.	2—Apalatchicolas	2	64	71	42	37	214
140 W.	3—Apalachees	4	275	248	65	555	643
150 Westerly	4—Savanos	3	67	116	20	30	233
180 W.N.W.	5—Euchees	2	130	270	*	*	400
250 W. & by N.	6—Ocheeses or Creeks	10	731	837	417	421	2,406
440 W.	7—Abikaws	15	502	578	366	327	1,773
390 W.S.W.	8—Talliboosees	13	636	710	511	486	2,343
430 S.W. by W.	9—Alabamas	4	214	276	161	119	770
		..	3,032	3,451	1,816	1,703	10,002
	Cherokees (viz.)						
450 N.W.	10—Upper Settlement	19	900	980	400	480	
390 N.W.	11—Middle Settlement	30	2,500	2,000†	950	900	11,530 (10–12)
320 N.W.	12—Lower Settlement	11	600	620	400	480	
640 N.W.	13—Chickesaws	6	700	1,200	*	*	1,900
200 N.N.W.	14—Catapaws	7	570	900	*	*	1,470
170 N.	15—Sarows	1	140	370	*	*	510
100 N.E.	16—Waccomassus	4	210	400	*	*	610
200 N.E.	17—Cape Fears	5	76	130	*	*	206
70 N.	18—Santees	2	43	60 (18–19)	*	*	125 (18–19)
120 N.	19—Congarees	1	22				
80 N.	20—Weneaws	1	36	70	*	*	106
60 N.E.	21—Seawees	1	57	‡	‡	‡	57
Mixed with the English Settlement	22—Itwans	1	80	160	*	*	240
	23—Corsaboys	5	95	200	*	*	295
Total							26,731

*Women and Children both included in figures for Women.
†Probably 2,000 women is too small. Men usually fewer, due partly to war.
‡Men, women, and children.

Tallaboosees in the spring of 1726, when Spanish and Yemassees were trying to win over the Creeks, the Tallaboosees burned the Spanish present and likewise the rattle sent by the Yemassees, "and said they would never make peace with them whilst any of them was living; for they was the first founders of the last war, and that if they should be ruled by the Spaniards, they would be brought to nothing in a little time for they was sensible that the Spaniards could not supply them with necessaries or what they wanted, nor was they to be made slaves by them as the Yemassees are."[2]

The Opening Fury.—The conspiracy involved so many Indian nations —fifteen, the Assembly stated—extending from the coast to the middle of the present State of Alabama, that only lack of Indian co-operation saved the whites. Of the numerous tribes over which South Carolina had

[2] "Samuel Sleigh's Journal," in South Carolina Council Journal, April 20, 1726.

exercised sway, with the exception of trivial numbers near the coast only the Cherokees and the Chickasaws remained friendly. The tribes involved were supposed to number 15,000 warriors, but only a fraction of them ever took any further part than to massacre the traders.

A friendly Indian warned of the rising. A delegation sent to promise the Yemassees correction of their grievances, after having been hospitably entertained, were treacherously slain at dawn, April 15, 1715. Governor Craven, on his way to aid in the negotiations, immediately assembled the militia and defeated the Yemassees at the head of the Cumbahee. His messengers to the various tribes brought news that all had slain almost all whites among them, including those sent to solicit aid.

The war thus inaugurated falls into three periods. The first, attempting to overwhelm the colonists with a sudden onslaught, ended with Governor Craven's checking the Yemassees in his campaign concluded June 6. The second extended from the invasion by the northward Indians in early June, 1715, to the decision of the Cherokees to help the English, January 27, 1716. The third dragged its course in vexatious raids until formal peace was declared with the Creeks in November, 1717.

Governor Craven proclaimed martial law, laid an embargo on all vessels, impressed men and property, and appointed a deputy governor to administer during his own absence at the front. The Assembly confirmed his measures and even consented that commanders in the field should have power of death over their men when the Governor submitted letters from officers which "will sufficiently show you how necessary martial law will be amongst our deserting army."

The Second Phase.—The second phase of the war opened with an attack by Indians from the north. Craven marched with seven hundred men across the Santee to meet Colonel Maurice Moore coming from North Carolina and to strike the Cheraws and their neighbors. But the Governor was hardly across the Santee in mid-July when six or seven hundred Indians rushed across the Edisto and wrought havoc to within a few miles of Charles Town, only to retreat to parts unknown as Craven hurried back.

The militia proved so unsatisfactory that the Assembly provided for a "standing army" of 1,200 men to consist of 600 white South Carolinians, 100 Virginians, "400 negroes or other slaves," and 100 free Indians. So weak was the province that 1,400 or 1,500 fighting men was the number regularly spoken of as its available strength. Nervousness at having a body of armed slaves in the province (for there had been a slave conspiracy in 1713) is suggested by the request in February, 1716, that they be disbanded.

The Yemassee War was not a short, sharp, conflict of a few weeks, but as a matter of fact, with its aftermath, was a terrible strain for years. Not only were agents sent to urge aid from the Proprietors and the Crown and to beg the latter to take over the colony, but appeals were sent to North Carolina and Virginia, and agents were sent to purchase arms and ammunition in Virginia, New York, and Boston. Governor Craven praised Governor Robert Hunter of New York and New Jersey, who had sought to rouse the Senecas to aid South Carolina, and Governor Eden of North Carolina, who sent skilled officers and men. Six hundred arms were purchased in Boston; but the attitude of the Massachusetts authorities was "ungenerous." The help from the Virginia Assembly was on hard terms; but Governor Spotswood wrote the Governors of Maryland, Pennsylvania, and New York to watch their Indians and took steps to restrain his own. The British government sent 1,000 muskets, 600 pistols, 2,000 grenades, and 201 barrels of powder, but no soldiers, though one or two warships came from northern stations.

The Proprietors shriveled up under their responsibility and forfeited almost the last remnant of South Carolina attachment. They ordered the arrears in quitrents and quitrents to May 1, 1718, to be given the province, but their feeble efforts to ship munitions failed. The British government urged that they surrender their province which they could not defend; but this they "absolutely refused" unless the King would purchase. The Carolinians struggled against destruction while the politicians 3,000 miles away dickered over the value of their tar and pitch and their usefulness as a spear point for England's thrust to the south and southwest

The Cherokees Join South Carolina.—Vital was the attitude of the Cherokees. They had so far taken little part beyond the murder of a few traders. The nation wavered for months. Maurice Moore with 300 men was sent up the eastern side of the Savannah River into the heart of the Lower Cherokee settlements. The Lower Cherokees were for helping the English, but there were great searchings of heart, especially among the Middle Towns in the Little Tennessee Valley. Creeks lurked in the forest to fall upon the white men as diplomacy strove in the council house. An act of passionate impulse decided the crisis in favor of the Carolinians when, on January 27, 1716, the Creek envoys were suddenly slain and the red stick of war was dispatched through the villages.

The war thus entered upon its third phase. The Lower Creeks, unable to stand before the Cherokee-Carolina combination, withdrew from their homes in central Georgia back to the Chattahoochee. Winning the friendship of the Cherokees, Governor Craven considered winning the war. He sailed April 23, 1716, leaving Colonel Robert Daniel deputy governor. Daniel's skill in the war and his assistance in long-needed legislation won the praise of even the enemies he had made in the factional quarrels of former years. Skulking murders were common into the mid-summer of 1717. For £960 currency Governor Daniel bought for frontier garrisons thirty-two of the Scottish rebels being sold into servitude for the rebellion of 1715 and urged the public to buy more from others soon to arrive.

The Cherokees proved invaluable allies. They brought numerous tribes to make peace and put an end to the supplying of other Indians with arms by the Cheraws, who were actively in trade in Virginia. The ugly business charged against Virginia traders of seeking to engross South Carolina's old Indian trade during her prostration was a feature of the long and bitter rivalry for this lucrative business.

The Cherokees knew their advantage, and "the last time they were here" in Charles Town in January, 1717, "they insulted us to the last degree, and indeed by their demands (with which we were forced to comply) made us their tributaries." The Cherokees had saved the colony, even though at the cost of its humiliation. They had acted shrewdly in their own interest, for the spirit of the whites laid them under no obligation to act otherwise. All Indians were merely pawns in the white man's game of trade and empire.

Peace with the Creeks formally closed the war. The Creek "Emperor" Brims was shrewdly playing his policy of keeping the French, the Spaniards, and the English all suitors for Creek support by keeping on good terms with all but in subjection to none. This very summer of 1717 the French built Fort Toulouse in the heart of the Upper Creek country, and seven Lower Creek chiefs went to Mexico and swore allegiance to Spain. In November, 1717, the last treaty with the Creeks, closing the Yemassee War, was signed in Charles Town; but how precarious a peace it was the next ten years were to show.

Some Incidents and Results of the Yemassee War.—The war left South Carolina impoverished. About four hundred colonists had been slain. St. Helena and St. Bartholomew parishes were desolated. Paper money had deranged every economic relationship and laid the train for more than a decade of enmity between debtors and creditors which finally threatened to break into armed violence.

Virginia's rivalry for the Indian trade was complicated by an ugly dispute over the aid rendered by her during the war. South Carolina considered that the most powerful of the English colonies should have saved her as South Carolina had saved North Carolina in the Tuscarora War. Governor Spotswood was well inclined, but the Burgesses met his pleas with the narrowness of view typically provincial. Spotswood sent about one hundred and thirty men of poor quality. South Carolina was unable to send to Virginia Negro women to take their places as laborers as had been promised, as this threatened to rouse their husbands to rebellion. After mutual recrimination, South Carolina, considering herself unfairly dealt with, flatly refused to make good her contract.

More serious was the charge that Virginia traders were permitted to supply goods and arms to the warring Indians. The South Carolina agents in London asserted that "if the Virginians are allowed to trade in the bounds of South Carolina, we are ruined, for only by holding the Indians in dependence on us for goods can they be kept in control." South Carolina retained the bulk of the trade, but the British government declined to exclude other subjects of the Crown from South Carolina's western grounds. These intercolonial rivalries were never settled until the royal government took over the regulation of the trade in 1756.

The emphasis upon control of the Indian trade as essential to South Carolina's safety was not exaggerated. No truer illustration could be found of pushing of English imperialism into vast barbarous areas by means of creating in the natives the craving for goods that they could obtain only by dependence on the English trader. As the Indian covered his nakedness with the white man's cloth and found his safety against other Indians in possessing the white man's gun, the dependence on the white man superseded his ancient dependence upon himself alone.

One result of the Yemassee War was that South Carolina had to reconstruct her whole Indian system in the face of renewed attempts of Spain to win back her place in the Southwest, and a new and more dangerous interference by France on the Mississippi. South Carolina had previously sought to keep all the Indians under her influence friendly with each other and had encouraged the slave-catching wars only against Indians adhering to France or Spain. But the sudden eruption of practically all her red allies except the Cherokees and the Chickasaws planted the fear that peace among the Indians might afford the opportunity for combination against the white man. After the Yemassee War she pursued the policy of keeping her two greatest nations, the Cherokees and the Creeks, at enmity—a policy which some in closest touch with the savages thought, to the end of the colonial period, was essential to safety. Wrote a South Carolina leader on April 25, 1717, "It is a delicate matter to keep both friendly with us and assist them in cutting one another's throats without offending either. This is the game we intend to play if possible, . . . for if we can not destroy one nation of Indians by another, our country must be lost." The terrible experience of the Yemassee War, which might easily have annihilated South Carolina and spread indefinitely northward, demonstrated the necessity of unified imperial control of Indian relations and Indian trade. It is one of the examples of the sloth of England's colonial administration that this was delayed until 1756.

A station for garrison and trade was founded in 1716 at Congarees five miles below the mouth of the Saluda. Like Savannah Town at the head of navigation of the Savannah, forecasting the later Augusta, Congarees pointed to the later Granby and Columbia, which were to enjoy a similar situation.

Seeking to Get Rid of the Proprietors.—The events of 1715 and '16 helped rouse the British colonial administration to the danger to the whole South Atlantic region from a possible combination of French, Spaniards, and Indians.

For all practical purposes, the Proprietary government might have been ended with the war. The colonists in 1709 had petitioned the Queen to take them under her immediate protection. From the moment the Yemassee War proved that the Proprietors were even a hindrance to their being given protection by the royal government, the colonists never relaxed in determination for their overthrow. Early in 1717 the Carolina agents had their case laid before both houses of Parliament. Emphasis was laid on the colony's importance as a barrier on the south of England's North American possessions and on the quantities of stores that it supplied the navy. Through the whole series of appeals from South Carolina and the consideration of them in England run iterations of the amounts of pitch, tar, timber, etc., that were produced there, on the assumption that no aid was expected unless it was proved that it would pay. Help as a mere matter of humanity and justice is little stressed by either side. Of the ardor to save distressed fellow-countrymen with which we are familiar in our more patriotic age there was hardly mention. How far it was taken for granted we can only guess.

The war was over, but its effects were to operate powerfully through more than a decade of confusion, distress, and conflict.

CHAPTER XIII

THE PIRATES, 1718

Economic Conditions in About 1719.—The growing commerce of South Carolina was a tempting prize for pirates. Governor Johnson estimated in 1719 from muster rolls, etc., 1,600 white men sixteen to sixty years of age and a total white population of 6,400. This is more reliable than the estimate by the Assembly of 2,000 fighting men and a white population of 9,000. Agents Joseph Boone and John Barnwell, on August 23, 1720, give the whites as 9,000 and the blacks as 12,000. The most reliable figure we have is from the tax returns of January, 1722, where the assessors swear to 9,570 slaves between seven and sixty years of age and 1,163,817 acres. This accords fairly with the estimate of 12,000 slaves of all ages.

About sixty ships came annually from England and returned loaded with deerskins, rice, pitch, tar, etc. The English bounty on naval stores greatly benefited South Carolina. In the year 1718 the collector's books showed exports to England of 6,773 barrels of rice of 350 pounds each, 18,414 barrels of pitch, 27,660 barrels of tar, 43 chests of deerskins, and considerable lumber; and to other colonies 2,333 barrels of rice, 4,187 barrels of pitch, 5,677 barrels of tar, besides deerskins, beef, pork, butter, naval stores, lumber, leather, raw hides, corn, and peas. The northern colonies paid in flour, beer, cider, and fish, and the southern in slaves, rum, sugar, molasses, cotton, etc. This trade engaged eighty ships besides the sixty that plied from England. Growing industry absorbed a thousand new Negroes annually. The trade with Great Britain alone amounted to about £160,000 sterling annually. There were only about twenty small vessels owned in South Carolina, some built here and some bought in New England.

Pirates Before 1716.—South Carolina lay between two of the chief pirate haunts—the West Indies and the North Carolina inlets. The naval wars of the period filled the sea with freebooters. The character of the privateers authorized to prey upon enemy commerce is indicated by the common use then of the words privateer and pirate as synonymous. In the New World, where mutual fears and hates continued little abated during the intervals of official peace, the change was easy from the privateer receiving his pay by plundering the enemy in war to the pirate earning his living the same way against former enemies or his fellow-countrymen.

That pirates were often suffered in colonial ports in the early period is not to be denied. Several instances are charged of pirates, either on account of the terror of their guns or because of the lure of their coin, being tolerated in South Carolina; but the charges of Hewat and Edward Randolph are wildly imaginative. Morgan, for example, is said to have been allowed in Charles Town harbor. Charles I knighted Morgan and made him lieutenant-governor of Jamaica. It might seem to the Governor and Council of the frontier province more heinous, as well as more dangerous, to exclude their best defenders against the Spaniards than to admit them. Lord Craven, the Palatine, in 1684 reported that the only undoubted pirate he knew of was hanged in chains with two of his crew at the harbor mouth as a warning. We know of several convictions during the next decade. But such instances, aside from the fact that South Carolina's very existence depended upon the safe transport of her staple products, made her the enemy of sea robbers. Not only is her record in abstention from collusion with pirates among the best, but her achievements for their destruction stand unrivaled.

The reign of James II saw more earnest efforts for the suppression of piracy. Sir Robert Holmes was sent with a small fleet to suppress the sea robbers of the West Indian and adjacent waters. In 1687 South Carolina enacted a more elaborate law. Still later, Governor Blake wrote, June 20, 1700, that eight pirates would be hanged on the twelfth. Nothing but such examples, he said, would end the evil. Would not the King send a frigate here to protect Carolina and the Bahamas, for a ship couldn't stir for them in this part of the world?

The Pest of Pirates, 1716-18.—A sudden pest of pirates resulted from throwing seamen out of employment by the cessation in 1713 and '14 of the War of the Spanish Succession. September 15, 1716, the King ordered the warships in America to aid in their suppression. Every pirate who surrendered before September 5, 1718, was offered pardon for his piracies committed before January 5, 1718. Captain Woodes Rogers so well executed his commission that the sea robbers transferred their bases chiefly to the Bay of Honduras and the inlets of North Carolina, then thinly settled and poorly governed.

South Carolina did not lag behind the royal government. Chief Justice Trott, acting under his commission as judge of vice-admiralty, held the first of his piracy trials in November, 1716. The nine men on trial were acquitted. The captain of the warship *Shoreham,* despite the plea of the Commons that he remain to protect against another attack of which there was definite warning, departed, and thus, as in her desperate war against the savages of the forest, South Carolina was destined to depend on her own resources against the savages of the sea.

In June, 1717, four pirates were executed; but the outlaws grew worse. On May 22, Edward Thatch, alias Blackbeard, appeared in sight of the town and after taking eight or nine ships sent messengers to say that unless a chest of medicines was immediately furnished he would kill all his prisoners, burn all the shipping in the harbor, "and beat the town about our ears." The medicines were sent.

Governor Johnson's appeal for protection was unheeded, and the hard discipline of self-help that was soon to make the colonies too strong for the mother country to govern went on to a crucial test.

Thatch had hardly gone when another pirate, Charles Vane, or Vaughn, before June 13 took the best Negroes from an Angola slaver and plundered a ship approaching from Boston. These insults, said Attorney General Allein, "roused our spirits, and we sent out a force to suppress them." Colonel William Rhett, experienced seaman and first-rate fighting man, was commissioned vice-admiral. Thus when Stede Bonnet put into Cape Fear River to refit in August, 1718, he ran straight into the wrath prepared for another.

Rhett Captures Stede Bonnet.—Bonnet was a man of good education, a retired major of Barbados, and a man of some wealth. Charles Johnson, the historian of the pirates, thinks that a disordered mind, harassed by an unhappy marriage, drove him early in 1717 to the sea. On September 15 Rhett, with two vessels, sailed out to find Vane, but after several days' search sailed for Cape Fear. Upstream could be seen the masts of Bonnet's ship and his two prizes. All night both sides prepared for battle. As the sun rose on the twenty-seventh the pirate sailed around the headland in an attempt to escape. Rhett made for him from both sides with intent to board. Ignorance of the shoals ran the vessels aground. Bonnet's *Royal James* and Rhett's *Henry* careened in the same direction so as to turn the pirate's deck away from Rhett and to leave Rhett's deck fully exposed to the pirate's fire.

Rhett kept up the battle at pistol range for nearly six hours. Victory would be with the vessel that first floated on the rising tide. Slowly the *Henry* righted, and the pirate was at last at her mercy. Seeing Rhett preparing to board him, Bonnet sent a white flag and after some short time surrendered on Rhett's promising he would intercede for mercy. The dead Carolinians appeared finally as sixteen. The pirate's advantage of position had held his losses to seven killed and five wounded, two mortally.

After the capture of the pirates there occurred a strange episode as related in Thomas Hepworth's speech to the jury as co-prosecutor with the Attorney General: "I believe you can't forget how long this town has labored under the fatigue of watching them and what disturbances were lately made with a design to release them and what arts and practices have lately been made use of and effected for the escape of Bonnet, their ringleader, the consideration of which shows how necessary it is that the law be speedily executed on them to the terror of others, and for the security of our own lives, which we were apparently in danger of losing in the late disturbance, when upon a notion of the honour of Carolina, they threatened to set the town on fire about our ears."

Was this evidence of a strong element financially interested in the pirate trade, or an example of the same sort of maudlin mob hysteria that today makes heroes of dashing criminals? Does the "notion of the honour of Carolina" refer to some supposed obligation to Bonnet from Rhett's pledge to solicit mercy for him? War with Spain was announced to South Carolina in a dispatch of December 31, 1718, an anticipated conflict for which some of the opponents of executions might have desired to reserve such fighting men; for with a few exceptions they all had good English, Scotch, or French names.

Attorney General Allein and Thomas Hepworth, who assisted him, were leaders in public life, both of them later chief justice. With Nicholas Trott, chief justice and judge of the court of vice-admiralty, who was as well qualified for the duty before him as any man living, sat (as the law required four) ten assistant judges, all laymen and for any part in the proceedings mere ciphers. Trott's charge defining the law of piracy is quoted at some length with approval, as General McCrady points out, by Phillimore in his *Commentaries upon International Law.*

Under the English law of the time the accused were denied counsel except in cases of treason. The prosecution had to contend against the same sentimentality that had threatened to release the prisoners by force. Of Major Bonnet it was urged "that he is a gentleman and a man of honor, a man of fortune, and one that had a liberal education." "Alas, gentlemen," said Allein, "all these qualifications are but several aggravations of his crimes."

The accused were tried for the specific crimes of pirating the two vessels found with them in Cape Fear River, but had apparently taken over thirty-eight since the 5th of the past April. Of the thirty-three men then on trial all but four were condemned and hanged. Two days later Stede Bonnet went to trial and pleaded guilty. Trott sentenced him to death in a discourse reviewing his education, etc., and emphasizing that after the noose there awaited him the second death in the eternal torments of hell. Before his execution this brave soldier and desperate pirate so completely lost courage as to plead abjectly for life. Rhett, according to tradition, offered to carry him to England for a personal appeal to the King; but Governor Johnson knew his responsibility to the province that had been threatened with ruin and the empire whose colonies had been afflicted from Newfoundland to South America. Bonnet was hanged on the tenth of December.

Governor Johnson Defeats Worley.—Even before the trial of Bonnet's men had been completed word came that the notorious Moody was before the harbor. Because Governor Johnson had refused to regard Rhett's unwarranted promise to intercede for mercy for Bonnet if Bonnet would surrender, Rhett refused to take any part in the expedition against the new danger. Equipping four vessels with a total of seventy (not sixty-eight) guns, Governor Johnson himself early in November sailed over the bar with his ships disguised as merchantmen. As the *Revenge* and the *New York Revenge's Revenge* fired upon Johnson their decks were swept with a broadside from the Governor's concealed guns. The pirates maintained a desperate four hours' fight ending with the loss of both their ships and twenty-six men, including their commander, who proved to be Worley, and not Moody. Moody, hearing of Governor Johnson's preparations, had fled to New Providence to receive from Captain Rogers the King's pardon.

Worley's ship the *New York Revenge's Revenge,* which he had captured on her way from England, contained 106 convicts, 36 or 37 of them women, being sent as indentured servants to "Virginia or Maryland." Trott as judge of vice-admiralty divided the property captured from the pirate between their captors and the plundered owners. The 106 convict servants afforded a first-class sensation and a legal complication. Trott decreed that they should be sold for their respective terms of service and the proceeds divided half to the captors and half to the owners. This accidental importation of convicts is one of the few instances in the history of the province.

On November 19 the twenty-four survivors of Worley's men came to trial. Nineteen were hanged and five acquitted. Of Bonnet's gang of thirty-six (including him), one turned state's evidence, one was shot in escaping, thirty were hanged, and four were acquitted. This execution of forty-nine outlaws in a month stands unparalleled in American history as an attack of an aroused community on crime.

Virginia played an honorable part completing the work. Thatch had gone to North Carolina, where Governor Eden and Attorney General Knight were virtually his partners. Defying such protectors of crime, Governor Spotswood sent into North Carolina waters after "Blackbeard," as he was called, where, on November 22, 1718, his men slew the greatest of the pirates on their own deck which he had boarded and where he fought until he fell under twenty-five wounds. Lieutenant Maynard sailed back to Virginia with Blackbeard's head swinging from his bowsprit and with fifteen prisoners, thirteen of whom were hanged.

Would South Carolina's hanging forty-nine pirates deter the horde of desperadoes still at large, or stir them to a bloody revenge? There were other acts of piracy, but no organized retaliation, though the South Carolina coast was still occasionally disturbed. The activity of the British government was breaking up the outlaw haunts in the West Indies. The warship *Station* in 1724 carried a number of pirates into Charles Town. In 1727 President Middleton commissioned a sloop to cruise against pirates who had recently taken ships off the coast. A pirate was executed in 1728.

Although piracy long continued to plague the northern colonies, South Carolina's relentless repression gave her comparative immunity. The successive sea fights, further prostrating the finances of the southern frontier province just emerged from her desperate Indian war, testify to a high degree of moral as well as physical courage. South Carolina's part in exterminating this age-long scourge of civilization is one of the most honorable passages in that story.

It was impossible that such an experience should fail of important political results. Battling to desperate success against the savages of the forest and the savages of the sea, South Carolina's indignation rose at the Proprietors as a superfluity and a hindrance. She longed for direct union with the royal government as alone adequate in power and dignity. And yet the events of 1715 to 1718 must have had their influence along with other experiences during the next fifty years in leading her to question the utility of any authority three thousand miles away.

CHAPTER XIV

THE PROPRIETORS OVERTHROWN, 1719

To THE long-standing grievances against the Proprietors there was now added the veto of more than a dozen laws, several of them touching the most vital interests of the province. On July 22, 1718, the Proprietors vetoed the import duty act, the act in force since 1709 guaranteeing the Commons the right of electing the public receiver (or provincial treasurer); the act of 1716 for electing representatives by parishes instead of electing twenty for the northern section at Charles Town and ten for the southern section at Willtown; the act encouraging white immigration; the act looking to the distribution of the Yemassee lands for that purpose; and the act of 1716 placing the Indian trade in the hands of a commission to be conducted on public account. They also ordered the Governor to dissolve the Assembly and have another elected on the old plan.

The infrequency of vetoes during recent years had increased the unwillingness to submit to them in such wholesale fashion. Since the veto in 1693 of the jury act of 1692, there had been several vetoes at the order of the Crown, but no others so far as is known. This was evidently because "Archdale's Law" of 1695 forbade the repeal of that law or of the one regarding the payment of quitrents without the consent of the Assembly, or of any other act assented to by the Proprietors' deputies except such as related to the Crown and royal prerogatives, or the lands, rents, revenues, or charter rights of the Proprietors. Though they are said never to have assented to "Archdale's Law," the Proprietors had until 1718 observed it.

These irritating vetoes arrived at a most unfortunate time. Economic distress and Proprietary negligence in the Yemassee War were still irritating memories as was also the recently settled paper money controversy. Although the colonial spokesmen insisted that the issue had been closed, many passages in the correspondence on the events of 1719 indicate that the opposing views of the colonists and Proprietors on the paper money question formed a background hostile to Proprietary authority, even though it might not be classed as a direct cause of rebellion.

The Governor and Council felt obliged to announce the veto of the duty act, since that had been ordered by the King because it included a

5 per cent tariff on British manufactures; but they agreed to keep the others secret until the Assembly, now near the expiration of its term, had been induced to pass a revenue law free from the King's objection. But the news leaked out and "produced prodigious heats." Trott, as the private correspondent of the Proprietors, had for years been a power behind the throne, at times thus frustrating both the Governor and the Assembly and securing valuable benefits for himself. The fact that the vetoes struck down one measure which he had unsuccessfully opposed convinced the people that his secret influence was behind this Proprietors' action. So unpopular was Trott at this time that the Commons and the Council had shortly before united in sending to England thirty-one complaints against him, including partial judgments; multiplying his fees by delays, etc.; giving advice in cases before him; holding the offices of judge of the pleas, of king's bench, of vice-admiralty, member of Council, and member of chancery court—hence no prohibition could issue against him.

The Commons met the vetoes by denying the right of the Proprietors to veto any law to which their deputies had assented. They omitted referring to Archdale's Law to this effect, doubtless because the Proprietors had never ratified it, although for twenty-four years they had observed it.

On February 27, 1719, the Proprietors, at the urgent request of London merchants, sent their veto to two other acts, one favoring South Carolina as compared with English ships and the other seeking to check the influx of blacks.

The Governor and Council now sent to London one of their number, Francis Yonge, to explain the situation, but the Proprietors did not see fit to seek further information from one who had sailed 6,000 miles to serve them, and preferred to accept without investigation whatever Trott wrote. "Thus," says Yonge, "a whole province was to be governed by the caprice of one man," to whom, however, in the next sentence he adds Rhett.

A further example of the unfitness of the Proprietors to preside over the destinies of the province is found in their conduct regarding the Yemassee lands, revealing indifference to their word and to the people's safety. At the close of the recent Indian war, Proprietors and people agreed on the necessity of settling the Yemassee lands with a barrier of immigrants. The Proprietors announced their intention of granting the lands rent free for five years to actual settlers, but, when the Assembly legislated on the subject, they vetoed the laws for restricting slave importations and drawing in province-aided white settlers. Although hundreds of settlers had arrived on these promises, the Proprietors in September, 1719 (not after the revolution as they later stated), ordered land grants stopped. The Yemassee lands were ordered surveyed in tracts of 12,000 acres each for the several Proprietors.

Inaugurating the Revolution.—Under the positive orders of the Proprietors against further delay, Governor Johnson proclaimed the veto of the laws, the dissolution of the Assembly, and the election on November 26 of another on the old plan.[1] The revolutionary leaders organized before the election. On the night of November 17 "the chief [men] of the country subscribed to repair the fortifications of [Charles Town], and to an association to the following effect: That the Proprietors having pretended to repeal laws contrary to the charter and offered other hardships to the inhabitants of this country, they do resolve to choose an Assembly pursuant to the writs issued out and to support their representatives with their lives, and fortunes, and to stand by such resolutions as they shall take at the next Assembly."

The new Assembly refused to recognize the recent vetoes, and the revolutionary leaders requested Governor Johnson to "hold the reins of government for the King till his Majesty's pleasure be known"; for the people are determined "to get rid of the oppression and arbitrary dealings of the Lords Proprietors."

Johnson stood loyally to his employers and ordered the Assembly dissolved. The "Convention" thereupon unanimously chose as governor to hold the province for the King General James Moore (son of the former Governor Moore), a successful soldier and a man of the highest honor.

Governor Johnson had ordered a review of the town companies for Monday, December 21, because of an anticipated Spanish attack, and the popular leaders planned to take advantage of this to proclaim their Governor. Johnson hurried to town only to find the militia drawn up. Going up to Colonel Parris he commanded him in the King's name to disperse his men. Parris "commanded his men to present their muskets at him and bid him stand off at his peril." Governor Moore was proclaimed, and on the 23d the Convention, with the Governor and Council they had elected, enacted that dating from the 21st they were the Assembly of "this settlement" until the arrival of a royal governor.

Even Colonel Rhett, who with Trott had been the mainspring of the Proprietary faction, failed to come to Governor Johnson's assistance. Rhett's conduct soon proved that, good mariner that he was, he knew a sinking ship when he saw it. His refusal to uphold Johnson was a great service to the revolutionists. Rhett was not only receiver general for the Proprietors, but was surveyor and comptroller of the customs for the

[1] See p. 34, above.

King. He now refused Johnson's request to use his authority as a royal officer as the last means of sustaining Johnson as governor. So highly did the revolutionists appreciate this that they made an exception to their resolution that no employee of the Proprietors should hold office and awarded Rhett the lucrative post of overseer of the repairs of the fortifications. Rhett explained to the Proprietors that he accepted Governor Moore's commission because it gave him an opportunity to bring back the people to their interests, and apparently succeeded in getting them to swallow the story.

Governor Johnson soon made two more attempts and later a third to regain his authority. He was willing, he wrote the Assembly, in view of the Spanish danger to consult with them as a commission for the public defense. The Assembly, as the Convention declared itself, made no reply and continued to make laws and levy taxes and to enforce its authority on everyone except Governor Johnson. The Spanish danger passed with the repulse of their expedition against the island of Providence and the wreck of their "retreating fleet in a storm."

The captain of the *Flamborough,* who came to Charles Town, "thought himself obliged to declare for Mr. Johnson," and attempted to awe the people into submission by parading the men of the *Flamborough* and the *Phoenix;* but the Carolinians' seventy guns and five hundred defenders of the fortifications rendered this a failure.

Schemes to Restore the Proprietors.—The long delay of the royal government in taking charge afforded opportunity for plots by the small but capable Proprietary faction in the province to regain control. Colonel William Rhett gave serious trouble. This willful and unscrupulous man continued in office by double-dealing. Though accepting a lucrative office as reward for his services to the revolutionists, he sought secretly to undermine them in England and actively opposed them in Carolina.

Governor Johnson, after being quiet for some months, sought to rally "the remaining one-third" of the people who had not actively rebelled, to refuse taxes except to the Proprietors. They gave no support when, on May 9, 1721, the deposed Governor, backed by 120 armed men, demanded the government. Three cannon discharged in their direction ended their attempt. Documentary evidence of Governor Nicholson's appointment brought Johnson to promise no further resistance.

The royal government's unwarrantable negligence to take charge of the situation promptly was at last ended by the arrival of General Sir Francis Nicholson as provisional royal governor. Taking charge May 30, 1721, or a day or so before, his firm though often arbitrary hand, aided by the desire of the colonists to make a good impression on the royal government, held the ship during his four years on an even keel.

The real cause of the revolution was not so much the immediate grievances which became its occasion as the fact that the Proprietary organization had failed in the purpose for which governments exist. A degenerate commercial stock company retained none of the virtues even of money-makers. So negligent had they become that they had not had a settlement with their own receiver-general in ten years and had permitted their rents to fall into arrears for about that period. The corruption of contemporary politics they extended to Carolina by the outright sale of offices and honors. The impatience and contempt of the Assembly's address of December 24, 1719, to the British government expressed more truly the reason for the revolution than the labored document in which they later piled up every possible charge.

It was a thoroughly orthodox English revolution, seeking to conserve rather than destroy. It was led by the most substantial citizens for the definite purpose of correcting grievances that pressed most heavily on their class. Nonetheless it was unfortunate that a good change was accomplished in such a way. For more than a decade the life of the province suffered from the disorganization, confusion, and lawlessness which were in part the legacy of the overthrow of a government by force, as well as in part the results of mistakes by the colonists themselves and of the neglect of its duties by the British government.

Debit and Credit of the Proprietary Government.—The Proprietary government in South Carolina was ended, although it continued in North Carolina until the surrender of the Charter to the Crown in 1729. It had been a mixture of good and bad, with the bad part continually growing worse. The only justification for the gift of huge blocks of the royal domain to Proprietors was that, under the existing indifference of Crown and Parliament to developing or defending the empire, it was better for it to be done imperfectly by the King's favorites than not to be done at all.

So long as the energy and liberalism of Shaftesbury directed, there was a beneficent force without which the infant settlement might have perished. Even after Shaftesbury's death the Proprietors were at times more just than the colonists, as, for instance, in defending the Huguenots against social, religious, and political prejudices, and in restraining to some extent the tendency of early comers to engross the best lands. But as the shares passed to indifferent or narrow men, the Proprietary form of government became more and more of an impropriety. A narrow-minded Palatine was largely responsible for the bitterness of the religious factionalism of the early eighteenth century. The indifference to the peril of the colonists in the Yemassee War and the paralysis of the Proprietors in the face of problems and dangers proclaimed their authority a nuisance of which a high-spirited people would soon be rid in order to replace it by a national government that had become more conscious of its duties.

Summary of the Proprietary Period.—The events of the fifty years of the Proprietary period may be summarized as a struggle for existence against external foes and an effort for internal development and progress. Practically from the moment of landing there was the constant necessity of guarding against destruction by the Spanish, who regarded the existence of South Carolina as a trespass. Though Spain frustrated attempts to expel her from Florida, she was steadily forced out of the later Georgia. Her influence among the Indian tribes between the Savannah and the Mississippi received its first serious blow when Dr. Woodward opened the Carolina trade on the Chattahoochee in 1685. The great superiority of English goods and the restless energy of the South Carolina traders soon almost destroyed Spanish influence north of St. Augustine and Pensacola and laid the foundation for the successful assertion of British supremacy to the Mississippi.

The outstanding calamity of the Proprietary period—the Yemassee War—was the punishment for South Carolina's own neglect and her traders' wrongdoings in the ruthless exploitation of the natives. She was still too weak to be unjust with safety. She had hardly rallied from this threatened destruction from the rear in 1715 to '17 when called upon to face the peril of virtual subjection to organized bands of pirates in 1718. With splendid energy and courage she rendered a public service matched in this respect by no other colony, and wrote one of the heroic chapters of American colonial history.

Along with the struggle against external enemies went the working out, more or less effectively, of internal problems. The economic foundations were deepened and broadened. The Indians were made the subjects of an extraordinarily profitable trade. This, with cattle raising, agriculture, and forest industries, supplied the basis of a society early marked by wealth and culture.

Out of the Spanish and Indian wars came the plague of inconvertible paper money, the injustice and confusion of which were in the early part of the royal government to involve a prolonged conflict, at times almost approaching anarchy.

Another vexing problem was presented by the determination of the Anglican element to establish its religion as the state-supported church—a measure which, both by the unscrupulous method of its being done and the unfair relationship which it established, intensified the religious animosities of an intolerant age. Whether this means of more quickly bringing in a considerable body of Anglican clergy did more harm than good is difficult to decide. Certainly the effect of dependence on state aid reduced their instinct of self-help so low that the withdrawal of government support in 1778 paralyzed the Episcopal church for a generation.

The dominant political fact of the Proprietary period is the growing power of the Commons House of Assembly. The later negligence of the royal government went by no means so far as that of the Proprietors; but the very nature of English institutions and of the people and their situation made this growth of popular power inevitable. Governor after Governor was forced to recognize that he could only lead and not control, and that free exercise of even the veto power of the Crown was likely to react unfavorably on its ability to have its own policies supported. The persistence of self-government resulted in 1719 in the overthrow of the Proprietors; and the same instinct, continuing under similar circumstances, we shall find, made the people's representatives more and more the dominant element under the royal government and, as naturally resulted, after another fifty-five years, in that government's overthrow.

CHAPTER XV

THE PROVINCIAL CONSTITUTION, 1719-1776

A GENERAL view of the government under the King shows the Commons House of Assembly as the motive force of the provincial Constitution. Although the relative power of the royal and popular elements varied with the strength or weakness of important leaders, and most of all with the constantly growing assertion of authority by the Commons, the institutions and agencies of government continued with little change of external form. The change of the inner realities constitutes a large part of the history of the province.

A question of fundamental importance concerns the nature and origin of the authority of the provincial government from 1719 to 1776. Neither under the Proprietors nor under the direct government of the King did the colonists admit that they were subjects of unlimited power. On the contrary, they claimed the rights of Englishmen as a birthright and regarded the Charter merely as confirming them. For instance, the Commons, March 28, 1735, resolved, *nemine contradicente,* "that His Majesty's subjects in this province are entitled to all the liberties and privileges of Englishmen (*vide* Charter to the Lords Proprietors; *vide* Statute 31 Ed. I, Chap. 1 and 4); [and] that the Commons House of Assembly in South Carolina, by the laws of England and South Carolina, and ancient usage and custom have all the rights and privileges pertaining to money bills that are enjoyed by the British House of Commons." On December 2 or 3, 1762, they asserted that their rights were "originally derived as British subjects" and "confirmed to them by charter." But the Charter or any other document was regarded as the witness, and not the creator, of their liberties. There was a tendency to regard the King as governing under the limitations of a living principle that their liberties were inherent.

In the Act of 1721 acknowledging the legal title of George I to the throne, the Commons inserted the clause, "saving to your Majesty's liege subjects in South Carolina the rights and privileges by law to them granted and of right accustomed." Although this assumption of sharing along with their fellow Englishmen their inherent liberties, unconferred by anybody, was dropped at the request of the Council, they insisted on passing a resolution that nothing in the bill "does, can, or ought to be interpreted, extended or construed to abridge" their rights. Loyalty and gratitude were thus tempered with this truly British reservation.

The royal element in the government on the other hand emphasized the power of the prerogative; but this contrast must not be taken to imply that the Commons denied that there were certain prerogatives of the Crown which, when lawfully exercised, must be respected in South Carolina as in England. Nor did the royal servants conceive of the colonists as slaves of the prerogative. The difference was one of emphasis on the conflicting elements in the English Constitution, which were not fully understood in England itself until much later.

The most logical presentation of the prerogative view was elaborated by Chief Justice Whitaker of South Carolina in 1743 in advice to a provincial official, which did not become public. All the powers of government in the royal province, said Whitaker, were derived from the King; even the existence of the Assembly and its right to make laws depended upon the royal prerogative.

The Commons.—Theories aside, the motive power in the government was the Commons House of Assembly. The earliest laws extant (1685) denominate them the Commons. The word Parliament is used in 1685 for the entire legislature, and in 1692 the term General Assembly to include both houses and the Governor. Several instances occur during the Proprietary period of calling the whole legislature by this name, which it still bears. The lower house was before 1719 called the House of Commons, the Commons, or the Commons House of Assembly, but under the royal government the last was almost continuously used.

The sessions of the Assembly were frequent and long, for four reasons. First, throughout the colonial period it insisted on attending to every sort of detail. Second, there had not yet occurred any sharp division of spheres among the executive, legislative, and judicial departments. Third, there was not allowed to executive or administrative officials the decision of details or the application of the general laws to specific cases without which modern government would be impossible. Fourth, the details of local government fell largely upon the Assembly, as there were few local agencies.

The burden of time required caused many to decline membership, and it was sometimes hard to maintain a quorum. The ruling class were too proud, wrote Bull, to receive pay. Self-interest in controlling public policy, interest in public affairs, and enjoyment of social life in Charles Town contributed to membership's being sought.

The act of 1721 remained the law on suffrage, terms, etc., until the Revolution, acts modifying it being invariably vetoed by the King. The voter must be a resident of a year, a free white man professing Christianity, twenty-one years old, possessing fifty acres or paying 20 shillings currency (about a half dollar 1940 value) tax. The representative must be for a year a resident of the province, but not necessarily of the parish, and own 500 acres and ten slaves, or £1,000 currency (about $425) value in other real estate. The term was three years unless shortened by dissolution. Not more than six months must elapse between sessions. From 1716 (except in 1719), elections were held by parishes at the Anglican churches, the wardens of which were the managers. Catholics were not forbidden to vote, but they could not accept the oaths of membership.

The custom before 1721 of allowing persons having religious scruples against swearing on the Holy Evangelists to swear "according to their profession" (which generally meant by holding up the hand) was guaranteed by the law in 1717; but it was taken away by the Act of 1721 under the influence of the bigoted Nicholson; and, despite the earnest and persistent efforts of the Anglicans in the Commons in behalf of their brethren of other denominations, it could never be restored over the opposition of the Governor, the Council, or the King, although even in trials involving men's lives this right was accorded witnesses. Numbers of Dissenters were thus excluded in the earlier years, though later few seem to have observed this scruple.

The Commons were frequently arbitrary and violent, and in many instances where their own property interests were involved were far less regardful of right and justice than was the Crown with its aloofness from local influences. The ideal of a good King as father of his people often broke down as the part was directed by inferior ministers; but nothing could be more contrary to historical truth than the assumption that the Commons were always just and the King always an enemy of the people's rights.

Imprisonment at the pleasure of the Commons, so long as their session lasted, was inflicted with great frequency for anything from disrespect toward them in tavern gossip to attempts to defend legal rights by appeals to the courts. For such arbitrary imprisonment there was no remedy. Until adjournment, perhaps months away, nothing could secure release from a filthy, sweltering prison except an abject apology and payment of the officers' fees. The Council and the courts were helpless, and rarely did a Governor dare to jeopardize important public measures and the annual insertion of an amount for his own salary by offending the body whose good will was essential to carrying on the government.

The King's instruction to the Governor enjoining that the Commons House of South Carolina was to enjoy no greater privileges than those possessed by the British House of Commons was taken as an acknowledgment that they did possess in full those rights. The Commons' knowledge of parliamentary history and their skill in the long battle for more authority against the upper house make the state papers and political skill of the leaders of the American Revolution seem quite natural.

Not only were the Commons continually threatening the privileges of the Council, but they encroached on the rights and duties of the executive. Having control of the purse, they exacted the right to supervise the expenditure of what they granted to a degree that vexed the Governor, and even absorbed completely the control of extensive executive functions through the device of naming commissioners to expend certain appropriations, etc.

The Council.—The other house was His Majesty's Council, appointed by the King without limitation of term. Its position as the upper house of the legislature, as the executive council whose consent the Governor was obliged to obtain for many of his acts, and as the highest provincial court of appeal as well as the court of chancery, gave it great importance. Its multiplicity of duties rendered membership a burden, and to recompense themselves for this the Council, on at least one occasion under Broughton's administration, made themselves and the Lieutenant-Governor a present of six thousand acres apiece of public land. The membership of twelve was seldom complete, and frequently the smallness of the number in commission rendered it difficult to secure a quorum.

So confused were the executive and legislative characters of the Council that until the accession of Lieutenant-Governor Bull the elder (1737), the Governor always sat with the Council, signed messages to the lower house, and spoke of himself and the Council as "we." At one moment a bill would be under discussion, at the next a chancery case, and at the next the settlement of an orphan's estate (the last by the Governor alone as Ordinary).

Until about 1756 membership in the Council was a prized distinction. "Integrity, fortune, and ability" were the characteristics sought. Few resigned; hence there was at times a troublesome proportion of the infirm. The Charles Town merchants, whose interests often clashed with those of the planters, were generally stronger in the Council than in the Assembly, although the upper house also included great planters and lawyers. It was the great conservative element in the government. But as the Council was transformed largely into a body of placemen in the years toward the Revolution, less and less did it supply the need of a wise and public-spirited upper house.

By the royal instructions, the Council possessed a complete legislative equality with the Commons, but the latter successfully disputed this and imposed restrictions similar to those on the British upper house in regard to money bills. In fact the Council was at times, beginning as early as 1745, obliged to defend its right even to veto a money bill.

It was to vindicate its character as a legislative body that the Council in 1739 excluded the chief executive from its sittings as an upper house and some years earlier adopted the practice of having separate minutes recorded for "the Upper House of Assembly" and for "the Council." Over only the latter during those periods of controversy was the Governor allowed to preside, or at times even to be present.

Governor Glen had the mortification of seeing the Council, to enforce its legislative character, leave the room and go into the garret, from whence it sent for its papers when this failed to cause him to leave his chair, where he continued alone for several hours. He was finally allowed to be present during legislative business when he "declared that he never would enter into the debates of the upper house or interfere with them, or receive nor make answer to any message which might come to them, but that he thought that most proper to be done by the eldest Councillor present, as was the practice."

The Governor.—The Governor was appointed by the King during the royal pleasure. He acted under an elaborate set of instructions, which in large part formed the Constitution of the province and were largely the historical antecedent of the later-written State constitution. The parts directed to officers holding by royal appointment were legally obligatory, and generally, but not always, effective; but many passages amounted only to requests, often unheeded, as the action of the Assembly was necessary for their realization. As our story progresses, we shall find how often and in matters of what importance the King's own appointees preferred to brave the displeasure of his distant and perhaps preoccupied ministers rather than to incur social or financial persecution by the people and Assembly with whom they were obliged day by day to live. Royal officialdom in the province was never so large or so united in itself as to be able to brave public opinion with impunity.

One point on which the King insisted futilely was that fixed salaries should be settled by law on royal officers and particularly the Governor. The dependence of the executive on the annual granting of a gift by the Assembly, which they insisted was not a salary but a gratuity, and the fear of losing this, were believed to have on various occasions prevented the Governor's strict observance of the orders of the Crown. The King could discharge him, but the Assembly could stop his pay. Governors were in fact at times accused by the Council of joining the Commons, against them and the King's instructions, out of dread of offending those who controlled the purse strings. Governor Glen complained of social displeasure visited upon him for supporting unpopular or resisting popular measures.

In 1769 the Assembly willingly made the judges independent of them by affixing salaries to their offices, and under compulsion did the same for the Attorney General and Clerk of Court, and strove unsuccessfully to induce the King to make the judges independent of his influence also by appointment during good behavior instead of during the royal pleasure.

The constant conflicts between the popular and royal elements were inevitable in a system that left neither power enough to control the other or to feel itself secure against being controlled. This system, typical in colonial America, now exists only in the Bermudas, Bahamas, and Barbados. The tendency has been toward securing harmonious co-operation of the appointed and elected factors by making one or the other so strong that it can welcome the advice of the other without fearing encroachment.

Under both the Proprietary and the royal government all executive and judicial officers were largely paid in fees. The act of 1736, e.g., allows the Governor fees from four shillings to two pounds currency for fourteen different acts, such as signing marriage licenses, land warrants, land grants, certificates for ships, commissions, etc. The royal government allowed Governor Nicholson £1,000 sterling as commander of the troops that he brought out, which was more than the stipend bestowed by the province. After Georgia was established, this handsome perquisite was transferred, along with the command of the troops, to Oglethorpe. On Glen's complaint, he was allowed, in addition to what the Assembly gave him, £800 by the royal government, an amount increased before the Revolution to £1,000. When to these were added the fees and the one-third share in condemned vessels and cargoes, the Governor's income rose to a princely sum. Glen states that his predecessor's official income totaled £3,000 sterling—a sum equal to perhaps over $100,000 in 1940. In the land boom years Robert Johnson's and Broughton's fees equaled the province-paid "salary"; but Governor Glen complained that his fees never exceeded £300 sterling a year, although he had been led to expect £1,000.

The Governor of an American colony was generally paid half the amount promised from the King for such time as he was not actually in his colony. The Lieutenant-Governor, as the chief executive was called when a South Carolinian served in the absence of one sent from Britain, received all the fees and apparently half the royal stipend and such amount as the colonial Assembly chose to grant, which was usually £2,500 in the early part of the royal period and £3,500, the same as to the Governor, to the beloved Lieutenant-Governor Bull the younger in the later period.

The encroachment of the Commons on executive functions was encouraged by the habit of even the strongest governors of constantly consulting them on appointments and on Indian and Spanish frontier affairs, etc. The Commons even formulated for the Governor "talks" to the Indians. The closeness of relations of a small community, the imperfect differentiation of departments, and the necessity of keeping the good will of the purse-holders led the Governor to treat the Commons almost as a second executive council.

With a few glaring exceptions under the Proprietors and several less evil ones under the King, the province enjoyed good governors. They were generally men of character and often of high ability. All the more important ones under the Proprietors except Archdale were either permanent settlers or residents of such long time as to bring them into full sympathy with the people. Under the royal government, Robert Johnson, virtually all but a native, Glen, who thoroughly identified himself with the province, and the Carolinians Moore, Middleton, Broughton, and the Bulls father and son, held office for about forty of the fifty-seven years between 1719 and 1776.

With the consent of the Council, and for certain reasons without, the Governor could for cause suspend any executive or judicial official appointed by the Crown; but the numerous officials elected by the Assembly were beyond even his power of reproof. Two good things may be said of the governors. They frequently restrained, or as best as they could opposed, the paper money excesses or arbitrary conduct of the Commons; and they very often strove to defend the interests of the people against the selfish policies urged on the home government by British merchants and the mistaken policies of the royal government itself.

Relations with England—The Agent.—A law passed by Assembly and Council and signed by the Governor was at once of force unless it contained a clause suspending it until the King's approval. Such a suspending clause was enjoined upon the Governor regarding laws touching the King's prerogative, the property of his subjects, including private acts, or laws prejudicial to British trade or shipping, or laws repealing an act to which the King had assented.

The King's veto was called his "repeal" or "disallowance." Repeal was logical because the law became of force (except as specified above) with the Governor's signature. Laws were sometimes thus repealed after many years of operation. In 1734 the King repealed a law enacted forty years before.[1] But a law which the King had once approved he could not repeal. Delay in acting on laws with a suspending clause was a grievance. In June, 1754, the Lords of Trade were considering whether to recommend approving or vetoing nine South Carolina acts from two to sixteen years old.

Although bad laws, especially on finance, were frequently vetoed, good laws sometimes met the same fate. Even to this day, American indignation is stirred by the policy of the London merchants in running the colonies through their influence with the Lords of Trade as though their own commercial profits were more to be considered than the rights and interests of the inhabitants. The colonists begged, generally ineffectually, that their laws might not be vetoed without their being allowed to defend them, which was one of the duties of their salaried agent in London.

Provost Marshal—Prisons—Local Government.—Among the upward of forty administrative and judicial officials we must note the Provost Marshal. This official, acting as sheriff for the whole province until the Circuit Court Act of 1769 went into effect in 1772, was generally the absentee owner of the patent. His deputy in South Carolina discharged the duties while the patentee in England drew a large part of the profits. Under the Proprietors the Governor was regularly allowed to sell the office for half or more of the perquisites. A patentee who had mortgaged his right or, as in one instance, had four or five mortgages out on it, would naturally take little interest in his duties.

There was an official strong box; but so long as the treasurer, ordinarily a man of wealth, was solvent, there does not appear to have been any question raised as to whether public funds were mingled with his own. One of the leading treasurers of the Proprietary period died a heavy defaulter, but his son loyally paid the debt. Two treasurers of the royal period, of eminent social standing, died deeply indebted to the public. They or their heirs put their property at the disposal of the public in settlement. That graft was practiced at times by public officers cannot be doubted from certain specific testimony. The best type of gentleman today would scorn some of the practices, public and private, then taken for granted by men of the highest social class.

Historians have called Francis Fidling (named by the law of 1698) the first postmaster of South Carolina; but the law of January 17, 1695, confers that position on William Smith, to whom three pence three farthings were to be paid for every letter that he delivered.[2] Smith's main duty was collecting the toll of powder from incoming ships.

[1] The king's veto is now limited to one or two years in the self-governing colonies. Lowell's *Government of England,* II, 405.

[2] I thank Miss Mary A. Sparkman for the citation on Smith.

Liquor-selling licenses were issued by the Governor until 1711, when the duty was laid on the public receiver with approval of commissioners, with some resulting laxity. Liquor was allowed to be sold by planters, not to be drunk on the plantation, and the peddling of intoxicants was forbidden as it was "observed to be mischievous, and to impoverish the otherwise sober planters."

Until the parishes were created in 1706 there were virtually no subdivisions for local government. The four counties created by Proprietary order served for assigning and electing representatives, organizing the militia, designating the residence of magistrates, and locating in the most general way land grants, and as territorial units for a short-lived county court system. The parishes were so laid out as not to cross county lines. These ancient counties virtually ceased to exist with the Circuit Court Act of 1769, which set up the first real subdivision of the back country. The townships created in the 1730's were merely temporary agencies for settling the frontier, though they were sometimes used for other purposes. The parishes served as agencies for poor relief. Both the poor and the insane were aided in their own homes or boarded out, except such as were sent to the workhouse or "hospital" in Charles Town.

The parish was the principal division for what little local government existed, for authority was so centralized that the Assembly even passed laws for running a drain in a particular street. There was no municipal corporation until after the Revolution except "Charles City and Port" for about a year, 1722-23, after which the royal veto restored the unincorporated Charles Town.

The workhouse in Charles Town is mentioned in 1744 as a recognized institution. It held anybody from runaways to prisoners of war. There was no publicly owned jail until after the Circuit Court Act of 1769. The Provost Marshal held prisoners in his own home or in such prison as he provided at his own expense. The sufferings of indigent prisoners were denounced in 1730 as inhuman. Conditions of crowding were at times revolting almost beyond belief. Thieves, murderers, debtors, women, were herded in rooms in which the sexes had to meet the calls of nature before each other.

From 1703 the Chief Justice was a trained lawyer, but until the Circuit Court Act of 1769 the assistant judges were laymen, though often laymen whose breadth of mind and strength of character were valuable additions to their chief's legal knowledge.

The colonial laws under the royal government early regulated the criminal court of general sessions and the civil court of common pleas. Both functions had been performed since the founding of the province. These and other laws merely regulated their time, functions, etc.

The method of selecting the jurors was at first, we may presume, similar to that then in use in England. The Proprietors deserve credit for insisting on drawing jurors individually instead of in blocks of twelve made up by the sheriff. The act which became the basis of our jury law from that day to this was passed January 17, 1695. Previous historians have said that it could not be found, overlooking the fact that it is given in full as No. 119, in Trott's manuscript volume of South Carolina laws. It is omitted from his printed laws, as having been repealed by later law incorporating its provisions. This act of 1695 provides that no person shall be a juror unless his name is on the annexed list. The judge shall cause to be written on separate slips of parchment, all of the same size, the names of all qualified persons. For the court of common pleas, a child under ten years of age shall in open court draw from a bag or box as many names as the judge thinks will be needed for the next term of court. When that term comes, a child under ten shall draw for each case from those previously drawn a jury of twelve names. Jurors challenged according to the laws of England shall be replaced from the box or bag. For the general sessions jurors, the procedure was somewhat, but not materially, different. The jury list was supplemented from time to time by the General Assembly.

The Jury Act of 1731 re-enacted and codified many existing laws and provided improved machinery in some respects. The jury list thereto annexed was to be revised every three years by the chief justice, the public receiver, and the coroner, if the Assembly did not itself make the revision, by placing on it as petty jurors all new names paying twenty shillings currency taxes and as grand jurors all paying £5, provided only half as many should be in the grand as is the petty jury box. A healing of technicality that might well be imitated was the provision that any man on the list was legally qualified even though it might be found that he did not meet the property qualification.

It was because of the law of 1731, which made practically impossible the operation of an exchequer court, that this agency for correcting encroachments on public lands and other royal rights could not be established. The abuses connected with the land engrossing of the 1720's and 30's called loudly for this means of protecting the King's rights, which meant in effect the rights of future settlers to whom the King alone could grant lands; but the land-engrossing element, powerful in the provincial government, were determined that no such impediment should be put in their way. In addition was the set aversion of the colonists to the very nature of such a court, operating without a jury. In spite of the King's undoubted prerogative, the plan broke down before public hostility.

Chief Justice.—Chief Justice Whitaker, in a letter to the collector of quitrents in 1743, complained of the inferior position of the Chief Justice, from two causes: the restrictions of the provincial laws and the power of the assistant judges. All acts of Assembly, he said, were made by authority derived from the Crown, which authorized Governor, Council, and Assembly to make laws provided they were as near as might be agreeable, but not repugnant to the laws of England. Sometimes laws had been made in the colonies not only contrary to the King's prerogative but repugnant to the laws of England. The question was whether these laws were void when they were first made or were only voidable by his Majesty's disallowance and might therefore be put in practice until his Majesty repealed them. Ought the judges, when they were brought up in cases, to declare them *ipso facto* void, or only voidable, and so to be put in practice until repealed by the King?

The Chief Justice had raised the same question in a memorial to the Lieutenant-Governor and Council on September 16, 1742, and concluded that the King had reserved the annulling power, and hence that the courts should, until he acted, regard such laws as only voidable but not void.

The Judicial Annulment of Legislation.—The above is one of the earliest and clearest discussions by an American jurist of the American doctrine of the judicial annulment of unconstitutional statutes and thus holds an interesting place in that development. The idea stems back, as Professor McGovney points out,[3] to the classical and medieval idea of the moral law, or the law of nature, limiting government's right to enact injustice. This found clear statement in Chief Justice Coke's dictum in 1610 in Dr. Bonham's Case: "When an Act of Parliament is against Common Right and Reason . . . the Common Law will control it, and adjudge such Act to be void." The idea was repeated by English judges and law writers until it lapsed before the modern doctrines of the unlimited power of Parliament and the dubiousness of "natural rights."

As steps in the development of the American practice of the judicial annulment of legislation, let us recall the protest of the South Carolina Commons on January 18, 1693, "that inferior courts take upon themselves to try, and judge and determine the power of assemblies, or the validity of acts made by them," and that the Commons in 1726 and '27 protested against the Charles Town judges' decision of August 12, 1724, denying the validity of a law passed by the Assembly.

Reference to the case of 1724 in the three-volume edition of my

[3] D. O. McGovney, "The British Origin of the Judicial Review of Legislation," *University of Pennsylvania Law Review*, 93 (September, 1944), 1-49.

History of South Carolina, the first historical mention apparently ever made of it, led Professor D. O. McGovney into an investigation proving that the court had, in deciding the case of *Dymes* against *Ness,* August 12, 1724, definitely overruled an act of the Assembly. The Assembly's protest of January, 1693, that inferior courts presumed "to try, judge and determine . . . the validity of acts made by" the Assembly seems to refer to the actual adjudication of a case or cases; but, as no further facts are known, Professor McGovney concludes that the case of *Dymes* against *Ness* in 1724 "is our earliest known instance of a judicial annulment of a statute on a constitutional ground" in deciding a litigated case.[4]

Power of Assistant Judges.—The power of the assistant judges, generally laymen, was a serious limitation, as it was intended to be, upon the Chief Justice. In their hatred of Trott's autocracy, the revolutionists specified in the commission of their Chief Justice, Richard Allein, that he should not hold court without the presence of at least two assistant judges; but the King's Commission later authorized him to hold court alone if they failed to attend.

Now occurred a serious encroaching on the King's prerogative. An act of February 26, 1732, and one of April 9, 1734, set up the assistant judges with individual commissions making each of them equal in power to the Chief Justice. These were vetoed on March 4, 1735, and a more modest law of April 5, 1740, authorized the assistant judges to hold court without the Chief Justice only in case of his absence, sickness, or death. Whitaker denies their equality with the Chief Justice, but his own protest in 1741, like that of Chief Justice Wright in 1735, proves that the assistants each had an equal voice with the chief and at times overrode him.

Appeals.—The first royal Governor and Council were authorized to hear appeals in civil cases involving over £100 sterling. Further appeal lay in the King in Council if the value exceeded £300 sterling. Toward the close of the royal period the amounts were raised to £300 and £500 sterling respectively. Appeals were allowed irrespective of the sum concerned if important points of law or the King's prerogative or revenue were involved. Appeal was never perfected from the Governor and Council in South Carolina during the whole royal period. An instance begun about 1763 or '64 was dropped before inquiry could ascertain the proper method.

Governor Glen was instructed to allow petitions directly to the King's mercy in cases involving fines of £100 or over; but petition to the

[4] *Ibid.,* p. 48.

Governor alone to grant reprieves or pardons was the usual procedure in criminal cases. Sentences for treason or willful murder he could if he saw fit reprieve, but pardon for these rested only with the King.

Petty Courts.—As soon as settlement extended beyond easy reach of Charles Town there arose the difficulty of affording justice to the remoter parts. The first attempt to establish courts outside Charles Town, except the sheriff's courts before 1700, was the county, or more correctly precinct, court act of 1721, which ordered five courts to be established outside the city, well distributed throughout the then settled area. Their jurisdiction extended to criminal cases not involving life or limb and to civil cases of £100 sterling. Five designated justices of the peace were to preside, and for a while the Chief Justice "rode the circuit." They exercised also sundry administrative functions. They were tried at a period of economic distress and political confusion and by the early 1730's had been virtually abandoned. The extraordinary difficulties of the period, the sparseness of population, and the legal incompetence of their judges combined to wreck an experiment which if properly fostered might have prevented much subsequent hardship and injustice.

Justices of the peace existed practically from the first. Almost every man of first-class prominence was on the commission, and some, unhappily, as time went on, who should not have been. An act of 1747 to create minor courts of two justices and three freeholders to try cases involving over £20 and less than £75 currency, which would have been of great convenience to the back country, was vetoed, largely, it appears, because of the efforts of patent office holders who strove for the sake of their fees to force everybody to come to the one court of common pleas and general sessions in Charles Town.

The court of vice-admiralty functioned directly under the authority of the King from the appointment of Joseph Morton in 1697.

In concluding this summary of the frame of government, we may drop a warning against the error of inferring that the colonists were always right and the King or his representatives always wrong, as some crude American writing tends to represent. The royal government, as sometimes the Proprietary before it, by its detachment from factional quarrels or special interests, was frequently more just and upright, more regardful of the permanent public good and of the rights of the colonists as a whole, than was the particular faction in control of the Assembly.

The means of royal control were the appointing power, the granting of honors or favors to influential individuals or concessions to the province as a whole, the right of veto, and the powerful spirit of the people's loyalty. The rival powers of King and people resulted in developing, long before the term was applied to our Federal Constitution, a government based on the ideal of checks and balances—a form of government in which a free people sharply restrained encroachments by an executive regarded as a possible danger, and the executive, being separated from the legislature, became the powerful but frequently frustrated combination of co-operator and opponent of the legislature, as we continue in state and nation to this day. So strong are the hands of the past.

CHAPTER XVI

GOVERNOR NICHOLSON'S STRONG HAND, 1721-1725

General Sir Francis Nicholson, selected as the first royal Governor of South Carolina, had the widest experience of all living colonial executives. He had made a poor show in New York, but redeemed himself by a wise administration in Virginia. Transferred in 1694 to Maryland, he began to display his qualities of bigotry and violence. He was returned to Virginia in 1698, where he quarreled with Commissary Blair, threatened to cut the throats of the groom, the magistrate, and the parson concerned in the marriage of a lady whom he desired for his own, and recommended that the colonies should be placed under a viceroy with a standing army supported by taxes on the people. He displayed the same faults in Acadia. He assumed the government of South Carolina on May 30, 1721, and seemed determined to redeem a bad reputation; but before his four years were out he had shown his worse as well as his better qualities. In one respect he was the man needed by South Carolina. He had the soldier's strength and promptness of decision. Despite his faults, he deserves credit for bringing a situation bordering on anarchy immediately into order.

Nicholson's character was a bundle of contradictions. A contributor to the building of churches in many colonies, who constantly referred to "our Holy Mother the Church of England," he quarreled violently with her official heads in both Maryland and Virginia. A liberal contributor to education and ecclesiastical libraries, and the author of two pamphlets, he bitterly opposed the introduction of printing into South Carolina. He gave prayer books to the members of the Assembly at the beginning of his administration and Bibles at its end. The most fanatical of Anglicans, only Sir Nathaniel Johnson is comparable to him for his railings at the Dissenters, and no colonial governor approached him in rudeness to the legislature; but before adjournment he invited them all to breakfast or dine with him whenever in town. When, despite his storming, he had to yield, it would probably be with the warning that "the blood lies at your doors" if it results in harm.

Reviving Religious Intolerance.—By ancient law and custom in South Carolina, members of Assembly took the oath on the Holy Evangelists or by holding up the hand "according to their profession." By no means all Dissenters claimed this privilege, but some rigidly refused as a matter of conscience to swear on the Bible. At Nicholson's first assembly he refused the "state oaths" to Captain Robert Fenwick, Captain Thomas Lynch, and Michael Darby, as they desired the privilege of swearing by holding up the hand. The plea of the House for these and others to be indulged in a privilege which was, they said, as old as the province, and perhaps a doubt as to the legality of his action, led the Governor temporarily to relent. It was doubtless not by chance that the House the next day sent to inform the Governor that they were ready to reply to his "speech" by a committee consisting wholly of members whose right had been questioned.

The average churchman was more liberal than the Governor or the clergy, many of whom brought from England the factional feelings still so fierce. Yet the Anglicans were weak enough to consent to Nicholson's insistence on the repeal of the right guaranteed by the act of 1717 and to prescribe the rule of swearing on the Evangelists. Repeated efforts by the Commons to restore the Dissenters' privilege failed. Charles Pinckney (father of Thomas and Charles Cotesworth) illustrated his breadth of mind and character in a noble protest against this petty persecution in 1745. The clause was justly inserted by the Commons, he said to his fellow Council members, for preserving to those of scrupulous consciences regarding oaths the civil rights to which as Englishmen they were entitled, which were confirmed to them in the original contract in the Constitution of this province, and which they enjoyed for many years with few interruptions until unjustly deprived of them under the influence of General Nicholson. The discrimination was utterly unreasonable, he continued, as the Dissenters had no principle detrimental to the government, but were as faithful as any of his Majesty's subjects. Prescribing a particular form for an oath, which is a religious act, was an infringement of the rights of judgment and conscience in religion and was as truly an act of exclusion as if it was such in set terms. It was unreasonable here, as it was not required of a witness in the highest capital cases. It stirred ill feeling between Churchmen and Dissenters and deprived the public of the services of many a good man. "And finally," continued Pinckney, "because I conceive that keeping out any good man from a share in the civil rights of the government merely because he has a religious scruple of conscience, not in taking the oath itself, but in the form in which it is administered, seems to border too near . . . upon a spirit of persecution for conscience sake, and is consequently unbecoming the honor and dignity of the Upper House of the Assembly."

Pinckney fought unremittingly, but the Council could not be convinced until the act of 1747, and that was vetoed by the King.

The Anglican clergy seized the opportunity offered by a Governor of Nicholson's views to stop Dissenter "teachers" (i.e., ministers) from solemnizing marriages, which hurt both their consciences and pockets. But Governor Nicholson, they lamented, hesitated to offend a party really less numerous than he supposed. The provincial secretary refused a marriage license to John Bee because he specified a Presbyterian minister, the Rev. Archibald Stobo; and Stobo was warned by the Rev. Commissary Bull in September, 1722, under threat of legal punishment, not to perform any more marriage ceremonies. Stobo was not a man to be browbeaten. He prepared a petition to the Assembly for the equal establishment of the Presbyterian Church by law with the Anglican. The Act of Union, he pointed out, guaranteed equal rights to Scotland, including the Scottish established church. There was no such thing as the Church of Great Britain. In a British colony the national church of each nation had an equal right, as in the two parts of Great Britain. Mr. Kinloch, to quiet strife, dissuaded Mr. Stobo from a contest before the Assembly; but Stobo's strategy served its immediate purpose. Governor after Governor rejected the attempt of the Anglican clergy to monopolize marriage ceremonies.

Assembly Surrenders a Right—Other Legislation.—The elimination of the uncertainties of a revolutionary government, the joyous loyalty of the people, and the strength of the Governor enabled Nicholson to leave his name on many important laws. A county or precinct court act (1721) establishing courts of inferior jurisdiction in five places represented the first effort to meet the needs of the settlers at a distance from Charles Town; settlement around frontier posts was encouraged.

The high tide of loyalty led the Assembly to surrender an important right it had gained under the Proprietors. In 1707 the Commons had forced the recognition by statute of their sole right to elect the provincial Treasurer, or Public Receiver as he was called during the Proprietary period, and every other officer supported exclusively by their taxes.[1] The Commons consented in 1721 to an act placing the election of these officers in the hands of both houses by the method of a statute, thus allowing executive veto. But, as Professor W. R. Smith observes, throughout the royal period Governor and Council were frequently forced, however much against their will, to accept the nominees of the Commons, who held the purse strings.

An Administration Ending in Quarrels.—No degree of loyalty could

[1] The Public Receiver and his successor, called Treasurer, handled only the Assembly's own revenues, and were entirely different from the Receiver General of the Proprietors and similar financial officers under the King.

long keep the peace between the arbitrariness of the passionate Nicholson and the calm determination of the Commons to be their own masters. In some points he was the winner, as in defeating for the time the effort to bring in a printer. He had his way to a degree unequaled by any other royal Governor, though the Proprietary Governor Craven's firm and courteous wisdom was more compelling. The Governor's wrath ran over when they proposed to give him a present of only the same amount as they had given Governor Moore, a mere appointee of the people. Nor did it soothe his irritation for them to defeat his efforts to continue the Assembly beyond its legal three-year term in order to avoid the choice of a new body in the cooled state of loyal enthusiasm. This very constitutional people would be a party to no such usurpation. To their suggestion that the sooner a new Assembly is called the better, he replied, " 'Tis my opinion that the later another Assembly is called the better, . . . for you can't but be sensible that I have an account of what sort of men are intended to be chosen and parties raised to choose them, which if ever accomplished the country may date its ruin from that time. . . . I thank you for your last compliment, but to return you the same is a very great trouble to

"Francis Nicholson."

The assembly replied that they were sorry that he had such a poor opinion of the people as to think they would elect an Assembly that cannot be trusted. "We know well that our King, who builds his happiness upon the liberties and privileges of his subjects, will not think the worse of us for supporting them." Then, differing with the Governor by one day as to the end of their legal term, they chose to regard the law rather than his prerogative of dissolution, and declared themselves ended as an Assembly.

Such defiance required a report to headquarters. "The Commons House of Assembly, as they style themselves," are "upon all occasions insisting on their old privileges, as they call it, in the Proprietors' time, some of which I think very inconsistent with the King's Government. . . . I should fail in my duty to his most sacred Majesty if I did not observe to your Lordships the very great trouble I have to find the spirit of Commonwealth principles both in church and in State increase here daily and (as supposed) partly by the influence of the New Englanders." These political vagaries, he thinks, may be due partly to "the uncertainty of the weather both in respect to heat and cold."

Governor Nicholson was tried not only by the "Commonwealth principles" of the Assembly but by the old Proprietary leaven of the Rhett-Trott faction. Rhett had already been criticized because his wife was a merchant while he served as surveyor and controller of customs and because, contrary to law for one in his position, he maintained wharves and ships. He was charged with harassing shipowners who used other wharves and granting useful official favors to his own patrons. But more serious were the charges of smuggling two hogsheads of tobacco and of disloyally and illegally selling provisions and guns at St. Augustine while Spanish privateers were ravaging English ships off the South Carolina coast. Rhett sought to lay the blame on Captain Hildersley, from whose warship, the *Flamborough,* he had borrowed his crew. Rhett's insolent retort when Nicholson charged him before the Council with smuggling, that the Governor was as much a smuggler as he was, roused such wrath that the old pirate fighter complained to England that the Governor towered above him with bent hands as though he would strike him down, and brought upon Rhett a prosecution for slander. The fine of £400 currency imposed by the Court of General Sessions was the result, he charged, of the Governor's bribing the jury. He lay in jail for a time rather than pay the fine or procure sureties. But before the Governor had brought the other prosecutions that he threatened, he ended the story with the laconic report that "old Rhett died of an apoplex" on January 12, 1723.

Thus at fifty-six passed one of the most striking personalities in our history—a willful, brave, rough-grained soul. There are few men in South Carolina history of such contradictory character as this greedy, violent, vulgar, lawless, brave, impulsive, generous, loyal churchman and pirate fighter. Greedily violating law and propriety for bigger profits, insulting the noble and courteous Governor Craven too vulgarly for quotation, trying to kill Governor Daniel in a quarrel over authority, fighting Stede Bonnet to the finish, magnanimously offering him mercy and refusing before the court to share in the prize money, he represents the raw material of violent passions, powerful personality, and untamed willfulness. But he met his match in the calm, dignified, and equally courageous Governor Robert Johnson and in the stormy General Francis Nicholson.

Governor Nicholson had made enemies, especially among the powerful merchants on both sides of the water, largely on account of taking sides with the planters for the £120,000 paper money act. Also thirty-nine articles against him were said to have been signed by three hundred persons in South Carolina. Many testimonials cited his devotion to the church. He was promoted to lieutenant-general on his arrival home to defend his administration and remained governor to his death on March 5, 1728, but South Carolina saw him no more. Nicholson was narrow, blustering and autocratic; but the firm hand with which he maintained order in domestic affairs and safety in Indian, French, and Spanish relations marks him as a successful executive.

Regulating the Indian Trade.—In reviewing Governor Nicholson's administration of the domestic affairs of the province we passed over for the moment his part in the relations with its Indian and foreign neighbors in the period from the close of the Yemassee War to the founding of Georgia, so as not to break the continuity of that subject.

The secret of South Carolina's Indian control lay in her ability to supply better goods than could France or Spain to satisfy the newly awakened desires of the savages. A well-regulated trade was her strongest fortification, and fair traders her best garrison. The Yemassee War was not over when the plan that the planters had long urged against merchant opposition was enacted. The commissioners named in the act of June 30, 1716, were to conduct the trade as a public monopoly. "Factories" were to be maintained at Winyaw, Fort Moore, and the Congarees, to which the Indians were to bring their skins. Agents might by special permission be sent among the tribes.

The public monopoly roused loud criticism. The Indians grumbled at the long journey to the trading posts and turned to the Virginia traders in their own towns. The Charles Town merchants charged that the new law drove the Indians into the hands of the Spanish and French, and that quantities of goods were taken by ship from Charles Town to Pensacola and Mobile to supply the traders of hostile powers with the means of ruining Carolina. Though distrust of the private traders was still profound, it proved necessary still to employ these efficient and dangerous characters. By 1721 the whole trade was back in private hands. In 1724 a single commissioner system for supervising the trade was adopted, which, except for a few months during 1751 and '52, continued until the Crown took over supervision in 1756.

The South Carolina act of 1731, closely copied by that of Georgia in 1735, formed the southern frontier trading code so long as colonial control continued. Its principle was an open trade under strict regulation, such as strict prohibition of credit, which was a temptation to the Indians to institute war as a means of wiping out desperate debts. The savages were not allowed to come into the settlements to trade, as they sometimes offered to do with bodies of armed men. Liquor offered a serious problem. It was destructive of every legitimate interest; but any nation which refused to supply it found its Indians turning to rivals who would. South Carolina engrossed the bulk of the southern Indian trade even after the establishment of Georgia, and by 1725 Virginia competition had become negligible.

Keeping France and Spain Out of Georgia, etc.—Intertwined with

Indian trade were the relations, friendly or hostile, with the various tribes and with England's rivals for American dominion, Spain and France. Fear of French aggression stirred by the founding of Mobile in 1702 and of New Orleans in 1718 determined South Carolina's foreign policy. Boone and Barnwell (agents sent to London) urged the ministry to imitate France's policy of securing the frontiers by a line of forts. Reviving in less ambitious form Thomas Nairne's program of 1707 and '08 for sweeping out the French and extending South Carolina's control over the Indians as far west as the Mississippi and from the Gulf to the 36th parallel of latitude, they cited Nairne's map of the western country for particulars and as proof of English alliance with the southwestern Indians. The French, they said, should be prevented from corrupting the Cherokees. The Lords of Trade, partially roused to the necessity of meeting France's threat to the empire on the southwest, adopted these suggestions along with those of Governor Spotswood of Virginia and Governor Burnet of New York as part of their elaborate representation of the state of the plantations completed in September, 1721. But, as Professor Crane points out, Spotswood borrowed even his words from South Carolina sources.

The Lords of Trade, in closest touch with the provinces, thus at last realized the significance of what far-seeing provincials had long urged; but the Privy Council was still lethargic. The building of a fort at the mouth of the Altamaha to forestall the rumored French intention of seizing that river was the only part of the program for which they chose to assume the expense. The plan included a settlement to be fostered around the fort, and in fact was the first definite move that was to lead a decade later to the founding of Georgia partly as an enterprise of philanthropy and partly as a bulwark against France and Spain. It was against French aggression primarily, although its location was a direct affront to Spain, that Fort King George was to be placed upon the Altamaha. "Not Oswego, in 1727," says Professor Crane, "but Altamaha in 1721, saw the inception of the British eighteenth century scheme of frontier posts to counteract French expansion." "The provincial origins of that policy," he continues, "were indubitable."

Governor Nicholson on his arrival in South Carolina promptly took up the problem of defense. Though peace was signed with Spain in November, 1719, Indians on both sides, with white encouragement, continued their forays. The fort on the Altamaha, it was hoped, would not only stop any French plans of aggression in that quarter but would also end these Spanish vexations and make good England's title to the disputed territory as far south as St. Augustine. Colonel Barnwell was selected for the task of building Fort King George. In June, 1721, he left Port Royal with a band of scouts "all drunk as beasts" on the liquor that helped induce them to enlist. The labor of getting the cypress out, wading waist or even neck deep in the swamp, was a veritable slavery, and the mosquitoes a torture. He built his 26-foot-square fort on the north side of the north branch of the Altamaha, five miles below its branching from the main stream, of four-inch plank between uprights, making removal easy if a change of location were desired.

The Carolina Assembly maintained that Spain had never held the Altamaha country since 1670 and that an English fort there was necessary to counteract the Spanish forts threatening South Carolina's territory in the west. It may be frankly admitted that Spain's title to the country south of the mouth of the Savannah was superior to England's; but to South Carolina such claims were of small weight compared with the necessity of erecting an effective barrier between herself and St. Augustine. Service in the swamp-surrounded fort, where the men died like flies, was so trying that soldiers deserted even to the Spaniards. It burned about January 1, 1725, was rebuilt about 1731, and had a garrison as late as 1734 and possibly as late as 1736.

The hundred men brought by Governor Nicholson to garrison Fort King George were the first British regulars sent to South Carolina. This was the beginning of a garrison of from one to three British companies (later largely recruited in the colonies) that with intermissions, including one of ten years from 1736 to '46, did duty in South Carolina. Until the French and Spanish danger was removed in 1763, they were welcome, but not after that.

As a further defense to the South and Southwest, a small fort was built on the lower Savannah, and a trifling little fort at Beaufort, replaced by Fort Frederick made of oyster shell, lime, and timber in 1732-34, on the extreme southeastern corner of Port Royal Island.

Keeping Cherokees and Creeks at War as a Means of Carolina Safety.—For more than a decade following the Yemassee War South Carolina faced a triangular Indian problem cornering with the Yemassees in Florida, the Creeks in the West, and the Cherokees in the mountains. The Yemassees, though now weak in numbers, were protected by Spain and presented the most immediate danger. As in all Indian wars, save the Westo affair, the purpose of the province was to teach the Indians their place, not to exterminate or expel them. They were essential as consumers of trading goods and as bulwarks against the province's enemies.

South Carolina now entered in 1717 upon a desperate eleven years' diplomatic struggle against the French to reclaim her position in the Southwest which had been shattered by the Yemassee War. From Fort

Toulouse in the fork of the Alabama, France had established a strong hold upon the upper Creeks and for the first time had gained influence with the Lower Creeks of the Chattahoochee. The Spanish were not behind, though less formidable, and in the same year sent seven Creek and Apalachee chiefs to swear allegiance to Spain in the grandeur of Mexico. The Lower Creek "Emperor" Brims, "wilderness politician extraordinary," took the position which his people were for years to occupy with such benefit to themselves—that he would trade with French, Spanish, and English alike, and profit by their differences. Up to the expulsion of France and Spain in 1763, Brims' policy of the balance of power prevailed with a consistency worthy of European statesmanship.

In November, 1717, the Creeks made peace with South Carolina, thus becoming the last tribe concerned to close the Yemassee War. Later Governor Nicholson promised the Creeks by treaty that English settlements should not extend west of the Savannah.

South Carolina's policy from 1717 to '28 was to pretend friendship to both Creeks and Cherokees, while secretly favoring the latter and holding both in check by stimulating the war which began with the Cherokees' murdering the Creek envoys in 1716 and joining South Carolina in the Yemassee War.

The Creeks were thoroughly cynical regarding Carolina professions of friendship and for years kept the province on the ragged edge of war with unpunished outrages. South Carolina was beginning to realize that her feeble and transparent double-dealing game was sowing danger rather than security.

To bring about a peace between the Cherokees and the Creeks was the only alternative to open war with the Creeks and the Yemassees. The chiefs of Cherokees and Creeks were induced to meet in Charles Town January 26, 1727, with due precedence arranged for the Cherokees as punctiliously as though they were European diplomats. Royal healths were drunk amid the roaring guns of all the forts, and the Indians went off to smoke the pipe of peace together.

But the old Spanish leaven still worked among the Lower Creeks, warriors from some of whose towns joined the Spanish-Yemassee raids on the southern parishes. Sometimes, led by two or three Spaniards, the Yemassees would murder a planter, sometimes kill and sometimes capture the women, burn the buildings, and be off with stolen valuables and slaves before pursuit could be organized. Finally Colonel John Palmer, who as a stripling had won fame for one of the most daring acts of personal heroism in the Yemassee War, with seventy-nine whites and ninety-odd Indians at daybreak of March 9, 1728, crushed the

Yemassees under the very shadow of the Castle of St. Augustine. This was a language that could be understood. The Governor of Havana assured President Middleton of his desire for peace, which he emphasized by sending all his English prisoners. Palmer's victory was effective not only in Havana, but likewise in the Chattahoochee-Alabama wilderness, where Glover had been buying Spanish scalps and preferably Spanish captives. Says Professor Crane: "After ten years of uncertain peace, after three anxious years of increasing tension, something like stability had been restored in Anglo-Creek relations. Fitch and Glover[2] had helped notably to make possible the later frontier achievements of James Edward Oglethorpe."

Sir Alexander Cuming and the Cherokees.—But while Creek relations were thus slowly mending, Cherokee affairs were growing worse. Under the incessant attacks of the Illinois and other French Indians, the Overhill Cherokees, most exposed of their nation, were yielding to the French offers of alliance. It was at this critical juncture that one of the strangest incidents in American Indian relations occurred to bind the Cherokees to the English. The erratic Scotch baronet and Fellow of the Royal Society Sir Alexander Cuming, in obedience to a dream directing him to the Cherokee Mountains, was in 1729-30 in South Carolina on a private voyage of scientific discovery. As he approached the home of the Cherokees, he learned of the machinations of the French. The scientist instantly became the statesman. His superb audacity, endorsed apparently by the most violent thunder and lightning ever known, won the submission of the whole nation.

Two chiefs and five warriors accompanied Cuming to England, apparently merely as individuals and not as Indian representatives. The British government, at last alive to the importance of the southwestern frontier, improved this opportunity. The Indians were presented at court, witnessed the grandeur of installing two Knights of the Garter, the treasures of the Tower, the maneuvers of troops, etc., were paraded as "Kings" and "Generals" in the press, and lionized in society, in all of which they bore themselves with dignity. "Articles of friendship" and commercial agreement were prepared with three purposes: peaceful trade with the Cherokees, their alliance against England's enemies, and the establishment of England's claim against any other European nation to the vast Cherokee territory which France planned to absorb. On September 7 the proposed agreement was read to the Indians before the Lords of Trade.

Two days later the Indians replied. In words instinct with native

[2] Colonel Tobias Fitch, who persuaded the Creeks to come to the peace conference of January, 1727, and Colonel Charlesworth Glover, who skillfully cemented the peace.

eloquence and personal dignity their spokesman represented the Cherokees as nothing in comparison with the greatness and power they had witnessed. "We look upon King George as our brother," he said, "and will carry the chain of friendship to our people. In war King George's enemies shall be ours, and we will die together. Your white people may very safely build houses near us; we shall hurt nothing that belongs to them."

Whether it was barbarian ignorance or shrewd design, the Indians omitted all reference to the King's right over their lands or the exclusion of French traders. Nothing ever happened in later years to indicate that the Indians or the English considered the former to have surrendered title to their lands. For practical purposes they regarded themselves as having become allies of a power much greater than themselves, and the English treated the sovereignty clause as what it was proposed for —a basis for excluding the rival territorial claims of France. The unauthorized act of the seven Indians in England seems to have received the tacit assent of their people. For over twenty years the tremendous impression communicated to the Cherokees by their tribesmen who had seen the majesty and the power of the Great King held them in the English interest.

CHAPTER XVII

DEPRESSION AND PAPER MONEY, 1725-1730

ARTHUR MIDDLETON, the eldest member, as president of the Council assumed the administration on May 7, 1725, a few days before Governor Nicholson's departure at the beginning of a period of difficulty and confusion. The fortunate outcome of Middleton's management of the critical Spanish and Indian problem as related above was not paralleled in his handling of domestic affairs.

Sale of Offices, Defaults, etc.—Middleton rendered his position, trying enough amid prolonged economic depression and popular passion, worse by his lack of sympathy with popular distress, his hauteur, and his practicing in a more than usually offensive form the bad custom of selling offices. Benjamin Whitaker, at this time Attorney General and later Speaker of the Commons and Chief Justice, was one of the ablest and most rigorous opponents of public abuses. On January 28, 1726, he wrote to Governor Nicholson in England that President Middleton had sent word to Mr. Killpatrick that he might have Clerk of the Crown and Court Coulliette's place for £300 currency. To his plea of no money, Middleton replied that he would take his bond endorsed by a friend who had married a rich widow. An attempt was then made to sell the office to another, whom Middleton caused to petition him to remove Coulliette for incompetence; but the simple gentleman offered no money, and the President bestowed the office on Childermas Croft for £200 cash.

The place of vendue master went to a favorite without the other applicant's having a chance to bid. The attempt to run the price of the provost marshalship up £100 by deceit failed, and it went at half price for £200. Such corruption, Whitaker continued, is condemned in a native South Carolinian who formerly denounced the Proprietors for such practices. He did take £200 for the office, Middleton wrote Nicholson, but he did it openly, and discharged Coulliette only on the judge's complaint. This place and the other two "have been looked upon as perquisites of the government, and something has always been given for them, and how it now comes to be a crime in me, I can't tell. Indeed your Excellency did not, but that was your own goodness, and you spent many thousand pounds in the country more than you got," but, he added, he could not afford it.

The Commons unanimously resolved that the selling of places connected with the courts, punishable by the laws of England as peculiarly heinous, was "of the utmost ill-consequences to his Majesty's subjects in this province and very much to the dishonor of His Majesty."

To report President Middleton to Secretary of State Newcastle for selling offices was the joke of the season. The enormously wealthy duke was not a bribe-taker, but was the most prodigal corrupter of public men. Naturally what shocked the more primitive South Carolina, already started on the upgrade that in a few generations was to make public life a synonym for honor, was perfunctorily put to sleep by the Lords of Trade. And despite improvement, we shall find, later than this, public men in South Carolina doing, without general condemnation, what men of the same standing would not do today.

Though the Commons' severe rebuke to Middleton doubtless made sentiment against an ancient abuse, it did not end sales. When Governor Robert Johnson in 1732 heard of an effort to make the post of naval officer a patent place, he protested to the Duke of Newcastle that it always had been in the nomination of the Governor, and "I humbly hope that this hardship won't be put upon me"; but he indignantly denied in 1732 that he had profited by appointing a deputy provost marshal. When Jacob Motte was running for Treasurer in 1743, he denied that he had offered to bribe members and explained he had merely offered his opponent part of the perquisites if he would withdraw. In 1806 the Richland clerk of court was credibly reported to have agreed to sell his office for $800; but the Governor would, of course, have no part in the profits.

Sources of Public Revenue.—The returns for January, 1722, showed only 1,163,817 acres in private ownership—less than six per cent of the present area of the State.

The colonists paid to the British government slight import duties imposed by Parliament which went toward supporting the officials in the colony necessary to administer the laws of navigation and trade but not for revenue, and were recognized as a legitimate charge for imperial regulation. The royal government, like the Proprietors, collected quitrents, which were recognized as a legitimate though unwelcome charge in return for the gift of the land. The quitrents amounted at the best under the Proprietors to about £500 sterling. They used them partly to pay their officers, and never on but one or two distressful occasions gave any, and then small sums, for general provincial defense. Governor Robert Johnson wrote in 1729 and again in 1731 that none had been paid in over twenty years, a surprising statement which I am not prepared to sustain or deny.

The rent was to begin ten years after the grant; but it proved, to the last, impossible to overcome, with regard to a large part of the land, the passive resistance to payment. Collectors who persisted in pressing the King's claims found themselves subjected to social and even stronger hostility. The act of 1731 remitted all quitrents due before that date. The lands returned for provincial taxation in 1742 were 2,349,129 acres. And yet in 1773, after extraordinary efforts to complete the quitrent roll, the number of acres on the roll was only 811,761. Many large estates are absent, which is doubtless accounted for in part, but only in part, by their having descended from grants under the Proprietors on which quitrents were remitted as a favor or because the lands were bought quitrent free. The quitrent book for 1768 notes many estates from five to thirty years behind, the law enjoining forfeiture for five years' delinquency being a dead letter. In 1772 various large owners are recorded as paying up arrears of from five to thirty-eight years. Some of the outstanding large owners, as Lieutenant-Governor Bull, Elias Ball, N. and A. Broughton, Henry Laurens, Elias Horry, and John Colleton, are recorded as paying on time. It is evident that the vast majority of the lands due to pay quitrents escaped.

The King expended the entire income from quitrents in supporting his officers or similar services in South Carolina. The collections for the years ending March 26, in sterling, were as follows: 1769, £1,916; 1770, £1,793; 1771, £1,727; 1772, £2,173; 1773, £3,671.

The province's budget was small, equaling, in 1724-25, £16,658 currency, and for 1726-27, £27,452. But in addition to the ordinary expenses of government normally met by the land and slave tax, there were the salaries of Anglican ministers and various special services to which the import duties imposed by the colonial Assembly were appropriated. The duty on Negroes, imposed to discourage importations, was for long dedicated, to double the desired effect, to aiding poor white settlers.

Money bills occasioned many clashes between the two houses. That of 1725 began the process of encroachment by the Commons which ended only with the Revolution. In December the Commons struck out without conference the Council's amendments to the tax bill. The Council asserted their equal rights in legislation as based on precedent and the King's instructions. The Commons now passed beyond their original objection to the method of amendment, and denied that the Council had any more right to amend a tax bill than did the lords in England. The King's forbidding the Commons of South Carolina to possess greater privileges than possessed by the Commons of England, they contended, was the same as guaranteeing them the same privileges, one of which was the sole right of originating and shaping money bills with only the right of approval or rejection in the upper house.

The Council submitted, as the only means of securing a tax and appropriation bill (for the two were always in one measure), and referred their violated rights to the Crown, which pursued decade after decade the temporizing policy of placating the purse-holders.

Paper Money.—The dominant internal question under President Middleton was that of paper money. There are in American history few such examples of the havoc wrought by this deceptive agency as that afforded by South Carolina from 1715 to 1730. The tendency of new countries to manufacture money or to attract metal by giving it a fictitious value appeared in the South Carolina acts of 1700 and 1701 grossly overvaluing foreign coins. Complaint was made to the Lords of Trade that creditors were thus defrauded of 30 per cent of their dues. This fraud was continued until about 1712, when the royal veto ended South Carolina's only attempt of this kind.

On May 8, 1703, in order to pay the debt left by the St. Augustine expedition, the Assembly issued £6,000 of bills of credit, to be legal tender under double-value penalty for rejection. They were to be retired by taxes in two years (soon extended to three) and meanwhile to bear twelve per cent interest. The notes were of large denomination—50 shillings to £20—a wise precaution against expelling specie that was soon abandoned. From 1703, says the elder Bull in 1740, gold and silver were dealt in as merchandise.

The redemption promise and even the interest pledge were soon broken and new quantities of bills printed. There had been issued through November 10, 1711, £29,000, of which £9,000 had been redeemed.

The depreciation of the bills in 1710 was only £150 of currency to £100 sterling. The process now entered a new stage in the act of June 7, 1712, called the bank act. By declaring it impossible to pay in any tolerable time the debts represented by the existing bills of credit due to the St. Augustine expedition, fortifying Charles Town, repelling the Franco-Spanish invasion, and assisting North Carolina in the Tuscarora war, it virtually declared the existence of a permanent public debt. This act also introduced government loans to private persons for their own business purposes. New bills to the amount of £32,000 were issued as loans on real estate to be repaid by twelve annual installments of 12½ per cent of the face of the loan. This was the "bank." The bank bills were faithfully destroyed on being repaid except the last installment of £8,000.

The Yemassee War added £5,000 of new bills, bringing outstanding legal tender paper to $106,000. The law for gradual redemption was slighted, and in 1722 a bill was launched to print a new issue of £120,000,

£80,000 of which was to retire the existing paper and £40,000 of which was to be a clear addition to the amount already outstanding. The argument was that floods had destroyed the people's power to pay taxes. In December, 1722, twenty-eight South Carolina merchants presented a memorial against the bill, exposing the evils that had flowed from twenty years of inflation and the habitual breaches of the public faith as to redemption. The Commons voted that this was false, scandalous, and destructive to the interests of the province, and threw the twenty-eight merchants into prison for contempt. Only after repeated petitions, descending lower and lower in submission, were the last of the offenders freed, after having been confined almost a month, and then only after the house had raised the fees that must be paid their clerk and messenger for the formalities of release. Thus passed one of the worst examples of the tyranny by which, until the Revolution, this haughty Assembly was accustomed to silence opposition. With their growing power only the direct authority of King and Parliament was able to stand before them, and even that not ultimately.

On February 23, 1723, Governor Nicholson, contrary to the King's instructions and much to his injury with the higher powers, signed the £120,000 bill, but it was vetoed by the King at the instance of the London merchants, who largely directed England's colonial policy. However, a large part of the new money had already been issued when the veto arrived. The act of February 15, 1724, virtually provided for it to remain outstanding on the pledge of rapid retirement. On the bitter complaint of the South Carolinians that their laws were vetoed at the instance of persons who knew nothing of their conditions without their having a chance to state their side, and on Governor Nicholson's warning that the planters would be driven to put their slaves to making woolen and linen cloth for lack of a medium for buying goods, the royal government let the matter stand. The pledge of redemption was very partially kept. But it should be remembered in judging the passion for paper money among the colonists that they lacked the facilities for bank credit expansion by which England could and we do now inflate the circulating medium by creating "deposits" out of nothing but credit.[1]

To relieve the scarcity of money, private agencies emerged. Thirteen merchants are known to have issued their own notes. In May, 1730, some prominent planters with a cash capital of £10,000 had currency

[1] *An Essay on Currency,* written in August, 1732, and printed in Charles Town in 1734, is perhaps one of the earliest books on the subject published in the United States. It abounds with the standard follies of the blessings of fiat money. Public expenses, the author thinks, should be met partly by paper money to ease the burden, and partly by taxes lest people get "resty" (lazy); "but too high taxes eat out their very victuals."

printed and issued as a partnership, without legal authority, their circulating notes to the sum of £50,000 currency, lending them at the legal rate of 10 per cent, to relieve the stress of 15 per cent, which was being charged. They professed that their notes were redeemable in currency or the equivalent in silver, but a hostile critic charged that the issuers openly said they would give out no silver, and sneered that it was proposed even to give their promissory notes for their stock subscriptions. Yet, he said, we merchants will have to accept the paper, which we fear will still more depress currency value. The fact that it did not, seems to indicate a need for more currency.

Thus the paper money stood at the end of President Middleton's administration. We must now notice some of the effects of the agitation. The following, from official statements or trustworthy letters, etc., indicates the varying values of South Carolina currency:

Year	*Currency*		*Sterling*	*Year*	*Currency*		*Sterling*
1710	150	=	100	1735-36	750-760	=	100
1714	200	=	100	1736	740	=	100
1715	400	=	100	1737	740	=	100
1717	575	=	100	1738	800	=	100
1720	400	=	100	1739	700-720	=	100
1722	520	=	100	1748	700	=	100
1724 (Feb.)	600	=	100	1749	700-725	=	100
1725	710	=	100	1755	700	=	100
1726-29	700	=	100	1764 (Sept.)	721	=	100
1730	675-700	=	100	1764	775	=	100
1731	700	=	100	1767 (April)	700	=	100
1733	700	=	100	1770-73	762	=	100
1734	700	=	100				

The familiar phenomena were observed: clergy and public employees reduced to distress because their incomes were sharply reduced in purchasing power, with belated relief through increased pay much less than in proportion; business relations disordered; creditors defrauded; contracts made payable in commodities; interest rising to 30 per cent, as creditors sought to secure themselves against the diminished value of the paper in which they would be repaid; and debtors protesting with almost revolutionary violence against being sacrificed to merciless money-monopolist creditors, until at last the strong hand of the royal government checked the flow of paper. From the time that paper became the ordinary medium of business, appropriations, taxes, etc., were regularly stated in "currency" (i.e., paper money), often without anything to indicate the distinction. Overlooking this fact often causes modern writers to represent colonial sums as much larger than they really were. After the paper medium had become stabilized by about 1725 at about one-seventh the value of sterling, the disturbance of business and social relations on account of violent fluctuations largely ceased.

The Courts and the Debtors.—The courts became involved through foreclosures and imprisonment for debt. Judges and grand and petty juries joined in protests that the proposal to force payment of debts in proclamation money (three-fourths the value of sterling) would amount to a clear gift of enormous sums to creditors. The Commons took advantage of every necessity of the administration. For instance, when Fort King George had to be rebuilt, the only means they would supply was to enact that the paper due to be burnt should instead be used for the fort. President Middleton could only plead necessity for violating the King's instructions in submitting. For conduct impeding their course the Provost-Marshal was jailed for contempt by the Commons and the Chief Justice himself was saved from being dragged from the Council chamber to answer for contempt before the Commons by President Middleton's indignantly ejecting their messenger and dissolving the Assembly. For over four years before August, 1731, the only laws enacted were two in the face of an expected Indian war. There was not a tax or appropriation act, and, since the jury lists were exhausted, there were no courts. The breaking open of the jury box and the taking out of nearly all the names was evidently a part of the plan to block the courts. There was widespread resistance to all legal process, and officers seeking to serve papers dared not venture into the country after several had been beaten and rolled in ditches by slaves who were set upon them.

The breach between the Council and the Commons was complete. The former represented the merchant interests as defended by the royal prerogative, and the latter were fully in sympathy with the debtor planters. In an elaborate historical memorial the Council accused Governor Nicholson of having agreed to new issues of paper money to win favor with the Commons who controlled his pay; "nor is it any secret in any of your Majesty's plantations where paper credit is made," they wrote, "why your Majesty's Governors evermore join with the people [in favor] of these projects." But for us, they continued, the £120,000 act would have been for £200,000.

Debts and Paper Money Threaten Civil War.—Following severe contraction of the paper circulation for the past three years, and the spread of counterfeiting, the popular movement for more paper money assumed definite shape in the bill sent up by the Commons on December 15, 1726, by a majority of two. When the Council refused a conference on an issue involving disobedience to the King's instructions, the agitators sought to accomplish, said the Council, by mob violence what they had failed to do by law. The Council was denounced as opposing the public good, and Thomas Smith, a leader in the Commons and among the people, declared "that now there was necessity for a bold stroke, and that some men (meaning your Majesty's Council) must be put in bodily fear." The agitators bound themselves to defend each other in refusing to pay taxes, and prepared "an insolent and intimidating" address to the President and Council. The gist of the address thus described is that the opponents of issuing more paper money were conspiring to deprive the people of their lands. We are forced by grasping lawyers, base judges, and extortioners, it said, to pay three or four times our just debts because of the lack of a law for the tender of produce or a sufficient amount of paper money for the trade of the province.

President Middleton stirred the petitioners' anger by a proclamation on April 21, 1727, denouncing their meetings as riotous assemblages to withdraw the people from obedience to the King, and ordering their dispersion or arrest. When the meetings continued, Thomas Smith, son of the Landgrave, was arrested. This only led to worse disturbances and the release of Smith. Early in May, 1727, about two hundred men rode into town, while two of their leaders delivered to the President and Council their petition, with swords at their sides and pistols under their arms. They did not intend to be arrested as Smith had been.

The meetings continued and grew in size. Landgrave Smith, boldly defiant always of what he considered wrong, now entered the scene. One of the wealthiest and most active men in the province, he had abandoned his seat in the Council since a dispute with Nicholson. His letters to John Croft, now laid before the Council, related that the great meeting was postponed to give time for assembling more people. Charles Town, he hears, thinks the country people are coming to make a revolution. He cannot tell what may be in time. "The laws of God and man forbid obedience to an usurper."

President Middleton thereupon caused the Landgrave to be arrested at three o'clock in the morning in his bed by constables and man-of-war sailors, on a charge of high treason, accused of seeking to have himself put in Middleton's place by force. Militia were summoned but did little but beat the Marshal for trying to arrest one of their leaders and send in papers, "full of invectives," which cited the vote of the British Commons in 1681 on the right of petition, denounced the arrest of Landgrave Smith by man-of-war's men, and demanded the calling of the Assembly. Militiamen threatened to take two of the Council in reprisal for the Smiths.

The Assembly, summoned for August 1, afforded a constitutional channel for the discontents. The event of the session came when the Assembly, its doors and windows crowded with the populace, permitted ex-Chief Justice Trott, as Smith's attorney, to argue his case. This President Middleton's command had failed to stop. "I will not suffer his Majesty's royal prerogative nor his courts trampled upon," he declared as he prorogued them to mid-September.

The worst of the domestic crisis was over, although the bitterness and deadlock lasted until the long-delayed first definitive royal Governor arrived in 1731. Landgrave Smith was never prosecuted, but lived long enough to give the Commons, through his being further, and apparently illegally, persecuted, another of those dangerous things—a grievance.

The Indian danger served to draw some of the inflammation from internal troubles. When President Middleton recalled the Assembly to face an apparently unavoidable Creek war, co-operation was excellent except on how to secure the funds. They could devise no way of providing the funds except to re-issue the £20,000 reserved for burning, said the Commons. They had their way. The Council could only plead to the King the necessity of saving the province and complain of the refusal of the Assembly to fix standing salaries by statute for the Governor, judges, and Attorney-General and thus be able to intimidate them.

A Creek war was avoided, and the legislative quarrels were resumed, the Commons seeking vainly to stop the retirement of the paper money as provided by law or to force bills for more paper and for giving it a false valuation. To trace the wearisome squabble is useless. Newly elected Assemblies refused to form quorums or walked away without leave. Sir Alexander Cuming found South Carolina in 1729 and '30 a land where every man did what he thought fit, without security for life or property. Unpaid garrisons threatened to quit, and but for the fee system, civil administration might have collapsed.

President Middleton, losing any faith he might have had in popular government, wrote Newcastle urging that the Governor to be appointed should be furnished with British funds and troops and "that some means may be found out for punishing these disorderly people that are grown frantic with their own licentiousness and fancy themselves out of the reach of the power of the government."

But the ministry, largely responsible through their neglect for the disorders, were at last better advised. They considered South Carolina's extraordinary expenses—four times as great as any other colony's, they were told by Burrington of North Carolina. Even the British merchants relented and requested the Lords of Trade to allow the continuance of the £106,355 of paper for seven years, during which the taxes that would have retired it should go to buy tools, etc., for settlers.

It can hardly be doubted that in this is seen the wise and healing hand of Robert Johnson, who had never ceased to love the Carolinians nor they him. He had now been selected for governor and was active in urging concessions.

In 1729, the King, having bought the province, was preparing to conciliate the people and make a new start under an exceptional leader. Middleton's administration was over. One of the most beloved of all the governors was coming to supersede one of the most unfortunate. The paper money agitation would have taxed the strongest and most tactful executive, and Middleton's stiff pride made it worse. The Commons cut his pay severely. Yet he showed courage and determination during one of the most difficult periods, in which passion disorganized every branch of the province's life and brought within hailing distance the dissolution of government. He and his Council, who stood loyally by him, were commanded by the King to defy the people without being much helped in the task.

Barring the early error of duplicity toward the Creeks and Cherokees, which was the province's and not his personal policy, Middleton showed skill and courage in Indian and foreign relations. He was not a great executive; but many a man counted as such would have a smaller fame if he had been tried under such circumstances.

CHAPTER XVIII

ECONOMIC AND POLITICAL RECOVERY, 1731-1735

THE HAPPIER era which began with the arrival of Colonel Robert Johnson for his second term as governor on December 15, 1730, was due partly to his own wisdom, moderation, and skill, but also largely to the awakening, however tardy, of the British government to the situation of the province. In 1729 Parliament bought out at £2,500 sterling apiece seven of the Proprietors for both Carolinas, and on account of £9,500 rents estimated due the corporation compensated them for these credits up to £5,000. Lord Carteret, refusing to sell, shared with the King the income from rents and land sales until 1744, when he was given as his one-eighth the land lying between Virginia and latitude 34 degrees 34 minutes. The Proprietors were a bankrupt company, indebted since 1708 for their own annual quitrents of £13 6*s*. 8*d*. to the Crown. The sale price constituted practically all they ever made.

As though the orphan on the King's doorstep for the past ten years had just been found, the government now overflowed with kindness. The solicitation begun in 1712 resulted in 1730 in Parliament's permitting exportation of rice to any port south of Cape Finisterre, thus saving to the planter the British duty and the middleman's profit.[1] In consultation with Governor Johnson, who was the owner of 19,000 acres in South Carolina and so long a resident as to amount almost to a native, favorable instructions were prepared on paper money, quitrents, land grants, and immigration.

Land-grabbing and Frauds.—A pressing necessity was the re-opening of the land office, virtually closed by the Proprietors in 1718 and absolutely on September 4, 1719. While would-be settlers were thus barred, inheritors or purchasers of old patents direct from the Proprietors were staking out some 800,000 acres of the best lands. There now followed a bitter controversy on the legality of these patents or warrants, by means

[1] After rice was allowed to go directly to ports south of Cape Finisterre it was nevertheless required to pay half the duty that it would have paid had it entered Britain, i.e., the duty less the drawback, or the part of the duty returned on re-exported goods.—E. C. Kirkland, *History of American Economic Life* (1946), p. 103. Re-exported goods were allowed a drawback ranging from half to the whole of the duty paid on entering Britain.

of which a few persons were given such advantages at the expense both of the Crown and of actual settlers.

The regular method provided safeguards lacking in these cases. The applicant secured from the Governor and Council a warrant, directing the Surveyor-General to lay off the stated number of acres designated loosely as "in Craven County," "on Cedar Creek," etc. On viewing the plat made by the surveyor, the Governor and Council issued a grant describing the land, which the owner recorded with the Secretary of the province. Orders had frequently been obtained from the Proprietors to issue on such patent alone a grant to such and such quantities of land. But the situation in 1731 presented two peculiarities: many of the patents were for very large tracts, and many of great age, specifying no particular land, had passed from deceased persons into later hands.

In 1730 the Lords of Trade asked the opinion of the King's Attorney-General and Solicitor-General on the legality of a patent for 24,000 acres in 1686 to Sir Nathaniel Johnson, the father of the new Governor. The law officers advised on July 28, 1730, that such a patent was void, as it failed to specify any particular land. On November 24, 1735, they gave a similar opinion on another patent. The chancery court in South Carolina (i.e., the Council, generally laymen and some probably interested in this question) had on August 12, 1726, sustained for the son such a patent dated 1698 for 48,000 acres to the deceased Landgrave John Baily, against the strong protest of Attorney-General Whitaker—an opinion in which Whitaker was sustained by Attorney-General Pinckney (1732-33).

The question now became one of extraordinary violence in connection with the law by which land titles and arrears of quitrents were to be settled. On the advice of those uncrowned sovereigns, the British merchants, in whose interests the colonists were so largely governed, the King had allowed Governor Johnson to consent to suspend for seven years the process of retiring the paper money and to use the sinking fund for helping poor Protestant settlers, and had agreed also to remit all arrears of quitrents, provided the Assembly would repeal "Archdale's Law" of 1696 and enact an effective law for the future payment of quitrents in proclamation money. The quitrent act of August 20, 1731, enacted this bargain into law, and in addition confirmed the whole body of the old Proprietary patents that the Attorney-General and Solicitor-General had declared void. Within eighteen months these and all other land titles must be registered, in order to secure a record of landholdings for what there had never been and never came to be—a complete rent roll.

There followed a period of feverish anxiety during which the King was urged to approve or veto the law, as the possibilities of making or missing quick riches roused passions between factions in South Carolina. Greed was stirred the more deeply as men emerging from a long period of depression and debt visioned wealth through engrossing the land that would soon sell at higher values on account of the rapid growth of population through government-aided immigration. Many members of the Council and Assembly were themselves deeply interested as holders of old patents, with the effect on their public action that might be expected. Governor Johnson defended the law to the Board of Trade on grounds of equity and necessity. "I would have fain excluded the large grants of landgraveships, cassiqueships, and baronies as being prejudicial to the well settling of the province; but so many people have during the long time the land office has been shut up purchased under these titles that almost everybody in the province are more or less concerned in the support of them, so that the Council and I found it impossible to carry the point so necessary for his Majesty's service without confirming those titles, however deficient they may be in law. They claim equity as having paid considerable sums for their purchases under those titles . . . and they further plead that every government in America has one time or another passed acts to determine and secure titles to land; and as the reserved quitrents are continued to his Majesty, which consequently makes it no detriment to his immediate interest, the Council and I consented to this part of the law as what was absolutely necessary for the peace and tranquility of the province."

The critics of the law had the advantage that it was inconsistent with the King's instructions seeking to prevent land-engrossing that would hinder the plans for bringing in settlers. Governor Johnson's instructions empowered him to grant fifty acres for every man, woman, or child, white or black, dependent on the grantee. The looseness of the instructions left the way open for speculators to obtain vast tracts in addition to their already large holdings, contrary to the whole intention to place the land in the hands of actual users. The requirements of settling were met under the friendly eyes of the Assembly by cutting notches in boundary trees.

Benjamin Whitaker, now the deputy of James St. John, Surveyor-General, and Inspector and Controller of Quitrents, wrote, September, 1732, that those whose duty it was to aid the Surveyor-General in ascertaining the land due quitrents, etc., intimated it would not be well for him to interfere with their interests, and that his tranquillity was to be purchased only by his silence or connivance. Not acceding, Whitaker was subjected to treatment "not fit for the most mean or abject of all his Majesty's subjects." Great abuses, he continued, "are practiced under the clause of the law that permits grants on old purchase receipts and old deeds burnt or lost. The law enables any common surveyor to perpetrate frauds for his employers through not having to turn his survey into any office. As an example, a poor cattle hunter picking up a little income from showing people untaken lands was imprisoned by the Assembly under a pretext of contempt and threatened by the Governor, which afforded me the occasion to inform the Governor that I hoped the tranquillity of the province did not depend on confirming the possessions of those who had unlawfully intruded on the King's lands. I am sure much of the greater part of the people would like to see the King's instructions on the land question obeyed; but the places of authority are filled with those who prefer a present and selfish advantage."

The Lords of Trade recommended a veto; but the Privy Council hesitated to throw the recovering province back into uncertainty. Warrants were issued for 600,000 acres in about two years. A moderate man, Surveyor-General George Hunter, years after the excitement, wrote that Governor Johnson on November 27, 1731, signed for more land than Governor Glen in his first four and a half years, 1744 to '48. There was such a greed, he said, that the King's instructions were misconstrued, and a man with 10,000 acres was granted 10,000 more for his head rights. They engrossed these lands with intent of selling them to newcomers; but, he continued, most of them could not sell for the fees they paid and the quitrents without the 10 per cent interest on the money they borrowed. Governor Glen himself reported that "many thousand, I may say hundred thousand, acres . . . have been granted directly contrary to his Majesty's instructions, . . . to the ruin of numbers of poor Protestants" coming to settle the townships. In 1751 he wrote, "A great many stand possessed of more, and some of exceedingly more, than they are entitled to" by family right.

Punishing Critics of the Land Policy.—The question presented two aspects: first, of the public interest, including the fair treatment of the actual settlers; and second, the facilitation of actual frauds. So far as the public interest was concerned, it was ruthlessly sacrificed in the interest of holders of the old patents or their assignees. The cry that the approval of the act was necessary for securing all land titles was specious, as this was united in the same bill with the questionable patents for the same reason that the new quitrent arrangements were—to force the acceptance of the whole bill. Sanctifying these questionable patents was entirely out of harmony with the principle on which land had regularly been granted. The Lords Proprietors until their degeneracy had often granted lands on condition they be settled in a short time, after which the grant lapsed. Consideration was primarily for the actual settler. "Archdale's Law" of 1696 specifically guaranteed the titles of persons actually holding lands on a mere survey, and of squatters without even a survey.

The act of 1731 sacrificed in favor of the patentees even the immigrants who had been invited by Governor Robert Johnson under the act of Assembly to settle around Port Royal to defend the province against the Indians and Spaniards. Numbers of these swore that they had come on these official guarantees, that they had occupied their lands for years under official warrant and survey, but had been prevented from getting grants because of the closing of the land office for thirteen years. Yet during those years they had defended the border until forced away by prolonged Indian raids. Colonel Beamor swore that he presented to Governor Johnson the warrant for land for George Beamor, signed by Johnson himself, praying to have again his lands, but that Johnson threw the warrant aside and refused all relief. Bitter was such treatment, as Johnson had had some of these very lands run out for himself under the old 24,000-acre patent to his father, though he dropped them and took out new head-right grants when the patents were declared illegal, a needless technical change, as he was soon to sign the act validating his patents. If defects in titles were to be healed by legislative act, surely those of the Port Royal defenders, brought in under public promise, might have been considered.

The Lords of Trade were advised by their legal counsel that these people had a good case; but the Assembly resisted the establishment of an exchequer court to correct such abuses. An exceptional opportunity was presented for the Crown to exercise its function as trustee for the public, as Archdale had done in 1696; but reluctance to prolong confusion and conflict dictated swallowing the draft so mixed of good and evil.

Passing from consideration of the act as a moral fraud, what of the acquisitions of lands contrary even to the act itself? That there were such under the virtual invitation of the act, by rich and poor alike, is certain; but they were doubtless less than either contemporary or modern critics charge. Men sometimes swore to nonexistent head rights. Officials shamelessly granted vast tracts to themselves or their favorites who already held all they deserved on head rights. Governor Johnson reported that the Council had taken up 6,000 acres apiece, but that most of them had head rights for so much. On another occasion Governor Broughton and the Council voted to each of themselves 6,000 acres apiece, on the theory, perhaps, that their public labors deserved it. From 1731 to '38, says Professor Meriwether, over a million acres had been added to the tax books in the feverish land speculation. And in approximately the same period 15,600 Negroes had been imported. The prosperity which was to last with some interruptions to the Revolution had begun.

When the people who had been driven from the southern district by the Indian raids of 1715-27 returned to find their lands assigned to the holders of ancient patents, they and others wishing to test the matter prepared to appeal to the courts. Their leader, Dr. Cooper, was thereupon committed to prison by the Commons for action tending to litigious disputes involving the country in confusion. During the five weeks that he lay there he was elected to the Commons by the people whose rights he had sought to protect. Graeme, his attorney, the Commons imprisoned for contempt for seeking a habeas corpus for him, as they did also Attorney Vaughn for applying to the Chief Justice for a habeas corpus for Graeme, and spoke of punishing the Chief Justice himself. Chief Justice Wright, whose authority was thus so contemned, protested to the Council; but that body, for once in harmony with their traditional opponents through a community of plunder, published an elaborate defense of the Commons and arrested for comtempt persons who applied to members of the Council for habeas corpus papers for the imprisoned.

The Commons wreaked their revenge on Chief Justice Wright by petitioning for his removal and by stopping his salary, or, as they insisted, his "donation," or "gratuity." For his remaining six years the royal insistence finally secured him about one and a half year's pay. The matter resulted in 1737 in the King's placing the office of judge permanently in the royal pay.

Surveyor-General St. John, whose paper against the land act Governor Johnson showed the Assembly, had meanwhile suffered a long imprisonment for contempt of the Commons. But why give further details of these elected despots, except their attempted statute to prevent persons suffering their tyranny from obtaining redress against members or officers of the Commons, which died by royal veto—one of numerous instances of the forgotten virtues of the Crown?

Townships for the Frontier.—Into this maelstrom of passion and land-grabbing was launched Governor Johnson's plan for defense and expansion by bringing new settlers into a series of townships girdling the entire frontier. This important forward move was the culmination of efforts to increase the white population in the face of the internal enemies (as they were frequently called), the slaves, and the external enemies red and white. Repeated acts requiring planters to purchase a few white servants in proportion to their slaves had proved disappointing. The number of indentured servants imported remained small until the importation under the laws of the 1730's and especially of the 1760's.

Nor is the assumption warranted that our "poor whites" had this origin. The only certain conclusion (and to that there are some early exceptions) from an immigrant's being an indentured servant is that he was poor. Their descendants today are often persons of high standing and character. Economic and social conditions hostile to the small independent farmer account for a great part of our depressed population. We made our "poor whites" rather than imported them. A more effective means of depressing the small white farmer and filling the country with Negroes could hardly have been devised than the land system. The planter could buy Negroes on credit; for the merchant knew that for every slave from pickaninny to patriarch his debtor would receive free fifty acres of land from the government, which increased his ability to pay. Modern capitalism has its sins; but rarely has capitalism so trodden under foot the permanent interests of the masses of the population as did the pushing men of affairs who were appropriating colonial lands.

Another immigration device was offering large tracts to persons bringing in large numbers of white settlers; but such ventures were usually of small success.

Settlement had lagged during the Proprietary period and had almost ceased under the closing of the land office and the general uncertainty of the 1720's. The Governor stated the population in 1708 as 9,580, of whom 1,360 were free men, 900 free women, 1,700 free children, 120 white servants, 4,100 Negro and 1,400 Indian slaves. Governor Glen estimated the population in 1724 as about 14,000 whites and 32,000 slaves. In 1730 the settlers occupied "a squat triangle" whose base extended from Port Royal Sound to Winyaw Bay, and whose apex rested about fifty miles inland at the great bend of the Santee. Settlement was thin at both ends, particularly north of the Santee. Rev. Varnod wrote in 1724 that settlement ended and the Indians began about fifteen miles above his church of St. George, Dorchester. The inhabitants north of the Santee were so alarmed by Indians in 1733 that they considered removing "into the settlement."

Since 1716 suggestions had been made for protective frontier settlements, but nothing had been done to realize these plans when Governor Johnson took them up in earnest on an enlarged scale. South Carolina needs nothing so much, he wrote, as white inhabitants. In February, 1730, twenty-one British merchants, generally owning land in South Carolina, presented to the Lords of Trade a proposal for using for seven years the funds that, under the law of 1724, were to be used for sinking the paper money, for the encouragement of poor Protestant settlers. Who first suggested this diversion of the sinking fund we do not know, but there is no doubt that Johnson was the effective formulator of the plan. The whole scheme was included in the King's instructions to Governor Johnson. There were to be eleven townships of 20,000 acres each, two each on the Altamaha, Savannah, and Santee, and one each on the Edisto, Wateree, Black, Peedee, and Waccamaw. Each settler was to have fifty acres for each head, white or black, and a lot in the town at the center of each township. The province promised transportation from the landing place to the settlement, tools, and food for a year. Six miles were reserved on every side for future development. When there came to be 100 heads of families, the township should be organized as a parish with two members of Assembly. Every means should be used to annul large uncultivated grants.

The grand plan got on the rocks of human nature from the first. Officials quarreled over fees, non-settlers were allowed to take up lands, often the best, ahead of settlers, and the Assembly violated faith with the King in providing that only a small part of the Negro duties diverted from sinking the paper money should go to the township service. But normal political and economic life had been restored, never again, except during periods of war, to approach so near anarchy as was witnessed during the years of transition to the permanent royal authority while that authority so neglected its duty to the province.

CHAPTER XIX

SETTLING THE LOWER MIDDLE COUNTRY, 1732-1760

By November, 1732, six of the townships had been laid out. As Georgia soon absorbed the Altamaha, only nine of the eleven originally ordered were established by South Carolina: Purrysburgh, on the Great Yemassee Bluff on the Savannah, about twenty-two miles in a direct line from the mouth of the river; Orangeburg, comprising a narrow strip along the northern bank of the North Edisto almost wholly above the town; Amelia, comprising the area between Orangeburg township and the Congaree-Santee; Saxe-Gotha, comprising a good part of the present Lexington below the Saluda; New Windsor, opposite the present Augusta; Williamsburg, comprising the middle of the northwestern part of the present Williamsburg County; Kingston, within the present Horry; Queensborough, a square on the southern side of the Great Peedee; and Fredericksburg, east of the Wateree at Camden.

Purrysburgh.—A few Swiss arrived in South Carolina between 1685 and 1691. Twenty-four Swiss (some of them the remnants of Purry's first attempt) reached South Carolina in 1726. Purry persisted, and in 1732 secured the King's promise for himself personally of 48,000 acres quitrent free for ten years on condition that he settle, at a place to serve the safety of the province, six hundred Swiss Protestant men, women, and children. The South Carolina government promised to pay him £400 sterling for bringing one hundred men and two hundred women and children in two years, to be settled together on the Savannah River, with a view to making hemp, indigo, silk, wines, cotton, etc., and affording defense on this most threatened frontier. The immigrants would be carried there from their landing place free, and be given cows, hogs, food, and ammunition. Purry selected the Great Yemassee Bluff, a narrow plateau rising from surrounding swamps, but for convenience of trade the town was located in a marsh by the river, where the Alpine mountaineers sweltered and died. By 1738 he had landed the six hundred promised the British government. The ill-located settlement never prospered. Prominent persons took up land contrary to the King's directions inside the six-mile belt ordered to be reserved around the township for expansion, thus, charged Purry's son, making it impossible for the settlers to support themselves. In 1763 the German Swiss were the more numerous.

These French and German Swiss were of good quality, furnishing some later distinguished names and many of modest excellence, such as Holzendorff, Brabant, Dominick, Huguenin, Henry, de Saussure, Richards, LaBorde. Few were illiterate; but the inevitable degeneration under an unprofitable and unhealthy situation soon set in. A hundred soon died. Many departed to find better land. The idea of raising silk, olives, and wine proved visionary, although until the Revolution there continued some silk culture.

The Reverend Abraham Immer, Purrysburgh pastor from 1760 to 1766, said that the original settlers "shine with a sufficiently ample knowledge. They excel in a deep and solid sort of piety; but the younger ones, in the deepest darkness of ignorance, rarely show forth works from which true and wholesome faith is apparent. Nor could this in any way be expected to be otherwise," as they had lacked proper teachers. Almost all were ignorant of the alphabet. All, he says, were very poor. They paid more attention to cattle than agriculture. He taught the young three times a week, few of the French or English and none of the German youths being able to read.

In 1747 the government heeded the Purrysburghers' long-continued pleas by erecting St. Peter's Parish. In the Revolution Purrysburgh remained a settlement, and is listed as a village in 1826. It is one of the most disappointing of the townships.

Williamsburg.—A sprinkling of settlers were to be found here, near Winyaw Bay, before the township movement. Hunter's map of 1730 says that "Georgetown was laid out in lots and sold last year to people who are obliged to build a house in fifteen months," and Governor Johnson recommended on January 2, 1730, that a town should be laid out there and be made a port of entry.

The opening of the seaport greatly helped Williamsburg, the second township to be established in the ring that was to push back the whole frontier. Centering at "The King's Tree" on Black River, it was designed primarily for Scotch-Irish Protestants. The Assembly, contrary to the King's idea, omitted the word "foreign" before "Protestants," and so drew in large numbers from the old country and the northern colonies.

Grants, contrary to the King's instructions, to large planters and officials, lawyers, and merchants who sought a profit from the expected growth of population took up the best lands. The settlers complained that there was little good land left. After Governor Johnson's death Lieutenant-Governor Broughton and the Council abandoned all pretense of reserving the townships east of the Santee for new settlers. By the end of 1737 the township contained 500 to 550 white inhabitants. After 1737 surveys in Williamsburg almost ceased. Beginning shortly before 1760, the Scotch-Irish fairly swarmed into the up country unpre-empted by speculators and physically more attractive.

The Williamsburgers produced valuable industries based on hemp, flax, weaving, provisions, and indigo, and socially and morally were a stimulating influence. They represented, says Professor Meriwether, the best success of Governor Johnson's township plan.

Orangeburg and Amelia.—What has been said of Purrysburgh and Williamsburg shows that the great influx of population beginning in the early 1730's was soon flowing into several townships simultaneously. Orangeburg was the third to be settled as a part of the township plan, although several South Carolinians had already obtained grants and were probably living there when, on July 13, 1735, a shipload of 250 German Swiss arrived from Rotterdam. Of these, 220 were promptly sent there. Dr. Meriwether finds only a few indentured servants, agreeing with my own observation that the number of indentured servants among the poor Germans of this period was smaller than later. Their early success with wheat diminished the province's dependence on the northern colonies, particularly Pennsylvania, for flour.

Dr. Meriwether points out that although the English and the Germans were friendly, they intermarried little. Of one hundred names to an Orangeburg petition in 1749, sixty-six are German, twenty-five are apparently English (with possibly five or six really German), one is French; eight I cannot decide.

Amelia township, lying between Orangeburg township and the Congaree-Santee, and two or three times the area of its neighbor, covered roughly the present Calhoun County. Through it lay the Cherokee path, a determining factor in its settlement. Orangeburg remained a region of small German farmers, while Amelia early developed into a region of large planters, mainly of English stock, who advertised for private tutors and dominated the location of the church and the politics of the parish when the two townships were erected into St. Matthew's Parish in 1768.

Germans on the Congaree and Saluda.—As early as 1704 the Proprietors were planning to bring in immigrants from Germany, but German immigration was negligible until organized under the township plan. Saxe-Gotha township, ordered laid off in 1733, consisted of the greater part of the present Lexington County southwest of the Saluda and Congaree and already contained a few inhabitants. In 1735 the first German Swiss bounty settlers arrived. By 1748 Saxe-Gotha probably contained two hundred inhabitants, gratefully thanking the Assembly for raising them from their depressed condition in Germany. But the richer coast region owed gratitude in return; for these poor Saxe-Gothans were the first line of defense thrown directly across the path of the Cherokees, through whose country often came marauding Indians from as far north as central New York.

The peace of 1748 was followed by a new and larger influx of Germans. John Jacob Riemensperger was paid a shilling sterling a head for bringing, in October, 1749, about six hundred "Palatines," some of them, thinks Dr. Meriwether, Württembergers. An English firm brought in fifteen hundred. They succeeded in selling a fourth of them as indentured servants, and had to take promises of future payment by the others. No such numbers continued, and the Seven Years' War brought a further decline. The English, says Dr. Meriwether, were less than half of the eight or nine hundred settlers in the upper Congaree valley, but were dominant in politics and trade.

The Dutch Fork (i.e., the country between the Broad and the Saluda, including the lower third or more of the present Newberry County), settled largely by Germans, not Dutch, received a few settlers as the better lands in Saxe-Gotha were pre-empted.[1] The Germans pressed up to within three and one-half miles of the later county seat, while the upper portion awaited the coming of the English and Scotch-Irish from Virginia and Pennsylvania. The two elements still give their distinctive characteristics of readier social co-operation and of stiff individualism to the two sections respectively. Settlement was swinging into the later Laurens County by 1753.

To return to Saxe-Gotha, the contradictory reports of moral and intellectual conditions are largely due to various witnesses' reporting half truths. Like other back-countrymen, the Saxe-Gothans were much neglected by the government. Rev. Christian Theus, ordained in the Presbyterian form, brother of the Charles Town artist, served the Saxe-Gothan Swiss and Germans from 1739 for over fifty years. He was barely saved by a canoe from the hands of the Weberites, a sect of fanatics whom he reproved for their nakedness, lust, etc. Jacob Weber was accepted by his followers as God Almighty, and John George Smith Peter as the Son of God. But Weber discovered after a quarrel that Peter was the devil, without whose death there would be no peace; so Peter was chained and piously beaten to death. For this and an accompanying murder (Febru-

[1] The tradition that John Adam Summer was the first white settler in the present Newberry County is proved by Professor E. B. Hallman to be erroneous. He names seven settlers shown by the land records to antedate Summer, but which was the first to come cannot be stated. E. B. Hallman, "Early Settlers in the South Carolina Dutch Fork" (MS, M.A. thesis, Wofford College).

ary 23-24, 1761) Weber was hanged. The sect spread, says Bernheim, to the Germans of North Carolina, Virginia, and Maryland.

The Saxe-Gothans and Dutch Forkers suffered for lack of schools and ministers and complained of the prevalence of ignorance and vice, made worse by the arrival of new German immigrants in 1755, "poor and of the meaner sort." Giessendanner from Orangeburg acceptably supplemented the steady ministration of Theus, as did Rev. John Gasser.

Number and Character of the Germans.—Sweeping statements made by grieving ministers that there was not a Bible in the region, and of black ignorance and depravity almost universal, are proved excessive by such facts as Stephen Creel's dying in Saxe-Gotha in 1763, leaving books including a Hebrew Bible and a Greek Testament, and Herman's dying in the Congarees section in 1752, leaving Psalters, a sermon book, and a Bible. I am convinced that much of the ignorance, superstition, and vice were the result of degeneration in unfavorable frontier conditions. The Württembergers left a country of good parish schools, says Dr. Gilbert P. Voigt, although the Swiss schools of the eighteenth century had fallen into decay. He finds in a list of seventeen German immigrants in 1756 only two (both being women) making their mark, and only one (a woman) doing so among seventeen or eighteen in 1755. Two-thirds of the signers of certain land papers in the Dutch Fork in the same period signed their names. He also found that in about a hundred representative cases slightly over 70 per cent of the Germans signed their Revolutionary receipts, while not quite 90 per cent of the non-Germans signed their names to about a hundred such papers. I must believe that the ignorance of which Judge Nott complained in 1812 was largely a degeneration of a naturally stolid isolated population. Dr. O. B. Mayer, Sr., stated in 1891 that many Dutch Forkers clung to the German language until a couple of generations before that date.

Dr. Meriwether thinks that at least 3,600 Germans (including German Swiss) came to South Carolina from 1748 to 1759. Professor Voigt thinks 5,000 or more landed here from 1732 to 1765, and were perhaps increased to 7,500 or 8,000 by those coming from other colonies. How considerable was the German element is indicated by the fact, says Dr. Voigt, that over a fourth of those paying quitrents in 1771 bore German names; but it was commonly supposed that not over a third of the lands were included on that roll. The Germans were not well situated for evading payment.

Though the Swiss and Germans were generally humble folk, they supplied from the first some men of culture and prominence. Michael Kalteisen's efficiency as wagon master general in the Cherokee War, 1760-61, led to his appointment to the same position in 1775 and as commissary of military stores in 1776. He died in 1807 as commander of Fort Johnson. Jeremiah Theus became "one of the very best of the colonial painters," accumulated wealth, and bought a pew in St. Michael's. Two Theuses were officers among the South Carolina Continentals. John Frederick Holzendorff became a militia captain in the 1730's and was a surgeon in the parish hospital, Charles Town. The engineer John William Gerard (originally von) Brahm, who had formerly served in the army of the Emperor Charles VI, planned and built the fortifications of Charles Town after the destructive hurricane of 1752, and was Surveyor-General of South Carolina and of Georgia. The Grimkés early came into prominence. The grandfather of the poet Timrod is thought by some to have been Henry Dimroth, a 1765 immigrant to Charles Town from the Rhenish Palatinate.

German musical talent made its contribution to a city notable in this art. John Tobler of New Windsor knew enough astronomy to issue almanacs. The highly educated Christian Gottlieb Priber, who came to grief with the South Carolina and Georgia governments for seeking to establish Cherokee independence in a sort of Platonic republic, was for a while a resident of Amelia. The Germans took little part in politics. Professor Voigt says Frederick Grimké was the only German in the Assembly before 1766, and Governor Glen wrote that the Purrysburgh foreign element had never been able to persuade one of their number to stand for election. Some, however, held subordinate positions.

The Germans came generally to better their economic condition. But from Switzerland and the Palatinate, clearly, some came from religious pressure and some from the desire, as they said, to live in a free country. Their descendants form a very large portion of the population of the regions which they first settled, and are found in all sections. The names of some were originally indistinguishable from English and others were soon Anglicized. Muller or Mueller became Miller; Fredagh, Fridig, Friday; Stroather, Strother; Fulmer, Fulmore; Flohr, Flory, Flora, etc. Their contribution to South Carolina life has been varied and substantial.

The Northeastern Townships.—Since the rice and indigo lands of the Georgetown County of today attracted settlers without special public aid, the townships in that region (besides Williamsburg, already treated) were roughly, in order of settlement (although the movement was in general contemporaneous) as follows: Kingston, between the Waccamaw and the Little Peedee, crossed near its northern point by latitude 34; Queensborough, a little west and almost equally divided by the Great Peedee; the Welsh Tract, joining Queensborough on the northwest; and Fredericksburg, surrounding the later Camden on the eastern side of the Wateree. In addition, although not a township, the future Richland County was being taken up. Large slaveholders immediately began to take up considerable holdings and defeated the plan for a numerous white farmer settlement.

The Welsh on the Peedee.—The Welsh Tract (not strictly a township) originated in August, 1736, from the petition of Daniel Lewis, Samuel Wilds, and Daniel James representing a colony of Welsh Baptists in Newcastle County, Pennsylvania, later a part of Delaware. The country was found suited to hemp, flax, wheat, barley, etc., and their request was granted for a great tract exceeding a thousand square miles including much of the best land of the province. This was reserved for the Welsh ultimately into 1745.

Dr. Meriwether finds no evidence of migration direct from Wales, but from Pennsylvania Welsh came in numbers: Griffith, David, Gillespie, Evans, Ellerbe, Wilds, Rowland, Greenwood, Lewis, Jones, James, and many others whose descendants have spread throughout South Carolina. The moderate size of their grants indicates they were immigrants generally in early manhood and without slaves.

These Pennsylvania Welsh built their first Baptist Church in 1744, having previously met in private houses. The Anglican element remained much less numerous, despite the creation of the parishes of St. Mark's to the southwest in 1757 and St. David's with its church at Cheraw in 1768. A little later the lack of adequate ministerial supply, and the fact that this was Asbury's path from north to south, made the Peedee one of the chief Methodist strongholds.

Kingston (sometimes called the Waccamaw township) was opened to settlement in 1735 and was long a small, poor community with a sprinkling of Scotch or Scotch-Irish and much land owned by outsiders. The little town occupied the same bluff on which Conway now stands.

Filling Out the Line from Camden to Augusta.—We turn now to the English and German settlement in the fork of the Congaree and Wateree, later to become Richland. Grants were being taken out in 1740 for lands six to ten miles below the present Columbia. In 1757 the English and German settlers supplied 133 militiamen.

In December, 1737, or January, 1738, Fredericksburg township was laid off on the east bank of the Wateree at the later Camden. Even after the reservation for several years for Scotch settlers expired, growth was slow, partly on account of the hostility of the Catawbas, who still claimed the lands. Thieves, some so notorious as to be advertised for in the *Virginia Gazette,* plagued the magistrateless settlement as they did other South Carolina frontiers of the period. The later town of Camden originated with a store founded by Joseph Kershaw representing a Charles Town firm in or a little after 1758.

Two other outposts complete the settlement movement of the 1730's and 1740's, those at New Windsor opposite Augusta, and one in the southwest. The township of New Windsor, around an old settlement, was laid out in 1735, the same year as the founding of its vis-à-vis Augusta.

The last area to be considered in the settlement movement of the 1730's and '40's was along the rivers in the southwest from the Salkehatchie-Combahee to the Savannah. This was part of the land and slave boom in the 1730's of the old English element, and so dotted the region with large plantations. For security against slaves and outside enemies a few score German families were settled on the upper Salkehatchie. Cattle raising continued a leading industry there until the Revolution.

The period of 1733 to 1760, which began with an attempt on the part of the government to strengthen the province against its mounting number of Negroes by state-aided white settlement, was marked also by a wild orgy of land-grabbing and slave importation by the planter class, in which the greed for private gain counteracted efforts for the public good. The net result was disappointing. It was not a period notable for public spirit, and the capable and willful knot of planter-politicians who dominated the Assembly exercised their authority at times for their own class interest rather than for the interest of the whole people. The Commons themselves resolved that failure had been due to great quantities of land being taken up in the townships by non-residents (in violation of the King's instructions), and to many Negroes' being taught trades. But, as Dr. Meriwether points out, the people from the mountains and semi-mountainous parts of Europe soon got enough of the swampy region of the lower townships. In the spontaneous movement of the next generation they took to the hills above the fall line.

What, finally, was the significance of the township plan fostered by Governor Johnson? The government's efforts artificially to populate such unfavorable locations as Purrysburgh and Kingston attained scant success. Population generally took the natural course that it would have taken without government interference along the great Congaree-Wateree systems and the rich Peedee basin, but the amount of immigration there was greatly stimulated through government aid. By means of its propaganda, its definite location of townships, and its financial aid, the government exercised a powerful influence on the nationality, the location, and the time of the settlement of the middle and lower middle country. The next great influx in the 1760's saw still greater numbers of Germans introduced into the lower and middle country with government aid and a far greater spontaneous influx of Scotch-Irish into the up country.

CHAPTER XX

BOUNDARY TROUBLES AND BORDER WARS, 1732-1748

Disputes Over the North Carolina Line.—The fact that the earlier settlements in North Carolina lay near the Virginia line and that the early South Carolinians were along the faraway Ashley destined the development of two provinces instead of one imperial Carolina. The expansion of the two colonies toward each other rendered a dividing line between them a necessity for establishing the certainty of land titles and the authority of one government or the other in border regions. An increasing class of frontier outlaws took advantage of the uncertainty and retarded the coming of desirable population.

In January, 1730, the Lords of Trade, to divide the provinces, adopted a line "beginning at the sea thirty miles distant from the mouth of the Cape Fear on the southwest thereof," paralleling the river to its source, and thence west to the Pacific. They added in June, "but if the Waggamaw River lyes within thirty miles of Cape Fear River, then that river to be the boundary from the sea to the head thereof and from thence to keep the distance of thirty miles parallel from Cape Fear River to the head thereof, and thence a due west course to the South Sea."

Here was a fatal ambiguity; for, although the mouths of the two rivers are over fifty miles apart, they approach in their upper reaches nearer than thirty. South Carolina claimed that the instruction referred to their separation at their mouths and that therefore the line was to lie thirty miles west of the Cape Fear and so to its source, while North Carolina contended that the Waccamaw was to be the boundary if at any point it was within thirty miles of the Cape Fear. In 1735 commissioners were appointed by both provinces to run the line. An agreement was made by them, unauthorized by the King's instructions or the action of the Assembly, to run northwest in a straight line from a point on the coast thirty miles southwest of the mouth of the Cape Fear up to latitude 35 and thence west to the Pacific. Both provinces accepted this compromise, but the surveyors erroneously stopped in 1737 eleven miles south of latitude 35.

The steps in settling the line between the Carolinas have been as follows:[1] From the sea to a point twenty-two miles southeast of the angle over Marlboro County at which the line turns west was surveyed in 1735, and the twenty-two miles onward to the angle in 1737. The line running west sixty-two miles to the point at which the boundary turns north was surveyed in 1764. The eight-mile line running northward was substituted in 1813 for the road lying mostly a little west of that line, the road having been regarded as the boundary since 1772. From the point on the boundary of Lancaster County at which the line turns northwest to the point at which Spartanburg and Greenville counties join, the survey was made in 1772. From there to the point on latitude 35 at which the line meets the corner of Georgia was surveyed in 1815. Locating the 1772 line north of latitude 35 was intended to compensate for the error of having placed the line of 1764 too far south.

Georgia as Friend and Rival.—A loss of territory destining South Carolina to the role of a small instead of a large State was suffered by the founding of Georgia in 1732. But so great was the immediate advantage in defense against Spaniards and French that this stroke of fate was warmly welcomed. The infant colony was assisted by public and private South Carolina gifts. Georgia as a refuge for ruined debtors was a feature of the religious-humane movement which so greatly changed eighteenth-century England. Georgia now took the place of South Carolina on the English frontier against the Spanish and even more against the newer French effort to restrict the English colonies.

The trustees of Georgia assumed the right to regulate trade with the Indians within their borders, and as philanthropists they enacted regulations for the protection of the Indians and for ending the abuses which tended to provoke Indian wars of revenge. No one was to trade without obtaining license from Georgia and giving bond to abide by her regulations. As Georgia seized South Carolina boats in the Savannah, the controversy involved the question of whether the eastern bank, the western bank, or the middle of the stream was the boundary, a question which was not finally settled until the decision of the United States Supreme Court in 1922, which, construing the agreement of 1787 between the two States, fixed the line at the middle of the stream or midway between islands and the eastern bank. South Carolina in the 1730's merely contended for the free navigation of the river as a common highway.

South Carolina's complaint against Georgia's assuming the exclusive control of the Creek trade was sound. Georgia at that time embraced only a strip between the Savannah and the Altamaha and a strip running

[1] Cf. Skaggs, *North Carolina Boundary Disputes Involving Her Southern Line* (University of North Carolina Press, 1941).

west from their sources. The great body of the Creeks thus lay west and south of Georgia, and the Cherokees nearly all beyond her northern line. Not until 1763 was the territory from the Altamaha to Florida added to Georgia. Until 1763 it remained a part of South Carolina. The Lords of Trade, following the same principle as when they condemned South Carolina's exclusion act of 1711 against the Virginians, declared the Indians were independent nations living on lands under British sovereignty with whom all British subjects had the right to trade. Neither did Georgia have any right to obstruct the navigation of the Savannah, or to seize rum unless it was being imported into Georgia, or to interfere with trade south of the Altamaha, that area being still a part of South Carolina. The incident bulks large among the many proving the need for imperial regulation of Indian relations.

Priber and the Cherokees.—Several recent incidents had emphasized the constant Indian danger. Forgetting the promises of eternal friendship made in England in 1730, young Cherokee warriors in the spring of 1734 were threatening death to traders unless they sold their goods cheaper than at officially agreed prices; they were also reported to be urging the Catawbas to join in war against the whites. South Carolina stopped her trade for six or seven months and planned placing a garrison near the Cherokees for the protection of the frontiers and the traders—the first mention that I have found looking to the later Fort Prince George. On November 23, 1734, the tract for a fort was ceded on payment of a few goods in a treaty signed by twenty-three Indians from all four divisions of the Cherokee Nation. It comprised a strip in the southeastern part of the present Oconee County and the western tip of Anderson, running about twenty miles along Tugaloo River between Chauga Creek and Seneca River, and a line connecting Chaugee Town two miles up the former and Seneca Town ten miles up the latter, just below the mouth of Concrass (Connor's) Creek.

In 1734, or more probably 1735, arrived in Charles Town "a little ugly man," a Saxon social philosopher and utopian reformer—Christian Gottlieb Priber. He was steeped in the current humanitarianism and idealism concerning "the noble savage." Driven from France in 1734 for attempting a communistic community, he now planned to found among the Cherokees a utopian socialistic state modeled on Plato's Republic.

Priber settled at the Overhill Cherokees' head town of Great Tellico at the western foot of the Unakas and soon was almost indistinguishable from the Indians. A genuine humanitarian who was willing to risk his life for the rights of the humblest, he acquired enormous influence by teaching the Indians by the use of weights and measures to protect themselves from the cheating so common with the traders. The white man's governments themselves were to be watched and kept at a distance, he taught, as the only means of maintaining Indian freedom. Both English and French were invaders of Indian rights. But the fact that his policy of Indian independence operated principally against the English led the Cherokees to consider him an emissary of France. Priber did teach them that opening a connection with New Orleans would afford a means of preserving their liberties against the English. Above all, they must jealously guard their lands. But he did not seek to stir up war. War, he taught, was folly.

Priber set up the head man of Great Tellico as emperor and himself as prime minister. A defiant letter signed by him determined the government of South Carolina in 1739 to arrest him; but the Indians sternly forbade Colonel Fox to touch the "great beloved man."

Priber now felt strong enough to propose "a confederation among all the Southern Indians" for their common defense against all white nations. Along with this was to go a communistic society of complete equality, the "Kingdom of Paradise." Only the laws of nature were to rule. Women were to be as free as men. Marriage was to be completely superseded by freedom of sex relations as in Plato's Republic, and the children were to belong to the state.

In 1743 he was seized among the Creeks while going, it was believed, to the French. Georgia held him a prisoner in Frederica for the few remaining years of his life. To the gentlemen who came to enjoy his discourse he said, "It is folly to repine at one's lot in life. My mind soars above misfortune. In this cell I can enjoy more real happiness than it is possible to do in the busy scenes of life. Reflection upon past events, digesting former studies, keep me fully employed, whilst health and abundant spirits allow me no anxious, no uneasy moments. I suffer, though a friend to the natural rights of mankind, though an enemy to tyranny, usurpation and oppression; and what is more, I can forgive and pray for those that injure me. . . ."

With Priber (who spoke fluently six languages) were captured a dictionary of the Cherokee language and the manuscript of his description of the ideal republic which he hoped to set up in France after its success with "the noble savage." His death after several years in his Frederica prison ended the career of one deserving a page in the history of humanitarian idealism.[2]

Foiling the French and Indian Danger on the Southwest.—The explanation of why the Priber episode so deeply stirred South Carolina and Georgia was the growing menace of the French. The Natchez-Chicka-

[2] Priber was grotesquely misrepresented by historians until Professor V. W. Crane in 1919 published the first fair-minded sketch of him. *Sewanee Review*, XXVII, 48.

saw-Choctaw conspiracy of 1729 to root the French out of the lower Mississippi Valley ended in the return of the powerful Choctaw nation to their old French alliance and the ruin of the Natchez. The Creeks' attitude toward South Carolina was one of cynical self-interest toward the best buyers of their skins and suppliers of European goods. They continued to resent the province's treatment of the Cherokees as their favorites, on whom, "under God," South Carolina considered her safety depended. Governor Johnson secured a new treaty of trade and friendship, binding the Creeks against intercourse with Spain and pledging them to "encourage" none but English to settle among them; but the old Brims policy of the balance of power made it impossible to secure any pledge against the French. The Creeks were inclining alarmingly toward the French in 1736.

South Carolina and Georgia were both sure that France was planning their conquest. The large forces assembled at Mobile in January, 1736, were turned against the Chickasaws, thought Broughton and Oglethorpe, only because peace was declared in Europe. The French were defeated from 1736 to 1742 by South Carolina's faithful friends the Chickasaws.

Though South Carolina's attempts to attach the Choctaws in 1729 and again in 1738 to 1742, as the basis for a union of the southern tribes powerful enough to root the French out of the lower Mississippi Valley, failed, the French plan for an irresistible anti-English alliance of the Choctaws, Chickasaws, Creeks, and Cherokees had likewise failed. There thus remained the old stalemate, with the Creeks maintaining their traditional policy of balancing the Europeans against each other lest either should become so strong as to endanger Indian independence. The danger zone for South Carolina and Georgia for the time being shifted to the Spanish at St. Augustine.

Georgia and South Carolina Attack St. Augustine, 1740.—The rival claims of England and Spain to the territory between Charles Town and St. Augustine rendered formal peace between the two Crowns hardly more than a truce. These were the circumstances when General Oglethorpe's letter arrived informing Lieutenant-Governor Bull that the King had ordered him to annoy the Spaniards the best he was able, since war had been declared on Spain by England in October, 1739. Oglethorpe's request for co-operation could hardly be refused. He had secured the co-operation of the Cherokees, not too strongly attached at that time to the English, and of the Creeks, who were still less compliant. It was essential to impress these savages with English power in order to prevent their shift to France or Spain. General Oglethorpe built St. George's Fort on the northern bank of the St. John's, to which

Spain replied by renewing her claim to Georgia and southern South Carolina. As these provinces were almost sure to be attacked if they did not themselves attack, the argument was strong for an aggressive war in the enemy's territory for the destruction of that standing menace, the castle of St. Augustine. South Carolina pledged £120,000 currency and 400 men. A British fleet also co-operated.

High hopes were cherished for an expedition commanded by an officer of Oglethorpe's prestige; but the enterprise, launched in May, 1740, the first with which he had been entrusted as an independent commander, proved him so lacking in the qualities of organization and strategy as to nullify his enormous energy. To take the castle in any event would have been difficult; but he rendered it hopeless by committing almost every possible blunder, the details of which have little value except for a military treatise on how not to do it. When the fleet, in terror of autumnal storms, though assured that the earliest known had occurred on August 2, refused to remain beyond July 5, the fate of the expedition was sealed. The last troops to leave were the South Carolina regiment under Colonel Vander Dussen, who was left to bring off or destroy the artillery; and he brought it off.

Spain Invades Georgia, 1742.—Spain's counterstroke was a powerful expedition from Havana. On July 5, 1742, a large Spanish fleet entered St. Simon's harbor, Georgia. The Spanish landing force, reported as 3,000, was repulsed at the battle of Bloody Marsh with the aid of some Chickasaws and other friendly Indians, and re-embarked on hearing that English ships and a strong body of South Carolinians were approaching.

The South Carolina Assembly voted an unlimited credit and arranged for securing a thousand men from North Carolina. The alarm was acute, for it was found that the Spaniards had planned to take and fortify Port Royal, and it was feared they would rouse a servile insurrection, for which their considerable number of Negro and mulatto soldiers would well serve. The South Carolinians and British arrived in Georgia too late to cut off the Spanish retreat.

The Energetic Governor Glen.—Governor James Glen landed in Charles Town, December 17, 1743. Amid the booming of the batteries along the waterfront, preceded by the Provost-Marshal bearing the huge sword of state, descended from the Proprietary period, that still typifies the authority of our Senate,[3] he passed through two lines of soldiers to the Council chamber. James Glen, formerly a Scotch high sheriff, thus began his administration of almost thirteen years, the longest in

[3] In 1941 the sword, left exposed during recess of the senate, disappeared and has not so far been recovered. It is interesting to recall that the silver mace of the house was once stolen, but was long afterward recovered.

South Carolina history and one of the best. The apprehension of the merchants, upon the announcement of his appointment in 1738, that the interests of trade would suffer at the hands of the young lawyer without business experience proved groundless. He was the most progressive and active of any of our royal governors. He gave his whole time to the governorship, unlike the large planters who had held office since 1725. His restless activity offended the jog-trotters, and his ardent desire to check the alarming encroachment of the Commons on the royal prerogative (though he was liberal for a governor), and of the Council upon his own rights, at times brought sharp passages with those bodies. He traveled through the province oftener and farther than any provincial governor before or after him to see "what improvements have been made" and what ought to be done, and to win the friendship of the Indians and encourage the back settlers.

Glen had the defects of his qualities. He had none of the dignity that depends on stolidity; but of direct efficiency that neglected conventionality he had plenty. The watch of Charles Town, he early reported, consisted of forty-five men and three officers paid highly for doing little. Two were to act as nightly guard for the powder magazine. Glen went inspecting and found not a soul near, and was told that the guards had never been placed, although there was an additional allowance to pay for them. He remedied this. Observing the inefficiency of the watch at fires, he handled the buckets himself and had the watch instructed as fire fighters.

The incidents are typical of Glen's whole character and administration: definite ideas as to what needed to be done, direct and prompt action for the end in view, and boyish bragging about his success, which was sometimes not so great as he imagined. These qualities got him in hot water with Council and Commons. The sweeping statements into which his exuberance sometimes led, and his open frankness with the Assembly as almost co-partners in his commission, irritated London officialdom. Yet his realization of the dangers threatening the English colonies and the means of meeting them, his insistence on strengthening the Charles Town defenses, his activity in tying the Indians to the British interest in the face of the French advance from Louisiana, and his fostering of the back country settlements rank him as one of our most statesmanlike leaders.

War with France and Indian Relations.—France declared war on England on March 4, 1744. "I shall publish the declaration of war," Glen wrote, with a regiment of foot and one of horse in the presence of the Creek chiefs in town as a means of securing their aid "in our immediately intended attack" on France's Alabama Fort Toulouse. The Council was ardent for the expedition, but the Commons balked at the £20,000 currency expense. This many-times-contemplated destruction of France's most threatening outpost, the Creeks, true to their policy of maintaining their own independence by balancing one power against the other, would never encourage.

The presence of two Frenchmen and twenty French Indians among the Cherokees moved Governor Glen to summon the head men to meet him in May at the farthest English settlement, Ninety Six. The Cherokee Emperor, with sixty of his head men, was impressed with meeting the Governor surrounded with several hundred white men far in the interior. The Cherokees complained of the danger to their towns on the western waters, to which canoes often brought the French and their Indians. These exposed towns inclined therefore to the French. Glen proposed that he build a fort for their security, to be garrisoned by the English; but they were jealous of any such threat to their independence. Glen refrained from pressing for his desired fort among the Overhills (his later Fort Loudoun), to be, as he wrote the Lords of Trade, an effectual bar to the French and a bridle in the mouth of the Indians themselves. But he hoped he had damped the French, as the Cherokees promised to make no engagement with them without his permission.

On February 12, 1747, Governor Glen succeeded in buying from the Cherokees all their lands south and east of Long Canes Creek in the later Abbeville County and a line running in general northward and northeastward from its head. With the exception of the small tract for a fort in 1734 in the present Oconee County, this is the first sale of land by the Cherokees to the Crown through the government of South Carolina.

At the same time the Cherokees offered to give the land for a fort, help build it, and feed the garrison for two years. The Cherokees had definitely chosen to stick to the English. The penuriousness of the Assembly and of the British government delayed the execution of their promise of the fort (Fort Prince George at Keowee) until 1753 and of the one most needed (Fort Loudoun on the Little Tennessee) until 1756.

The years 1746 and 1747 seemed about to witness a renewal of the brief English alliance of 1738 with the powerful Choctaws, whose loss by the French would have ruined them along the lower Mississippi. But the delay of over a year in getting supplies to the Choctaws enabled the French faction to overpower the Anglophiles and restore the French alliance.

The Choctaw debacle was a severe disappointment marked by bitter reproaches as to the blame. While the Council, more far-seeing than the Commons, strove to checkmate the French by building forts in the far west, the Commons would consent only if allowed to issue more paper money. Forbidden by the King to consent to more paper money, the Council was obliged to drop its plans.

Governor Glen Finds the South Carolinians Very Independent.—The declaration of peace in 1748 suspended the plans of both the imperial government and the South Carolina authorities for consolidating an assured position against the French by means of adequate forts among the Creeks and Cherokees. The costly results of this negligence were soon apparent, but for the moment it seemed enough to rejoice over relief from the ruin of the rice market and the burdens of war taxation. Scarcity of shipping depressed the prices of Carolina exports and raised those of imported goods. People complained they could not pay their taxes. The middle and lower classes swore that rather than stand the hardships of another Indian war, they would leave the province.

Eight weeks after landing Governor Glen wrote England that he found the whole frame of government unhinged and the Governor divested of the power placed in him, because, he thought, of the indolence of some governors and the continual absence of others on their private affairs. Five years' experience confirmed his conviction that "our Constitution should be new modeled." The public treasurer was named by the General Assembly, he said, and could not be replaced but by them. They also appointed the commissary, the controller of the duties imposed by law, the powder receiver, etc.

Much of the executive function of the government was lodged by law in various commissioners, Governor Glen continued. All ecclesiastical preferments were in the hands of the people, contrary to direct instructions of the King that the Governor should collate to all livings of which the King was the patron. Because of this perhaps the Governor was not prayed for in any parish—the only such instance in America, although the Assembly were prayed for during their sittings. The Governor had no power to reprove or remove the officers elected by the Assembly. "Thus by little and little the people have got the whole administration into their hands, and the Crown is by various laws despoiled of its principal flowers and brightest jewels. No wonder if a Governor be not clothed with authority, when he is stripped naked of power," and can neither reward the deserving nor displace the unworthy. A former Governor, for instance, sent a message to the Assembly telling them that Fort Johnson was in a ruinious condition and desiring them to give directions to repair it instead of asking them to raise money with which *he* might repair it. Such messages led the Assembly into thinking they had the sole direction in everything. "And a Governor will

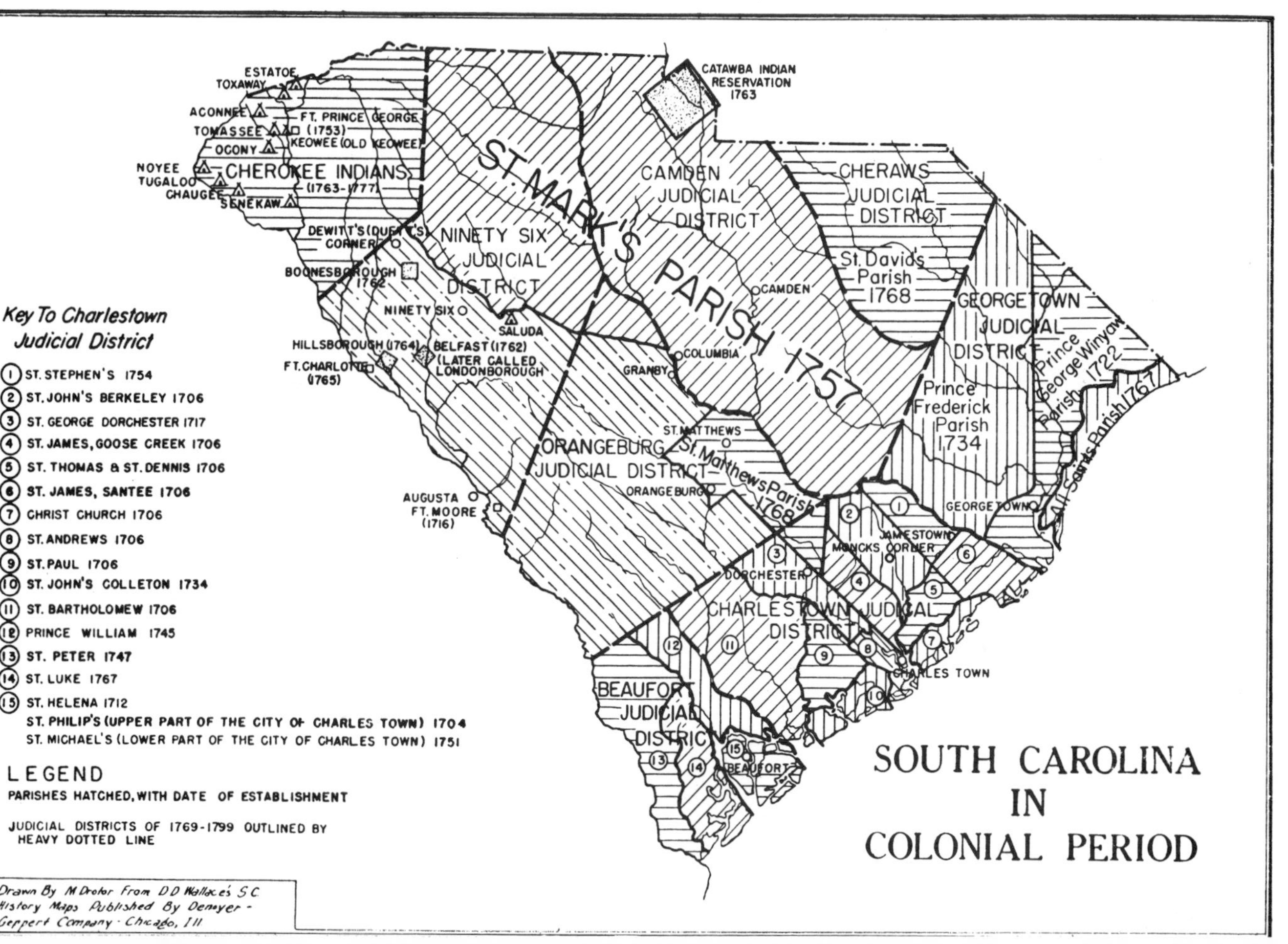
SOUTH CAROLINA
IN
COLONIAL PERIOD
CATAWBA INDIAN RESERVATION 1763
ESTATOE
TOXAWAY
ACONNEE
FT. PRINCE GEORGE (1753)
TOMASSEE
KEOWEE (OLD KEOWEE)
OCONY
NOYEE
TUGALOO
CHAUGEE
SENEKAW
CHEROKEE INDIANS (1763-1777)
DEWITT'S (DUFF'S) CORNER
BOONESBOROUGH 1762
NINETY SIX
SALUDA
HILLSBOROUGH (1764)
BELFAST (1762) (LATER CALLED LONDONBOROUGH)
FT. CHARLOTTE (1765)
AUGUSTA
FT. MOORE (1716)
ST. MARK'S PARISH 1757
NINETY SIX JUDICIAL DISTRICT
CAMDEN JUDICIAL DISTRICT
CAMDEN
COLUMBIA
GRANBY
CHERAWS JUDICIAL DISTRICT
St. David's Parish 1768
GEORGETOWN JUDICIAL DISTRICT
Prince George Winyaw Parish 1722
Prince Frederick Parish 1734
All Saints Parish 1767
GEORGETOWN
ORANGEBURG JUDICIAL DISTRICT
ST. MATTHEWS
St. Matthews Parish 1768
ORANGEBURG
JAMESTOWN
MONCKS CORNER
DORCHESTER
CHARLESTOWN JUDICIAL DISTRICT
CHARLES TOWN
BEAUFORT JUDICIAL DISTRICT
BEAUFORT
Key To Charlestown Judicial District
1 ST. STEPHEN'S 1754
2 ST. JOHN'S BERKELEY 1706
3 ST. GEORGE DORCHESTER 1717
4 ST. JAMES, GOOSE CREEK 1706
5 ST. THOMAS & ST. DENNIS 1706
6 ST. JAMES, SANTEE 1706
7 CHRIST CHURCH 1706
8 ST. ANDREWS 1706
9 ST. PAUL 1706
10 ST. JOHN'S COLLETON 1734
11 ST. BARTHOLOMEW 1706
12 PRINCE WILLIAM 1745
13 ST. PETER 1747
14 ST. LUKE 1767
15 ST. HELENA 1712
ST. PHILIP'S (UPPER PART OF THE CITY OF CHARLES TOWN) 1704
ST. MICHAEL'S (LOWER PART OF THE CITY OF CHARLES TOWN) 1751
LEGEND
PARISHES HATCHED, WITH DATE OF ESTABLISHMENT
JUDICIAL DISTRICTS OF 1769-1799 OUTLINED BY HEAVY DOTTED LINE
Drawn By M Drotor From D D Wallace's S C History Maps Published By Denoyer-Geppert Company · Chicago, Ill

not be listened to that shall afterwards tell them that all castles, forts, etc., are the King's."

These are the observations of a governor, he concludes, "but I can not but make this short, disinterested reflection, that though a virtuous person might be trusted with a little more power, perhaps there may be as much as can safely be delegated to a weak or wicked man, and such in ill times may happen to be employed, and therefore a wise prince will guard against it."

Governor Glen here expresses exactly what South Carolinians and Americans in general already felt and still feel regarding the superior value of security against oppression to efficiency in administration. It is an impressive illustration of the rooting of our institutions in colonial as well as in older English experience. The Lords of Trade agreed with Glen that the Assembly's encroachments on the royal authority would bring confusion and anarchy unless checked. The war of 1739 to '48 seems to have begun the stirring of the British government out of its colonial policy of "salutary neglect," which the next war definitely ended. Abandoning their previous brief and general letters, the Lords of Trade, about 1748 to 1750, became minute, voluminous, exacting, alert, authoritative, and fault-finding. Their very tart letter of November 15, 1750, to Glen, for example, is distinctly of the meddling, censorious, dictatorial type bent on maintaining the royal prerogative that a few years later became so common in the art of empire-destroying.

Despite his uniform moderation, even in controversy, Glen suffered sharp rebuffs from both houses of the Assembly, each particularly jealous just then of even an apparent trespass on their rights because of bitter conflicts with each other over their respective powers. The Council, to maintain its position as an upper house of the legislature, went into the attic to get rid of the Governor's presence, and when he continued to sit for hours, sent for their papers to be brought up to them. In 1748 the Commons sharply reproved him for violating their sole right of shaping the tax bill by sending a message during its framing protesting against a tax on his and other officers' salaries and asking an increase on certain allowances because of the depreciation of paper money. They paid him far more than they used to give Proprietary governors, they replied; and why should he have any special favors against the depreciation of money more than any other officer? And as for his house rent, though the committee favored stopping it as he had moved to his own house out of town, they did, after much bickering, continue that.

Yet the Commons as a matter of course trespassed on the executive to the point of habitually writing for him addresses to the Indians and virtually dictating his appointments for diplomatic agents to the tribes.

The rudest rebuff from the Assembly was occasioned by Governor Glen's criticism of South Carolina's time-honored jury law. Neither in England nor in any other colony of which he knew, he wrote the Commons on April 18, 1751, were jurors drawn by ballot. If this method was to be continued, some way should be adopted to prevent abuses. The Commons replied that the ancient and approved method of drawing juries by ballot was established in South Carolina nearly sixty years ago and informed him that England had recently adopted a similar law. "We think ourselves in duty bound to acquaint your Excellency that we are firmly of opinion that any person who shall endeavor to deprive us of so glorious a privilege of trials by juries drawn by ballot in the method hitherto practiced in this province is an enemy to the same."

When the Governor was thus downfaced, it is natural to find that the lower officers were so intimidated by suits that they dared not prosecute the clearest cases of the then numerous violations of the navigation laws.

In the 1750's a statehouse was built on the site of the present Charleston County Courthouse, northwest corner of Broad and Meeting streets, partly over the old moat around the town (as was discovered too late to avoid the expense thus occasioned). It was still unfinished in 1759, although the Commons moved in on March 25, 1756.

Perennial Struggle over Paper Money.—The effort of the Commons to increase the paper money and the stolid refusal of Governor and Council under the royal instructions to permit any such law without the King's previous consent was a standing source of irritation. Need of repairs, a new fort, war service, a public building, hard times—any excuse—served to persuade or force consent to more paper money as the price for which the Commons would consent to something the Governor, King, or Council wanted. The fall in rice prices under war conditions in the 1740's occasioned angry conflicts. Members of the Assembly even offered what Glen considered a large bribe, to be paid under the guise of reimbursement for his expenses on his tour to the Indians—expenses which were honestly due him, and were never fully paid. Glen, though personally strongly favoring more paper, and though assured by the Assemblymen that they had no other way of paying, rejected the offer with scorn. Private "banks" were formed as at earlier dates, whose members contributed (or sometimes it was charged merely promised) small amounts of capital, on which the group issued ten times as large a sum in their joint notes and lent them out at 10 per cent. The grand jury in 1743 presented as a grievance the issue of small notes by persons not good for the amounts. Bankrupts learned thus to meet their difficulties. A joint committee of the two houses reported on December 9, 1749, total paper money outstanding £133,044, equal to £19,006 sterling. The French and Indian War forced consent to issues of £33,600 in 1755; £204,300 and £25,000 in 1757; and £371,693 in 1760, each retired in four or five years. The custom continued of issuing certificates in advance of taxes, diminishing quantities of which remained out for eight or ten years. These certificates, legal tender only for taxes, but virtually a violation of the royal prohibition, and the £106,500 legal tender, equaled in April, 1767, £446,673, and in 1770, £497,653. The £70,000 issued to pay for the new circuit courthouses and jails were disallowed; but £69,274 had already been handed the commissioners.

It is often represented that the colonies were drained of metal money to pay for their excess of imports. Rather let us say that these ambitious colonists were converting their balances into slaves, other capital equipment, good house furnishings, and luxuries. Considerable sums of gold and silver were in the province in 1748, for instance. In August, 1773, there were £10,000 in gold and silver (in currency value apparently) in the South Carolina treasury, and, although gold was very scarce, the usual influx to pay for rice and indigo was expected by November. Metal was, of course, driven into wholesale and foreign trade, as always where there is an abundance of paper.

Fortifications.—Part of the large paper issues during the war of 1739 to '48 was for fortifications. The defenses of Charles Town and other crucial points were a frequent and heavy expense, with generally small results. The commander of Fort Johnson, when required in 1737 to pass his garrison in review, paraded three men, and explained that, of the other three, two were working his private plantation, and the other was his son, two years old, for whom the captain, accused of various misconduct, doubtless drew the pay. Two of his twenty-one cannon were fit for use. The shot were rusting in the sand, and half were of the wrong size. The incessant discussion of forts and garrisons had to continue until the long contest of the Latins and the Britons over the huge prize of North America reached some definite settlement. We pass now to South Carolina's part in that final struggle.

CHAPTER XXI

FRONTIER POLICY AND INDIAN WARS, 1746-1761

Building Fort Prince George.—Glen's conference of 1746 and purchase of the lands below Long Canes in 1747 barely held the Cherokees from the French. The Franco-British peace of 1748 was hardly more than a truce. The American forests during the following years teemed with the emissaries of both governments seeking to secure the aid of the powerful Indian nations for the coming grapple for supremacy. By 1750 the French were thus undermining South Carolina's western wall, the Creeks; her northwestern barrier, the Cherokees; and her outlying defense, the Chickasaws. In the war that followed between the Creeks and the Cherokees South Carolina had to witness the weakening of her two chief bulwarks and also endure the danger of becoming involved herself. The danger from the Cherokees, as the nearer, was attacked first. Governor Glen and Council stopped their trade and secured similar orders from Georgia and Virginia. Glen, while smiting the Cherokees with the embargo with one hand, offered with the other goodwill on the basis of the mutual righting of wrongs.

These firm measures brought immediate results, for, of all things, the Indians despised weakness. Tacitee, the Raven of Hiwassee, alias the Mankiller, and other headmen requested a meeting at Saluda Old Town and promised to surrender the leaders in the outrages. Still mingling conciliation with firmness, Glen refused to stir from his capital, but assured them of the falsity of the reports of his intention to harry their country. On November 13, 1751, he assured an enormous delegation from the whole Cherokee Nation, who had come to him instead of his going to meet them, that none but the guilty had anything to fear, but that those must be punished. On November 26 was signed an elaborate treaty, and the one hundred and sixty-two Indians departed, loaded with the largest presents ever given and captains' commissions to several for their unbroken fidelity to the English.

Glen in 1752 successfully urged peace between the Cherokees and Creeks. The Six Nations of New York had made peace with the Cherokees and the Catawbas, and Glen successfully pointed out to the Creeks the folly of continuing at war with the northerners, who could now direct their strength at them alone. The gaps in the English western defense were being closed.

In 1753 the Assembly at last enabled Glen to redeem the promise to the Cherokees to build a fort, as they had requested on definitely deciding to repel the French. But the location of the fort at the eastern foot of the mountains was a confession that it was the Cherokees themselves, rather than the French, against whom it was to guard.

In October, 1753, Glen departed for the mountains accompanied by one of the King's Independent Companies and fifty other armed men. With the death of the Old Warrior of Keowee and the Good Warrior of Estotoe, leadership had passed to the Overhill towns—an ominous change big with results in the next few years. Yet over a hundred miles to honor the Governor came Tacitee, King of the Valley, that rich land of inexpressible beauty where the Valley River winds its way beneath the Unakas, behind whose towering protection the Overhill towns insolently reposed.

Refusing the land as a gift, Glen bought several thousand acres in the fork of Keowee River and its eastern tributary Mile Creek and a right of way to it nearly 200 feet wide from there to the Cherokees' southeastern boundary at Long Canes Creek. Here, before returning to Charles Town, he built his Fort Prince George, a square earth and wood structure almost 200 feet on each side, about a half mile above Crow Creek on the eastern side of the Keowee, a few hundred yards above and opposite to the Indian town of Keowee. Three years later it was a weathered ruin, though the guardhouse and barracks were serviceable.[1]

Peace with the Creeks.—Along with these achievements went negotiations with the Creeks, more unmanageable because of their distance and their traditional policy of maintaining a balance between the English and the French. If satisfaction could not be obtained for the Creek crimes the only alternatives were a Creek war, or, worse, Carolina's sinking into a contempt that would invite attack by every Indian nation. Boldness succeeded when the terrible Acorn King died by the action of his fellow chiefs in fear of vengeance by the English, and the Creeks delivered up their stolen goods. France and Spain were thrown upon the defensive, but South Carolina was forced to enjoy her triumph in moderation, for her attempted treaty of alliance with the Creeks in 1756 failed because it sought too much and because the Creeks were alarmed at Georgians' encroachments on their lands. Trade with the English

[1] The words of the treaty show how erroneous is the statement often made that Glen in 1753 bought about half of up-country South Carolina. The confusion has arisen from ignorance of the treaty of 1747 treated at page 164 above and that of 1755 presently to be described.

continued on improved though unsettled terms, but with the Creek attitude uncertain.

The French and Indian War beginning in 1754 and officially proclaimed two years later, of which these Indian affairs of the forest fastnesses were a preparation or a part, called also for fortifying the coast. The hurricane of September 15, 1752, wrecked the "shadow" fortifications, as Glen called them, and led to the erection of the strongest defenses the city had ever had, designed in 1756 by John William Gerard De Brahm, formerly an engineer in the German Imperial Army, at this time surveyor-general of Georgia. The Commons, as generally in crises, finally had their way in issuing paper money to pay the expense.

Struggle of France and England for the Southern Indians.—In the spring of 1753 Governor Glen was asked by Governor Dinwiddie how many troops South Carolina could furnish in a united effort of the colonies to oppose the French, now moving to dispossess the Virginia English in the Ohio region. An independent company of the King's troops, largely recruited in South Carolina, was at the King's order sent to Virginia and joined Colonel Washington on June 29, 1754.

Glen urged a conference of colonial governors to devise plans against the French, but negotiations of Virginia with the Cherokees and Catawbas aggravated his unsympathetic attitude toward Dinwiddie. "We have no proof," Glen wrote in August, 1754, "that the French plan a fort on the Ohio, where I would be sorry to see them, but infinitely more sorry to see them on the Tennessee." He proposed that the Indians cede all their lands east of the Mississippi, after which Virginia, New York, Pennsylvania, Maryland, and the Carolinas, could jointly build such powerful forts in the forks of the Tennessee and the Ohio and where the Wabash meets the Ohio as to isolate Louisiana and Canada. The government of South Carolina ended by pledging its aid to Virginia if the French encroached upon her.[2]

Conditions among the Cherokees were bad. The traders continued their cheating, and the Indians in the spring of 1755 were showing leanings toward the French. Glen determined to execute his plan of binding the Cherokees to England by securing a cession of all their lands to the Crown. Conocautee (alias Old Hop), Emperor of the Cherokees, pleaded his lameness, and hence Glen, though in poor health, acceded to his request to meet him halfway. Hearing when he was near the Congarees that the Indians were coming five hundred to seven hundred strong, in order to calm the fears of the people and to maintain the dignity of the government he summoned between four and five

[2] In my original edition, II, 9, note, I misplace the French Fort Assumption. It was built in 1739 on the Mississippi near the center of the later Memphis. South Carolina's allies the Chickasaws destroyed it in 1740.

hundred armed men and proceeded to Saluda. With solemn ceremonies on July 2, 1755, at Saluda Old Town, the Indians transferred to the King of England what a European would consider the feudal overlordship of all their lands. For this imperial domain of some 360,000 square miles Governor Glen handed them presents worth about $325.

How much the Indians meant beyond an acknowledgment of the King's sovereignty, or whether they intended to permit the Governor to grant to settlers their lands above the line of Long Canes Creek established in 1747, was a question rendered merely academic by the swift tragedy of the next few years. The Cherokees' lands were acquired piecemeal by later treaties that took no account of this one. But apart from questions of the King's right to grant the soil to settlers, Glen felt that his treaty prevented the Cherokees from abandoning the English after Braddock's defeat, in which he thought they would have been followed by the Creeks. If he was correct in that, his efforts had indeed been worth while.

The outbreak of the French and Indian War found the Cherokees cooled in their attachment to the English because of the unfulfillment of the promise of a fort among the Overhills for protection against the French and their Indians and the retaliation they suffered for what little aid they gave the English. South Carolina, having built Fort Prince George, was not hasty to incur a greater expense for a fort beyond her own borders that would be of substantial value to Georgia, North Carolina, Virginia, and the whole British imperial interest. Dinwiddie and Glen realized the necessity of co-operation, but could not agree upon the amount of the funds, entrusted by the British government to Dinwiddie, he should advance for the fort. So threatening was Cherokee discontent that South Carolina determined to act alone. Since the Commons and Council were deadlocked over their respective rights in another matter, private citizens advanced the necessary funds. Glen sent De Brahm ahead to select a location and followed with about three hundred men. In June, 1756, at Ninety Six, he was recalled by news of the arrival of his successor. Lyttelton found a Council dissatisfied with Glen for what they considered his slighting treatment of them and at their advice disbanded the expedition, but told the Indians not to doubt the fort would be built.

In June, 1756, Dinwiddie's Virginians arrived among the Overhill Cherokees and offered to join the Carolinians in building a fort. But the Indians insisted on a fort by each, and the Virginians built a 105-foot-square log structure a mile above Chottee (variously spelled) on the north side of the Little Tennessee. It gained only seven Cherokee warriors for the Virginians, and, being ungarrisoned, was soon destroyed by the savages.

Governor Lyttelton's South Carolina expedition, backed by a £4,000 sterling gift from the province, finally reached the Overhills in October, 1756. The approximately 500 miles were covered with infinite toil. De Brahm perched his strong and rather elaborate fort on several levels of a narrow ridge overlooking the Little Tennessee from the south and a few hundred yards above the mouth of the Tellico River, in the present Monroe County, Tennessee.

The execution of this promise to the Indians had the immediate effect of sending Cherokee aid to the English on the Ohio and in Virginia; but even as the fort was building, emissaries of the French-inclined faction were in Fort Toulouse and New Orleans plotting to destroy the garrison. On December 13, 1756, Kerlerec, Governor of Louisiana, wrote his government that the Cherokees had been making overtures, especially for the past three years. With five chiefs here at New Orleans from their leading towns, he wrote, "I have just concluded an alliance, ratifying of which I am delaying until they send their proposal to Vaudreuil in Canada. I fear the defeat of my plan by the English Cherokee partisans' informing Carolina of chiefs being here; for our treaty would put Carolina within two fingers of ruin and leave New England in a critical situation. These chiefs have also sought to get the Alabamas [Creeks] to join us. This is sent you, my lord, by le S[ieur] Duplessis, who will tell you by mouth what I ought not even confide to paper."[3]

The treaty pledged the Cherokees to destroy Fort Loudoun, promised trading supplies, and planned a general Indian war against the English. Right wisely did Kerlerec urge on his government haste and adequacy in sending the promised trade, for otherwise, he warned, the Cherokees must of necessity cleave to the English.

Kerlerec's diplomacy, pulling the Cherokees toward France, adds to the credit of Glen for having held them to the English interest until after France had been defeated in America. If the Cherokees had joined France earlier they would have enormously added to British difficulties. When the Cherokees did finally strike they were confronted by an already victorious Britain.

The Acadians.—In 1755, with its hands full with the Indian complications, the government of South Carolina had dumped upon it by Governor Lawrence of Nova Scotia, without previous notice or information as to whether they were French or British subjects, almost a thou-

[3] Kerlerec to ———, December 13, 1756 (apparently added to later); photostat obtained for D. D. Wallace from British Pub. Rec. Office, 5, Vol. 375, K 64. Treaty, etc., ditto, *passim*. They were captured with the French vessel bearing them and brought into Charles Town.

sand Acadians under the description of "French neutrals." The Assembly provided for their necessities. Some earned a living on the fortifications then building. The arrival of some 200 from Georgia and 106 Frenchmen from captured prizes brought the total French to 1,200, 400 of whom were men. The fear of what they might do, either in firing the city or rousing the slaves, threw the community into a panic, which was not helped when some of the Acadians predicted that the French King would release them. After futile plans for migration, etc., those of the 645 Acadians still present in July, 1756 (for deaths and migration had reduced them), who were unemployed were sold as indentured servants, the adults for three years and the children for a longer term; but many flocked back to the city. In November, 1763, those remaining in Charles Town went to Haiti, but were not pleased there. Of the very few families who stayed in South Carolina, that of Lanneau gave the State one of her brightest jewels—Basil Lanneau Gildersleeve.

Estimate of Glen.—Governor Glen, through his administration of twelve and a half years, proved a useful executive both to the province and to the empire. The Assembly struck the true note in valuing him on his Indian policy. No governor of the province before or later was so active and so constant in his duties. No other governor advanced so liberally his own funds for the public service. It was largely this restless activity, coupled with a readiness to criticize inefficiency or what he considered trespasses on the legitimate rights of the Crown, that brought him into conflicts with both houses. At the same time his frank and cordial confidence in the Commons and his consenting to certain of their measures offended the Lords of Trade. His propensity of magnifying his own achievements invited criticism of even his best accomplishments, and his sanguine temperament betrayed him into raising hopes, as with the Choctaw treaty, the dashing of which exposed him to official resentment; and his interminable letters wearied his superiors.

Seeking to Destroy the Legislative Character of the Council.—The closing years of Governor Glen's administration saw the most serious dispute as to the legislative powers of the Commons and Council respectively that occurred until their final deadlock in the years just before the Revolution. It will be recalled that the dispute of 1737 to '39 over the sole right of the Commons to model or amend money bills had been settled by the compromise that the Council might send down on a separate sheet suggestions of amendments which they would like the Commons to make. Peace continued on this basis until 1754.

The next serious dispute arose as follows: When James Crokatt, Agent since 1749, proposed on July 6, 1753, to resign, the two houses disagreed as to insisting on his continuance or choosing another. The Council struck from the appropriation bill the £1,400 currency which the Commons had inserted as the annual allowance for Crokatt, whom they insisted on retaining. The Commons resolved that the people's representatives, since they paid the Agent, had the right to say whom they would pay. In order to take from the Council any power in future to do more than accept or reject the tax bill as sent to them, the Commons resolved, "That no account, petition, or other paper that shall be laid before this House for the future of, for, or concerning any claim or demand whatever for any matter or thing done or to be done for the service of the public shall be sent to the Council for their inspection."

The clamor of the public creditors, the urgent necessity of aiding Virginia in the war, and Governor Glen's insistence impelled the Council to submit.

So bitter was the dispute that the Commons determined if possible to destroy all legislative authority of the "upper house" and reduce it to a mere executive council to advise the Governor. On reassembling in November they appointed a committee to search the records and resolved that no recognition of any legislative character in the Council should be taken as a precedent. The Council meanwhile compiled an interminable defense, fortified by precedent, of their right to inspect the accounts.

It was evidently to this dispute that Lieutenant-Governor Bull alluded in later years in saying that leading members of the Commons privately inquired of the Governor whether he would sign the tax bill if it was presented to him by the Commons alone. The grievance was aggravated by the condition, now almost chronic, into which the upper house had fallen. Through deaths, removals to England, resignations, physical infirmities, or distance from town, Glen wrote in 1746, chancery cases (the Council was the court of chancery) had been waiting for years, "and for many months past there has been a total failure of justice." It was this often almost nonexistent body whose character as a legislative house the Commons questioned. On July 2, 1756, the Council, in order to give Lyttelton, who arrived on June 1, a good beginning waived their right to inspect the public accounts.

Governor Lyttelton Takes Over a Troublesome Situation.—William Henry Lyttelton, a baron by two separate elevations, who at the age of thirty-one superseded Glen, had been ambassador to Portugal and was a graceful writer and a scholar of some distinction. He was the favorite of the Lords of Trade. Their gall for Glen became honey for him, which they poured over even his egregious blunders. Governor Lyttelton has the distinction of dealing the declining Council almost its deathblow in public respect by expelling from it William Wragg, one of the most esteemed characters in the province, for the reason that he could not endure Wragg's frank and courageous opposition to his policies. From that time it became difficult to induce South Carolinians of standing to accept membership in the Council, which declined more and more into a group of royal placemen.

The arrival of the new Governor itself became the occasion of new embitterment. The Council, aping the House of Lords, ordered the Commons to withdraw into the lobby with the crowd during their reception of the Governor. Many of the Commons received no invitation to the dinner, but they agreed to pay the expense, though so contemptuously that the councillors felt shamed into paying it from their private pockets. With a powerful savage enemy at the gates, the Commons refused to transact business because a bar was erected at which, instead of at the table, their commissioners were to deliver papers to the Council. The bar removed, the wheels of government again revolved. South Carolina was proving what has before and since been proved all over the British Empire—that satisfactory government is not possible unless either the popular or the prerogative element is strong enough to listen to advice from the other without fear of its power.

South Carolina had welcomed British troops, small numbers of whom were in the province almost constantly from 1721, for she obtained, for the portion of their pay which she contributed, garrison services at less than cost. For the British regulars (largely recruited in America) and Virginia colonials arriving in 1757 the Assembly provided additional barracks for a thousand men besides a liberal appropriation for powder and supplies, though General Lord Loudoun's orders to Colonel Bouquet to quarter his men in private houses by his own authority if proper provision was not made caused resentment. Governor Lyttelton also snuffed out the Commons' bill for an artillery company and organized one himself, lest their permission might seem to imply his lack of right. The province, on Lord Loudoun's appointment, added 500 men in addition to her existing force of 200. There were, in January, 1758, 1,500 British regulars in South Carolina, of whom Lieutenant-Colonel Montgomerie's battalion of Highlanders was the main portion. The Assembly voted for military purposes, between 1755 and 1760, £100,656 sterling.

Lyttelton and the Cherokees.—We must now trace through the course of several years the relations of the province with the Cherokees. The Indians were slow in going to Virginia. In 1758 the frontiers were in danger because of the anger of the middle settlements that some of their warriors returning from the north had been killed by the frontiersmen of Virginia and the Carolinas in retaliation for thefts and murders committed in Bedford and Halifax counties, Virginia. Soon the Cherokees and Creeks seemed to be concocting a joint revenge. Before July 31 all the Cherokees deserted General Forbes in Pennsylvania. The spy of Lieutenant Coytmore at Fort Prince George brought the news that the Lower Cherokees had agreed for war on the English provided the Creeks would commit themselves by first killing all the English traders in their nation. The Cherokees would then apply at the English forts for ammunition to punish the Creeks and use it to massacre the English themselves.

In September, 1759, the Cherokees laid siege to Fort Prince George. On October 6 the Council advised an immediate declaration of war; but the arrival of a large delegation of the tribe seeking ammunition moved Governor Lyttelton to ask for a further opinion. The Council advised that if the Indians now in town were authorized to treat of the murders, a specific number of guilty Cherokees should be surrendered, pending which an equal number of the delegates now in town should be held as hostages for the delivery of the murderers. The Governor replied that he considered this unwise and perhaps unlawful, and that he would shortly set out on the expedition to the Cherokee country authorized by the legislature.

Half the Council now advised retaining the Indians as hostages, and half advised the expedition. To the Indians the Governor reviewed the Cherokee crimes and said that he was going up to take satisfaction if it were not granted, but promised to them the safe return to their country guaranteed to diplomatic representatives.

It is thus evident that historians, neglecting the Council records, have unjustly shouldered Governor Lyttelton with the whole blame for the bungled and perfidious action in seizing the Indians a few days later. A majority of his Council were guilty of originating the immoral and stupid scheme, while he has the right to the excuse, as a young and inexperienced executive, of adopting the advice of older men long accustomed to Indian affairs.

Governor Lyttelton arrived at Fort Prince George on December 9, 1759, with fifteen hundred men. To measles and sickness from bad weather was added on the twenty-eight smallpox, brought by Cherokees from the Catawbas. Since November 19, 1758, when Lyttelton had compensated the Indians for their warriors killed by the Virginians, the savages had murdered twenty-four whites. Three of the murderers were now surrendered, and one a little later. By the treaty signed on December 26, the Indians renewed their old relations with the English and agreed to Lyttelton's retaining as hostages twenty-two Indians, many of them of high standing, until the surrender of the other murderers. In the danger of a general desertion before the smallpox, the Governor returned to Charles Town.

Cherokee War, 1760-61.—The peace thus proclaimed was entirely illusive. The Indians had not been overawed by an army marching home under disease and desertions. Their already alienated minds were inflamed by the breach of faith in seizing their ambassadors as hostages. On January 19, 1760, they murdered a considerable number of traders throughout the nation (24 in all, report says), and attempted to surprise Fort Prince George. "A Cherokee wench" and fleeing traders warned the settlers at Ninety Six; but upward of 75 persons (25 of them as far south as the present Lexington) were slaughtered. Georgia also suffered. On February 16 the Great Warrior enticed the commander of the beleaguered Fort Prince George out for a conference and killed him in ambush. Firing rained from the hills, and cannon replied from the fort all day. The Indian hostages in the fort, having killed a soldier seeking to bind them, were, against orders, all shot to death.

Governor Lyttelton sailed for England on April 5, leaving leadership to the firm, wise, and able Lieutenant-Governor Bull, the Second, who now began the first of his five administrations.

The war thus rashly begun by the Cherokees was for them fatally late, for France had already lost the war. The traditional Creek policy of maintaining their own independence by a trimming attitude toward both English and French, and denying any control over them by either, held, though severely strained; but they massacred many of the English traders and gave a few men and much encouragement to the Cherokees. The Catawbas, as usual, aided the province.

The causes moving the Cherokees to war were the abuses by the traders, the encroachment of white settlements toward their hunting grounds, the killing of their warriors for horse stealing, etc., in Virginia as they were returning from defending Virginia herself, and French intrigues. The treachery and mismanagement of Governor Lyttelton and his Council fanned these embers into flame. The rapid influx of settlers in the past few years, swelled by the movement from western Pennsylvania after Braddock's defeat left that frontier open to the French Indians, for the first time roused the Cherokees to the danger of losing their lands. The Long Canes line of 1747 was in effect a mere truce at the point then of greatest danger. The whites, complained the Indians in 1758, have settled so near that the deer have become so scarce we can hardly feed or clothe our wives and children. This, they said, is our great grievance.

Montgomerie Against the Cherokees, 1760.—Lieutenant-Colonel Archibald Montgomerie, after his service against Fort Duquesne, reached Charles Town with his 1,200 Highlanders on April 1, 1760. Adding to his force 350 South Carolina troops, he reached Fort Prince George early in June. The lower Cherokee towns were quickly burned, some of the Indians killed, and many driven in destitution across the mountains. Indian chiefs were now sent out to persuade the nation to peace; but the treachery to the hostages caused even the best inclined to distrust any English promises.

On June 24 Montgomerie struck for the Little Tennessee Valley by War Woman Creek and Rabun Gap. On the 27th the Indians attacked in the mountains from ambush at a point about eight miles south of the present town of Franklin, North Carolina. After two days of litter-making, he began his retreat. Attacked twice on the way, his army arrived at Fort Prince George totally exhausted.

South Carolina, with the situation made worse by Montgomerie's failure, was astounded at his announcing that his orders required him to return to the north after having "chastised" the Indians. This sealed the fate of Fort Loudoun, whose garrison surrendered on August 8 on promise of safe conduct to Fort Prince George, only to see thirty murdered in revenge for the massacre of the hostages at Fort Prince George and other prisoners brutally mistreated.

Grant Crushes the Cherokees, 1761.—Lieutenant-Governor Bull, convinced that nothing would serve but thoroughly to crush the Indians, now contemptuous of the weakness of both South Carolina and Virginia, wrote to General Amherst for troops. On January 6, 1761, Lieutenant-Colonel James Grant, who had been with the 1760 expedition, arrived with 1,200 regulars, who, with those already here, made 1,600. His well-equipped force of British and South Carolinians, consisting of 2,250 effectives (besides detachments to secure communications), reached Fort Prince George at the end of May, 1761. The Virginians were again too late for action, and the North Carolinians were not ready until the fight was over.

On June 7 the army marched into the mountains by Montgomerie's old route. On June 10, when they were two miles south of the last year's battlefield, the Indians attacked from ambush. In a month of devastation Grant destroyed fifteen towns and all growing crops in the rich and beautiful Little Tennessee and Tuckaseegee valleys and drove the Indians into the high mountains to starve. The provincial regiment behaved well, Grant reported. Attakullakulla (the Little Carpenter), faithful throughout to the English, was sent to Fort Prince George to seek peace. The treaty of December 18, 1761, provided for the surrender of all English property (including slaves) held by the Cherokees; the restoration of trade; the right of the English to build forts anywhere; the exclusion of all Frenchmen; the prompt execution by the Indians of murderers of white men; surrender for punishment by the province of white criminals among the Indians. No Indian, unless accompanied by a white man, or by special permission, was to come more than forty miles below Fort Prince George. The boundary was fixed as described below. The campaign over, the South Carolina troops who, Grant had reported, fought well, deserted rapidly. They were good, said Bull, for quick fighting, but soon became insubordinate if held inactive in camp.

The boundary thus so loosely indicated was not actually marked until 1766, and then only partially. As extended, it remains as the line south and east of Anderson and Greenville, except where below the Enoree Greenville was in 1792 pushed over on Laurens. It was the first line definitely established between the Cherokees and the South Carolina whites, except the Long Canes Creek line in 1747, and a temporary arrangement in 1765. It formed a part of the line established after the general peace which extended into every province on which the Cherokees bordered.

A trivial personal incident was the Middleton-Grant duel. Thomas Middleton, as colonel of the South Carolina Regiment, thought he should outrank Grant, as lieutenant-colonel of the British army, as he might have had technical grounds for claiming but for General Amherst's having definitely guarded against such claims by a special commission to Lieutenant-Colonel Grant. Middleton secured permission from Bull to return if he found the service disagreeable. This he did after the actual fighting, feeling a grievance, the justice of which Grant denied, in not being duly consulted. A duel followed, the injuries from which were confined to the wounded feelings of the factions into which it violently divided a considerable portion of the province's public men. Gadsden, for example, strongly supported Middleton; Henry Laurens, as strongly Grant. Middleton's correspondence with Bull beforehand seems to reveal the trouble as the outcome of Middleton's temperament rather than, as General McCrady, who apparently did not see these letters, surmises, an outcropping of the jealousy between regular and colonial officers as such. No other South Carolina officer seems to have fancied himself mistreated.

Middleton was one of the last great aristocrats to continue in trade at the period when amassed mercantile wealth was transforming itself into landed estates and sneering at those who still followed commerce.

Organizing Indian Relations for Justice and Peace.—The royal government was determined to avoid further wars by respecting Indian rights, a policy which helped alienate the land-hungry Americans. The

Treaty of Paris, removing France from North America, so angered the Creeks, thus deprived of their power of balancing the rival Europeans against each other, that there was danger that they, like Pontiac, might seek to destroy the English. It was to extinguish such perils that the King ordered a congress to be held by Southern governors and the Superintendent of Indian Affairs. These gentlemen, on November 3, 1763, opened the congress at Augusta with about seven hundred Indians of the Cherokees, Chickasaws, Choctaws, and Creeks.

The Creeks were promised that the settlements would extend only as they had agreed.

The Cherokees were told that the abuses by the South Carolina traders were ended, as the King had ordered goods to be kept at Keowee at low prices by a man of character. South Carolina could now send no private traders. Virginia's few traders could do as they pleased; and North Carolina had no Indian traders.

The Catawbas were satisfied with their spot fifteen miles square, the survey of which had already begun.[4] Friendship was pledged by the tribes to one another, and a treaty of perpetual friendship signed with the King. The Indians departed with abundant presents, and a Cherokee-Creek war was averted.

Despite the treaties, the Cherokees and Creeks, deeply stirred by the fear of encroachments on their lands, never settled into their old-time quiet until a later day when what they feared had come upon them so heavily that it was no longer to be resisted. After the French and Indian War, which removed the barrier that had held the English east of the mountains, life could never be the same in America to either white or red. The year 1763 opened a new era in the history of the world. A larger portion of the earth's surface changed hands in that year, and vaster racial streams seeking opportunity had their courses changed, than at any one time before or since in history.

[4] On December 15, 1943, by agreement between the State and federal governments, the 250 Catawbas, mostly living on a 652-acre tract in York County, were made American citizens and promised an extension of lands, to be State-owned and therefore tax free, of several thousand acres.

CHAPTER XXII

ECONOMIC AND SOCIAL CONDITIONS IN THE MID-EIGHTEENTH CENTURY

Health and Mortality.—Smallpox, yellow fever, diphtheria, and malaria broke out with frequent violence during the colonial period; but the high death rate is not so much a part of South Carolina history as an illustration for the general medical conditions of the times. The infant mortality recorded in old graveyards, church registers, and family records is appalling. Diphtheria was a frightful scourge, "the sore throat" sometimes sweeping away almost all the children of a family. All sorts of bacterial diseases worked havoc in an age that was ignorant of cause, and therefore of prevention. In time the planters learned there was a causal connection between residence on plantations in summer and malaria and invented many fanciful theories, which were believed until the guilt was fixed on the mosquito a few decades ago.

Christian Work among the Slaves.—From about 1710, when the number of Negro slaves began greatly to exceed the number of whites, apprehension of these "internal enemies" was frequently expressed. Lieutenant-Governor Broughton warned in 1737 that "our negroes are very numerous and more dreadful to our safety than any Spanish invaders. I am also sending for some Cherokee Indians to come down to the settlements to be an awe to the negroes."

The standing tragedy of Southern life was already disclosed. Men saw the peril they were creating for themselves and their posterity, but were morally unable to take the obvious course for permanent well-being. Only a society of philosophers could have resisted the temptation, and they probably only if legislating for some society other than their own. The immediate gain to the planter outweighed the permanent interests of the State, as is the custom when the class receiving the benefit holds the power.

The Society for the Propagation of the Gospel in Foreign Parts made the Christianizing of the slaves an active aim. All but a few masters at first opposed religious instruction, lest making the slave a Christian brother might tend toward manumission. Other objections were that religion injured him as a laborer or involved danger of insurrection by facilitating assemblies. In 1724, Alexander Skene, his wife, and his sister assumed leadership in having their slaves instructed and baptized. But opposition was long in abating. In 1745 there were three or four Christians among the 2,600 slaves of St. John's, and in 1762 the Rev. Mr. Martin estimated 500 Christians among the 46,000 Negroes in the province. The Anglican and Presbyterian clergy were too few to serve adequately even their widely scattered white parishioners. After the greater value of the Christian slaves became evident, the work of Christianization was fostered even by irreligious masters; but the conversion of Negroes on a large scale awaited the later work of the Baptists and Methodists.

In 1740 Hugh Bryan, a well-to-do and deeply pious Presbyterian, on the advice of the Rev. George Whitefield, opened a Negro school with the later Rev. William Hutson as teacher. Bryan's conduct, often indiscreet, now showed him well within the bounds of insanity. On February 16, 1742, the Commons were informed of frequent great assemblies of Negroes in St. Helena parish with the countenance of sundry white persons, to the terror of the neighborhood. Bryan explained that the invisible spirit, whose intimate converse he had thought, until three days ago, to be for the public good and his own soul's welfare, was none other than the devil, whom he in remorse abjured. He pleaded that his proofs of devotion to the public good might wipe out his guilt for having assembled great bodies of Negroes under pretense of religious worship and having prophesied the destruction of Charles Town and the freeing of the slaves. The grand jury presentments against Bryan and his associates seem not to have been pressed to trial.

Dr. Alexander Garden, commissary of the Bishop of London and rector of St. Philip's, was of earnest but better regulated mind. In full harmony with the zeal of the Society for the Propagation of the Gospel for the conversion and education of the Negroes, he opened in Charles Town, on September 12, 1743, a school for educating Negro children. Private philanthropy in Charles Town built the schoolhouse. "E'en the very slave parents themselves would gladly . . . pinch it off their own backs and out of their own bellies," wrote Dr. Garden, "but no such charge shall either the one or the other be put to in my time." Neither did he nor these self-sacrificing parents realize that they were undermining slavery just as truly as Bryan; but South Carolina in time came to realize it and forbade teaching slaves to read. Dr. Garden's school, having at one time upward of sixty pupils, ended in 1764 or a little later.

Danger of Insurrection, Etc.—There were frequent complaints of the laxity with which the slave code was observed, until a plot, a murder, unbearable insolence, or disorderly assemblages led to greater strictness. Plots and conspiracies were more frequent while the mass of the slaves remained African barbarians ("new Negroes") than after many of the plantation population had become "country born." The conspiracies ranged all the way from mere plots of a group to run away to plans of general murder. One band of Negro bandits and five slave conspiracies are found between 1702 and 1737.

Spain's policy of offering freedom to slaves fleeing to St. Augustine was a constant danger. It was therefore not surprising when a serious insurrection occurred on the night of September 9, 1739, on Stono River. A great number of Negroes rose, wrote Lieutenant-Governor Bull, broke open a store, got arms, and killed twenty-one persons. They marched the next morning for Florida, killing all they met and burning several houses. To subdue the rebels Bull called out the militia, who in a few hours entirely suppressed the movement. Forty-four of the Negroes were killed or executed.

With a Spanish invasion expected the situation was indeed alarming. Said the legislature in addressing the King, the rising of 1739 was "no sooner quelled than another projected in Charles Town, and a third lately in the very heart of the settlements, but happily discovered time enough to be prevented." Sixty-seven were tried for the latter. There were intermittent alarms and little plots for nine years as well as some unusual crimes, such as two slaves' raping a white woman, and two others beating their overseer to death, and numerous poisonings of masters.

But soon the accustomed carelessness returned—negligent paroles, Negroes possessing arms and crowding into gambling and grog shops and disturbing the Sabbath. In 1759 two Negro fanatics prophesied destruction of the whites, and in January, 1761, the *Gazette* reported that "the negroes have again begun the hellish practice of poisoning." Scores of slaves had run away in 1765, a large camp of whom was dispersed by military force, and a general insurrection was so feared for Christmas that Indians were brought in to terrorize the Negroes, and the whites of the back country were solicited to be ready to march toward the coast.

Only the desperate shortage of whites can account for the province's employing Negro soldiers. Their use in the Yemassee War will be recalled. Seventy-three slaves served on ships against the Spaniards in 1742, and the law of 1747, renewed from time to time, continued to authorize in time of alarm or invasion slave soldiers up to one-third the number of whites. But the insurrection of 1739 did afford the needed impetus for temporarily stopping importations.

Slavery Regulations—Miscegenation.—The early slave code was brutally harsh, first, because criminal law was then harsh all over the world;

and second, because an even sterner cruelty was needed to rule the savages fresh from Africa. Bloody statutes remained on the books long after they were actually employed. Particularly heinous crimes were punished in South Carolina as in New York and elsewhere, by burning alive. Several slaves were burned in South Carolina after the 1720 conspiracy, one each in 1741, 1748, 1754, 1772, and a few after the Revolution. Until well into the eighteenth century slaves were frequently branded for identification. Slaves legally executed were paid for by the public, lest masters should be tempted to conceal slaves' crimes.

For several years before the insurrection of 1739 a demand had grown for more humane treatment as a safeguard against insurrection, murders, and runnings. The revised slave code of 1740, which remained the basis of the Negro law while slavery lasted, added to the rules for the benefit of the slave.

The free Negro very early emerged, manumitted by a kindly master or at public expense for some signal public service, such as revealing conspiracies or fighting against invaders. A noted instance was that of the sexton of St. Philip's Church (not St. Michael's, as misrepresented thus and otherwise by Whittier), Charleston, in 1796, freed by the church officials for his heroism in tearing burning shingles from the roof. Free Negroes owned slaves in 1754 and doubtless much earlier. Such sometimes owned their wives.

The economic and social evils of slavery soon became evident even to the eighteenth-century conscience. In 1734 Governor, Council, and Commons protested against the British merchants' seeking to defeat the province's efforts to check slave importations, which, they said, were sacrificing white handicraftsmen and driving off white settlers. The white shipwrights' protest in 1744, e.g., pointing out the injury of Negro competition to themselves and the public interest, is merely one of numerous such complaints that continued as long as slavery and failed of any material effect, for the private interests of the ruling element as slave owners soon obscured their view of the welfare of society as a whole.

The most troublesome phase of the Negro question, the phase against which, as the ultimate peril, the social barriers were to be maintained long after slavery had disappeared, was racial interbreeding. Marriages of whites with mulattoes or blacks in a very few instances occurred, this not being unlawful until 1865.

Numbers of Free, Slaves, and Indentured Servants.—In the absence of any census, estimates of population before 1790 are mere approximations. The number for various dates may be found in the appendix.

White indentured servants never formed such a large part of the population of South Carolina as of Virginia, Maryland, and Pennsylvania. The planters preferred slaves to white servants, who were inclined to insubordination and became free almost as soon as trained. The ship captain or the merchant, and in some cases the colonial government, who assumed the risk, looked to reap a profit by selling at a price the services of these white people for a term of years, varying from two to seven. An English firm was unable to sell more than a fourth of 1,500 Germans whom they sent to Charles Town in about 1750, and had to be satisfied with the personal notes of the others to pay passage. Some were underfed on the voyage and otherwise mistreated. Henry Laurens denounced the cruelty to a body of Irish imported in 1768 that "would make your humanity shudder."

The poor Swiss and Germans of the migration of the 1730's to 1760's were the principal source of our indentured servants; yet it is easy to overguess the proportion. Out of hundreds of applications for land grants from about 1745 to 1756, I noted only thirty-five or forty ex-indentured servants, compared with hundreds who say they paid their passage and scores who say nothing of their status. Most of them apparently signed their names. But I suspect that the proportion of servants was generally much larger than among the lists referred to.

The master received at once fifty acres "head right" for an indentured servant, and the servant the same amount on becoming free. The master could sell the servant for the remainder of his term of service. The master's power of control was harsh, but the indentured servant, unlike the slave or the free Negro, was under the protection of the ordinary courts and not subject to the juryless courts of magistrates and freeholders. At the expiration of his term of service he must be given a certain equipment of clothes, etc. A freeman who married a woman servant had the right to buy her freedom. A bastard born of a servant woman remained a servant until twenty-one years of age if male, or eighteen if female. The whole system was an expression of the inhumanity then common. It was a natural development from the system long common under which an apprentice was legally bound to his master for seven years.

Mr. S. C. Hughson, in his misnamed monograph *The Carolina Pirates* (for few indeed of them were connected with Carolina in any way except to be hanged for robbing her), explains the tolerance of pirates by remarking that "a large part of the first settlers in many parts of America were banished criminals of the lowest class." South Carolina and all other continental colonies in 1697 rejected the offer of a number of criminals awaiting deportation from England, and in 1712 South Carolina penalized the importation of criminals under the pretense of their being indentured servants, and in 1716 protested against some having been sent here and forbade the repetition of the practice. Eighteen male and six female convicts were sent to South Carolina in 1729. How 106 were accidentally imported in 1718 has been related in the chapter on the suppression of pirates. The province suffered nothing from the thirty-two "traitors" whom she bought in 1716 to defend her frontier as they had been defending their convictions when captured at the battle of Preston. Over a score of most excellent Scotch "criminals" were sent in 1684 to Lord Cardross' settlement at Port Royal for clinging to Presbyterianism in preference to Episcopacy.[1]

Rice and Indigo.—Some account has already been given of lumber, rice, pitch, tar, turpentine, cattle, deer and other skins, which formed the economic foundation of the province, and of other conspicuous products also, as wheat, hemp, flax, silk, and fruits. From the beginning numerous experiments were conducted. Indigo culture was almost abandoned. It was revived in the 1740's as a great staple, as cotton was still later. From about 1750 to 1776 rice and indigo were much the most important sources of wealth. Great fortunes were made by merchants who handled the great exports and the imports for which these paid.

Rice was at first cultivated on dry lands, but early in the eighteenth century swamp lands beyond the reach of high tide (for salt water kills rice) began to be used. Governor Glen's remark, a little after 1748, that "the very best lands may be meliorated by laying them under water at proper seasons," shows that systematic floodings had not then been universally adopted. Impounded rain or streams (called "reserves") were first used for this purpose. McKewn Johnstone led the way in 1758 near Winyaw Bay, says Dr. U. B. Phillips, in utilizing the tide to back the river water over the rice fields. In 1783 Gideon DuPont of St. James Goose Creek sought compensation from the State for inventing the method of water cultivation; but clearly this was an adaptation or improvement of the earlier method.

Water cultivation not only promotes the growth of the rice, but kills the weeds and grass, which formerly had to be laboriously cleared with the hoe. Until long after the Revolution, with enormous labor, swamps were cleared and the network of dykes constructed, whose sluice gates admitted, retained or discharged the fresh water which rose many miles up the rivers with the tide, and excluded the salt water which dry weather or storms sent abnormally far upstream. It was the driving of

[1] Mr. St. Julien Ravenel Childs in his *Malaria and Colonization in the Carolina Low Country 1526-1696* (J. H. U. Studies Hist. and Pol. Sci. Ser. LVIII, No. 1, 213-14) states that 35 of the 148 Scots brought for Cardross' colony in 1684 were convicts and that 150 more prisoners (character not stated) were sent from Scotland to Charles Town during 1684, besides 74 or more other "servants."

salt water over the embankments or through breaks as well as the beating of the winds that made the August or September storms sometimes so ruinous, converting today's wealth into tomorrow's rotting straw.

The best rice lands are the black, greasy mould of cypress swamps with a clay bottom, writes Governor Glen about 1750. The heaviness of rice led the planter to seek lands on navigable streams. This and the tidewater backing twenty to thirty miles inland led to the extraordinary concentration of a wealthy and cultured country gentry within a short distance of Charles Town, Beaufort, and Georgetown.

The Act of 3d and 4th Anne (1705 or '06) placing rice on the list of "enumerated" articles permitted to be exported only to England was a severe blow to the Carolina planter. His Spanish and Portuguese market was destroyed and the price of his commodity depressed, thus magnifying the complex economic difficulties of the province at a very trying period. A part of the tardy measures of relief ending the depression of the late 1720's was the permission granted in 1730 to ship rice to points south of Cape Finisterre, as previously mentioned.

Rice suffered severely in the war of 1740 to '48, dropping in 1745 to a fourth or fifth of former prices. During the later years of the war the development of indigo culture was a godsend. But in 1752 rice was selling so high that indigo was neglected, although prudent planters were planting it for seed as a standby, for the rice market was more easily glutted than that for indigo. The rice crop in 1754 approached 100,000 barrels of about 600 pounds each.

In the fiscal year 1747-48 the province exported 55,000 600-pound barrels of rice, 39,308 bushels of Indian corn, 1,764 barrels of beef, 6,107 bushels of peas, and 296,000 oranges, a fruit whose cultivation was being extended in disregard of the frequency of heavy frosts. In 1760 flour was extensively manufactured in the back country.

In the 1740's South Carolina developed her second great staple crop —indigo. Like many another semitropical plant, it was very early tried, but the better profits from rice caused its neglect after about 1695. In 1722 little or no indigo was being cultivated. Under depressed rice prices in the 1740's the planters were casting about for any substitute. In 1744 the Assembly offered bounties for native wine, olive oil, flax, hemp, wheat, barley, cotton, indigo, and ginger. Eminent among South Carolina agricultural leaders was a young girl, Eliza Lucas, one of the principal creators of a virtually new industry. Her father, Lieutenant-Colonel George Lucas, stationed at Antigua, acquired lands in South Carolina because of the feeble health of his wife. When the war of 1739 called him back to Antigua, his South Carolina plantations were left under the management of his seventeen-year-old daughter, Eliza. This remarkable young woman, who by her marriage in 1744 to the later Chief Justice Charles Pinckney, became the mother of Charles Cotesworth and Thomas Pinckney of the Revolution, found time for every social duty and for the experiments with indigo, ginger, cotton, lucern, etc. In 1741 or '42 she planted her first indigo seed in St. Andrew's parish. In 1744 she made seventeen pounds of good indigo. Andrew DeVeaux, also of St. Andrew's, who, she says, observed and improved part of her process, was soon making far more than she.

Cultivation increased so rapidly that, in the fiscal year ending in 1746, 5,000 pounds were exported; in the year ending November 1, 1747, 46,674 pounds; and 1748, 134,118 pounds. The province repealed the bounty in 1746 in dread of the expense. Great Britain, detesting paying money to the French, in 1748 established a bounty of six pence a pound (reduced in 1764 to four pence, and enjoyed to the end of the colonial era) for every pound sent to her from her colonies. By 1754 the new staple had people in high spirits and the slave market booming.

The indigo plant is of about the size and limbing of good cotton, but slenderer, and thrives on the same land as cotton. Though the loss of the bounty by the Revolution destroyed the industry, indigo was raised, especially in Orangeburg, long afterward for domestic use. Coal tar dyes have now almost supplanted it everywhere. Cotton was a welcome successor to indigo, for the harvesting and preparation of the latter was a great burden on both the master and the slave. Peter Sinkler, says Samuel DuBose, would not see his family for three weeks during the indigo-making season, as he rose before they waked and returned after they were asleep.

The progress being made in England in retaining or restoring fertility by manuring did not spread to South Carolina until considerably after the Revolution. Hence the loose, light soil of the coast country soon began to show signs of exhaustion. Rev. Robert Stone wrote on March 6, 1750, that the lands in Goose Creek parish were worn out, many inhabitants were dead, many were running away to new settlements, and health was so bad that forty-five was considered the common age of man. Essentially the same economic conditions were described for Christ Church parish by Rev. Levi Durand in 1749.

Cotton, Silk, Etc.—Manufactures.—The "corn, cotton, and tobacco did well" in 1670. In 1693 reference is made to the export of cotton to other colonies; but before 1722 it and indigo had been abandoned on account of "too severe a climate." In 1731 it was being raised and woven with coarse wool for slaves' garments. In 1747 Governor Glen wrote that some gentlemen themselves wear such cloth made in South Carolina. Seven bags of cotton were exported in 1748. In 1768 Henry Laurens ordered two bushels of cotton seed from the West Indies.

The early expectations of making silk were defeated by the higher profits available from other industries. "Everybody has planted mulberry trees to feed their worms," wrote Edward Randolph in 1700. Sir Nathaniel Johnson named his home plantation Silk Hope. The Proprietors in 1699 thanked him for a present of silk. Mr. Godin in 1716 imported into England from South Carolina several bales of silk which he considered as good as that from Piedmont. There were Parliamentary and provincial bounties. Ten thousand pounds were produced in 1759. In 1766 or '67 a silk-spinning factory was opened in Charles Town and another in Hillsborough in the later Abbeville, where the French were the province's most successful silk raisers.

The high hopes based on the skill of the French immigrants for grape culture met the same conditions: splendidly successful horticulturally, but financially unprofitable compared with staples.

Little manufacturing existed in colonial South Carolina except a few handicrafts, the preparation of tobacco for use, the making of rice and other mills, the home weaving of some cloth, the necessary preparation of pitch, tar, turpentine, etc., for market, and the making of a few necessities such as salt and potash. William Mellichamp had by July 31, 1731, manufactured 14,000 bushels of salt.

Low agricultural prices and high prices for manufactures due to the war led many planters in the middle 1740's to bring in sheep from northern colonies and for a few years to make coarse cloth from wool and cotton mixed for their Negroes or even for themselves. The Assembly offered prizes for the best South Carolina-made cloth. The ministry in alarm ordered Governor Glen to discourage manufacturing. Booming prices for rice and indigo after the war ended the movement. In 1729 there were started a rope walk and a sugar house, the product of the latter being as good as the London product and far cheaper.

Commerce, Roads, Etc.—The merchants accumulated some of the largest fortunes in the province. Many landed estates were in fact commercial fortunes converted into the form of wealth which carried the greater social distinction; but many a merchant found in the years of the booming rice and indigo prices that his lands netted more than his trade. In the mid-country, good planters bought Negroes largely on credit and paid for them in three or four years and sometimes less out of their product. Before 1720 most South Carolina trade was conducted by London merchants through their factors or agents in South Carolina. In both the Proprietary and the royal period women merchants doing a good business were frequent. Madam Sarah Rhett, wife of Colonel Rhett the pirate-fighter, was a notable trader. Of the sixty-six persons and firms licensed in 1763 to retail liquors in Charles Town, thirty-four were women, indicating apparently eating-house or tavern keepers.

Some merchants in South Carolina traded on commission only; others both on commission and on their own capital. The ordinary commission was 5 per cent. For selling imported slaves it was 10 per cent less coasting fees, loading, and other incidentals. Before 1732 imported slaves were sold for rice, the factor remitting the rice when it was delivered by the purchaser of slaves. After 1732 the stricter requirement prevailed that the factor was to remit two-thirds of the price within a year and the balance by the end of the second year.

The number of vessels leaving Charles Town annually between Christmas, 1735, and November 1, 1749, varied from 317 to 190, and was usually well above 200. The following sailings from Charles Town for the year ending December 25, 1751, indicate the directions of trade:

	VESSELS	TONS	MEN
For Great Britain	96	10,262	1,034
For British Islands in America	81	2,294	503
For British American Continental Colonies	57	1,896	292
For ports of Europe south of Cape Finisterre	26	2,900	289
For Bay of Honduras	4	299	36
For St. Augustine	1	20	5

Ten per cent was allowed as legal interest by the act of 1720. In 1748 it was reduced to 8 per cent and in 1777 to 7 per cent. Before 1720, 25 per cent had been common. These rates were in the eighteenth century charged on open accounts, and were compounded if not paid yearly. Lands were commonly overvalued; slaves were mortal, and buildings were generally uninsured; hence personal security was preferred, as, in addition to the above, fees, etc., on foreclosure were high, and delinquent quitrents might convert the loan into a loss.

In 1735 there was organized "The Friendly Society," a mutual fire insurance company, which thus antedated by almost seventeen years the next oldest such organization in the United States, the one organized in Philadelphia in 1752 with Franklin at the head of its directors.

Whatever banking functions existed (except issuing paper money) were exercised by large merchants. Bills of exchange were sold by them on their foreign correspondents. Remittances of cash were made in metal, of which there was more (mainly Spanish) in the colonies than is commonly supposed; but the superabundance of paper caused metal to be confined almost solely to foreign trade. One warship carried 100,000 dollars from Charles Town to England in 1748, and much that missed that ship still awaited safe transportation. The Treasurer in 1752 held

£14,136 currency value, in Spanish dollars and pistoles, and on October 22, 1771, £61,269 currency value of gold and silver. Attempts were made to draw metal by giving it an unwarranted value, even after Queen Anne's proclamation to the contrary. In 1701 a proposal to coin silver was declined by the Assembly for the lack of sufficient bullion. A ton of the detested Wood's half-pence, which Ireland had refused to use, was dumped off on South Carolina. After they had lain unused for more than twenty years, the South Carolina Assembly took the loss (about £41 sterling) rather than use them on any terms.

South Carolina depended almost entirely on outsiders for seagoing craft. The possession of the finest oak, pine, and cypress for ships made no difference when labor and capital brought larger returns in naval stores, rice, and indigo.

After 1740 there was a stronger tendency toward ship building. Ramsay's statement that there were twenty-four square-rigged vessels built in South Carolina between 1740 and 1773, besides sloops and schooners, Miss Leila Sellers finds partly confirmed from the *Gazette*. The building of less than one ship a year in a province possessing every natural advantage is impressive evidence of the superiority of other roads to wealth.

River and small coasting boats, required in great number by coast country life and industry, were built at home, and often with artistic skill. Until the settlements had extended beyond the myriad arms of the sea and the numerous navigable streams of the coastal region, water transportation was, for many settlers, of more importance than roads. The heavy products of forest and field were thus carried to Charles Town, long the only market.

The periagua (or "pettiauga") was the common large boat. Originally an Indian canoe hollowed from a large tree, it was enlarged to a boat forty feet long or more. Some were decked and made voyages as far as Virginia. There were sometimes two removable masts, and oars according to size. The office of patroon over such a craft was one of the most coveted honors of the better slaves.

As settlement extended inland the opening of roads became one of the most important duties of government. Where the government, out of touch with frontier conditions, lagged, neighborhood enterprise met the necessity. Innumerable ferries were vested in certain individuals, frequently after sharp contests for the possession of the valuable privilege, besides many operated without legal authorization. The coastwise road from Georgetown through Dorchester to Beaufort was built after numerous shorter highways radiating from Charles Town. Trade with the Creeks early made the path from Charles Town to Savannah Town.

about opposite where Augusta later rose, an important route, while the growing Cherokee trade a little later gradually developed the trading path that was to become the great highway skirting the southwestern side of the Santee-Congaree-Saluda, through Ninety Six and De Witt's Corner and on to Fort Prince George on the Keowee River.[2] A fork running north through Camden reached the Catawbas, while the path from the lower Cherokees to the Catawbas and on to Virginia paralleled the routes that the main lines of the Southern Railway and the Seaboard Air Line were to follow long after. A road map of the eighteenth century compared with a highway or railroad map of today reveals how rivers, ridges, and shoals that fixed the head of navigation early prescribed the principal centers of commerce and lines of travel.

Classes and Customs.—Along with the stimulating environment there were the cultural influences of intimate contact with the older society across the sea to which South Carolinians, more than perhaps any other colonists, continued to refer as "home." Many large merchants resided for years first on one side of the ocean and then on the other. Planters frequently spent long periods in England, where a few owned estates, and many kept up family and friendly contacts. Notwithstanding this clinging to England as "home," there early developed a genuine local public spirit, as manifested in bequests for schools, etc.

In 1728 merchant Allen was reputed to be worth £20,000 sterling. The imposing Charleston houses surviving from the colonial period are generally of the decades immediately before the Revolution, built under the combined influence of swelling wealth and the improved architectural taste evoked by the classical revival. The broad piazzas, frequently two and sometimes three stories high, were an adjustment to the hot summers. It became common to string out the dwelling one room broad, with immensely long piazzas on the garden side, and the end of the house toward the street. In the country even well-to-do planters in the mid-eighteenth century (and many at a much later period) built wooden houses that were more commodious than imposing. By 1775 the general country style of large, plain houses for over a hundred years had been set as a two-story wooden structure with narrow eaves and with a broad one-story piazza extending across the front, two rooms up- and two downstairs in the main body, two one-story rooms behind, and often an "L" running back from these. In many, a hall ran from front to back. On the other hand, some planters built mansions of brick worthy of an English country estate and comparable to the best American houses of the period, like (to name several surviving) Mulberry, Fenwicke

[2] De Witt's (sometimes spelled Duett's) Corner was about six miles northwest of the present Due West, a corruption of the name, on the road to Keowee.

Hall, Drayton Hall, and Middleton Place, of which last the remaining wing and the gardens (planted about 1753) are among the most imposing colonial memorials, as is also Drayton Hall, notwithstanding the demolition of its two flankers. Yet generally the life of the early and mid-eighteenth-century planters was lived in simple and often hard conditions.

The isolated life on the plantation impelled to hospitality. Most people, said De Brahm shortly before the Revolution, kept a Negro at the gate (for the house was often far from the road) to invite travelers to refreshments and lodgings, helped them forward with their own conveyances, and in foul weather accompanied them around bad places, having their slaves cut away trees, etc.

The lonesomeness of the country was increased by the tendency of successful planters to live in town. The attractions of the city and its better health (except for the frequent scourges of smallpox and yellow fever, the latter of which left the country immune) were draining the country of its white inhabitants.

The wholesale merchant in 1750 enjoyed an unquestioned social standing, although there was already the higher esteem, later so much more strongly emphasized, for the large planter. The superior social distinction of the latter, as well as the profits from land, led successful merchants very commonly to invest a large part of their profits in settled landed estates. By 1770 the disdain of the landed aristocrat for the merchant was well developed. As classes became more rigid in the nineteenth century, the social status of even the prosperous wholesale trader sank relative to that of wealthy planters, lawyers, and bankers. Snobbish youths as late as the 1890's sneered at one whose "grandfather was a ham-slinger on the Bay" (i.e., a wholesale grocer).

The dress and manners of these mid-eighteenth-century South Carolinians were those of the best English society. Whitefield in 1740 found "an affected finery and gaiety of dress and deportment which I question if the Court end of London could exceed."

Manners were dignified, not to say formal. Henry Laurens wrote to a would-be son-in-law whom he disliked that "when [in 1750] I paid addresses to the lady my daughter's mother . . . I scorned to attempt an attachment of her affections, 'till I had obtained the consent and approbation of the other parties [her family] so nearly interested. I should have deemed a contrary conduct a species of dishonorable fraud." Marriage contracts were common among the upper classes, bonding the gentleman in heavy sums to "intermarry with" so and so. Marriage settlements were not uncommon, settling property upon trustees for the bride, whose property otherwise came into control of her husband.

The huge importations of liquor testify to the absorbent habits of our ancestors. Dr. Ramsay says that only a physician could know the extent of the ruin wrought on health and family welfare by intemperance in the late eighteenth and the early nineteenth century.

Dueling seems to have grown worse as the eighteenth century advanced. The men of the Proprietary period quarreled abundantly, but not with such deliberate deadliness. Ramsay thought (to glance forward) that the Revolution strongly encouraged dueling. In this, as in so many things, the colonists were merely acting out the customs of the mother country.

Colonial Aristocracy.—The aristocratic cast that prosperous society assumed in South Carolina was also a reflection of English custom, and some distinguished Carolina families were offshoots of British aristocracy. Historians generally agree that American aristocracy is an American product. The most forceful grasped wealth and power—the essential original basis always of aristocracies. The Proprietors encouraged the coming of men of wealth and initiative, on the theory that they, by bringing in others, white or black, to serve them, would best develop a prosperous colony. Such representatives of the English gentry or knighthood as the Colletons, Sir Hovenden Walker, and Sir Nathaniel Johnson gave a tone of distinction to South Carolina society far back in the Proprietary period. The early Barbadian element furnished a remarkable number of distinguished names. Such families, early assuming prominence, settled into positions of wealth and refinement and frequently conspicuous public service which marked them as a nobility in everything except title. Several intermarried frequently with English nobility.

Mr. A. S. Salley, widely versed in South Carolina family history, tells me that there have been at least eleven South Carolina families who had the right to bear the arms of British noble families. Many had the right to arms from the English gentry. A few other families, equally distinguished in character and public service, during the eighteenth century paid the fees to the College of Heralds for the registration of their newly adopted coat-of-arms, and others as a mere matter of course adopted arms quite informally.

Eighteenth-Century Charles Town.—Colonial South Carolina was dominated by a city to a degree that gave a peculiar character to her history. This condition indeed continued long after the Revolution. For long South Carolina's only city, and even to this day in a true sense her only real city with a character of its own, Charleston, in which circumstances caused marked concentration of talent and wealth, largely determined the politics of the province and State. This made her of incalculable importance when South Carolina became the leader of Southern interests in the generation preceding the War of Secession.

Mr. Joseph W. Barnwell in 1913 ventured the opinion that the little group who had led the politics of Charleston thus had had, for good or evil, a larger influence on American history than any similar number of people in the country.

On November 18, 1740, about two in the afternoon, a fire broke out and, fanned by fierce winds, in less than four hours laid in ashes the most valuable parts of Charles Town. The loss of £61,400 sterling falling on 171 persons came as a terrible blow to a community which had been afflicted with the expense of preparation against expected Spanish attack in 1737, the smallpox in 1738, yellow fever in 1739, and the heavy outlay for the St. Augustine expedition in 1740, soon to be followed by defense of Georgia against Spanish attack in 1742, and the rebuilding of the fortifications.

Calls were sent to other provinces and to England. Of the total American contributions of £7,094 sterling, Barbados sent £146 18*s.* 6½*d.*; New England, £144; and Philadelphia (including the Quakers outside the city), £726. Parliament appropriated £20,000. The town as rebuilt assumed the architectural trend which has led travelers of the present day to describe it as the most perfect Georgian city in the world, the distinction, individuality, and beauty of whose residences and gardens have a unique charm. De Brahm thought it in 1770 the wealthiest and most elegant city in the South, and Josiah Quincy in 1773 placed it above every other American city. Yet, as was common in that age, the streets were cluttered with filth no village would tolerate today. Bull reported its population in 1770 as 5,030 whites and 5,833 blacks. It had 16,359 in 1790, of whom 8,085 were white and 8,274 colored.

Literacy, Libraries, Printing.—The illiteracy that ran to such high percentage at a later day seems to have been the result of two causes: the pressing back of new settlers into a rude frontier, and the withering influence of the slave economy on the poorer whites. The number of persons making their marks on any of the various classes of papers requiring their signatures is astonishingly small during the entire eighteenth century. Very rarely is an illiterate public official or church warden found. Only four out of the 113 men signing a Charles Town petition in 1722 made their marks. Even petitions for small allotments by land grant rarely bear a mark. Investigators who have been through Court of Ordinary records of 1672 to 1692, and Revolutionary pay receipts, report that fewer than 10 per cent made their marks. Eight (with one or two cases doubtful) of eighty-eight settlers of the Saluda and Enoree back country signed a petition of 1755 with their marks. Sixteen out of fifty-six who signed by marks some petitions of 1756 is the worst proportion I have found.

The clear, incisive English of the South Carolina public papers during the whole eighteenth century, even before the publicity achieved by the defenders of American rights from 1765 to 1775, and the wide knowledge of English law and parliamentary history attest a highly intelligent upper class.

The South Carolina custom of educating the sons of the wealthy in England has been overemphasized. It was a confession of the impossibility of collegiate training for those unable to go to a distance. The South Carolinians educated abroad did not outshine the Jeffersons and Madisons, the Wilsons and Franklins, the Hamiltons, and the Adamses of colonies that supported their own colleges. That residence in England gave the South Carolinians the bearing of the finished man of the world is true; but from other standpoints prolonged contact with eighteenth-century English society involved dangers against which there may be found warnings in the correspondence of South Carolinians.

The custom of sending boys to England, or sometimes, in the case of the very wealthy, of the whole family's residing there for years, began before 1740 and grew with the rapidly increasing wealth of the third quarter of the century. That it had not become common by 1753 is indicated by Governor Glen's longing for it to become so, as it had in Jamaica and Barbados, since acquaintance with the British Constitution would lead the colonists to obey the royal instructions for fixing a salary on their Governor. Of a list compiled by Professor J. G. de Roulhac Hamilton of ninety-five South Carolinians (several, however, being Englishmen temporarily here) admitted to the bar in England, only fifteen (and several of them not South Carolinians born) were before 1750.

The earlier history of libraries is traced in Chapter XI. In 1748[3] a number of young men in Charles Town associated themselves to import the current British pamphlets and magazines. On December 28 they organized as the Library Society (still functioning as a very important institution) for acquiring books as well, thus postdating the oldest such institution still existing in the United States, Franklin's Philadelphia library, by only sixteen or seventeen years. Two-thirds of a collection being held for a contemplated college by the society were saved when in 1778 fire destroyed all but 185 of the more than 5,000 other volumes.

In 1763 George Wood, bookbinder and stationer of Charles Town, advertised that he had just imported a collection of miscellaneous books intended for a circulating library, to which he would add all new books

[3] McCrady, II, 510, unfortunately has 1743.

published. The Charleston Museum, a remarkable example of intellectual activity, dating from 1773, will be discussed in connection with its post-Revolutionary history. Georgetown possesses the distinction of having had almost the only other library apart from colleges south of Philadelphia before the Revolution. The Winyaw Indigo Society, formed about 1740 as a social club, found itself by 1753 possessed of funds with which it founded a school and soon a library. The school, intended at first only for the poor, soon served all classes.

Although paper money from its beginning in 1703 was engraved and printed in South Carolina, the introduction of types and printing press was delayed until 1731. The Commons voted in 1717 to encourage a printer to come to print the laws compiled by Trott. They resolved in 1722 to advance a printer and bookbinder £1,000 currency and pay him 25 per cent advance on London prices. The Council concurred. The paper money act of February 23, 1723, vetoed by the King, provided £1,000 currency for a printer. When the Commons persisted in 1724, Governor Nicholson retorted: as to "the thousand pounds of the said money for a printer, such an offer is not proper to have at this juncture, and you can't be insensible to what trouble those people put his Majesty's government in Great Britain to, and I suppose it will be very difficult to get an honest one hither, and as for those that have been already convicted of crimes against the government, I hope you would not have such fellows here. As for the honest ones, I suppose they have work enough there."

In response to an offer of £1,000 currency bonus outright in May, 1731, three printers were soon in Charles Town. On November 18, 1731, George Webb, "printer in this province," petitioned the Council. Mr. D. C. McMurtrie found in the London Public Record office a document published in Charles Town on November 4, 1731, by George Webb and another published by Thomas Whitmarsh in Charles Town dated November 27, 1731.[4] On January 27, 1732, Whitmarsh prayed consideration on account of the expense he incurred in coming from Philadelphia in response to the action of the legislature, and on February 2, 1732, Eleazer Phillips, Jr., a native of Boston, petitioned for the £1,000 and the public printing on the same ground. As Phillips had come on the invitation of the Commons only, Governor Johnson favored Whitmarsh, who, he said, had a better equipment. But Phillips got the public printing and the exclusive right to publish the votes of the Commons, while Whitmarsh received only £200 currency for the expense of coming.

Eleazer Phillips, Jr., founded the *South Carolina Weekly Journal* and Whitmarsh the *South Carolina Gazette*. Copies of Phillips' paper

[4] McMurtrie, *History of Printing in the United States,* II, 308-10.

and the day of its origin are alike undiscovered. He died in July, 1732. Some time later his father, a bookseller and stationer, advertised that six months' subscriptions, etc., due the deceased should be paid to him.

Whitmarsh was an English compositor whom Franklin had taken into his office and now set up as the first of his partners in establishing a newspaper here, as others later in Antigua, New York, Lancaster, Jamaica, and Georgia. Franklin supplied the equipment, paid one-third of the expense, and received one-third of the profits, and the younger man usually bought control at the end of six years. Whitmarsh's *Gazette* appeared on January 8, 1732, and continued through September 8, 1733, when his death, apparently on the twenty-first, caused its suspension. Lewis Timothée, another protégé of Franklin, recommenced the publication on February 2, 1734, but numbered it Volume I, Number I. Timothée, the son of French parents, it seems, who had fled to Holland and thence to Philadelphia, had worked with Franklin, who promptly sent him on to take the place of Whitmarsh.[5]

Timothée anglicized his name to Timothy with his April 6, 1734, issue. After his accidental death on December 29, 1738, his widow Elizabeth, announcing herself as burdened with several "small children and another hourly expected," continued the paper with the help of her half-grown son Peter, who bought the paper after six or seven years. Mrs. Timothy is the first known woman in American journalism, says Mr. A. S. Salley.

Timothy also printed books. His magnificent Trott's *Laws* (1736) is his most ambitious enterprise; but his first edition of John Wesley's hymnbook (1737) is the most valuable of all South Carolina imprints among collectors.

[5] JCHA, February 3, 4, 5, 8, 1731-32; JUHA, December 8, 1732; W. J. Rivers, "Printing in South Carolina," *Russell's Magazine*, September, 1858; A. S. Salley, Jr., *First South Carolina Presses*, Bibliographical Society, American Papers, 1907-08, II, 28-69; Salley, "History of Charleston Journalism," *News and Courier*, 1904 Centennial Edition; Mrs. Marion Reynolds King, on *South Carolina Gazette*, in *Journalism Quarterly*, September, 1932; Franklin, *Autobiography, Works* (1907), I, 307; VI, 243; X, 171.

Mrs. King, by discovering the partnership agreement between Franklin and Timothée, proves Franklin correct in speaking of their being partners. Professor Hirsch's view that printing existed in Charles Town in 1725 because a "pressmaster" was paid by the public is inconclusive (*Huguenots of Colonial South Carolina*, 239). The pressmaster had doubtless been printing money from engraved blocks. The committee reports in 1731 indicate that there had never been a printer in South Carolina.

Franklin states that Mrs. Timothée was Dutch, and more systematic than her husband. The Dutch element in South Carolina is infinitesimal. (The people of the "Dutch Fork" are, of course, German.) I note these names: D'Arsens, Vander Horst, Van Velson, Hendrick, Schuyl, Haes, Nergeles, Welhuysen, Gillon, Van Shajct, Visser, Ioor, Smoor, Viet, Vander Heydon; also allusion to Dutch ladies in business, and to thirty Dutch imported for two years to erect and operate mills. The latter left the province on account of being drafted for the Yemassee War. Transients, also, some of distinction, there have been, as the distinguished Houkgheest.

The vulgarity common in the press during the 1730's and 1740's and continuing less grossly almost to the Revolution would be incredible to those not familiar with English Restoration and early eighteenth-century writings. In the earlier period occur words of the grossest filth. But, after all, how much more corrupting are these, and the jesting comparisons of the capacities of white and Negro women for night work, than the smoother vulgarity of today's fiction and drama?

Science, Law, Art, and Drama.—The learned professions of the law, medicine, and the ministry were represented in the province from an early date. In 1771 there were thirty-four members of the South Carolina bar. Sixteen of the twenty-four in active practice here were natives of South Carolina.

The intellectual life of the province was fostered by the physicians, who were present from its settlement. Dr. Henry Woodward, of the first settlers, was a man of brilliant and active mind. I find twelve others called "Doctor" by 1718, after which physicians became more numerous. Dr. Thomas Dale, born in 1700 of an intellectual English family, arrived in Charles Town in 1725 shortly after having graduated in medicine at Leyden. He published English translations of Latin works as follows: Dr. John Freind's *Emmenologia,* 1729 (second edition, 1752); Freind on *Fevers and Smallpox,* 1730; and Dr. Jodocus Lommius's *Continual Fevers,* 1732. In 1731 appeared his translation from the French of Le Dran's *Methods of Extracting the Stone of the Bladder.* Dale's literary propensities broke out in violent controversy against Dr. James Kirkpatrick's introduction of inoculation into South Carolina, and in at least one prologue (1735) in the early history of the Charles Town theatre. He found time from his practice and his duties as a judge of the highest court to make a collection of natural history specimens before his death in 1750.

Mr. A. S. Salley tells me that Dr. James Killpatrick (who changed his name to Kirkpatrick), after being educated in medicine abroad, introduced inoculation into South Carolina. This greatly reduced mortality in the epidemic of 1738—a result which Dr. Ramsay notes without mentioning Kirkpatrick. Ramsay records his own introduction of vaccination in 1802, since which time the smallpox has been so far controlled as never to have mounted to a general terror. Ramsay records the second Lieutenant-Governor William Bull, who received his degree in medicine at Leyden in 1734, as the first native-born American medical graduate. In 1749 John Moultrie received his medical degree from Edinburgh, as did ten other native South Carolinians between 1768 and 1778.

The earliest scientific work here was by physicians, unless we except the correspondence of Mrs. Hannah English with English scientists on birds, about the last decade of the seventeenth century, and the work of

Edmund Bohun, Jr., and the transient Mark Catesby. Dr. John Lining experimented in electricity, and in 1753 made the first scientific report in the United States on yellow fever. Dr. Lionel Chalmers made weather records and published works on South Carolina weather and diseases from 1750 to 1756. Dr. Alexander Garden (the physician, not the clergyman) was honored for his botanical work when Linnaeus named a brilliant flower the gardenia. Dr. J. M. Toner says that Carolinians from a comparatively early period furnished numerous valuable contributions to the literature of medicine and natural history, and for some years led all the colonies in the natural sciences.

Several works on money (1734?), religion (1752 and 1756), and antiquities published by persons at some time resident in South Carolina show the literary interest which our limits prevent us from tracing. As schools were treated in Chapter XI and will again be noticed in Chapter XLVI, further treatment for the colonial period is not here necessary.

Henrietta Johnston, the earliest American woman pastelist, began her work in 1707 or earlier in Charles Town, where she died in 1729. Her delicate pastels, never exceeding 14 by 16 inches, charmingly portray beautiful women, but her pastel of William Rhett and her two oils of Governor Sir Nathaniel Johnson and his son Governor Robert Johnson, if the oils are really by her (on which I express no opinion), fail to exhibit capacity to master the strong masculine face. About twenty of her portraits (including the oils) are identified.[6]

The frequent visits of wealthy merchants and planters to England diminished patronage of artists at home except as they may have stimulated taste. Nineteen painters in Charles Town before the Revolution are known by name, though some were clearly amateurs. B. Roberts advertised to paint either portraits or the exterior of houses—an arrangement by which at least a certain general harmony of the premises might be assured. His "Charles Town Water Front" was frequently copied by later artists.

The most prolific of the Charles Town painters was the German Swiss, Jeremiah Theus, who arrived in 1739. His faces give the impression of formal resemblance to the originals, but both features and figures are lamentably stiff, and his coloring is without richness or delicacy.

In 1883 Dr. Gabriel E. Manigault listed nineteen portraits of eighteenth-century South Carolinians by Ramsay, Zoffany, Reynolds, West, Romney, Gainsborough, Copley, and Gilbert Stuart, all, with one exception, then still owned by the descendants of the subjects.

Charles Town early cultivated music. Two concerts were advertised in 1732. Frequent notices follow through 1735, after which there are few or none advertised for some time, dancing and theatres perhaps

[6] Miss Eola Willis has written fully on Henrietta Johnston.

having distracted attention from music. In 1762 the St. Cecilia Society was formed as a musical organization. Ambitious programs, with orchestra and Italian and German artists, were provided; but ultimately the ball which followed became the chief feature, and the society was transformed into a social organization of the city's most exclusive circle.

To Charles Town apparently belongs the distinction of being the first American city to witness a theatrical performance. In 1702 Tony Aston, player, poet, soldier, wanderer, joined the ill-fated expedition against St. Augustine, whence, he writes, "We arrived in Charles Town full of lice, shame, poverty, nakedness, and hunger:—I turned player and poet, and wrote one play on the subject of the country."

On January 24, 1735, the tragedy of *The Orphan* was performed in the courtroom, ushered in by the first American-written prologue. Seven performances completed the season of 1735. During 1735 a theatre was built, which was used for the 1736 season, with twelve entertainments. This was the third theatre erected within the United States, being preceded only by that at Williamsburg in the 1720's and that in New York in 1732. The year 1773 saw the most brilliant season in colonial America. There were during the five months 118 performances, says Seilhamer, including eleven of Shakespeare's masterpieces, eight of Garrick's, and all the contemporary popular operas.

Such a round of gaiety at such a time inevitably drew censure. "Cleopatra" denounced the theatre in the *Gazette* as "the Devil's synagogue," though she later decided she had spoken in haste. The minister of the newly organized Methodists preached against it, and the grand jury requested the legislature to suppress the playhouse as an extravagance, a promoter of robberies and "of vice and obscenity." These were a continuation of the invective of Sophia Hume, a remarkable Quakeress born in Charles Town. Returning to her native city in 1747 after an absence of seven years, she published in 1752 a 152-page book written in 1747, *An exortation to the Inhabitants of the Province of South Carolina to bring their deeds to the light of Christ,* and in 1754 a 114-page *Epistle to the Inhabitants of South Carolina,* in which she voiced the ideals of a religious devotee.

In the stress following the Revolution the theatre appeared to many an unwarranted frivolity. The Continental Congress strongly denounced it, and the South Carolina legislature in 1787 penalized "all persons representing publicly for gain or reward, any play, comedy, tragedy, interlude, or farce, or other entertainment of the stage, or any part thereof."[7] The prohibition was removed by the law of 1791, which permitted theatrical exhibitions under an annual license of £100 sterling in Charleston and of £25 elsewhere.

[7] I thank Mrs. Marion R. King for calling my attention to this prohibition in *Statutes at Large of South Carolina,* V, 41.

CHAPTER XXIII

THE CHURCHES IN SOUTH CAROLINA, 1706-1778

General Morals.—Nothing of the past is more difficult to judge than its morals. Yet, with due caution, some just comparison is possible. The eighteenth century inherited the cynicism and filth of the Restoration. Healthier conditions in the colonies prevented such a degree of coarseness as developed in England; and there was never an approach to the looseness of morals among women. More of Commonwealth Puritanism extended to colonial America than of Restoration license. Yet there was even in the best eighteenth-century colonial society a rough and vulgar strain.

Defalcations were comparatively rare; but public men of high standing used their opportunities for enrichment in ways that men of the same standing in the community would not now, as was amply illustrated in the land frauds of the 1730's, and in some aspects, especially during the Proprietary period, of the Indian trade. Governor Sir Nathaniel Johnson's trick for excluding the Dissenters in 1704 and his outright lie about the Presbyterians in the election of 1707 savor today of men of far lower standing. Arthur Middleton's selling offices and under false pretenses bidding up prices in the 1720's was condemned, as was Jacob Motte's securing the treasurership in 1743 by promising a part of the emoluments if his opponent would withdraw. Governor Glen rejected with scorn the proposal (apparently from interested merchants in Charles Town) to make a large graft on buying arms. On another occasion, numbers of the leading members of the Commons, he writes, offered him a large sum in repayment of certain expenses he had personally incurred in the public service if he would consent to the passage of a paper money bill. Though he rejected both propositions with scorn, he did not expose his tempters. In short, the eighteenth-century public standards savored somewhat of the coarseness which in contemporary England ran into widespread corruption. The finer type of public honor of a later day developed in the generation immediately before the Revolution; and at the climax of Southern civilization, before the War of Secession, it developed still higher.

The Reverend Levi Durand, rector of Christ Church, reports in 1744 that "this country is more infested with free thinkers than it is with enthusiasts," and in 1747 he is appalled at "this province, where infidelity, profaneness, heresy, blasphemy and the most offensive breaches of common morality have scarce ever appeared with more insolence."

Superstition, of course, was present. That a man who pulled a rattlesnake out of a hole by the tail was saved from the resulting bite by eating of the snake's broiled liver and broth from its flesh, was believed in 1711 by the Reverend Francis Le Jau of Goose Creek. Belief in witchcraft has already been alluded to.

There were other fanaticisms. In 1715 and '16 "two pestilent fellows" were dispensing in St. Thomas' parish an extravagant fanaticism imported from France by way of England. This or a kindred fanaticism took tragic form in 1724 in the same parish. The Dutartres were descended from French refugees. From a strolling Moravian preacher they came to conceive themselves the only family on earth with knowledge of the true God, who communed directly with them. Peter Rembert, husband of the eldest Dutartre daughter, who had been a widow, was their prophet. Soon there came a message to the prophet to put away his wife, whose husband God would restore from the dead that the holy family might be complete, and to take in her place her youngest sister, a virgin. A sign was vouchsafed the astonished father, and he gave his daughter accordingly.

Divinely forbidden to bear arms, to work the roads, or to obey any human law, they nevertheless were divinely ordered, their prophet assured them, to resist by arms the wicked men who came to serve a warrant on the holy man with two wives. A part of their sincere fanaticism was the belief that no weapon could harm them. The captain of the militia summoned to assist the constables was killed and several of his men wounded in effecting their arrest. With perfect faith that they would be raised on the third day, Father Dutartre and his sons-in-law went calmly to the gallows. When they did not rise, the two young Dutartre men, aged eighteen and twenty, became gloomy and repentant, and were pardoned. One later manifested his insanity by killing a man at the divine command, and died on the gallows a saved penitent.

A few inconclusive data may be given on the subject of sex morals. Out of 810 children baptized in the country parish of Prince Frederick between 1713 and 1794 sixteen are recorded as bastards, a percentage of 1.97 per cent. Probably bastards were withheld from baptism oftener than legitimate children. In some cases several illegitimate children are of the same parents, indicating concubinage. One couple married the day their child was baptized. All the illegitimate recorded are between 1736 and 1753. Well into the nineteenth century, men of high social standing occasionally made provisions by will for their colored concubines and their children.

On May 5, 1704, George Frost was granted permission by the Commons to bring in a bill for dissolving his marriage, his wife to appear to defend herself. I find nothing further on the case, so that it doubtless remains true that except for a few cases during Reconstruction there was never a divorce in South Carolina until the constitutional amendment of 1949. The *Gazettes* from 1730 to '56 contain not infrequent advertisements warning against crediting absconded wives, none, however, of any known social standing. The wife of a Charlestonian of some prominence departed to England with Governor Boone, as his mistress.

A tax on rum was imposed in 1720 and 1730 to help build St. Philip's Church, and in 1752 on rum and other goods for Prince George, Winyaw. Although private lotteries were forbidden from 1751, lotteries were authorized as late as 1814 for Episcopal churches; for Presbyterian, 1814; for Catholic, 1828.[1] Gambling debts and bets of every variety were made uncollectible in 1752.

General Religious Conditions.—The broad religious tolerance maintained in South Carolina has already been described at page 66. Jews were kindly treated, and in 1750 organized one of the earliest congregations in the United States. Dr. Elzas says that in the years following 1800 the Charleston Jews were the most numerous, cultured, and wealthy of their religion in the United States, and that the movement for reforming the rigid formalism and tyrannical parental authority of primitive orthodoxy originated there about 1824 to '33. Numbers of South Carolina Christian families are descended from the brilliant Spanish, French, or Portuguese Jews who for over two centuries have illumined the history of their people by their patriotism and intellect, and who offer a high ideal for their later-coming kinsmen from northern Europe.

The small number of Catholics before the Revolution held no services. Mass was first said in Charleston in 1786 for a congregation of twelve by an Italian priest en route to South America. A year or two later mass was celebrated for a congregation of about two hundred in an abandoned Methodist church renovated as St. Mary's Church. This was without sanction of law until the Constitution of 1790, which established complete religious equality. The "State oaths" prevented Catholics from qualifying for office before the Revolution. The vetoed act of 1759

[1] *Stat. at Large,* 3, 729; 8, 258, 365; 6, 246; 5, 602, 725; 7, 128. Lotteries were authorized to erect "a suitable house of public worship" in Greenville in 1809 and in Conwayborough in 1819.—*Ibid.,* 5, 601; 8, 306.

The reference to a lottery for the Savannah River Baptist Association in the index of the Statutes is entirely erroneous.

attempted to narrow the voting qualification from "Christian" to "Protestant Christian."

The Dissenters long endured petty vexations, as well as exclusion from the Assembly of those whose scruples forbade their swearing upon the Bible. The Anglican clergy's attempts to deprive the Dissenters' ministers of the right to perform the marriage ceremony long failed to secure the assent of even the most devoted Anglican governors; but at what date between 1760 and 1777 I have not ascertained, they apparently won their point, for the Rev. Mr. Tennent in 1777 complained of the injustice of refusing marriage licenses to any except the Anglican clergy. It is hardly likely that this prevented frontier Dissenter preachers from performing the marriage ceremony. The Assembly was habitually liberal toward Dissenters, who generally composed a large part of its membership.

The presence of two strong religious factions stimulated both. The Governor and Council said to the Bishop of London in 1717 in complaining of a bad minister, "We have just cause in this country, which abounds with Dissenters, to wish for gentlemen of the highest probity and circumspection."

The antagonism among Dissenters toward the establishment law (and not toward the presence of the Anglican Church, as Anglican extremists believed), and the latter's detestation of Presbyterians and "Anabaptists," gradually subsided from 1706 to 1730. There was always a strong liberal element among the Anglican laity. Charles Burnham offended Commissary Johnston in 1716 by refusing to carry his [Burnham's] children three-fourths of a mile in fine weather to be christened in church; he wrote the Commissary that as God is "a lover of all Christians" he was confident that with Dissenter baptism "they will git as sone to Heaven that way as the other."[2]

In 1723 and 1724, for lack of a rector, Anglicans were going to the Dissenting minister at Beaufort to be married and to have their children baptized. Many Anglicans in the frontier and back country, which the Established Church with slight exceptions neglected, naturally were won by the Presbyterian, Baptist, Lutheran, and later Methodist ministers. The Reverend John Fordyce of Prince Frederick parish, after a trip among the Baptists along the Great Peedee in 1745, reported that "There is almost as many ignorant preachers among them as there was in *Oliver's* Camp, that one can scarce beat a bush, but out comes a preacher; and they and every one of their number, are so *presumptious* and *self-willed,* that they are neither afraid nor ashamed *to speak evil*

[2] Dr. Anne King Gregorie shows me that this was apparently Charles Burnham, planter, not Dr. Burnham, as I stated in my three-volume *History of South Carolina.*

of dignities." If the society would send an itinerant missionary among them, he "might in time remove that inveterate enthusiastical spirit of prejudice which prevails so much among these Baptists." Send me, he writes, "The Ax Laid to the Foot of the Tree, or the Baptists Ministry Examined, because it exposes the error and deeds of those false prophets and emissaries of Satan."

While the back country, almost totally neglected by the Anglicans, was being Christianized by the Presbyterians and Baptists and later the Methodists, there was near the coast a steady drift from those denominations to the Anglican, which by 1730 or '40 had given the latter a clear numerical superiority there. The old Dissenter families of Elliott, Morton, Lynch, Fenwick, Bee, Landgrave Smith, etc., not to mention some of wealth and distinction whose names are less well known because of the extinction of the male line, had pretty generally become Anglican before the Revolution.

The Anglican Clergy.—The establishment act of 1706 conferred an enormous advantage for the time being upon the Anglicans, although in the long run it brought them almost to ruin through their dependence upon government aid, the withdrawal of which in 1778 left them prostrate for a generation. Out of the tax bill of about £40,000 currency for 1722 the amount for the church was £9,208. Funds were appropriated for church buildings, parsonages, and glebes, which the congregation frequently supplemented. The usually small churches were inadequate for any considerable attendance, and frequently left little or no free seating space when their two or three dozen pews were sold.

Of the thirteen parishes in 1723, six, including several rich and populous, were served by missionaries of the Society for the Propagation of the Gospel. Four were vacant. It is an interesting speculation what would have been the fate of the Anglican Church but for the interest of this great missionary society, which made South Carolina one of its favored fields; for the bland tolerance displayed by such a large proportion of the ruling class was the outcome, by all contemporary testimony, of a considerable indifference to religion. The society, after long aiding wealthy parishes that deserved no such charity, decided in 1759 to fill no more vacancies in South Carolina.

The Society for the Propagation of the Gospel was indeed of inestimable value in guarding the colonies in which it worked from the dregs of the ministry in that corrupt age of the Anglican Church; but many an unworthy clergyman slipped by the society and the Bishop of London, who exercised jurisdiction over the colonies. St. Helena's in 1756 discharged the Reverend William Peasley as the keeper of concubines or mistresses. He also refused to attend the dying, beat one man, and threatened others. In 1772 this vestry shut the church against their pro-rector, the Reverend Edward Ellington, as "extremely offensive to the generality of the inhabitants."

The Reverend Michael Smith carried disgrace to the lowest depths, plaguing the excellent people of Prince Frederick's beyond measure. A liar, a thief, a multiple adulterer, he had the effrontery to justify himself on the church door by the example of Abraham and Hagar, and, when taxed with bringing a concubine to the rectory, replied that, being a priest, he needed no one else to perform the ceremony. Prince Frederick's was one of the most unfortunate parishes and had to discharge another minister in 1772 for "infamous behavior." Christ Church also was much afflicted. There was bitter complaint by the country parishes at having inferior men sent them, while the best went to the city churches. The worst that appears of the latter was one shortly before the Revolution whose gross heartlessness, violence of temper, plagiarism of sermons, and roistering company rendered him wholly unfit.

How frequently the Society for the Propagation of the Gospel and the Bishop of London were imposed upon by unworthy priests is attested by the fact that of the one hundred and thirty-two Episcopal clergy in South Carolina from 1670 to 1775, five are reported, in the correspondence with their authorities or in the parish records or in one case the *Gazette,* to have been guilty of actual or attempted sex immorality, five besides these of drunkenness and twelve of other unacceptable conduct. Twenty-six Anglican clergymen before 1776 were here a year or less; twelve for less than three years; twenty-three for five years or more, and forty-two for ten years or more. None of the serious offenders was here over six years. The twenty years preceding the Revolution saw decided improvement in the character of the clergy.

Such blots on a clergy, the bulk of whom were upright men, and many of whom were patterns of devotion and piety, is not surprising, for the eighteenth century was one of the worst in the history of the church. It was these conditions that the Wesleys and the Evangelicals within the church, and the now-sneered-at mid-Victorians reformed. John Wesley, then rector of Christ Church in Savannah, attended the annual visitation of the clergy of South Carolina on April 22, 1737, and wrote in his *Journal* that "there was such a conversation for several hours on 'Christ our Righteousness' as I had not heard on any visitation in England, or hardly on any other occasion." And as to clerical coldness, it was a time of decline in the Dissenting denominations also, among whose ministry until well into the nineteenth century lapses of morals or sobriety were far more common than today. The heavy drinking of the eighteenth and the early nineteenth century led many a minister to his ruin.

Anglicans suffered for want of a bishop or any outstanding leadership. Under such circumstances the tendency toward congregational government natural to the frontier assumed great strength. Unhappy experience led the people quite generally to refuse to elect ministers except after many years' trial, if indeed they ever consummated formal election; for there was no way short of London for getting rid of an unacceptable minister once vested with his parish. This keeping the clergy on trial subject to discharge at any time (as was practiced also in Virginia, for example) was denounced by the ministers as a plan to keep them in fear and dependence; but this was an exaggeration, for pious Episcopalians lamented the frequent long vacancies in the country parishes. On June 28, 1757, the Prince Frederick vestry wrote the Reverend John Andrews, who was departing for England, "to quicken his Lordship's motions in our favor, remonstrating" against prolonged vacancies and the sending of unworthy men, both of which were driving the people to the Dissenters. To the same effect is the letter of the excellent Reverend Lewis Jones of St. Helena to the Bishop of London. But even Lieutenant-Governor Bull, who lamented the rising of Dissent, thought that the government was doing enough in supporting the existing ministers.

Indicative of Low-Church tendencies was the fact that in 1766 only the town ministers wore surplices, a practice which the town Dissenting preachers also followed. In 1808 the Beaufort Episcopalians sent delegates to the State Convention only on condition that no action of the body should bind the congregation unless it confirmed it by its own vote. There is said to have been a distinct dislike of the authority of bishops even as late as 1808.

Support from the public treasury so enervated the Anglicans that disestablishment in 1778 involved them almost in ruin for a generation. Not a native South Carolinian was ordained to their ministry until 1795, nor the second until 1806. Eight more followed by 1820, when the church was well on the way to revived life. But we must remember that a very large proportion of the Baptist and Presbyterian ministers up to this time came from outside. The South Carolinians were not notably spiritually-minded before the Great Revival about 1800.

Presbyterians and Methodists.—The Presbyterians, the Baptists, and the new denomination of the Methodists were of approximately equal numbers in 1810. The Methodists were experiencing the marvelous growth accounted for by their early zeal. They were having an almost unbelievable multiplication of their ministry and supplied an emotional element which helped to vitalize all the other churches. The great Baptist growth later in the nineteenth century left the Presbyterians only about a third the numbers of the Methodists and a fifth of the Baptists.

Presbyterian numerical decline had several causes, apart from the fact that there is only a limited portion of any population to whom the rigorous Presbyterian system appeals. Adherence to an educated ministry made filling their pulpits impossible. To this was added the fact that their able and educated ministers were often drafted into academic positions to the benefit of the culture of the community at the cost of the denomination. The Presbytery of South Carolina, embracing about a third of the State, reported in 1799 twenty-eight congregations with ministers and twenty-nine unsupplied. The Presbyterians lost popular touch also by discontinuing camp meetings in the early nineteenth century and by bitter doctrinal disputes in the 1830's.

Methodist history falls so largely into the post-Revolutionary period as to call for only brief notice here. John Wesley, while visiting Charles Town from his Savannah parish, preached in St. Philip's Church so earnestly on April 17, 1737, that a gentleman exclaimed, "Why, if this be Christianity, a Christian must have more courage than Alexander the Great." The next year Commissary Garden showed similar courtesy to Whitefield; but on the great evangelist's return to Charles Town in 1740 he fell afoul the instructions of the Bishop of London, condemning his preaching to open-air congregations without the Prayer-Book. Dr. Alexander Garden preached against him from the text, "These that have turned the world upside down are come hither also," forgetting apparently that these were the words of "certain lewd fellows of the baser sort" seeking to slay Paul. Whitefield replied from the words of Paul, "Alexander the coppersmith did me much evil; the Lord rewarded him according to his works." The affair ended in a prolonged newspaper controversy, bitterly dividing the evangelical and formalistic elements of the town, the suspension of Whitefield by Commissary Garden, and an appeal to England. Whitefield was too absorbed by his orphanage in Georgia and his evangelism in two continents to trouble further with the affair, which had little significance save as an illustration of how new wine was bursting old bottles. His frequent visits to Charles Town, where he preached to crowded houses in the Dissenting churches, continued to be heralded by the *Gazette* as prime news. The Reverend William Peasley, not yet run out of St. Helena, who declined to leave his mistresses to visit the dying, wrote the Society for the Propagation of the Gospel that he found Whitefield very troublesome, as the people of Prince William parish were much led astray by him and his preachers; but, Mr. Peasley reported, he was finding the comparing of their enthusiasm to that of the Papists a good antidote against their enthusiastic spirit. The stirrings of religious revival in the 1740's and '50's brought in strolling preachers denounced by Dissenters as well as Anglicans as Egyptian caterpillars, "such unclean beasts, such an insolent brazen crew of raggamuffins and polecats."

Joseph Pilmoor in 1773 was the next authorized Methodist preacher in Charleston after Whitefield; but like Whitefield he left no organization, and so his work redounded mainly to the benefit of the Presbyterians and Baptists. Asbury was of different genius, and organized a church and left a preacher in charge in 1785. In 1787 the South Carolina Conference was organized. It might be remarked here that the antislavery activities of Dr. Coke stamped the Methodists in popular opinion with being abolitionists and increased the opposition to them as religious enthusiasts. Charleston was troubled by the tumultuous shouting of the Negro members. Preachers were several times subjected to minor personal violence. The church was stoned, and in 1807 the congregation was expelled from Bethel in Charleston by the militia. Though no explanation was ever given, the reason was perhaps partly the noise of the Negroes in the galleries, as numbers of these were marched off to the (not sweet) "sugar house."

Baptists Before the Revolution.—Under the leadership of Rev. William Screven the Baptists became so active by 1703 that Judge Trott wrote the Archbishop of Canterbury for literature, as "we are here very much infested with the sect of the Anabaptists." But despite the ignorance and violence of the extremer type of wandering Baptist preachers, and their denunciation of the Episcopal and in New England of the Congregational clergy as "a hireling ministry," they were answered in South Carolina by contempt and slander rather than persecution. The whippers of the Rev. Joseph York roused much public indignation. In 1700 the South Carolina Baptists adopted the "Century Confession" of faith of 1677, known also as the "Philadelphia Confession," which is still their standard. This proves them to have been thus early "particular," and not "general" Baptists. For many years they called themselves Anti-paedo Baptists, thus emphasizing their adherence to believers' baptisms only.

The whole Baptist belief, policy, and outlook were inharmonious with monarchical and aristocratic institutions. It was in fact the conviction of the more intolerant Anglicans that Baptists and Presbyterians were at heart republicans and at least potentially disloyal to the royal government. The Baptists, Miss Townsend points out, made a strong appeal to persons of direct, literal, definite minds. Their dramatic declaration of faith by immersion, their simple, rigid theology, their tonic discipline, their system of self-government, their strong democratic appeal, destined them to be a power. It was not until the nineteenth century that there came the great Baptist growth that made them the most numerous denomination in the State; but they were active on the frontier from the beginnings of the influx of settlers. The few Society for the Propagation of the Gospel missionaries who visited the back settlements reported that they found there swarms of Presbyterian and Baptist "teachers," whom they plentifully denounced but did little to supplant except to seek to have the government discourage their coming.

In 1733 William Elliott, Jr., led a secession of Arminian (his enemies said of Arian) character from the Charles Town church. William Elliott, Sr., a pillar of the old church, was said by some always to have been a "general" (that is, Arminian) Baptist. The general Baptists, after years of weakness, were extinct in this region by 1791. The Baptist church in Charles Town soon split; one party actually deposed the minister, and the other replaced him by force. Long and bitter quarrels had almost ruined the coast country Baptists when Whitefield's preaching in Charles Town, 1738 to '41, turned them to twenty-five years of revivals, but the great inland immigration had already shifted the Bap tist center of gravity into the up country, where the establishment of many churches between 1765 and 1772 began by about 1777 to stimulate the coast country.

A large factor in the Baptist mid-century revival was the Reverend Oliver Hart. Hearing of the situation in Charles Town, Hart, at the age of twenty-six, came from Pennsylvania in December, 1749. Although many disliked his gown and bands (regalia which Richard Furman also later wore), his ability, zeal, piety, and appeal to young people, and a generous personality that won the friendship of ministers of the established and other churches, made him a power. "Realizing from his northern experience the benefits of cooperation, he formed in 1751 the Charles Town Baptist Association, the second Baptist Association in America, consisting of four churches (Charles Town, Ashley River, Euhaw near Beaufort, and Welsh Neck.)" Every forward movement was almost surely his suggestion or execution. He was in effect a veritable bishop of the Baptists; and so great was his work, says Furman, that the South Carolina Baptists of the time considered his advent as a special interposition of Providence.

In 1774 Hart married the young widow of Charles Grimball. She was already a Baptist. The incident suggests the common error of supposing that the early American Baptists were confined to the lower classes. Governor Blake's wife and her mother Lady Axtell were members of the Rev. Mr. Screven's church. William Elliott in 1699 or earlier was a Baptist leader. An Anglican minister rejoiced in 1724 that he had "proselyted" from the Baptists Mrs. Guerard, daughter of a considerable planter. Paul Grimball, of the early eighteenth century, was a Baptist, as was the Reverend Henry Heywood, "esteemed one of the greatest scholars in America." The tendency of the Dissenters, through frequent intermarriage with the best Anglican families, etc., to drift into the Anglican connection had, says Miss Townsend, before 1800 pretty well drained the coast-country Baptists of their aristocratic elements. But it is to be noted that Jonathan Maxcy, first president of the South Carolina College, was a Baptist preacher; that Baptists were prominent in the early St. David's Society; that the Reverend Henry Holcombe was president of the Beaufort District Society and trustee of Beaufort College; that the Baptist John Waldo, the Georgetown teacher after 1792, became a prolific writer of textbooks; and that Dr. Richard Fuller (1804-76) of Beaufort contended with such learning against Catholic Bishop England that the latter's biographer thinks (doubtless erroneously, since he did not know the cultural resources then in South Carolina) both must have received outside aid.

The Baptists have never in South Carolina or the United States occupied political positions in proportion to their numbers. Said Dr. Richard Furman in 1791: "But a great part of the ministers as well as members are very illiterate men, which is a great hindrance to the Baptists having that weight in the State they would be entitled to, and has in many instances opened the door to enthusiasm and confusion among them."

Welsh Neck, constituted in 1738 with thirty members, was the first Baptist church of the deep back country and became the mother church or inspirer of a wide-spreading circle of churches. Fairforest, in Union County near the Spartanburg line, founded in 1762 or '63, is the oldest Baptist church in the far up country. From Fairforest, Baptist principles spread far and wide.

Despite the slurs of the Anglican clergy, without specifications, on the character of "ignorant" and "wandering" preachers (who included men sent on regular missions from the North), and notwithstanding the comparative ease with which men obtained ordination, the proportion of the unworthy, so far as available records go, was small. Ordination was easy; but the ordainers were the neighbors of the applicant and knew him of old. Drunkenness and adultery were usually the sins into which the erring ministers fell—falls far more common then in all the churches than they are today. But Baptist discipline was rigorous. The Bush River Baptist Church, from 1772 to 1804, tried sixteen persons, a majority of them on charges of drunkenness, slander, adultery, and rape; two on questions of church doctrine or polity; one for planting tobacco on the Sabbath and justifying it.

The Baptists, as did others, long depended largely on ministers from outside. All the Anglicans until 1795 were from abroad. Many of the Presbyterians were from Britain, particularly Scotland, or from Northern provinces. The Charles Town Baptist Association in 1756 began a movement for raising funds for ministerial education. This was the first partnership for the purpose among American Baptists. Dr. Richard Furman's rise to leadership a few years later gave the movement new impetus. It met sharp opposition in the back country. The Separate Baptists, who were strong for some years after 1755, shocked the Particular Baptists by allowing any man, however ignorant, to preach if he felt called by the Spirit. "Separates frequently harbored an idea that education and religion were hostile forces," says Miss Townsend, and—what is more important—carried these ideas over into the Regulars when they joined them.

The coast-country organizers of the American Revolution realized that the possession of the back country by Presbyterians and Baptists called for a political mission by leaders of these groups. Accordingly the Reverend Oliver Hart of the Baptists and the Reverend William Tennent of the Presbyterian-Congregational group accompanied William Henry Drayton on his memorable tour. Dr. Richard Furman (then of the church in the High Hills of Santee) was so active in the American cause that, like Hart, he had to flee the country as the British advanced.

In April, 1776, a meeting of Baptist churches was held at the High Hills of Santee to choose delegates to attend the "Continental Association . . . in order to obtain our liberties and freedom from religious tyranny or ecclesiastic oppression." This was part of the movement for overthrowing the system of an established church throughout the United States. One result of the meeting at the High Hills of Santee was evidently the choice of the Reverend William Tennent of the Independent Church in Charles Town to present the case of the Dissenters against the establishment. How ably Tennent performed the duty is attested by his address before the legislature, which in the Constitution of 1778 placed all Protestant churches choosing their own ministers on the basis of equality as maintaining the "established religion of South Carolina." The Constitution of 1790 established religious equality for all creeds.

The Revolution thus marked an era in the religious development as well as other aspects of the State's history. The activities of the past century had laid down the main lines on which the religious history of the State was to continue except as to the Methodists and the Catholics, who were present only in small numbers before the Revolution. While the missionaries of the Society for the Propagation of the Gospel, supported in part by the society and in part by the provincial government, were serving the wealthy older settled portion of the province and confining their back-country activities mainly to complaining of the intrusion of Presbyterian and Baptist "fanatics" there, these denominations by their spontaneous activity carried religion, morality, and civilization to the farthest bounds of the province. The Established Church meanwhile suffered the enervating influence of public support, the withdrawal of which left her for a generation in a ruinous prostration from which, adjusting herself to the more wholesome conditions of self-reliant life, she was to emerge into a more vigorous life than she had ever known. Meanwhile the vulgarity of thought and speech that had characterized even polite society in the eighteenth century, and the irreligion, coarseness, and violence of the frontier, yielded, particularly after the Great Revival about 1800, to the benign influence of an ardent evangelical spirit that pressed into the remotest quarter.

CHAPTER XXIV

THE SETTLEMENT OF THE BACK COUNTRY, AND THE CIRCUIT COURT ACT OF 1769

Governor Boone Offends the Commons.—Thomas Boone, formerly Governor of New Jersey and a nephew of Joseph Boone of a prominent family in South Carolina from 1694 to 1725, arrived on December 22, 1761, as Governor of South Carolina. He soon showed a determination to warp long established practices to his own ideas that plunged him into conflicts with the Commons, blighting his administration and precipitating one of the angriest of the chronic quarrels between the two houses. In accord with the immemorial custom of the Commons' participating in Indian relations, on being prorogued on May 29, 1762, they appointed a committee to sit with the Governor and Council in distributing Indian presents. Governor Boone informed the Commons that he would regard this committee merely as private gentlemen not to be consulted on executive business.

Boone's criticism of the election law was ignored until in September, 1762, he made a sharp issue. The Commons, in examining the returns for a by-election for St. Paul's, observed that the church wardens had not, as the law required, taken an oath before opening the polls. They overlooked this, as there was no doubt as to the intention of the voters, declared Christopher Gadsden elected, and sent him to the Governor to take the state oaths.

The Governor refused to administer the oaths and summoned the Commons into his presence. He was astonished, he said, that they were seeking to dispense with the law to which they owed their existence as an Assembly. "To manifest in as public a manner as I can my disavowal of so undeniable an infraction of the election act, I hereby dissolve this present General Assembly."

Boone's newly elected Assembly consisted of almost exactly the same old members. The ardent Gadsden and the conservative Wragg, in a committee headed by John Rutledge, united in a long report exposing Boone's political folly, not to say illegality. The existence of the Assembly, they said, did not rest upon the election act, but upon the known and ancient Constitution of Great Britain. The Commons alone were the judges of the election of their members. The Governor could not constitutionally take cognizance of any of their acts until regularly notified. Therefore his refusal to administer the oaths to Gadsden was a breach of their privileges, and his dissolution of the Assembly a violation of the freedom of elections and a blow at the liberties of the people.

Boone replied angrily and drew a reply from the house, written by Gadsden himself, maintaining that the repeal of every election law would not prevent popular representation, which was guaranteed by the Charter, but did not rest upon it, since the Charter itself was but a recognition of the natural right of freemen to representation. On Boone's reply that forty such messages would have no effect, the Commons voted to enter upon no business with him until he did them justice. Only after months was a quorum at last obtained. Gadsden and Moultrie were sent with a new member (as was customary), Sir John Colleton, to take the state oaths. Boone requested Colleton to remain and be sworn and ordered Gadsden and Moultrie from his house. Such stupid insolence was answered by a petition for Boone's removal and the circulation by the Commons of a seventy-eight-page account of the affair in England and America. The Assembly virtually suspended, despite Indian outrages on the frontier, until Boone departed on May 14, 1764, virtually driven from office.

Lieutenant-Governor Bull promptly summoned the Assembly; but Boone absent proved as great an impediment as Boone present. Soon after his arrival the Assembly had paid him £86 6*s.* currency for the last few days of 1761. The Council insisted on amending the tax bill by adding £7,000 currency, his salary for two years. This revival in a particularly offensive connection of the claim of the Council to amend money bills brought the most insulting message ever received by that body, openly denouncing them as composed largely of placemen with "no natural tie or connection whatever with the province."

The ministry were displeased with Boone, whom they privately reprimanded while upholding him to the Commons. The withholding of his pay alarmed the government as likely to intimidate future governors. In 1766 the Assembly, in deference to the King's request, and in good humor at the repeal of the Stamp Act (as Professor W. R. Smith remarks), sent Boone the balance of the usual amount.

Filling Up the Back Country.—In 1731, the province had sought to draw white settlers, both as a step of general progress and as a means of safety against the constantly mounting proportion of Negro slaves. Lieutenant-Governor Bull gave the strength of this "intestine enemy" in 1760 as 57,253, of whom he estimated 15,000 must be adult males. "Our white males of sixteen years and over cannot be more than 6,000," a circumstance, he commented, which "must raise in our minds many melancholy reflections." These "melancholy reflections" bore fruit in the law of 1761 for a bounty to Protestant European immigrants and in an attempt to lay an additional duty on Negroes. The latter died in a quarrel over the Council's right to amend, but there soon was enacted the prohibitive duty law of 1764, to last through 1766, 1767, and 1768. Greed for quick wealth, with the planters full of money, brought in 5,438 Negroes in the first eleven months of 1769. Timothy's *Gazette,* a steady opponent of importations, warned in italics on July 6, 1769: *"This scarcely needs comment; every man's own mind must suggest the consequences of such enormous importations."*

After a spasmodic restriction during 1770 the flood mounted higher than ever, piling up simultaneously private riches and public weakness. The first five months of 1773 saw the unprecedented number of 11,641, more than a fifth of the total of 55,606 imported from January 1, 1753, to May 31, 1773. When Henry Laurens refrained from re-entering the trade on its reopening in 1769 (thus joining his brother James and also Gabriel Manigault, who had always refrained, with trivial exceptions on Manigault's part), he was twitted with entertaining scruples. His pretense of other reasons reveals the fear of one of the wealthiest merchants to face sneers which almost the whole community would have visited upon anyone considering the slave trade immoral.

Not only the slaves, but the Indians also were a danger. In 1765 Fort Prince George was practically rebuilt against the Cherokees, and a new fort called Charlotte was built of stone to guard the South Carolina end of the ford of the Savannah two miles below the mouth of the (Georgia's) Broad, by which the Creeks frequently made their inroads. To meet the Negro and Indian danger and strengthen the province in general, the law of 1751 had imposed a duty of £10 currency on imported Negroes 4 feet 2 inches tall, and less in proportion on smaller. Three-fifths of the income was for bounties to poor Protestants, foreign or British. They must settle between the Santee and the Savannah rivers within forty miles of the sea during the first three years. The policy was to secure a continuous body of settlements and strengthen the coastal region. Hence, no encouragement was offered those who were already settling the upper region, but so strong was the push there that in 1752 the limitation of location was removed.

It is customary to speak as though the tide of migration from Virginia and Pennsylvania into South Carolina originated from Braddock's defeat in 1755, which left those frontiers exposed. As a matter of fact the Virginia migration was considerably before that. Matthew Lyons with his family of eleven from Virginia asked for land in New Windsor in 1742. The application of the Virginians and Pennsylvanians in 1745 clearly afforded the immediate urge for Glen to buy the Cherokee title up to Long Canes Creek in 1747, thus freeing the lands around Ninety Six, which had been a trading place as early as 1730. In 1752 there were about forty Virginia and other northern families between Stevens Creek and Ninety Six.

How long continued and extensive was this migration from the northward to South Carolina is evidenced by a Revolutionary pension roll of about the years 1835 to 1840, which shows that almost every one of the pensioners living in the low country had served in the South Carolina Continental line, whereas a large proportion of the pensioners living in the up country had served as North Carolina, Virginia, or Pennsylvania Continental soldiers.

The great stream of immigration overland from the northward came unaided by bounties and spread over the northwestern half of the province. The roll of Colonel William Thomson's regiment in 1775 consisted of 121 men born in Virginia, 52 in South Carolina (only 20 of whom were 25 years of age), 33 in Ireland, 28 in North Carolina, 22 in Pennsylvania, 16 in Maryland, 8 in England, 5 in Scotland, and one each in New England, New York, New Jersey and Delaware. Sixty-seven were under twenty-one. Virginia, North Carolina, Pennsylvania, and Maryland thus furnished by birth almost 65 per cent of the whole, and probably a good proportion of those who were born in the British Isles had come through those provinces to South Carolina.

The movement of the 1750's to 1770 filled in the space of the middle country but mainly pushed forward into the country including and above the present Lancaster, Fairfield, Newberry, Saluda, and Edgefield counties, up to the Indian line bounding Greenville and Anderson on the east and the southeast. A few settled in the old parishes as overseers, etc., but the north Europeans generally avoided that region on account of the summer heat, the malaria, and the long-established system of great slave-worked estates, conditions which had so seriously hindered the township settlement movement of the 1730's and 1740's.

For the immigrants who were expected as a result of the bounty encouragement, three square-shaped townships were, in 1762, laid off west of Ninety Six: Boonesborough, 20,500 acres on the headwaters of Long Canes Creek two miles east of the present Due West; Hillsborough, 28,000 acres centering near where Long Canes enters Little River and containing the town of New Bordeaux; and Belfast (later often called Londonborough), comprising 22,000 acres and lying on both sides of Hardlabour Creek above its junction with Cuffeetown Creek.[1] Though these townships received English, French, German,

[1] In my large *History of South Carolina* (1934) I stated that there were four town-

and Scotch-Irish immigrants, this was mainly the Scotch-Irish era, as the 1730's and '40's were mainly the German.

The picture had its darker side. Commercial greed led to cruelty to the helpless poor, and importers drew on indentured servants the bonus that was intended to bring in freemen. Hundreds more were obliged to transfer their bounty to the shipowners as their only means of coming. "I will not help your friend collect his claim," wrote Henry Laurens, November 9, 1768. "If you knew the whole affair, it would make your humanity shudder"; worse than he had ever witnessed in the African slave trade. Such abuses swelled the traffic in indentured servants to its highest point. "The bounty to foreign poor Protestants having been much abused," wrote Laurens January 28, 1768, "will be discontinued." Expiring by limitation that year, it was not renewed; but the independent movement from the northward, largely Scotch-Irish, continued unabated.

A plat for one hundred acres on Padget's Creek in the southern part of the present Union County bears the date July 31, 1753, and the grant a year later. Its "path to Tiger River" suggests a white man's road rather than an Indian trading path. The Pacolet, a little farther north, was settled by 1759. Professor Meriwether's investigations show the whole country east of the Indian line of 1763 settled by 1760. Along with thousands of grants for small tracts to immigrants in the 1760's went a number of very large up-country grants to planters on account of their new slaves, or to settlement promoters.

In 1762, one hundred and fourteen of the still-persecuted French Huguenots who had fled to England petitioned to be sent to some southern colony. The group, led by Revs. Jean Louis Gibert and Moses

ships in this region. My long uncertainty as to whether there were three or four, because of the ambiguities in the records, was finally decided in favor of four by the large map of North America (two sheets, each twenty by forty inches, London, 1777, found also in *The American Atlas* of 1776), which gives four townships, with Belfast and Londonborough separately and distinctly outlined and named. Dr. R. L. Meriwether, in his intensive studies in land grants in the region (*The Expansion of South Carolina,* p. 251), was led to the conclusion that Belfast was later called Londonborough. Examination of his evidence and that supplied by Mr. Wade C. Harrison of Troy, S. C., especially his map of the region, leads me to the following conclusion: Belfast Township was surveyed in 1762, and lands within it continued at times to be described as late as 1775 (I have not searched later) as in Belfast Township. But when in 1765 Lieutenant Governor Bull placed some Germans in the northern part of Belfast, and named their settlement Londonborough in honor of London gentlemen who had aided them, it became common to describe lands in or near that settlement as being in Londonborough Township. There was never any formal change of name. At least as late as 1775, both Belfast and Londonborough are used in surveys and grant book records, with the gradual diminution of use of the name Belfast.

I thank also Miss Nora Davis of Troy, S. C., for valuable information on the township locations and names.

Boutiton, arrived in Charles Town in April 1764. They were given arms, tools, cows, etc., and encouraged to make wine and silk, as the Irish and Germans had been to raise flax and hemp. A small number, separating for "disgust" and quarrels, were settled in Purrysburgh. There were three hundred persons around New Bordeaux in 1765. The total Huguenot immigration of 1764-72 appears to have been about 475. The early success of Gibert and others with silk was abandoned for more profitable and easy occupations.

The Germans began to come in numbers on the 1761 bounty in 1764. Some settled in the new townships and some in the low country.

When Spain's title to Georgia south of the Altamaha was extinguished in 1763, the great South Carolina planters or rich merchant would-be planters grasped for the new means of wealth. Few requests were for less than a thousand acres, some for many thousands. It was a great planter movement sparkling with a large proportion of the distinguished names of the period—to him that hath the slaves shall the land be given. On April 5, 1763, petitions were presented for 318,040 acres, and on May 3, for 203,700 acres. The Lords of Trade severely condemned a movement contrary to their plans for a well-regulated Georgia—another instance of the British government's higher regard for the general interest of the province than was felt by the local governing class. Many South Carolina families secured valuable estates, some of which were cultivated by their families until after 1900, says Mr. A. S. Salley, although none that he is aware of moved there.

Neglect of the Back Country.—The concentration of social, political, and commercial interests in Charles Town naturally led to neglect of the interests of the back country, which just as naturally resented it. The rapid flow of a non-slave-owning white farmer class into the middle and far back country during the twenty years before the Revolution shifted the preponderance of population to the newer region while leaving an equal preponderance of wealth and culture near the coast. This accentuated the attitude of disdain on the part of the older section and of resentment on the other, and constituted for generations one of the most striking instances of intrastate sectionalism in American history.

This antagonism was not primarily one of regions, but of conditions and therefore of classes. The "missionaries" of the Society for the Propagation of the Gospel were almost all sent to the old coastal region, but poor back settlers were left to supply their own churches while being taxed to help support the ministers of the wealthy. In 1741 the grand jury for the whole province presented as a great hardship that persons were obliged to travel long distances to Charles Town for even small causes, whereas in other colonies justice was near at hand through county courts and "circular judges." Petitions of 1743, '46, '52, '58, '62, '66 kept the government informed of this crying need. Each section seemed to think the other extremely wicked. Strong views were founded on very partial knowledge.

In 1757, with Indian massacres threatening the frontier, the Assembly, while voting £10,000 currency to repair Fort Johnson in Charles Town harbor, £3,500 for Georgetown, £10,000 for Port Royal, and £5,000 for a magazine at Dorchester, refused a petition to aid the people between Broad and Saluda rivers in erecting a fort, because "other inhabitants living in the back settlements have, heretofore, erected small forts to defend themselves against the inroads of the Indians, without ever applying to the government of this province to defray any part of the expense; and as the granting of the sum prayed for by the petitioners, though but a small one, may be a bad precedent by opening a door to great impositions from people who live so very remote, we can not agree to make provision for the same."

And yet the lands of these "people who live so very remote" were taxed exactly the same sum per acre as the richest rice and indigo plantations of the planters in the Assembly. These were the back-country men who were in 1765 asked to be in readiness to march to save the plantation region in case of an anticipated slave insurrection.

Governor Glen planned, on his trip to build Fort Prince George in 1753, to investigate the proper location for courts in the back country, and on his return strongly urged their establishment. In consequence a bill for courts at Beaufort, Georgetown, and Congarees was introduced in the Commons, but died after the first reading. The Peedee people in 1758 asked that the County Court Act of 1722, as a permanent (though sleeping) act, be put in force, and that the laws be printed in one volume, instead of in many little inaccessible tracts. Lieutenant-Governor Bull, like Governor Glen, was in 1765 urging courts upon the Assembly. The Commons promptly passed a bill for courts at Beaufort, Georgetown, and Congarees, but the Council took no action.

On February 27, 1766, the Commons read a more general petition for redress of grievances sent up from the people of Congarees, Ninety Six, Broad and Saluda rivers, "and places adjacent," praying for relief from paying the same taxes per acre as paid by the richest rice lands, and relief also from the lack of the commonest government services and of any representation in the Assembly; all of which was pigeonholed while the Assembly considered building a chapel of ease at Wambaw and the grievances of the dray owners of Charles Town against traffic regulations.[2]

[2] JCHA, Feb. 27, 1766, *passim.* All lands outside of towns were taxed at the

The failure of the government to provide the agencies of orderly government for the back country led to the aggravation of the disorders natural to the frontier. Outlaws driven from other provinces swarmed in. For several years, wrote Lieutenant-Governor Bull on September 10, 1768, the back country had been infested with horse thieves and robbers, who banded themselves together and formed alliances with "hedge taverns" which helped them elude officers. The great distance made it difficult to bring them to Charles Town. Hence, says Bull, the people, irritated beyond the bounds of law, hunted out and whipped the thieves and destroyed the principal houses that harbored them. At the suit of some of the scoundrels, honest "regulators" were thrown into jail and mulcted in damages.

About June, 1767, back-country agitation for redress of grievances took on a more widely organized and determined form. There appeared a remarkable leader who cried aloud for justice and scourged the indifferent and selfish like a veritable Amos. Charles Woodmason, as a layman residing in the back country, read prayers for the people for some time before 1762 or '63. In 1766 he abandoned the prosperous position of leading justice of the peace in Charles Town to become an Anglican clergyman. His lack of the learned languages was overlooked, as well it might be with his command of eloquent English. He sought the hard appointment on the Wateree for which no one had applied since its creation nine years before. Burning with a zeal which whirled him into exaggerations less harmful because so patent, he carried the liturgy fifty miles beyond its previous inland penetration.

Woodmason wrote, at least in large degree, the petition presented to the provincial government in 1767 by the people of his vast parish of St. Mark's, which included about a third of the province, consisting as it did of everything northwest of Williamsburg between the Great Peedee and the Santee-Congaree-Saluda. "Though we contribute to the support of government," said the petition, "we do not share the benefits enjoyed by our fellow-provincials. We are practically denied trial by our peers, as few persons north of the Santee are on the jury list. Forty-four members of the Commons are elected south and six north of the Santee. It is the number of *free men,* not *black slaves,* that constitute the strength and riches of a state." The failure to divide the back country into parishes "we conceive to be due to the selfish interests of those in and near Charles Town, who seek to have everything center there. To our absence was largely due the voting of £60,000 for an exchange for

same value; but town lots were taxed at their real value. The back country in numbers of colonies suffered similar injustices in representation, but South Carolina was an outstanding instance. Taxing all lands the same amount had been practiced in England and was later in some Western territories.

the merchants and a ballroom for the ladies of Charles Town, while nearly 60,000 back settlers have not a minister or a church, as if we were not worth the thought of, or deemed as savages and not Christians! As loyal subjects and true lovers of our country we beg leave to sum up what we conceive necessary to afford us our equal right as British subjects." They noted the following rights (among many others):

Circuit or county courts, as in neighboring provinces; subordinate courts in each parish consisting of justices and freeholders; provincial laws to be digested into a code and printed; the interior and upper parts of the province, and all beyond Black River, to be laid out in parishes, and churches or parsonages to be founded among them; public schools to be founded in the back settlements; the lines of all counties and parishes to be run to the Cherokees' boundary, "that we may no longer wander in the maze of supposition."

Four thousand men backed the petition, according to Woodmason, who were restrained by their leaders in deference to a letter of Lieutenant-Governor Bull from marching to Charles Town to present it in a body. The unhappy sectional antagonism that was for so long to blight South Carolina was already deeply planted. The consideration of the petition was marked by passion on both sides. When assemblymen ridiculed the suggestion that the money for Pitt's statue should have been spent for Bibles for the back country, there was posted on the State House:

Inscription for the statue of Mr. Pitt:

What love to their adopted sons
Is by our fathers shown?
We ask to taste the Bread of Life,
And, lo, they give a stone!

The demand for the arrest of the deputies and the burning of their petition was calmed by the reminder that but for the interposition of the Lieutenant-Governor, whom the people trusted, the 4,000 who backed the petition for 50,000 would have been at the door. The deputies were dismissed with promises.

The Regulators.—The rapid realization of all the requested reforms was impossible. The greatest result was the enactment of the Circuit Court Act, one of the epoch-making laws in South Carolina history. The codifying of the laws was committed to John Rutledge, but, so far as appears, was pushed aside by the Revolution.[3] Six new parishes were promised, but not created, this and other reforms soon falling foul of a quarrel between Commons and Council that ended legislation

[3] On the later history of codification, see Chapter XLII.

until the Revolution. Jury reform was promised. A number of public schools with free tuition to twenty scholars each were designed, but only on condition, says Woodmason, that a college be created in Charles Town.

Unfortunately the delay in the performance of some promises stirred the back-country men's distrust, while the delay of two years in passing the court act, and prosecutions of Regulators by rascals whom they had whipped, again threatened the province with internal violence. The unauthorized arrest of Regulators after Montagu's order of *nolle prosequi* of April, 1768, destroyed faith in the indemnity, says Bull. "They are not idle vagabonds," he continues, "the canaille, the mere dregs of mankind. They are mostly the tenants of his Majesty's, landholders, though poor. They are in general an industrious, hardy race of men, each possessed of and expert in the use of fire arms, each master of one horse, many of several, besides cattle and slaves." It is impossible to suppress them by force, as "the only resource where a military force for such service can be raised must be among our maritime settlements, where white inhabitants are few and a numerous domestic enemy is thick sown in our plantations and require our utmost attention to keep them in order. . . . I humbly apprehend that the surest and only method of quieting their minds is the treating them with moderation and their complaints with attention, and their grievances with reasonable redress."

Some of the Regulators were men of considerable property. Woodmason asserts that over 3,000 armed North Carolinians offered to come to their assistance if the government sent regular troops against them. The last item indicated the sympatthy in grievances of the frontiersmen irrespective of provincial boundaries.

A constable with thirteen men seeking to seize chattels of Regulators on the Peedee had a battle with Regulators under Gideon Gibson in which one of the posse was killed and several Regulators were wounded. The Regulators won, cruelly whipped some, and threatened to hang one if Gibson's brother died. The people had come to the determination to permit no process from Charles Town.

The Lieutenant-Governor issued a strong proclamation against the outlaws and three days later another, offering pardon to all who would disperse but Gibson. On August 9 the Provost Marshal, Roger Pinckney, with Colonel G. G. Powell of the regiment of the region, started with a posse for Mars Bluff on the Great Peedee. The three hundred militia present informed the Marshal and their Colonel that they would stand by their fellow-Regulator. Colonel Powell's influence sufficed to save Provost Marshal Pinckney from being "grossly abused" as had been planned; but Colonel Powell in mortification resigned his commission.

In 1767 apparently six or seven hundred desperate men marched against the outlaws to suppress whose crimes the Regulators had been organized. Several lives were lost before prominent gentlemen arrived just in time to prevent a bloody battle on the Saluda. There was wild talk of marching against the plantations, whose owners' words in defense of liberty against the Stamp Act were scornfully turned against their injustice to their fellow provincials: "The oppression you pretend to fear you make others feel."

"The Regulation," by which principally the South Carolina back-country men at last forced attention to their rights as the only alternative to armed rebellion, was of more than local significance. The malcontents of New England complained of grievances in some respects similar to these. A similar movement was feared in the Wyoming Valley, Pennsylvania. The fear of further irritating the Dissenter backwoodsmen throughout the colonies appears to have played a part in the hesitation of the Virginia Anglican clergy to press their desire for an American episcopate. The culmination of "The Regulation" in North Carolina in the battle of Alamance in 1771 must have derived its inspiration in part from the movement in South Carolina, for many North Carolina back-country men had manifested sympathy with the South Carolina movement. It is significant that early in the Revolution the King's adherents who fled from the Carolinas to join the British in Florida were called Scoffelites (or Scovelites), as synonymous with the vermin who had constituted Scoffel's posse sent against the Regulators in 1768. The outbreak of the Revolution witnessed strangely conflicting cross currents of feeling in the back country, some resenting injustices by the royal government, and others blaming the neglect of back-country interests equally on the coast-controlled Assembly. "The Regulation" played its part in creating the perturbed state of mind without which revolution is impossible.

Circuit Courts Created.—At last an act for circuit courts was signed by the Governor on April 12, 1768, providing for seven circuit courts; but the King disallowed it because it attached salaries to the particular attorney-general and clerk instead of permanently to the offices, because it confined the Governer's selection for sheriffs to the three nominated for each circuit by the judges, and (most serious of all) because it provided for commissioning judges during good behavior, this being considered "indecent and disrespectful to his Majesty." An attempt of New York thus to establish judicial independence had occasioned a special instruction to all governors to permit no change in the commissions of judges.

The province was dismayed at the veto and widely demanded that relief be obtained by meeting the King's conditions. When Governor Lord Montagu sailed for England he carried the act of July 29, 1769, identical with the former act except that it met the essential objections. The King assented on November 25, 1769. The act instituted a new era, both in the courts and in the general history of the province. Seven circuits (or "precincts") were created, the basis from which all subsequent political and judicial subdivisions have developed. The parishes remained in the low country as election districts until 1865, but the old Craven, Berkeley, Colleton, and Granville counties, formerly used to locate land grants, magistrates, etc., virtually ceased. Court was to meet thrice annually in Charles Town and twice in Beaufort, Georgetown, Cheraw, Camden, Orangeburg, and Ninety Six.

The ancient office of provost marshal for the whole province was superseded by that of sheriff for each district. Richard Cumberland, an English dramatist, held lifetime patents to the South Carolina offices of provost marshal, clerk of the crown, and clerk of the peace, which he administered by deputy, keeping a share of the income for himself. He secured through his patron's influence the King's consent to the extinction of the patent, a valuable prerogative by which His Majesty might buy or reward supporters. To cut short a long story of private versus public interest thoroughly characteristic of eighteenth-century England, the province, on establishing circuit courts, bought out Cumberland's marshalship for £5,000 sterling, but left his clerkships on his hands, apparently to be swept away by the Revolution.

The easy habit of making the King and the ministry scapegoats has led at least one eminent historian to emphasize the patent-holder as long preventing the establishment of circuit courts.[4] This is not warranted by the records. The delighted patentee was easily disposed of. The back-country men, while condemning patent-holding, laid much more stress on the colonial Assembly's ignorance of their needs and the greed of Charles Town lawyers and other legal interests seeking to keep all possible revenues centered in the city. It was even suggested in bitter sarcasm that everybody should be required to come to Charles Town to obey the calls of nature.

Striving for Better Representation—Starting the Courts.—Nor is it possible to unload on the King the responsibility for delaying the other reform—the granting of legislative representation for the back country. For decades protests had come from the townships at unfulfillment of the King's pledge of parish organization and representation when they should come to contain a hundred heads of families, only to find the

[4] General McCrady was apparently overly influenced by Plowden J. C. Weston's publication of the Cumberland negotiations and was unacquainted with the abundant MS sources on the matter.

Assembly unresponsive. The Purrysburgh region was erected into the parish of St. Peter in 1747, and during the next twenty years several of the old parishes were subdivided. In 1757 St. Mark's parish was created, to include everything northwest of Williamsburg between the Great Peedee and the Santee-Congaree-Saluda, with two members of Assembly, and its church in the extreme southeastern corner, where resided a handful of Episcopal planters.[5]

The creation of back-country parishes demanded in 1767 was prevented by several causes. The existing parishes were unwilling to divide their fifty members with the back-countrymen, an issue which intensely embittered the sections until 1808 and to a lesser degree even until 1865, when the old scapegoat the King could no longer have the sin cast upon him.

The Court Act ended a bitter struggle between up country and low country; but the memory of it made many a man a few years later scorn to follow, against the sovereign who had given him his land, the coast-country politicians from whom he felt he had suffered far greater wrongs than any imposed by Parliament or King.

With the Court Act at last on the statute book, Lieutenant-Governor Bull urged the sending of trained lawyers from England, as he found the salaries of £500 and £300 sterling for the chief justice and the four assistant judges insufficient to secure competent lawyers in South Carolina, though "there are many who are ready to accept the offices." Laymen would not suffice as formerly, as their integrity and common sense could not, when on circuit, lean on the help of books or friends. "As they go in pairs," said Bull, "one will hold criminal and the other civil court. Could not your Lordship find among the attorneys of London gentlemen bred to the law who are arrived at a time of life when the sanguine hopes of rising to eminence or a comfortable share of practice in the profession are extinguished by a very moderate employment therein, who could be prevailed on to accept employment here, where our mild climate would cherish their advancing age, give dignity to their office, and authority to their decisions?" So English lawyers were sent over.

Another result of the Court Act was a pardon for all the Regulators, some of whom, Bull reported, still languished in prison for "illegally though deservedly" punishing criminals. Finally, in November, 1772, were held the province's first courts of common pleas and general sessions ever convened outside of Charles Town. The lawyers and judges,

[5] General McCrady, in describing St. Mark's as extending to the Wateree, overlooks the fact that the law of 1721 creating Prince George Winyaw extends its bounds as far west "as it shall be inhabited by his Majesty's subjects," not to speak of the fact that the Santee was then and later frequently understood to include the Congaree and Saluda.

returning from their first circuit, expressed themselves as amazed at what they had learned of the back-country men, who, they said, with proper advantages would make as fine a population as any on earth.

One of the progressive measures planned shortly before the Revolution was the Assembly's order in 1766 of a survey by Tacitus Gaillard and James Cook for a large map of the province, to be engraved on copper. Four thousand back-country men (half the men of the province, wrote Bull), on the strength of private surveys or those of Gaillard and Cook, planned to ride to the churches, in some cases a hundred and fifty miles distant, and vote in the election of October, 1768. Much confusion and alarm accompanied their effort, but Moses Kirkland was the only back-countryman elected. John C. Calhoun relates that his father, rifle in hand, led his armed followers almost across the province and was by them elected to the Assembly in 1769. Benjamin Farrar, elected in 1772, was the third back-country member.[6]

[6] The eastern half of Gaillard's and Cook's map of South Carolina is in the archives of the South Carolina Historical Society, hand-drawn and colored on cloth seven feet eight inches from north to south. It is dated February, 1770. It was engraved and printed in London in 1773. Very rare. A copy is in the Library of Congress. Gaillard's and Cook's work is evidently largely the basis of the handsome map of the Carolinas "by Henry Mouzon and others" published in London in 1775.

CHAPTER XXV

RESISTING THE STAMP ACT AND IMPORT TAXES, 1765-1771

The South Carolina Commons, during practically the whole royal period, as during the Proprietary period, had steadily encroached upon the executive and in lesser degree upon the judiciary. In refusing to permit the Council to amend money bills they had since 1725 disobeyed the express instructions of the King. The Stamp Act presented a more serious question. What would be their reaction to an act of Parliament which they considered transgressed their rights?

Peter Timothy, steady supporter of the American side, filled his *Gazette* with anti-stamp material from the North, and mercilessly exhibited Wells as the steady prerogative supporter for sneering in his *General Gazette* at Massachusetts at "what they call their grievances." In July the Commons, on the invitation of the Massachusetts House of Representatives to send delegates to a Congress in New York on October 7, 1765, elected for that purpose Thomas Lynch, Christopher Gadsden, and John Rutledge, and ordered the Treasurer to advance their expenses.

News of resistance to the northward enabled the more aggressive leaders to add to the popular determination to petition for relief a program of protest by violence. The stamped paper arrived on October 18, 1765, in preparation for the law's taking effect on November 1. Bull first placed the stamps in the warship *Speedwell,* but, fearing that she might be attacked at her wharf, he transferred them to Fort Johnson and increased the garrison, for the people swore to destroy the stamps that night. The fort was not attacked, but for nine days the city was filled with threats, house-searchings, manifestoes, mobs, and vast funeral processions ending in the burial of "American Liberty." The homes and furniture of the stamp officers were considerably damaged. The great merchant Henry Laurens expressed his detestation of such "burglary and robbery" as strongly as he did his condemnation of the Stamp Act, the repeal of which, he said, should be sought through constitutional means. Refusal to use stamps would ruin every man of property, he thought, and mobs would destroy orderly government. He was accordingly suspected of concealing the stamps. The night of October 23 a masked and armed mob at midnight beat upon his door, which he opened to prevent its being burst. They searched the house and sought to force oaths upon Laurens for an hour and a quarter.

All these acts of the populace, said Bull, were evidently animated by some prominent men who stood behind the curtain. He was convinced, he continued, that attempting to execute the law by force would mean bloodshed without accomplishing the purpose. On the 28th the stamp officers were brought from Fort Johnson in a boat flying a "Union flag" (i.e., the British Union Jack) bearing the word "Liberty." Before a concourse estimated at seven thousand was read their pledge not to act until Parliament had acted on the petition of all America.

No colony, says Bancroft, was more ably represented in the Stamp Act Congress at New York than was South Carolina with Lynch, Gadsden, and Rutledge. Gadsden was largely responsible for placing American liberty on the basis of the colonists' natural rights and rights as Englishmen instead of on charters. The importance of South Carolina's influence is further seen in the fact that two of her delegates were chairmen of two of the three principal committees. One result of the Congress was to open the eyes of an astonished world to the resources of intelligence, legal knowledge, and literary expression existing in the colonies.

The South Carolina delegates on their return met an Assembly which had been chosen under pressure to elect only native Americans fit to save American liberties and lives. A passionate appeal, signed "A Native," upbraided the people for allowing sometimes a single voter to elect a representative. In the coming election, he said, "the Assembly to be chosen may be the men with whom our liberty or lives may rest. Reject all smooth politicians, all narrow-minded men, all timorous, all ambitious men, all of narrow fortunes. Men in public employment ought not to be chosen. Vote only for firm men who stand for the constitutional liberty handed down to us by our fathers." "A Native" was not disappointed, for the election showed the choice of a long line of later revolutionary leaders. On November 29 the Commons adopted by a unanimous vote, save that of William Wragg, the report of their committee headed by Gadsden, stating their duties and rights as British subjects in virtually the language of the resolutions of the Congress, with slight changes expressive of local conditions. "Sincerely attached as we are to his Majesty," ran the resolutions, "we insist that we are entitled to all inherent rights and liberties of his natural born subjects within the Kingdom of Great Britain," and that taxes may be imposed only by the Assembly of this province.

The *Gazette* appeared as usual on plain paper with the words across the top, "No Stamped Paper to be had." "Though [their interest] is greatly affected by it," wrote Lieutenant-Governor Bull to the Lords of Trade, "that inconvenience is submitted to however with great perseverance and constancy. The courts of common law, admiralty and ecclesiastical jurisdiction are all silent; no grants of land are passed; all the ships remain in the harbor as under an embargo; every transaction requiring stamps is at an end."

The harbor of Charles Town was congested with ships. In December, 1765, Lieutenant-Governor Bull allowed a ship to clear without stamped papers to take food to the troops. The people seized on this and demanded the same privilege for every ship. Bull found it easier to yield when Surveyor General of Customs Randolph reported that on his advice customs officers to the northward, unable to obtain stamps, had cleared vessels without them. Bull consented that captains might leave without formal clearance papers, but with a "permit" for which they paid what stamps would have cost. The surplus of shipping depressed freights to an unheard-of figure. Said Laurens, "Our rice planters have gained a vast ascendant over the British owners and fairly turned the edge of the stamp tax upon them."

The contest now entered the courts. In 1765 court was held by Chief Justice Shinner alone, as the only assistant judge, Robert Pringle, rarely acted. Shinner adjourned court, on November 13, as no stamps were to be had. The lawyers, before the next term time, presented to the Chief Justice a petition to hold court without stamped paper, in which they placed both American and British liberty on very high ground. We "have ever thought," they said, "the principal excellency of the British constitution consists in the subject's not being bound by any law to which he himself doth not consent by his representative. We claim our rights," they continued, "under Magna Charta, the Petition of Right, etc., . . . which were made of force here by Act of our Assembly. . . . We cannot think ourselves bound by the Stamp Act, which annihilates our natural as well as constitutional rights."

They secured from the Lieutenant-Governor the appointment of three assistant judges. When, on the morning of the 3d of March, the Chief Justice walked into court, he was astonished to see Messrs. Rawlins Lowndes, Daniel Doyley, Benjamin Smith, and Robert Pringle take their seats beside him. "I knew how it would go with me," he tells us.

Mr. Bee, attorney for the plaintiff in *Jordan* vs. *Law,* moved for judgment by default, as the defendant had not appeared. The court reserved its opinion and adjourned to April 1, when it declared that, since it was against Magna Charta to deny or delay justice, and since it was impossible to obtain stamps, business should proceed on plain paper despite the Act of Parliament.

Chief Justice Shinner read a contrary opinion, but the assistant judges refused to allow it to be recorded. The Chief Justice held that the court had no power to question the authority of an act of Parliament and that the plea of impossibility to get stamps was specious, since it was impossible simply by the unlawful demonstrations of the people. It was a principle of law, he said, that no man should derive benefit from his own offense.

The impolicy of the Stamp Act led to its speedy abandonment; but with the repeal went the Declaratory Act, to the effect that Parliament could legislate for the colonists in any respect whatever. It was against this as a threat to the liberty of Americans that Gadsden warned the company who called on him for a speech in rejoicing under the great oak, thenceforth called the Liberty Tree, at the repeal of the Stamp Act.

May 5, two days after unofficial news of the repeal, "the mob," said Shinner, declared that they would insult any house not illuminated that night in their grand demonstration. The King's other servants, glad of an excuse, seized upon the news and opened their offices of admiralty, chancery, etc., but not so Shinner. On July 1, 1766, he announced in court that he had received such information as satisfied him of the repeal of the Stamp Act, and that he was ready to proceed to business. The assistant judges refused to allow his paper to be recorded. Similarly the Chief Justice's order rescinding his order of November 13 closing the court was denied entry, since it would have implied the validity of the original order.

Two of the King's servants requiring a word of comment are Chief Justice Shinner and Lieutenant-Governor Bull. The Chief Justice, deprived of his income, the most hated man in the province, his personal safety threatened, was yet unyielding in what he conceived his duty. Persecuted by every means short of actual physical assault, proudly refusing to claim the Stamp Act in any process that his creditors might seek against him, he had nothing but contempt for officers who sought loopholes to escape the popular fury without offending their royal master. It is impossible to judge fairly the conflict that was to divide the British Empire without recognizing the sincerity of those who took the position of the Chief Justice. His stubborn opposition to the popular leaders may have played its part in the petition of the Commons in May, 1767, that sought his removal, urging both his faults of ignorance of the law and lack of judicial dignity. He admitted ignorance of the law of South Carolina, as it could only be obtained in rare pamphlets. On May 11, 1767, by the unanimous advice of Council, he was suspended by Governor Lord Montagu as ignorant and unfit.

To judge the position of Lieutenant-Governor Bull is less easy. His appointment of the assistant judges afforded, as he must have foreseen, the means of resisting the law and can hardly be explained by saying that the bench needed to be filled. His conduct was typical of his long public life—the moderate man, determined on doing his own duty, but singularly free from any aggressive or combative attempt to control the conduct of others.

The Commons House of Assembly in May, 1766, voted £1,000 sterling for a marble statue of William Pitt in gratitude for his exertions for the repeal. The statue, made by Joseph Wilton in England, was erected on July 5, 1770, in the crossing of Broad and Meeting streets. It is thus the first in the United States to a public man. New York erected her statue of Pitt on September 7, 1773.

The Stamp Act profoundly disturbed traditions of loyalty and produced a sensitive state of mind toward future violations of ancient custom. Said Henry Laurens, who was thoroughly loyal to the Crown, "Glad I am upon the whole that the act is repealed, though I know not yet what cause to ascribe it to, nor am I clear about the durability of our present seeming happiness." Instead of this vague uneasiness, there remained in minds like Gadsden's an ineradicable suspicion of future aggressions. Ignorant of the perils it ran, the British government proceeded for the next decade to force one irritation after another upon the colonies before the wounds from the last had healed. This was particularly true of South Carolina. Governor Boone, the violator of the rights of the Commons, had hardly departed when the Stamp Act came. The year after that was repealed came the tea and other taxes. The next year saw bitter public controversy in which Henry Laurens, representing the best element of the mercantile community, exposed the greed, the double-dealing, and the injustice of admiralty courts and even the corruption of customs officers, and the grievances against selfish and narrow laws for exploiting colonial trade. Tea riots and new importation agreements were accompanied in South Carolina by a prolonged quarrel over the right of the people's representatives to dispose of the people's money without the consent of the royal appointees and the Council, and were accompanied, too, by a degeneration in the latter body which supplemented anger with contempt. Even this did not complete the list of grievances. In 1766 a Commons House committee formulated these desires: judges should be appointed during good behavior as in England; the holding of inconsistent offices by the same man should be ended; prohibition of paper money should be removed; permission should be granted to export rice north of Cape Finisterre directly to foreign countries (instead of only to England) as south of that point; they should be allowed to export lumber and provisions directly to any country. The strong light turned upon constitutional and natural rights in seeking for defenses against the Stamp Act served to stimulate resentment at other grievances.

Attitude toward the Laws of Trade.—The acts of trade, restricting the natural course of commerce so as to give England a middleman's profit at the expense of the colonists, and the laws limiting manufactures were a constant source of irritation; but until their more vigorous execution was undertaken after 1763 they were generally accepted as regulations which were legitimate, or at all events inevitable, between the mother country and her colonists; those whose thinking extended further regarded them as proper means for imperial power and unity.

South Carolina enjoyed certain advantages counterbalancing the losses she suffered through these measures. Her indigo received a liberal bounty; her rice was permitted export direct to consumers south of Cape Finisterre; the British navy was recognized as the salvation of a society dependent upon the export of staples; and the whole economic and social system led to an intimacy of personal contact between the wealthy Carolinians and the mother country that fostered strong affections. The phenomenal prosperity enjoyed by her since 1748 left South Carolina satisfied that the benefits received more than counterbalanced the cost. But the new rigor of enforcement soon laid an irritating emphasis upon the disadvantages, and especially the abuses, of the system.

Commercial Restrictions and Unworthy Officials.—In 1765 some naval captains deputized by the Commissioners of Customs announced their intention of seizing decked pettiaugers found at sea with rice on board, although clearly bringing it from plantations to Charles Town. These vessels carried 100 barrels of rice, were decked to protect cargo, and went by sea because the inland passage was too shallow. The rule of 1762 that such boats must clear at a custom house (because in some colonies the enemy were being supplied with food) was a great hardship on them and on those carrying lumber or merchants' shipments within the province. On May 23, 1767, a South Carolina mob beat the crew sent from a sloop of war to inspect a schooner and prevented the performance of the duty prescribed by Parliament. Customs officers were intimidated by threats of suits. Searcher Roupell had to be defended by the Attorney-General, as no lawyer would take any customs officer's case. This endangered the customs service, as the Attorney-General was hampered by being also Judge of Vice-Admiralty.

In 1767 occurred several prosecutions of ships belonging to Henry Laurens, accompanied by acts of personal spite and fraud by officers and injustice by Vice-Admiralty Judge Egerton Leigh that resounded far beyond the province. The Judge's embarrassment at having given advice as a paid attorney which he could not stand by when his client, a customs official, stood before him in court, and his squirmings to secure his fees out of a perfectly upright shipowner, involved the customs administrative and judicial machinery in contempt. In a venomous pamphlet controversary, Leigh was exposed in England and America. "What claimant and owner," wrote Laurens, "conscious of their own integrity, acquitted from all suspicion of fraud, 'trepaned' and 'surprised' by the custom house officers, thus cunningly dismissed with compliments upon their conduct and character, with partial restitution, exorbitant fees, and with effectual bar against recovering satisfaction for damages, could refrain from expressing the highest dissatisfaction at the proceedings and final sentence of a double-minded judge thus greedily running after the error of Balaam, or could forbear complaining as we complain against judge and officers all, who juggler like, trick us and trick one another." "An American," he wrote, "thinks it hard that he should be obliged to purchase almost all the articles he makes use of from Great Britain at an high price, and at the same time be prohibited from carrying his own produce to the most advantageous market; whereby the British merchant is enabled to set his own price, not only on British goods, but also on the produce of America. By this means, the American pays a much greater tax than any person of equal fortune on the other side of the Atlantic, exclusive of the sums he is bound to contribute towards the support of the provincial government under which he resides.

"He esteems it an additional hardship that, super-added to the high price he is obliged to pay for British goods, he should be saddled with an heavy duty payable on many of them; particularly at a time when, for the reason above mentioned, of not being suffered to carry his own produce to the best market, he is not able to pay the first cost of them in Britain."

Further grievances, Laurens continued, were the rapacity and dishonesty sometimes found among the customs officials and the autocratic power of unjust judges of admiralty. These were the sentiments, he concludes, of one "whose heart bleeds at the idea of the separation of the interests of Great Britain and America even in idea, and who would wish to preserve and perpetuate that Empire and the Constitution great and inviolable to latest times." Disgust at unworthy royal officials unquestionably helped to alienate the minds of the colonists from the British government itself. This feeling was intensified when a native American of the highest character, such as the father of Charles C. and Thomas Pinckney, was displaced as Chief Justice to make a place for a low British politician.

Resisting Parliamentary Taxation, Billeting, etc.—This was the state of mind on which was imposed the order for sending to England for trial persons accused of treason; the law requiring a colony to supply quarters and barrack necessities to royal troops; and the Townshend law of 1767 taxing imports of several articles of wide consumption—glass, red and white lead, painters' colors, paper, and tea. Said Townshend, the Americans in condemning an internal tax (the Stamp Act) had acknowledged the legitimacy of external duties. So many of them had; but they had in mind duties for regulating commerce in the general imperial interest, and not tariffs for revenue; and moreover their state of mind had changed.

The billeting act required colonial assemblies to provide quarters, fuel, and lights for British troops quartered within their bounds. This was a departure from the old practice of requesting such provision and amounted to an assertion of the right of Parliament to force taxes upon the colonists or to order colonial assemblies to legislate at command. If this were admitted the colonial assemblies were reduced to administrative boards taking their orders from a supreme legislature of a consolidated empire. To meet this assumption underlying the whole new British policy the more radical colonial leaders, driven from their inconsistent halfway distinctions between the right of Parliament over taxation per se and its right of commercial regulation, ultimately formulated the theory that the Empire consisted of separate units, each with its own legislature, united under a common sovereign. The existence of a separate Irish Parliament and of a separate constitution of Hanover, and the fact that the King, and not Parliament, had chartered the colonies or granted them to favorites as appanages of the Crown, lent plausibility to the contention. As a matter of fact, the relations of Crown and Parliament had long been legally such as to negative the colonial theory. Justice was on the side of the colonists, but the stupid conduct of Parliament was undoubtedly within the law.

New York in 1766 was the first to protest against the billeting act, because the issue first arose in that colony as the military headquarters. The landing of soldiers at Boston soon involved Massachusetts, and the quartering of the 21st Regiment and a company of artillery at Charles Town from the fall of 1768 to September 6, 1769, raised the issue in South Carolina. The Commons declined to meet an expense incurred without their consent whose threat to their liberty, they said, was increased by the unlawful taxes imposed by the Townshend Act.

The refusal of South Carolina was much more pointed than that of New York, which had in part met the demand; but in South Carolina no disciplinary action followed as it did in New York. The Assembly resented with equal decision the determination of the government to revive the ancient statute of Henry VIII for carrying Americans accused of treason to England for trial.

The first official act against the Townshend taxes was that of the Massachusetts lower house on February 11, 1768, inviting the other continental colonies to co-operate in bringing Parliament to rescind an act of such dangerous tendency. Their circular letter and their petition to the King admitted the general supremacy of Parliament and repudiated the charge that Americans aimed at independence. The Virginia House of Burgesses, on receiving the Massachusetts letter, unanimously resolved that only their own assemblies possessed the right of taxing the colonists, and directed their speaker to communicate to each Assembly their proceedings and their opinion that the colonists should unite in firm opposition to every measure injurious to their rights and liberties. Speaker Peter Manigault replied to Speakers Cushing and Randolph that the South Carolina Commons in their last session had ordered the province's Agent to join with the other provincial Agents for securing the repeal of the laws in question, and for all matters concerning general American interests.

The ministry, on hearing of the action of Massachusetts, dispatched an order that it be rescinded, and directed every Governor to warn his Assembly against seditious communications tending toward unwarrantable combinations or inflaming the people against their sovereign, and to dissolve his Assembly instantly on any sign of sympathetic action on any such communication. To this the Massachusetts Assembly replied that their action bore no such character, and by a vote of ninety-two to seventeen refused to rescind.

These events excited the keenest interest in Charles Town, though apparently little disturbing the country parishes. The element that had led the Stamp Act agitation organized for capturing the Assembly on the new issue. On October 1 the mechanics nominated candidates for the October election. The favorites were Gadsden, Thomas Smith, Sr., and Hopkins Price from St. Philip's, and "Broad Street" Thomas Smith and Thomas Savage from St. Michael's. The caucusers, having partaken of a hearty meal provided by one of the candidates, adjourned to the Liberty Tree, where they drank toasts to "the glorious ninety-two anti-rescinders of Massachusetts Bay," etc.

Joined with this was the cause of constitutional liberty, represented by John Wilkes in his defense of some of the most precious rights of freemen, as involved in his prosecution at the instance of George III for criticizing in No. 45 of his newspaper, *The North Briton,* the King's speech at the opening of Parliament in 1763.[1] Charles Town had "The

[1] See pages 243-44 below.

Friends of Liberty Agreeable to the English Constitution, Club No. 45." Forty-five thus became another sacred number. The mechanics decorated the Liberty Tree with forty-five lights and drank toasts from ninety-two glasses to numerous British and American patriots. The election found Gadsden acceptable to both factions, and Henry Laurens and Charles Pinckney won despite the mechanics' opposition.

Thus when the new South Carolina Commons assembed in November, 1768, they were met by the communications from Massachusetts and Virginia, by their speaker's reply, by the continental excitement over "the glorious 92" anti-rescinders of Massachusetts, and by the question of supporting British and American liberty as represented by "the intrepid patriot John Wilkes." They promptly aligned South Carolina with Massachusetts and Virginia. The Governor's reply was a series of prorogations for fourteen months, which began a conflict between the royal and the popular elements in the province that lasted until the Revolution.

Non-Importation, 1768-70.—Lieutenant-Governor Bull wrote on October 18, 1768, that the letter from Boston inviting the merchants of Charles Town to join in refusing to import goods from Great Britain was handed about from man to man in silent neglect, but that there were many who favored it and might be able to carry their point. The most ardent supporters of non-importation practiced it and patronized home manufactures long before the general adoption of any agreement, as witness the total disuse of mourning at the funeral of Mrs. Christopher Gadsden. *The South-Carolina Gazette* of February 2, 1769, warned that unless the revenue acts were speedily repealed the people of this province would strictly adhere to the non-importation resolutions. During June and July a bitter newspaper controversy raged, which clearly revealed many merchants as strongly against an arrangement, destructive to their prosperity, which public opinion sought to force upon them.

The proposed agreement, although to the general population merely an inconvenience, was indeed to many merchants a threat of ruin. An "Association" dated June 28, 1769, was numerously signed, pledging non-importation of any of the products of Great Britain except Negro cloth, duffle blankets, osnaburgs, plantation and workmen's tools, powder, lead, shot, canvas, nails, salt, coals, wool cards, card wire, printed books, and pamphlets, and denouncing as no friend of the province any person neglecting within one month to sign. A meeting of the general population of the town was held on July 22, at which this Association was unanimously adopted, along with these additions: Not to import or sell Negroes from Africa after January 1, 1770, nor from elsewhere after October 1, 1769; goods sent here contrary to these resolutions to be returned or stored; after November 1, 1769, to deal in no European goods except salt and coal; after January to import no wine; to trade with no person who after one month had failed to sign this agreement.

A striking feature of the movement was that the General Committee of Thirty-Nine to enforce the Association was deliberately composed of thirteen planters, thirteen merchants, and thirteen mechanics, as though these classes constituted the three estates of the realm. It is an interesting feature of the democratic movement which we shall see immediately after the Revolution, and again at later dates, running so strongly in Charleston. This prominence of the working class in politics intensified the disgust of young William Henry Drayton, at this time as staunch a supporter as later an opponent of the royal prerogative and the authority of Parliament. No man who could "boast of having received a liberal education," he wrote in *The South-Carolina Gazette,* would consult on public affairs "with men who never were in any way to study, or to advise upon any points, but rules how to cut up a beast in the market to the best advantage, cobble an old shoe in the neatest manner, or to build a necessary house." Gadsden contemptuously answered Drayton as a conceited, inexperienced youth guilty of folly and falsehood. The mechanics also replied, reminding him that his boasted exemption from the necessity of labor arose from his having married a rich heiress rather than from any merit of his own.[2] Neither in manners nor ability did any of these contestants rise to the dignity of their cause.

An exception to the rough and commonplace interminable controversies that filled the press was the article in which William Wragg stated his opposition to the Association and its methods. He and Drayton were among those whose names were circulated in hand-bills containing the names of non-signers. He neither cared nor inquired for the motive of publishing his name, said Wragg, but took it, contrary to their design, "as an honorable certification of me; by representing me as one upon whom neither fear, interest, or the prevailing desire and seeming security of swimming with the stream could operate to do violence to his judgment. . . . Had I no other resources than what a plantation affords, I would endure everything rather than have the freedom of my will or understanding limited or directed by the humors or capricious proscriptions of men not having authority."

Manufacturing received temporary stimulus from non-importation. *The South-Carolina Gazette* of August 24, 1769, says that proof that "we can if necessary manufacture our own commodities is afforded by a gentleman living near one hundred miles in the country who was in town wearing a costume produced on his own place, except his hat,

[2] Drayton later inherited a fortune from his father.

which was made by a neighbor. His shirt was of fine linen, his coat of fustian, his jacket of dimity, his breeches buckskin, and his stockings thread. The flax and cotton grew on his own place and were spun, woven, and knit by his own people; the buckskin was dressed there, and the leather of his shoes was made and tanned on his place."

Less admirable were the tyranny and the inequity as between the weak and the powerful with which the general committee, upheld by frequent mass meetings beneath the Liberty Tree, enforced the Association. A poor widow in trade with her living jeopardized failed to see why she should be deprived of the use of her goods ordered before the Association, while John Rutledge, conspicuous in defending American rights, should be allowed to retain his carriage horses bought in England under similar circumstances, or why wealthy merchants on the committee were permitted to sell certain English goods.

Dissatisfaction increased as hardships pressed on merchants and inconveniences irked customers, who saw that other colonies were breaking over. By the autumn of 1770 it was evident that non-importation was disregarded everywhere else, and South Carolina merchants complained that there was no sense in their holding out in this province alone as a mere point of honor. On December 13, at a large concourse of merchants, planters, and mechanics, it was voted that the non-importation agreement cease, despite the tears of Lynch and the maneuvers of Gadsden and Mackenzie.

Nevertheless non-importation had achieved a large measure of success. In the face of reduction of her exports Britain in 1770 repealed all the duties except that on tea, which the King insisted on retaining "to try the matter with the Americans"; but that was reduced to a point making tea cheaper in America than in England. Under the Liberty Tree, on May 23, 1771, a general meeting of the people resolved, *nemine contradicente,* that no tea should be imported while the duty remained on it, and that no goods on which there was a duty for purposes of raising a revenue should be purchased by the subscribers to the general resolutions while such duties remained.

CHAPTER XXVI

GENERAL CONDITIONS ON THE EVE OF THE REVOLUTION, 1769-1775

South Carolina Aids John Wilkes.—South Carolina became deeply involved in the Wilkes dispute, which stirred the British Empire during the decade preceding the American Revolution—a dispute involving the personal liberty of the subject against the King and Parliament, and in America the degree to which a colonial government should be allowed to manage its own affairs without interference by the central authority. The issue arose as follows: on April 23, 1763, Wilkes attacked in No. 45 of his newspaper, *The North Briton,* the speech from the throne. George III determined to punish him for criminal libel. He was arrested on an illegal general warrant not containing his name, and during the next ten years was subjected to protracted violation of his lawful rights in the government's attempt to crush anyone who dared so boldly to oppose the King. Despite his low character, Wilkes thus stood as the individual who must be upheld in order to preserve the liberty of the press, protection against unlawful arrest and general warrants, and the right of the people to elect to Parliament any man not legally disqualified.

This was why William Pitt, though despising Wilkes's character, defended his cause, London made him lord mayor, and friends of "the Society for the Support of the Bill of Rights" in England and America contributed £17,000 sterling to free Wilkes from his debts and enable him to carry on his fight. Franklin surmised that, had Wilkes had a good character and George III a bad one, the politician might have pushed the monarch from the throne, so intense was the excitement which raged through ten years over the personal and public rights centering in his contest with the Crown. Those who supported Wilkes believed in the right of the press to criticize the King's speech (which was merely the ministry's declaration of policy), in the right of the people to choose whom they would as their representative, and in the illegality of general search warrants. This dissolute man thus became the symbol of constitutional government and personal liberty. To support Wilkes was therefore considered by the South Carolinians as part of their resistance to arbitrary rule by the same Parliament that had imposed unconstitutional taxes on America. "Bill of Rights Societies" were organized in England and the colonies for raising funds to pay Wilkes's debts, thus defeating the plan of squelching him in debtors' prison, and to defend the constitutional principles involved in his conflict with the Crown. These considerations explain the action of the South Carolina Commons House in ordering the public Treasurer on December 8, 1769, to advance £10,500 currency (£1,500 sterling) to their committee "to remit the same to Great Britain for the support of the just and constitutional rights and liberties of the people of Great Britain and America." It further "Resolved that this House will make provision to reimburse the Public Treasurers the said sum."[1]

Appropriation of Money on the Sole Authority of the Commons.— The King's indignation at the action of the South Carolina Commons can be imagined. The British Attorney-General de Grey, instructed to report on the legality of the Commons' appropriating money by their sole authority, found, of course, that the King's instructions to the Governor, constituting the basis of the provincial Constitution, permitted no such practice, but placed the Commons and Council on an absolute equality in law-making, including the amending and passing of money bills.

Lieutenant-Governor Bull, ordered to report on the same subject, produced a paper of much greater historical significance. He took, of course, the same legal ground as de Grey; but, recognizing that the Constitution was a matter of custom as well as formal law, he traced the growth of the superior power of the Commons over finance. In emergencies, the Governor, Council, and Commons sometimes concurred in an order on the treasury, at the same time resolving to replace the money by the next tax bill. As the Commons absorbed more and more power, their passing alone such orders and resolutions for replacing the money was sometimes allowed to pass *sub silentio,* wrote Bull, on account of the obvious propriety of the purpose. As the Commons broadened the practice, objections by the Council were overborne, with the result of the constant decline of their authority and the fortifying of that of the Commons by successful precedent. Thus, what had been allowed the Commons as an irregularity for the public good came to be retained as a legal right. The Commons based themselves on their historic Constitution and made the rights of the British Commons their model.

On the strength of de Grey's and Bull's reports, the King issued his "Additional Instructions" of April 14, 1770. This denied the claims of the Commons and reaffirmed the co-ordinate authority of the Council in

[1] Wilkes-Barre, Pennsylvania, founded in 1769, honors Wilkes along with Colonel Isaac Barre, the defender in Parliament of American rights.

amending and passing money bills. The Governor and Council were forbidden on pain of instant removal to assent to any tax bill appropriating money for any purpose except for specified services of the King's government in South Carolina or on his direct requisition for his service elsewhere. Nor were the Governor and Council to assent to any tax bill that did not inflict a penalty of treble the amount on any Treasurer in future paying out public money except as above. The treasurers were thus not only left exposed to suit, as existing law provided, for the £10,500 currency unless the Commons should succeed in replacing it, but were threatened with severer penalties in future.

The Council had not waited for the Additional Instructions to check the Commons; for this last instance of aggression by the latter could not be suffered if the Council were to retain the reality of legislative authority. On April 5 they returned the tax bill to the Commons with the message that they were surprised at the provision for reimbursing the treasurers for the £1,500 sterling sent to England, which they considered neither "honorable, fit, or decent." All moneys are granted, they said, for the King's service; but this "tacitly affronts his Majesty's government. We do not wish to raise contests as to the constitutional rights of the houses," they continued, "or our rights to amend money bills, but merely intimate that if the bill retains this item it will likely fail of our assent. We cannot let the affair pass, as it would result that our legislative power would finally be interpreted away, according to the ingenious distinction of a Governor many years ago."[2]

The severity of the reply of the Commons, and the fact that it was approved by men of the standing of Lynch, Lowndes, Gadsden, Laurens, Mackenzie, and C. C. Pinckney, indicate the extent of the breach between the royal and popular elements. The resolutions they prepared accused the Council of falsification and denied their being an upper house. The contention of the Council that it should control money bills was, they continued, a "seditious doctrine . . . for the interposition of some power to raise money upon the inhabitants of this province other than their own representatives." The defense of the constitutional liberty of the people of Britain and America was a proper, and not a disloyal, purpose.

The deadlock dragged on year after year with legislation at a standstill. Governor Lord Montagu wrote home that conditions were most alarming; that the Commons had made three innovations that would revolutionize the "very nature of the constitution": they had for three years maintained their sole right over the public money; they had proceeded with business after being summoned by the Governor; their com-

[2] See the incident apparently referred to in Glen's administration, page 167.

mittee of correspondence had continued to act after the Assembly's dissolution, thus making it impossible for him to check agitation hostile to himself or the royal interests. In September, 1773, the Commons unanimously endorsed the position that the Council was merely the Privy Council of the Governor and not a house of the legislature.

After having several times ordered the payment of public money on their sole authority, the Commons, on June 1, 1774, ordered that their clerk issue certificates of indebtedness, to be signed by himself and five members, for the public debts to January 1, 1773, to which time the house had audited the accounts. The certificates included past and future interest until the certificates were paid, which they promised to provide for in the next tax bill. Thus were settled the long-standing debts of the years 1769-72. The action brought an immediate prorogation and a protest from the Council; but the certificates were eagerly accepted even by the members of that body, and by every other Crown officer with the exception of Lieutenant-Governor Bull, to whom over £2,000 sterling was due. His independent fortune enabled him to enjoy the satisfaction of consistent loyalty to the Crown.

On August 2, 1774, the Commons called for a loan of £1,500 sterling to pay the expenses of their delegates to the Continental Congress. The dispute over the control of money solely by the Commons was merging into the wider question of general American rights. What might otherwise have been the outcome in South Carolina's internal constitutional development can only be surmised.

In February, 1775, the Council finally abandoned their resolution to transact no business with the Commons until the Commons recognized their right to amend money bills. They therefore joined in enacting two laws: one for punishing the counterfeiting of the paper money of other colonies, and one for reviving for one year and until the end of the next session a long list of expiring laws, and for one year only the general duty law. Thus, says John Drayton, "the staff of government was virtually transferred; for at the end of one year complete surrender to the Commons would be unavoidable as the only means of income." These acts, the first passed since March 20, 1771, were the last enacted under the royal government.

The embittered councillors vented their wrath on their fellow-member William Henry Drayton, whose published protest had rallied public opinion against them. As a member of Council, as a pamphleteer under the name of "Freeman," and as a judge in his charges from the bench, Drayton had become one of the most advanced popular leaders. On March 1, 1775, Lieutenant-Governor Bull sadly suspended his nephew subject to action by the King. Drayton improved the incident with his talent for propaganda by urging the people further on the path along which they were hurrying toward open rebellion. Men alert to trespasses upon their rights on both sides of the Atlantic were defending the common heritage of British subjects, whether dwelling in the old home or the new. Even after the conflict had assumed the character of secession and was called the Revolution, thousands of Americans remained who clung to the authority of the King and Parliament. The conflict over the adjustment of the relations of the local to the central government continued until 1865 in America, where it received a decision confirming the tendency toward greater consolidation. Within the British Empire the theory of the absolute centralization of authority in the imperial government was ultimately so modified as to transform the Empire into the British Commonwealth of Nations. In 1776 the tendencies of centralization had gone too far in the Empire for local liberty; in 1861 the tendencies of State rights had gone too far in the United States for national safety.

Agriculture and Commerce.—The South Carolina which was manifesting such understanding of the nature of political liberty, and also the determination to meet at the gates any attack upon it, clearly must have possessed great moral and material resources. Lieutenant-Governor Bull reported on December 5, 1769, that there were about 45,000 white inhabitants (doubtless an underestimate, as the back country was filling rapidly) and over 80,000 Negroes. Charles Town in 1770 contained 5,030 whites and 5,831 Negroes. The land returned for taxation in 1768 was 2,591,762 acres. From January 1 to December 5, 1769, 5,438 slaves were imported and sold for £200,000 sterling. The increasing hemp crop, receiving the provincial bounty, amounted in the year ending November 1, 1769, to 526,131 pounds, almost three-fifths of which was worked up in the province. Good silk and some wine were made. Exports from Charles Town in the same year equaled £402,238 sterling, of which £326,451 were sent to Europe. Of this, all except the £54,594 worth of rice sent to Portugal and the £11,353 worth to Spain went to Great Britain.

Exports included 123,317 barrels of rice, 1,624 barrels of rough rice, 65,751 bushels of corn, 2,754 barrels of flour, 2,170 barrels of pork, 39 barrels of oranges, 100 gallons of orange juice, 7 hogsheads of rum, 6,106 barrels of pitch, 1,646 barrels of tar, 80 barrels of rosin, 4,616 barrels of turpentine, 24 barrels of spirits of turpentine, 229,500 staves, 678,350 feet of timber and lumber, 1,987,000 shingles, 42,800 bricks, 14,470 pounds of beeswax, 116 boxes of candles, 309,570 pounds of indigo, 214,210 pounds of tobacco, 290,095 pounds of hemp, 1,014 pounds of raw silk, 183,221 deerskins, and 269 horses. The prosperity of the twenty years just before the Revolution, says a student of Charleston architecture, is exemplified in the numerous fine houses of the period, as, for instance, the Brewton-Alston-Pringle mansion.

Commerce, when unable to utilize watercourses, suffered from execrable roads. Inhabitants of the Ridge, "Saludy," Stevens Creek, Long Canes, Ninety Six, Raburn's Creek, Little River, Bush River, and the western parts of the province prayed the Assembly in 1775 to make the Edisto navigable, as the road to Charles Town was almost impassable.

Between 1765 and '76 a number of inventions were made, some of them rewarded by Assembly bounties, for preparing rice for marketing, making high-grade potash, and breaking hemp. In 1769 snuff and tobacco were being manufactured almost as well as in England, and South Carolina silk, apparently carried through the stage of winding the fibre, was selling in London in small quantities. Silk raising, Bull wrote, languished because labor was so dear that planters were obliged to confine it to the most profitable enterprises. Shortly before 1771 "sea coal" (i.e., brought by sea) had become common in Charles Town. Mineral springs had been found in the back country, though the low-country men, complained Rev. Charles Woodmason, refused to give up going north for their health in summer instead of breathing the pure air of our Appalachian Mountains. The Charles Town Chamber of Commerce was organized in 1773 and reorganized in 1784. On October 22, 1771, gold and silver in the public treasury amounted to £61,269 currency (1/7 the value of sterling), consisting mainly of Spanish doubloons (£27,984) and English guineas (£13,641).

The easygoing way of the Treasurer, mingling his own and the public's money, embarrassed the finances at the death of Jacob Motte in 1770 as it had at the death of Alexander Parris in 1736. In Motte's advanced age his office fell into confusion. His estate owed the public a large sum, which the colonial records at their close showed was being paid.

Political, Religious, Social, Educational.—On November 30, 1770, Lieutenant-Governor Bull sent Lord Hillsborough by command an elaborate description of the province. There should be eighteen or twenty new parishes in the back country, he said. "There are about five thousand men living westward thereof beyond a moral possibility of being represented in Assembly while elections are made at the parish church." There were nearly thirty lawyers, though five or six carried the bulk of the business. Several earned from £1,000 to £1,200 sterling annually.

"Literature is but in its infancy here," he continued. "We have not one good grammar school, though foundations for several in our neighboring parishes. All our gentlemen, who have anything of a learned education, have acquired it in England, and it is to be lamented they are not more numerous. The expense, the distance from parents, the danger to morals and health, are various objections against sending children to England. Though there are many gentlemen well acquainted with such branches of knowledge as can be derived from the English language. We have a provincial free school, the master and usher whereof are paid by the public, but their salaries being established in the early age of the province, are insufficient to engage and retain fit men. The masters when tolerably well qualified have frequently quitted the laborious task of teaching boys, for the more easy office of preaching in some country parish. It is proposed by increasing the salary and building a convenient house for boarders to put the master above the seductions of any ecclesiastical benefice here, and to invite able men, perhaps ushers from some of the great schools in England." The Charles Town Library Society was accumulating funds by which they hoped ultimately to employ professors of arts and sciences. Their collection of books was nearly two thousand. Teachers there were of mathematics, fencing, French, drawing, dancing, music, and needlework.

General McCrady collected from the *Gazette* from 1733 to 1774 over 412 advertisements relating to schools and schoolmasters in South Carolina, proving that there were in the province during that period almost two hundred tutors, schoolmasters, or schoolmistresses. Moreover, there was a wide variety of subjects taught, of both a practical and a cultural character. This evidence may be compared with the testimony of Lieutenant-Governor Bull, who through a long life had observed the actual conditions of education.

South Carolinians contributed liberally for the founding of Princeton in the 1740's and of Brown in the 1760's; they also contributed to what is now the University of Pennsylvania. In 1764 the South Carolina Commons ordered a bill and appointed a committee for devising a college. A writer in 1765 surmised that in thirty years £50,000 sterling had been sent abroad for the education of South Carolina youth, and that £2,000 annually was then going.

On January 29, 1770, Lieutenant-Governor Bull sent the Commons a message devoted entirely to education. He recommended that the free school be put on a better basis, that a college be created, and that schools be established at Waxhaws, Camden, Broad River, Ninety Six, New Bordeaux, Congarees, or any other place needed for most general use. The Commons committee supported these recommendations and suggested that the master of each of the eight schools they proposed (substituting Enoree for Broad River and adding Orangeburg and

Cheraws) should be required to teach twelve (and later twenty) pupils free. A draft to these effects, apparently in the hand of John Rutledge, the chairman, still exists. Benjamin Smith, who died about this time, left £500 sterling for a college, and John Mackenzie (educated at Cambridge), who died May 30, 1771, bequeathed £7,000 currency and his library.[3]

The spirit of self-sufficiency of the non-importation Association stimulated the movement, but the Wilkes fund deadlock checked all legislative action, and the Revolution necessitated postponement.

Population, Lands, etc.—To return to Bull's general account: 75,178 slaves and 2,678,454 acres of land were returned for taxation, although several hundred thousand acres more had been granted. Many officials, he said, served without pay—a fine example of public spirit which, however, made it difficult to call them to account for neglect of duty. The Commons disdained to accept pay, although those of Virginia and North Carolina received a per diem.

The South Carolina of 1769 thus described was clearly a vigorous, alert, wholesome community; one sufficiently fortified economically to defend its rights with confident strength, but not sufficiently sunk into luxury to fear to stake its fortunes on defending its liberties lest it might lose the enjoyment of material comfort. The province was loyally attached to the British Crown. It recognized the disadvantages imposed upon its commerce and industry by the laws of navigation and trade, but it frankly acknowledged the advantages derived from the protection and assistance of the great empire enlisting its affection and pride. The planters and merchants of the coast country had enjoyed for a generation extraordinary prosperity, and the hardy farmers of the back country were laying the foundation for a satisfactory personal and political self-sufficiency. Upon this diverse community was about to come a test which it could not with self-respect avoid.

[3] The statement regarding Smith is correct, though treated as an error in the errata of my *History of South Carolina,* III, 509. The bequest was in a codicil.

CHAPTER XXVII

EMERGENCE OF THE EXTRA-LEGAL ORGANS OF REVOLUTION, 1773-1775

Resisting the Tea Tax.—When Parliament yielded to the demand for the repeal of Townshend duties, George III insisted on retaining the tax on tea; for he was determined "to try the matter with the Americans." An additional circumstance was the fact that the difficulties of the East India Company were highly alarming to the numerous stockholders of the corporation prominent in British social and political life. To save the company by increasing its trade with America would thus serve those influential private interests and at the same time afford a means of vindicating the right of the British government to tax the colonies. The Company was freed from certain burdens in England and was relieved of a duty there on tea sent thence to the colonies; and the duty on tea thus imported into the colonies, to be paid in America, was placed at only three pence a pound. Hence tea was offered cheaper in the colonies than in England, and even cheaper than the Dutch smuggled tea.

Two hundred and fifty-seven chests, consigned by the East India Company to prominent merchants to be sold on commission, arrived at Charles Town on December 1, 1773. Smaller quantities had already been imported undisturbed in general cargo, but this shipment specifically raised the issue. Handbills called for a mass meeting, on Friday the 3d, of all South Carolinians, especially landowners, in the great hall over the Exchange. This meeting is of great importance, for from it, in a sense, has lineally descended the government of South Carolina. The legislature of the State had its legal predecessor, the colonial Assembly, but it actually developed without a break from this mass meeting of December 3, 1773. The meeting resolved not to import or buy any tea taxed for raising a revenue in America. The consignees resigned amid applause. Christopher Gadsden was appointed chairman of a committee to secure signatures all over the province not to import or use tea, and an agreement was put into circulation threatening boycott of non-signers.

Conservatives contended that this hasty act did not represent the true sense of the meeting. Accordingly another was called for the 17th, which revealed strong division of opinion. Many of the opponents of British taxation held that the East India Company was a mere private merchant and should no more be discriminated against than other traders had been who had imported tea since the breakdown of non-importation and had even carted tea bought from private merchants in England past the public meeting. "Let us await word of the action in the North," they said, "where the people have been more stirred by oppressive measures."

Despite these counsels, the meeting resolved "That the tea ought not to be landed, received, or vended in this colony," nor should any be imported while the law imposing this unconstitutional tax remained unrepealed. Notice was given of business to be discussed at the next general meeting, which was thus growing into a continuous institution.

The law directed that if after twenty days no consignee received the goods, they should be landed and stored by the customs officers. Anonymous letters threatened the burning of the wharf and of the tea ship *London* if she were not removed to the middle of the river, but no violence occurred. Early December 22, to circumvent the committee, who did not expect such action until noon, the officers unloaded the tea and stored it in the basement of the Exchange, rented for this purpose, from which it emerged three years later to be sold by the South Carolina government to support the liberties the tea had been intended to violate. On June 26 more tea arrived and was similarly stored. Captain Maitland was pursued by a mob of several hundred men who entered his ship from one side as he escaped to a man-of-war on the other. His ship was removed from the wharf the next morning for fear of its being burned. Another lot arriving in July was also stored. That arriving November 1 was emptied into the water, as was a small quantity in Georgetown. A quantity smuggled in was shipped away November 3 to emphasize the principle.

The mass meeting for January 7, 1774, was sparsely attended and was adjourned to the 20th, when it took a step of importance in making its organization permanent by appointing a large committee with power to fill its own vacancies which was to digest business for the "General Meeting" which it was authorized at any time to call. The first "General Meeting" summoned by the standing committee was for March 3 (postponed to the 16th), when all the citizens of the province were invited to assemble at the Liberty Tree. The General Committee was by this General Meeting authorized to enforce non-importation, boycotting, or other resolutions of the General Meeting.

The anti-tea agitation had up to this time been mainly the work of the leaders of the mechanics and small merchants and of those planters who were infected with the growing ideas of American democratic control. The great importing merchants, naturally conservative, were uneasy as to possible losses on tea they already had on hand or had ordered.

We may here carry the narrative of the tea to its conclusion. It lay in the storehouse for almost three years, when the President of South Carolina wrote to the State's delegation in the Continental Congress to secure permission to sell it for the benefit of the State. But a strong opinion developed in Congress that it should be sold for the benefit of Americans whose property had been confiscated in England. The South Carolina delegation thereupon secured permission to withdraw the question and wrote advising the State authorities to sell the tea at once. The legislature accordingly ordered its sale for the benefit of the State. The advertisement by the commissioners announced the sale for October 14, 1776.

To return to 1774: In the early summer there arrived news that rallied new adherents to the policy of resistance. The account of the act of Parliament closing the port of Boston in punishment for the destruction of the tea, the call of the Bostonians for a complete stoppage of commerce with Great Britain, and other Northern resolutions, caused a General Meeting of the Charlestonians. So solemn was the occasion that at the order of this meeting the General Committee called a General Meeting for July 6 of representatives to be elected throughout the province.

Letters to the back country urged resistance and recommended a meeting of the landholders of the parish or region to elect representatives for the General Meeting of July 6. Some districts elected ten delegates, others fewer. The meeting was thus the first in which back-country men participated in the government, except that Patrick Calhoun had been elected to the Commons when his supporters marched (needlessly armed) 150 miles to the polls in 1769, and Moses Kirkland had been elected in 1768 and Benjamin Farrar in 1772. Meanwhile subscriptions for the relief of Boston were taken, which exceeded in amount those from any other province, not excepting Massachusetts.

The fifth or sixth General Meeting since the arrival of the tea in December, in session July 6, 7, and 8, 1774, marked a new departure. Its 104 delegates represented every region except Granville County (between the Combahee and the Savannah) and St. John's Colleton and Christ Church parishes. But the representative character of the meeting was seriously impaired at the outset by allowing all who might attend to vote.

The meeting rapidly adopted resolutions condemning the current violations of American rights, and then considered the two questions: whether to adopt the Boston resolution of commercial non-intercourse with Britain; and whether to send delegates to a general congress. On the latter all were resolved; but on commercial non-intercourse there was such sharp division that the question was left undecided. The radicals, however, were victorious in carrying the motion that the delegates should have unlimited power to concert legal measures for the redress of grievances. The argument of Rawlins Lowndes against this is worth noting, for, says Drayton, it represented the existing views in South Carolina and illustrates how great was the change they were shortly to undergo. "Our delegates should be strictly limited," argued Lowndes, for the Northern colonies denied the entire legislative authority of Parliament, a position which South Carolina rejected, but to which she would be bound if a delegation of unlimited powers were outvoted on the question.

The conflict therefore centered on the election of delegates, July 7. The Chamber of Commerce had resolved not to accede to commercial non-intercourse. They therefore assembled their clerks and marched to the ballot box in a body to support a designated conservative ticket. The radicals thereupon rushed in men and secured the election of Thomas Lynch, Christopher Gadsden, and Edward Rutledge, though permitting the election of Henry Middleton and John Rutledge of the merchants' ticket. The conservatives thus won a partial victory on instructions, but lost a majority of the delegation. This divided victory, or absence of victory, was significant of the division of opinion which was to make South Carolina the most stubbornly contested region of the Revolution.

On July 8 the meeting elected a General Committee of ninety-nine with virtually unlimited powers, to correspond with other provinces and do anything necessary for carrying into effect the orders of the General Meeting. The Meeting chose, to represent the city, fifteen merchants and fifteen mechanics, and to represent the rest of the province, sixty-nine planters. This General Committee immediately elected Colonel Charles Pinckney (father of the later Governor Charles Pinckney) chairman, and in very large measure proceeded to act as though it constituted the government of the province. The Commons ratified the action of the meeting of July 6 through 8 and provided for the expenses of the delegates to the Continental Congress.

The First Continental and the First Provincial Congress.—On September 5, 1774, met the first Continental Congress, including representatives from all the colonies except Georgia. In order to concentrate blame on the administration of George III, they resolved, in deference to the view of Virginia, to confine their protests to grievances arising since 1763.

The injustice of the acts of navigation and trade was thus passed over, though South Carolina urged putting this forward. The Virginia plan was better strategy, in view of the fact that such a late complaint against an ancient system would have lacked the impressiveness of a protest against unaccustomed wrongs unfortified by acquiescence. The old fiction of a good King misled by bad ministers was maintained. Besides addresses to the British King and people and the people of Quebec, the Congress adopted an Association pledging the colonies to commercial non-intercourse with Great Britain, Ireland, and the British West Indies, and to abstention from use of their products and of East Indian tea. But rice might be exported to Europe. No slaves would be imported. Non-importation should take effect December 1, 1774, and, unless grievances were redressed, non-exportation September 10, 1775. The laws which must be repealed were stated to be the following: those imposing duties on tea, etc.; those extending the powers of admiralty courts, including substituting the authority of the judge for that of a jury; those that required transporting Americans to England for trial for certain offenses; the Boston Port Act; the act altering the charter of Massachusetts; the act for trying out of the colony persons prosecuted for acts committed in enforcing certain British laws; and the Quebec Act, which, though conciliatory toward the rights and customs of the new French subjects, alarmed the Protestant Americans by making Catholicism the state religion of that vast region.

Events had assumed a gravity which demanded the judgment of a wider representation of the people and called for measures calculated to draw support of the back country to a movement which so far had been the work of the radical party of the coast, and mainly of the city itself. Accordingly the General Committee issued its call for "A General Provincial Committee" for January 11, 1775, to be composed of delegates from every quarter, to be elected by freeholders and payers of taxes of 20 shillings currency (about 65 cents). The term "General Provincial Committee" distinguished it as a representative body of definite membership from a "General Meeting" of inhabitants.

The General Committee settled the question of apportionment of delegates as follows: Colonel Charles Pinckney proposed thirty for the city (apparently on the basis that it had thirty in the committee), and that the country should take as many as they pleased. Country members suggested that their parishes would not send over six, which number was accordingly adopted for each parish outside of Charles Town, the two parishes of which (St. Philip's and St. Michael's) were given unitedly thirty. Thus originated the custom, enduring until after the War of Secession, of treating the city as a political unit. After that time it was merged into the county, which it dominated, though the county was allowed two senators through 1895. Saxe-Gotha (approximately the later Lexington) was given six representatives, like a parish, and the rest of the back country (including the recently created St. Mark's of enormous dimensions, which was thus disregarded) was divided into four large districts with ten members each. The vast importance which events were to give the apportionment of this supposedly temporary expedient was unanticipated. The 184 delegates thus to be elected were, the call explained, to consider the action of the Continental Congress, to carry its recommendations into effect, to elect delegates to another congress to meet in May, 1775, to elect a new General Committee, and to take such other action as they deemed necessary.

The writs for the election were sent to "influential gentlemen," who were of course favorable to the cause, and the members constituted consequently a rally of the radical faction.

Sectional Differences over Non-Exportation.—The body called as a "General Provincial Committee" met January 11, 1775, and declared itself the Provincial Congress. The back country, including the new St. Mark's parish, had 46 delegates, though it probably possessed the great majority of the white population. The Revolution had at least begun the representation for the section which was gradually, through long and bitter contests, to attain an approximate equality. About forty out of a total membership of forty-eight of the Commons House of Assembly were members.

The clause of the Association adopted in Philadelphia that permitted the exportation of rice so offended producers of indigo and other commodities as to threaten a revulsion of the interior, which considered itself sacrificed to the interests of the rice planters. Gadsden disclaimed responsibility for the exception and explained that the proposal to permit the exportation of rice and indigo had greatly shocked the Continental Congress, but that, in order to secure a united America, the exception of rice was at last allowed. In his view, the exception should be abolished.

John Rutledge defended his having secured the exception of rice. The Northern colonies, he explained, insisted on continuing to send to the continent of Europe their flour and fish, by which their debts to England would, as usual, be indirectly paid. Thus their usual export business would be little affected. The affair seemed to him, he said, like a commercial scheme among the flour colonies to find a better vent for their flour through the British Channel, by preventing, if possible, any rice from being sent to these markets; and that, for his part, he would never consent to the South's becoming dupes to the North and yielding to their unreasonable expectations. Our delegates, he said, considered that the rice planters, having had their interests protected, should compensate the indigo planters.

There was indeed strong ground for Rutledge's insistence on the disproportionate burden which the policy of non-exportation would impose upon the South, and especially upon South Carolina; for these were the colonies having large exports to Great Britain. Exports from South Carolina to Great Britain (including those sent from North Carolina through South Carolina ports) for years before the Revolution far exceeded the combined exports to Great Britain of all the colonies north of Maryland, and in 1768 and 1769 they exceeded those of Virginia and Maryland combined. The coastal region of South Carolina was so dependent upon the exportation of rice that its cessation would mean ruin.

It was on these grounds that the Rutledges, the Lynches, and Drayton defended the exception in favor of rice. After angry demands for justice to other crops it was voted that one-third of the rice brought to port was to be delivered to commissioners, who were to buy with it one-third the produce of other kinds at prices fixed by the resolutions. The course of events prevented the plan's being tried, but, says John Drayton, its adoption secured the harmony so essential to the Revolutionary movement. The delegation to the First Continental Congress was endorsed by its election to the Second.

Seizing the Arms and Powder.—The Provincial Congress adjourned on January 17, 1775, and the General Committee organized the next day. In March arose the puzzling case of furniture and horses that had been used in England by a returning family. By the chairman's casting vote they were declared not to be "goods" or "merchandise" in the sense of the Association. The cry arose that "the Association is broken," and a crowd, invading the committee meeting, converted it into a tumult. The mob threatened to kill the horses if they were landed. The committee sought the support of the military companies, but most of the militia refused to serve. The committee, in the presence of a large throng, heard its action argued, and by 35 to 34 reversed its order admitting the horses—the first instance of the leaders' being overridden by the mob.

April 14, 1775, news arrived that Parliament had acceded to the King's request for increased forces to execute the laws against which the Congress had protested. Great offense was roused by the announcement that the colonies must seek redress individually. In the existing state of American opinion the British plans meant war. The General Committee at once ordered the seizure of the public arms and munitions. For their conception of their rights within the empire they would fight, as Englishmen had often fought before. On the night of April 21 the Secret Committee of five, provided for by the Provincial Congress and headed by William Henry Drayton, seized, with the assistance of some of the most eminent citizens, the public powder in the Hobcaw and "Neck" magazines and the arms in the State House. No disguises were used, and night was chosen merely to avoid mortifying the Lieutenant-Governor. That beloved gentleman informed the Commons House of Assembly of the "very extraordinary and alarming" disappearance of about 800 guns, 200 cutlasses, 1,600 pounds of powder, and some minor stores. The Commons solemnly informed him that all the inquiry they "had made" failed to reveal those removing the arms and powder, "but [we] think there is a reason to suppose that some of the inhabitants of this colony may have been induced to take so extraordinary and uncommon a step in consequence of the late alarming accounts from Great Britain."

Moderates and Progressives.—News of the battle of Lexington reached Charles Town on May 8.[1] The General Committee summoned the Provincial Congress for June 1. A letter arriving on May 3 from London from Arthur Lee, that mind ready, almost to the point of aberration, to believe any evil of an opponent, charged that the British contemplated raising an Indian war and a servile insurrection against the colonists. "This most infernal falsehood" spurred the revolutionists, from mob to Provincial Congress. That body in its second session now assumed extensive governmental powers. It ordered 1,500 special troops raised; formed an Association to "go forth and be ready to sacrifice our lives and fortunes against every foe" in defense of the liberty outraged "in the bloody scene on the 19th of April last, near Boston"; ordered all non-signers to be dealt with "according to sound policy"; authorized the issue of £1,000,000 paper currency; created a Council of Safety, to consist of thirteen members and the members of Congress when present, of almost unlimited executive authority; and committed legislative authority during the adjournment of the Congress to the General Committee. Having ordered its own life to be terminated in favor of a second Provincial Congress to meet December 1 unless sooner summoned, the First Provincial Congress adjourned.

The Association thus adopted, pledging men to war against their sovereign and to treat non-signers as enemies, was a grueling test for

[1] Both the newspapers and Drayton's *Revolution* give May 8 for the news by sea, though the latter's extensive notice of the efficiency of the land courier service, arriving May 11, has led some writers to mistake the latter as the date of the first news. Ramsay (*Revolution of South Carolina,* I, 30) makes the powder-seizing the result of the arrival of the news, thus having a horse or ship fly from Massachusetts in a day and a half.

the conservative friends of liberty. There were in truth men of the highest character and patriotism who either condemned the course taken to right American wrongs or considered that the movement was going so far as to threaten greater evils than it sought to remedy. In addition, as General McCrady remarks, the back-countrymen were largely indifferent, and many of them, such as the Germans and the recent French arrivals in the present McCormick County, were busy improving the lands they had received in the King's name. The relations of divided factions were indeed ominous for the future.

Raising Provincial Troops.—On June 18, 1775, Lord William Campbell, the new Governor, landed in Charles Town. Although he was married to Sarah, the daughter of Ralph Izard, of one of the most distinguished South Carolina families, instead of being greeted by the welcoming boom of cannon and joyous shouts, he was received almost in silence. On the 20th, hesitating between legality and expediency, he received a deputation of the Provincial Congress, who presented a formal address praying his interposition to disabuse the King's mind of the slanders against his loyal subjects, falsely accused of lust for independence.

The new Governor met the Assembly on July 10 and entreated them "as the only legal representatives of the people of this province—the only constitutional guardians of its welfare—to reflect that the happiness or misery of generations yet unborn will depend on your determinations." The Commons replied with an elevation and dignity comparable with the best state papers of the period so notable for these qualities:

"We want words to give an idea of our feelings at your Excellency's expression, *'If there are any grievances that we apprehend the people of this province labour under'*; as if you doubted their existence. The world resounds with the catalogue of them. We should have esteemed it an high obligation if your Excellency had pointed out to us what effectual mode for the redress of those grievances could have been pursued, or what steps we have omitted which we ought to have taken in order to avert the inevitable ruin of this once flourishing colony. Every pacific measure which human wisdom could devise has been used—the most humble and dutiful petitions to the Throne; petitions to the House of Lords and House of Commons of Great Britain, have been repeatedly presented, and as often treated not only with slight, but with rigour and resentment. We, therefore, with all due deference to your Excellency's judgment, beg leave to observe that the present are the only measures which seem best calculated for our preservation and removal of our intolerable grievances. However, not confiding in them alone, we wait the event, and leave the justice of our cause to the great

Sovereign of the Universe, upon whom the fate of kingdoms and empires depends."

The Commons on July 12 unanimously resolved to make provision for paying the £1,000,000 paper currency to be issued by the Provincial Congress. This was the last action of the Provincial Assembly, which, on August 31, merely ceased to meet.

The regular militia organization of the province, of from ten to fourteen thousand men, was loosely organized territorially into twelve regiments of foot and one of cavalry. Apart from its ineffectiveness for quick action, its own division of sentiment rendered its dependability precarious. It, like everything else, was split, and men were gravitating toward their desperate choices, out of which new organizations would arise. But the Congress by no means contemplated disregarding the militia in favor of entire dependence on the three regiments of regulars which they created and which were known as provincial troops, the basis of the later "Continentals." The militia colonels were ordered to hold a third of each company in readiness for instant service, and many of the militia, without change of organization, served the Revolutionary authorities. This one-third arrangement was practiced extensively in the low country and to some extent in the upper. The raising of the regular troops in and near Charles Town progressed so well that 470 were there recruited in a month.

John Stuart and the Indians.—False rumors that John Stuart, Superintendent of Indian Affairs for the Southern Department, was plotting to bring the savages upon the frontier, stirred intense indignation. With news of Lexington heightening excitement, Stuart fled, late in May, 1775, from his Charles Town sick bed to his Lady's Island plantation and soon thence to Savannah and then to St. Augustine.

The Revolutionists stopped the Indians' regular powder supply in order to serve their own desperate need. This threw both the Cherokees and the Creeks into a dangerous state of mind. To the Indians, long adjusted to the white man's arms, powder and lead were their very foundations of life. Stuart's and Cameron's conduct in this crisis was honorable and humane. In sending sufficient powder to the Creeks for hunting, Stuart wrote them on August 15, 1775, "There is an unhappy dispute between the people of England and the white people of America, which however can not affect you. Nothing is meant by it against you or any other nation of red people, but to decide a dispute amongst the white people themselves." He wrote the Cherokees to the same effect and reproved them for having aided the Shawnees (old enemies of the English colonists) in attacking some Virginians. Cameron, on November 9, 1775, expressed to Stuart his horror of the idea of an Indian war, "though my duty to my sovereign exceeds all other considerations."

We must return now to June, 1775. The South Carolina Secret Committee learned that several tons of powder were expected at Savannah which Stuart and Governor Wright intended to seize for supplying the Indians, thus holding their allegiance and serving the King's cause. The committee therefore secretly commissioned Captains John Barnwell and John Joyner to seize the powder. They sailed with forty men for the mouth of the Savannah. An armed schooner to aid them was commissioned by the Georgia Congress. The powder ship was captured, and the 7,000 pounds destined for South Carolina and St. Augustine merchants were appropriated for South Carolina, and the 9,000 for Georgia merchants, for Georgia.

The importance of this capture was emphasized by news of the battle of Bunker Hill and a request from the Continental Congress for powder while Barnwell and Joyner's enterprise was in progress. The South Carolina Council of Safety obtained a loan of 5,000 pounds from Georgia and dispatched it to Philadelphia. It was used in invading Canada and conducting the siege of Boston.

In July, 1775, the Secret Committee dispatched Clement Lampriere to capture powder expected from London at St. Augustine. Boarding the armed brigantine outside the harbor he secured 11,900 pounds, thus increasing South Carolina's supply to 21,974 pounds.

Non-importation from Britain and the contemporary disregard for British law stimulated a brisk smuggling trade carried on openly with the French, Spanish, and Dutch West Indies. Military stores constituted part of the goods received.

Violence Against Ordered Freedom.—In June (apparently), 1775, occurred the first tarring and feathering by the South Carolina Revolutionists. James Dealy and Laughlin Martin, for damning the Committee of Correspondence and rejoicing (it was charged) that Catholics, Negroes, and Indians were to be armed, were by the Secret Committee stripped, tarred and feathered, carted about the streets, and banished, though Martin, on expressing contrition, was allowed to remain. In August the gunner at Fort Johnson was tarred and feathered and carted ten or twelve times around the town (apparently by mere mob motion) and exhibited before the doors of the most obnoxious royal officers. Dr. Milligen of the garrison fled to avoid the same fate.

These incidents fell in with and supplemented the excitement caused by Arthur Lee's tale that the ministry was plotting massacre by slaves and Indians. Some Negroes' parrot-like shouting, "Liberty," stirred such dread that a number were imprisoned. Some, says Lord Campbell, were terrified into accusing themselves and others did so in order to escape punishment. Jerry, a free Negro pilot worth £1,000 sterling and owning several slave fishermen, was sentenced to be hanged and then burned. Lord Campbell, straining every effort to save his life, was warned that if he interfered he would raise a fire the waters of the Cooper could not extinguish and would find the Negro hanged at his door. Jerry was hanged on August 18 on the testimony that he had said that, if British warships came, he would pilot them across the bar.

Henry Laurens, president of the Provincial Congress and of the Council of Safety, considered that tar and feathers did the cause of liberty more harm than good and deprecated the excitement against the Negroes. He stood as the best single representative of the conservative friends of liberty, ready, though with grief, to break the strongest ties for its preservation, but not ready, as were the aggressive young Drayton and Arthur Middleton, to visit violence upon sincere opponents or, except under extremest necessity, to precipitate civil war. The Council of Safety itself represented the divided state of opinion in the province. Standing with Drayton and Middleton for aggressive measures were Colonel Charles Pinckney, suspected, however, of veering toward moderation, and Thomas Ferguson. For moderate measures could usually be counted Rawlins Lowndes, James Parsons, Miles Brewton, Thomas Heyward, Jr., and Thomas Bee, while John Huger, Benjamin Elliott, and William Williamson acted with one or the other on the merits of the question. As president of the Council of Safety, Henry Laurens held a sort of balance, though generally inclining toward the moderates. Though the party of action had made the daring strokes we have noticed, the general population presented even more extremely these divisions, to the consideration of which we must now turn our attention.

CHAPTER XXVIII

WAR IN THE BACK COUNTRY, 1775

Suppressing Anti-Revolutionists in Charles Town.—Slight opposition was met in the low country to enforcing the Association. William Wragg, one of the most estimable South Carolinians, met harsh treatment. He refused to rebel against the King who had honored him with the chief-justiceship (though he had declined the appointment); "and in addition," he said, "he had a right to exercise his own judgment in the premises, although in doing so his sentiments might differ from the general voice." He was banished to his plantation in the unhealthiest season of the year and cut off from his friends and from his wife, soon again to become a mother. "Finally leaving the colony with his son for England, he was shipwrecked and drowned, and his son barely escaped with his life. Some other persons of respectability and fortune would not take the oath; and like Mr. Wragg, went away, leaving their fortunes to the hazards of a civil war, and their claims for indemnity to the liberality of a sovereign whose allegiance they preferred."[1]

The attempts to sequester the estates of the non-jurors failed, but they were published as public enemies, confined to Charles Town, and forbidden all business except obtaining provisions and visiting the public offices. Prudence and kindly feeling combined led to the abandonment of the demand that Lieutenant-Governor Bull be disciplined when he pointed out the unreasonableness of expecting from him any declaration savoring of disloyalty to the sovereign with whom his official relations had been so prolonged and devoted.

Drayton's and Tennent's Back-Country Mission.—Much more serious was the disaffection to the Revolutionary movement in the back country. The mere isolation of these regions prevented their feeling British wrongs as did coast city dwellers or planters in constant contact with the restrictive laws. The deep-seated resentment at the long delay in granting courts and representation, for which the back-country men held the coast-country planters and merchants more responsible than the King, and resentment at the disdain with which the backwoodsmen were often treated, were a poor preface for an invitation to join in war against a King from whom the settlers had recently received greater values in

[1] Drayton, *Memoirs,* I, 315-16.

land than they were now asked to pay in taxes on tea that they rarely used. To these frontiersmen, who had been consistently refused representation in the colonial legislature because the low-country planters and merchants declined to meet the King's requirement of dividing the existing number of representatives with the new parishes, and whose lands were taxed the same amount per acre as the richest rice fields contiguous to market, it seemed rather farcical for the persons who had denied them their rights and taxed them without representation to invite them to make war on account of taxation without representation against the King from whom they had received great benefits. Nor did the tarring and feathering of dissidents and the proscription of honest men for their opinions present the new freedom attractively. There was, to the minds of many, at least as much prospect of liberty on one side as on the other. Whatever liberty the Whigs were clamoring for they had derived from the British government against which they were contending. Taking all this into consideration it would have been strange had there not been a large loyalist faction.

Another dissident element in the interior had never been British and had not yet become American. The Germans of Orangeburg, Saxe-Gotha, and the Dutch Fork, enjoying their new unprecedented freedom and a substantial economic independence under grants of land from the King, could not be expected to resent the foolish acts of their sovereign violating ancient principles of liberty with which they were not familiar. The German George Wagner and the Swiss Felix Long were appointed to enlighten their fellow-Teutons. Their mission was a failure.

Most alarming was the situation among the Scotch-Irish between the Broad and Saluda; for they were men as much accustomed to fight for their political opinions as were the English of the coast, with whom they now differed. When agents of the Council of Safety seized the powder, etc., in Fort Charlotte on the upper Savannah, for instance, Robert and Patrick Cuningham and Major Robinson, with 200 men, recaptured the ammunition and jailed Major Mayson on the charge of having stolen it from the King's fort.

This large body of dissidents from the Revolutionary movement was led by men of energy and influence, some of them of high intelligence and determination. Such were the Cuninghams, who illustrate the virtues as well as the better-known cruelty of the Tories. The family had struggled for religious freedom in Scotland. About 1681 they migrated to Virginia, whence, in January, 1769, Robert and Patrick moved to South Carolina and at once assumed prominence. Robert, at Island Ford on the Saluda, became one of the first magistrates of the new judicial district of Ninety Six, and Patrick became a deputy surveyor. They condemned England's taxing the colonies, but they considered the tyranny of the Revolutionary faction dominating South Carolina more odious. The opponents of the Revolution as truly staked all on their convictions as did its advocates, and their cruelty was often in retaliation for outrages by which the dominant party sought to force conformity on men as sincere as themselves, actuated by a profound love of ordered constitutional liberty, and proud of risking life in loyalty to their oath of allegiance.

Had Lord Campbell gone boldly into the back country to lead the loyalists he might have struck a serious blow at the Revolution in South Carolina. The moderates in the Council of Safety were holding the movement in a feeble posture of defense, which, if continued, would have ended in collapse. The aggressive young aristocrats, Arthur Middleton and W. H. Drayton, and the determined Gadsden (his influence absent on account of service in Philadelphia), depended largely upon the readiness of the party of the mechanics, the successors of the old Liberty Tree faction of Stamp Act and non-importation days, to suppress opposition by violence. Peter Timothy, sleepless watchman over popular rights, who throughout his long career rendered inestimable service through his *South-Carolina Gazette* to the party of liberty, wrote on August 22, 1775, that the merchants and the Charles Town Germans were dissatisfied, and that "in regard to war and peace, I can only tell you the plebeians are still for war, but the noblesse perfectly pacific." It was a situation in which bold leadership on either side would count much. How feeble the Council of Safety had become through divided views was indicated by the impossibility of moving it to active measures for defending Charles Town and its difficulty in agreeing to face the defection in the northwest of the province. However, on July 23 it was determined to send W. H. Drayton and the Congregational minister Rev. William Tennent to explain to the back-country men the causes of the quarrel with England, to settle disputes, "and to enforce the necessity of a general union in order to preserve themselves and their children from slavery."

The commissioners, after complete failure among the Germans of the middle country, passed north into the Scotch-Irish country. In upper Newberry County of today, Drayton was confronted by Patrick Cuningham and Thomas Brown. Brown was a Scottish gentleman of some fortune, settled in Augusta. For ridiculing the Liberty Boys he was tarred and feathered and otherwise misused, all of which failed to reveal to him the superiority of the new American to the old British freedom. Made a British lieutenant-colonel, he many times over avenged his wrongs.

On August 17, at Fletchall's residence on Fairforest, the commissioners found Brown, Cuningham, and Robinson exploiting the old grievances of the back country toward the governing class of the coast. Unless a dozen leaders were seized, wrote Drayton, there would be civil war. Tennent, he wrote, had been successful east of Broad River, and was now in the New Acquisition (the present York) "where they were very hearty in our cause."

On August 23 the commissioners faced a small hostile or indifferent crowd and violent abuse by Kirkland and Brown. About seventy signed the Association; but the election for provincial congressmen was for a second time postponed.

In addition to contradicting, in some important particular, Drayton's report (heretofore generally treated as the sole authority besides Tennent's brief journal), Brown's letter of October 18, 1775, to Lord Campbell is necessary for the complete picture. Tennent and Drayton, says Brown, not meeting with the success which the reports of their partisans had led them to expect, met with a spirited opposition from the inhabitants, whom "we had prepared for these incendiaries." Stung with disappointment and fear of losing their influence with their associates, they resorted to every artifice and deception. The subscriptions to the Association which they sent to Charles Town contained names clearly duplicated. They then hit upon the method of intimidating the non-signers by seeking to arrest their leaders.

Drayton recognized that he was in a position of grave danger to his person, his reputation, and his cause. When advising the arrest of a dozen leaders, on August 21, he assured the Council that the insurrection this would cause could be easily suppressed. The Council of Safety was alarmed lest the hot-headed young man of thirty-two should inaugurate a civil war. But as news came of his boldly meeting one crisis after another, there was nothing to do but back him up or let the whole movement back down. On August 31, by a vote of four to three, with two of the four in danger of reversing themselves, he was sustained.

To return to Drayton's narrative: From the meeting at Ford's he proceeded to the country opposite Augusta and to the Ridge (between Augusta and the present Columbia), while Tennent visited the Long Canes settlement, where he found that most of the inhabitants were for the Association, but were paralyzed for want of ammunition.

Drayton, having driven out Kirkland, proceeded (according to Brown) with his plan of arresting the Anti-Association leaders by seizing nine of the "King's men." From his headquarters at Ninety Six he sent squads who broke open the houses and searched the papers of those opposing the Congress. "Captain Cuningham and I," continued Brown, "then embodied about 2,200 men."

Drayton records regarding these events (to take up his narrative) that, as Cuningham and Brown continued to raise men, he marched for Ninety Six Courthouse with 225 men. To meet an expected night attack September 10 and 11, he ambuscaded Island Ford (corner of present Newberry and Laurens), where the loyalists would cross the Saluda from Colonel Fletchall's district. No attack occurred, but both sides assembled forces, until Fletchall on the north of the Saluda had 1,200 and Drayton on the south 1,000 commanded by Colonel William Thomson and Major Andrew Williamson. On September 13 Drayton sent a proclamation to be read before Fletchall's men disclaiming all intention to force any to associate and warning of the armed vengeance that would follow resistance.

The King's men replied (according to Brown): "We have as true and real regard for liberty established on constitutional principles as any men on the continent by whatever name distinguished and shall take every proper legal step in our power for its preservation and support." They stated their conditions as follows: no Revolutionary bodies or forces to be established among them; no person to be disturbed on account of his opinions or to be deprived of trading rights; Governor Lord Campbell to be unmolested; and Fort Charlotte, as fully equipped as when seized by the forces of the Congress, to be restored to him. Fletchall, accompanied by several other cowardly fellows, without even mentioning these instructions, signed terms of submission dictated by Drayton on September 16, 1775.

It was fortunate for Drayton that Fletchall had not been accompanied by Cuningham and Brown, who too much distrusted Drayton to enter his camp. The King's men were furious at Fletchall's having arranged for them to remain neutral, but nearly all accepted the terms. Drayton drew from Cuningham by letter a declaration of his continued hostility as a means of justifying his possible arrest.

When Kirkland, fleeing from Drayton, arrived in Charles Town, he succeeded in entering Lord Campbell's residence. But the fact that the Governor smuggled him aboard the *Tamar* inflamed the suspicion already entertained of Campbell's sincerity in his assurances that he had discouraged proposals from back-country men to raise 4,000 men for the King. To a spy of the Revolutionists professing to be a loyalist from the back country, Campbell urged that the loyalists should keep organized and assured them of early assistance, as South Carolina would soon be attacked by the King's forces. The motion to seize the Governor failed, but he feared to remain. On September 15 he dissolved the Assembly and fled to the *Tamar*. The last vestige of the royal government thus expired, and the Revolutionary Congress was obliged to assume the complete administration if for no other reason than for preservation of order.

South Carolina Captures a Fort and Adopts a Flag.—Forcing Lord Campbell into the open was followed by decisive action on both sides. The Revolutionists' taking of Fort Johnson originated the South Carolina flag. Colonel William Moultrie, directed by the Council of Safety to provide a flag, chose, before leading his men against the fort, the blue of the uniform of the 1st and 2d Regiments and the silver crescent adorning their hats. After Moultrie's defense of the palmetto log fort in 1776, to which his name was given, the palmetto tree was added.

Cuningham Rallies the Loyalists.—There now followed a struggle of more than two weeks between the moderates in Charles Town, alarmed at the danger of conflict with the two British ships in the harbor, and the advanced party who were seeking that very thing. The situation was so serious, including the unwillingness of the city militia to fight, that the General Committee called the Second Provincial Congress to meet November 1 instead of December 1. After the Congress was well under way the militia "recovered from their delusion."

Drayton was voted into the chair, supposedly to prevent his agitating on the floor of the Congress; but he made his position a tribune from which to propagate his views, thus enhancing the power of the most important leader in the Congress for carrying the province into revolution. The transfer of official leadership from Laurens to Drayton was doubtless a source of supreme satisfaction to both.

The first day of its session the Congress was informed that Captain Robert Cuningham had been arrested and brought to town on the charge of having spoken seditiously. His imprisonment sent a wave of indignation among a wide circle in the back country, with alarming repercussions.

Shots Exchanged in Charles Town Harbor.—President Drayton was seeking to involve the hesitant Congress in some overt act of war that would rally public sentiment and render retreat impossible. When Congress ordered the blocking of Hog Island channel, Drayton supervised the sinking of four hulks in the channel on November 11. Thornbrough, to save his British honor, fired six shots, which fell short, and Drayton replied with his nine-pounders. About dawn on the 12th the *Tamar* and the *Cherokee* fired ineffectively about 130 shots. The effect of rousing public opinion to the fighting point was temporarily as desired. But warlike measures were taken by very narrow majorities. On November 29 the Congress adjourned to February 1, 1776.

These divided counsels were natural. South Carolina had been mildly treated by the mother country and could not easily forget the advantages of membership in that powerful empire, notwithstanding both old and new grievances. Hence representation of the moderate party was deliberately continued in her councils, so that each step of resistance might be carefully weighed. How truly the moderate leaders expressed the general view is proved, Drayton says, by the high stations to which many of them were called during the most critical times of the Revolution.

War in the Back Country.—We must return now to the civil war threatened in the back country by the arrest of Robert Cuningham and the retaliatory seizure of public ammunition by his brother Patrick in October and November, 1775. The backwoodsmen's fear that the Council of Safety had been sending the ammunition to the Cherokees for attacking the loyalists was hard to allay. Major Williamson marched his Revolutionary force to Ninety Six and had hardly thrown up breastworks near the courthouse to shield his 562 men when about 1,890 Tories appeared under Major Joseph Robinson and Captain Patrick Cuningham. The Tories knew that Whig reinforcements were approaching and therefore agreed that both submit their case to their respective civil authorities. In the three days' battle, November 19 to 21, the Whigs lost one killed and twelve wounded; the Tories, several killed and about twenty wounded. Thus in the second battle of the Revolution in South Carolina was the first blood in this State shed.

Colonel Richardson soon arrived with 3,000 Whigs, "unkennelled" Fletchall from a hollow tree, and received the submission of large numbers of the King's men who now saw how badly they had been deceived as to the strength of Congress. But the most determined of the King's men refused to submit. Retreating into the Indian country west of the present Spartanburg-Greenville and Abbeville-Anderson line, the principal aggressors formed a camp of about 130 men at the Great Cane Brake on Reedy River, in the southern part of present Greenville County, and sought unsuccessfully to induce the Cherokees to join them. Three-fourths of them were captured and some killed by a detachment of Richardson's Whigs. The next day began a thirty-hour snow, covering the ground two feet deep and giving the expedition the name "the snow campaign." After suffering severely in their light clothing, without tents, and drenched with rain and sleet, the army reached Granby on January 1, 1776, and were dismissed.

Richardson's prisoners, including almost every important Tory leader, were almost all released by the Council of Safety and the region was reorganized with increased representation as a bid for its support. Thus originated as one of the new divisions "the upper or Spartan District," apparently in honor of Colonel John Thomas' "Spartan regiment." These acts and the humanity with which Richardson had acted in the disaffected country between the Broad and the Saluda had a most beneficial effect. A spirited, suspicious people, loyally attached to their King against whom in their remote homes they cherished no wrongs, resentful of unlawful attempts to control them, were convinced of the overwhelming power of the Provincial Congress, of the humanity of its officers, and of the falsity of the charges that the Revolutionists planned to subject them to Indian massacre. The result of the political and military operations of 1775 was to strengthen the party of action and to carry the province into the new year in a more nearly united condition.

CHAPTER XXIX

THE BATTLE OF FORT MOULTRIE, 1776

While South Carolina was committing herself more and more deeply by overt acts, the Continental Congress was even more boldly plunging into courses that would, according to the outcome, attaint them of treason or crown them as the founders of a new nation. But all were still fighting for their rights as Englishmen. The idea of independence, peering out of the future, was as yet a dread shadow instead of a bright hope.

The Second Provincial Congress reconvened on February 1, 1776, and on the third received from the Continental Congress copies of captured letters from royal officers in the South to General Gage and others revealing the plan of bringing the Indians upon the frontier. During January, February, and March the Revolutionary movement was strengthened by the defeat of the Scotch loyalists at Moore's Creek, North Carolina, and by the seizure of Governor Wright by the Georgia Council of Safety and the assertion of the authority of the latter, supported by some 300 South Carolina troops under Stephen Bull, against the British vessels and the powerful loyalist element in Georgia.

The Constitution of 1776.—While "everything was running into confusion," the Continental Congress, at the request of New Hampshire and South Carolina, advised those colonies on setting up a government. The "Convention of South Carolina" was recommended "to call a full and free representation of the people" for establishing a form of government to "effectually secure peace and good order in the colony, during the continuance of the present dispute between Great Britain and the colonies." The constitution of New Hampshire, adopted in January, and that of South Carolina in March, 1776, were both intended merely for the temporary administration of public order until the regular royal government should function constitutionally.

The South Carolina Provincial Congress, with its apportionment accidentally arranged for a temporary purpose, itself assumed the duty of framing a constitution, as did similar bodies in two other colonies.

A written constitution was the natural development from colonial conditions. In a royal colony the King's instructions to the Governor outlined the frame of government and defined the duties, powers, and limitations of its parts. These instructions were spoken of as "the constitution" of the colony, and were recognized as the will of the sovereign to which the governmental agencies must submit. Custom supplemented this written constitution; and this custom, as we have observed, the popular element in the government was continually seeking to magnify to its own advantage. As an act of the colonial Assembly contrary to the King's instructions was annulled by the sovereign as unlawful, so, after independence, the courts, as the best available representatives of the sovereign, developed the practice of annulling unconstitutional acts. The preamble of the South Carolina Constitution of 1776 actually mentions, as necessitating its adoption, the fact that Lord Campbell had carried away the royal instructions to governors. In a colony possessing a charter the analogy to the written constitution of the later State is even more obvious. Connecticut continued her colonial charter as her State Constitution until 1818, and Rhode Island hers until 1842.

Gadsden and Drayton were the farthest advanced of South Carolina leaders along the road to independence. Arriving from Philadelphia on February 6 with a copy of Paine's *Common Sense,* Gadsden advocated that the Constitution should, as Paine recommended, declare South Carolina independent. Even the few in South Carolina desiring independence considered the suggestion premature, and the majority were so outraged as to threaten to withdraw from the Provincial Congress. The arrival of news, on March 21, of the parliamentary act declaring the Americans in rebellion and the royal proclamation declaring their ships and cargoes lawful prize dampened the moderates seeking a reconciliation with England. On March 26, 1776, the Constitution was signed, and the *de facto* Congress adjourned to reassemble in the afternoon as the General Assembly. With the Declaration of Independence a little later, this became the government of the State. The extra-legal organs of revolution, beginning with the mass meeting against the tea in December, 1773, had merged without a break into the legal government of the State.

Colonial experience was practically the sole source of this Constitution. The long preamble, anxiously justifying the step being taken, declares the Constitution established "until an accommodation of the unhappy differences between Great Britain and America can be obtained (an event which, though traduced and treated as rebels, we still earnestly desire)." South Carolina is spoken of as "this colony." The apportionment of the General Assembly (a regular colonial term) was fixed at the existing membership of the Congress for the lower house. A legislative council, or upper house, was to be elected by the lower house. The parish region thus had 138 members of the lower house, and the much more populous back country, 64. The accidental apportionment of the First Provincial Congress for a temporary purpose thus became fixed in the Constitution to vex public life until 1865. The executive, chosen by the two houses, was called president. The absolute veto was continued; but the power of prorogation and dissolution, so abused in the past five years, was withheld. Courts and law were continued virtually unchanged, except that the long-desired judicial tenure during good behavior was established. The resolutions of the Continental Congress and the orders of the Provincial Congress were declared to be of force.

The feature most sharply distinguishing this from other early American constitutions is the great power of the chief executive. John Rutledge was elected president, William Henry Drayton, chief justice, and an entire roster of officers was chosen. On the reopening of the courts, April 23, after they had been closed for almost a year, Chief Justice Drayton delivered to the Charles Town grand jury another of his flaming political charges. With sweeping eloquence he depicted the stupidity (which he represented as malicious tyranny) of the British government toward America, and maintained a free people's right to expel monarchs who had violated the mutual compact of protection and obedience between King and people. His model was the English revolution of 1688. The people of South Carolina in 1719 had overthrown the Proprietors and "called upon the House of Brunswick to rule them. . . . The King accepted the invitation and thereby" vested in "us a clear right to effect another revolution. . . . Our ancestors by act of Assembly passed on the 18th day of August, 1721, *recognized* the British monarch."

These audacious misrepresentations were, in the spirit of the moment, greedily swallowed by a people hungry for justification in sound theory and legal precedent. Gladly they followed Drayton's analogy between the conduct of James II and that of George III and his conclusion that "the Almighty created America to be independent of Britain. Let us be aware of the impiety of being backward to act as instruments in the Almighty Hand, now extended to accomplish his purpose, and by the completion of which alone America, in the nature of human affairs, can be secure against the craft and insidious designs of *her enemies who think her prosperity and power already by far too great.* In a word, our piety and political safety are so blended that to refuse our labors in this divine work is to refuse to be a great, a free, a pious and a happy people!"

The address is remarkable from every standpoint, and not the least in its assumption, more than two months before the Declaration of Independence, by a man so largely responsible for bringing South Carolina to readiness to accept independence, that the fact of independence had already occurred.

The Battle of Fort Moultrie.—The public mind, relieved by the departure of the British fleet, the cessation of disorders in the back country, and the settlement of government into more ordered form, enjoyed until the spring a period of repose.

Lord Campbell had long pleaded for a powerful expedition against South Carolina to crush the rebellion in the South. Sir Henry Clinton sailed from Boston for Cape Fear with part of Howe's troops, intending to join there the fleet from England and erect a royal government in the interior of North Carolina. The plan was wrecked by the overthrow of the Scotch loyalists at Moore's Creek Bridge. Therefore, after the arrival of Parker's fleet in May, the combined expedition sailed for Charles Town.

To meet the threat Congress sent the English soldier of fortune Charles Lee to command the Department of the South. General Lee condemned the palmetto fort on Sullivan's Island as a slaughter pen, and only Rutledge's refusal prevented his abandoning the post. Colonel Moultrie, with the confidence of the amateur and the carelessness that marked his bold disposition, was unconcerned and disposed his troops with skill. The fort was a square structure, its wall formed of two rows of firmly joined palmetto logs sixteen feet apart, with the space between them filled with sand.

Preparatory to a combined land and naval attack Clinton landed between 2,000 and 3,000 men on Long Island, immediately to the northeast of Sullivan's. The Americans held the adjacent end of Sullivan's Island with 780 men under Colonel William Thomson. Within the fort were Moultrie's 2d South Carolina Infantry (413 men), and 22 of the 4th South Carolina Regiment. In Fort Johnson on the opposite side of the harbor were Christopher Gadsden and his 1st South Carolina Infantry, to whom, as it turned out, the location of the battle afforded no opportunity. In and near the city, guns and troops were disposed to meet a possible attack should the fleet pass the forts.

Between ten and eleven o'clock on June 28, the nine British ships began shelling the fort. Though Moultrie was so scantily supplied with powder as to have to suspend firing for two hours and fire slowly during the whole action, the British withdrew at night, completely defeated. For his heroism in replacing the Fort Moultrie flag at the peril of his life, Sergeant William Jasper was presented by President Rutledge with the President's own sword. Lord William Campbell died from a wound received in the battle.

Of inestimable service to Moultrie was Colonel Thomson's preventing Clinton's overwhelming force from crossing from Long Island to Sullivan's Island.

For about ten days or so after the battle Clinton remained on Long Island. On August 2 the last British ship sailed for New York. Thus ended the first attempt to conquer the South, deprived of whose co-operation it was supposed that the New England colonies could easily be beaten out of their ideas of independence.

CHAPTER XXX

INDEPENDENCE AND A NEW CONSTITUTION, 1776-1778

THE BATTLE of Fort Moultrie was followed by the fiasco of the American campaign toward Florida. It was at this period that the South Carolina regulars were turned over to the Continental service, and that Gadsden and Moultrie were elected, on September 16, 1776, Continental brigadiers.

Declaration of Independence.—While the guns were booming at Fort Moultrie, Congress was discussing the question of independence. To this they were being driven, not from choice, but by the belief in its necessity as the only means of preserving liberty. Even John Adams recorded that "there was never a moment during the Revolution when I would not have given everything I possessed for a restoration of the state of things before the conflict began, provided we could have had a sufficient security for its continuance." The reluctance thus expressed by Adams was even more powerfully felt by South Carolinians. Henry Laurens, e.g., wrote in February, 1776, "One more year will enable us to be independent. Ah! that word cuts me deep—has caused tears to trickle down my cheeks," as a dutiful son "thrust by the hand of violence out of his father's house," whose children must be called by some new name. Though he never wavered in his "duty to posterity" after independence was declared, he wrote, while a prisoner in the Tower of London, of the Declaration of Independence, "I wept that day as I had done for the melancholy catastrophe which caused me to put on black clothes —the death of a son, and felt much more pain."

The Declaration was formally adopted July 4, signed by the President and Secretary, and on August 2 signed by the then existing membership, including some who had not even been members on July 4. The young South Carolina delegates, without waiting for authorization, all voted for independence. Edward Rutledge was twenty-six; Thomas Heyward, Jr., twenty-four days under thirty; Thomas Lynch, Jr., thirty-two days under twenty-seven; and Arthur Middleton, thirty-four years of age. News of the Declaration reached Charles Town on August 5, at the psychological moment. The spilling of blood at Fort Moultrie had prepared South Carolina's mind for the separation it had formerly abhorred. Though there remained many secretly dissatisfied, the words of the popular branch of the legislature on September 20, 1776, doubtless expressed the sentiment of the mass of the people: "It is with the most unspeakable pleasure we embrace this opportunity of expressing our joy and satisfaction in the Declaration of the Continental Congress declaring the United Colonies free and independent States . . . an event unsought for and now produced by unavoidable necessity and which every friend to justice and humanity must not only hold justifiable as the natural effect of unmerited persecution but equally rejoice in, as the only security against injuries and oppressions and the most promising source of future liberty and safety."

The Constitution of 1778.—Both the severance of allegiance to England and the crudity of the temporary Constitution called for a new instrument. On October 12, 1776, the House appointed a committee to report needed revision and amendment. Unfortunately mere lethargy in the one case and sectional selfishness in the other delayed for years the adoption of the committee's enlightened plan for judicial reform and a just apportionment of representation. Since the legislature's term expired October 21, they could only publish their proposed changes for public information and leave final action to the legislature soon to be elected.

The South Carolina legislature at this session unanimously declared in favor of the union of South Carolina and Georgia into one State, and sent William Henry Drayton and John Smith to urge the plan. On its rejection by the Georgia convention, January 23, 1777, Drayton entered upon an active propaganda, but had to return before Governor Treutlen's offer of a reward for his arrest.

Crushing the Cherokees.—General Gage ordered Stuart on September 12, 1775, that, as the colonists had used Indians against Boston, he should have the Southern Indians "take up arms against his Majesty's enemies, and distress them all in their power." But even then Stuart interpreted his orders to mean only co-operation of the Indians with British troops against the organized troops of the colonists. And he included the warning to his subordinates: "You will understand that an indiscriminate attack upon the provinces is not meant, but to act in the execution of any concerted plan and to assist his Majesty [*sic*] troops and friends in distressing the rebels and bringing them to a sense of their duty." This was, of course, good policy as well as humanity, as a general massacre would have turned the divided frontier against either side provoking it. The impossibility of such limitation of Indians deprived Stuart of any credit with the colonists.

The Cherokees were irritated not only by the stoppage of their supplies from Charles Town, but by the encroachment of the Watauga settlers in the present Tennessee upon their lands, contrary to both the King's proclamation of 1763 and the Treaty of Hard Labor of 1768. Such was the inflamed sense of injustice among the Indians when they learned that the British fleet was off Charles Town. On July 1 the Lower Cherokees poured across the South Carolina frontier, massacring all ages and sexes. The news either set off or encouraged the overhill warriors against the Wataugans. A few Creeks joined, and the frontiers of Georgia, the Carolinas, and Virginia were aflame.

Collecting his militia, Williamson destroyed most of the Cherokees' towns, orchards, crops, and animals east of the Blue Ridge. Throughout the war Georgians, Carolinians, and Virginians appropriated deerskins, sold captives as slaves, scalped living Indians, killed women, even lame or fleeing, and destroyed every means of sustaining life with a savagery equaling and a thoroughness surpassing their enemies'. Far more Indians probably perished of starvation and exposure than by arms.

Colonel Williamson had destroyed the lower towns before General Griffith Rutherford led his North Carolinians through Swannanoa Gap to destroy the middle and valley settlements along the Little Tennessee and the Hiwassee, or Colonel William Christian moved down the Holston with his Virginians. For weeks the 6,000 Carolinians and Virginians reduced to ruin the log cabins, the orchards, the granaries, the cultivated fields and gardens of one of the most advanced Indian nations, who generally fled to the forests before the overwhelming force. At Dewitt's Corner[1] on May 20, 1777, South Carolina and Georgia concluded a treaty (the first in America after independence) by which the Cherokees retired behind a line which may be roughly described as running southwest from the eastern end of the straight part of the present Pickens County's northern boundary to South Carolina's extreme western point. South Carolina thus obtained practically the present Greenville, Pickens, Oconee, and Anderson counties. Immediately there was a rush of settlers into the beautiful hills and valleys of the ceded territory. In 1790, though only 8 per cent of the area, it contained over 10 per cent of the State's free population. Two months after the cession to South Carolina, the Cherokees in a treaty with Virginia and North Carolina ceded about four times this area in North Carolina and Tennessee. In 1817 the Cherokees were removed entirely from South Carolina.

Church Disestablishment.—The new legislature of December, 1776, and January, 1777, met amid an atmosphere of security unknown for the past year. A matter of immediate importance was the completing of the new Constitution begun in October, 1776. The political apathy of the

[1] About six miles northwest of the modern Due West, to which Dewitt's has been changed.

masses, both before and after the Revolution, is surprising. Two or three voters in a parish, or even the returning officers alone, sometimes named the members to the house.

There was no demand in the legislature for a constitutional convention. Judge Pendleton, a man of unusual activity and progressive ideas, sought to stir interest in the framing of the Constitution through his charges to the grand juries, an agency then frequently employed in the absence of local agencies of public opinion. In the autumn of 1776 he urged the grand juries on the circuits of Beaufort and Ninety Six to make recommendations, as the views of such bodies would doubtless be considered. Ramsay says that the election was conducted with the understanding that the legislature would frame a constitution; this may be true, for he witnessed what was passing. The judges besides Pendleton merely extolled the Constitution of 1776.

Rev. William Tennent now urged a constitutional change not included by the committee of October, namely the disestablishment of the Anglican as the State church. He was supported by a petition signed by many thousands. The meeting at the High Hills of Santee in April, 1776, of Baptist churches for choosing delegates to a "Continental Association" for the evident purpose of overthrowing union of church and state throughout the country is said to have selected Tennent to lead the fight in South Carolina. Tennent, thirty-six years of age, "of majestic and venerable presence," the leading Presbyterian or Congregational minister of the province, was, like Rev. Richard Furman and Rev. Oliver Hart, the leading Baptists, an ardent Revolutionary leader, and as a member of public bodies and in the pulpit and press had industriously promoted the cause. His powerful speech in the Assembly advocating religious equality, January 11, 1777, was his last important public act; for he died on August 11 at the High Hills of Santee while bringing his recently widowed mother from New Jersey.

The petition was introduced by Christopher Gadsden, in conformity with the breadth and moderation of his character, which are much less well known than his fiery opposition to autocratic authority and his appeals to the masses as affording the best support during conservative inaction. Said Tennent, laws "which make odious distinctions between subjects equally good ought not to be tolerated. Under a reputedly free government, licenses for marriage are refused to any but the established clergy. The sums advanced by the public treasury for the support of the Church of England for the ten years preceding the 31st of December, 1775, amount to 164,027 pounds, 16 shillings, 3 pence. The religious estate, drawn more or less from the purses of all denominations by law, would probably sell for 330,000 pounds. If the Dissenters have always made more than half of this government, the sums taken taken from their pockets . . . must amount to more than 82,013 pounds within the ten years aforesaid; and the very large sums of their property in glebes, parsonages, and churches, lies in the possession and improvement of the Church of England. Meanwhile the established churches are but twenty in number, many of them very small, while the number of dissenting congregations are seventy-nine, and much larger, and would pay 40,000 pounds annually could they be furnished with a clergy. . . . Would it content our brethren of the Church of England to be barely tolerated, that is not punished, for presuming to think for themselves? . . . With the new Constitution, let the day of justice dawn on every rank and order of men in this State. Many of [the Anglicans] have signed the petition. Many more have declared their sentiments in the most liberal terms. . . . Yield to the mighty current of American freedom and glory, and let our State be inferior to none on this wide continent in the liberality of its laws and in the happiness of its people."[2]

Lowndes and Colonel Charles Pinckney argued strongly for supporting the Anglican establishment, but C. C. Pinckney advocated religious equality. Efforts to retain some sort of privilege without financial support failed, and disestablishment was voted unanimously.

The Constitution as framed early in 1777 was printed in pamphlet form and left for public consideration for a year.

Rutledge Resigns Rather Than Accept Independence.—On January 9, 1778, President Rutledge submitted the Articles of Confederation. South Carolina proposed over twenty amendments, including one putting the army primarily under State control, all of which were rejected; but her delegates signed the Articles on July 24, 1778.

The new Constitution of the State, after having been before the people for a year (without apparently stirring much interest), was given its third reading in March, 1778. It deprived the President of the veto. In the upper house, now called the Senate and popularly elected, the city of Charles Town, as it consisted of two parishes, was given two senators, which the later Charleston County retained through 1895. Other parishes or districts had one senator except that in a few instances two combined to elect one. The old parish region continued to enjoy the vast prepon-

[2] General McCrady, III, 211-12, while commending Tennent's view, falls into a strange error in criticizing his figures by saying, "The low country, in which was the great wealth of the province, paid all the taxes." One of the grievances of the back country was that their lands bore the same tax per acre as the richest rice fields contiguous to market. General McCrady also overlooks the fact that a large share of the wealth of the low country belonged to the Dissenters. The Anglican clergy's salaries were paid from the general duty taxes. Parochial charges were levied by the church in each parish on all property owners. Church buildings were erected from province general taxes, supplemented by private contributions.

derance in both houses over the much more populous back country. But it must be remembered that representation on any proportional basis was then practiced hardly anywhere. Suffrage was left virtually as it had been since 1721—the requirement being the owning of a lot or fifty acres of land or paying a roughly corresponding tax.

At the end of seven years and every fourteen years thereafter representation was to be reapportioned on wealth and property combined. The existing provision that the resolutions of the Continental Congress should be of force in South Carolina was omitted. The agreement to create a separate court of appeals, to abolish the equity jurisdiction of the Privy Council, and elect a chancellor, as adopted in October, 1776, was rescinded. But the former vote to establish probate courts in each of the seven judicial districts instead of having only the one in Charles Town was maintained.

Only Protestants could be legislators or governor, though all acknowledging a God who awards future rewards or punishments were not denied the vote on religious grounds. The Anglican Church, though disestablished, retained all its property. Protestantism was declared to be the "established religion" of South Carolina, as a unit of which any Protestant congregation electing its own pastor could incorporate. South Carolina thus followed Maryland (August, 1776) and North Carolina (November, 1776) in abolishing her state church, a step in the practice of American democracy which New Hampshire, Massachusetts, and Connecticut did not take until well into the nineteenth century.

On March 5 President Rutledge, in a special pleading speech, explained to the legislature why he could not assent to the new Constitution. He overlooked the fact that the old Constitution (like the new one) was a mere act of the legislature, repealable like any other mere statute. His contention that "the people" had delegated to the government certain powers was mere fiction, for the people apart from the legislature had taken no action whatever. Equally forced was his objection to having a popularly elected Senate substituted for a Legislative Council elected by the lower house, and to having the executive veto destroyed, on the ground that "the people also preferred a compounded or mixed government to a simple democracy, or one verging toward it," because democratic power is "arbitrary, severe, and destructive."

However serious were these points, Rutledge's real objection seems to have been surrendering the hope of reunion with Britain. "We still look forward to such an accommodation," he said, "an event as desirable now as it ever was . . ." And yet he hoped in strange contrast for "a peace which will secure the sovereignty and independence of America." President Rutledge therefore resigned. His vacillation between independence, which he had so recently heartily endorsed, and reunion with England, on which he now insisted, reveals an element of indecision in Rutledge's character which bears directly on the question of his willingness to have South Carolina return to her old place in the British Empire at the time of the attack on Charles Town in 1779.[3] It was a manifestation of his moderation of character and his philosophical habit of mind, which viewed the contest for American rights from a broader standpoint than that of local or even American patriotism.

The legislature's supplanting one "constitution" by another may be regarded as an act of usurpation or as a mere practice stroke in the development of constitutional law before its nature had come to be well understood. Both constitutions were declared by the Court of Appeals in 1823 mere legislative acts.[4]

Arthur Middleton was elected to succeed President Rutledge, but declined. Rawlins Lowndes was then elected and served until Rutledge was again made chief executive as governor in January, 1779. The Constitution went into effect at once, though Lowndes was called president instead of the new title "governor" to the end of his term, and the old legislature served to November 29. Gadsden, after Parsons had declined, was made vice-president. He could not refuse without throwing the State into confusion; but it was a scheme to get rid of him, he wrote angrily, by making him ineligible (for governor?) for the next election. Gadsden, having in a huff eliminated himself from the army by resigning the ranking commission among the South Carolina Continentals, saw himself threatened with elimination from political leadership through being shelved by his conservative enemies. Rutledge, able, moderate, broadminded, ever willing to serve in humbler places even after the distinction he was yet to earn, was sent by Charles Town to take the place in the legislature vacated by Gadsden's elevation to innocuous desuetude.

Campaign in Georgia—Character of Militia and Continentals.—The repulse of the British invasion from Florida in February, 1777, gave Georgia so little respite from British and Tory raids that in May, 1778, the South Carolina Continentals had been advanced far into Georgia to assist that State. Sickness and quarrels with Governor Houston of

[3] See page 290.

[4] 2 McCord, 360. The still-current arms on the seal of the State, bearing the palmetto, ordered in 1776 and put into use in 1777, were the design of W. H. Drayton; the reverse, being the woman, the design of Arthur Middleton. The symbolism, elaborately explained, is drawn from the Declaration of Independence and the victory of Fort Moultrie.—Drayton, II, 372-76.

The legislature in 1924 made the yellow jessamine the State flower and in 1939 made the mocking bird the State bird. In 1948 the Carolina wren was substituted.

Georgia resulted in the Americans' retreating to await the British counter blow.

The tedium of regular service after the stirring events of 1776 rendered it hard to fill the ranks of the regular (i.e., Continental) army. The dwindling of pay, as the State's paper money plunged rapidly toward worthlessness, and the terrible hardships of the Georgia expedition, repelled men from a service requiring enlistments for long terms. On March 28, 1778, the legislature ordered to the Continental Regiments vagrants, harborers of deserters, and night hunters attracting deer by fire (unforgivable to sportsmen though useful to the hungry). Persons voluntarily enlisting were promised 100 acres in the portion of the recent Indian cession between the Keowee and the Tugaloo, in addition to the 100 acres offered by Congress. On January 29, 1779, a bounty of $500 was added, increased September 11, 1779, by a note of the State for $2,000 bearing 10 per cent interest on the completion of twenty-one months' service. In 1778 the militia law was revised. The colonial law for constituting, in crises, half the militia in Charles Town and one-third elsewhere of slaves was modified to allow one-third of the men to be slaves used as hatchet men and pioneers.

The difficulties that confronted South Carolina were experienced everywhere by both British and Americans. Yet, in the face of them, South Carolina before 1777 had organized six Continental regiments and furnished large numbers of militia. The conduct of Sergeant Jasper and many others, both before and after the drafting of vagrants, attests the presence of soldiers of the highest quality among the Continentals. The numbers of South Carolina's Continentals (called State regulars before September, 1776) and militia respectively in active service during each year of the war are given as follows by Secretary of War Knox's report of May 10, 1790, the militia numbers being conjectural: 1775, 1,500 and 2,500; 1776, 2,069 and 4,000; 1777, 1,650 and 350; 1778, 1,650 and 2,000; 1779, no Continentals reported (clearly an error, as we have accounts of them), 4,500 militia; 1780, no Continentals reported (clearly an error, as we have accounts of them), 6,000 militia; 1781, no Continentals, 3,000 militia; 1782, no Continentals reported (but there were a few), 2,000 militia; 1782, 139 and none.[5]

Naval War.—After the repulse of the British from Fort Moultrie, June 28, 1776, South Carolina enjoyed, save for the Indian war of July

[5] American State Papers, Military, I, 14-19. J. F. Grimké's order books, SCHM, XVI, *passim*, relate to South Carolina Continentals August, 1778-May, 1780.

It is painful to criticize an historian for whose work I have such respect as for General McCrady's; but I cannot refrain from expressing the conviction that his strong predilection in favor of the militia led him into unfairness to the Continental soldiers. The following *(South Carolina in the Revolution, 1775-80,* p. 302) appears grossly to October, 1776, and the Georgia expeditions, all but complete peace for more than two years. As the war in the North interrupted commerce there, Charles Town's trade so flourished, says Ramsay, that fortunes were never made more quickly. Wagons hauled to the North the sup-

exaggerated against the character of the troops to which Sergeant Jasper and many another brave and true patriot belonged: "Ranks which were filled with sturdy beggars, lewd, idle and disorderly men, and deserters were not the place for patriots and decent citizens. If the militiaman was insubordinate and would leave the ranks when tired ot the service, the hired and vagrant continental soldier, without patriotism or pride, engaged in a desperate cause, and often apparently a losing one, would desert when opportunity offered and circumstances invited. The militiamen when he left, with or without leave, would go home. The continental regular when he deserted would go to the enemy if he could."

The contrast is too complete. Large masses of men of the same blood and environment cannot differ so radically. And as to deserting to the enemy, General McCrady's own book gives ample evidence thaat militiamen often fought on both sides. The Continental ranks were not "filled," but only supplemented, and apparently very slightly, with vagrants under the act of 1778. As to the "hired" Continentals, thousands of vouchers in the State Archives prove that the militiamen did not neglect to apply for their pay. The matter of pay for the militia was attended to promptly after the Revolution. Those who had fought for the State presented their claims as did also those who had furnished supplies and were given indents which, like a great part of the pay due the Continental soldiers, mostly awaited redemption until the passage of Hamilton's funding measures under President Washington, as will be related in our chapter following the Revolution. Since the question of the relative willingness to serve without pay has been raised, we must remember the fact (narrated elsewhere by General McCrady) that plundering by the militia soon assumed enormous proportions, and led them to go home with their plunder when their remaining in the ranks was imperatively needed. The Continentals were not only without pay, but were also without sufficient food and even without clothing sufficient to prevent actual suffering or indecent exposure in many cases for long periods, whereas the militia, after a few days' service, returned home to eat and rest. General McCrady emphasizes that it was necessary for them to do this in order to care for their families; but the Continentals, so far as they had families, stayed with the colors instead of going home; and if it is objected that many of them had no families, it may be replied that refraining from that luxury to remain in the army was itself a not inconsiderable sacrifice to their country.

Since General McCrady has attacked the character of the Continentals, it is well to ask why were militiamen, who refused to bind themselves to serve for any specific period, superior in patriotism to Continentals who deliberately agreed to fight to the ending of the war or for long specified terms? As we trace the history of the Revolution, we shall find the Continentals enduring incredible hardships for prolonged periods, often in almost hopeless defeat, and yet remaining with the colors—hardships a tithe of which would have soon dissolved any militia force that was ever assembled.

Fortunately General McCrady's own work supplies material demonstrating the unfairness of his attitude toward the Continentals in his reaction against the neglect and unfairness with which the militia had been treated by some writers. He is obliged continually to praise the services of the Maryland and Delaware Continentals who were sent to South Carolina after our own Continentals had been made prisoners, and to glory in the magnificent conduct of our own South Carolina Continentals at Savannah in October, 1779, months after the passage of the law concerning enlisting vagrants, etc., which he makes the basis of a sweeping reflection upon the Continental troops, and only a few months before they began their heroic defense of Charles Town, which ended their organized existence.

plies that ships brought from Europe or the French and Dutch West Indies. Brief blockades and occasional naval fights occurred between the British and the State's small navy or Continental vessels; but Charles Town continued until 1780, except for brief periods, an open port near which passed large numbers of richly laden British ships, from which there might be expected a rich harvest of prizes. For Charles Town's own commerce the presence of powerful frigates would be a welcome protection. These considerations led the legislature in February and March, 1778, to enlarge its naval plans by ordering $500,000 worth of indigo to be purchased for public account and shipped to Europe, the proceeds to be used to build or buy three frigates, and to elect as commodore Alexander Gillon, and also three captains. Gillon was a Charles Town merchant born in Amsterdam. To accept this service with his State he gave up a contract with Congress by which he had expected annual profits of £7,000 sterling. He was further to prove his patriotism, as well as his faith in prize money, by supplementing the State's credit with his entire fortune. Before sailing for Europe, Gillon, having projected the plan, actively participated in capturing off Charles Town bar, on June 19, 1778, two British vessels carrying together more men and guns than his two vessels.

Refusal to Swear Allegiance to State.—The division of parties flared up in June, 1778, over the question of enforcing the oath of allegiance to the independent State of South Carolina. When many neglected to obey, President Lowndes proclaimed an extension to June 10. The radical supporters of independence in Charles Town prevented the reading of the proclamation by seizing it from the sheriff and returned it insultingly to President Lowndes.

Gadsden was so furious at this "mob" defiance of authority that he resigned the vice-presidency in protest, but consented to continue on the legislature's request. He was doubtless right in believing that the conservatives rejoiced at the embarrassment of the party who had forced through the new Constitution establishing independence and disestablishing the church. But it is hardly fair to accuse him of inconsistency in denouncing these abusers of the Liberty Tree tactics as "more danger than . . . exportable Tories." Though Gadsden had boldly opposed

The desertions, flight under fire, and other unpatriotic conduct which he so fully exposes in the Northern militia were by no means entirely lacking among those of South Carolina. The truth seems to be that there was an immense amount of indifference and a good deal of downright meanness among the population of 1775 to 1783, so largely without the stiffening power of pride in a great and long-loved country. So much the greater credit to those who, having not seen, yet loved, the nation that was to be.

For discussion of General McCrady's attitude toward the Continentals for the latter part of the war, see note at the end of Chapter XXXIII.

royal governors and King and Parliament, he had always done so in defense of what he considered constitutional rights. Now, as in 1784, in opposing the lawless violence of mobs against reasonable liberty, he was true to his principles. His talent was for opposing unconstitutional aggressions, and as these were eliminated, his own importance declined.

Many "malcontents" still failed to swear, and the legislature extended the time to the spring terms of court, 1779. Many, of course, still refused, as the State plunged into the civil war of 1780 to 1783, of which these tumults were the prelude.

CHAPTER XXXI

GEORGIA AND SOUTH CAROLINA CONQUERED, 1778-1780

The French Alliance and British Conciliation.—Before the events just related had ended, important military and political developments had occurred at the North. Sir Henry Clinton and Commodore Sir Peter Parker, abandoning attempts to conquer South Carolina, had had better success in New York, where they co-operated under General Howe and Admiral Lord Howe in taking the city in September, 1776. Washington's gloomy experience of defeat was relieved by his brilliant capture of the thousand Hessians at Trenton on December 26, 1776, and his victory at Princeton eight days later. The long monotony of defeat was interrupted on October 17, 1777, by the capture of Burgoyne's army. Its vast significance was appreciated by both France and England. The former ended her secret aid and on February 6, 1778, signed a treaty pledging her and the United States to make no peace save a joint treaty acknowledging American independence. Parliament, anticipating this, enacted the three conciliatory acts of March 11, 1778, abandoning every practice that had driven the colonies to rebellion.

British hopes of reconciliation were not unreasonable. We may estimate that about a third of the Americans cared enough for the Revolution to sacrifice something for it. Probably about as many preferred to remain in the British Empire. About a third were unwilling to sacrifice anything one way or the other. The suffering at Valley Forge was due, not to the poverty, but to the indifference, of the country. While Washington's soldiers endured cold and hunger, Pennsylvania and New Jersey farmers exchanged their abundant supplies for the metal money of the British in Philadelphia. It was thus in America's darkest hour that Britain offered conciliation. But conciliation came too late. On April 22, ten days before news of the French alliance, Congress, hearing of the British acts, unanimously agreed to hold no conference unless the British should first "withdraw their fleets and armies, or else, in positive and express terms, acknowledge the independence of the said States." Nevertheless one commissioner addressed letters to influential public men, holding out to some of them hopes of great rewards for effecting a reconciliation.

Repulsed by Congress, the commissioners sought the defection of the States individually. On October 20 a vessel delivered at Charles Town the commissioners' appeal to the President, the leaders, and people of South Carolina. These advances were unanimously rejected by the available officials and a hastily summoned group representing the various classes.

Georgia Conquered.—The rejection of conciliation inaugurated a new era in the war. Britain now determined to renew the plan of 1776 of rolling up the States from South to North. The weakness of Georgia, the proved readiness of Southern Tories to fight, and the remoteness from the forces under Washington offered an inviting prospect. The stalemate at the North settled into a few raids and a watching game after the drawn battle of Monmouth, July 28, 1778, and the fiasco at Newport in August. In South Carolina there now followed three years of war of a constancy and severity unparalleled in the North.

Lieutenant-Colonel Archibald Campbell was ordered from Long Island to Savannah with 3,000 men, to be supplemented by Prevost's from St. Augustine. Campbell drove Howe's 600 or 700 men through Savannah on a run on December 29, 1778, and captured nearly his whole force. General Benjamin Lincoln of Massachusetts now relieved Howe, whose monotonous bad fortune had led South Carolina to secure his removal. Colonel Campbell's moderation and wisdom, supplementing his military ability, soon had lower Georgia out of the war, but in North Georgia Andrew Pickens dispersed near Kettle Creek a large body of Tories. Pickens' victory was followed by a most lamentable vengeance. A number of the Tory captives were tried by the circuit court at Ninety Six for treason against their State. Five were hanged and the rest pardoned. There was thus set the example of executing captives which both sides were later to practice with no result beyond brutalization and bitterness.

Question of Negro Troops.—How woefully Congress failed to recognize the desperate situation was exhibited by their discussing, during the early months of 1779, terms of a triumphant peace. New England demanded as an ultimatum the recognition of equal American rights in the Newfoundland and Canadian coast fisheries. John Mathews of South Carolina opposed as unjust forcing our suffering country to fight for this. Henry Laurens and W. H. Drayton, frequently quarreling on the merest trifles, were thrown into fiercer antagonism when the latter joined the North Carolina delegates in condemning Laurens' defense of the New England demand. "The censors from the land of turpenpine" outraged Laurens by threatening to request the withdrawal of North Carolina troops from South Carolina, as she could not need aid if her leading delegate was willing to continue the war for a purpose in which the South, they said, had no interest. Laurens' and his colleague's enmity disappeared in an affecting scene at Drayton's deathbed on September 3, 1779, when, just short of thirty-seven, one of the most brilliant, influential, and daring leaders of the Revolution fell on sleep.

All that Congress could do in answer to South Carolina's plea for aid was to send young Lieutenant-Colonel John Laurens, the engineer DeLaumoy, and Count Pulaski with his "Legion" of about 120 men, along with the advice that South Carolina and Georgia should arm 3,000 trusty slaves. The suggestion was not so absurd, for the South Carolina law had until 1778 allowed this in crisis. North Carolina, true to her traditions from early days, sent 3,000 or more militia and her remaining Continental battalion that was not in the North.

The Laurenses, father and son, both favored emancipation. John wrote, on February 17, 1779, "It will be my duty and my pride to transform the timid slave into a firm defender of liberty, and render him worthy to enjoy it himself." General Isaac Huger (sent to secure aid from Congress) and both Laurenses urged the plan of enlisting slaves. Though Washington pointed out the folly of teaching the British a game at which they could beat us, Congress recommended the arming of 3,000 slaves. The South Carolina legislature in 1779 rejected Congress' proposal with contempt and considered their State not only abandoned but insulted. Henry Laurens met this defeat with the determination of the convinced emancipationist. Reminding John of the same principles in the youth's grandfather, he wrote, "The work will at a future day be efficaciously taken up, and then it will be remembered who began it in South Carolina." In 1780 the house rejected General Lincoln's plea for armed blacks, but ordered enrolled 1,000 as pioneers, fatigue-men, oarsmen, or mariners. John Laurens renewed his proposal in 1782, and secured twice as many votes as in 1779.

Disorderly Militia.—General Lincoln's handful of Continentals at Purrysburgh were reinforced by militia until the whole amounted to 4,000 by February 8. The militia, courageous for a rapid movement, proved thoroughly undisciplined under the law whose severest penalty was a small fine. Moultrie wrote on January 20, 1779, "They are worse than nothing, as they absolutely refuse General Lincoln's orders." How extreme was the opposition to the slightest abridgment of the liberty of freemen, even with the enemy at the gates, appears in the act of February 13, 1779, tightening up the law. For the next eighteen months a third of the militia were made liable to go into any threatened State. Refusal to serve might incur a small fine. Assaulting an officer or deserting incurred from four to twelve months' sentence to the Continental line. Offenders were to be tried by a court martial containing a majority of privates.

Charlestown Besieged and Saved.—There now followed a period of several months during which the British and Americans alternately attempted the invasion of the State held by the other, with little result except further to exhibit the ineffectiveness of the militia. Lincoln determined upon an incursion into Georgia near Augusta. Prevost countered by invading South Carolina. Moultrie stupidly allowed himself to be besieged in Charlestown instead of fighting at some strong position behind the Ashley, where even a serious defeat would have left him free to join the other American forces.

On May 11, General Prevost summoned the besieged Moultrie to surrender, the fate of those captured to be the same as that ultimately of the other "colonists." Governor Rutledge, supported by 5 to 3 of his Council, now sent to Prevost, according to Moultrie, the following proposal: To propose a neutrality, during the war between Great Britain and America, and the question, whether the state shall belong to Great Britain, or remain one of the United States be determined by the treaty of peace between those two powers.

John Laurens refused to carry the message, and others were prevailed on with difficulty. Moultrie, writing in 1802, says he had the signed message in his possession; but both the wording and the style of his quotation marks indicate he does not give the exact words. But John Laurens' and his father's account (derived presumably from John) gives the following as the Governor's and Council's proposal (again, as apparently with Moultrie's statement, the exact words not being given): "That he should be permitted to take possession of it [i.e., Charlestown] provided the state and harbor should be considered as neutral during the war, the question whether it belonged to Great Britain or the United States to be waived until the conclusion of it, and that whenever that should happen whatever was granted to the other states, that [South Carolina] should enjoy."

This evidence of Rutledge's vacillation on independence, rather than endorse which he had the year before resigned as president, again exhibits his hesitant mind. Either version of his proposal disqualifies him as a good partisan of independence; and yet there was much to be said in favor of his proposed neutrality. British victory over South Carolina appeared almost inevitable. There was a strong feeling that the abandonment of South Carolina by Congress deprived the other States of any right to complain at anything she might do. To secure the exemption of the people from the obligation of military service in the British army would be a great benefit for them and for the American cause. The Laurens version of Rutledge's proposal would be preferred to that of Moultrie by Rutledge's friends, for it did not leave South Carolina's independence at the disposal of others. But why should Rutledge object to leaving South Carolina's fate to be determined by Congress and Great Britain? Moultrie, writing with Rutledge's signed document before him, is supported by Rutledge's former declaration against independence.

Gadsden, violating the injunction of secrecy, openly spread the hateful proposition and threatened that those responsible should answer with their lives. General Prevost refused to treat with anyone but General Moultrie, responsible commander of the garrison. Moultrie snapped back into his true character of the South Carolina bulldog and declared, "We will fight it out." This in truth was his proper role, for, though possessed of some good military qualities, he was so careless and slothful that only this prime virtue of a soldier redeemed his faults.

Lincoln, at last unable to doubt that Prevost would soon be before Charlestown, had left Georgia; but his incredible slowness saved Prevost's 2,400 regulars from being "Burgoyned" between him and Moultrie. Prevost retired along the sea islands as stepping stones to Beaufort, where he took a position too strong to be attacked.

Prevost's invasion had cost the citizens dear in plundered plate, jewelry, horses, slaves, and other movables. Few houses were burned, an exemption purchased by the ready abandonment of the rebellion by "the planters, who," says Ramsay, "were more attentive to secure their property by submission than to defend it by resistance." The invasion proved that incapable or careless generals and fickle militia, though far outnumbering the enemy, were no match for competent professional officers and trained regulars. It revealed the deep rift in opinion among South Carolinians, and the feebleness in the government itself. Americans could derive little encouragement from the operations of 1779 for the more serious struggle sure soon to follow.

Americans and French Fail Before Savannah.—Count D'Estaing's presence in the West Indies offered an opportunity for a blow at the British in Beaufort and Savannah. He arrived about the beginning of September, 1779, with a fleet of forty-one vessels. Lincoln brought 4,000 South Carolina and Georgia troops, all of them militia except 600 Continentals, who, with the French, made a land force of about 6,500. Prevost took advantage of the allied delays by assembling 2,500 men. After five days of cannonading, at D'Estaing's demand that the place be stormed, or he would leave for fear of hurricanes, there was a general assault. Without reflecting on other combatants, we may say that the South Carolina loyalists and the South Carolina rebels shed glory on their State. Sergeant Jasper and Count Pulaski were among the slain as the defeated Americans withdrew.

The Siege of Charlestown.—D'Estaing's abandonment of the American coast after his failure at Savannah invited the British to launch their plan for taking Charlestown, rolling up the southern States, and crushing Washington between their northern and southern armies. Sir Henry Clinton, now in supreme command, had on December 1, 1779, 39,569 men. Washington had nominally 27,000. Strengthening New York beyond the possibility of assault, Clinton sailed on December 26 with a powerful expedition for Savannah.

The condition of South Carolina before this onslaught was most discouraging. On Washington's recommendation Congress ordered some 3,000 Virginia and North Carolina Continentals on the long march to Charlestown. Expecting more militia from Virginia and the Carolinas than he ever received, Lincoln agreed with the civil authorities in drawing his forces into Charlestown for a siege. The only alternatives were thus complete victory or the utter loss of practically the entire American army in the South. The determination to hold the city was based more on political and sentimental than on military reasons. Having determined to hold the city, Lincoln proceeded in the worst possible way, i.e., by merely walling himself up in the tip of the peninsula. Instead of using the numerous islands and marshes, natural defenses by which the Confederates held back the Federal forces from 1862 to 1865, he allowed the British to employ them to seal him up.

On February 3, 1780, the legislature by ordinance conferred on Governor Rutledge and Council additional powers, but by no means such as, on Ramsay's statement, have passed into tradition, sustained by the veneration for Rutledge, the romanticism of the idea, and the ringing sound of the word "Dictator." The very idea of dictatorial powers was inconsistent with Revolutionary South Carolina's distrust of all power, especially one-man power, which caused her to refuse in the greatest peril even to sanction laws capable of enforcing military discipline. Instead of granting the "Dictator," as he was afterward romantically called, astonishing powers, the powers allowed were astonishingly limited. "Whereas, in times of danger and invasion, it has always been the policy of republics to concentrate the powers of government in the hands of the supreme magistracy for a limited time," ran the ordinance, the Governor, with consent of the Privy Council, could until ten days after the next meeting of the legislature call forth any part of the militia, provided not over one-third be called out at once except within eighty miles of an invasion; support families of poor militiamen; suspend trade and civil courts; provide vessels, forts, etc.; seize provisions at current prices; "and to do all other matters and things which may be judged expedient and necessary to secure the liberty, safety and happiness of this State, except taking away the life of a citizen without legal trial. Provided it does not extend to subject the militia to articles of war for the regulation of the Continental or State troops." As Mr. Robert W. Barnwell, Jr., points out, these powers were continued on the retirement of Rutledge to the two governors who filled out the time until the signing of peace. They might also therefore be given the romantic title of "Dictator."[1]

The whole siege was a chapter of irresistible resources and minute thoroughness on the part of the British against the errors and weakness of the Americans. Clinton began with 6,000 men, raised during the siege to 11,000, the largest force employed in any operation of the war except the capture of Philadelphia and possibly the battle of Long Island, and controlled the sea. Lincoln commanded about 5,150 or 5,775 men, according to American and British figures respectively. The besiegers included the flower of the British army. The defenders included over 1,600 militia.

On February 11, 1780, Clinton's army landed at the southern end of John's Island, whence it passed with perfect safety to James Island, whence with ease it passed to the mainland. Arbuthnot's fleet was allowed to cross the bar without opposition by Commodore Whipple's fleet inside. Of the 7,975 soldiers with whom Clinton embarked at New York in December, 1779, 2,020 were Hessians under their own officers.[2] Governor Rutledge and three of his Council left Charlestown on April 12 in order to avoid the demolition of civil government by their capture. Gadsden, appointed acting lieutenant-governor, remained, only to add confusion to Lincoln's weakness. The bombardment began on the 13th.

Clinton seized successively the garrison's every avenue of escape.

[1] In the *Journal of Southern History* of May, 1941 (VII, 215-24), Mr. Robert W. Barnwell, Jr., objects to my calling Rutledge's powers under the law of 1780 "astonishingly limited." "Astonishingly limited" is not an exact term, but it described my feeling on finding how excessive had been the idea of "dictator" derived from Ramsay's statement. Mr. Barnwell admits that "the powers of the dictator while in exile [i.e., we may interject, during the struggle for driving the British from the State] were very limited and amounted to little more than the appointment of militia officers." Mr. Barnwell's conclusion is: "It must be admitted that the powers wielded by South Carolina's 'dictator' seem slight when compared with those of famous dictators of other days. Nevertheless, it is true that John Rutledge was vested with broad powers, that he was virtually the government of South Carolina during the most critical months of the British occupation, and that at times he exercised his powers with severity, albeit with discretion and sound judgment. It can also be maintained that the exercise of these powers by Rutledge was a factor in the recovery of the State. Thus, in the main, the traditional view of Rutledge 'the dictator' is sustained."

[2] B. A. Uhlendorf (translator and editor), *Siege of Charleston* (diaries and letters of Hessian officers), (University of Michigan Press, 1938), p. 105.

Conspicuous in the fighting for these approaches was one of the most brilliant cavalry leaders of the war whom this campaign had brought to South Carolina, Lieutenant-Colonel William Washington of Virginia. Every possibility of reinforcements or escape having disappeared, the surrender of the town with freedom of the garrison to withdraw armed to the northward was offered to Clinton on April 21 and immediately rejected.

The remnant of the American cavalry having been cut to pieces on May 6, and Fort Moultrie having surrendered on May 7 without a shot, Clinton renewed his demand for surrender. Bombarded by 200 British cannon from without and by petitions of the citizens and militia within, the luckless Lincoln surrendered on May 12. The garrison had the satisfaction of having the enemy compliment them on their gallant defense.

American figures (admittedly inexact) appear to make the number of captured 5,058. Clinton's minutely detailed report says 5,683.

The articles of capitulation provided that all public property, including 50,000 pounds of powder, should become the victor's; that the Continentals should remain prisoners until exchanged; that the militia should go home as paroled prisoners not be disturbed in their property so long as they observed the parole; and that all persons in the town, whether they had borne arms or not, should be prisoners on parole on the same terms as the militia.

In addition to public losses, inhabitants of the whole region were plundered of enormous wealth by systematized official stealing lasting far beyond the siege and estimated to total £300,000 sterling. Commissioners of captures administered the plunder and assigned it by rule. The quota of a major-general approached four thousand guineas, but individuals often secured in addition by private plunder more than their allotment from the commissioner. Tarleton, having lost by bad weather the horses of his legion on shipboard, restocked from the famous stables of South Carolina. Thousands of slaves were sold in the West Indies, and thousands more flocking to the British, as in 1779, perished of disease.

CHAPTER XXXII

SOUTH CAROLINA BEGINS THE SECOND WAR OF THE REVOLUTION, 1780

THE SITUATION in South Carolina after the fall of Charlestown could hardly have been gloomier for the Americans. The British had not only taken the capital but had virtually conquered the State. An appreciable proportion of the population viewed this situation with pleasure. The great majority of those feeling regret accepted it as inevitable. To the annihilation of their army was added the destruction of their civil government save for a peripatetic governor in headlong flight.

Clinton ordered three expeditions to the interior, one to hold Augusta, one Ninety Six, and one Camden. Lord Cornwallis dispatched Tarleton after Colonel Buford* who was retreating with Virginia Continentals whom he had intended for the relief of Charlestown. On May 29 Tarleton overtook Buford six miles south of the North Carolina line and eight miles east of the present town of Lancaster, and, when surrender was refused, attacked with such suddenness and fury as utterly to ruin his foe. After the Americans had surrendered, thrown down their arms, and begged for quarter, the British continued their slaughter. Only about 30 of the 350 Americans escaped capture, severe wounding, or death. The compassion stirred in the inhabitants who nursed the wounded and the cry of anguished rage that greeted the savagery throughout the State turned Tarleton's victory into a British disaster, for it planted in the hearts of thousands who had accepted renewed British rule the determination to expel a power which could be guilty of such cruelty.

James says that "Tarleton burnt the home of General Sumter near Stateburgh, and roused the spirit of the lion." The era now opening was for South Carolina her second war of Revolution. She had entered upon the first in resistance to unconstitutional taxation, made more irksome by other well-recognized grievances. She was driven into the second by Clinton's breach of his plighted faith of May 12, 1780, soon to be noticed, and the barbarity with which the arrogant conquerors expressed their contempt for beaten rebels. The folly with which British politicians precipitated the first Revolution was now paralleled by the stupid cruelty

* Full names of Revolutionary officers will be found in the Index of this book.

with which British soldiers roused the second. In this rising the old questions of constitutional rights were revived; but they were for practical effect overshadowed by the grim determination to expel a conqueror under whose perfidy, cruelty, and tyranny free men refused to live.

Clinton Violates Paroles.—Clinton apparently contemplated from the first treating the general population of the province (as he considered it) as subject to all the obligations of British allegiance, for his proclamation of May 22, offering pardon to all who submitted, threatened the severest punishment to any who still maintained rebellion and, promising the earliest possible restoration of civil government, commanded all persons whenever they should be required to aid the king's forces. On June 1 followed a proclamation offering pardon to all except those still in rebellion and those having under the forms of law executed loyalists for treason, and promising civil government with exemption from all taxes except those imposed by their own Assembly.

Clinton was pleased with the effect of his proclamations. The militia around Beaufort asked to be accepted as prisoners on parole on the same terms as the Charlestown garrison. The rebels of Camden met Lord Rawdon with a similar request, those of Ninety Six District accepted the same status, and so on. This acceptance by the conqueror of thousands of men as prisoners on parole who could neither oppose the conqueror nor be molested by him was inconsistent with Clinton's apparent intention of requiring all to recognize the King's authority and of transforming the South Carolina militia into a British army. Whether his act of June 3, soon to be considered, was intended to correct his error in accepting paroles, or whether the proceedings merely expressed a contemptuous carelessness of the rights of rebels, that act went far to undo all that had been accomplished by his victory and his two mild and just proclamations. This proclamation of June 3 abolished the status of prisoners on parole for all except the actual Charlestown garrison and citizens and declared them, unless they returned to their allegiance by June 20, enemies and rebels. Prisoners of war were thus notified they might be forced to choose between acting as British subjects, even to the point of fighting against their fellow-Americans, or fighting for independence. Even Rutledge dismissed the idea of reconciliation and declared that the achievement of independence at the earliest possible moment should be the object of America and our ally. But no general rising occurred until the outrages by British troops and the dragooning of men out of their rights forced the Whigs to choose between fighting for or against a government which now presented itself to them as a despotism.

The British, having broken the parole agreement, proceeded to persecute the unwilling into acceptance by an astonishing extent, variety, and shamelessness of perfidy which destroyed the age-old tradition of English freedom sanctioned by law, honor, and custom. The Charlestonians, who were specifically guaranteed their parole rights, were dragooned into accepting British allegiance by being denied the right to sue in court, by being restricted in their movements, by being forbidden to sell the stocks of goods the conquerors had encouraged them to buy, by being subjected to soldiers quartered on almost every family, by being robbed by British soldiers who were permitted plundering as a compensation for their labors in the siege, and by being refused restoration of seized property. Hundreds of American prisoners were taken from the prison ships and forced to serve in Lord Montagu's regiment in the West Indies. To the poor it was to submit or starve; to the rich, to submit or lose their estates. Added to this was the groundless belief, encouraged by the British, that Congress had determined to abandon the two southernmost States. Thus, for one reason or another, except in the present York County, the inhabitants after the fall of Charlestown generally preferred submission to resistance and accepted British protection, as acquiescence in the proclamation of June 3 was called, by acknowledging their allegiance to the King. Among those accepting British allegiance were Henry Middleton, for a few days President of the First Continental Congress, old Mr. Manigault, and Colonel Charles Pinckney, formerly president of the Provincial Congress. Colonel Andrew Pickens surrendered the fort and munitions at Ninety Six, marched in his men, and like them acknowledged British allegiance. Pickens ultimately re-entered the war and fought at the risk of hanging for treason should he be captured. General Andrew Williamson kept his renewed allegiance and ultimately resided near Charlestown, but he rendered the British no service. There is on the contrary some ground for believing that he was one of those who toward the end of the war supplied Colonel John Laurens, in charge of General Greene's secret service, with information of affairs in Charlestown. Nevertheless rumor, attacking even his early brilliant services, blighted one of the noblest reputations of the earlier years of the Revolution in South Carolina.

Clinton, having, as he imagined, pacified South Carolina, leaving Lord Cornwallis in command, sailed for New York with the greater part of his army in order to face with adequate forces General Washington after the arrival of expected French reinforcements. There were few men in South Carolina, he wrote on June 4, who were not "either our prisoners or in arms with us." The re-establishment of normal life was to most a welcome boon. Wagon trains from the mountains even resumed their commerce through their natural port. English money supplemented the worthless paper, and life for a while flowed normally.

The Rising Under Sumter and Hill.—Sumter's leaving his burned home on May 28 to rally the people may be taken as the beginning, only two weeks after the fall of Charlestown, of the new resistance. Thomas Sumter (1734-1832) was born of poor parents in Virginia and came to South Carolina in 1762 in charge of Cherokee Indians whom he had escorted from Virginia to London and thence home by way of Charlestown. Of extraordinary strength and quickness, bold in fight, rash both in battle and business, he was typical of the climbing American of the age making his own way. Marrying a rich widow considerably his senior, the young man of thirty-three swung into the landed gentry. He was soon obtaining large grants on his own account, manifesting a love for land that kept him speculating and debt-burdened while his life lasted. As a captain in the Snow Campaign of 1775 he began under suspicion of Tory sentiments but won distinction and confidence. As lieutenant-colonel commanding a regiment in 1776, he helped hold Clinton off while Moultrie battered Parker's fleet, and looked out on the *Acteon* stranded and burning on the shoal where later was to stand the fort bearing his name. In 1778 he resigned his commission as a Continental lieutenant-colonel, but continued in civil life as a legislator. Though he could hear the guns at Charlestown, he did not go to her help. Like the State at large, he was roused only by the enemy's later conduct.

Another leader of the new rising was William Hill of the New Acquisition, i.e., the later York County, whose Aetna Furnace, erected in partnership with Colonel Isaac Hayne, employed 100 men making tools and cannon. Hill was surrounded by Scotch-Irish Presbyterian neighbors of the same opinion. General McCrady is doubtless justified in interpreting the conduct of these men as inspired by their long history of organized resistance to royal and ecclesiastic tyranny in the old country, and the republican principles of their church government. The British understood the situation in the same sense, for Major James Wemyss burned Presbyterian churches as "sedition shops." Presbyterian ministers were insulted, their houses and libraries burned, and Bibles with the Scottish version of the Psalms consigned to the flames as indicating a rebellious sect.

At all events the Scotch-Irish Presbyterians of the New Acquisition now made good the long tradition of a people characterized by the grim defense of their liberties. They elected Hill and Andrew Neel their colonels, formed a camp, raised the American flag, and thus became the first community to move to redeem the State, though they themselves had experienced no British violence.

The British captain Christian Huck at Rocky Mount struck promptly and burned Hill's iron works, saw- and gristmills, workmen's houses, etc. In the following months the British hanged as traitors men taken in arms after renewing allegiance, and turned women and children of affluence from their burned homes into the woods. "The enemy seem determined, if they can, to break every man's spirit, and if they can't, to ruin him," wrote Rutledge of these and other inflictions.

Sumter was now east of the Catawba at Tuckasegee Ford with a few followers who on June 15 elected him their general, though Rutledge continued to call him colonel until officially raising his rank. The men found their own supplies and agreed to serve under Sumter to the end. Hill and his men joined Sumter. The expiration of the time for accepting British protection brought in more recruits as Sumter lay just within the South Carolina line. Sumter was in his fortified camp at Old Nation Ford on the Catawba below the North Carolina line with 500 men, when Captain Huck of Tarleton's Legion with 105 men, raiding the country a little south, encamped on July 11 at James Williamson's in southern York. On July 12 men from Sumter's and others' forces slew Huck and drove off his troops with heavy losses. This, the first success of the South Carolinians since the fall of Charlestown, brought men flocking to Sumter.

Partisan War in the Northwest.—Sumter's operations have been first noticed because they began first, and because they served to inspire others. His activities along the Catawba stirred the Whigs of the present Cherokee, Spartanburg, and Union counties. The Whigs of Ninety Six district had to overcome a difficulty from which their compatriots elsewhere were free—wise and conciliatory conduct by the British leaders. On June 22, 1780, Colonel Patrick Ferguson, already a distinguished soldier, with his British regulars from the North, the "American Volunteers," joined Colonel Balfour at Ninety Six, with the special mission of inspecting the back-country militia and winning over the inhabitants. Flattering the backwoodsmen and endearing himself to them by conversing with them by the hour on public affairs, this aristocratic Scottish gentleman soon had large numbers of young men, already prepared by Cuningham, Fletchall, Robinson, and Pearis, drilling in his camps. Little battles were almost continuous in and near the later Spartanburg County, until Ferguson himself with 1,500 men sought unsuccessfully, on August 8, to crush the 1,000 men under Clarke and Shelby in the running second battle of Cedar Springs.

Sumter and Davie on the Catawba.—Clarke's and Shelby's most important and final action of this campaign was now only eleven days in the future, but the previous events elsewhere must first be narrated. Let us turn first to Sumter on the Catawba. His men deserting rapidly when inactive, Sumter, on July 30, unsuccessfully attacked Rocky Mount in the southeastern corner of the present Chester, while William Richardson Davie attacked Hanging Rock in the south of the present Lancaster.

On August 6 Sumter failed at Hanging Rock, but even Rawdon and Tarleton recognized that the moral advantage was with Sumter, for, said the latter, men "flocked from all parts of South Carolina" to him as "his reputation for activity and courage was fully established by his late enterprising conduct."

In these operations in which the courage and initiative of many shone brilliantly, conspicuous was William Richardson Davie (1756-1820). Born in England, he was reared in the home of his uncle, the Presbyterian minister of the Waxhaws, Rev. William Richardson. He left Princeton College to join Washington's army but later graduated. He had settled in Salisbury, North Carolina, when, in 1779, he re-entered the war with a North Carolina commission. His soldiers now were from South Carolina. His marvelous voice thrilled men upon the battlefield as later in legislative halls. As General Greene's commissary general he rendered invaluable, though less conspicuous, service in the desperate struggle of 1781. After notable public honors, despite his Federalistic contempt for the Democratic politics and politicians of North Carolina, he served as governor and as peace commissioner to France. In 1805 this aristocratic gentleman of wealth and culture retired to Tivoli, his plantation in Lancaster district, South Carolina, near the scenes of his boyhood.

Marion Emerges as Leader in the East.—The inhabitants along the west bank of the Peedee were roused by the barbarity of Major James Wemyss as those along the Catawba were by Tarleton's. Shortly after the patriots along the upper Catawba and Broad had formed their voluntary organizations under officers whose commissions were virtually their sheer power of leadership, similar spontaneous assertion of the spirit of independence arose in the country between lower Lynch's River and the Santee. Several brushes with Tories and British marauders had already occurred when Marion arrived on August 10 or 12 from the approaching Continental army to take command.

Francis Marion (1732-95) had the most continuous record of service of all those leaders now organizing the new war of independence. This scion of the Huguenots, born in St. John's Berkeley, as a young man settled in his permanent home, Pond Bluff in his native parish. A veteran of the Cherokee war of 1760-61 and a member of a Provincial Congress of 1775, he fought as a major at Fort Moultrie and shared the battles of the 2d Regiment until the siege of Charlestown in 1780, from which he was sent before the surrender because of a sprained ankle.

He repaired to North Carolina to join Gates's approaching army. He thus, as a Continental lieutenant-colonel, began the phase of his effort in which later, as a South Carolina militia brigadier, he was to render his greatest service.

His men quickly sensed the personal and military worth of their new leader, small of stature, taciturn, less dashing and perhaps of a less fertile mind but far more cautious, than Sumter, rigid in discipline, but always imposing on himself more than he demanded of others, and destined to prove himself under circumstances tempting to every license singularly pure, merciful, upright, and just. Marion immediately dispersed Major Ganey's Tories at Britton's Neck (southern modern Marion) and held himself in reserve for other opportunities at the enemy whose superior numbers enforced caution.

This was the situation in South Carolina when General Gates arrived north of Camden with the Continentals sent by Washington. Clinton had the answer to his breaking his plighted faith to the men on parole, and Tarleton and other officers, to their cruelty and arrogance. As Tarleton remarked, Clinton's vision of converting the South Carolina militia into a British army had vanished. More correctly, it had been transformed into the disconcerting reality of a people roused in unconquerable determination to expel his British army. The military victory which he had won with such extraordinary care and thoroughness he had flung away with equally notable political folly. Men who would not submit to such treatment were already stinging his army to death. The war assumed in this new phase a character of terrible ferocity. Instead of embodied armies maneuvering for position and fighting pitched battles, little bands slaughtered each other as they could, and neighbors virtually crept upon neighbors to commit murder. Within three months of the fall of Charlestown, and in much less time since the abuse of their victory had become evident, the British armies were faced with formidable bodies of fighting men from the Peedee to the upper Savannah. The way had been prepared for Gates, and a widely flung force of light cavalry had been provided for his attempt to recover the State.

The Battle of Camden.—Conditions in South Carolina moved Washington, at some risk to his own position, to advise Congress to send a portion of his Continentals to South Carolina. Accordingly, DeKalb led from Morristown, New Jersey, nearly 2,000 Continentals, mainly Marylanders, but including also the Delaware regiment. Gates, crowned with his undeserved Saratoga laurels, was made commander instead of Greene, whom Washington preferred. After a grueling march the army united in the present Chesterfield County with the North Carolina militia.

Lord Rawdon advanced from Camden to the west fork of Lynch's River, but Gates, instead of smashing through as he probably could have done, detoured by right, and reached a point about thirteen miles north of Camden on the main road to Charlotte on August 13. Here Gates approved the offer of Sumter west of the river to cut off British supplies from Charlestown at the ferries. This Sumter accomplished brilliantly, and retreated with his booty up the river, so that he was far away in the hour of supreme need about to strike.

But more important events were about to happen on the eastern, or Camden, side of the river. Cornwallis, having concentrated his forces, and having himself arrived in Camden from Charlestown early August 14, determined on a night attack for August 15-16. Gates had formed the same determination. The advance guards collided after midnight just north of Sanders' Creek seven miles north of Camden.

Gates believed that he had 7,000 men, but returns showed only 3,052 fit for duty. Not only had his army been thus reduced by sickness and exhaustion, but two-thirds or a little more were militia, and the army, being sent upon a difficult night attack, had never been exercised together as a whole. The British numbered about 1,700 regulars and 300 loyal militia. At the first attack Gates's militia fled, sweeping along their general, whose only order had been permission to begin the battle. Tarleton's legion pursued, "glutting themselves in blood." The Maryland and Delaware Continentals were thus left at the mercy of greatly superior numbers and outflanked, but their steady fire held back the enemy until Cornwallis threw overpowering forces upon their front and flank. The Americans lost their artillery and ammunition, almost all their baggage, probably 600 killed and wounded, and perhaps 1,300 prisoners. The remnant collected at Hillsborough totaled 777 Maryland and 175 Delaware Continentals and 50 Virginia militia. The British admitted the loss of 300 killed and wounded.

With the composure of the professional soldier, Cornwallis immediately turned to Sumter. That officer, so much more brilliant in attack than cautious in repose, had retreated "slowly and carelessly up the Catawba." On the 18th at midday, although informed on the 16th of Gates's disaster, he had traveled only forty miles in three nights and almost three days. Suddenly Tarleton dashed with a shout on the careless camp with 160 men, and captured 310 men, 800 horses, 44 wagonloads of stores and two of ammunition, and two cannon. One hundred and fifty Americans were reported killed and wounded, and many drowned. Sumter fled without coat, hat, or saddle. But such was the devotion to him that three days after his arrival in Charlotte from his disaster at Fishing Creek he again had a considerable force.

The terrible disadvantage of militia under untrained officers, fighting against regulars commanded by competent professional soldiers, could hardly be more pathetically illustrated than at Camden and Fishing Creek. But the confidence they had gained by their victories over British regulars in July and August was not destroyed even under these terrible blows, which tended rather to forge them into veterans.

The Militia Keep the Field.—Contrasted with Sumter's carelessness at Fishing Creek was Marion's alertness in capturing 150 of Cornwallis' prisoners at Nelson's Ferry and part of Wemyss's force at Kingstree, and on August 28, when the enemy grew too strong, skipping untouched into North Carolina. In a few weeks he was back, defeating the Tories at Black Mingo Creek and Tarcote Swamp with lightning-like strokes.

Musgrove's Mill.—After the second battle of Cedar Springs (or Wofford's Iron Works) on August 8, Major Ferguson was called to the upper Catawba to reinforce the British posts against Sumter's attacks. This invited Whigs on the upper Broad (all North Carolinians except a few Georgians and South Carolinians) to strike at Musgrove's Mill on the Enoree. Riding all night southwest across the present Cherokee and Union counties, they arrived near dawn, August 19, in the southern tip of Spartanburg, opposite Musgrove's Mill. Astonished at finding the British reinforced, the Americans were forced to fight or be cut to pieces in futile flight on their tired horses. A half mile or more north of the river, Shelby, Williams, and Clarke hurled back the British, whom they had skillfully lured into a disastrous charge against their strong position. About 200 American frontiersmen with a total loss of 13 inflicted a loss of 223 killed, wounded, and captured on an enemy of double their number. In the choice of their ground, the skill of their strategy, and the fortitude of their combat, the Americans at Musgrove's Mill illustrated the best qualities of militiamen and volunteers as notably, although on a smaller scale, as at King's Mountain, to which this action directly led.

It was the plan of the Americans to press on thirty miles south and take the weakened British post at Ninety Six, but news that Gates was defeated at Camden forced immediate flight. A terrible day's ride following the all-night ride to the battle took them to North Carolina.

The contest for the northwestern districts thus joined between the British and the men of the western portion of the Carolinas and east Tennessee was to move rapidly to a conclusion as astonishing as influential, having a vital bearing on the outcome of the Revolutionary War in the country as a whole.

Rebels to Be Executed, etc.—For the second time in a little over three months South Carolina was conquered, and from a military standpoint even more thoroughly. But spiritually she was not now conquered at all as she had been on the fall of Charlestown in May. The people had then passively accepted the fall of their capital, and a majority had preferred submission as prisoners on parole to further resistance. Though not an organized body of resistance remained in the State after the ruin of Gates's army at Camden, hovering on its borders were leaders whose return to head resistance thousands would welcome.

Cornwallis failed to understand the deep forces that were working against him. To him it remained merely a task of beating armies and intimidating subjects into obeying their lawful sovereign. Besides this deep spiritual opposition and the constant attrition of partisan attacks on every expedition or garrison separated from his few strong centers, Cornwallis had to fight against a climate whose diseases science had not then mastered. The numbers of his sick were portentous, and frequently valuable officers were incapacitated for weeks by fever.

All this was very irritating, as it was delaying the execution of his fundamental aim—the march to crush the army of Washington between himself and Clinton. To speed up the pacifying of South Carolina he therefore entered upon measures to force submission by threat of death or the loss of men's entire estates.

A few days after his victory over Gates, Cornwallis issued the following order to his post commanders: All who had signed paroles and had afterward borne arms against the King "should be punished with the greatest rigour"; all who refused to bear arms for the King "may be imprisoned and their whole property taken from them or destroyed. . . . I have ordered in the most positive manner that every militiaman who has borne arms with us and afterwards joined the enemy shall be immediately hanged. . . . You will obey in the strictest manner the directions I have given in this letter." Executions began at once, while numbers were imprisoned for refusing to fight for the King. The British thus, and with more cruel rigor, began to follow the example of the South Carolinians in executing their opponents for treason.

The St. Augustine Exiles.—Dragooning into submission assumed a different form in Charlestown, where the civil population had been specifically included among those guaranteed the rights of parole at the capitulation. As Cornwallis' vexation rose at the derangement of his plans his persecutions stiffened. In August and November, 1780, sixty-three prominent men, mostly civil or military officials at the time of the capitulation, were sent to St. Augustine "to secure the quiet of the province," which was, Cornwallis charged, being disturbed because some persons on parole were fomenting a spirit of rebellion. No accusation was made against these men specifically. The act of expulsion was clearly intended not as a punishment for any offense, but as a threat of what those might expect who persisted in exercising their parole right of refusing to accept British allegiance.

General McCrady appears correct in maintaining, contrary to Americans generally, that Cornwallis was within his legal rights in banishing these men to St. Augustine, for the articles of capitulation promised that prisoners should be unmolested in their property, but did not guarantee security for their persons. Gadsden refused to give a second parole to the authority that he considered had violated the first, and so spent forty-two weeks in a cell in the castle at St. Augustine.

On May 3, 1781, representatives of Generals Greene and Cornwallis signed a cartel for the exchange of prisoners in the Southern Department. The St. Augustine exiles were accordingly shipped to Philadelphia in July, 1781. Many were soon joined there by their families, who were ordered by Commandant Balfour, on June 25, 1781, to leave Charlestown. Governor Rutledge retaliated by ordering all loyalists to leave their plantations and repair to Charlestown. The miseries of the wretched inhabitants of Rawdontown, the suburb outside the city for such refugees, were thus increased.

Sequestrations and Defections—Moultrie's Integrity.—September 16, 1780, Cornwallis issued from the Waxhaws his proclamation sequestering the estates real and personal of (1) all who had abandoned their plantations to join the rebels; (2) all not included in the capitulation of Charlestown acting under the authority of Congress; and (3) all by words or acts desperately opposing the re-establishment of the King's authority. A wife was to receive a sixth, and a wife and children a fourth, of the income from such an estate. The estates were not confiscated, but only taken from their owners for the time being, the question of their ultimate disposition being reserved for the future.

A different attack was made on General Moultrie. If General Moultrie would merely desert the American cause he might leave the "colony" for a while, wrote former Governor Lord Montagu, and take command of his Lordship's own regiment. "Thus you would avoid any disagreeable conversations, and might return at leisure to take possession of your estates for yourself and family." Moultrie replied, on March 12, 1781: ". . . Good God! Is is possible that such an idea could arise in the breast of a man of honor? . . . You say, by quitting this country for a short time I might avoid disagreeable conversations, and might return at my own leisure and take possession of my estates for myself and family; but you have forgot to tell me how I am to get rid of the feelings of an injured honest heart, and where to hide myself from myself; could I be guilty of so much baseness I should hate myself and shun mankind. This would be a fatal exchange from my present situation, with an easy and approved conscience of having done my duty, and conducted myself as a man of honor."

Men of less resolution yielded. With all occupations closed, on March 25, 1781, to any but loyalists, and loyalists forbidden to employ any but those who had accepted British allegiance, many were conquered, bowing to the necessity of feeding self and wife and children. In addition there was the force of example. There had all along been a strong loyalist party embracing men of all ranks of society. On June 5, 1780, 206 persons in Charlestown presented a long address congratulating General Clinton and Admiral Arbuthnot on their victory. Continued British success drew others into the circle of congratulators. On September 19, 1780, 164 persons styling themselves "loyal inhabitants of Charles Town" congratulated Cornwallis on his victory at Camden and execrated "the contemptible remains of that expiring faction" opposing "that government under which they formerly enjoyed the highest degree of civil and political liberty." Foremost was the name of Daniel Huger, one of the Council who had accompanied Rutledge from Charlestown. There, too, were the names of Colonel Charles Pinckney, Gabriel Manigault, Wade Hampton, and others of the highest standing or of past Revolutionary service who now considered that independence was hopeless. But Hampton, says McCrady, was yet to render notable service to the American cause, which he joined for the first time shortly before April 2, 1781.

Thus were added to the horrors of war the barbarities inevitable in a genuine civil war. To the casualties of combat were added the dangers of death by hanging for treason and of whole families being reduced to poverty by the seizing of the estates of men whose politics displeased the party in power. All this was added in South Carolina to a war in which the number of combats, the communities ravaged or fought over, the continuous period of conflict, and the suffering inflicted, were not approached in any other state.

CHAPTER XXXIII

DRIVING THE BRITISH FROM THE UP COUNTRY, 1780-1781

About September 7 or 8, Cornwallis marched from Camden to Charlotte. After the stinging defeat by the back-country Whigs of the British at Musgrove's Mill, Ferguson repaired to headquarters for consultation and received Cornwallis' order to pursue the North Carolinians into their mountains. He entered North Carolina on September 7, marched beyond Old Fort, and, returning, camped on September 23 at Gilbert Town (Rutherfordton), from which on his advance he had sent a message to the "men of the western waters" threatening to hang their leaders and waste their country with fire and sword.

On September 30 he learned from two deserters that the mountain men, instead of being intimidated, were advancing upon him. He was thus transformed from the avenger, dispatching threats of destruction to the overhill men, to the fugitive, fleeing from their wrath. He accordingly recrossed Broad River to the east, a little below the mouth of the Green, and struck for Charlotte to join Cornwallis.

Shelby and his associates, on retreating from Musgrove's Mill, had agreed to raise sufficient forces to attack Ferguson. Colonel Shelby of North Carolina and Colonel John Sevier of Tennessee at once began to assemble at Sycamore Shoals on the Watauga the host that was to strike Ferguson before he could strike them.

Besides the North Carolinians, almost the entire military force of the later Tennessee were present, and 400 Virginians from the later Kentucky. More came than could be allowed to leave the frontier, for an attack by the Indians was expected as part of the British campaign. The Indians did rise, and for it were signally punished in fights running through two years. But that is Tennessee history, except the Cherokee outbreaks in northern Georgia which Pickens aided in suppressing.

Few more colorful scenes mark American history than these thousand frontiersmen, clad in moccasins, coonskin caps, and hunting shirts, and armed with tomahawks, scalping knives, and unerring Deckhard rifles, bowing in prayer beside the rushing mountain stream, accompanied by their mountain preacher's exhortation on "the sword of the Lord and of Gideon," and riding away to meet the enemy at the mountain gates.

They had been unmoved by quarrels about tea taxes (though of principles of free government they were by no means uninformed); but now the representative of lawless power had spoken a threat they would not ignore.

Having in four days passed through these magnificent mountains and at Gillespie's Gap crossed the Blue Ridge dividing the eastern from the western waters, they were joined on September 30 at the eastern foot by Colonel Benjamin Cleveland's and Major Joseph Winston's North Carolinians. Campbell of Virginia, as the only colonel not a North Carolinian, was selected commander. At Gilbert Town (Rutherfordton) General James Williams came in with a few North and South Carolinians.

The Battle on King's Mountain.—By the evening of October 6, 1780, the retreating Ferguson was within about thirty-five miles of Charlotte, where his messengers arrived the next morning, too late to secure assistance from Cornwallis. Selecting an eminence in the King's Mountain range, he camped on the top. This little rocky mountain in York County, South Carolina, a mile and three-quarters south of the State line, is part of a range some sixteen miles long, the imposing "Pinnacle" of which lies about six miles to the northeast in North Carolina. The hill selected by Ferguson rises about two hundred feet above the plain to a ridge a thousand feet above sea level, so narrow at places "that a man standing on it may be shot from either side"; but its length of six hundred yards affords ample rolling ground. Here Ferguson rested, willing to fight alone if he must, but hoping for reinforcements for inflicting upon the attacking mountaineers a defeat that would wipe away the discredit of Musgrove's Mill and end the rebellion in the northwest.

Lest Ferguson escape, 910 mounted infantry from Virginia, North Carolina, and South Carolina, rode all night and to three o'clock on the afternoon of October 7. Concealing their horses, they proceeded on foot to surround the mountain and particularly to enclose its eastern end so as to intercept Ferguson should he run for Charlotte. The advancing Whigs were repeatedly forced to retreat before the British bayonet charges, but the accuracy of the frontiersmen's rifle fire was decisive. Seeing his defeat complete, Ferguson sought to dash through the lines toward Charlotte but fell pierced by several bullets. The slaughter continued after the white flag was raised, as the Whigs, crying, "Buford's play," killed and wounded men as Tarleton had in the Waxhaws. The British lost in killed or captured every one of their 1,104 men engaged. The Whig loss was 28 killed and 62 wounded.

Ferguson was the only man present not an American, for his 122 regulars had been recruited in the North, and his 982 Tory militia were from the South. King's Mountain was one of the turning points of the Revolution, for the American victory necessitated Cornwallis' falling back from North Carolina to Winnsboro, depressed the spirits of the Tories, put a new courage into the Americans, and completed the derangement of the great south to north movement for crushing Washington between Cornwallis and Clinton. The conquest of South Carolina had to be begun over again in a series of campaigns that led Cornwallis straight to his surrender at Yorktown.

Cornwallis Returns to South Carolina.—General Leslie, who had been sent from New York by sea to crush the rebellion in Virginia and form a junction with Cornwallis, now had to be shipped to Charlestown to help hold South Carolina. Marion was so seriously threatening the communications between Charlestown and Camden that Tarleton was sent to drive him off. Marion had barely escaped from Tarleton's superior numbers when Tarleton was recalled to check Sumter's threats against Cornwallis at Winnsboro.[1]

On October 6, 1780, Governor Rutledge commissioned Sumter as brigadier-general in command of all the State militia, thus adding legality to election by his men. Marion's brigadiership soon followed. Sumter was directed by Governor Rutledge to hold the entire militia ready to co-operate with the Continentals and in the meantime to act according to his own judgment. He was instructed to accept the services of men who had served with the enemy under compulsion, but to hold for trial for treason by the civil court all who had voluntarily aided the enemy. How the State authorities could, after this, protest against the execution of Colonel Hayne and others is difficult to explain except on humanitarian grounds.

As Sumter moved down Broad River with 425 men, Cornwallis at Winnsboro dispatched Major Wemyss on a night march against him as he lay on the eastern side of Fishdam Ford in the southwestern corner of the present Chester County. Only his officers' watchfulness prevented a complete defeat and the capture of the General in the night battle at one A.M., November 9. Both sides retreated, Sumter to the western side of the Broad. As already mentioned, Cornwallis summoned Tarleton from his pursuit of Marion. Sumter disposed his men with unimpeachable skill on an advantageous terrain at Blackstock's in the present Union, November 20, and, skillfully leading Tarleton to attack too soon, gave him a sharp defeat. But Sumter was obliged to retreat up the country

[1] Tarleton, pp. 170-72; James, *Marion*, pp. 61-63. Tarleton is said, when abandoning his pursuit of Marion through the swamps on this occasion to obey the order to go and attack Sumter, to have said to his men, Come on and we shall soon catch the game cock (a name Sumter had had for some months), "but as for this damned old fox, the devil himself could not catch him."

from the superior forces available for Tarleton and also to retire for weeks because of a severe wound.

Summary of Events from June to December, 1780.—The first seven months of the second war of the Revolution in South Carolina thus came to a close in December, 1780, just as a new phase was about to open with the arrival of General Greene and his Continentals. General McCrady excellently summarizes the results: Not including the three actions yet to come in December and belonging in the coming campaign, there had been thirty-four battles in South Carolina during 1780, counting the siege of Charlestown as only one. While Washington's feeble army was inactive, and the French fleet was blockaded in Newport, there had been fighting in South Carolina about one day in five during the whole year. Twenty-six of these actions had been fought by volunteer bands without the aid of Continental officers or troops and had inflicted upon the enemy far heavier losses than had actions by the Continentals. This warfare had inflicted on South Carolina greater suffering than any other State endured, and more and longer suffering was to follow. The civil war from which the State thus suffered for three years degenerated into a savagery in which professedly legal execution of prisoners by both sides on charges of treason passed into the frequent massacre of prisoners with little or no investigation.

The British policy of contemptuous disregard for the guaranteed rights of the paroled, and their attempts to persecute men into returning to allegiance, had not only failed, but had raised a popular war in three States that utterly wrecked the plan of Cornwallis' marching north to crush Washington between himself and Clinton. Cornwallis' forces were dissipated in a long line of posts from Charlestown and Georgetown, through Camden, Winnsboro, Ninety Six, and Augusta. It was necessary to maintain strong guards along the lines of communication. The partisans, springing from the soil, held the British engaged until the Continental forces, wrecked along with the militia at Camden, could be reorganized and brought back into the field for their united task of finally expelling the enemy.

Greene Takes Command in South.—At Charlotte, on December 4, 1780, General Greene took command of the little army of Continentals, threatened through destitution with "death, desertion and the hospital." Fewer than 800 men were fit in health and equipment for duty. To increase the gloom, General Leslie, commanding 2,300 British troops, well armed, fed, and clothed, landed in Charlestown nine days later to find orders awaiting him to march to Cornwallis' assistance with 1,530 men.

Greene moved, on December 20, to a training camp opposite and just above Cheraw. Here he received reinforcements including Lee's Legion of 300 Continentals, thus securing a commander and troops rivaling in dash and celerity Tarleton and his famous British Legion. General Greene desired to direct the militia of Sumter, Marion, and others in continual attacks as likely to produce better results, while he held his Continentals ready for a heavy blow at Cornwallis, who would thus be held in South Carolina instead of marching north to join in attacking Washington. The conception was bold and good, and, despite the limitations in numbers and the undisciplined character of the militia, which necessitated that events should string along rather loosely, it determined the general character of his operations. Cornwallis was at the same time forming his own aggressive plans. His greatly superior numbers encouraged him to renew the invasion of North Carolina from which he had been forced to withdraw by King's Mountain.

On December 16, 1780, Greene ordered Morgan, with about 600 men, to join a large force of North and South Carolina militia west of the Catawba and thus, he hoped, tie Cornwallis to Winnsboro. While Pickens, McCall, and other Carolina leaders, including Governor Rutledge himself, were heartily falling in with this plan of the Continental commanders, a rift had opened between Sumter and the Continental leaders. Sumter, still incapacitated by his wound, had himself desired to undertake the very campaign that was assigned to Morgan, an officer for whom he entertained a strong dislike on account of his reflections upon the militia. A letter from Greene, appearing to convey similar reflections, so offended him that he prevented his men's participation in the Cowpens campaign now opening. The difficulty between Greene and Sumter was smoothed over, and the head of the Southern Department learned to adjust himself to the high-spirited head of the South Carolina militia as much by yielding as by commanding; but the rift between Sumter and Morgan was permanent.

That a powerful army of regulars would have been preferable to partisan militia, as Greene and Washington insisted, cannot be denied. But it is equally true that, in the absence of such an army, the militia had rendered and were to continue to render services of inestimable value. The militia (often styled the "partisans"), without the support of even their own State government, had so harassed the British army as to render impossible Cornwallis' movement to Virginia at the time that he might have gone there with the prospect of carrying to success the plan of crushing Washington between the armies from the South and the North, and by the delay thus occasioned they caused him to go at such a time as to lead to his surrender at Yorktown and to recognition of American independence.

In my opinion, General McCrady in praising the services of the militia unjustly depreciates those of the Continentals and unwarrantably charges Greene with ungenerous conduct toward Sumter. The resolution of Congress of January 13, 1781, thanking Sumter for his actions at Hanging Rock, Fishdam Ford, and Blackstock's was adopted at Greene's suggestion. It is true that his relations with Sumter were marked by difficulties and that those with Marion and Pickens were perfect except for a brief misunderstanding with Marion originated by Lee. Not only the situation of the individuals but their personalities entered. McCrady, Sumter's most ardent defender, in commenting upon his clashes with various men, surmises that there may have been something in his bearing to rouse antagonism. To the end of his life Sumter, in his personal relations, was combative and sometimes violent.

Such were the personal difficulties, added to discouraging material drawbacks, when Morgan, opposed by powerful, trained antagonists united in purpose and authority, marched on his perilous expedition so critical for the course of the war. Cornwallis, surprised at Greene's boldness in dividing his force by the wide space separating Cheraw and the Spartan District and leaving the British army between his two divisions, dispatched Tarleton in pursuit of Morgan, while he himself prepared to invade North Carolina and, if Greene followed, to chase him out. The reinforcements brought by Leslie, he considered, would render the British force in either Carolina overwhelming. Tarleton forced Morgan to retreat northward to prevent being trapped between himself and Cornwallis. At Cowpens, in the present Cherokee County, four miles south of the North Carolina line and only five miles south of Broad River, which here runs from west to east, Morgan took his stand on January 17, 1781.

Perilous indeed was Morgan's situation, far beyond the possibility of help from Greene and confronted by a superior force under the most formidable of British partisans with the main British army within forty miles in southern York. He has been criticized from that day to this for accepting battle in such a situation; but, having allowed Tarleton to come so close, he had no alternative except a retreat that would have incurred the virtual destruction of his force, the annihilation of confidence in the newly arrived Continental army, and the swing of the region toward the King. Having allowed himself to be maneuvered into this position, and having determined to fight rather than have his army cut to pieces on the run, he fought what Fiske calls the best-planned battle of the Revolution.

Tarleton arrived with about 976 to 1,050 men, all but his 50 militia or thereabouts being regulars. Morgan had 940 to 970, including 370 Continentals and 600 militia of Virginia, and the Carolinians and a few

Georgians. When criticized for fighting with Broad River five miles in his rear to cut off a retreat (and the river moreover swollen by rains), Morgan said he did this to keep the militia from running away. This insulting afterthought or subterfuge of self-justification might well have been omitted in view of the militia's splendid conduct in the battle. Morgan fought there because he had to. Tarleton had outmaneuvered him, and now he had to outfight Tarleton.

As the British pressed toward the American main line, which they outnumbered almost two to one, they met the fire of Howard's Maryland Continentals and William Washington's charge upon their flank. Tarleton now threw his reserve against Howard's right, forcing upon him a perilous reformation at right angles to his old position, which his veteran Continentals so skillfully executed as to receive the British with a crashing close-range fire. Pickens now charged with the militia. A panic seized these crack British regulars, who fled in as utter confusion as did Gates's militia at Camden. Tarleton lost three-fourths of his force compared to the American loss of 12 killed and 60 wounded.

To brilliant victory Morgan had now to add rapid and skillful retreat; for his battle had been against Tarleton, but his campaign was against both him and Cornwallis. The afternoon of the battle he crossed the Broad in a race to join Greene in central North Carolina. Cornwallis started in pursuit two days later.

Transferring operations into the far interior had thus proved as disastrous to the British in proportion to the numbers involved as the fate of Burgoyne in the depths of the State of New York. At King's Mountain and Cowpens two of the best officers and some of the best soldiers in their army had been overwhelmingly defeated when they ventured into the shadow of the mountains. The militia and the Continentals had proved how essential to final victory were the services of each. King's Mountain called Cornwallis back from his first movement northward; Cowpens led him upon a course which ended twenty months later in his ruin at Yorktown. In the view of the English historian Stedman, "The defeat of his Majesty's troops at the Cowpens formed a very principal link in the chain of circumstances which led to the independence of America."

Sumter Along the Congaree—His Plan for State Regulars.—Before taking up Greene's operations in North Carolina we must narrate Sumter's and Marion's activities in South Carolina. Sumter, still suffering from his Blackstock's wound, called his men for a dash at the British posts along the Congaree before the spring planting would require their presence at home. On February 9 he attacked Fort Granby, about a mile and a half down the Congaree across the river from the present

Columbia, but was driven off by reinforcements. After unsuccessfully attacking several British posts lower downstream, with his men rapidly deserting, he suffered a sharp defeat on March 6 by Major Fraser and escaped to the Waxhaws only because the enemy lacked cavalry.

The scarcity of dates in James's *Marion* renders it impossible to know whether Marion's operations were at this time such as to prevent his going to Sumter's aid. Marion habitually showed little regard for his official superior's desires. He was much less given than Sumter to large, sweeping plans and may have thought that he could do more good by his rapidly moving little columns. At all events, Rawdon's rapid dispatch against him and Sumter of detachments stronger than either left very few days in which he could have come into touch with Sumter.

Despite its boldness, the failure of Sumter's expedition exhibited glaringly the defects of the partisan system. The men were volunteers for the immediate occasion, coming and going when they pleased. It was doubtless largely this failure of the temporary volunteer system that moved Sumter at once to formulate a plan for a regular standing force of State troops similar to the Continentals. Men were being forced to recognize that the unregulated plundering by the Whigs as well as the Tories threatened civilized existence. After the evacuation of Ninety Six, murders along the frontier, wrote Pickens, "made no distinction of sexes." All over the State murder, house burning, and stealing directed against their enemies were tolerated by the party in power. Friends' property as well as enemies' was taken for the necessities of war. In addition was mere stealing under the pretense of public service.

To check these terrible conditions Sumter, in March, 1781, proposed a plan for a State force of regulars supported by property taken in an orderly manner by public officials. Governor Rutledge and his council approved, as did Greene. The results were most unhappy. Plunder degenerating into petty thievery demoralized good men and drew to the ranks low characters. The British retaliated by plundering the property of the Whigs. Governor Rutledge arrived at the High Hills of Santee from North Carolina by August 1, 1781, and as his first official act issued a proclamation against plundering.

Sumter apparently raised 1,100 men by this plan. As the whole proceeding was probably illegal, "Sumter's Law" was enacted in 1784 and at the same time a similar one for Pickens immunizing them and their officers for their seizures. The statute was attacked in the courts. The judges charged that the law protected Sumter and other officers from suit, but did not extend to protect purchasers of the property seized by them. The juries rejected this inconsistent position and found that the law fully protected purchasers of the seized property also.[2]

[2] *Stat. at L.*, IV, 598-600; I Bay 53, 269. McCrady, IV, 145-47, n., digests the cases, but erroneously represents Sumter's proclamation as "Sumter's Law."

Marion at Georgetown, Fort Watson, etc.—Marion was already active before Greene's retreat into North Carolina in January, 1781. Made a brigadier shortly after Sumter, but still under his command, with the lower country assigned to him and the upper to Sumter, he now gave a more systematic organization to his force and formed a base at Snow's Island in eastern Williamsburg. On January 24 Marion and Lee dashed into Georgetown and captured Colonel Campbell but failed to oust the garrison.

About March 1 Rawdon ordered Colonel Watson against Marion and sent Colonel Doyle from Camden to trap Sumter in his retreat up the eastern side of the Wateree and then to co-operate in crushing Marion between himself and Watson. Marion met Watson, harried him up and down the labyrinth of swamps and water courses, repeatedly defeated him, and drove him to seek the safety of Georgetown by a long circuit, and Doyle was recalled to meet danger from another direction.

Guilford Courthouse and Hobkirk's Hill.—During Marion's and Sumter's operations in South Carolina in February and March, 1781, Greene was equally busy in North Carolina. After Cowpens the army of Morgan on the Broad and that of Greene on the Peedee raced north in an attempt to unite before Cornwallis, marching between them, could crush them separately. Uniting at Guilford Courthouse, five miles from the present Greensboro, on February 9, 1781, they continued into Virginia. Returning to Guilford Courthouse, Greene fought Cornwallis on March 15. Though Cornwallis won, he had suffered such losses and exhaustion then and earlier as in effect to lose the campaign. His withdrawal to Wilmington was virtually a retreat.

Greene's militia, going home, ended a pursuit by which he might have turned the tables. Turning to the right, he headed for Camden, where a strong British force had been placed under Lord Rawdon to dominate the center and north of the State. On April 25, 1781, Greene determined to attack with his 939 men Rawdon's 900 on Hobkirk Hill in the outskirts of Camden. Greene's daring plan was to envelop both Rawdon's flanks, take him in the rear, and crush his center; but Rawdon outmaneuvered him and forced him to an orderly retreat, although his army remained a disciplined force ready for further combat. Sumter, Marion, and Pickens were stronger than ever, and the British were deeply discouraged. Cornwallis had already ordered Rawdon's retirement south of the Santee, and the withdrawal of Cruger from Ninety Six would of necessity soon follow. Toward this end, the partisans' cutting off British supplies, capturing outposts, and exacting a constant toll of killed, wounded, and captured, and Greene's army, threatening at any moment a major disaster and rendering it impossible for the

British to disperse their forces to hunt down the partisans, both contributed.

Greene's Difficulties and Services.—His disappointment at Hobkirk Hill, the enormous difficulties of feeding his army and securing effective co-operation with the partisan leaders, dependent as they were upon their fluctuating voluntary forces, and the hope of easier and more glorious service in Virginia, led Greene to consider leaving South Carolina, an idea which to his credit he soon abandoned. He adjusted himself with patience, skill, and regard for the public interest to the independence of Marion and the still stronger inclination of the hot-tempered Sumter to direct his own movements. As an officer officially above all others, he supplied the only central authority for co-ordinated effort. To argue, as does Judge Johnson, that Greene conquered the British with some help from the partisans, or, as does General McCrady, that the partisans conquered the British with some help from Greene, is to dispute about which blade of the scissors did the cutting.[3]

Fall of the British Posts.—After the American and British armies had for two weeks after the battle of Hobkirk Hill unsuccessfully stalked each other for an advantageous attack, Lord Rawdon withdrew from Camden, accompanied by a mass of loyalist families, many of whom perished miserably in the huts of "Rawdontown" outside Charlestown. The evacuation of Camden marked the turning of the tide. Orangeburg surrendered to Sumter on the 11th, Fort Motte to Marion and Lee on the 12th, and Fort Granby to Lee on the 15th. Augusta and Ninety Six were tottering on the west. Disappointment and hardship had so undermined British authority even in Charlestown that Balfour feared that the loyalists there might join the American army if it should attack the city. The taking of the posts above mentioned was accompanied by dramatic incidents. Mrs. Rebecca Motte willingly agreed to her house's being burned to drive out the British, who surrendered to prevent themselves from being blown up by the stored powder when the roof was ignited by burning arrows. The Americans then extinguished the flames.

[3] Judge William Johnson's *Life of Greene* and General Edward McCrady's *History of South Carolina during the Revolution* are marked by neglect of the services of the militia by the one and gross unfairness toward the Continentals by the other. General McCrady says (IV, 63), to cite one of innumerable slurs, that Greene brought no army to South Carolina, when as a matter of fact he came as the commander of a Continental army greatly augmented by reinforcements from Washington's army. General McCrady constantly contrasts the hired Continental with the patriotic Confederate soldier, overlooking the fact that the Continental soldier bound himself by a long enlistment, while the militiaman retained his freedom to come and go except for short campaigns.

In the making of his monumental contribution to the history of the American Revolution of commanding attention to the vital service rendered by the partisans, General McCrady's depreciation of the Continentals is as needless as unfair. The services of both were essential, and there is glory enough for both.

The Fall of Augusta—Barbarities.—Colonel Thomas Brown, holding Augusta for the British, found himself by May 15, 1781, besieged by Pickens, who had been made brigadier-general after Cowpens. Fortunately the jarrings which so seriously disturbed the relations of Sumter and Marion with the Continental officers never arose with Pickens. The triumph of the Americans on June 5 was stained by the murder of Colonel Grierson, hated for his cruelties, and several other prisoners. The same day that Augusta surrendered Marion took Georgetown.

The Siege of Ninety Six.—Greene, who began the siege of Ninety Six on May 22, did not enjoy similar success. The place was defended by a strong earthen star-shaped fort commanded by one of the most gallant officers and admirable gentlemen in the war, Lieutenant-Colonel John Harris Cruger of New York. He had done much to counteract the unfavorable effect on the royal cause produced by the tyranny of Lieutenant-Colonel Balfour, whom he succeeded.

Colonel Cruger's garrison of 550 regulars were all Americans. The siege by Greene's more than 1,100 men was going well when the approach of British reinforcements rendered taking the fort by immediate assault the only hope. On June 18 the costly and futile attempt was made, and Greene rapidly retreated toward Winnsboro. The British evacuated Ninety Six, as had been ordered before the siege. It was largely their expecting the French at Beaufort that influenced the British to abandon the interior posts, but the French fleet went to Yorktown, with results of the utmost importance.[4]

The evacuation of Ninety Six closes a definite period of the war. The partisans had rendered the British hold on the middle and back country precarious and unprofitable by cutting communications, seizing supplies, and capturing posts. The presence of Greene's army, supplying a central force and a co-ordinating authority, added the danger of major disasters to the most important garrisons. The spirit of the loyalists even in Charlestown had sunk while those of the Whigs throughout the State had risen. Both in Virginia and in South Carolina events could easily take a decisive turn.

[4] It was while on this retreat, legend relates, that Greene sent a message to Sumter by eighteen-year-old Emily Geiger. The existence of almost daily dispatches between the generals renders incredible the story of her rendering that particular service. It is impossible for me to doubt that Emily Geiger rendered some such heroic service as tradition holds, though it might not have been between the two officers named, or, if between them, might have been without authorization, as was Mrs. Mary Dillard's carrying to Sumter at Blackstock's information of the approach and forces of Tarleton. The absence of documents, particularly at the time and place, is not presumptive evidence of fraud. But for Tarleton's mentioning that "a woman" rode to tell Sumter the character of the former's force approaching Blackstock's, Mrs. Mary Dillard's ride would have rested merely on tradition.

CHAPTER XXXIV

INDEPENDENCE ACHIEVED, 1781-1783

Marching from Ninety Six to the low country, Rawdon united with Stewart at Orangeburg on July 8 and awaited reinforcements. Greene accordingly withdrew his infantry north of the Santee and turned over his cavalry and the mounted State infantry to Sumter for a daring raid conceived by the latter on the British posts near Charlestown.

Sumter's Campaign toward Charlestown.—Sumter's plan was to attack the garrison at Monck's Corner 30 miles north of Charlestown, Dorchester 19 miles north of Charlestown, and the Quarter House five miles from the city. It was the most extensive operation that Sumter had ever attempted and included, besides Lee's Continental cavalry, all the State troops except Pickens' brigade and a small party with Harden. Lee took Dorchester, and Captain Read, under Colonel Wade Hampton, brought away 20 prisoners from the Quarter House.

Sumter moved toward the main object, Colonel Coates at Monck's Corner. The first slip was that Marion's men so imperfectly destroyed Wadboo Bridge in the face of Coates's attack for saving it that it was easily repaired. The second was that they abandoned their picket posts there and so deprived Sumter of knowledge of the route Coates had taken. The third was that Sumter allowed Coates to conceal his flight.

Coates considered that such boldness as Lee's and Hampton's indicated the presence of Greene's whole army below him. As he fled from Charlestown he was overtaken by Lee's cavalry on July 18 at Quinby Creek. Sumter arrived in the afternoon and found Coates strongly placed in and around the Shubrick plantation houses. Marion considered the place impregnable but was overruled by Sumter, the prudence of the one and the impetuosity of the other being illustrated as usual. The American losses were heavy and the dissatisfaction of Sumter's leading officers extreme. The ammunition was exhausted; British reinforcements were coming. Sumter sought safety north of the Santee.

But despite Sumter's failure, the British had suffered, too. The important post at Monck's Corner was temporarily abandoned, enormous stores and about 150 men were lost, and their prestige was flouted at the very gates of the capital. Sumter had displayed his characteristic failings as well as his virtues as a leader, but he had accomplished a large part of the purpose of his brilliantly conceived, though imperfectly executed, campaign.

The Execution of Colonel Hayne.—During the military lull following the battle of Quinby Bridge, when the intense heat almost prohibited operations, occurred the most shocking of the executions for treason by which both sides enforced their contention of sovereignty over the individual. The eminence of Colonel Isaac Hayne, his elevated character, and the deliberation with which he was hanged by the highest British authorities in the State, in the face of earnest pleas by important elements for his life, have tended to obscure the fact that in his cruel death he shared the fate of many. Moreover it was the civil courts of South Carolina in 1779, and not the British commander in 1780, who began the practice of hanging for treason. Both sides finally came to killing prisoners with no semblance of even military trial.

Colonel Hayne, on the fall of Charlestown, had been included in the parole of the militia throughout the State. Upon Clinton's revocation on June 3, 1780, of all paroles except those of persons surrendered with the city, Hayne was ordered to accept the obligations of a British subject or submit to imprisonment. He signed the declaration of allegiance because only thus could he avoid being separated from his dying wife and his children ill with smallpox. To his protest against the clause requiring him to bear arms, General Patterson, it is said, replied that it would never be required, as it would be time for the British army to leave when it could no longer defend the province.

General Patterson's comment had, of course, no legal significance. Hayne, however, regarded it as a vital part of his contract. Accordingly, when he was later called upon under threat of imprisonment to bear arms for the King, he considered himself released from his oath of loyalty. The additional fact that Colonel Harden was overrunning the region afforded him ground to consider that under the law of nations his allegiance was now due to the American government as having conquered the country. Yielding to the solicitations of his neighbors and exacting a pledge that they would act humanely, he consented in the summer of 1781 to become their colonel. After a dash within five miles of Charleston, he was pursued and taken on July 8.

For six months the British had been irritated by men who had accepted British allegiance taking up arms against the King. Lieutenant-Colonel Balfour, commanding in Charlestown, requested the opinion of Lieutenant-Colonel Lord Rawdon, supreme commander in South Carolina, on Hayne's case. Rawdon approved the necessity of making Hayne an example. Without a court-martial, they jointly ordered the execution. Hayne with perfect calmness and dignity faced death on the gallows August 4, 1781. Knowing from the moment that he resumed his arms the fate that might befall him, if captured, he had pursued his duties without permitting this terrible possibility to influence his conduct or movements, and thus exhibited the noblest virtue as a patriot. The policy of such severity by his captors may be doubted, but its legality, though adding to the horrors of civil war by both sides, can hardly be questioned.

The immediate effect of Hayne's execution in the low country, says Governor Rutledge, was to drive many of those who had followed Hayne's course to resubmit to the British. Marion found Harden reduced to fifty men threatening to desert. Greene's pledge to retaliate on British officers was not carried out, though all his officers, disdaining the horrible danger it would impose on them, urged it. Reflection forced him to relinquish a plan that would have sunk an already barbarized war still lower.

Eutaw Springs.—While Greene was refreshing and training his army in the High Hills of Santee, Colonel Alexander Stewart, having succeeded to the command of Lord Rawdon's army, lay south or southwest of the mouth of the Wateree. The next major move in South Carolina, the battle of Eutaw Springs on September 8, 1781, was forced by the course of events in the North. The appearance of the French and American armies threatening New York caused Clinton to order Cornwallis, who had been overrunning Virginia, to take a strong position on Chesapeake Bay from which he could either move to the relief of New York or proceed against the States around the Chesapeake, as developments should dictate. It is easily perceived, remarks General McCrady, in view of the situation in Virginia and New York at this critical moment, how influential in general American affairs were the operations in South Carolina which led Colonel Gould in June, 1781, to land his reinforcements in South Carolina instead of northward, and, we might add, how important was the presence of Greene's army, which General McCrady so constantly depreciates, in rendering Colonel Gould's action necessary.

In August Washington learned that de Grasse, long expected, was approaching with the second division of the French fleet and 3,200 soldiers, to remain until the middle of October. He therefore left part of his army before New York, moved the balance toward Yorktown, had the French fleet to blockade that harbor, and instructed Lafayette to prevent Cornwallis from marching toward Charlestown. Greene had already planned to attack any British army outside of Charlestown as soon as he was reinforced. Information of Washington's plans necessitated prompt action to prevent the British in South Carolina from sending aid to Cornwallis.

It was, therefore, now imperative for Greene to attack Stewart south of the Santee. The numbers on each side in the battle, September 8, are uncertain, but apparently, with his 1,250 Continentals and the militia and 145 ten-months State "regulars," Greene had about 2,092. The best estimate of Stewart's force is 2,300 regulars largely enlisted in the North. With the two veteran armies thus matched, it is not surprising that the battle proved one of the most bloody, stubborn, and well conducted of any during the war and was claimed by both as a victory. Both sides were victorious at opposite ends of the line, but the British success was last. Wade Hampton saved the Americans from rout while Greene withdrew in good order seven miles back for the necessity of water. Stewart the next day destroyed vast stores and retreated for Charlestown.

The British were from now on confined to Charlestown and a few near-by posts. Yorktown six weeks later assured independence and should instantly have ended the war everywhere. The war was indeed over except in South Carolina, but, while statesmen dickered over peace terms, fighting dragged on here for another dreary year.

Taking refuge from the low-country malaria, Greene returned after Eutaw Springs to the High Hills of Santee, where his camp resembled a vast hospital. Greene wrote on December 14, 1781, "Near one half of our soldiers have not a shoe to their foot, and not a blanket to 10 men through the line." South Carolina relieved their mortification by a gift of clothing to every Continental commissioned officer in Greene's army. The Continentals had not been paid for more than two years, at a time when difficulty was experienced in keeping the militia for more than a few days because of their going home to carry their plunder.

Watching Charlestown—The Negro Troop Question.—The dominant factor in the situation in South Carolina during the month following Eutaw Springs was the possibility of the return of Cornwallis' army. Since early June he had entertained such a desire, which his movements in Virginia and those of Stewart in South Carolina led Greene to suspect. The capture of Cornwallis' army at Yorktown on October 19, 1781, so raised American spirits that the British in Charlestown constructed fortifications across the neck, brought in the garrison from Wilmington, and enlisted Negroes as soldiers.

The British fear of an attack on Charlestown was unwarranted. Greene had less than four rounds of ammunition per man. It was under these difficulties that he wrote Governor Rutledge urging the enlistment of Negroes, as his opponent was already doing. The legislature heard the proposal with indignation, but Lieutenant-Colonel Laurens' motion to embody 2,500 confiscated Negroes as soldiers received twice as many votes as had his similar motion in 1779.

John Laurens in France.—Allusion to Lieutenant Colonel Laurens' legislative activities recalls another important service away from the field—his diplomatic mission as special minister to secure immediate aid from France. After his arrival in Paris about mid-March, 1781, the British ministry sought to have his father ask him to retire in order to secure milder treatment for the father, then a prisoner in the Tower of London. Henry Laurens scorned the proposal as incompatible with his own and his son's character.

Young Laurens' ardor served to hasten French action, though his undiplomatic manners, due, he confessed, to inexperience and a soldier's habits, alarmed Franklin and irritated the French ministers.[1]

Laurens' aid to Commodore Gillon of the frigate *South Carolina,* unable to sail because of unpaid debts, by buying a quantity of his goods is related elsewhere. Laurens, having completed his mission with remarkable swiftness, arrived at Boston on August 25, 1781, with two shiploads of military supplies and 2,500,244 livres in specie (half a million dollars). Half the latter was used to start the Bank of North America which Morris was launching for Congress. Another shipload of supplies arrived apart from Laurens, and a fourth was driven back by storm.

Laurens did not obtain the 10,000,000 livres gift made us by France at this time, almost half of which he carried back in goods or cash. Franklin had shortly before secured the promise of this; but Laurens' energy, and his information fresh from the army, expedited France's actual delivery of the funds. The supplies arrived just too late for the Yorktown campaign; but that campaign was made possible by his securing the prompt dispatch of the French fleet. Laurens did, moreover, secure in Holland a loan of 10,000,000 livres. Though less to his taste, Laurens' diplomatic mission rendered by far his most valuable service to his country and was performed with a brilliancy rivaling the heroism of his career as a soldier.

Rutledge Reorganizes Militia—Sumter Resigns.—During his enforced absence from the State, Governor Rutledge had been striving to secure help from Congress and to encourage the South Carolina leaders. Arriving at the High Hills of Santee by August 1, 1781, from Philadelphia,

[1] According to the testimony forty-one years later of his secretary Captain Jackson, Laurens resented Vergennes' patronizing manner as well as delays, and informed him that "the sword which I now wear in defense of France, as well as my own country, unless the succor I solicit is immediately accorded, I may be compelled to draw against France, as a British subject." His next memorial, he declared, would be delivered to the King in person—a threat which brought prompt compliance with his requests. This incredible narrative, representing Laurens as saying to Vergennes what he perhaps said to his own secretary, has been changed by later romancers so as to have Laurens make some such representation to the King.

he renewed the close personal associations with Greene which dated from the General's arrival in the South. Since his flight from Charlestown Rutledge had had so little opportunity to employ extra powers granted him (called later a "dictatorship") as to have been hardly more than a peripatetic diplomatic agent of a hypothetical government.

His most difficult tasks now were organizing and bringing out the militia, in neither of which he succeeded with these men of almost unregulated independence. His proclamation against plundering attacked a great evil which, by tempting men to go home with their plunder, was defeating the purpose of maintaining a force in the field. His proclamation of September 17, 1781, pointed out the worthlessness of State and Continental paper money, suspended, until the legislature had an opportunity to act, their legal tender, and forbade suits for small debts. Deep offense was caused by his order that the militia serve on foot. This violated the whole custom of the volunteers, whose quick movements and short terms of service and facilities for plunder all required horses.

Rutledge's reorganization also brought the resignation of Sumter. The order that the militia serve on foot was enforced against Sumter's brigade, but was relaxed for Marion's. This deepened the conviction of Sumter and his men that they had in many respects been unjustly treated. The old hero resigned late in February, 1782, and was succeeded by Colonel William Henderson.

Thus passed out of military life the most important of the South Carolina partisan leaders. His enormous energy, his daring, and his impetuous temper rendered him sometimes careless in defense, and often rash, but always formidable, in attack. His quickness to perceive the weak situation of an enemy and his readiness to dare enterprises beyond his resources incurred risks legitimate for a leader accustomed to the sudden dispersal and reassembling of his small forces, but not always permissible for a commander-in-chief responsible for maintaining a steady regular force that could not be replaced and whose destruction might mean national calamity. Sumter was supremely suited to his role and justly earned Cornwallis' tribute as his greatest plague. He did not fit readily into a subordinate place, and hotly resented real or supposed indignity. Says Mr. Joseph W. Barnwell, he never fought an action under another's command. In refusing to permit the co-operation of his men with Morgan in the Cowpens campaign unless orders came through him, he was within his legal rights, though he thereby hindered a movement of the highest moment for the American cause.

Greene, while irked by Sumter's independence, recognized his essential value as not only screening, but often as actually feeding, his army, and, while improperly criticizing him to others, shrewdly maintained harmony along with a fair amount of authority. Wrote Colonel Henry Lee, Sumter's fellow-soldier and critic: "His aspect was manly and stern, denoting insuperable firmness and lofty courage. He was not over-scrupulous as a soldier in his use of means, and apt to make considerable allowances for a state of war. Believing it warranted by the necessity of the case, he did not occupy his mind with critical examinations of the equity of his measures, or of their bearing on individuals; but indiscriminately pressed forward to his end—the destruction of his enemy and liberation of his country. In his military character he resembled Ajax; relying more upon the fierceness of his courage than upon the results of unrelaxing vigilance and nicely adjusted combination. Determined to deserve success, he risked his own life and the lives of his associates without reserve. Enchanted with the splendor of victory, he would wade in torrents of blood to attain it."

The Jacksonborough Legislature.—The feeling that the war was won disordered the army. Colonel Lee retired dissatisfied in February, 1782. Bickerings over rank by officers and conspiracy among the men, the lawless custom of officers' taking public horses for their own use, and even selling them, an abuse fostered by two years' lack of pay, were sternly suppressed by Greene.

On November 23, 1781, Governor Rutledge wrote the brigadier-generals directions for conducting an election for legislators to meet on January 8, 1782. Only persons at the time loyal to the State were allowed to vote. The membership was of great distinction, including almost every available civil and military leader of the Revolution in South Carolina. With a quorum at last present at the village of Jacksonborough on the Edisto, the House began business on January 17, 1782.

The legislature agreed that "Generals Sumter, Marion, and Pickens, with the brave militia, . . . are deserving of the highest commendation," and heaped upon General Greene extravagant praise, bestowing upon him an estate of 10,000 guineas sterling value. While the disproportion of reward to Greene is obvious, it is hard to escape the conviction that the men then present must have had a vivid realization of the value of his having afforded a continuous disciplined force amid shifting State volunteers, of having sustained the hope of the long-continued resistance, and of having co-ordinated the efforts of the State's own officers.[2]

[2] Georgia and North Carolina gave Greene 5,000 guineas and 2,400 acres respectively (McCrady, IV, 575). Boone's Barony, a valuable plantation south of the Edisto, was purchased by South Carolina and conveyed to General Greene. He had to sell it on account of debts incurred in endorsing for Banks and Company, to enable them to feed and clothe his army. He settled on the plantation given him by Georgia and died there on June 19, 1786, from undue exposure to the sun.—Johnson's *Greene,* II, 401, 420.

Christopher Gadsden was elected governor, but declined on account of infirmities of age when the times demanded the highest vigor. Another act sounded true to his long record of disinterested patriotism. Though he had suffered extraordinarily in the St. Augustine dungeon and in the sequestration of his property, he, like Marion, opposed the confiscation of Tories' estates and urged "that sound policy required to forget and forgive."

John Mathews, of creditable abilities and excellent State and Congressional record, was made governor. The next year the courts were again opened. Assent was given to Congress' laying a 5 per cent duty on certain imports. Laws were passed for improving the militia and raising Continental troops; and for contributing, in supplies to Greene's army, Congress' requisition on the State; for ending the legal tender of paper money; for staying units; and for punishing conspicuous Tories.

Tories Afflicted and Restored.—The hardships following the Revolution stimulated war-bred hatred toward the Tories. These internal enemies were not always submissive. The House of Representatives in 1783, finding that certain Tories were too numerous to be taken or "drove off," recommended the Governor to offer 300 guineas for William Cuningham, dead or alive, and 100 for certain others. In the *Gazette* of April 29, 1784, seven men signed a statement of why they basted the stripped carcass of Tory William Rees for his misdeeds with fifty stripes of juice of hickory, without the slightest fear of punishment for their lynch law. Christopher Gadsden, whose unfailing pleas for justice and moderation from the end of the Revolution added to the fame he deserves as a protagonist of unlimited resistance to British wrongs, regretted that the government had not in fair and open trials made examples of several Tories of conspicuous position, but condemned this "retail tyranny" of mob law under which no man was safe. In the noble work of pacification, from his opposition to extreme measures by the Jacksonborough Assembly onward, none labored more zealously than General Marion. Young Charles Pinckney also urged the repeal of the confiscation acts. In April, 1784, twelve active Tories who had returned to their homes on Fishing Creek were given twenty days to leave. Three days after this limit eight were killed and the other four allowed to bear the news to other Tories.

At the Ninety Six court on November 7, 1784, Judge Aedanus Burke liberated Love, the cruelest of "Bloody Bill" Cuningham's lieutenants, as the treaty of peace required. Relatives of men whom Love had murdered at Hayes's Station waited until the Judge had reached his lodgings and hanged their enemy from a tree. Secret organizations, etc., were used to prevent Tories from voting lest their participation in government disturb the holders of confiscated estates or endanger republican institutions.

The desire to fill the public treasury and the private hope for personal gain added zest to the plans for punishing the Tories. The most guilty suffered confiscation of their entire estates and banishment under pain of death for returning. Others were amerced 30 or 12 per cent of their estates. These acts of confiscation encountered strong opposition in and out of the legislature as more unjustly condemning large numbers of persons without trial than had the British acts against persons supporting America. If judicial process had been allowed, many a man condemned because an influential politician placed his name on the list through prejudice, as was openly charged was common, could have proved that his acceptance of British protection, etc., had been under virtual compulsion, while his heart was really with the State. There was injustice, relatively speaking, also on the side of mercy, as was inevitable with a political body undertaking duties belonging properly to a court. Indeed a letter of Edward Rutledge, the author of the bill, who stood for moderation, reveals the vast power of mere personal influence in the whole matter of the inclusion or omission of names and the extent of the penalty.

Judge Aedanus Burke is the supposed author of a fiery pamphlet against these laws, signed "Cassius," Charlestown, January 14, 1783. "Cassius" denounced as "high treason against the sovereignty and liberties of a people" the action of a legislature in whose election almost half the people were disfranchised, taking away without trial the inheritances and dowers of innocent women and children. Unless the gentlemen were checked who in private declared that the people were incapable of governing themselves and that there should be set up an aristocracy of certain families, success would crown "the fierce and jealous aristocracy which has been gaining ground for seven years past." Better if Governor Rutledge had remained away from the State and a convention of the people had been assembled in due time to settle the State in serenity. No other State had acted so tyrannically as had South Carolina in these laws, which in many cases placed persons under the ban for the private vengeance of individual legislators. It was idle to talk of liberty unless these laws were repealed.

The fierce democracy of this appeal forecasts the movement of the next few years which was the natural development from the events since 1765. The enlisting of the support of the Charlestown mechanics by the Revolutionary leaders had taught them their power. In another direction, the back-country men had been deeply stirred to the assertion of their rights. It is therefore reasonable to believe that there really may have been something of sectional and class dissatisfaction, though confused in the reporting, behind the statement of the *Royal Gazette* of December 26, 1781, that for the governorship "the aristocratic party as they are styled are strenuous for Mr. Ralph Izard, Senior—to whom Mr. Sumter is opposed by a considerable body of Back Country people."

"Cassius'" demand for the repeal of confiscation and amercement voiced a growing sentiment. Possibly the protest of General Leslie (when the British commander here) had influence in contrasting the absolute confiscation of the estates of loyalists with the British government's policy of stopping at sequestering the estates of rebels and using part of the income without depriving the proprietor of ownership or, presumably, ultimate repossession. It is easy to prove that Leslie's picture of the careful preservation of the property was untrue; but the greater American severity could not be denied. Confiscation and banishment failed to justify themselves either as revenue producers or as medicine for treason. In some instances the effect was to disinherit heirs who themselves had been loyal to the American cause. Subsiding passions brought realization of the impolicy of deepening feuds and fostered moderation. In 1783 seventy-seven of the banished were allowed to return, and the sale of their estates was halted. Mercy was shown 125 more the next year, and those who had suffered confiscation were indemnified. Almost yearly similar acts restored confiscated property and welcomed back the banished with the exception of the worst offenders.

The Frigate South Carolina *and the Luxembourg Claims.*—We may conclude here the narrative of South Carolina's plans of 1778 noticed at page 285 for spending $500,000 in Spanish silver for three frigates. Commodore Alexander Gillon sailed to France about August or September, 1778, to build or buy vessels. After every effort seemed futile a fine new frigate dropped into his hands through an act of personal favoritism by Louis XVI to the Chevalier Luxembourg. The same day that the King lent the frigate to the Chevalier, May 30, 1780, the Chevalier formed the following contract with Gillon as representing South Carolina: The State should have the frigate for three years to cruise against the common enemies of France and America. Half the proceeds of all prizes was to go to the officers and crew, a quarter to South Carolina, and a quarter to Luxembourg, who acknowledged in addition receiving in cash 100,000 livres. Should the ship be lost he should receive 300,000 livres more. For the 300,000 livres Gillon pledged, in addition to the credit of the State, his own estate. The frigate, renamed the *South Carolina,* was the best of her class and of 1,350 tons. Gillon at last slipped to sea in August, 1781, to avoid his vessel's being seized by his creditors.

The *South Carolina* participated in the capture on May 8, 1782, of the Bahama Islands for Spain. Andrew DeVeaux, the South Carolina Tory, soon recaptured the Islands for England. After discharging her cargo in June, 1782, at Philadelphia, the *South Carolina* put to sea to avoid seizure for debts in Europe and was captured by the British on December 20, 1782.

The "Luxembourg claims" against the State, growing out of the frigate *South Carolina,* were not fully paid for seventy-three years, but not because of any desire to avoid the obligations. The $115,000, said to have been received by the State as prize money, exceeded her expense by little if any. As for Gillon, at his death in 1794 his once ample estate was heavily insolvent on account of the ship.

War with the Indians, 1781-82.—In the latter part of 1781 the Cherokees attacked Georgia and upper Ninety Six district, while Robert Cuningham made his eruption from Charlestown into the back country in November. General Pickens with 394 horsemen from South Carolina and Georgia visited destruction upon the villages of Oconee County, South Carolina, and northeastern Georgia. Colonel Robert Anderson of Pickens' brigade dealt them a final blow when a few rose in April, 1782.

Tory Skirmishes—The Cuninghams.—On February 27, 1782, the British Commons voted to stop the war, and accordingly, on May 23, General Leslie proposed that hostilities cease and he be allowed to purchase supplies. His request was refused on the ground that he might accumulate surplus stores to supply the British in the West Indies against our French allies. This fatuous idealism without resources for enforcement deprived the famished commerce of the State of the stream of gold and silver which Leslie was ready to pour into its veins under safeguards that the State could have provided, and cost some precious lives.

Lieutenant-Colonel John Laurens, in charge of intelligence service near Charlestown, so thirsted for action and fame that he rose from his sickbed, abandoned his post without permission, and obtained command of a small force to oppose a British food expedition up the Combahee. The British were informed of Laurens' movements. As he rode before sunrise on August 25, 1782, toward the redoubt near the northern end of the loop of the Combahee at Tar Bluff before it takes its final course to the sea, the enemy's 140 men rose from the tall grass and poured a deadly fire into his 50. Laurens, one of the most brilliant and gallant figures of the Revolution, fell at the first fire, a costly and almost the last sacrifice to months of senseless war.

Privations of the Army.—The suffering of Greene's army from hunger and from the want of almost every article for the sick grew worse after the enemy had been beaten. The support of the army was entrusted by Superintendent of Finance Morris to the four southernmost States, but among the first acts of the restored legislatures were laws which almost destroyed the army by ending food impressments before the States were prepared to deliver supplies.

During the whole war South Carolina far exceeded, in proportion to population, any other State in her contributions to the common cause and in 1782 was doing incomparably better than the others. "The commissioners who finally settled the accounts for expenses of the respective States during the Revolution," says McCrady, "found that the little State with at the utmost but 100,000 white inhabitants had expended in the common cause $11,523,299.29, and that after charging her for all advances, including the assumption of the State debt by the United States at the end of the war, there was still due her as overpaid $1,205,968." Massachusetts, with three times her white population, exceeded South Carolina's contribution by only $42,823, and all others were far below her in their proportionate contributions.

In 1782, when the support of Greene's army was almost wholly thrown upon South Carolina, she contributed in supplies her entire Congressional requisition of 373,598 Mexican dollars out of $8,000,000 for the whole country, while by August 1, 1783, Superintendent Morris reported, the other States had contributed as follows: Rhode Island nearly one-fourth; Pennsylvania about one-fifth; Connecticut and New Jersey, each about one-seventh; Massachusetts about one-eighth; Virginia about one-twelfth; New York and Maryland each about one-twentieth; New Hampshire about one one-hundred-and-twenty-first; North Carolina, Delaware, and Georgia, nothing.

At this time, while testifying to the earnestness of Governor Mathews and Council, Greene wrote that "We have three hundred men without arms, and more than a thousand men are so naked for want of clothing, they can only be put on duty in cases of a desperate necessity." The fortitude of the Continentals, many of whom had enlisted at the first for the whole war, in enduring cruelties of hunger and cold that would have dispersed any militia or volunteers in a few days should be kept in mind in considering comparisons of patriotism and character disadvantageous to the regulars.

South Carolina Diplomants.—The diplomats were at this moment in Paris framing the treaty of peace between Great Britain and the United States. Of their number was Henry Laurens, formerly president of the South Carolina Council of Safety and of the Continental Congress. On October 21, 1779, Laurens had been elected commissioner to obtain a $10,000,000 specie loan in Holland. To this was added on November 1 the duty of negotiating a treaty of amity and commerce.

He was captured at sea, with the draft of such a treaty drawn by William Lee and de Neufville, without authorization on either side to do so. This formed the pretext on which England declared upon Holland the war she had desired as a means of preying upon the republic's rich commerce and stopping the supplies that flowed to the United States through the Dutch West Indies Island of St. Eustatius. Charged with high treason, Laurens was confined in the Tower of London from October 6, 1780, with absurd and at times unmerciful restrictions, under which his health declined so alarmingly as to lead the government to release him on December 31, 1781. He was soon exchanged for Lord Cornwallis. Appointed a commissioner for framing the peace treaty, he arrived in Paris on the last day of the negotiations and added nothing to the document but the clause forbidding the British to carry off property, a provision primarily to secure payment for the thousands of slaves appropriated. He gave his hearty support, as in Congress, to American fishing rights and used his wide acquaintance in London to convince the Ministry of the futility of their hope for a peace with America separate from France. Although he signed the preliminary articles of November 30, 1782, his name does not appear, because of his absence, on the definitive treaty signed in identical words on September 3, 1783.

We may here notice the diplomatic services of another South Carolinian, Ralph Izard, who at the outbreak of the Revolution had been living in London since 1771, apparently as a permanent resident. He was elected United States minister to Tuscany on July 1, 1777, one of several whom Congress appointed without any agreement for their being received. Dissuaded by the Tuscan minister from going where the affront of rejection was inevitable, he remained in Paris until his mission was terminated by Congress on June 8, 1779, and carried on quarrels with other American envoys, especially Franklin, in which then and after returning home he expressed himself with imprudent violence. Like the Lees and Adamses, Henry Laurens, and some other South Carolinians, he valued the fisheries highly and feared that Franklin would sacrifice them. He so strongly preferred England to France that in January, 1778, he urged the English agent Hutton to hasten to London to save his country by having it acknowledge American independence and so allow him to urge on Congress an Anglo-American alliance, *"but that it must be done within ten days."* Hutton sped to London to inform the ministry that "there is something brewing between France and America." Faÿ's statement that Izard "dabbled in treason" has no further basis than this monumental imprudence.

Charlestown Evacuated—Peace.—The British fleet carried away from South Carolina 5,333 Negroes, and the total number taken off during the war was "computed by good judges," says the contemporary Ramsay, perhaps with some exaggeration, to total 25,000. The white civilians leaving on the British fleet numbered 3,794, including many British who had come before or during the war and a much larger number of South Carolina loyalists who, for their virtues or their vices, refused to desert the British flag. Hundreds of British soldiers deserted and remained in the State.

General Leslie, fearing an attempt of some of his Tories, inflamed with injuries, to fire the city, suggested to General Greene mutual safeguards in the evacuation, which he set for December 14, 1782. Governor Mathews and the Council, fearing outrages against Tories, forbade the presence of the militia. This discrimination was so painful to General Greene that he explained he was not responsible. Not one of the distinguished partisan leaders was present. The prudence of the Governor and Council in not permitting the presence of militia is commendable; but no harm, only deserved honor, extending beyond the officers to their men, could have resulted from the presence of militia officers in conspicuous positions.

It was a scene of grief and joy. Many of the Tories, permanently bereft, so far as they knew, of every possession, were men and women of culture and character leaving forever their homes under the stern compulsion of a sense of duty. Among the throng who followed the American army into the city were many who had suffered equally for the opposite principles and whose joy at returning to their homes was mingled with grief at the ruin they witnessed.

Into this struggle South Carolina had entered far more on principle than for relief from burdens. Those in control of her government in 1776 accepted instead of seeking independence as the only means of maintaining their ancient liberties. South Carolina suffered comparatively little in the era of the war antedating the fall of Charlestown, but in the second war of the Revolution, forced upon her by British cruelty and the violation of paroles, she suffered incomparably more than any other State. General McCrady catalogues 137 battles and skirmishes in the State, scattered over almost every present county. The number of men in proportion to population engaged in battle, and the duration of actual hostilities far exceeded what occurred anywhere else. Without detracting from the services of the armies sent by Congress and the help of volunteers as militia from outside, well might Bancroft write:

"Left mainly to her own resources, it was through the depths of wretchedness, that her sons were to bring her back to her place in the Republic, after suffering more and daring more and achieving more than the men of any other State."

CHAPTER XXXV

STABILIZING THE GOVERNMENT, 1783-1790

Hardships and Unpopularity of the Army.—The people of South Carolina resumed control of a State suffering from the prostration and passions of a long and bitter civil war. When protection by the army was less needed, its taking of food and clothes by force and paying with certificates of Federal indebtedness inflamed the hatred toward the military that had been growing ever since the approach of peace. A crisis was reached when, on January 10, 1783, Greene was informed that the State would no longer permit impressment of supplies. Forced to endorse for contractors as the only solution, Greene lost a considerable portion of the fortune that southern legislatures had bestowed for his services. Greene's warning that the hungry army might become dangerous was perverted and made to appear a threat that he would make himself dictator. The quarrel bore directly on the proposed amendment allowing Congress to collect 5 per cent import duties. South Carolina rescinded her ratification as Virginia had done. Rhode Island and Georgia had refused to ratify. The amendment was dead, and congressional bankruptcy confirmed.

Stay Laws, Debt-Scaling, Tender Laws.—In 1782 South Carolina repealed the legal-tender character of the Continental and of her own millions of paper money. Nothing was done to correct injustice in debts already paid, but for the equitable settlement of those still unpaid the law of 1783 enacted a scale of depreciation.

Speculators bought confiscated estates or lands, sold under distress, that failed to resell at the expected profit or to produce the revenues necessary for final payment. The distress of debtors led the legislature, itself largely composed of sufferers, to work the government for the benefit of their class. Planters and merchants, debtors and creditors, were arrayed as hostile classes, and the conflict was the sharper as many of the merchants were outsiders. The act of 1784 forbade suit for old debts before 1786, at which time a fourth (later diminished to a fifth) could be sued for annually.

Stay laws and paper money, adopted to relieve distress, were seized upon as means for fraud or quick speculative wealth. Speculation or other means of attaining wealth by *coup de main* possessed almost every man. No price was considered too high for lands, slaves, or British luxuries if they could only be gotten on credit. Men who refused to pay their suffering creditors sported the finest clothes, furniture, and equipages. At no period, says Ramsay, were fortunes of attorneys made so rapidly and easily; never were so many planters ruined or forced to sell at extraordinary sacrifices.

The legislature passed acts permitting the tender of any property for debt until 1787 and emitting "paper medium" to the amount of £100,000 sterling to be lent on mortgage over land or silverware. The paper medium was a success compared with most of the expedients of the time. It was in essence a land bank, whose paper money capital was, despite efforts at further inflation, rigidly limited to the original £100,000 sterling. It furnished loans of not over £250 each to something over four hundred persons and a welcome circulating medium to everybody. Though a legal tender only to the government, the government paid it out again, and an organized pressure on merchants and mechanics prevented much depreciation. The pledge of five-year redemption was not kept, nor was the five-year repayment of the loan enforced. Many tracts were sold for the interest, the borrowers having virtually sold their lands to the State at exaggerated values; but the great majority of the loans were paid in full. As late as 1815 the paper medium was still being taken in and burned, and the last loan was collected in 1829 or perhaps a little later. Most of the loans seem to have been made in the middle and low country. The names of prominent public characters among the borrowers suggest political favoritism in the whole scheme.

The unsettled claims for supplies and military services during the Revolution presented a stupendous burden. Accounts for every pound of food and every day's service of a militiaman were carefully audited, and certificates of indebtedness, called indents, were issued bearing 7 per cent interest. Each State's official report of its debts in 1789 shows South Carolina's greater than any other. Only Massachusetts ($5,226,801) and Virginia ($3,680,743) carried as much as half of South Carolina's ($5,386,232). South Carolina was therefore deeply interested in the success of Hamilton's plan for the assumption of State debts. William Loughton Smith of South Carolina argued in the House that unless State debts were assumed the South Carolina soldier would get one shilling in the pound from the State on his indent while the holder of a Continental certificate would receive full value. Smith showed his faith by his works by buying up the depreciated South Carolina indents and advising his Charleston friends to do the same, all of which reinforced their enthusiasm for assumption as a public benefit.

Aedanus Burke said that, if the assumption bill failed, South Carolina would almost certainly be bankrupted, as she could no more cope with her huge debt than could a boy with a giant. Her obligations, he said, had sunk from one-sixth of face value to one-eighth even while the speculators sped in swift ships from New York to Charleston.

The long wait of the South Carolina soldier for his money (if he had not already sold his indent at a discount) was now soon ended. By September 30, 1791, the Federal government had taken over South Carolina paper to the extent of the full $4,000,000 allowed. Further Revolutionary expenditures by the State to the extent of $1,965,756 were said to be unprovided for. These figures were in excess of those of any other State.[1] The Federal government, after balancing off sums advanced by Congress during the war, gave South Carolina $1,447,173 in certificates of funded stock. The State's treasury was thus raised from prostration to the strength which it was almost uniformly to maintain for seventy years.

South Carolina paid pensions to her wounded militiamen and their widows and orphans until the United States took them over in 1832.

Democratic Stirrings.—Out of the pre-Revolutionary and Revolutionary disorders there emerged a democratic agitation against the old ruling class, especially in Charleston.[2] The parties taking form were essentially a continuation of the divisions, of ten or fifteen years before

[1] *American State Papers, Finance,* I, 150. South Carolina's creditors from 1775 to 1790, soldiers and others, received pay in various forms. So long as there was paper money in the treasury, this was paid. The receipt of such money (even though greatly depreciated) settled the debt beyond readjustment. But in the confused period from 1780 to '82, while there was no civil government, there was not even this form of payment. Officers gave certificates to persons furnishing supplies or military services. On March 16, 1783, the legislature ordered that all accounts be audited and certificates be issued to public creditors. These certificates (or indents, as they were also called, because of the indented stub for identification) were to bear 7 per cent interest until paid.

So prostrate was the treasury that it was unable to pay even the interest, and accordingly issued "special indents" annually for the purpose. The State did however, after the Federal assumption was over, pay in cash some old indents, the time limit under the assumption law, March 1, 1793, having expired, and the amount assumed for South Carolina having been taken up.

The indents, ranging from tiny amounts to large sums, entered extensively into trade during the lack of currency. Speculators bought them up. The books of the United States Treasury show merchants presenting large totals, composed of hundreds of little certificates.

Even the Federal government under President Washington was not able to pay its own or the States' debts to their soldiers in cash in 1790. Under the act of August 4, 1790, it gave the holder of a Federal or a State indent or certificate United States stock to the amount due, however small. These odd denomination stocks, bearing interest, were not converted into round sums until later funding measures.

The Federal government assumed only the still unpaid debts of the States, and did not reimburse the States for debts already paid. This, like other features of assumption, was criticized as inequitable and was defended as humane and practical.

[2] Cf. the two paragraphs beginning "Judge Aedanus Burke," page 326 above.

the Revolution, between the more vigorous elements among the masses and the merchants and planters. The city mechanics, led by a scattering of men of the upper and middle classes, sought combination with the back-country farmers against the dominance and little-concealed disdain of the coast-country planter and merchant. But, said John Lloyd, December 7, 1784: "The gentlemen of property, to preserve their necessary consequence in the community and in order to prevent anarchy and confusion, have almost unanimously exerted themselves in opposition to them, and it is with particular pleasure I inform you they have pretty generally carried their point, especially in the city, so that we shall have exceedingly good representation, and by that means support the honor and credit of the country."

The long conflict of up country against low country was a manifestation of the same class antagonism and was only incidentally sectional, since the two classes dominated the respective sections. Local attachments, always so powerful in sentimental appeal, of course accentuated the class conflict and gave it the character of a sort of local patriotism. In the 1790's the same class alignment developed into Federalists and Republicans, and, except when disturbed by outside influences, has persisted to this day as the dominant fact in South Carolina politics next to the necessity since 1865 of all white men's standing together against the Negro in politics. John P. Grace was the successor of Alexander Gillon, and B. R. Tillman of Governor Charles Pinckney.

Charleston witnessed an anti-Tory riot in 1783, and distinctly class riots in 1784, when, charged the radicals, an armed Tory mob was called out by the nabob city government against an unarmed Whig mob. The Marine Anti-Britannic Society and the Secret Committee of Correspondence of the Whig Club of Six Hundred organized the radicals against everything aristocratic and British. Christopher Gadsden, never in truth a radical except in being radically opposed to all tyranny, denounced in the press the policies of the democratic leader Alexander Gillon, which he condemned as stirring strife between classes and factions and enmity against England. Let there be no Dutch, German, Irish, or any other class of citizens, he urged, but only Americans.

The anti-aristocratic, anti-nabob, anti-Britannic, anti-Tory, super-Whig party were noisy and emotional. Rough words by Captain William Thompson to John Rutledge's servant, and Rutledge's saying (Thompson charged) that he would believe the slave before the captain, led to Thompson's so insulting Rutledge (a member of the House) that he was imprisoned for contempt—clear evidence to the democrats of the peril of free institutions. The imprisoned tavern keeper complained to the public: "The NABOBS of this state, their servile Toad-eaters, the BOBS,

—and the servilely-servile tools and lickspittles to *both,* the BOBBETS, are the *lofty* criminals I allude to." He did not consider it a breach of the privileges of the House for a common citizen "having dared to dispute with a *John Rutledge,* or any of the NABOB Tribe . . . even though they should have degraded him, in his testimony below the rank of a Negro." He had been punished because *"the great John Rutledge* was individually offended by a *plebeian."*

The proceedings of the Sons of Liberty in New York on March 26, 1784, were reported in the Charleston press, and thus the radicals from end to end of the country kept in touch. The conservative "Another Patriot" sneered at "the solemn-oath-of-secrecy-societies. . . . Shall a contemptible smoking, bacchanalian club have the unheard of assurance to press upon us societies subversive of all society, and the annihilation of government?" The democrats were denounced, too, for their affiliation with Catholic priests. So early was this still active Charleston alliance. The elections revealed that, because of the peculiarities of the system of representation, the conservatives, who were ready to continue moderation toward the "rich Tories," were to remain in power by a 3 to 1 majority.

It was in the midst of this partisan furor that the country was stirred by the controversy over the Cincinnati, organized in 1783 on the basis of descent through the eldest male line from Continental army officers. Governor Guerard, in his annual speech to the legislature on February 2, 1784, earnestly attacked the plan. The pamphlet in 1783 of Judge Aedanus Burke of South Carolina under the pseudonym of "Cassius the slayer of tyrants," violently attacking this supposed attempt to create an hereditary aristocracy, was so closely reproduced by Count Mirabeau that the author accused him of plagiarism. It was part of the revulsion against the scheme, foolishly voiced by a few, of making Washington king and placing government in the hands of a landed and moneyed aristocracy. The democratic movement in South Carolina continued to assert itself vigorously until its partial victories of 1808 and 1810, after which, though from time to time finding a voice, it was submerged for three quarters of a century through the entanglement of the State in quarrels with the Federal government and the abolitionists and their post-bellum consequences.

Amid the laws reorganizing the life of the State after the Revolution was that of 1784, classifying land into town lots and nine classes of country land according to its value for taxation, thus ending the abuse so bitterly resented by the back-country men of having their new grounds 200 miles from Charleston taxed at the same rate per acre as the richest rice fields close to market. The taxable values thus established ranged from 20 cents to $26 an acre—one to 130 instead of the former equality. Modified during the next 31 years, such classification lasted through the War of Secession. Although they were equitable when adopted, the unchanged valuations, through the generations, themselves became an injustice. Merchandise, income, and other objects were also taxed.

Another forward step was the law of 1785 creating counties and county courts. The seven districts of 1769 continued to serve for the circuits courts, but were divided into thirty-four counties, in each of which its justices of the peace were to hold court quarterly. Hence originated also almost all the present county seats except a few pre-existing towns, such as Beaufort, Georgetown, Orangeburg, Camden, and Cheraw, and those of later created counties, such as Bamberg and Bishopville.

The county courts were given certain administrative as well as judicial duties. The old parish section disliked the new system. The county courts were apparently never established in Charleston and Georgetown districts. Though abolished at the end of 1799 because of the inefficiency of their bench, they constituted an important step toward a better judicial system, and their areas have supplied the territorial basis for local government and representation to this day.

Despite the bitter cleavage between Whig and Tory, the lawless aftermath of war, the disorganization of industry, and the threat of financial collapse, the State was moving to surer ground.

Boundary Dispute with Georgia.—The boundary dispute between Georgia and South Carolina, which had existed since the younger province was set off, assumed new significance as settlement pressed toward the mountains. To the old question as to whether the boundary lay in the middle or at one shore line of the Savannah was added the question as to what branch of the upper waters was to be considered the dividing line. The charter of 1732 defined Georgia as extending "from the most northern stream" of the Savannah, and along the coast southward, "unto the most southern stream" of the Altamaha, and west from their heads to the Pacific.

Here was room enough for dispute. Did Georgia own the islands in the Savannah? Did she even own the entire stream to its northern shore? Further, which of its branches was the head of the Savannah? Each side claimed at one time or another the whole of the river bed, if an occasional inferential passage in South Carolina laws can be taken so seriously. Georgia claimed what is now Oconee County, South Carolina, and South Carolina claimed what is now Rabun County, Georgia, and a strip of the width of Rabun County to the Mississippi.

The dispute was temporarily ended by Georgia and South Carolina in the Convention of Beaufort, April 28, 1787. This very confused document defined, in the opinion of the United States Supreme Court in 1922, the boundary as being the middle of the Savannah, the Toogaloo, and the Chattooga, reserving the islands and the bed to midstream between them and the South Carolina shore to Georgia.

On August 9, 1787, South Carolina ceded to Congress the imaginary strip bounded on the north by latitude 35 degrees to the Mississippi, and on the south by a western line from the head of the southmost branch of the Toogaloo. As the head of that branch is north of 35 degrees, this strip of course had no existence. Its inclusion to this day on historical maps indicates mere ignorance of geography.

South Carolina in the Federal Constitution Convention.—South Carolina's record in the Congress of the Confederation was a natural prelude to the part she played in the Constitutional Convention of 1787. As Mr. C. G. Singer remarks, she had usually favored a stronger Federal government, a tendency in her ruling class that continued until long after the Revolution. This tendency was largely due, as he surmises, to realization by a community so largely devoted to foreign commerce and staple agriculture for a world market that rights in international trade depend on a strong central government. It is doubtful, says Mr. Singer, whether any other state with the possible exception of Virginia had continuously such able representation in the Continental Congress.[3] Governor Guerard speaks in 1784 of the United States as a "national" government, a term which the Constitution makers themselves did not venture to use. The amendments proposed by Congress for strengthening its powers over commerce were approved by the South Carolina legislature, sometimes three to one, though the legislature, in resentment at General Greene's urgency, which they construed as a Cromwellian threat, repealed in 1783 their ratification of the impost duty amendment. Undoubtedly the masses, deprived of control by a restricted suffrage and the small representation of the populous back country, were antinationalist, as was shown a little later when they voted almost unanimously against ratification of the Constitution.

South Carolina sent an able delegation to the Federal convention in 1787 in the persons of John Rutledge, Charles Cotesworth Pinckney, Charles Pinckney, and Pierce Butler. Rutledge's and C. C. Pinckney's previous services ranked them with the distinguished men of the Revolution. Pierce Butler, an English ex-army officer, an impulsive, haughty aristocrat, contributed to the Constitution only the clause for the rendition of fugitive slaves.

[3] C. G. Singer, *South Carolina in the Confederation* (Philadelphia, 1941), pp. 162-3, 166-7.

Charles Pinckney, the youngest member of the convention with the exception of Jonathan Dayton of New Jersey, was to earn the highest fame of his delegation in the framing of the Constitution. This brilliant young statesman (1757-1824) had already been active in seeking to remedy the weakness of the Confederation. Though a connoisseur in art and literature and very wealthy, this advocate of a strong Federal government was to become the chief leader of his generation of the democracy of South Carolina and to be rewarded by an affection which elected him four times governor, and by a hatred from his own class which denounced him (with disappointed class hatred rather than justice, so far as any evidence that I have seen reveals) as "blackguard Charlie." On May 29, 1787, he presented to the Convention a complete outline of a constitution. It comprised thirty-one or thirty-two of the provisions of the Constitution as finally adopted, including many of the most fundamental. Nineteen or twenty of its proposals were not in any other plans or resolutions, such as counting slaves for representation, the control of the President over the military forces, Federal power to order the militia into any State, and the powers of the House over impeachments. Others, while of importance, were found in the Articles of Confederation or in other plans, or were the common thought of constitutional reformers.

The two supreme virtues of the Federal Constitution were its settling (so far as was then possible) the relations between the States and the Union, and the establishment of a Federal judiciary with ample powers over individuals. To the first of these Pinckney's plan contributed strongly. On the other hand, several unwise proposals of Pinckney were rejected, while he contributed to doing good and preventing evil in numbers of points not included in his draft. We may accept Mr. James M. Beck's conclusion, when considered with due regard for the work of others, that Pinckney's plan "did not differ in principle from the Virginia plan, but was more specific and concrete in stating the powers which the Federal government should exercise, and many of its provisions were embodied in the final draft. Indeed, Pinckney's plan was the future Constitution of the United States in embryo. . . . It is amazing that so young a man should have anticipated and reduced to concrete and effective form many of the most novel features of the Federal government."

Mr. Richard Barry in *Mr. Rutledge of South Carolina* (1942) shows that John Rutledge's influence in shaping the Constitution was considerable, a fact which should be recognized despite Mr. Barry's exaggeration of Rutledge's part in everything in which he participated.

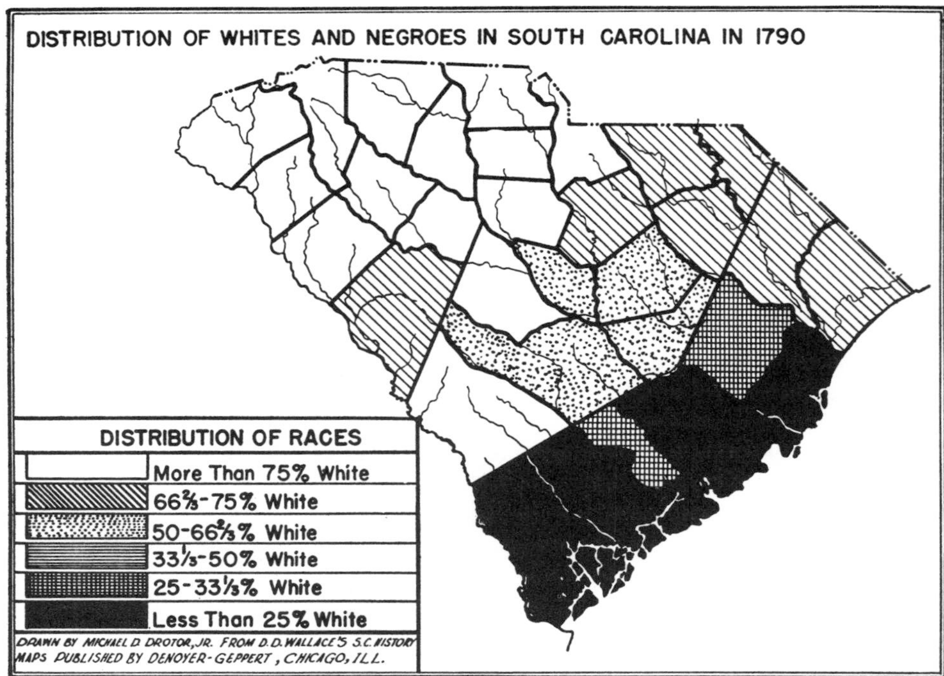

Rawlins Lowndes's opposition to the Constitution in the legislature was taken up in the convention called for its consideration by Judge Aedanus Burke, Dr. Peter Fayssoux, and General Sumter; but the Constitution was ratified May 23, 1788, by 149 to 73. In only a few of the more remote parishes was there a low-country vote against it; except in Greenville County and the soon-to-be-created Pendleton there was scarcely an up-country vote for it. The people of the State were evidently against the action of the convention, in which the low country was represented several times as strongly in proportion to numbers as the up country.

Movement for a New State Constitution.—This was the first constitutional convention in the history of the State, and served to strengthen the feeling that a convention should be called to supersede with an improved and genuine State constitution the mere act of a wartime legislature in 1778. The democratic element strove for years for a convention against the aristocratic element, which feared the diminution of its power. Out of the discussions of the years 1784 to 1790, on the need of a new State constitution and how to obtain it without risking the loss of liberty through the imposition of an unrestrained body, there grad-

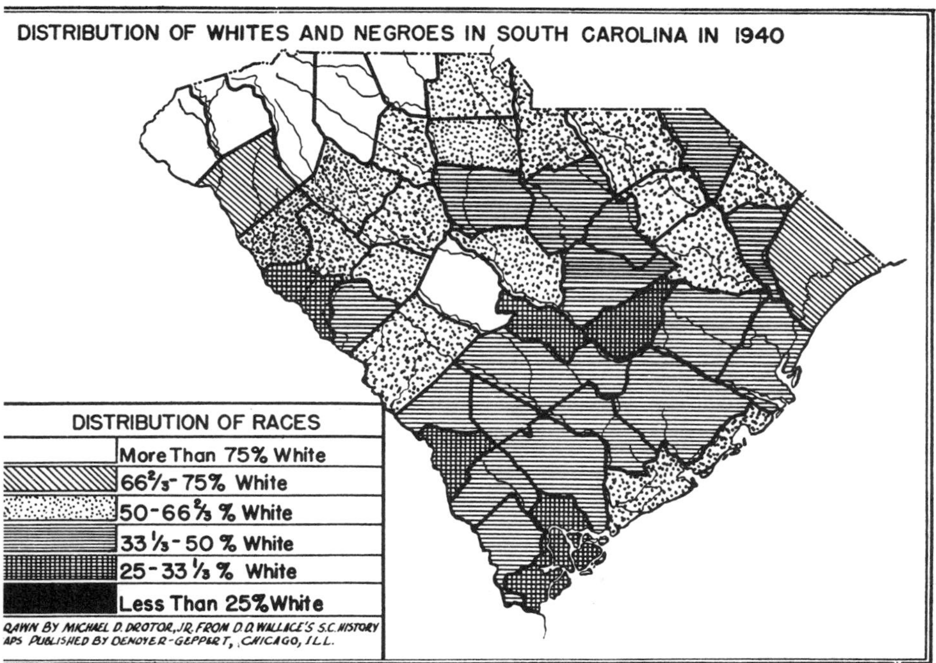

ually emerged the South Carolina conception of the omnipotence of the convention as embodying the sovereign people, accompanied by the idea that the convention ought to act in accordance with the manifest will of the people. Put into practice in 1790 and found of the highest utility in the subsequent difficulties with the Federal government, though questioned by dissatisfied elements in the 1830's and 1860's, this conception has never been modified by South Carolina, though the plan of popular ratification was forced upon her during Reconstruction.

The argument of the up country that "a convention brings the people back to first principles, according to which all are equal," could not persuade the low-country minority to surrender its control. It was accordingly enacted that the existing voters of each election district were to send as many delegates as equaled its representation in both houses of the legislature. The parish or low-country section was thus left in complete control. This, the "lower division" as officially defined by the compromise of 1790, consisted of the judicial districts of Georgetown, Charleston, and Beaufort, and in 1790 contained 28,644 white inhabitants. The "upper division," consisting of the judicial districts of Cheraw, Camden, Ninety Six, and Orangeburg, contained 111,534. One-fifth of the white population, possessing over three-fourths of the wealth, were in control. The terms "lower" and "upper division" will be used in the strict sense. The terms upper and lower country may at times indicate different areas as the civilization of the old low country spread upwards toward the fall line.

The unhappy conflict of upper and lower country, dating as a definite movement from the 1760's, was to reach in the convention of 1790 an alarming crisis, not allayed until the compromise of 1808, which may be called the completion of the Constitution. The fight, begun in 1780, to remove the capital to the center of the State had been won in 1786 by making the Taylor plantation the site of the present capital, to which was given the nationalistic name Columbia. Since the State House in Charleston had burned in 1788, the legislature first met in January, 1790, in the unfinished wooden State House in the new capital.

Here the convention of 1790 met on May 12. It was a battle of the sections, the upper division coming to win its rights, the lower division to hold its privileges. The personnel was comprised of a series of social and historic strata. Among the old parish delegates there were five Pinckneys, four Draytons, a Moultrie, a Grimké, a Bull, a Pringle, two Rutledges, a Porcher, a Huger, a Laurens, a Heyward, a Seabrook, and a Washington. From the upper division appeared hardly a name that had been famous before the Revolution; but bright potential stars of the younger aristocracy, many of whom had won their places in the struggle for independence, shone in Kennedy, Manning, Kershaw, Hampton, Pettigrew, Simms, Earle, Bratton, Anderson, Pickens, Calhoun.

Governor Charles Pinckney, though president of the convention, was one of the most active members on the floor of the committee of the whole. He had brought to Columbia a complete plan for a State, as to Philadelphia a plan for a Federal, constitution, though of its outlines we are ignorant.

Contest of Up Country Against Low Country in the Convention of 1790.—The work of the convention had two aspects. On the general principles of government there was such agreement that a Constitution was framed which with a few changes served until 1865. But on the conflicting interests of the two socially and economically contrasted sections there was such antagonism as to threaten the disruption of the convention. The long conflict between the wealthy planter and slave economy of the low country and the small white farmer economy of the up country now reached one of its three great crises, as in 1768-69 and in 1808. This antagonism, found within so many of the old coast States, manifested itself again and again.

The just demands of the up country were neglected because of the low country's ignorance of conditions as well as because of the human propensity of those possessing power to retain it and the equally natural tendency of an old, wealthy, and cultured society to feel contempt for the new. The "upper division" had long been more populous than the "lower," and in 1790 contained four-fifths of the white population.[4]

The convention of 1790 was the arena for the battle still waging over the re-apportionment of representation. The up-country men were constrained to modify their demand for representation according to population in favor of the unfulfilled promise of the constitution of 1778 of representation according to wealth and population combined; but even this was refused. Christopher Gadsden, who was not the democrat he has been thought, but in effect an orthodox English Whig opposing the power of the Crown in favor of Parliament, wrote, "but [I] am now apprehensive from a conversation last evening with one of the select committee, that a most unreasonable advantage to the back country in regard to representation will be reported to the convention and attempted to be carried."

The new counties of 1785 were made the basis of representation in the up country, while the parishes remained the basis in the low country. The increase of 67 per cent given the "upper division" in the House, and some increase in the Senate, still left the "lower division" with a majority in both houses. The size of the lower house was reduced by almost half to 124, the figure at which it still remains.

Democratic ideas were still so immature that the moderate property qualification for suffrage hardly raised debate. The contest over the location of the capital was even warmer than that over representation, another illustration of the fact that old Whig principles of justice were more prominent than the newer ideas of democracy. Should the capital be fixed in Columbia or should it be moved back to Charleston? Columbia won by 109 to 105, but the legislature by a two-thirds vote could change the capital. The low-country men, defeated by defection from their ranks, now sought so far as possible to have two capitals. A committee of four from each section was appointed to devise some compromise. Their unanimous recommendation was adopted:

1. There should be two treasurers, one for the "lower division" to reside in Charleston, and one for the "upper division" to reside in Columbia. (But the public funds were the possession of the State as a whole.)

2. The Secretary of State and the Surveyor-General should maintain offices in both places.

[4] See further explanation pages 356-57, 359.

3. The Court of Appeals should meet in Columbia to hear cases from the "upper division" and in Charleston for cases from the "lower division."

4. The Governor might reside where he pleased except while the legislature was in session.[5]

The Constitution of 1790—Aristocratic Stability.—The dominant English Whiggery spoke also in denying, as did the first constitution of South Carolina as a State, any veto power to the Governor, and in having him elected by the legislature. Liberal provisions were the order to abolish primogeniture (which was done in 1791) and the establishment for the first time of complete religious equality in place of the favored position of Protestants.[6]

It is needless to say that there was no submission to popular vote of this Constitution, which gave control of both houses of the legislature to one-fifth of the citizens, and, through the legislature's election of practically all officers from the Governor down, gave to the legislature the control of local government in each county as well. But few constitutions were submitted to popular vote at that period. The South Carolina Constitution of 1790, like the Federal Constitution, closed the period of experimentation, and was mainly the work of the conservative classes, definitely protecting property and institutions against "the mob." It placed control in the hands of a propertied, slave-holding aristocracy, where it remained to a degree unexampled in any other State until 1865. Representatives should own in the district 500 acres of land and 10 Negroes, or real estate of £150 sterling value clear of debt, or if a nonresident, £500 sterling value. Double these values were required for a senator. A man might vote in any district in which he owned fifty acres of land or a town lot, or in the district in which he lived if he paid three shillings sterling tax.

After the fashion of the time, the legislature was left almost unrestricted power. In addition to its law-making functions, it elected the governor, presidential electors, United States senators, of course, and almost every other official down to county tax-collectors, though the choice of many of the local officials was, without great delay, surrendered to the people. South Carolina had a more fortunate experience with

[5] He did in fact customarily reside at home before the War of Secession. The attorney-general did not take up his residence regularly in Columbia until even later.

The divided locality of government provided by the Constitution of 1790 recalls that Newport and Providence were both capitals of Rhode Island until 1900 and that New Haven and Hartford were both capitals of Connecticut from 1701 to 1874.

[6] Several of the following paragraphs are taken, by permission of the Lewis Publishing Company, from Chapter XXXIII, contributed by D. D. Wallace to the *History of South Carolina,* edited by Dr. Yates Snowden, written by Mr. H. G. Cutler.

this system of legislative near-omnipotence than most other States. This was probably because circumstances secured here, during the period under consideration, a higher average of legislative ability. First, the slave-holding class realized that their most vital interests were constantly under the necessity of protection, both from outside and even from inside the State. Hence they sent into public life men to whom they were willing to entrust such power. In the second place, the existence of a semi-leisure class, particularly in the low country, supplied to some extent men of ability who had the time and inclination for political life, a tradition which still operates more strongly to the public benefit in the lower than in the upper country, where most men of ability are so busy establishing their own fortunes that they neglect public service. And, lastly, the ideals of the ante-bellum period stimulated in young men the ambition of a public career. The classic models upon whom their minds and characters were formed were senators and generals and patriots. The mere business man was long made to know and keep his place by the landed aristocracy and the bar, to a degree, indeed, that was injurious to the interests of the State.

The Governor, without the veto and for four years ineligible for re-election, was greatly limited in power. His office was regarded as being, in addition to a position for public service, a sort of civic crown with which to honor exceptional public men. But let us not suppose that this excluded personal candidacies and political maneuvers. The proud disdain of submission to personal power thus registered in the restrictions upon the Governor is exemplified in the almost unbroken refusal of South Carolina to appropriate money for the statue of any individual from that of William Pitt in 1766 to that of Wade Hampton in 1903.[7]

The Constitution of 1790 provided South Carolina with just the government which her ruling class were satisfied she needed; and, whatever may have been the errors or shortcomings upon which it was founded, under it and largely by means of it the aristocratic republic attained a phenomenal influence and distinction among her sister States.

[7] Statements by Judge Simonton and others overlook the fact that the legislature in 1858 appropriated the money to buy the copy of Houdon's Washington that stands before the capitol. Would they have done so if Governor R. F. W. Allston had not already assumed personally the obligation of $8,000 so as to be sure not to miss securing the statue?

CHAPTER XXXVI

POLITICS AND CULTURE ABOUT 1800

South Carolina enjoyed the honor in 1791 of entertaining President Washington on his southern tour. The president entered the State from North Carolina on April 27 and, passing through Georgetown, reached Charleston on May 2, and remained there until the 9th. After visiting Savannah he returned to South Carolina by way of Augusta and on the twenty-first reached Columbia, whence he passed through Camden and Lancaster into North Carolina.

Enthusiasm for France.—Genêt, appointed minister to the United States on the eve of the long war between France and Britain, landed in Charleston in April, 1793, and roused a storm of pro-French enthusiasm. The population was divided into Francophile and Francophobe; but the conservatives retained control of the legislature and, on December 2, 1793, ordered an investigation of the reported raising of forces under foreign authority. South Carolina enthusiasm was punctured by this and by the discovery that Genêt and the Girondists were "friends of the blacks."

The zeal for France, fanned by the insolent captures by British vessels and the rich rewards of trade as neutral carriers between Europe and America and the French West Indies, survived the fall of Genêt and the brutalities of the Terror. There were two Jacobin Clubs in Charleston. In the celebration in honor of the French National Assembly, January 11 and 12, 1793, the Governor, judges, and other distinguished citizens participated. French privateersmen paraded the streets of Charleston waving long swords with an air of dominance, and recruiting headquarters were opened, but these the governor closed in April, 1793. So insolent did the French become that a privateer that had captured a British vessel in American waters threatened when arrested, it is said, to batter down Charleston, but changed her determination when cannon were trained upon her for many critical hours.

Upon this revelry of republican enthusiasm and quick riches fell the shadow of Jay's treaty threatening the lucrative commerce with France and offending the South by denying it the British West Indian trade and forbidding its exporting cotton—clauses which, however, the Senate deleted. John Rutledge, Federalist though he was and honored friend of Washington, denounced the treaty so violently as to incur his rejection as chief justice by the Federalist Senate. The Jay treaty had its part in turning South Carolina from Federalism.

France was so angered at our treaty with her enemy that she began a series of insults that soon developed into informal war. Charles Cotesworth Pinckney, whom Washington had sent to displace Monroe in Paris, was refused recognition. Marshall and Gerry were then sent to supplement our mission, only with the result of drawing new insults. To the demand of a bribe of a quarter of a million dollars for the pockets of the Directors, Pinckney replied, "No, no; not a sixpence," a sentiment given its popular form of "Millions for defense, but not one cent for tribute," by Robert Goodloe Harper. France's insolence had gone too far, and public opinion would no longer brook her insulting American sovereignty by preying upon British commerce inside the Charleston bar. The State had already begun to arm. Workmen donated their labor for erecting Fort Mechanic, and popular subscription built and, on June 5, 1799, launched at Charleston the frigate *John Adams*.

On overthrowing the Directory, Bonaparte brought the informal naval war with America to an end by agreeing in 1800 to abrogate the Revolutionary treaty of alliance and form a new treaty of commerce—a conclusion advantageous to the United States to which C. C. Pinckney had contributed by firmly maintaining the honor of his country in France. In the crisis South Carolina Republicans and Federalists stood together.

Eminence of South Carolina Federalists.—The leading Federalists were the brothers Charles Cotesworth Pinckney and Thomas Pinckney, dignified, highly respected, moderate; John Rutledge, of the same character; Ralph Izard, the haughty aristocrat; and lastly William Loughton Smith and Robert Goodloe Harper, vigorous in mind and the most active in leadership. Active on the same side were Governor Arnoldus Vander Horst, Henry W. DeSaussure, General William Washington, Gabriel Manigault, David Ramsay, and Judge Elihu Bay.

The South Carolina Federalists stood very high in the nation. On May 24, 1791, President Washington wrote to C. C. Pinckney and Edward Rutledge, offering to either one who would accept the Supreme Court judgeship which John Rutledge had resigned. Both declined. Pinckney declined the secretaryship of state in 1795, but accepted the mission to France in 1796. Edward Rutledge was selected by Washington, it is said, to command the artillery in case of war with France, and C. C. Pinckney was one of the three major generals Washington selected for the anticipated French war. In the unpleasantness regarding Hamilton's primacy, Pinckney acted with perfect magnanimity. John Rutledge, who had resigned as associate justice of the United States Supreme Court in 1791 to become chief justice of South Carolina, was appointed by President Washington chief justice of the United States in 1795, the only instance, it is said, of a second appointment to the Supreme Court until that of Charles E. Hughes. Thomas Pinckney was the Federalist candidate for vice-president in 1796, and C. C. Pinckney the Federalist candidate for vice-president in 1800 and for president in 1804 and 1808.

So fearful were the Federalists of losing South Carolina, and thus the election in 1796, that they nominated Thomas Pinckney for vice-president without his solicitation. South Carolina voted for Jefferson and Pinckney, and Adams won by a majority of two. Edward Rutledge drew the scorn of his class by turning Republican, and the legislature, despite the preponderant representation of the Federalist districts, in 1796 for the third time elected as governor Charles Pinckney, one of the most loved and hated Republicans. "What a disgraceful condition are we reduced to when such a wretch is to be Governor?" exclaimed William Loughton Smith. "What a scandalous tool is E. R. become when he coalesces with such men." But the time was not far distant, he comforted himself, when they would draw the curses of good citizens.

When Smith left Congress to go as minister to Portugal, "Federal management in South Carolina," says Phillips, "passed entirely to a more moderate man, Robert Goodloe Harper, who differed greatly from the local Federalist type both in origin and residence, though not policy. A Virginia-born North Carolina graduate of Princeton, he had settled in Ninety Six district and entered Congress as a Republican. Drifting with the socially and politically prominent in Philadelphia, he was from the time of Jay's treaty as strong a Federalist as he had been a Republican and was soon the leader of the House of Representatives." The rally to President Adams' spirited defiance of France carried every South Carolina congressional district but Sumter's for the Federalists. Edward Rutledge, so moderate as to be acceptable to both parties, was in 1798 elected governor.

South Carolina Turns to Jeffersonianism.—The fact that the Federalists were compacted in the narrow coast strip and were so dominated by Charleston afforded both the material for leadership and the facility for organization. Much more difficult was the task of the Republicans, although there was never a doubt that by majority of citizens the State had always been anti-Federalist, with the possible exception of the brief reaction against French insolence in 1798, when she sent five Federalists to one Republican to Congress. What leaders the South Carolina Republicans possessed were largely from the wealthy planters. In 1796 Ephraim

Ramsay was, according to Harper, "the ablest, the most artful and most dangerous of all the supporters of antifederalism in South Carolina." Charles Pinckney, first cousin once removed of Charles Cotesworth and Thomas, soon assumed a Republican leadership which proved so strong that he was four times elected governor between 1789 and 1806. Bitterly hated for the unforgivable crime of treason to his class, the control of which he overthrew in favor, so it then seemed, of that of the masses, his name comes down to us covered with opprobrium by the one and affection by the other.[1]

Charles Pinckney was the outstanding Charleston democrat. Edward Rutledge, author of the act abolishing primogeniture, had been a Federalist of liberal leaning and voted for Jefferson in 1796. Pierce Butler, haughty aristocrat and individualist, in revolt against Northern selfishness in Congress, now co-operated with the Republicans. "The Jeffersonian movement, however," says Professor Phillips, "combining the principles of individual and state rights, welcomed from the beginning by the Charleston radicals, and vigorously organized by Charles Pinckney with Pierce Butler, Thomas Sumter and Wade Hampton as his colleagues, had strength enough even in the lowlands to keep the Federalists in fear of losing all their Congressional representation at each recurring election." Sumter was the typical back-country Republican. He was of humble origin, an individualist, an extreme State rights man, and a popular hero, and Jeffersonianism was his political mother tongue.

The possession of a majority of the seats in both houses by the three coast judicial districts containing about a fifth of the citizens made the capture of the legislature in 1800 a desperate task for the Republicans. Charles Pinckney wrote Jefferson that never before had the Federal interests connected with the British, the banks, and the Federal treasury made such a fight. Non-taxpayers voted. "The lame, the crippled, diseased and blind were either led, lifted or brought in carriages to the polls." Watchers scrutinized to see whether men voted the green, blue, red, and yellow ballots as directed.

When it was clear that the legislature was Republican, friends of C. C. Pinckney, Adams' running mate, sought a compromise by which the State's vote should be given for Jefferson and Pinckney, but the Republican caucus refused any compromise, and General Pinckney is

[1] I cannot agree with Professor U. B. Phillips' view of Charles Pinckney as of "no principles in particular"—a strange view of a man of positive and aggressive turn, from his activity for a stronger Federal government in the 1780's to his unyielding position on the constitutional rights of slavery before most Southern men realized the significance of the issue of 1820. The rumor that he had acted dishonorably in some money matters has never been supported by a word of proof. His challenge of proof when this was rumored in the campaign of 1818 brought none, says Mr. T. D. Jervey in his *Robert Y. Hayne*, p. 76.

said, by a tradition which his character makes it easy to believe, to have refused to be a party to any such arrangement. By 82 to 87 for the various Republican electors, as against 63 to 69 for the Federalist electors, the entire Jefferson-Burr ticket was elected. In the Federalist attempt in Congress to settle the tie by bringing in Jefferson over Burr, the South Carolina delegation, Federalist to a man except Sumter, voted for Burr. Later Huger, apparently the only Federalist in the House who took this course, is thought to have voted for Jefferson.

Federalism was later again to assert itself vigorously among the Charleston merchants and the great coast-country planters; but forces as yet not fully manifest were to bind South Carolina more and more strongly in national politics to Jeffersonian principles.

Cultured Charleston.—Charleston was instinct with life as one of the country's chief commercial centers with exports almost equal to those of Massachusetts or Pennsylvania. The already astonishing expansion of cotton culture seemed to promise her the third place among American cities, a promise which would have come nearer fulfillment had not the invention of the steamboat neutralized her natural advantage from the Gulf Stream and the trade winds for European commerce. Only fifteen miles of road were needed in 1795 to connect the city with Knoxville. Her long fight for this connection began that year by the creation of a commission to confer with the Governor of the Southwest Territory on a wagon road over the mountains, a purpose for which South Carolina voted an appropriation in 1796.

"The small society of rice and cotton planters at Charleston," says Henry Adams in describing America in 1800, "with their cultivated tastes and hospitable habits, delighted in whatever reminded them of European civilization. They were travelers, readers, and scholars; the society of Charleston compared well in refinement with that of any city of its size in the world, and English visitors long thought it the most agreeable in America." Ebenezer S. Thomas, one of four book dealers in Charleston, in 1803 brought from England 50,000 volumes in every department of science, art, and literature; but the re-opening of the foreign slave trade the next year was disastrous to literature, for the planters were so absorbed in buying Negroes that they would have even a little paper or pens charged. In 1807 there were said to be in the city thirteen teachers (all French) of feminine accomplishments. The mere exuberance of luxury was such that Mrs. Royal said in 1831 that the dry goods, millinery, etc., imported into Charleston were superior to anything in New York or Philadelphia.

The grandeur of a royalist past had not disappeared. Many of these men, educated in English universities, says Fraser, were a peculiar race.

Born and reared under royal government, they were impressed with the exclusive feeling which rank and fortune create. In the most exclusive society in America, "such men were, in their proper element, at the head of society—it was theirs to maintain and transmit the ancient character of Charleston for intelligence, refinement, and hospitality." The Duc de Liancourt in 1796 found that nowhere in the world was hospitality better exercised than in South Carolina. These gentlemen after the Revolution loyally accommodated themselves to republican institutions. One of their first measures was the abolition of primogeniture.

Along with this elegance went a good degree of coarseness, as all over the world at the period. The table, wrote Fraser, was then and for the next half century a great center of attraction in Charleston. "The conversation of gentlemen, at the table, *now* [in 1854] is without the least blemish of freedom or impurity, which was not always the case; for I remember when licentiousness was almost the fashion," which might be illustrated by Rabelaisian instances most astonishing in gentlemen of the very highest standing. Christopher Gadsden in the *Gazette* in 1784 sneered at his opponent in a phrase too repulsive for quotation—a hangover from the coarse wit of the mid-eighteenth century.

Neither had morals undergone the discipline under which they were soon to be improved. Mrs. Louisa A. Aikman (*née* Wells), a Tory refugee from Charleston, was shocked at the case of "that infamous woman, S—— R——," who had wrecked the life of a youth and had afterward lived openly for years with the merchant, Mr. J—— S——, who subsequently married her. In 1791 the beautiful creature was at the top of the fashion, and vied with the British consul's wife in elegance of equipage and entertainments. "I need not add that there were found plenty of people to admire and frequent them."

Intemperance was a general vice. William J. Grayson's manuscript autobiography relates that well into the nineteenth century it was the custom for the host to lock the doors and refuse to permit any guest to leave the table until he was drunk. In 1805 a group from both houses of the legislature went hilariously by night with drum and fiddle "to set the town to rights." This consisted in part in smashing the doors of those who did not rise to join them. Practical jokes were rough among the high as well as the low, such as tricks to induce a gentleman to smash his fine hat, or hanging the bed of a bridal couple to the ceiling. The pre-Revolutionary custom of raising blooded horses continued. The February races were the social event of the year. "The enthusiasm produced by their recurrence pervaded all classes of the community to such a degree as scarcely could now be conceived," wrote Fraser in 1854.

"Schools were dismissed. The judges, not unwillingly, adjourned the courts," and the legislature excused members.

"I would not venture to say that religion had no place in the hearts of our people at that time," wrote Fraser referring to the early nineteenth century, "or that it did not exercise an active and vital influence over very many of them. But I think its general manifestation consisted rather in a decent respect for outward observances, and in a formal compliance with its social requirements, rather than that deep and devotional sense of its sacred obligations, which now characterize so large a proportion of our community."

There were then but two churches termed such in Charleston, the others being called meeting houses and their members męet-ners. It was at this period that an intelligent traveler observed "that devotion is not a prevailing fashion in this country." It is not surprising that Bishop Asbury continually inveighed against the wickedness and frivolity of Charleston, saying that nowhere in England or Ireland was pleasure so eagerly sought; but when, on February 5, 1800, he visited the Charleston Orphan House, he had to record: "There is no institution in America equal to this; two or three hundred orphans are taught, fed and clothed and put to good trades."

The growing love of dancing, says Fraser, made it difficult for the St. Cecilia Society to cultivate a love for music after the war. After struggling from 1815 to about 1822 the concert yielded to the balls, which have since continued under the patronage of the highest society of the city. The chartering of the Philharmonic Society in 1810 carried on the city's musical traditions.

It was impossible that a society so rich, so polished, so ignorant of the State except in its own then-favored region, so haughtily despising any sort of labor, and so constantly praised, both by itself and by others, should entirely restrain its sense of distinction from at times splashing over into arrogance toward the back country even after it had emerged from its early crudity. And there was much in the early years of the up country to invite disdain. Though there were numerous exceptions, it was in general strongly marked by the rudeness of the frontier.

Typical of the thousand illustrations of the contrast in wealth, culture, and intellectual interest that then marked the two sections are the numbers of subscribers to Mills's *Statistics of South Carolina* in 1825. The city of Charleston took 176; Columbia, 69; Union, 40; Edgefield, 15; Camden, 11; York, 10; Winnsboro, 9; Spartanburg, Beaufort, and Orangeburg, 7 each; and Georgetown, Chester, and Abbeville, 6 each. These are the largest subscriptions; and it must be noted that the numbers sold in the low country outside of Charleston are as pitifully small as in the very backwoods of the hill country; but probably some of those subscribing in the city were alternate residents there and on plantations. The number taken by State officials temporarily in Columbia may be disregarded. Union's, Edgefield's, and Camden's large subscriptions were expressive of their cultured planter and lawyer classes, in which they so long surpassed their up-country neighbors.

In the Charleston of that day, said Fraser, the merchant had not the recognition to which his services entitled him. "For, with the exception of the learned professions, no pursuit which yielded income from personal effort or employment, was properly respected." The "proscribed merchants" organized their own societies, with their balls, etc. Fraser lived to see before 1850 the ruin that overtook many of the elegant idlers and the acceptance of the sons of slighted merchants into the most exclusive circles.

The contempt for the merchant dated from shortly before the Revolution. In about 1761 we find Thomas Middleton, of the highest social distinction, retiring from trade, and in 1769 young William Henry Drayton sneering at mechanics, and about the same time merchants publicly set down as distinctly inferior socially. The Laurenses, Manigaults, Middletons, and numerous others high in the social register or the exchange were frequently no longer found in the latter after the Revolution, when merchandising came to be engrossed mainly by Northerners or foreigners, especially Scots; but by about 1822 natives were repossessing trade, though social recognition even for the large merchants was much longer delayed.

The Chamber of Commerce, founded in 1773 and said to be the first in the country, was revived in 1784, the year after the city received its charter. Back-country and plantation trade from 1790 to 1820, "the King Street trade," as it was called, drew wagoners from all over the State and beyond. It was centered on King Street between Hutson and Line, with warehouses containing everything from a needle to a millstone. There was in it no division into retailers and wholesalers. Retailers in 1803 occupied Tradd Street. The Carolina Coffee House, corner of Tradd Street and Bedon's Alley, was in 1803 a distinguished hotel. A gentleman living in 1935 remembered attending the St. Cecilia ball in a house in Bedon's Alley, whose handsome interior, but not whose surroundings, then still commanded admiration.

Other Towns.—Beaufort in 1796 was a pleasant village of about two hundred inhabitants. Little Camden was an important point for distributing the trade at the head of Wateree navigation, as was Granby on the Congaree. "Spartanburg Courthouse," "Lancaster Courthouse," etc., were accumulating a tavern, a smithy, a village store, and a few houses around their primitive buildings of justice erected under the court act of 1785. Some of the stone jails built about 1825 long remained as medieval disgraces, and at least one of these is still used. The era was fast approaching when the courthouses in Greek temple style, a number of which still remain to testify to the taste of the classical revival, were to dignify a number of public squares.

The Crude but Potentially Dominant Up Country.—The lack of transportation forced the up country to economic self-sufficiency. With few slaves, this independent, laboring farmer society much more resembled the North than the Carolina low country. The prevalence of household industries caused it to be known as a "manufacturing section." It was indeed a new and second South Carolina, which was to wage bitter conflict with the older and less populous South Carolina until assimilated by the spread of the slavery and plantation system.

Considering the coarser side of low-country life as described above, the frontier roughness of the up country is not surprising. The American frontier has been so idealized as to obscure its coarseness and brutality. Men drank heavily, ate greasy food gluttonously, talked vulgarly, and shouted with savage joy as the man on top gouged out the eye of his antagonist. The mountain and near-mountain inhabitants of the Alpine region were found in 1806 to be kindly, but marked by an extreme primitiveness that continued largely undisturbed until comparatively recent decades.

Captain Hall, journeying from Charleston to Spartanburg in 1804, found most of the up-country houses of logs, though their interiors usually displayed a pleasing neatness. Judge Grimké's seat at Belmont, Union County, was imposing, and Attorney Farrow in lower Spartanburg had an "elegant abode." Colonel Hampton's eight-room frame house of two stories in Spartanburg District was approached by an avenue of chestnuts and walnuts, and General Thomas Moore of that District had "a hospitable plantation." But it required a four days' journey of 120 miles to get a physician to set Hall's broken arm. Belfast, a handsome two-and-a-half-story brick mansion still standing in lower Laurens, was built by 1796. The stately Kincaid house in Fairfield County of a somewhat earlier date, now owned by the Winnsboro Granite Corporation and fittingly reconditioned by Mr. Dan Heyward, with its terraced gardens, etc., is another fine example.[2] The famous Cuningham home, Rosemont in Laurens County, built a few years earlier than Belfast, was unfortunately burned a few years ago. The exacting Professor Edward Hooker of Connecticut in 1806 found several handsome homes around Greenville and was charmed with piano and vocal music

[2] Mr. John T. Heyward to D. D. W., May 25, 1948.

in the home of the future Governor Pickens near Pendleton. With the influx of lawyers after the county court act of 1785, and the rapid advance of enterprising farmers and merchants, cultural conditions were progressing even to the foot of the mountains. But from that day to this a surprising proportion of the culture of the up country has come with settlers from Virginia or the low country. The up country has made many notable contributions of intellect and character to the coast region from before the days of Petigru to the present, especially to Charleston; but the heavy balance of the debt of polite culture is the other way.

Colonel Wade Hampton of the Revolution, the chief founder of a great name, by 1805 a leading citizen of Richland, was typical of the men of force who were making a newer aristocracy. Bold, original, foresighted, enterprising, judicious, of simple, clear-cut, positive, rather deistic religious ideas, he manifested the broad tolerance, independence, and fair-mindedness of a strong man that his namesakes in the crises of two generations were repeatedly to exhibit. He was a persistent builder of toll bridges. A great land accumulator, he had been one of the Yazoo speculators who sought to cheat Georgia out of an imperial domain. As probably the first user in South Carolina of Whitney's gin, the raiser of a cotton crop in 1799 worth about $90,000, and the owner of Mississippi sugar plantations, he was reputed the richest man in America.

CHAPTER XXXVII

THE SECTIONAL COMPROMISE OF 1808 ON REPRESENTATION

We have thus in the South Carolina of 1790 to 1800 two contrasted and in many respects hostile societies. The rich slaveholders definitely feared the possible hostility of a non-slave-owning democracy toward their most vital interest. The revelation of the census of 1790 that the "upper division" contained four times the white population of the lower intensified the determination of the former to remedy the injustice of having the smaller section hold a majority of both houses of the legislature. Therefore they formed the Representative Reform Association, whose leaders included Wade Hampton, Robert Goodloe Harper, Ephraim Ramsay, Abraham Blanding, and John Kershaw. In 1794 the Association issued a pamphlet "address" to the people of the State written by Robert Goodloe Harper, but signed "Appius."[1]

The existing representation had originated for the temporary purpose of organizing the First Provincial Congress in 1774, and, somewhat modified, had later been imbedded in the Constitution. In 1790 St. Stephen's parish, with 226 white inhabitants, elected three representatives and one senator, the same as Edgefield with 9,785 whites or Pendleton with 8,731. The entire "upper division," with 111,534 whites, elected 54 representatives and 17 senators, while the "lower division," with 28,644 whites, elected 70 and 20.

The legal term "upper division" means the judicial districts of Cheraws, Camden, Orangeburg, and Ninety Six; the "lower division" those of Georgetown, Charleston, and Beaufort. This legal distinction continued until 1865. Until the plantation system penetrated toward the fall line, the terms up country (or generally upper, or back, country) and low (or lower) country were frequently employed as synonymous with the terms upper and lower division; but after the assimilation of so much of the middle country to the civilization of the lower division, the term low country was understood to include the territory up to the

[1] "The celebrated letters of Appius written by Robert Goodloe Harper," said Abraham Blanding, himself active in the movement, before the Clay Club of Charleston, August 22, 1844.—R. Yeadon's newspaper scrapbook, University of South Carolina.

fall line. The old term, back country, as settlement progressed after the Revolution, gave way to the term up country.[2]

In wealth the relations were reversed. The "upper division" paid in 1790 £8,390 taxes, and the "lower division" £28,081, of which the city of Charleston contributed £10,671; for before 1800 the owner paid where he lived the taxes on all his property. Thus a few hundred men ruled the low country, and the low country ruled the State, whereas, argued Harper, the people should be represented proportionately; for wealth is naturally so strong that it should be restrained.

"Americanus" (a Charleston lawyer, Timothy Ford) answered "Appius" in able newspaper articles published in bound form as *The Constitutionalist*. When before the Revolution the free-labor strangers began to pour into the up country, he wrote, our ancestors allowed them the "natural rights" of individuals, but could not permit them political privileges. Had those immigrants professed half the doctrines of majority rule now published by "Appius," he continued, the low country would have regarded every arrival "as a reinforcement to an internal enemy." The low country must preserve its superiority in the legislature to protect its peculiar interests.

Henry William DeSaussure pointed out in 1795 that no Southern State had adopted the principle of representation in proportion to population, a principle incompatible with their circumstances, and that the Federal Constitution recognized the justice of concessions to slaveholders by its three-fifths rule. It had been asserted, he continued, that if control were turned over to the up country the next winter, the low country, conscious of having used their power to commit no wrong, would seek to be set up as a separate State; and a subject should not be discussed which might result in bloody civil war.

We should remember that the practice of representation in accordance with population was then generally recent, and that the combination of democracy and American sectionalism presented a new problem. Slaves were taxed, as were carriages and other luxuries rare in the up country, and from 1784 lands were taxed according to value, instead of as formerly all at the same value.

In December, 1794, after the legislature had rejected petitions for the readjustment for representation, sixteen senators and fifty-six representatives issued an appeal to the people of the "lower division." Disclaiming all methods of violence or any intention of fomenting riots or, as accused, even civil war, they presented a more moderate demand

[2] It is interesting to note that the sectional controversy in Virginia led to the legal division of that State into four divisions for purposes of representation, greatly to the advantage of the older sections.

under which the low country, though no longer holding a majority in the legislature, would have more than a third of the representatives. Thus, they said, the low country, being assured of more than a third of the House for blocking constitutional changes, would be secure against the danger of emancipation; and even the non-slave-owners of the up country would tar and feather any legislator who should vote for abolition. The address closed with a protest against dividing the State. "Be just on your part; be candid and wise. . . . We shall then accept as a boon what we might claim as a right, and make you a rich return in confidence and attachment; so shall the wounds of our country be healed, the source of our differences forever dried up, and our public prosperity and happiness be fixed on a basis broad as our soil and firm as the everlasting foundations of truth and justice."

It was largely to cure this sectional antagonism that the legislature in 1801, under the leadership of Governor John Drayton, founded the South Carolina College, in order that the leaders of the future by youthful associations might learn to understand each other. As Professor Schaper points out, the low country knew that ultimately it must yield; but it was determined to hold its power until education and the spread of slavery into the back country should transform that section from a possible enemy to an assimilated friend of the slavery system. And well did their plan succeed. But we should note that the up country heartily co-operated in the founding of the college, though the contrary has often been erroneously stated.[3]

The up country found a powerful advocate in Joseph Alston of All Saints. As one of the wealthiest of the planters, his pleas for justice were the more effective. Alston maintained that the assumption of an alliance between the two sections was a monstrosity, destructive of peace. Population, he held, is the only just basis for representation.

It was the force of economic changes rather than Alston's logic that won the day for reform. The spread of slavery up the State with the development of cotton culture had made the middle country in effect a part of the low country, though still legally classed as in the "upper division" until the abolition of the old division by the Constitution of 1865. Not only had slavery won the middle country completely and laid its hands powerfully on the far upland hills, but the old emancipation sentiment that had feebly lived in a few minds under the inspiration of the philosophical liberalism of the Revolution was practically

[3] Dean O. F. Crow, in his MS history of the government of the University of South Carolina, points out the inaccuracy of the memory of Chancellor DeSaussure as an old man on this point. His recollection that the up country opposed founding the college is contradicted by the contemporary record.

dead. Those to whom slavery was an economic necessity no longer had reason to fear attacks from within the State.

The "Compromise of 1808."—The constitutional amendment thus adopted and known until after the War of Secession as "the compromise of 1808" was as follows: henceforth each election district should have one senator (except that the city of Charleston should have two), and each should elect one representative for each one sixty-second of the white population and one for each one sixty-second of the taxable wealth of the State that it contained.

The new arrangement transferred to the legal "upper division" the control of the representatives by a majority of sixteen, and of the Senate by a majority of one. But the victory was really with the low country. The lower half of the upper division, already dominated by large planters, was steadily becoming more and more a slave-worked plantation section. In 1810 the black belt elected 26 senators and 62 representatives to the white belt's 19 and 62, an advantage steadily rising by 1860 to 38 senators and 97 representatives for the constantly expanding black belt to 8 and 27 for the white belt.

The terms low country and up country had acquired a new meaning more in accord with the topography of the State, and henceforth meant in effect the regions below and above the fall line, though the preponderance of Negro population gradually appeared in several districts above the line. Low-country ideals by the grace of white cotton and black slaves had conquered the State. True, sectionalism was to continue, but in softened form, as there was no longer the danger within South Carolina of a death grapple between a slave labor and a free labor society. But, as Mrs. Ravenel says, "the silent Negro vote of the parishes" continued to be a source of power to the white men of the black country.

"The compromise of 1808" continued to be regarded until 1865 as a pact to be guarded against even incidental modification, as, e.g., when it was proposed to distribute the free school fund on the basis of population instead of legislative representation. The hauteur of the older society long continued, angering or amusing its objects in accordance with their temperaments or social stations. The able and educated men whom Charleston sent to Columbia, often so much superior, in all that makes the successful politician or statesman, to many representatives from the up country, continued her power after its legal basis was removed. Mr. Joseph W. Barnwell was not far wrong when he said in 1913 that the small group constituting the ante-bellum governing class in Charleston had exercised a greater power in American history than any equal number of men; for they ruled Charleston, and Charleston ruled South

Carolina, and South Carolina shaped Southern policy in the tremendous years from 1830 to 1860.

Manhood Suffrage, 1810.—In 1810 manhood suffrage was established on the basis of every man's being permitted to vote where he resided. The legal right to vote wherever one held property, after bitter protests especially against Charleston owners of country estates who flocked out to turn close country elections, came by custom to be confined to a man's voting only for local officers in more than one district. The Constitution of South Carolina continued until 1865 to give wealth and conservatism a greater power than in the government of any other State.

CHAPTER XXXVIII

AGRICULTURE, BUSINESS, AND THE WAR OF 1812

THE REVOLUTION did not, of course, injure the self-sufficing agriculture of the back country as much as it did the coast-country system of producing staples for export. The bounty on indigo was gone. Plantations were disorganized; many fine properties were almost ruined. Coast planters on August 24, 1785, organized the South Carolina Society for Promoting and Improving Agriculture and Other Rural Concerns, which still functions as the Agricultural Society of South Carolina. In 1823 there were eleven such. In 1839 articles by Whitemarsh B. Seabrook in the *Southern Agriculturist* resulted in a call for all agricultural societies in South Carolina to meet in Columbia. Thus originated the State Agricultural Society. In 1840 it induced the legislature to appropriate $2,000 for a State agricultural and geological survey, and has continued its services to agriculture and other economic interests to this day.

Agricultural leadership was sadly needed. The sea island cotton planters, says Seabrook, followed the easy method of abandoning for new fields those they had exhausted except where necessity forced them to what experience proved more profitable. The large and fertile island of Edisto in 1822 contained not a plow or a scythe and only a few carts; but agriculture had greatly improved everywhere by 1843.

Colonel Thomas Shubrick's efforts in 1800 to encourage manuring were unavailing; but from 1808 the writings of John Taylor of Virginia on animal and vegetable manures became the gospel of South Carolina agriculture. John Palmer of St. Stephen's in 1808 was increasing his cotton yield fourfold by cattle manure, which he had used for ten years, and was growing wonderful corn by putting a pint of cotton seed around each hole. In 1800 and 1803 Kinsey Burden of St. Paul's derived great help from calcareous fertilizers, evidently marl, which was to remain neglected until the 1840's. Fertilizing was not systematically practiced in the State until about 1825.

Dyking the rivers out of the rich bottoms, the ordinary means of reclaiming tide-water rice lands, was occasionally practiced farther inland. David R. Williams, in about 1809, completed his five-mile dyke near Society Hill, and was almost beaten for Congress because a man who thought he could restrain the Peedee was considered a fool. But he was richly rewarded, as was Samuel Porcher for his large enterprise "Porcher's embankment" on the Santee, begun in 1817. By 1824 there were numerous embankments to reclaim the rich swamps of the Wateree or Catawba.

By 1805, when low-country agriculture had entered upon a program of large-scale production, the rich were buying out the less wealthy planters and uniting numerous old homesteads into one vast estate. The dispossessed owners sometimes bought new places in the up country, whose productive surface had not yet been washed off through careless cultivation. In the up country in 1796 the plow was in universal use, unlike the low country, where the abundance of cheap slaves made the hoe still a profitable and almost universal tool.

The landless white man of the better kind in the low country sought to become an overseer (for the overseer was distinctly above the "poor white"). In 1827 his wages were from $250 to $1,200 a year, with a house, a servant, and the use of various plantation supplies and animals. Though there were many planters who gave little attention to management, some of even the wealthiest vigorously supervised their plantations, with most beneficial results. Generally the ordinary farmer worked hard for his living.

Rice.—South Carolina's oldest staple, rice, experienced great expansion because of two improvements shortly after the Revolution. About 1786 Gideon Du Pont, Jr., developed the system of flooding the fields by river water backed up and later drained off by the tides, a method begun around Georgetown in 1758 but apparently not then attracting attention. The problem of preparing for market the greater crops thus produced was solved by Jonathan Lucas. In or about 1787 he erected upon the Santee River his first water-driven rice mill. By 1793 he was building mills run continuously by the incoming and outgoing tide and equipped with such labor-saving devices as endless conveyor belts, etc., so as to multiply six to ten times the previous output. In 1817 he or his son Jonathan built in Charleston the first steam-driven rice mill, which set the permanent model for the industry. Rice planting thus became more than ever a large-scale capitalistic enterprise.

The abolition of primogeniture in 1791 supplemented the greater ease and profit of the tidal cultivation, already supplanting the cultivation of rice in the inland swamps. Drainage of the whole inland swamp was necessary. When the great plantation was divided among several heirs, the neglect of one owner to maintain drainage forced the abandonment of the whole. At the time of the Revolution there were 128 settled inland swamp rice plantations in St. Paul's parish, but several decades later there were only eight.

In the 1830's and 40's, 110,000 to 140,000 tierces of 600 pounds were the annual crop. A prize field of 10½ acres and 13 compasses in 1851 yielded 888½ bushels. A good crop was 45 bushels per acre. Though rice enormously enriched a few hundred large planters, the total value of the crop could not compare in the generation before 1860 with that of cotton. Decade after decade more and more lands were devoted to the latter, while the area of rice lands was naturally limited.

Cotton.—Cotton came as a boon to the former indigo planters, for the two plants thrive on the same soil. It was experimented with by the first settlers. The renewal of interest in the 1740's was doubtless stimulated, as was the culture of indigo, by the crushing depression in rice prices during the war. Shortly before the Revolution some families raised enough to clothe their slaves. The necessities of the Revolution and the following years spread the culture. Hands picked four pounds a week from the seed, plantation wheels spun it, and the few weavers, notably a manufactory owned by Williamsburg Irish, wove the cloth.

The first post-Revolutionary cotton from Charleston to reach Liverpool arrived on January 20, 1785. Numerous experiments and failures finally selected the real green seed (short staple) and the black seed sea island (long staple) varieties as suited to South Carolina. Kinsey Burden of St. Paul's parish and his widow were pioneers with both varieties of cotton, as they were also with the long-staple gin. Mrs. Burden seems to have raised in 1788, with very slight success, the first crop of sea island cotton in South Carolina, a variety that had been introduced into Georgia in 1786. Kinsey Burden of St. John's, Colleton, by 1804-05 had extraordinarily improved the sea island staple by selecting seed from his best plants—a secret not generally known until in 1827 W. B. Seabrook surmised it, and numerous planters proved it. The improved quality thus became general.

Cotton was raised in Orangeburg in 1794, in the High Hills of Santee in 1796, in Richland in 1799, in Edgefield in 1802, and a little at least in Spartanburg in 1804. Tobacco-growing gave way by about 1816 to the fleecy staple, and "factors" developed to finance and handle the crop. South Carolina grew about 1,500,000 pounds in 1791; 20,000,000 in 1801; 40,000,000 in 1811; 50,000,000 in 1821; and 65,500,000 in 1834. Though greatly outranking all others until 1821, by 1834 she was far outdistanced by Georgia, Alabama, Mississippi, and Louisiana.

The whole economic life of South Carolina outside the rice area was revolutionized by the invention of the cotton gin, which made possible this enormous increase in production. Farmers gave up almost everything else. A society based on a self-sufficient varied agriculture and normal manufacturing development disappeared before the system of cotton raised almost exclusively and exported to buy everything else. Cotton was indeed king, and the gin was his throne. The opinion has been expressed that the cotton gin has been the mightiest single economic cause in human history, for out of it have come a whole social and economic system, a great war, and economic, social and political problems that are the most serious that still confront the American people. As to the South, she sank into a slavery to cotton of which the slavery of the African was a mere incident and which remains as a galling servitude of a whole section long after the African has been set free. Says Professor J. F. Turner, "Never in history, perhaps, was an economic force more influential upon the life of a people. . . . The price of cotton was in these years the barometer of southern prosperity and of southern discontent."

The Cotton Gin.—Following the invention of the cotton gin by Eli Whitney in 1793, the South Carolina legislature in 1801 ordered the firm of Miller and Whitney paid $50,000 to allow South Carolinians to make gins, two models of which should be furnished. North Carolina and Tennessee also voted generous sums, but disputes arose, and in 1803 South Carolina and Tennessee canceled their agreements. In Georgia, Whitney sought to maintain a monopoly of ginnings; but, not supplying enough machines, he found the planters making gins, an infringement which juries refused to penalize. Colonel Wade Hampton obtained three of the Georgia gins, which were the first in South Carolina to be operated by water.

The swift development of cotton culture not only withered the considerably developed tobacco industry introduced by Virginia immigrants but led to the neglect of fruits and breadstuffs. Corn continued to be extensively raised to feed slaves and animals until cheaper freight diminished that practice. Warnings in the 1820's against the danger of dependence on cotton were unheeded, and South Carolina swung definitely into exporting her two staples for the importation of almost every necessity, including even teachers, books, and other cultural agencies.

By about 1800, few horses were imported from the West, as the planters then raised their own. David R. Williams of Darlington claimed to have been the first in the South, if not in the country, to use mules in agriculture (perhaps about 1800). Washington had his jack "Royal Gift" (a present from the King of Spain) to cover mares a whole winter in Charleston. Panthers were killed in the vicinity of Camden in January, 1826. Very few had been seen since the Revolution.[1] In 1808 wolves still destroyed sheep, and bears attacked hogs in St. Stephens. Shad ascended to Cheraw, and in 1843 they were abundant far above where they are now found, as rivers had not then become so muddy.

The Foreign Slave Trade Reopened.—In 1787 South Carolina, concerned on economic grounds and very secondarily because of public safety, had stopped the foreign slave trade. From 1792 to 1802 importations from other States were forbidden. "Rusticus," of St. Andrew's, in about 1794, urged that justice, public safety, and better agriculture demanded immediate emancipation, which would be less dangerous now than later. David Ramsay in 1796 was opposed in politics because of his condemnation of slavery; but the feeble emancipation sentiment of the Revolution did not spread far or last long. Lewis DuPre issued two emancipationist pamphlets in 1810, and Mrs. Elizabeth A. Yates in a private letter in 182– bitterly denounced slavery. Some prominent South Carolinians in the 1840's expressed to confidential friends their condemnation of the system, and Mrs. Martha R. Roper (born Laurens), down to 1860, paid wages to her slaves on the ground that she had no right to such service free.[2] Large numbers of Quakers left the State in the 1820's, largely for Indiana, because of their abhorrence of slavery.

As a matter of fact, during the prohibition illicit trade by land and sea was active, and the law against domestic importation was at times resisted by force. The huge expansion of rice and cotton culture and the fabulous prices due to European war, because of which rice sold higher in 1805 than at any other time during the first half of the nineteenth century, led South Carolina, despite vigorous opposition, to reopen the trade in December, 1803, for the four years remaining before it could be forbidden by Congress.

Of the 39,075 Africans imported from 1804 to 1807, 21,027 came in British and French vessels and 18,048 in American. Native South Carolinians imported 2,006 in Charleston vessels, but most came from Rhode Island and British merchants. This was quite natural, as many Old and New Englanders were engaged in shipping, and few Carolinians. The attempt of later generations to throw the blame on outsiders overlooks the fact that South Carolinians alone authorized the trade. In the debate after which the House in 1805 voted to stop the trade and the Senate by

[1] Tyger River is apparently named from the panther, which the colonists often called and spelled "tyger." The name "Tyger" for a person does not occur in the State's grants of lands (searched to 1845 as sufficient) or in the Spartanburg records at any period. Byrd's *History of the Dividing Line* (about 1738) says South Carolinians called the panther the tiger. Dr. Anne King Gregory tells of an early up-country justice of the peace named Tyger.

[2] Francis Lieber details privately expressed opinions. The incident of Mrs. Roper and similar expressions by her were related to me by Mr. Henry Rutledge Laurens.

one vote dissented, economic considerations, the danger from more blacks, and moral reasons were all stressed, though the denunciation of the trade as immoral and unchristian gave some offense. After 1808 large numbers of slaves were brought to the lower South from the northward. It was estimated in 1816 that 60,000 were brought annually from Maryland and Virginia, half of them to South Carolina.

Nationalistic Sentiment.—South Carolina's prosperous staple-exporting system was sadly deranged by the War of 1812 and the antecedent commercial restrictions. As early as 1794-95 the Federal government decided to build an arsenal on the Potomac and one near the line between the Carolinas. On November 13, 1802, President Jefferson bought of Senator Thomas Sumter the 523 acres just above Rocky Mount in the southeastern corner of Chester at the Great Falls of the Catawba. The cornerstone of Fort Dearborn, as the arsenal there was called, was laid about 1803. The last soldiers left Fort Dearborn in 1817, tradition says, to join General Jackson against the South Georgia Indians. In 1825 it was an abandoned ruin. In 1829 Congress provided for retroceding Mount Dearborn (as it was officially known) to South Carolina.[3]

South Carolina, then strongly nationalistic, loyally supported the Federal government in resisting French and British aggressions, even when the embargo was ruining her agriculturists and merchants. David R. Williams, a supporter of the embargo as preliminary to war, bitterly denounced substituting nonintercourse, which would leave our commercial rights unvindicated and our impressed sailors in their "floating hells." As armed rebellion in New England seemed the alternative, he consented to repeal the embargo, though he wept as over a lost child. "I am for war," he said; "the people south of the Delaware are for war; but you have been humbled into an acknowledgment of the truth of the declaration, that you cannot be kicked into war, because the Eastern people will not follow you."

New Leadership.—The older South Carolina leaders who since before the Revolution had shed glory upon her name were now being succeeded by a group of younger men of even greater brilliance. David R. Williams, so notable as manufacturer, scientific agricultural leader, and lifelong nationalist, ended his six years in Congress in 1813 by becoming a brigadier-general in the War of 1812. In 1811 South Carolina sent to the House three of her most remarkable sons: Langdon Cheves (1776-1857, pronounced "Chivis" or sometimes "Chevis"), William Lowndes (1782-1822), and John C. Calhoun (1782-1850). Cheves, of humble birth, and Calhoun, son of a dominant character of old Ninety Six District,

[3] The groundless tradition that Rocky Mount narrowly missed being made the national military academy instead of West Point might easily arise from the above facts.

illustrated the resources of mind and character of the back country, but both so perfectly exemplified attachment to the State as a whole as to ignore the antagonism of up and low country that continued longer than they lived. Lowndes, a representative of the low-country aristocracy, was so broad-minded, so fair, so upright, so moderate, so wise, that he belonged to the State and the country. In contrasting Calhoun and Lowndes, Cheves said: "Mr. Calhoun is far more brilliant, and his mind more keen and rapid; he is a man of genius, and has the temptation of such men to leap to conclusions boldly, perhaps hastily. But in the power of looking at a subject calmly, dispassionately, in every light, Mr. Lowndes has no superior. I should have preferred his judgment to that of any man; and such, I think, was the feeling of their contemporaries. I will illustrate my view. If the nation were in great peril, and Mr. Lowndes recommended one policy and Mr. Calhoun an opposite one, I think that a majority of the American people would have said, 'Intrust our country to the guidance of William Lowndes; follow his counsel'; and in my opinion they would have judged wisely."

Calhoun.—No one ever better embodied the ideal of a united South Carolina than did Calhoun, nor, except to Hampton, has the State ever so unitedly rallied to any man; and Calhoun never experienced the alienation which Hampton, falling across a political revolution, could not escape. The embodiment of every virtue of the best type of up-country man, married to a low-country heiress (his cousin, Floride Colhoun),[4] Calhoun, realizing that the power of South Carolina in the Federal councils depended upon her acting as a unit, represented that the two sections lived in a beautiful harmony under an ideal compromise, although in this he was not sustained by the facts. Though a master in winning admiration and friendship except when he overwhelmed with his encyclopedic knowledge or his zeal as a propagandist, and a skillful manager of men of his own class, his outstanding quality was power. His self-esteem and self-confidence were in proportion to his abilities, and in political foresight he considered himself an almost infallible prophet. By power of argument, not by oratorical gift, he was formidable in debate. Said William J. Grayson: "The distinguished statesman from South Carolina was not a pleasing speaker. He was exceedingly angular in phrase as he was in figure. His manner was abrupt. His sentences were often left incomplete. He cut them short in the heat and hurry of his utterance. His ideas appeared to outrun his words and to leave them limping in the rear. His delivery was stiff and without grace, but it was impressive from its intense and eager earnestness. There was a glare, a fire, in his eye, the fire of a soul that seemed to burn within him. It fascinated the beholder and riveted his gaze. Mr. Calhoun's argument

[4] So spelled by that branch of the family.

was always vigorous, subtle and with ease. He was never muddy or confused. He was a powerful and skillful debater, not a declaimer or rhetorician. The arts of the rhetorician he seemed to despise. His mode of speaking suited important subjects only. On small occasions, in reply to a complimentary toast at a dinner for example, he was the least felicitous of politicians or men. Yet his conversation was attractive in the highest degree. But his conversation was always a disquisition."

Inheriting the rugged character, dauntless courage, fierce attachment to his rights, and vigorous intellect of his father, Calhoun naturally illustrated the same qualities in national politics. Graduating in 1804 at Yale, whose head, Dr. Dwight, predicted that he would be president, he spent a few years of active practice at the bar. His vigorous denunciation of the attack of the *Leopard* on the *Chesapeake* sent him to the legislature. Four years later he was overwhelmingly elected to Congress over a Revolutionary veteran, whose son Franklin H. Elmore was in 1850 to be appointed Calhoun's successor in the Senate.

Calhoun was placed second on the Foreign Relations Committee, at that time so important, and a few months later became chairman. He went to Washington with the fixed conviction that, if the country were unable to defend its independence, the sooner it was known the better. His speech urging adequate preparation for defense drew from the Richmond *Enquirer* the tribute, "We hail this young Carolinian as one of the master spirits who stamp their name upon the age in which they live."

Calhoun opposed the continuance of the policy of commercial restriction as a means of redress on the grounds that it was contrary to the active genius of our people and was making the government odious as the author of low prices and the instigator of corrupt means of evasion. War might incur as severe losses, but it would unite and elevate the people and feed patriotism. In taking this position Calhoun was opposing the accepted doctrine of his party; but he and the young group holding these new and aggressive views were soon to force their adoption by the administration.

Violent party differences over foreign policy revived the South Carolina Federalists, especially in the low country. The *Courier* was founded in 1803 as a Federalist journal. The *City Gazette* was the leading Republican paper. Prominent Federalists from 1810 to 1812 were Charles Cotesworth Pinckney their head, John Rutledge the Younger, Henry Laurens (son of the Revolutionary Henry), K. L. Simons, Daniel Huger, J. W. Toomer, and Stephen Elliott. Leading Republicans were Calhoun, Lowndes, Cheves, David R. Williams, John Geddes, and Joseph Alston. In 1812 the Federalists were beaten by about 50 per cent in the city, and were overwhelmed elsewhere.

South Carolina Defends Her Coasts.—On the outbreak of the War of 1812, Major-General Thomas Pinckney was placed in command in the Southeast. South Carolina's quota of 5,000 men was promptly raised. The Federal government, acknowledging itself unable to perform its duty, requested South Carolina to defend herself, relying on reimbursement by Congress. The government did send a few troops, and the State, wholeheartedly accepting the responsibility, appropriated a half million dollars, paid her direct taxes in advance, called out the militia for six months, and furnished arms, equipment, etc., for troops in Federal service. After the war the government haggled over details, sought to return in kind articles bought for it at war prices, and did not finally repay the State for nearly a hundred years. Private subscriptions supplemented appropriations.

Governor Alston's Militia and Political Troubles.—During 1813 British vessels infested the inlets on the South Carolina coast, looted plantations, captured ships, and kept Charleston in fear of attack. The unsuitableness of militia for dull routine, and the inadequacy of the militia law, were now strikingly exemplified. On May 28, 1813, Governor Alston ordered the Charleston militia to guard the magazines, esteemed to be in danger from the enemy. Though this duty would fall on each militiaman only three days in five months, in July members of two of the four Charleston regiments refused to serve. Governor Alston ordered the court-martial of about forty of their number.

The court-martial was interrupted by habeas corpus action, and the prisoner on trial was brought before Judge Bay amid a storm of indignation at the "tyrant's" "unhallowed libel" on the citizen soldiery. Judge Bay decided that the law provided no penalty for disobeying orders to defend the State, though it punished all lesser offenses. Governor Alston thereupon announced that since the militia law had been declared a mere rope of sand, all orders were countermanded. When the British landed on St. Helena Island, he revoked his order. Governor Alston at once summoned the legislature in order to obtain adequate powers. The legislature promptly placed the militia when in actual service anywhere under the same regulations as Federal troops and took other steps to meet the most serious threats yet experienced from the British.

That Governor Alston was right in his contention, though petulant and rash in disbanding the entire militia in the face of the enemy, is clear. It was of a piece with his action earlier in the year in jeopardizing the representation of the State in Congress because five Congressmen had not, as by law required, signified to him their intention to accept election. Alston was accused of seeking to unseat Cheves, whom he had designated a "political Jesuit." "I can but smile at the Governor's allusion to 'Political Jesuits,'" wrote "Argus" (in terms clearly intended to recall Alston's having aided with money the schemes of his father-in-law Burr) when I think of certain combinations in this State in the past four months by "the corps of worthies and choice spirits." He had charged Speaker Geddes with bribery. "If bribery and corruption are to be the objects of enquiry, the sooner his Excellency begins the investigation the better. There are facts which the people of this State should know and which are ready for their perusal when Governor Alston thinks proper."

Editor Thomas of the *Gazette* added to "Argus'" statement the charge that Alston, who was elected governor by the margin of his own vote,[5] had bought his election to the legislature from All Saints as a step toward the long-sought governorship. Alston accordingly had him prosecuted for criminal libel. The court postponed trial until the pardoning power was no longer in the hands of the prosecutor. The jury, then not being allowed by law to consider the truth of the charge, declared that "they found Mr. Thomas guilty, under the charge of the court, against their feeling as men and citizens." Judge Bay, since Alston's father had told Thomas that the Governor had spent $9,000 and his opponent $7,000 to be elected to the legislature from the tiny parish of All Saints, fixed sentence at a $200 fine and a month's imprisonment. The political nature of the whole proceeding was emphasized by the fact that Thomas's imprisonment was a continuous soiree, as admirers, doubtless remembering the strictures of the Governor on their beloved fellow-townsmen militiamen, overwhelmed him with gifts. Governor Williams, the new governor, ended Thomas's five-day confinement (since speeding horsemen instead of the telegraph required that much time in going and coming) by a pardon written on his saddle pommel the moment the application arrived. The editor was escorted home with a band by an enormous crowd, whom he addressed on the freedom of the press. So heated were politics that, as Thomas was awaiting trial, a rifleman fired at him through his window. Governor Williams' offer of reward brought no result, although the perpetrator (not Alston, Thomas graciously records) was generally taken for granted.[6]

[5] Or was it by two votes? I have not been able to ascertain.

[6] *Carolina Gazette,* April 1, 17, 24; March 1, 1813. Professor J. H. Easterby *(Dictionary of American Biography)* acquits Alston of knowledge of any criminal intention by Burr in the enterprise to which he contributed. Mrs. Alston (the frail and brilliant Theodosia Burr) left Georgetown December 31, 1812, for New York in a little vessel just in time for a furious storm off Cape Hatteras. The vessel was never heard of again—not so rare then. The stories of pirates taking her are gratuitously imaginary, and we may dismiss as equally wild the version that she was made away with by the North Carolina "bankers" when driven on their shore. Judge H. A. M. Smith is almost certainly right in saying she *sailed* "Thursday, December 31st," instead of the 30th (SCHM, XIV, 75). Unfortunately this extremely careful scholar, evidently writing from letters or diaries, omits at this point any citation. Mrs. Alston left her country home on December 30.

It is not surprising that the Federalist candidate for intendant of Charleston received 465 votes to 468 for his three Republican opponents, and that the Federalist William Crafts won a legislative vacancy there by 768 to 712. But Georgetown, formerly Federalist, went Republican by 176 to 78. Although there were only nine Federalists in the House and five or six in the Senate, the *Courier* rejoiced at the triumph of genuine American principles in Charleston.

Governor Alston, a man of cultivated mind and liberal principles despite his ambition and unpopularity, said, as he ended an unhappy administration, during which he had lost his wife and his only child, that he retired "undisturbed by the clamors of ignorance, or the calumnies and abuse with which every factious and intriguing spirit has felt himself privileged to assail me." Two years later he died at the age of thirty-seven or thirty-eight. The man who had been elected by the margin of one or two votes was succeeded by David R. Williams, of Darlington, the second back-country man to be made governor, who, without being a candidate, was virtually unanimously chosen under dissatisfaction with both the avowed candidates.[7]

"The Carolina Cincinnatus" (so called because he had been found employed in his fields by the delegation sent to inform him of his election) had already achieved a national reputation during three terms in Congress, had served creditably as a brigadier-general in the War of 1812, and had already made himself one of the notable men of our history as a pioneer in manufacturing and in scientific agriculture.

Peace came to a South Carolina that held a very creditable record. Colonel Nash's regiment of South Carolina volunteers suffered great hardships in the Creek war phase of the conflict. The President appointed a sixth of his new generals from South Carolina. Major-General Thomas Pinckney commanded the Sixth Military District. George Izard of the regulars served under Major-General Wade Hampton on the Canadian front and in March, 1814, was made brigadier to command around Lake Champlain. Major Arthur P. Hayne fought under General Jackson. The gallant Colonel Fenwick was severely wounded at Queenstown. Lieutenant John Templar Shubrick, who later distinguished himself against Algiers, was awarded a handsome sword by the South Carolina legislature for his gallantry against the *Guerriere,* the *Java,* and the *Peacock*. Thus South Carolina, patriotic and nationalistic, came through the War of 1812.

[7] In my larger *History of South Carolina* I speak of Williams as a Baptist. Professor H. T. Cook, author of the life of Williams, told Mr. J. W. Norwood that Williams was not a member of the Baptist Church so far as he knew. His associations were Baptist.

CHAPTER XXXIX

BANKING, TRANSPORTATION, AND MANUFACTURES, 1800-1835

THE HIGHLY specialized agriculture and commerce of the coast region called for banking. The failure of the primitive, self-sufficient farmer of the up country and the back parts of the low country to understand the situation appeared in 1796, when the "lower division" voted heavily for chartering the Bank of South Carolina (a private corporation in operation without a charter since 1792), and the "upper division" voted overwhelmingly against it. In 1796 there were in Charleston this institution; the Union Bank, capital $600,000, established 1796; and a branch of the United States Bank. The legislature, on chartering the State Bank (a private corporation) in 1802, elected three of the fifteen directors, delivered $300,000 of the State's bonds for an equal amount of the bank's $800,000 of stock, and required all State funds and public and court moneys of Charleston and Charleston District to be deposited there. The Union Bank and the Planters and Merchants Bank were incorporated in 1810.

All banks south and west of New England suspended specie payments early in the war of 1812. The distress of even the wealthy planters brought the State to the rescue by creating in December, 1812, the Bank of the State of South Carolina. The idea of a mere loan office like that shortly after the Revolution was dismissed in favor of a complete commercial bank chartered for twenty-three years. The State was the sole owner of the bank and delivered to it as its capital various securities. All State funds were required to be deposited in the new institution. The bank's debts were forbidden to exceed (over and above deposits) twice its capital under penalty of the directors' unlimited liability; but the State's faith and credit were unconditionally pledged. Loans, none exceeding $2,000, were to be apportioned according to representation in the lower house. Its notes were receivable in all dues to the State. The head office was in Charleston, with a branch at Columbia and later one also at Camden and one at Abbeville.

Thus began what was doubtless the most successful bank ever conducted by an American State. But the depression to which it owed its origin had hardly passed when the jealousy of its great powers, suspicion of favoritism, and fear of its possible domination of politics inaugurated a long period of bitter attacks. It made large advances to the State without interest, from its profits paid the interest and a great proportion of the principal of the State debt, and in addition turned into the treasury profits which greatly reduced taxes. In 1819 its capital was $1,373,250. Since State bonds from 1820 were secured by a pledge of the capital and profits of the bank, its intertwining with the finances and credit of the government rendered nugatory the decade of war against it in the forties led by Governor Hammond and C. G. Memminger. Recognized as essential in the anticipated clash of the State with the Federal government, it fully met the crisis and disappeared only in the cataclysm of war and Reconstruction that swept away the old South.

The Santee and Other Canals.—Another necessity for staple agriculture was transportation. Near the coast an intricate system of freshwater streams and deep tidal "creeks" and "rivers" afforded almost perfect means of travel from plantation to market. The rivers between the fall line and the coastal region were fairly suited for light navigation, but above the fall line they were broken by shoals.

In 1770 a Commons House Committee reported favorably on a plan for a canal from the Santee to the headwaters of the Cooper. The company was chartered in 1786. It accepted the badly located route of Colonel Christian Senf, of the Hessian forces captured at Saratoga, who had been sent by Henry Laurens to South Carolina for state engineer, instead of the proper route proposed by Henry Mouzon. Senf's route fatally lacked water supply and was of a topography that required miles of the canal's upper reaches to be built on trestles.

The canal was twenty-two miles long, thirty-five feet wide at the surface of its four feet of water, and twenty at the bottom. Two double and nine single locks raised it sixty-nine feet above the Cooper and thirty-four above the Santee.[1] It carried boats of twenty-two tons burden. The faulty location necessitated engines to fill the upper levels in the droughts of 1817-19, a circumstance that strengthened the movement for turnpikes. The building, completed in 1800, took eight years and from $650,000 to $750,000. This expense, so much greater than anticipated, limited the profits in even the best years to 2 per cent.

This was the second important canal in the United States and far exceeded its little local predecessors that had been built in South Carolina. Although it was projected as a food route, the agricultural revo-

[1] David Kohn, compiler and editor, *Internal Improvement in South Carolina, 1817-1828* (a monumental photographic reproduction of official reports, etc., privately printed, Washington, D. C., 1938), p. 257. F. A. Porcher, in *The Santee Canal,* a very informing pamphlet (1903), p. 7, says only eight single locks.

lution that followed the invention of the gin transformed it during its construction into primarily a cotton carrier. The canal enthusiasm, which tried to make the entire river system of the State available for transportation, lasted from 1791 to about 1825. The pathetic faith as to the possibilities of fleets on rivers that a child could wade for months during the year became a public delusion.

Road and Canal Building from 1819.—The rapid expansion of the cotton area and the slump in price soon after 1819 from the competition of the Southwest emphasized the desperate need of the older States, particularly South Carolina, for better roads, as well as water transportation, to the seaboard. The scheme took like wildfire. Mr. A voted to dredge Mr. B's swamp in return for B's vote for A's road over the mountains. In December, 1818, the legislature adopted as South Carolina's part of a nation-wide movement a bold program of public improvements which may be said to have run through 1828. The act of 1818 appropriated $1,000,000 to be expended during four years for cutting canals, improving rivers, and building turnpikes. Soon cotton could be sent by boat to Charleston from every district except Greenville. The present Columbia Canal, finished January, 1824, and then extending two miles below the city, and the Lockhart Canal (both now used for power), the Wateree Canal in Kershaw, the Rocky Mount Canal in southeastern Chester, and the Saluda Canal (near Columbia) were the principal ones. Sluices narrowed the currents of rivers at shoals. In some years the Columbia Canal carried over 60,000 bales of cotton and the Santee Canal 70,000. The importation of Irish-Catholic laborers, the heavy-duty men of American progress in those days, to build the Columbia Canal was the origin of that considerable element in the population of the capital. The planters were doing too well to hire out their Negroes for such work, as they had done gladly in their period of prostration for digging the Santee Canal.[2]

The towns that had grown up at those natural distributing points, the heads of navigation, were not disturbed by the attempt to place the whole State on a basis of transportation equality. Even below the fall line, upstream business was slight. A man placing his pole on the bottom of the stream walked as he pushed against it from the front to the rear of the boat. Fifteen men, walking in procession, could with heavy exertion pole a cargo of several tons ten miles upstream in a day. The high-sided "cotton box" of the rivers or the long narrow canal

[2] Men slaves hired out in 1850 for about 77 cents a day and their food, clothing, lodging, and medical care. A few years later the State paid $1.15 a day, whether with food, etc., in addition does not appear.—Miss Mabel Montgomery, research director on *South Carolina Guide Book*, to D. D. Wallace, October 20, 1937.

flats were often sold for lumber at the coast. But even so there were some regular up- and down-stream freight boats.

It is clear why the farmer preferred even the miserable roads. The Santee Canal was badly crippled by the completion of the railroad to Columbia in 1842 and ruined by the "Camden branch" in 1848. It was abandoned about 1858. Steamboats amounted to little except on the deep rivers of the Peedee system, where they were long important. Steamboats, painfully dependent on the stage of the river, plied from Augusta to the sea and between Charleston and Camden, which remained an important shipping point for a wide area until railroads reached Charlotte, Greenville, and Spartanburg in the 1850's. For some time before 1825 there had usually been two little steamers plying between Columbia and Charleston.

The insolvency of the Steamboat Company of Georgia in 1821 was the occasion of an attempt by Charleston to check her growing rival, Savannah. Charleston interests bought the company's property and sought for a brief period to make Savannah merely a way station in the commerce with the upper valley centering at Augusta. Henry Shultz in 1821 founded the town of Hamburg, South Carolina, opposite Augusta. Backed by Charleston, to whom he promised the trade of the region, he secured a loan of $50,000 from the State, a five-year tax exemption, and a bank charter. Hamburg gradually declined and after post-bellum Reconstruction reverted to fields and river bottom, for in 1852 Georgia gave the South Carolina Railroad permission to cross the Savannah and thus destroyed the reason for Hamburg's existence.

Turning now to the road part of the program, the State Road ran from Charleston by the later Holly Hill and Cameron and two miles west of St. Matthews on by Columbia, and thence up the western side of the Broad very near the river, and, crossing the Enoree, very near that stream on its eastern side, on over Saluda Gap in Greenville County into North Carolina. Disregarding what were little villages and are now large county seats, with uncompromising directness it stuck to the through route as it sought to draw the long-distance traffic in and beyond the State to Charleston.

The part above Columbia was a simple affair and under existing conditions so much less important that the term "the old State Road" is ordinarily taken to apply only to the part below Columbia, and therefore to that our further remarks will apply. This was completed apparently by 1829. Kept in bad repair, and charging a four-horse wagon nine dollars for the round trip from Columbia, it was neglected for the even worse, free parallel roads. Although a disappointment, and as a toll road a failure, it nevertheless later carried considerable traffic, and is included in the paved highway system of today. Appropriations continued longer for the branch road across the Santee swamp toward Camden, and for a branch across Vance's swamp leading toward North Carolina. Reaction against turnpikes and canals at public expense was strong by 1826. Small appropriations continued for a decade, but with 1828, after almost two millions had been spent, the system was all but abandoned. The act of 1825 systemizing road and similar legislation left the roads to the local authorities, who bungled them for almost the next hundred years.

The great river bridges continued until after 1865 (and in some instances much later) to be private toll ways, like the ferries which usually served, after the flood of 1796 destroyed Wade Hampton's bridge at Granby and many others. In the late forties and early fifties a small amount of plank road, then a popular hobby, was built in South Carolina. The longest, the Edgefield plank road from Cherokee Pond and Sweetwater to Hamburg, was a company-built toll road completed in 1852.

The Railroad.—The virtual abandonment of the internal improvements program in 1828 registered not only disappointment at its results but recognition of the significance of steam railroads. The decade 1820-30 witnessed in Charleston distressing decline. The average annual duties collected decreased by more than half. Said a committee of the Chamber of Commerce in 1828: "Industry and business talent driven by necessity have sought employment elsewhere. Many of her houses are tenantless, and the grass grows uninterrupted in some of her chief business streets."

A transportation system that would make access to Charleston cheap and easy was thought to be the remedy. Accounts of the success of railroads in England were seized upon as the solution. The hard, level surface of the rails was considered more important than the kind of power; and in fact when the South Carolina Canal and Railroad Company was chartered in 1827 to build a railroad or canal from Charleston to Columbia, Camden, and Hamburg, it was not certain what would be the means of locomotion.

The direction of the road was determined by two facts. The rivers and canals afforded some means of bringing cotton from the Santee-Broad-Saluda-Wateree territory, which moreover could hardly send its produce anywhere but to Charleston, except for the western Saluda valley, which might choose Augusta. And there lay the rub. Charleston had no canal or river to Augusta. A railroad built to that point would help to secure the great trade of the upper Savannah that was going to the city of Savannah.

Not a share was taken in Columbia, Camden, or Hamburg. Charleston, including the city government and the banks and insurance companies, supplied all the money. It was a Charleston enterprise to save Charleston. The company was fortunate in securing as chief engineer Horatio Allen (1802-90), formerly employed on the Chesapeake and Delaware and the Delaware and Hudson canals, who had been to England to study locomotives and railway construction. Rejecting former surveys, this young man gave the road practically its present location, advantageous for materials, more economical for construction, better for the contemplated branches to Columbia and Camden, and appreciably shorter. The State relieved its desperate need by a loan of $100,000. As a subscriber to about $3,000,000 of stock and a guarantor of about $4,000,000 of bonds the State aided almost every railroad built before 1860.

The South Carolina Railroad of 136 miles, completed to Hamburg opposite Augusta in October, 1833, at a cost of $951,148, was the then longest in the world. When construction was begun in January, 1830, there already existed the three-mile quarry railroad at Quincy, Massachusetts, finished in 1827; a nine-mile coal mine road in Pennsylvania completed in 1827; and a short road built in 1828 by the Delaware and Hudson Canal Company. The Mohawk and Hudson Railroad had built sixteen miles in 1831, and the Baltimore and Ohio had by 1833 constructed sixty-nine miles. "The Best Friend of Charleston," built in 1830 by the West Point Foundry, New York City, was the first American-built locomotive for public railroad service. In December, 1830, it ran twenty-one miles an hour with forty to fifty passengers in four or five cars, and, without cars, thirty to thirty-five miles an hour. This was thus the first steam power railroad in the United States. Substituting embankments for piling in 1834 and laying better rails a little later cost practically as much as the original construction.

The hopes that gave birth to the South Carolina Railroad were not fully realized. Georgia bestirred herself, and Savannah was soon served by rails that continued to draw her natural commerce. Not until 1842 did the South Carolina Railroad carry 60,000 bales of cotton a year; and not until 1852, after securing permission to enter Augusta, did it really begin to prosper.

Manufactures.—While these stirring changes of the staple-raising and foreign-commerce-sustained society were taking shape, there were developments in manufactures which were ultimately to modify the State profoundly. The Revolution while it lasted, and the difficulties of transportation afterward, rendered the making of heavy articles by the districts at a distance from the coast imperative. A nail- and hoe-making shop was started near Stateburg in 1789 or 1790. In 1802 there were two ropewalks near Charleston and one at Columbia, the latter of which, manufacturing 80 tons per year, supplied the cordage for the frigate *John Adams,* built at Charleston in 1799, and existed at least until 1811. Paper was being manufactured near Columbia in 1827 and probably for some years previously, and at one time or another at several places in the up country. Cottonseed oil was being expressed in Columbia in 1802—an industry which David R. Williams took up in 1829. In 1826 and apparently earlier castor oil was being made in both the low and up country. In 1800 some gunpowder was made in the up country, but this article was generally obtained from Tennessee and Kentucky. Clocks were being made or assembled in Charleston in 1812, and later excellent clocks were manufactured in Hamburg, Columbia, Laurens, and Chester —the last named made a fine grandfather clock.[3] This industry ended after Connecticut began to flood the country with her timepieces.

The beginning of systematic textile manufactures before the Revolution was stimulated by the war and by the subsequent interruptions to commerce. They were almost all household manufactures, but there were beginnings also of little factories. Late in 1776 a planter near Charleston had thirty Negroes spinning and weaving 120 yards a week of a cloth of wool and cotton. Daniel Heyward wrote his son on February 19, 1777, "My manufactory goes on bravely, but fear the want of cards will put a stop to it, as they are not to be got; if they were, there is not the least doubt but that we could make six thousand yards of good cloth in the year from the time we began." But the usual method then was to send the thread spun on the plantation to the nearest weaver. A weaving shop run by Irish near Murray's Ferry, Williamsburg, served the surrounding country. In January, 1789, Mrs. Ramage was manufacturing cotton cloth on James Island. A factory established about five miles south of Stateburg in 1789 or 1790 manufactured for some years a wide variety of plain and figured cloths. British workers were making excellent woolens in a Fishing Creek mill in 1790 or earlier, and in 1795 William McClure's petition for a lottery to aid in establishing a cotton mill was granted by the legislature. These little mills, until well into the nineteenth century, chose the falls on the creeks, for those on the rivers were too much for them.

South Carolinians had thus early begun the natural alliance between their product and its manufacture—a process which was checked only by the extraordinary profits which could be earned by planting the staple.

[3] To what extent clocks were made in South Carolina, and to what extent merely assembled, or even merely had the complete works placed in locally-made cases, I have not ascertained. Mr. A. S. Salley emphasizes the latter. See below, page 456.

We can hardly doubt, however, that the "factories" before 1800 were merely collections of hand looms, and perhaps of spinning wheels also, under one roof. When power-driven machinery was introduced does not appear, though spinning machinery was in use before 1810.

By 1810 all or most of these little mills seem to have disappeared except one more ambitious than its predecessors. In 1808 had been established in Charleston much the most ambitious enterprise so far, the South Carolina Homespun Company, with $30,000 capital, which, however, disastrously failed in three years.[4] The War of 1812 and the preceding commercial restrictions revived home manufactures even in the low country. John Palmer of St. Stephen's wrote in 1808 that they were increasing; that one planter clothed his Negroes in homespun, and that they were making cotton bagging. The figures gathered by the census taken in 1810 (though with many inaccuracies) showed that the manufactures of the country, valued at $127,694,602, were still almost wholly, excepting metals, hides, shoes, glass, and liquors, and a few others, in the household stage. South Carolina produced $2,147,147 worth, including 3,267,141 yards of cloth, nearly all cotton, all but 126,463 yards being in the up country. The census classifies it all under "families," but the presence of spinning jennies in Edgefield (154 jennies and 5,741 spindles), Fairfield, Barnwell, Abbeville, and Pendleton suggests how closely was approaching the development of little mills. The manufacturing districts were, in order of importance, Spartanburg, Pendleton, Edgefield, York, Abbeville, and Laurens.

By 1825 manufacturing in South Carolina had declined. Robert Mills mentions abandoned little establishments, as a cotton mill on Little River, Abbeville, and General Anderson's forge and firearms manufactory at Andersonville in the Seneca-Toogaloo fork. Makers of wagons and "chairs" (two-wheel sulkies) were found in several places. Sumter manufactured gins, and Winnsborough had "two considerable saw gin factories." Edgefield manufactured pottery; Greenville, iron; Pendleton, cloth and rifles; and Spartanburg, iron. The up country still largely wore its own homemade cloth. Even David R. Williams had suspended his mill, since it was more profitable to raise cotton than spin it. "The burnt factory" in Marlboro had early disappeared.

But Williams' suspension of his yarn mill, built on Cedar Creek near Society Hill, Darlington, apparently in 1812, was temporary. He had three or four hundred spindles in 1816, and six hundred more were being installed. The plant was enlarged in 1828. The machinery cost about $5,000 and would consume annually a hundred 300-pound bales of cotton and 8,000 pounds of wool. By November 16, 1828, the new equipment

[4] *DeBow*, VIII, 24; Shecut, *Essays*, p. 26.

was working, tended by Negroes, largely little children, under a New England superintendent. Williams was soon advertising cotton osnaburgs, coarse woolens, twine, bagging, and rope for baling cotton. Williams was one of the first to combat the doctrine that "South Carolina, from her climate, situation, and peculiar institutions, is, and must ever continue to be, wholly dependent on agriculture and commerce, not only for her prosperity, but for her existence," a doctrine which decried manufacturing as likely to degrade Southern society and to build up an interest friendly to the hated tariff. Williams' plan was to beat the Yankees at their own game by making better goods cheaper. How long his factory survived him (1776-1830) is not known.

Vaucluse had operated and burned before its rebuilding in 1832 and incorporation in 1833. The enthusiasm for Southern enterprises was then at its height, and the later opposition to manufacturing as likely to create a tariff element and undermine plantation slavery had not generally developed. Governor McDuffie and Christian Breithaupt subscribed $10,000 each, and Mitchell King, Seabrook of Edisto Island, Paul FitzSimons from the coast, and some up-country men $5,000 each. The Saluda Manufacturing Company was organized in 1832 and chartered in 1834 with $60,00 capital. A little later came the DeKalb factory at Camden. A similar movement was in progress in Maryland, Virginia, North Carolina, and Georgia. The Saluda Factory then used Negro labor, as did Vaucluse also; but Saluda was being operated by white labor when it was burned in 1865 by Sherman. Fisher Brothers seem to have had a cotton mill at Dent's Pond in Richland County, a short while before 1835, which was operated during the War of Secession. Lossing in 1849 mentions a cotton factory at Rocky Mount.

Manufacturing in the Piedmont.—We must now turn to the beginning of a movement that was to be more extensive and permanent in Greenville and Spartanburg. The legislature in 1812 granted a loan of $10,000 to Caruth and Thompson to establish a cotton factory on Reedy River. Caruth also made firearms in Greenville, as did Earle in Pickens.

Philip Weaver was a master textile mechanic of Coventry, Rhode Island. After March and before December 21, 1816, he, with his brother John, Thomas Hutchings, Thomas Slack, William Bates, and Wilbur Weaver, and perhaps others, moved to Spartanburg District to utilize its water power, ready material, and cheap labor for cotton manufacturing. His mill, the South Carolina Cotton Manufactory, contained 489 spindles, but had apparently disappeared by 1826. Philip Weaver was unhappy in his continual financial difficulties and his Southern environment. "Mr. Tatman Sir," he wrote, ". . . I wish to leave this part of the country and wish to settle myself and family in a free state, where myself and family will not be looked upon with contempt because I am opposed to the abominable practice of slavery." The letter reminds one of the welcome extended to Northern merchants, as they became slave-owners, and the aversion to Northern mechanics, because they opposed slavery.

Another Rhode Island group, the Hills, built four miles farther up the Tyger on the west side in 1816 or 1817, apparently just a little later than Weaver. With George and Leonard Hill came William Sheldon and John Clark, who at one time or another also owned part or all of this factory, a plant which in 1825 contained 432 spindles and 8 water looms, besides 2 gins and a sawmill. The Hill Factory, though twice burned, was rebuilt and operated by members of the group until its machinery was sold to other manufacturers in 1866.

A legislative grant to aid in building a cotton mill in Greenville District was made in 1812. John Weaver of the Spartanburg migration is said to have built his mill on Thompson's Beaverdam, a tributary of Middle Tyger just inside Greenville County, in 1820 or '21. It operated through the War of Secession, and a few decades ago was still standing. On its original foundation now stands a modern ginnery or gristmill.

In 1833 William Bates of the Weaver migration bought a site in eastern Greenville District, where before 1837 he had built "the Rocky Creek Factory," the later Batesville. Bates's daughter married Pinckney Hammett, who was for years President of Batesville and about 1850 founded the predecessor of the later Piedmont Manufacturing Company, still one of the leading cotton mills of the country. The Bateses and Hammetts afford an illustration of the prevalence of the continuous family group activity that has been conspicuous in Spartanburg and Greenville mill development.

Colonel John E. Calhoun of Pendleton in 1831 was selling at six dollars a pair, as fast as he could manufacture them, blankets of cotton warp and wool filling, and was also making flannel and carpet, while his factory carded wool for persons for forty miles around. Pendleton Factory at Autun (now called La France, the name of the present company) near Pendleton was incorporated in December, 1838, after having been in operation since February. Bivingsville (now the D. E. Converse Company at Glendale, Spartanburg County) was incorporated in December, 1837, and is thus apparently the oldest mill now in South Carolina. According to the memories of old people, handed down to the present generation, Bivingsville began operations in 1829 or 1834. Which (or whether either) is correct cannot be known because of the loss of the early records.[5] Whether it was the oldest in the South in continuous operation depends on the definition of continuous. The Rocky Mount Mills in North Carolina were built in 1817 or '18, were burned by Federals on July 20, 1863, were rebuilt in 1865, burned again in 1869, were at once rebuilt, and now, greatly enlarged, are operating on the original foundation.[6]

The up-country mills all used white labor. John Craig contracted in 1822 to weave for Hill and Clark from sun to sun for a house and $1 a day, one-third in cash and two-thirds in yarn or supplies at their store. Vincent Wilson in 1822 hired his two children for a year at $1.37½ a week each and 12½ cents extra for evening work if required, wages to be paid at the end of the year and to be forfeited for the time worked if the children proved unsatisfactory.

[5] President J. Choice Evans to D. D. Wallace, February 22, 1945.

[6] *Rocky Mount Mills,* published by the company, 1943; *Textile Bulletin* (Charlotte, January 15, 1944), No. 16, pp. 34-35. The Schenck and Warlick mill near Lincolnton, in which Dr. James Bivings bought a share in 1819, was built in 1813, but soon perished.

CHAPTER XL

THE LOOMING OF THE SLAVERY AND TARIFF CONTROVERSIES, 1815-1839

TURNING now to slavery, to which the manufacturing developments traced in the last chapter were inherently injurious, we find that in 1816 the rushing enthusiasm for more Negroes engendered by the cotton-growing era was subsiding sufficiently for philosophical minds to recognize the fallacy of the assumption that the slave could be relied on to remain nothing but a labor machine without the interests or possibilities of a human being. "Montesquieu" in the *Telescope* of December 3, 1816, lamented the hordes of Negroes being brought from Maryland and Virginia. Even a mind warped from virtue cannot but condemn slavery, he said. "It is to be regretted that when British tyranny was expelled from America slavery was not also abolished. The planters butcher their land and with the proceeds acquire more land and more Negroes, and so on in endless round. In the meantime, South Carolina is the victim." This is typical of several anti-slavery utterances in the early 1820's.

Southern opinion was tolerant on slavery, and generally acknowledged it an evil passively to be endured without much conclusive thinking on what the future would be, until roused by that "fire bell in the night," the Missouri debate. What was said then the South could not forget and accordingly assumed an alarmed attitude of self-defense. Charles Pinckney, performing in Congress his last public service, foresaw that the South was really defeated while winning a temporary victory in the Missouri Compromise, for she thereby acceded to the principle that Congress could exclude slavery from the territories.

Slave Conspiracies.—Local slave conspiracies were disagreeably frequent throughout the South, but rarely broke into action. A plot was feared in Charleston in September, 1793, and another in December, 1795.[1] A plot was discovered near Columbia in 1805, and in 1816 one at Ashepoo, and in June of that year another of more serious character near Camden. The Camden conspirators were possessed of "wild ideas about the rights of man and misconception of Bible passages." Two of the

[1] E. P. Link, *Proceedings of South Carolina Historical Association, 1943*, p. 33. That slave conspiracies were more frequent than is usually supposed is shown by J. C. Carroll, *Slave Insurrections in the United States, 1800-1865*.

leaders were literate and had borne good reputations. Six were hanged.

A drastic law was at once enacted stopping the importation of slaves from other States, which had been permitted since 1803. Humane sentiment, greed for gain, and prudential considerations were in indecisive conflict. The law against domestic importations was repealed as a farce in 1818. In 1821 Governor Bennett denounced unsuccessfully the inhumanity of the traffic, which continued as long as slavery. But in the same year a reproach was removed when, in place of the law that hanged men for stealing slaves but only fined and imprisoned them for murdering them, it was enacted that the willful murderer should be punished by death and one acting in sudden heat and passion by a fine of $500.

The Vesey Plot.—In 1822 occurred the most serious plot since 1739 and the last known in the State, except a little plot in Laurens in 1831. Charleston Negroes had developed a spirit of insubordination from laxity of discipline. The sight of large numbers of free Negroes there was also thought to have stirred aspirations. Vesey, the leader, was a remarkable man, who in 1800 bought his freedom with money from a lottery prize and became a prosperous carpenter. For years he had built up among the Negroes an admiration and fear of him amounting to adoration. A faithful slave's informing revealed that the stroke was to fall at midnight, July 4.

A court made up of the most respected citizens granted the accused all the rights of the common law that the statute permitted and conducted the trials with exemplary fairness. Horror crept over the community as it was revealed that Vesey had corresponded with Santo Domingo and had corrupted perhaps more than six thousand slaves in Charleston and the region for fifty miles around. The city was to have been burned, the banks robbed, the men killed, the women ravished, and the ships seized for sailing to Santo Domingo.

The conspirators were not cowed by the first convictions and even planned to rescue their companions at the gallows. In all, thirty-five Negroes were hanged and thirty-two transported from the United States. All were slaves except Vesey. Four low white men were given brief imprisonment for having encouraged the plot. This moderation contrasts with New York's severity in 1741 in burning alive thirteen Negroes and hanging eighteen Negroes and four whites and transporting eighty-five others for conspiracy.

It was most disconcerting that the slave leaders were with one exception of good reputation and that all were men of intelligence and subject to kind treatment. The ease with which a few natural leaders could, unsuspected, organize an extensive conspiracy vividly brought home to the South the reality of her danger.

What would be the reaction of South Carolina opinion? To seek a gradual elimination of slavery, or to determine more positively upon its extension and perpetuation? Governor Bennett's message to the legislature fairly expressed the helplessness of contemporary Southern opinion in the face of an admitted evil: "Slavery abstractly considered would perhaps lead every mind to the same conclusion; but the period has long since passed when a correction might have been applied. The treasures of learning, the gifts of ingenuity and the stores of experience have been exhausted, in the fruitless search for a practical remedy. The institution is established—the evil is entailed and we can do no more than steadily to pursue that course indicated by stern necessity and a not less imperious policy."[2]

The wavering utterance of Governor Bennett did not long continue to characterize South Carolinians. Opinion soon became hypersensitive to anything remotely involving slavery. Said Robert Y. Hayne in March, 1826, in opposing American representation at the Panama Congress, which involved association with the Negro republic of Haiti: "The question of slavery is one, in all its bearings, of extreme delicacy. . . . To call into question our rights, is grossly to violate them, to attempt to instruct us on this subject, is to insult us, to dare to assail our institutions is wantonly to invade our peace. . . . The very day the unhallowed attempt is made [to interfere with our domestic concerns] by the authorities of the federal government, we will consider ourselves as driven from the Union."

Shifting to Sectional View.—The decade 1820-1830 was critical for South Carolina. Her uprush of prosperity from cotton subsided as States to the west glutted the market. Slumping rapidly from twenty-eight cents, in 1825, down to eight-to-eleven, in 1826, cotton entered upon a long depression until 1832. Until about 1815, South Carolina had, since her foundation, steadily drawn immigration. The white majority of 31,283 in 1790 had been supplanted in 1820 by a black majority of 27,861, but the white increase, which had been slow since 1800, virtually ceased between 1830 and 1840. From the moment the tide of immigration shrunk and her own people began to leave, as a barometer indicating changed conditions, South Carolina as a State, whatever might be the condition of fortunate individuals, was fighting a losing battle. Nor did the tide turn for her until, late in the century, she had, by developing new economic resources, brought to a halt the terrible drain of her

[2] Jervey's *Hayne,* p. 135. Mr. Jervey brings out the contemporary unwillingness of Northern States to have free Negroes or to allow them civil rights, as do also several Northern writers.

lifeblood. The census of 1930 showed a white excess of 150,359 above the Negroes.

What South Carolina lost by the cessation of immigration aside from mere numbers may be conjectured from the contribution that she had received in such men as Ramsay, Lieber, Cooper, Shepard, Bachman, Maxcy, Howe of the Episcopal and Howe of the Presbyterian Church, President Wilson's parents, Sawyer, Enston, Wagener, Memminger, Jasper Adams, Manning, Hampton, England, Poppenheim, Dawson, Converse, Gonzales, and a host of other intellectual and moral leaders. The contribution of New England particularly to the spiritual and intellectual life of the province and State, until stopped by sectional antagonism, was enormous. Now, instead of receiving men and women as a gift, South Carolina began to raise human beings, free and slave, at immense cost and give them away to the rising West. Many of them like Dr. J. Marion Sims, Dr. Lawrence Smith, Dr. Gildersleeve, Yancey, Longstreet, were the most precious drops of her lifeblood.

It was a loss that South Carolina suffered in common with most of the old seaboard states, but she was one of those who suffered most severely. It would be a mistake to suppose that the population that she lost were the unprogressives, driven out by a competition they could not endure. On the contrary, there is every reason to believe that the emigration carried away a larger proportion of her most enterprising population than of the worser sort. The sowing down of the whole South from the Savannah to the Rio Grande with South Carolinians in the forty or fifty years before the War of Secession had its part in spreading South Carolina politics and ideals throughout the South.

Changed conditions soon manifested themselves in politics. The South Carolina legislature, still nationalistic in 1820, protested against the protective tariff because it would lead to sectional division threatening the safety and supremacy of the "general government." The House condemned "the practice, unfortunately become too common, of arraying upon questions of national policy, the states as distinct and independent sovereignties . . . with a view to exercise control over the general government." But by the middle twenties the era of prosperity and nationalism that had begun with the Federal Constitution was closing. Slavery, through which that prosperity had been so largely achieved, was meeting organized opposition in the North, and the decline of slave-supported prosperity was stimulating the anger of an already resentful South. South Carolina, whose national patriotism had never favored consolidation in the sense ordinarily understood, was losing her ardor for the Union.

Calhoun's Early Nationalism.—The understanding of these conditions explains why the startling action of South Carolina from 1828 to 1832 in resisting the tariff was not a bolt out of a clear sky but a collision of forces long preparing. The people of the State had from the time of the adoption of the Constitution been opposed to protective tariffs, despite occasional contrary action by her representatives. Calhoun's support of the tariff of 1816 was merely a feature of the broad-construction nationalism of his early years. He said, in defending that capital sin of protectionism, minimum valuation (on cotton goods sometimes amounting to a duty of 100 per cent):

"No country ought to be dependent on another for its means of defense. Behold the effects of the late war on them. When our manufactures are grown to a certain perfection, as they soon will, under the fostering care of government, we will no longer experience those evils. The farmer will find a ready market for his surplus produce; and, what is almost of equal consequence, a certain and cheap supply of all his wants. Manufactures produce an interest strictly American as much so as agriculture."

Of the National Bank Calhoun said in 1816 that the Constitution was not to be construed on minute metaphysical grounds. Nor was Calhoun alone among South Carolina statesmen of the period in deprecating narrow construction views. McDuffie thus expressed his devotion to nationalism in 1821:

"If after the National judiciary have solemnly affirmed the constitutionality of a law, it is still to be resisted by the State rulers, the Constitution is literally at an end; a revolution of the government is already accomplished; and anarchy waves his horrid sceptre over the broken altars of this happy Union. Be assured, then, the general government is not an object of dread.

"You assert that when any conflict shall occur between the general and State governments, as to the extent of their respective powers, 'Each party has a right to judge for itself.' I confess I am at a loss to know how such a proposition ought to be treated. No climax of political heresy can be imagined, in which this might not claim the most prominent place. It resolves the government at once, into the elements of physical force, and introduces us directly into a scene of anarchy and blood."

By the irony of fate the fiercest of later nullifiers, James Hamilton, in a preface to McDuffie's articles scoffed mercilessly at State sovereignty. As late as February, 1824, McDuffie was still holding this strain. To the same effect was the strongly reasoned minority opinion of Judge Nott, in the South Carolina appellate court in 1819, that "I cannot conceive of a more effectual source of domestic discord than a power in the States to resist or defeat the operation of a Constitutional Act of the general government," a government, he continued, which if too strong could be reduced by constitutional amendment, or if acting unconstitutionally could be controlled by the judiciary.

Just when the hearty nationalism with which South Carolina emerged from the War of 1812 began to wither under the blight of a tariff policy sacrificing her interest for the advantage of Eastern manufacturers cannot be exactly fixed; but by 1820 the efforts for higher and higher tariffs were rousing serious alarm as merely designed to take money from the farmer and merchant for the pocket of the manufacturer.

Efforts were made to boycott Northern products in retaliation against the tariff of 1824. McDuffie was reported to have given his broadcloth coat to his servant as a livery fit only for a slave, Judge Huger to have refused to eat Northern potatoes, and Judge Waddy Thompson to have declared he would walk his circuit rather than ride a Kentucky horse.

The Tariff and Economic Decline.—From 1823 South Carolina congressmen openly attacked the constitutionality of the protective tariff, and President Thomas Cooper of the South Carolina College, reversing his position of 1813, issued a pamphlet on its injustice and unconstitutionality.

The inconsistencies of Calhoun, McDuffie, and Cooper merely show that men are little concerned with the meaning of the Constitution in itself but primarily with it as a means of promoting whatever at the moment may be their vital interests. A written Constitution thus becomes a subtly immoral influence in our public life. For the constitutional arguments of politicians who could so completely reverse themselves for the exigencies of the occasion as did Webster and Calhoun we may have as much respect as for the opinions of a society of astronomers whose oil-stock-holding members maintained that the sun is illumined by superheated kerosene, and whose hydroelectric-owning members were sure that it is a giant arc light. Who can imagine that, if Calhoun had found that only by broad construction could slavery be protected, his reexamination of the Constitution would have revealed to him that his former constitutional latitudinarianism had been erroneous?

Webster and Calhoun bowed to the economic and social needs of their States, and in truth conditions had sadly changed in South Carolina. In 1801 New York's exports equaled $19,851,000; Massachusetts', $14,807,000; South Carolina's, $14,304,000. South Carolina had several big years after the War of 1812, being in 1816 second only to New York and then sinking to about half her old figures, later rising to $13,684,000 in 1836, and then settling down to about $8,000,000 a year through 1845. Making every allowance for coloring for political purposes, it was a gloomy picture which James Hamilton, soon to be governor, drew in 1828 of low-country conditions that had been developing for years:

"The consciousness that South Carolina was sinking had dawned upon them suddenly. Did they want the melancholy signs of coming decay, let them look abroad through the land and see the wilderness regaining her empire; let them look at the waste and desolate spots that had lately teemed with life and fertility. Where were the beautiful homesteads and venerable chateaux which once thronged the land? 'On the very hearthstone where hospitality once kindled the most genial fires that ever blazed on her altars, the fox may lie down in security and peace, and from the mouldering casement of the very window from which the notes of virtuous revelry were once heard, the owl sends forth to the listening solitude of the surrounding wastes her melancholy descant to mark the spot where desolation has come.' If such signs were not enough, let them look at this metropolis, designed to be the emporium of three States, lately visited by every flag of the civilized world, and where were the ships, the capital, the merchants? All gone in the ruin of its foreign trade; and with them, the hopes of the people."

Hayne in 1832 lamented "our merchants bankrupt or driven away, their capital sunk or transferred to other pursuits, our ship yards broken up, our ships all sold." Hayne frankly admitted that there were other causes of South Carolina's decline besides the tariff, that New York had better facilities, that cotton could be raised cheaper in Alabama. But those, the modern reader must remember, were not the results of human injustice by a government pledged to the equal care of all its members. There lay the root of bitterness. Sister Southern States have done South Carolina more harm than all the tariffs by the competition of their virgin soil and resources, impoverishing her cotton farmers, destroying her rice planting, and annihilating her phosphate industry. Men lament natural disadvantages, but resent the willful and (in their opinion) the unlawful unfairness of government controlled by the selfish interests of another section. South Carolina was suffering under the competition of new rich lands and the deadening weight of slavery; but even the few who realized this fundamental fact generally neglected it in their rebellion against man-made injustice.

In 1821, while Calhoun was seeking support for the presidency, the South Carolina legislature nominated William Lowndes. That miracle of modesty and unselfishness, whose expression, "the Presidency is not an office to be either solicited or declined," had a significance impossible for a mere politician, hoped that the State would support Calhoun if his chances appeared good. On Lowndes' death in 1822 the State endorsed Calhoun, but his disappointment by Pennsylvania, his main hope, relegated him to the vice-presidency.

"Time to Calculate the Value of the Union."—The year 1824 saw South Carolina moving definitely away from nationalism. Governor John Lyde Wilson's attack on the right of Congress to make internal improvements brought resolutions from the Prioleau committee denying the right of the legislature to impugn the constitutionality of acts of Congress or decisions of the Supreme Court. The report went over to the next year, when the House acted in the opposite sense, as it doubtless would have done less decidedly in 1824. The Prioleau report was completely discarded by "amendment," and opposite resolutions were adopted (72 to 38 in the House; 29 to 14 in the Senate). These "Smith resolutions," really those of S. D. Miller narrowly adopted by the Senate in 1824, were as follows, and became the platform of the State rights party: (1) Congress has no right to adopt a general system of internal improvements. (2) It is unconstitutional to tax the citizens of one State for roads and canals in another State. (3) Protective tariffs are unconstitutional.

But Dr. Cooper's declaration on July 2, 1827, that "it was time to calculate the value of the Union," shocked the State as had Gadsden's mention of independence in March, 1776. The same year Robert J. Turnbull of Charleston, in a series of articles in the *Mercury* called "The Crisis" and signed "Brutus," carried his recommendations to the very threshold of armed resistance. This planter, a wealthy retired lawyer, inaugurated a new era in Federal relations. His articles made the word disunion familiar in South Carolina. For the former hazy attitude toward constitutional questions he substituted one of rigid logic. Resistance, he said, is the proper course. If war should come we would conquer, for the South would not fight against us. "The Constitution is a compact between the States, and there are no parties to it, excepting the people of the different States in their corporate capacities." To allow the Supreme Court to decide would be to make the Federal government the judge of its own case; nor do political questions belong to courts. Between the sovereign States there can be no arbiter.

Turnbull's articles, republished as a volume, became the textbook of resistance. As Mr. David F. Houston says, we have here the South Carolina doctrine of nullification with everything except the word and some later refinements, particularly as to the substitution of the convention for the legislature. Turnbull is perfectly clear on the nature of the compact, i.e., that it was one to which the States only were parties, whereas even Hayne in his reply to Webster three years later fell into the blunder, destructive of the whole doctrine, of treating the State as one party and the Federal government as the other. The Federal government must be regarded under State sovereignty as a mere agent of the States. It was said at Turnbull's death in 1833 that he had wrought a change in South Carolina opinion almost unparalleled, tearing away the veil from Federal consolidation, and in the ablest exposition of the United States Constitution anywhere to be found had sounded the first bugle call to the South to rally. Taught by him, mass meetings sent up memorials against the tariff all over the State from 1827 onward. James Hamilton, Jr., superb as a leader for action, though not pre-eminent in mind, is said to have been, on October 21, 1828, the first to announce nullification by name from the stump.

The tariff act of 1828 roused the State to violent resentment. It was reported that the meeting of the South Carolina delegation (which Senator Smith refused to attend) after the adoption of this "tariff of abominations" was to concoct secession and indoctrinate with this their constituents. The truth is that Hamilton talked of withdrawing from Congress and said that persistence in protection would result in the dissolution of the Union and that South Carolina could not be coerced, all of which McDuffie endorsed and reinforced with more. The delegation agreed to meet at Columbia to inform the legislature and to seek means of preserving the Union.

South Carolina was not yet ready to try the issue, for she strongly hoped for relief through the election of Jackson, whom her legislature in 1826 had almost unanimously endorsed for the presidency. Conservatives deprecated rashness, and Unionists denied the right of opposition except through the ballot box and the courts. Said David R. Williams on July 20, 1828, "The tariff I consider unjust; but it has been passed by large majorities after mature deliberation, and the rule of the majority is the principle on which our institutions are based. To refuse to buy Northern and Western goods would cause intolerable friction. We could not exist except in misery outside the Union if allowed to secede peaceably. Suppose we are not allowed to go peaceably. Is there a discreet citizen . . . who would prefer to take his musket and shoot down twenty-three Kentuckians and Yankees (the destruction of life must be in this proportion, or it will be against us) rather than make his own coarse woolen cloths? I will continue to protest by constitutional means against the policy of protection, and meanwhile the proper method of defense against it for us is to make and wear our own clothes, and raise our own horses, mules, cattle, and hogs."

And to Stephen D. Miller he recounted how he was making himself free from the tariff: "I shall make within the year more than 20,000 yards of coarse cotton and woolen goods—have killed upwards of 500 head of hogs of my own raising and have young mules and colts enough to hinder me from buying a Western horse or mule for years."

But independence by such means was not generally acceptable. South Carolinians were attached to the system of raising cotton for foreign export and protested that they would not be forced either to change their occupation or abandon the homes of their ancestors. The latter, however, tens of thousands were doing in order to adjust themselves to the State's worst enemy, the rich lands of Alabama and Mississippi. The legislative committee of 1827 proceeded to report, as instructed, means of resisting the tariff.

Calhoun Abandons Broad Construction.—It was the report of this committee that first brought Calhoun into the controversy. Though denounced by extreme anti-tariff leaders like Cooper for his congressional and Cabinet record as a loose constructionist, he was honored by the mass of his fellow-Carolinians for the distinction which his ability, character, and eminence reflected upon the State. Removed from the floor of Congress since 1817 by his membership in the Cabinet and his vice-presidency, his public utterances on the revolution which South Carolina opinion was undergoing would naturally be few. The defensive phrasing of his reply as a presidential candidate in 1824 to the inquiry of Congressman R. S. Garner of Virginia reveals a decided weakening of the nationalism of the leader who had earlier scoffed at the timid souls who shivered at the broad construction of the Constitution. On the bank, he wrote, "I said nothing on the Constitution. I left each member to make up his own opinion on that point, but at the same time respected those who took the opposite view, for I have always considered the power the least clear of those which have been exercised by Congress." On internal improvements, he said, he was protected by the acts of Presidents Jefferson, Madison, and Monroe. "I have never yet committed myself beyond the mere right of making an appropriation. I have nowhere in my public capacity asserted[3] the right of applying money so appropriated without the consent of the States, or individuals to be affected. . . . It is, however, due to candor to say that my impression is that the power does exist to a certain extent, but as I have always believed that it should not be exercised without a clear necessity, and as I do believe that the mere right of applying our money, not as a sovereign without the consent of those to be affected, but as a mere proprietor with their assent, will be found sufficient in practice, I have carefully abstained from coming to any final conclusion until it becomes absolutely necessary."

In reviewing in 1825 to the people of his native Abbeville District

[3] Nor, he might have added, denied.

his "zealous efforts in favor of all such measures" for the security of the country, including "a due protection of those manufactures which had taken root during periods of war and restriction" and "a judicious system of internal improvements," the limitations "due" and "judicious" confirm this change of view. His casting vote as vice-president against the woolens bill of 1827, often taken as his open declaration of a shift to an anti-tariff and a general strict-construction position, was in fact the consummation of a long-maturing change.

Calhoun, as a brilliant mind of active and ardent patriotism long under the nationalizing influence of high executive office, and as an up-country man, had been slow to realize the danger to slavery of his earlier policies. But, having accepted the position into which South Carolina had settled, that abolition was impossible without the destruction of civilization, his policy inevitably became that of so restricting the Federal authority that it could not imperil slavery, and his abilities made him as certainly her champion; yet nothing can be clearer than that South Carolina led him into this self-defensive strict construction, and not he South Carolina. The contest would probably have taken much the same course without him, except that it would have been more swift and violent. In nullification as in the long slavery controversy he was constantly a conservative force, restraining the State from more precipitate action.

Calhoun's Exposition of the Constitution, 1828.—During the summer and autumn of 1828 many leaders sought the advice of the Vice-President at his Fort Hill home. Calhoun freely stated his views as at last determined by the tariff of abominations, and likewise his fear that the conduct of Jackson's supporters was such as to preclude hope of relief through Congress. At the request of William C. Preston, one of the legislative committee, he prepared a draft of an exposition of the State's wrongs and possible means of redress, and this, adopted "with considerable alterations" as the committee's report, was ordered published by the legislature. Accompanying it were resolutions in which the legislature declared that protection was unconstitutional, and that even if it were constitutional the tariff of 1828 was so grossly unequal and oppressive as to be incompatible with the principles of free government, and that the situation of South Carolina was such that only by the cultivation of certain few products by slave labor for export could she avoid derangement, if not dissolution.

Calhoun's authorship of the exposition was not generally known until July 26, 1831, when he addressed a long statement of his views to the *Pendleton Messenger,* though it had long been circulated at home that he was with the Nullifiers.

The Webster-Hayne Debate.—The Webster-Hayne debate in January, 1830, served as an enormous advertisement of the doctrine of nullification as well as an inspiration to the Unionists throughout the country. The resolution of Senator Foote of Connecticut for restricting the sale of public lands was attacked by Benton as typical of New England's policy of discouraging Western immigration in order to hold her own population. The West might be too weak to defend herself, he said, but she could look for help to the South, whom also the East wished to depress.

January 19 Hayne entered the debate, and, while not becoming "a responsible endorser," as Webster asserted, of Benton's charges against New England, treated them at least sympathetically. The Western lands, said Hayne, should be given out on more liberal terms as a means of fostering new States instead of being treated as a source of revenue to a rich treasury. He maintained that "the very life of our system is the independence of the States and that there is no evil more to be deprecated than the consolidation of this government."

Webster was convinced from recent events in South Carolina that there existed a more dangerous evil, one that threatened the very existence of the Union. He accordingly, on January 20, seized the opportunity to strike at this over the head of Hayne. Defending New England from the charge of selfishness both as to lands and as to tariff, he passed into his attack on the nullification movement: "I know there are some persons in the part of the country from which the honorable member comes who . . . declare that it is time to calculate the value of the Union. . . . The honorable member is not, I trust, and never can be, one of these."

The challenge, delivered in a style as provocative as the words, Hayne could not ignore. The real contest between the two greatest debaters in the Senate now began. In everything in the widely ranging discussion Hayne, to say the least, held his own, except, as his biographer Mr. Jervey points out, in the impossible task of defending slavery and nullification. Hayne contrasted Webster's denunciation of protective tariffs through 1824 and his eulogies of the justice and blessings of free trade with his reversal of 1828 in favor of the tariff of abominations. And as to the incipient disunionism which Mr. Webster visioned in South Carolina, why was he speechless in the presence of the widespread and open disloyalty which surrounded him in his own home in the days of the Hartford Convention? Hayne closed with briefly stating the South Carolina doctrine of nullification, for which he cited the precedents of the Virginia and Kentucky resolutions and the Boston resolutions of 1809; the Constitution was a compact among the several States, each of which retained its sovereignty, granting certain powers to their agent the Federal government. Any act of the agent exceeding those powers was without authority and might be annulled by any State within its own borders.

Webster could not leave either Hayne's attack upon him or his defense of nullification unanswered. He determined to make it the occasion, on January 26, for attacking the compact theory and defending the national theory of the Constitution as the supreme law of one united people. Hayne's argument demanded all Webster's powers, both for defending his tariff record and the Hartford Convention, in neither of which he shone very brilliantly, and for overthrowing the sovereignty of the States. In exposing as illogical and impracticable the South Carolina doctrine that a State could by the Constitution itself annul any act of Congress which it considered unconstitutional and yet remain a member of the Union, Webster had no difficulty; but it was another matter to disprove that the Constitution was a compact between sovereign States, every one of which retained the right to withdraw in case of willful, palpable, and persistent violation of the compact. That secession would be unwise, and to a growing majority intolerably hateful, he amply established. That, however, was not the question; but his baffled logic in a problem practically unsolvable was obscured beneath the glory of his immortal peroration which from that day to this has fostered in the emotions of the nation the passionate conviction that, whatever a written document, to which the mass of men give little examination, may have meant to men long dead, to living Americans what it stands for is dearer than life. Webster proved that the "Union, now and forever, one and inseparable," is greater than the Constitution.

Hayne's final reply to Webster was concluded on the 27th. Both speakers in effect merely proclaimed the two theories of the origin of the government and pointed the course which each section proposed in maintaining its views. The question was too deeply seated in interests and emotions for mere logic to decide whether the States had in the Constitution acted as sovereign nations adopting an elaborate treaty for common defense and the administration of a few concerns of mutual interest and still remained free to withdraw; or whether the States had in this momentous act given up with their other surrendered rights the sovereign right to secede.

CHAPTER XLI

NULLIFICATION, 1832

NULLIFICATION of unlawful government action, though not expounded in such fine-spun constitutional arguments, was an old American idea going back at least to the denial of the legality of the Stamp Act. The Continental Congress also declared acts of Parliament void. The Virginia and Kentucky Resolutions of 1798 and '99 advanced the argument into more metaphysical ground. Calhoun was now to carry it to its most thorough development. On the doctrines expounded by Calhoun, and proclaimed on the floor of the United States Senate by Hayne, South Carolina was more nearly ready to act than the rest of the country realized. And yet within the State, before such a result could come, there must be conflict all but as desperate as any that might be threatened with the Federal government. Nullifiers assumed that, if the one right for which they were contending were surrendered, the whole fabric of government was worse than worthless, for the Supreme Court, merely a willing tool, would rivet on them the conscienceless tyranny of an unlimited Congress. Said Francis W. Pickens, "I am for any extreme, even 'war up to the hilt,' rather than go down to infamy and slavery 'with a government of unlimited powers.' "

The danger of bloodshed was greatest in Charleston because of the concentration of opposing leaders and interests. At simultaneous mass meetings of the factions in the summer of 1830, "to one side the epithets submissionist, slave, sneak, coward, renegade, were freely applied; on the other with equal civility, the terms Jacobin, madman, fool, conspirator, were as liberally bestowed." Passions were so aroused that nullification leaders suggested that, as the Nullifiers could leave their hall only by King Street, the Unionists would use their Meeting Street instead of their King Street exits. This courteous and reasonable request so enraged the Unionists, treated now, they exclaimed, as well as denominated, as slaves, that they broke down fences in order to get into King Street. An agreement of the leaders and the concealment by Drayton, Petigru, and Poinsett of their bruises from brickbats got the parties off in different directions. In the legislative election, for which this was preparation. voters were bribed with money, liquor, riotous living, and promises of offices. Each side corralled its bought voters and kept them locked up drunk until marched to the polls.

In the parishes, persons classed socially as Negroes were voted. Everywhere communities and families were bitterly divided. Men went armed or procured dueling pistols for expected encounters. Bynum, seeking, his antagonist believed, to silence B. F. Perry, the leading Unionist editor outside Charleston, was killed in their duel.

Unionist and Nullification Leaders.—To Unionists, as Grayson said of Petigru, "the disruption of the Federal Union was to him an evil without remedy and without measure." The talent and the wealth of the State were sharply divided. Leading Nullifiers were Robert J. Turnbull, Chancellor William Harper, Robert Barnwell Rhett,[1] Judge Colcock, Eldred Simkins, R. W. Barnwell, A. P. Butler, F. W. Pickens, James Hamilton, Jr., H. L. Pinckney, Waddy Thompson, William C. Preston, F. H. Elmore, J. H. Hammond, R. Y. Hayne, S. D. Miller, Armistead Burt, D. H. Means, Nathaniel Heyward, and Calhoun, who remained in the background until July, 1831. McDuffie ridiculed nullification as constitutionally absurd but was extreme for any form of resistance. Robert Barnwell Rhett preferred the raw right of revolution, but deferred to advice for constitutional means. Langdon Cheves denied the constitutionality of nullification or that its doctrine was the same as that of the Virginia and Kentucky resolutions, denied that it would speedily remedy our grievances, or that the other Southern States were likely to adopt it. He urged instead the policy, from which he never swerved down through the later secession movement, of a convention of Southern States to save the Union by securing redress through united protest.

Prominent Unionists were P. F. Perry, James L. Petigru, Joel R. Poinsett, William Drayton, Henry Middleton, Daniel E. Huger, J. R. Pringle, Judge David Johnson, Judge William Johnson, Judge J. B. O'Neall, Judge Thomas Lee, Judge J. S. Richardson, Senator William Smith, Chancellor DeSaussure, Thomas S. Grimké, Governor R. I. Manning, Governor Thomas Bennett, Governor Taylor, Hugh S. Legaré, William J. Grayson, General James Blair, Governor David R. Williams, William Gilmore Simms, Pressley, Gaillard, Simpson Bobo, Allston, James Chestnut, H. A. DeSaussure, C. G. Memminger, Alexander Moultrie, S. H. Evins, E. J. Pringle, J. P. Richardson, Richard Yeadon, and William Aiken, whose death on May 5, 1831, removed him from the conflict.

The conflict between the State and the Federal governments in 1832 has been so emphasized, and the later struggle over slavery has so cast its shadow back upon 1832, as to obscure the fact that nullification en-

[1] Name changed from Smith to Rhett in 1837.

tailed a more extended and far more bitter conflict within than without South Carolina, and also the fact that the Nullifiers triumphed over the Unionists by a comparatively small majority. The anti-nullification vote in the legislature in 1830 embraced a block from Clarendon to Charleston and included a belt (except Calhoun's Pendleton) across the northern part of the State. Here Benjamin F. Perry was battling in Greenville, the chief stronghold of the Unionists, and in Spartanburg Calhoun was burnt in effigy.

Calhoun Openly Assumes Leadership, 1831.—In 1830 occurred the personal breach between Calhoun and Jackson. The breach, caused by the refusal of Mrs. Calhoun to recognize Mrs. Eaton, was widened by the President's and the Vice-President's clash of opinions at the Jefferson birthday banquet on April 13, 1830. To Jackson's toast, "Our Federal Union: It must be preserved," Calhoun returned the challenge, "The Union: Next to our liberty most dear. May we all remember that it can only be preserved by respecting the rights of the States and distributing equally the benefit and burden of the Union."

The next month came Jackson's sharp inquiry, prompted by the revelation of Calhoun's enemies, whether it was true that, while always professing friendship, Calhoun had as Secretary of War in 1818 urged in Cabinet Jackson's court-martial for conduct in Florida. Calhoun's elaborate explanation that his official duty had not lessened his personal esteem only deepened Jackson's conviction of his hypocrisy. It was therefore as a ruined presidential candidate that Calhoun at last openly aligned himself with the Nullifiers. He was forced, he wrote on June 16, 1831, to act by "the occurrence in Charleston, . . . caused by the accidental visit of McDuffie to that place," that is, evidently, by McDuffie's vehement speech scoffing at nullification as a constitutional measure, and defending it as a mere act of sovereignty. This denial of his remedy as a peaceful and legal act derived from the Constitution itself Calhoun met in a lengthy letter of July 26, 1831, to the *Pendleton Messenger*.

In the effort to secure a legislature two-thirds of whom would vote for a convention, Governor Hamilton in the campaign of 1832 asked Calhoun to amplify this letter. This Calhoun did on August 28, 1832, in his clearest statement of the doctrine. "The great and leading principle," Calhoun had said in the Exposition of 1828, "is that the general government emanated from the people of the several States, forming distinct political communities, and acting in their separate and sovereign capacity, and not from all the people forming one aggregate political community; that the Constitution of the United States is, in fact, a compact, to which each State is a party, in the character already described; and that the several States, or parties, have a right to judge of its infractions; and in case of a deliberate, palpable, and dangerous exercise of power not delegated, they have the right, in the last resort (to use the language of the Virginia Resolutions) 'to interpose for arresting the evil, and for maintaining, within their respective limits, the authorities, rights, and liberties appertaining to them.'"

Amplifying this in August, 1831, he continued, "There is no *direct* and *immediate* connection between the individual citizen of a State and the General Government." Whether the citizen shall or shall not obey any command of the general government rests entirely with his sovereign, the State, just as in case of his obligations under a treaty between foreign countries. There is no such entity as the American people, but only a confederation of States. It is objected to nullification, he continued, that it is merely implied from the Constitution. It is implied by inevitable logic; for the sovereign States retain every right not surrendered in the Constitution. The general government could not by any legal means punish an individual for disregarding a nullified law; and to exercise force against the State would be "folly or madness," which "will receive the execrations of this and all future generations."

Such was the vast and vague extent of the implied power of nullification insisted on as sun clear by the man who spent the rest of his life combatting implied powers. That a mind such as Calhoun's could imagine such a means of preventing otherwise inevitable secession is the strongest testimony to his love for the Union.

Right or wrong, Calhoun had taken his stand on the letter of the law, as under his new constitutional views he chose to imply its meaning, in defiance of the deeper laws of society and human nature. He had in effect denied the existence of any such entity as "the Union" in the sense that Webster used the word; and in fact it is a term of patriotism and not of law. But for the masses of men, both North and South, the patriotic conception of "the Union" was the reality for which their hearts throbbed, whether it was the Union of the whole country or the union under the growing conception of Southern nationalism contemplating a Southern Confederacy. It was for this emotional reality, and not for the gaunt thing, either in Washington or in Richmond, that Calhoun called an "agent," that in coming years over a million men were to die. Calhoun was enacting one of the saddest tragedies in our history as his powerful mind succumbed to an environment impossible of maintenance, and with inflexible logic, in obedience to his love for the Union, offered the negation of logic as the means of saving the Union.

The Nullification Convention.—The effort to secure a two-thirds legislative majority for calling a convention made 1832 a long, bitter campaign. The popular majority for Nullifiers was about 23,000 to 17,000; but the Unionists carried few districts, and the State rights party, or Nullifiers, had an overwhelming majority in both houses. The Unionists carried solidly Greenville, Spartanburg, Lancaster, Chesterfield, Darlington, Kershaw, and Clarendon, but secured only twenty-six members of the House of Representatives. Governor Hamilton summoned an extra session, which called a convention for November 19 to consider the acts of Congress for protective duties on imports and to devise means of redress.

Some demanded, quite naturally in view of four years' talk of the sovereignty of the people of South Carolina, that the convention represent only population, as wealth, which counted equally with population in apportioning the House of Representatives, certainly was not sovereign. The old fear of the low country for its privileges flared up in the face of demands that a convention represent only and wholly the white people of South Carolina, and not "the silent Negro vote" of twelve parishes casting fewer than 150 votes each, and three fewer than 50. Said the *Camden Journal:* "The oppression of a tariff, liable to repeal every year, is a trifle, to the degrading and overbearing usurpation of these Parish nobility. They ought to be *nullified,* and the free white people can do it constitutionally and peaceably too, for they have the power to keep the nobility quiet as lambs. Here is one instance, in which 'Nullification by Convention is the rightful remedy.' The evil is too flagrant to be *born[e] any longer."* Henry Middleton, though one of the wealthiest of "the parish nobility," also took strongly the ground that property, having no part in sovereignty, had properly no place in a sovereign convention. The protest was of course neglected, and the fiction was continued, as a matter of practical politics, by leaders professing the purest devotion to theory, that a convention, no matter how apportioned, is the people. Each district was assigned a number of delegates equal to its representatives in both houses of the legislature. The convention's life was limited to one year, a strange order for the servant to give; for it would seem that the sovereign might rule directly forever if he chose.[2]

The Ordinance of Nullification on November 24, 1832, declared the tariffs of 1828 and 1832 and all proceedings, judicial or otherwise, for their enforcement unauthorized by the United States Constitution and therefore null and void. Appeals to the Federal courts were forbidden, and all officers (except legislators) and all jurors concerned were to swear to enforce the ordinance and all laws supporting it. The passing of any act by Congress to employ force or to hinder South Carolina's

[2] Cf. the action of the Convention of 1861-62, p. 526 below.

commerce would be "inconsistent with the longer continuance of South Carolina in the Union."

A convention of Unionists met in Columbia on December 1, stated their view of the issue involved, and declared their determination, if compelled, to defend their rights by arms.

The legislature, meeting in regular session immediately after the convention, organized for war. Hayne was made governor, and his place in the Senate was filled by Calhoun, who on December 28, 1832, resigned the vice-presidency.

State and Federal Governments Prepare for War.—On December 10 President Jackson issued his proclamation, eloquent with affection both for his country and for his "fellow citizens of my native State," arguing at length the lawlessness of nullification and seeking to "use the influence that a father would over his children whom he saw rushing to certain ruin," led by designing men into treason, which must be put down by force.[3]

The President's proclamation brought general condemnation of nullification, though Southern States were the more lenient, and some requested Congress to modify the tariff. The legislature and the Governor of South Carolina met the threat of armed force with a defiant promise to meet force with force, and the President's imputation of the character of her leaders with indignation.

The President had already planned to send naval reinforcements to South Carolina and put the military on notice. The crisis brought the Unionists into the distressing alternative of foreswearing their convictions or being adjudged traitors to their own State. As desperate men they held to their convictions, and for almost two years South Carolina

[3] The question of whether President Jackson was born in North Carolina or South Carolina rests on whether he was born on the eastern (i.e., North Carolina) side or the western (i.e., South Carolina) side of the State line where it runs directly north and south as a part of the boundary of Lancaster County, South Carolina.

Mr. Marquis James in his *Andrew Jackson, the Border Captain* (1933), pages 268-74, reviews the evidence and concludes that neither side has conclusively proved its case, but that the probabilities favor the conclusion that Jackson was born in the Crawford home in the later Lancaster County, South Carolina, and not in the McKemey home in North Carolina. The late J. S. Bassett, of North Carolina, in his *Life of Andrew Jackson* (1916), pages 5-7, practically accepts the birth in South Carolina as established.

Jackson, who maintained that he was born in South Carolina, began as early as 1815 examination of the evidence, which he found to confirm what he had always understood to be the location of his birthplace, that is, the Crawford home in South Carolina.

See maps, document, etc., compiled by Mr. A. S. Salley, Secretary of the Historical Commission of South Carolina, *Charleston Sunday News,* July 31, 1904, and Bulletin No. 10 of Hist. Com. S. C., *The Boundary Line between North Carolina and South Carolina.* His material is depended upon and largely reproduced by Congressman W. F. Stevenson of South Carolina in his argument against Congressman W. C. Hammer of North Carolina. For both sides, see *Cong. Rec.,* February 23, 1922, p. 3,395; June 18, 1926, p. 11,534; May 24, 1928, p. 10,116; July 2, 1928, p. 11,312.

stood on the brink of civil war between her two factions. It was the President's desire that the Unionists defeat nullification without outside aid, as better in its effects on the country; but he stood ready to use force to any necessary amount. His confidential representative in South Carolina was Joel R. Poinsett of Charleston.

The Compromise Tariff.—While Jackson threatened force without limit for actual rebellion, he influenced Congress to modify the tariff. That the South was suffering severe injustice could not be denied, and was not denied by South Carolina Unionists. Prices of cotton had sunk for years. Says Professor F. J. Turner, with cotton at 30 cents South Carolina was nationalistic in 1816; with it at 20 cents in 1820 she found the tariff a grievance; with it at 14¾ cents in 1824 she found the tariff unconstitutional; and with it at 9 cents in 1827 she prepared to nullify. Moreover, prices of protected commodities had mounted sharply since the tariff of 1828, which constituted in effect taking millions of dollars from the pockets of the agriculturists, with no compensation, and giving it to the manufacturers. Severe as was the drain, added to South Carolina's losses in competition with the Southwest, the injustice of it was even harder to bear. A State already at a disadvantage from natural causes was to be beaten down for the sake of enriching another section already richer.

The 1832 congressional elections showed a strong leaning against high duties and fortified Jackson in urging tariff reduction, as he had done mildly for three years. The practical extinguishment of the national debt by January, 1833, operated in the same direction. As Congress was discussing bills for reduction, a mass meeting in Charleston on January 21, 1833, led by prominent Nullifiers and with full official countenance, suspended the operation of the Ordinance from going into effect on February 1, pending the outcome. This step, exhibiting so much more sound sense than adherence to any constitutional theory, was urged by President Hamilton of the convention, who added that if Congress should pass the force bill, he would re-assemble the convention for the purpose of secession—a threat which he did not execute.

Calhoun, habitually moderate and essentially conservative, supported Clay's bill as a reasonable compromise. The bill, enacted February 26, 1833, abolished minimum valuations and reduced all duties exceeding 20 per cent one-tenth of their excess after December 31, 1833, 1835, 1837, and 1839. After December 31, 1841, half their remaining excess should be removed, and six months later the balance of the excess. Calhoun surrendered two points: he consented to home valuation, although he declared it unconstitutional, and he accepted the flat rate of 20 per cent by July, 1842, although he desired 15 per cent by 1840.

Along with the compromise tariff went the force bill, removing every impediment which South Carolina had sought to throw before the Federal courts and authorizing the President if necessary to close or alter ports of entry and employ the armed forces of the government to suppress opposition to the law. Though opposed by Senator Calhoun and the South Carolina representatives as unconstitutional and an outrage, "the bloody bill" was signed the same day as the new tariff act.

The Commissioner sent by Virginia to urge South Carolina to rescind or suspend her ordinance arrived after suspension had already occurred but was an honored guest of the convention when it re-assembled to consider the compromise. Calhoun was present to urge acceptance. On March 15, 1833, the nullification of the tariff was revoked, and on the 18th the force bill was nullified. A few of the more determined and clear-sighted regarded South Carolina's acceptance of the "compromise" as surrender. Said James H. Hammond, with prophetic accuracy: "The tariff will be so lowered as to take away (it is hoped) the chief cause of our excitement, and render it impossible to get the people ever again to nullify. The principle, however, is to remain untouched, and after a few years of respiration the assault again to be made upon our purses and our liberty."

Rhett's Extreme Leadership.—There leaped into prominence at this time, with a fierce and ominous declaration of policy, the most radical South Carolina leader of the next generation, a young man of thirty-two, Robert Barnwell Smith, who in 1837, with all of his five brothers, took the name of his pirate-fighting great-great-grandfather, Colonel William Rhett. In opposition to declaring the compromise a cause for congratulation, he exclaimed, "South Carolina had no rights under this government but what she was prepared to assert in the tented field. . . . I ask the gentlemen upon this floor whether they can lay their hands upon their hearts, and say, that they are ardently attached to the Union of these States. . . . Sir, if a Confederacy of the Southern States could now be obtained, should we not deem it a happy termination—happy beyond expectation, of our long struggle for our rights against oppression? . . . It is the despotism which constitutes the evil; and until this government is made a limited government, and is confined to those interests which are common to the whole Confederacy, there is no liberty—no security for the South. . . . A people, owning slaves, are mad, or worse than mad, who do not hold their destinies in their own hands. Do we not hear the insolent assumption of our rulers, that slave labour shall not come into competition with free? Nor is it our Northern brethren alone—the whole world are in arms against your institutions. Every stride of this Government, over your rights, brings it nearer and nearer to your peculiar policy."

Rhett's ruthless sincerity had torn aside the veil beyond which moderate men did not wish to look. This most amiable and lovable of friends, the well-nigh perfect Christian gentleman, a man of the refinement and purity of a woman, with a single-minded devotion to truth as he saw it rare in politics, and a fanatical belief that he was right though all the world was wrong, by his unceasing advocacy of these ideas became for a generation one of the important characters in American history. Ominous indeed it was that South Carolina in a decade had passed from such leadership as that of William Lowndes, who had warned that in a generation the South must surrender control over the government and should be ready to adjust herself to the inevitable, to that of Rhett and the new Calhoun. For Calhoun differed in temperament and prudence but not in essential aims from Rhett, who staked all on defying the course of human history. They derived their power from the fact that they so truly expressed the determination of the State; for, despite Calhoun's ability, even he could not have turned South Carolina from her course. His real influence was manifested more in bringing the rest of the South to the South Carolina view than in any control over his own State.

This realization of the desperate stakes is largely responsible for the bitterness of South Carolina politics. We have campaigned and voted on our very destinies and often have been able almost to see ballots turn into bullets. Issues between Whig and Tory, coast aristocrat and upcountry farmer, slaveowner and abolitionist, on which the life of the State seemed to depend, developed an intolerance making difference of opinion seem treason to class or country or race; and the desperation thus bred gave factional politics the spirit of the vendetta. This, and not the fabled thundering of Gascon blood through our veins or the clashing of racial strains, has earned us the title of "the Hotspur State."

The Test Oath Struggle.—The crisis with the general government was past, but for almost two years longer that within the State imperiled peace. The dominant party, largely in the mere spirit of dictatorship, determined to force upon the minority the acceptance of a constitutional doctrine rejected by every other State. There was even talk of requiring an oath of all voters to obey the State in preference to the United States. On January 5, 1832, Unionists of Greenville resolved that they would never be deprived of their franchise, and that any attempt to force them to raise a fratricidal arm against the Union they would resist with drawn swords and fixed bayonets.

The convention, in annulling the force bill on March 18, 1833, ordained "That the allegiance of the citizens of this State . . . is due to the said State; and that obedience only, and not allegiance, is due" to the Federal government. The legislature was authorized to require oaths "abjuring all other allegiance" than that to the State. The legislature accordingly in December, 1833, enacted for all militia officers the much less provocative oath "that I will faithful and true allegiance bear to the State of South Carolina." To avoid doubts as to constitutionality, the legislature at the same time enacted a constitutional amendment (to be confirmed by its successor) prescribing the oath, but in less offensive form than authorized by the Convention. This "test oath," or "iron clad oath," required every official to swear "that I will be faithful, and true allegiance bear to the State of South Carolina, . . . and preserve, protect and defend the Constitution of this State and of the United States." Huger's amendment, "provided that nothing herein contained shall be construed so as to impair, or in any manner affect the allegiance now due by the Constitution of this State and of the United States," was voted against by every Nullifier but one. This was taken by the Unionists to mean that allegiance to the Federal government was intended to be denied. Said the report of F. W. Pickens' committee, showing how clearly it was recognized that slavery was the real and ultimate issue: "We have a peculiar and local institution of our own, as a people, of great delicacy and momentous concern to the very vitals of society. . . . The law of State sovereignty is with us the law of State existence. If there be any citizen of South Carolina who, forgetting all the ties of nature and sympathies that bind a man to the home of his childhood and the graves of his fathers, should refuse or hesitate to swear allegiance to the mother that has cherished or protected him, he deserves to be an offcast and wanderer upon the earth, without a home and feeling for no country."

The campaign of 1834 for a legislature to confirm or defeat placing this oath in the Constitution was embittered by continued talk of extending the oath to voters, and by the defeat of Huger's saving clause. A State-wide Unionist convention in Greenville, March 24-26, in which such men as Richard I. Manning and Alfred Huger pledged their lives and fortunes in the cause, and Poinsett advised those who contemplated leaving the State to remain and, if necessary, be buried in the bloody banner of the stars and stripes, protested against the "unconstitutional or ambiguous party test oath," which they would not take.

The militia oath of 1833, that the officer would "true allegiance bear to the State of South Carolina," had already been appealed to the courts. Judge John Smyth Richardson held in April, 1834, that General McMeekin was unwarranted in refusing to Colonel McDonald his commission because McDonald declined the oath. The oath, the Judge declared, was invalid as impairing allegiance to the United States, and thereby violating the Constitution and destructive of external safety and internal liberty and peace, and, on an abstract theory repudiated by twenty-three of the twenty-four states, sought to coerce men's opinions and "is apt, finally to take the form of civil war," in which men cease to fight for principle, but fight merely for revenge. The late controversy was ended by compromise except in South Carolina, he said, where there was no excuse for its continuance but local feeling. "Nine times have I sworn to support the Constitution of the State and of the United States, the State itself swearing me to support the Constitution of the United States. My country has in this decision the assurance of my fidelity to her complex government to which she has so often bound me. Let the mandamus issue."

In June the Court of Appeals upheld Captain McCready[4] for refusing to take the oath, on the ground that the legislature could not add to the oath prescribed by the Constitution. The decision was a foregone conclusion; for Judges O'Neall and David Johnson and the dissenting Judge William Harper had been long irrevocably committed as active partisans on the respective sides.

In the face of these judicial annulments the legislature in December pressed to confirmation the oath as a constitutional amendment. With it went a bill for defining and punishing treason with death, aimed, it was supposed, at the Unionist organization. But the prolonged bitterness threatening civil war had grown intolerable. The treason bill was dropped, and the House overwhelmingly voted down a resolution that the State had the exclusive right to define the obligation of the citizen to the Federal government, and then declared overwhelmingly that the new constitutional oath imposed no obligation inconsistent with the obligation of the citizen "to preserve, protect and defend the Constitution of the United States." The minority thereupon addressed the people of the State urging them to accept the oath, which, we may say, represented a more thorough backdown of the Nullifiers before opposition at home than the retreat of Congress before their threats. The individual's sovereignty over his own conscience remained unimpaired, and the legislative explanation was retained in mind as so sacred a compromise between factions that years afterward it was spoken of as a part of the Constitution.

One other feature of the conflict remained—the disciplining of the court which had presumed as a mere creature to defy the will of its creator and sovereign. The bill of 1834 sought to punish the judges who

[4] Old spelling of the name of the father of the historian, General Edward McCrady.

had annulled the test oath by so reorganizing the court system as to abolish their offices; but this was dropped to placate the anger of the Unionists, and unfortunately there was dropped with it the provision for uniting law and equity jurisdiction in the same Judges.

During 1835 the Court of Appeals again offended State-sovereignty men by upholding the act of Congress of 1825 giving State courts jurisdiction in punishing forcibly taking letters from post offices. The court, it was charged, adopted the Hamiltonian theory that the State and Federal governments form one system, and that the violation of a law of the United States is a violation of the law of South Carolina, thus as usual, prostrating the State before the Federal authority.

The act of 1835, attacking the courts for the Unionist decisions of a few judges, undid the admirable organization of 1824 by abolishing the separate Court of Appeals and re-establishing the old system by which the judges and chancellors assembled as an appeals court after riding the circuits, a plan which continued until 1859, when the Court of Appeals was recreated. The judges from beneath whom the bench was removed by abolition of the Court of Appeals were distributed among the other courts. When the Court of Appeals was recreated, Judge John Belton O'Neall, then aged sixty-six, received the tribute to his ability and integrity of being made its chief justice.

The Significance of Nullification.—Thus closed as a distinct episode nullification; but in truth it opened rather than closed an era. Cotton, adopted as a servant, had emerged as king, driving his subjects whither they would not have desired to go. The selfishness with which the manufacturers sacrificed other interests the more quickly to bring developments that would soon have come without the sting of injustice was as morally indefensible as the excesses with which South Carolina championed her views. She at least urged no government action in her own favor for the active injury of others. Unfortunately, and most of all so for herself, she insisted that she could do nothing but farm and repulsed the counsel of some of the wisest of her citizens like David R. Williams, who urged her to defeat tariff discrimination by practicing a varied industry. She futilely sought a political remedy for an economic evil.

Politically, nullification marked one stage in the century-long struggle beginning with the Stamp Act and ending with Appomattox to solve the problem of the relation of the colonies or States to the general government, an achievement the even partial accomplishment of which by the Constitution is its highest and most distinctive achievement. Nullification made even stronger Calhoun's long absolutism in State politics while it fatally blighted his national career; and it introduced to prominence Robert Barnwell Rhett, who was constantly to drive for secession as in itself desirable, while Calhoun sought to avoid it except as a last necessity.

Abolition developed just in time to confirm and magnify all the evils of the nullification controversy. From 1832 to 1860 South Carolina was in effect not so much a part of the country as a dissatisfied ally, for the last thirteen years of the period only awaiting a favorable opportunity to dissolve the alliance. The whole mental life of the State was most unhappily affected by continually dwelling on Southern wrongs. An enormously disproportionate amount of her abilities was drawn into politics for the defense of her peculiar and, supposedly, vital interest. The free sweep of the great South Carolina intellects of the Revolutionary and following decades was checked, and, in the expressive phrase of the brilliant South Carolinian, Professor Basil L. Gildersleeve, the South Carolina mind after 1832 became a foetus in a bottle.

CHAPTER XLII

THE COURTS AND THE LAW, 1783-1865

South Carolina colonial history supplies an interesting chapter in the development of the judicial nullification of legislation, as outlined above at pages 233-235. The development continued consistently after the Revolution. In 1789 the court declared that "It is clear that statutes passed against the plain and obvious principles of common right and common reason, are absolutely null and void," but avoided formal annulment by ruling that the statute of 1788 on which the case turned was not intended to apply, though by its words it specifically did, where it would work such manifest injustice.[1] In 1792 was decided the South Carolina case of *Bowman* vs. *Middleton,* the seventh instance (omitting a dubious case in 1778) of American courts after 1775 annulling legislation. In *Bowman* vs. *Middleton* the South Carolina court annulled the act of 1712 confirming the title of a grant of lands previously granted to another person as against common right and Magna Charta. This was a reaction against the colonial tendency to regard the Assembly as supreme in legislation (except for the limitation of the royal and parliamentary authority) and as warranted in encroaching according to its own ideas on individuals, the executive, and the courts. During the next six years our courts regularly assumed the right of annulling unconstitutional laws, though exercising it only against a Charleston ordinance. The trial judge in 1787, and again in 1792, declared features of "Sumter's law" unlawful, but both juries disregarded them, and their verdicts stood.

In the reorganizing of the courts in 1798, Governor Charles Pinckney, true to his democratic principles, combatted the courts' annulling power. Ably presenting the argument against that right, he urged that if it really existed, it should be taken away by Constitutional amendment.

Defects of Lower Courts.—The failure of the county court system of 1785-99 left a hardship in the lack of courts for small causes which the county court system of the twentieth century is just beginning to remedy. Governor McDuffie urged county courts in 1836, but this and many another call for such relief or the enlargement of the jurisdiction of magistrates produced no effect.

[1] McGovney as above, pp. 5-6; 1 Bay, 93.

The bench suffered from the large earnings at the bar from 1793 to 1815, when the fees in a single prize case growing out of the European wars might be enormous. Charles Fraser says that the four leading Charleston lawyers of that period earned from $10,000 to $12,000 a year.[2]

Admission to the bar in the later part of the colonial period was governed by rule of court, which required membership for five years in one of the four inns of court in England, and having kept commons for eight terms.[3] The act of 1785 required the judges to license as attorneys persons whom they found on examination qualified in knowledge and character. Study or clerkship in the office of an attorney, or study for three years in a law school, was evidently expected by the terms of the law (changed from time to time), but was not required. Examination by the Supreme Court now virtually continues the practice outlined above.

Impeachments—Life Tenure Attacked.—By 1812 serious discontent with tenure during good behavior developed. In 1828 Judge William D. James was removed for gross habitual drunkenness, sometimes extending through entire terms of court. Only the regard for him as a gallant Revolutionary soldier led to his being endured so long. Charges against Judge Waddy Thompson were postponed, and he resigned in December, 1828.

The crying scandal of Judge James's drunkenness and instances of less extreme intemperance raised a movement for limiting judicial terms to ten years or giving the legislature power of removal by two-thirds majority for any cause. Failure of impeachment of Grimké for tyrannical conduct convinced many of the inefficiency of that remedy. Those determined to shield the judiciary from "popular favor or popular rage" effected the compromise contained in the constitutional amendment of 1828. This contains two distinct parts, one for the removal of judges for permanent mental or physical infirmity by a two-thirds vote of each house after a hearing; and the other for easier and broader grounds of impeachment of any official, including "any misbehavior in office, . . . corruption in procuring office, or . . . any act which shall degrade their official character." The latter was not only a solemn warning to intemperate judges, but it registered disgust with executive irreg-

[2] Fraser, *Reminiscences,* p. 71. Major A. C. Spain of Darlington told the father of Mr. J. W. Norwood that he and Mr. Moise defended a man charged with murder for a fee of $1,000 each. Moise accepted a compromise of $500, but Spain sued for the full sum. Judge O'Neall charged the jury that he had never received a higher fee than $300. The jury awarded Spain $500. O'Neall was on the bench from 1828 to his death in 1863.

[3] W. H. Drayton, in Council Journal, October 5, 1774.

ularities or corruption in elections. John L. Wilson, a formidable man to offend, was so careless in finances that he allowed himself to be brought to the very verge of impeachment for not accounting for his contingent fee until 1826, two years after leaving the governorship.

The attack on the tipsy element in the judiciary co-operated with the nation-wide temperance movement then beginning to exercise force greatly to improve conditions. It is a question how much the rebellion against autocratic judicial methods accomplished; for it must be admitted that some of the old judges were arbitrary.

The amendment aimed at judges of failing powers was first employed in 1841 against Judge Gantt, a total abstainer. He at once resigned. At the same time two other judges were attacked for intemperance, but this amounted to nothing, "as they are considered two of the best judges in the State"; but the *Charleston Mercury* warned that unless the intemperate judges reformed they must be expelled.

It is difficult to realize the curse which intemperance then laid on every class, even ministers. Professor Maximillian LaBorde, while praising the integrity of the judiciary, said on the death in 1863 of Judge O'Neall, an outstanding total abstainer, "But yet it is not true that all have felt the full measure of their responsibility—that we have been aroused to a full sense of the dignity of their office—that in their personal lives they have exemplified the virtues which they have enforced from the Bench." O'Neall, he continued, was in this respect one of the most illustrious models. In 1901, Dr. James H. Carlisle (1825-1909) said of O'Neall, "It is impossible to measure the influence of such a man, of such a life. If each brother Judge, in addition to official integrity, had brought private worth, and true purity of life and character, like his, the condition of South Carolina would be different today."

Judge J. S. Richardson in 1847 admitted declining physical activity, but overwhelmed his attackers with unimpaired mental vigor. Failing powers, as illustrated by one judge who imagined himself a teapot and whose feebleness sometimes prevented a court, and another venerable judge, who had already made some ridiculous decisions, and was excused by legislative act from all but chambers duties for his last twenty-one years, stimulated the movement for shorter terms, easier removal, or retirement at a fixed age. The House in 1827 voted for a term of ten years. Of the six attempts between 1824 and 1844 to fix a retirement age, that of 1843-44 almost succeeded. Any tampering with the judiciary, it was feared, might end in degrading it by short terms or popular election.

The idea that in those days patriots always waited to be called is erroneous. Perry enumerates the candidates for judgeships in 1846, and Petigru in 1840 "thinks very poorly of the candidates for Judge." When in 1813 the salary for future-elected equity Judges was raised to that of law judges, that is from $2,400 to $2,572, all five equity judges resigned and were re-elected to get the higher pay. When in 1817 the salaries of judges and chancellors who should be thereafter elected were raised to $3,500, all resigned to be re-elected at the higher pay except Judge Bay, who was so aged that he was this year assigned to chambers duties only, and the intensely unpopular Judge Grimké, who could not possibly have won re-election. But Judge Abram Nott, whose words toward the legislature in annulling a statute were bitterly resented, went through "by a very lean majority."

Judge D. E. Huger persuaded his grand juries to petition for reduction of judicial salaries. This was enacted for future judges in 1828, bringing them down from $3,500 to $2,500 for several years. Huger resigned and was re-elected at the lower salary, but he had no imitators. The salary of judges elected in 1835 or later remained at $3,000 until raised to $3,500 in 1870. Large increases as expressed in the decreasingly valuable modern money have occurred since 1900.

Organization of the Courts.—The State, like the province, was slow in working out a good organization of its courts. The three great forward steps by 1800 were the act of 1769 for holding circuit courts at seven places (instead of in Charleston only); the County Court Act of 1785, which was allowed to go to ruin by making its bench ignorant magistrates instead of moderately paid trained lawyers; and the instituting of circuit courts on January 1, 1800, in each of the districts (called counties from 1785 to 1799 and since 1868). This last brought courts of the fullest civil and criminal jurisdictions within easy reach of every citizen. But efforts for a separate Court of Appeals (instead of the circuit judges *en banc,* existing on old English precedent since 1769) failed until 1824.

Until 1868 equity was administered by separate equity judges. Until 1784 these were the governor (or lieutenant-governor) and Council, none of them perhaps lawyers. Three equity judges were provided in 1784, elected by the legislature. Until 1791 they met only in Charleston; from then on in Columbia and Cambridge (at Ninety Six) also. Facilities were increased, and in 1808 an equity appeal court consisting of all the equity judges was created.

The equity courts were then and until 1824 exceedingly unpopular in South Carolina and some other States on account of their freedom in virtually making law (as they had been similarly unpopular much earlier in England), and their overruling even the constitutional Court of Appeals. Vexation and confusion followed. By the act of 1824 the Court of Appeals with its own three judges was created with complete powers in all appeals in law or equity, and with the right to order extra courts. The equity judges were reduced in number, the title chancellor given them, and larger use was made of masters.

The chancellors were never allowed their old uncharted freedom after 1824. A reform long unsuccessfully advocated had to await the Constitution of 1868—the uniting of the administration of law and equity in the same judge. The office of chancellor was thus eliminated.

The fruit of long hopes was dashed when in 1835 the Nullifiers abolished the Court of Appeals for annulling their test oath. Its judges were transferred to the law and equity benches, whose united judges *en banc* were to constitute the Court of Appeals for cases of law or equity. In 1836 this was abolished, and two Courts of Appeal were created, one in law and one in equity, each consisting of all the law or equity judges respectively. Above them was the Court of Errors, consisting of the two appeal courts combined, to which went all constitutional questions, all on which either appeal court was divided, or in which any two judges of a Court of Appeals made the demand.

Thus the courts stood until 1859, when a separate Court of Appeals of three judges was created, and the title of chief justice, extinct by law since 1798 and in fact since 1795, was revived, and, as mentioned above, conferred on Judge O'Neall, whose defiance of nullification excesses (with David Johnson's) had caused the abolishing of the Court of Appeals in 1835. The Court of Errors, consisting of all law judges and chancellors and the appeal judges *en banc,* was continued as a supremest court. The purpose seems to have been to prevent a small Court of Appeals, as far as possible removed from popular feelings, from repeating its defiance of the will of the people, as during the nullification period, in any future conflicts between the State and Federal governments. The words of the law of 1859 almost openly declare the intention of substituting for such purpose a sort of primary election court that could be relied upon to voice more correctly the will of the people than to uphold the letter of the law: "Whenever . . . there is any question of constitutional law or of conflict between the Constitution and laws of the State, and of the United States, or the duties and obligations of the citizens under the same, it shall be the duty of the presiding Appeal Judge to convene the Court of Errors for the determination of the same." There followed the provision also that any other question should be submitted to the Court of Errors on the request of two judges of the Court of Appeals.

South Carolina was one of the foremost States in improving the legal status of women. In 1824 a South Carolina statute made words imputing want of chastity to a woman actionable, as they were not by common law, nor, says a writer defending this move, at that time by the law of any other State except Kentucky. In various other particulars South Carolina much earlier than most States assured women valuable legal rights, although she awaited a judicial decision in the nineteenth century to interpret away the old rule that the husband alone possessed the right of disposing of his children.

In the extreme economy with which ante-bellum South Carolina was administered, allowing vast masses to grow up in ignorance, etc., her judges were overworked. Judge Richardson in 1847 doubted whether the dangerous condition thus produced existed elsewhere in Christendom. He contrasted South Carolina without county courts and with six judges and four chancellors, who did all appeal court duty also, with Virginia, which had a county court in every county four times yearly, twenty-two circuit judges, and a separate court of appeals. "P" (Edward J. Pringle) lamented in the *Southern Quarterly Review* in 1850 that the excessive labors of South Carolina judges were responsible for illogical, poorly written, ungrammatical decisions, and for the falling of the bench behind the bar in learning. Judge O'Neall once exposed conditions, but was said to have desisted because of offending his brethren. "Our conservatism cries out that change is dangerous," continued Pringle, "but so is stagnation."

Ante-Bellum Crime.—Stories of ante-bellum crime sound strangely modern; but, despite numerous miscarriages of justice, murder was by no means so safe as today. The ideal of a fair fight afforded immunity to the duelist and sometimes to other homicides, but ruthless murderers stood in grave danger of hanging. The standards of truth, honor, and fair play of a ruling aristocracy permeated other classes. All but the lowest classes regarded an oath as sacred. The Assembly jealously guarded against unfit jurors by itself making out the jury lists until late in the eighteenth century, and until after the War of Secession jurors were confined to taxpayers.

In 1820 incendiaries were frequent. Highwaymen, etc., sometimes occupied houses near Charleston and terrified, robbed, or murdered travelers. Desperate were John Fisher and his wife, keepers of the notorious Six Mile House. State Sheriff N. G. Cleary overpowered them with militia and a posse. They were hanged amid enormous excitement on February 18, 1820. Six persons were hanged in one day for murdering Nicholas John Wightman. A gang of organized slave stealers operated for years from the South Atlantic States to the West, murdering as a mere incident of trade until run down. "Lynching" was not uncommon in the form of whipping. In 1835, despite his threats of death to anyone who touched him, a buyer of stolen cotton in Charleston who was posing as a barber was taken by "The Lynch Club," led by ex-Governor John L. Wilson, was tarred and cottoned, and either (or perhaps both) jailed or banished.

Imprisonment for Debt.—The rigor of debt imprisonment was mollified by several colonial laws. In 1788 sincere debtors (on security furnished the sheriff) were given liberty to dwell anywhere within 250 yards of the prison walls. "Jail bounds" in Charleston in 1837 were bounded by Wentworth, Meeting, and Broad streets and the Ashley River. As the debtor could, if he chose, retain his property by living in jail bounds, many Charleston debtors continued to do business and live at home. This favor for city debtors was ended by the act of 1841 everywhere making the whole district (that is the present county) jail bounds. The stupid barbarity of debt imprisonment was finally forbidden by the Constitution of 1868.[1]

Humanizing and Codifying the Law.—Modifying the barbarous eighteenth-century criminal code went along with easing debt imprisonment as part of the general humanitarian movement. A strange modification of legal brutality was allowing "benefit of clergy" for the first conviction of a number of capital crimes, that is, branding instead of hanging the offenders. "Shall be hanged without benefit of clergy" meant (after the Protestant Reformation) hanged for the first conviction.

The barbarous custom of gouging out the eye in fighting, for which some toughs cultivated a special form of thumbnail, was declared by Judge Burke to the Camden grand jury in 1786 to be capital under the Coventry Act, made of force in South Carolina. Justice of the Peace Champion reinforced this to the Lancaster County grand jury in 1787; but the practice continued among the vulgar far into the nineteenth century.

Governor Vander Horst in 1796 told the legislature (and Governor Pinckney virtually repeated it in 1797) that, although our Constitution enjoined that our criminal code should be revised, "yet a sanguinary system still prevails among us, impregnated with the gothicism and barbarity of the rude ages in which it originated." Jurors, he said, acquit when they feel that the punishment made imperative by law is too severe. He urged a State prison on the Pennsylvania plan. Jails of medieval barbarity allowed prisoners in some districts to shiver without heat. Governor Paul Hamilton in 1805 repeated the arguments of his predecessor for reform of the criminal laws and lamented that the petty

[1] For General Sickles' decree on April 15, 1867, of an emergency homestead law and abolition of debt imprisonment, see Chapter LIV.

thief is hanged the same as the murderer. Governor Alston in 1813 urged penitentiaries (as Governor Seabrook did in 1849) instead of prescribing, as still in 1813, death for 165 offenses. Militia attended the execution of a man for horse-stealing in Barnwell in 1813, as it was rumored a mob would rescue him. As late as 1829-30 poor men sentenced to a small fine, and to lie in jail until it was paid, suffered protracted incarceration despite a long-existing law allowing them to swear out as insolvent, which various judges interpreted differently.

Governor R. Y. Hayne protested against barbarities in 1833. He and later governors, pointed out the gross injustice that frequently arose because the two magistrates and three freeholders (all sometimes ignorant and prejudiced) as both judge and jury determined the finest points in capital charges against slaves, and their protests finally led to the allowing of appeals and to other reforms in those courts. The penal law, said Governor P. M. Butler in 1837, is a choas of confusion and inequality. The people, wrote Professor Lieber in 1839 to Governor Noble, from mere neglect tolerate a system so faulty they have no intention of enforcing it; hence juries refuse to convict, or frequent corrective pardons undermine the certainty of punishment, the most effective of all deterrents. Let South Carolina, he urged, adopt the reforms worked out in Europe and some American States.

Governor Seabrook in 1850 helplessly rehearsed the old difficulties: there were still twenty-two capital crimes; fines were rarely paid under the law allowing early "swearing out"; hard labor should be substituted for whipping except for trading with slaves, for a Southern State could not afford to humiliate a white man. On the other hand, in 1850 so serious an offense as destroying another's will, be it ever so malicious, or breach of trust, be it ever so fraudulent and disastrous, was not a crime.

History of the Code of Statute Law.—The public printer of course published the sessions laws, which in time came to be a mass of confusion and contradictions and often not easily accessible. A promising movement for codifying the acts of the legislature was checked by the Revolution. The work of the commission of 1784-89 failed of adoption, but must have largely formed the basis of the publication in 1790, by a member of the commission, of his own compilation as a private venture —Judge J. F. Grimké's *Laws* (547 pages, 500 copies). In 1814 came Brevard's *Digest* in three volumes. Benjamin James's *Digest of the Laws of South Carolina* (710 pages) came in 1822. B. C. Pressly was paid by the State to digest the law relating to magistrates (1848); Judge Evans's

Road Law appeared in 1850; Judge O'Neall gave offense (and well might the truth hurt) by his *Digest of the Negro Law,* 1848.

Pausing for a moment in the history of codification, we must note the stupendous work of editing and publishing in ten volumes (1836-41; one volume is a splendid index) every law, with a few exceptions, enacted in South Carolina from her founding through 1838. The first five volumes are by Dr. Thomas Cooper, set to this task after his aggressive anti-Christian propaganda had forced his withdrawal from the South Carolina College presidency. Volumes VI to X are by David J. McCord. This great work sometimes includes laws vetoed by the King (because of the editor's lack of information now available), but few other errors exist in this monumental body of South Carolina history.

The growing necessity for a code eliminating obsolete, contradictory, or duplicated enactments, and arranging the existing statute law in one systematic whole by topics, led to the appointment of James L. Petigru for the task under the act of 1859. Petigru's creative mind yearned for larger powers, and so freely did he revise that his great work, presented in 1862, was rejected. Plans for revising his work crashed with the Confederacy; but his magnificent reduction of chaos to order, on Blackstone's method, became largely the basis of the work of the Republican commission headed by the able D. T. Corbin, which presented in 1872 in one large volume our first code, the *Revised Statutes of South Carolina.* Since then every year ending in 2 (barring one or two delays) has seen a new code containing the existing statute law through the year ending in 0.

Court Reports.—Connecticut began among American States the printing of judicial decisions, as a private venture in 1789 and as a State enterprise from 1814. But New York and Massachusetts were the first to order official publication. New Jersey followed in 1806. In colonial South Carolina the records of the court or the Journals of the Assembly preserved some important or controversial decisions in full. In 1799 the law ordered that every judge in the constitutional court of appeals should give for preservation in writing his opinion and reasons. In 1800 Judge E. H. Bay published Volume I of his reports of South Carolina law cases, followed in 1811 by Volume II.

In 1811 the law ordered the appeal court opinions recorded and indexed in books, appeals decided in Columbia to be kept there, and those decided in Charleston to be kept in that city. The judges often forgot while holding appeals court in one place what they had decided in the other and had to postpone decisions. In 1819 John Mill privately published two volumes of appeals court cases for 1817 and '18.

In 1816 the law ordered that one judge should write the court opinion and that the court should select the most important opinions for publication. In 1820 the first two volumes appeared, improved by the public printer's having Nott and McCord to edit them. In 1823 an official reporter was provided, who should report equity as well as law cases. Thus this forward step forms a part of the great judicial reform long striven for, culminating in 1824. A few private reports appeared after this.

CHAPTER XLIII

TARIFFS, BANKING, AND THE TEXAS QUESTION, 1833-1846

THE BITTER generation from 1832 to 1860: a generation of brilliant and swift absorbing drama with half a continent for its stage; for South Carolina a generation in which her aristocracy reached its highest splendor and her poor a deep degradation, and the proudest society in America desperately staked its all on an obsolete economic order against the power of modern life constantly upbuilding a mighty North; a period of large illiteracy, of absolutely or relatively declining commerce, of a ceaseless drain of population and capital to the West, of wasting soil; a period in which the intellect of South Carolina had ceased to grow. Such were the results of South Carolina's binding herself to slavery and committing her mind to the support of impossible ideas.

The hatred between Nullifiers and Unionists lasted into the 1840's, when it rapidly fused into common hatred of abolitionism. Poinsett in 1836 resented the strict partisanship of elections by the South Carolina legislature. A *Mercury* correspondent denounced the removal of Nullifiers by the Charleston Council as worse than the despotism of Russia or Algiers. F. W. Pickens told Congress on May 26, 1836, that Jackson's appealing to the heterogeneous mass of the people implied a brutal tyranny such as Janissaries sometimes found freedom from by bowstringing the Sultan; and Governor McDuffie in November warned the legislature that no South Carolinian could hold office under the Federal administration without being an accomplice in overthrowing his State's vital interests.

The Dictatorship of Calhoun.—Calhoun, all but dictator of South Carolina because he so truly and powerfully expressed her views, was becoming more and more the central figure of Southern politics. Yet, "when Calhoun took snuff, South Carolina sneezed," was only half true, for he perceived when he fell into the little irregularity of approving the Federal government's improving the Mississippi River that he must be careful to take the right brand. His power in Congress was greater than ever, because he was ready, unattached to party, to throw himself to either side. He was in effect an eclectic Democrat although professing to belong to that nonexistent thing, "the Republican party of 1799."

Despite his tendency to impeach the character of those who refused to accept his political views, he soon re-established friendly relations with many of the leading Unionists; for it was his cardinal principle that South Carolina's salvation rested on her remaining united in the face of growing tariff and abolitionist attacks. The national leadership of Virginia gave place to the sectional leadership of South Carolina, both because of South Carolina's consciousness of her interests at stake as the State most deeply involved in the fortunes of slavery, and because of her possession of Calhoun.

Calhoun failed to carry some of his colleagues, but overwhelmingly carried the State, in the contests over national finance. McDuffie was quite inclined to independence until his brilliant mind sank under the duelist's bullet in his spine. Hugh S. Legaré, Waddy Thompson, and William C. Preston could not be tamed, but they were all driven into private life. So hot did the contest become with the iron thrusts of Calhoun and the sarcastic eloquence of Preston that the two senators were for a time not on speaking terms. Everett pronounced a half-hour speech of Preston's in reply to some reflections upon South Carolina the most eloquent he had ever heard, and Grayson considered him the greatest natural orator in the country.

Calhoun's victory was for the State disastrously complete, thinks Mr. Gaillard Hunt. Death and the migration of crushed opponents to fill distinguished positions in other States settled the throne of the ruler the more firmly, but it also helped to settle a deadening rigidity upon the political thinking of South Carolina. Typical of this spirit was a toast at a celebration in 1838: "W. C. Preston: An alien by birth and a traitor to the State of his adoption." A strange sentiment was this for South Carolina, who owed the father of Calhoun himself and tens of thousands of her best sons and daughters to that same Virginia from which they and Preston came in the days when South Carolina was still the land of beckoning opportunity and freedom for men to think what they would.

South Carolinians had often spoken bitterly of one another, but from nullification dates their still-existent habit of stamping out as "traitors" their fellow-Carolinians who differ with the tenets of the majority. It is due to the long prevalence of this spirit and its permeation of our historical writings that the unheeded voices of Preston, William Gregg, David R. Williams, Huger, Poinsett, and others are almost unknown. Under the compulsion of standing together on slavery, and the imagined necessity of holding the low tariff wall as the outer line of defense, short work was soon made of the Whigs with their nationalizing policies. Calhoun looked on Whiggery as treason to the Constitution and the State. "What they regard as *treason,* we regard as patriotism," wrote a Greenville correspondent to the Whiggish *Charleston Courier* on September 3, 1844. But South Carolina Whiggism was a feeble shoot. Waddy Thompson was elected in 1838 as a Whig from Calhoun's own district, but Preston's effort to lead the State into Whiggism fell so flat that in 1842 he resigned from the Senate, and in 1844 the Whigs could rally only 6,000 votes to the Democrats' 52,000.

For curbing "corruption" through Federal patronage and extravagance, Senator Calhoun proposed the deposit of the surplus with the States, and a constitutional amendment for its authorization. The deposit was enthusiastically adopted but the amendment ignored, on the theory that the government had the right to deposit its money where it pleased. South Carolina received, during 1837, $1,051,422 as her share before the surplus disappeared in the panic, and long carried it on her books as a debt liable to be repaid on demand. She used the money largely for aiding railroads and internal improvements. The State refused to accept her share of Clay's public land money distribution of 1841 (not a deposit, but a gift) as unconstitutional and degrading; but when contemplating the probability of early secession in 1850, she applied for the money.

South Carolina Factions Make Peace, 1840.—The enmity of Nullifiers and Unionists soon began to lessen in the face of growing aggressions by the abolitionists. A little after midnight of July 29-30, 1835, a mob composed of both factions entered the Charleston post office and seized a sack containing copies of the abolitionist papers the *Emancipator* and *Human Rights.* A mass meeting of members of all parties followed, in which John Lyde Wilson sought to carry resolutions endorsing the mob action and Robert Y. Hayne succeeded in holding the crowd to more moderate action. Extremists even advocated taking possession of the post office. Postmaster Alfred Huger, a strong Unionist, was prepared with his double-barreled shotgun to resist to the death such action; but under the influence of Hayne no such conflict with Federal authority occurred. Postmaster-General Kendall ruled that the privilege of mailing abolitionist literature could not be denied, but that the postmaster was not obliged to deliver it.

Abolitionism was being pushed also by petitions to Congress for the abolition of slavery in the District of Columbia. These were met in 1836 by the first of the "gag resolutions," adopted by the House of Representatives on the motion of H. L. Pinckney of South Carolina. Congress had no authority over slavery in any State, said the resolutions, and ought not to meddle with it in the District of Columbia, and resolutions on the subject should be laid on the table without being printed or referred. Pinckney's apparent admission in the words "ought not" that Congress had the constitutional right to meddle with slavery in the District brought strong resentment at home. When in 1837 Slade of Vermont moved the abolition of slavery in the District of Columbia, the House almost broke up in riot. A meeting of the Southern members of both houses was called to concert measures of Southern defense; but so little had the South as a whole realized the nature of the struggle that only 64 out of 106 of her members were present, and the moderates were in control, despite the efforts of Senator Calhoun and Representative Rhett. The adoption by the House of gag resolutions similar to those of Pinckney was secured, but the Rhett program for calling a Southern convention to formulate constitutional amendments for the protection of slavery, adoption of which was to be the condition of continuance in the Union, proved impossible.

Since the South was clearly not yet ready to unite in self-defense, Calhoun and Rhett determined upon control of the Democratic party as the only available means of checking anti-slavery and high-tariff aggressions. The prospect that the Democrats would reduce the tariff to a revenue basis on the expiration of the compromise in 1842 appeared to Rhett so slight in 1839 that the only alternative was "the sword"; for, he said, "although we are too weak in votes, we are not too weak to do all that men can do in maintaining the very worst of these alternatives." But Rhett's extreme policy had few followers even in South Carolina, which had determined to stake its fortunes on the re-election of Van Buren in 1840 and the succession of Calhoun to the presidency in 1844. The defeat of Van Buren put the high-tariff Whigs into power and made Calhoun the rival of Van Buren for the next nomination. The adoption of the high tariff of 1842 so deeply offended Calhoun that he thought of nullification; but even extreme Nullifiers of 1832 realized the futility of a policy which had all but thrown the State into civil war. If resistance there should be, it must be resistance by a united South Carolina, and preferably by a united South.

The interplay of these views colored State politics. Rhett, close to Calhoun, and Rhett's ally at home, F. H. Elmore, made president of the Bank of the State in 1839, engineered a reconciliation movement backed by a large portion of the financial and landed wealth of the State. No important State office had since 1834 been bestowed upon a Unionist. Now this was to be changed, and the Unionist J. P. Richardson was to be governor. This offended the personal ambitions and nullification principles of James H. Hammond. But the weariness of ten years of internecine strife and the knowledge of the wisest leaders that the State must unite to maintain her rights operated strongly. A great mass meeting of Nullifiers and Unionists at Camden, on May 9, 1840, was the first open co-operation of the two parties since the settlement of the oath question in 1834.

Despite his declaration of neutrality, Calhoun was understood to sympathize with the reconciliation policy of making Richardson governor. He failed to compose the brilliant and bitter Hammond. Hammond wrote, "I do not believe that it is in my power were I ever so much disposed, or in any man to dry *those fountains of bitterness up*. The Union and nullification parties bear relations to each other that have not existed between any two parties in our country since the Revolution. They have stood opposed in arms. And prepared to shed each other's blood, the one for, the other against their native State in a struggle for all she held dear nay for her very existence. The Union men carried the matter to the very last and blackest die of treason. They invited a foreign enemy to our shore and received arms and commission at their hands. . . . The mass of those two parties can never exist together except as the conquered and the conquerors."

This last declaration was the negation of Calhoun's whole system. Not only could and must South Carolinians exist as united members of one party in opposition to abolitionist aggression, but so must the whole South, blind as he now found them to the necessity. Hammond was doubtless mistaken in his belief that a popular election by the masses, for whom he at the same time was expressing unmeasured contempt, would have given him an overwhelming victory. The legislature in 1840 gave Richardson 104 votes to Hammond's 47, with 13 scattering, a clear manifestation of a determination of South Carolinians again to be friends.

Democratic Mutterings, 1800 to 1850.—The allusion to popular election recalls the democratic movement that swept the United States in the 1820's but went to pieces in South Carolina. The movement of the Charleston radicals and up-country democrats quieted rather than ceased after gaining reapportionment in 1808 and manhood suffrage in 1810. Some State and local officers formerly holding office during good behavior were in 1812 limited to four-year terms. The legislature, though constitutionally entitled to the election of many officers, gave the people the election of sheriffs in 1808; of clerks of court, ordinaries (probate judges), and commissioners of locations in 1815; and of tax collectors in 1836. Partly because of Alston's unpopularity, suggestions were made in 1812-1814 for electing the governor by the people, and in 1824 H. L. Pinckney proposed in the legislature popular election of the governor and conferring on him certain powers of appointment.

Also significant of democratic feeling were the protests even before

1800 against the privilege allowed by the Constitution of 1790 that a citizen could vote in every district in which he held the qualifying amount of property. The attempt of the low-country members of 1800 to shelve, as usual, a House resolution to restrict the citizen to voting in his home district failed; but after passing it, the House a few days later voted 52 to 50 that the resolution was a sectional measure threatening "dissolving the social compact" and was not binding on citizens. In 1805 a resolution against plural voting was passed by both houses, but of course lacked the force of law. The constitutional right of plural voting continued at times to be exercised in some low-country parishes where a few votes might swing the election but was denied by the managers in others. Legislative resolutions at least as late as 1841 continued to condemn the practice, and an Attorney-General ruled that the voter might properly vote for local officers wherever he had property to be protected, but that he ought not to vote for legislators in more than one district, as otherwise he would be practicing double representation. The inconsistency of the Attorney-General in this last point is itself indicative of a democratic shift; for the Constitution specifically provided for the representation of property equally with people. So it continued until 1865, when the voter was restricted to the district of his residence.

Much greater was interest in the movement to give the people instead of the legislature the choice of presidential electors. The breakdown of the caucus system and the confusion of the campaign of 1824 moved Benton in the Senate and McDuffie in the House to introduce a constitutional amendment requiring the choice of the president directly by the people. The people were to vote by districts equal in number to the number of presidential electors allowed each State. Each district was to count as one vote, and a second election if necessary should be held between the two highest presidential candidates. The effort, renewed in 1825 and 1826, was supported by Hayne and Drayton.

In 1840 the question of popular choice of presidential electors was raised in South Carolina along with that of governor. "The electoral question," as that of the presidency was called, was agitated through 1856, on both the general ticket and the vote by district plan. In 1848 it failed in the State Senate by one vote. Calhoun's influence supported those who insisted on the legislature's wielding the State's power and discouraged the substitution of a "democracy" for a "republic."

The old conflict between up and low country appeared in the electoral question. It was urged, as to both the governorship and the presidential electors, that, however proper the compromise of 1808 in balancing the legislative power of the sections, it was contrary to justice for property to play a part in choosing the governor and the electors. On the other hand it was insisted that the compromise should not be undermined by indirection but, if attacked, should be attacked openly. J. J. Evans, wrote David R. Williams in 1821, calculated the strength of "the back country candidate," and relied on the help of certain southeastern parishes as "distinctly plebeian." Perry in 1837 deprecated denying the low country its due share of judges. In 1837 there was strong up-country resentment at the refusal to create Aiken a judicial district, as had been desired since 1827, lest this lead to its also becoming an election district. Through 1840 the conflict raged over whether the compromise of 1808 could be broken by creating another back-country senator. By the 1850's the disproportionate power enjoyed by the parishes was growing increasingly irksome. The fear was even expressed that in case of conflict with the North there might be up-country defections. "The courteous arrangement," begun in 1846, of alternating the governorship between the up and the low country, recognized the need for placating discontents.[1] This continued through the election of 1858.

But there had arisen an injustice to the low country in the system of taxation of which she now complained, as the back country had complained when the legislature of planters and Charleston merchants had, before 1784, taxed every acre of land in the province the same amount. But now the values of classes of lands, fixed in 1784 from twenty-six dollars down to twenty cents an acre and made permanent in 1815, worked a similar injustice to the low country, whose lands had not increased in value in proportion to those of the more rapidly growing up country. The city of Charleston suffered in addition from vast exemptions, some established by itself for encouraging railroads, banks, etc., and some enforced upon it by the State for similar purposes or in the interest of churches, etc., even to the extent of exempting their large productive holdings of real estate. The planter-controlled legislature exempted all buildings on rural land, though they might rank as palaces, while the cottage of the town mechanic paid its share. Here again it was said, by those having interests to protect, that the system of 1784 could not be touched, as it would disturb the compromise of 1808. These anomalies were not remedied until 1865.

Banking and the Bank War, 1837-60.—The panic of 1837 following Jackson's "bank war" stirred general anti-bank passions in South Carolina among the masses and a highly critical attitude among the upper classes toward "the money power." The first Bank of the United States had naturally not been popular in South Carolina except with the then-

[1] C. E. Cauthen, "South Carolina during War of Secession," citing *Carolina Spartan* of October 25, 1860.

powerful Federalists. South Carolina Congressmen had tried to kill it, but Calhoun drew the charter for its successor that was adopted in 1816. Charleston subscribed $2,598,000 to its capital—more, it is said, than either New York or Boston and exceeded only by Philadelphia and Baltimore. Cheves was soon called to its presidency to save it from insolvency, and the South Carolina legislature in 1821 almost unanimously endorsed its constitutionality and expedience. But by 1832 opinion had changed, and the United States Bank was charged with favoring Northern merchants to the great disadvantage of Southern, and of draining off specie from its Southern to its Northern branches.

In the crisis of 1837 the Charleston banks, with $8,000,000 assets above liabilities and $1,000,000 in specie, were, like the other banks of the State, solvent; for South Carolina never had a bank failure before 1860; but the suspension of specie payments in the North forced the Charleston banks, in order to avoid being drained, to suspend specie payments from May, 1837, to September, 1838, and again from October, 1839, to July, 1840.

This record did not prevent the development of strong anti-bank feeling. The law of 1840 prescribed regulations for safer banking and required all banks to accept the enactment as a part of their charters. The Bank of South Carolina, standing for the banks, refused to conform. "The bank case," one of the most famous in our history, thus went to trial as a test, in popular opinion, as to whether the State was to rule the banks or the banks were to rule the State. Amid deeply stirred public feeling, the bank won before the lower court, but lost in 1844 before the Court of Appeals, forfeited its charter, and received a new one embodying the law it had refused to obey. The effect was salutary. Henceforth the notes of South Carolina banks, always standing high, ranked with the best in the nation.

Memminger summed up the anti-bank sentiment in his closing words in the famous case: "The people of South Carolina will not submit to be governed by banks. . . . They will never endure arbitrary government of any sort, and least of all that meanest, most odious, and most degrading of all, the domination of an irresponsible monied oligarchy." Memminger, a brilliant lawyer prominently connected with banking, held that the State should not be entangled with financial institutions. He proceeded to turn this anti-bank sentiment against the great Bank of the State, the corporation chartered in 1812, owned by the State, and administered by directors chosen by the legislature.

James H. Hammond, elected governor in 1842, was already unfriendly to the great Bank of the State. He filled a large part of his 1843 annual message with an attack on the bank based largely on material supplied

by Memminger. He believed that the bank should be forced to pay off the State's public debt at the rate of half a million a year, and if it perished in the attempt, so much the better; two evils would be ended at once. The attack accomplished little.

Though, in my opinion, the charges that the Bank of the State was meddling in politics were exaggerated, its influence was great, and was actively exercised for its protection. Legislators were influenced, it was charged by men of the standing of W. B. Seabrook, by liberal accommodation, and at least potentially dangerous alliances were formed with important business and planting interests. Men were denounced for fighting the United States Bank as dangerous to purity and liberty and maintaining here an octopus still more dangerous to South Carolina finance and politics. Many maintained that there should be a divorce of government and banking here as in Washington, and that the funds of the State be withdrawn from the control of a corporation free to misuse or lose them. If the president of the bank should be a politician, was the cry, he could rule the State; and with the election of Franklin H. Elmore in 1839 there was a president active both in politics and in big business. Elmore was president of the Nesbit Manufacturing Company, whose heavy indebtedness at the time of its failure, however, cost the bank only a few thousands.

Legislative committee reports showed large but well-secured liabilities by officers and directors, with some forty men being liable for a total of $1,070,440, but showed also an unbroken record of integrity and fiscal services to the treasury in addition to accommodations to business. Even the names of all borrowers and the amounts of their indebtedness were read in public session as Memminger of Charleston and Perry of Greenville moved every stone to discredit the institution. The facts remained that the Bank had paid out of its profits enormous sums of interest and principal of the State debt, and had in times of stress made large advances to the State, and that it had not fallen into the abuses and losses common with State banks elsewhere.

The election of 1848 turned on the Bank question, and in 1849 Memminger failed, by only one vote, to kill the bank. But circumstances of wider import were leading public opinion to view the matter from a different standpoint. The mounting hostility toward the Federal government after the Wilmot Proviso attempt to exclude slavery from the Mexican cession made military expedience more important than financial and political differences. Calhoun said that if the South should be forced to defend herself, we would need all the assistance of our banks; and a resolution was introduced in the South Carolina House inquiring what assistance the Bank could render the State in case of conflict with the United States. "The Bank question" was submerged in a larger question, and the bank was left to bleed itself to death in financing the Confederacy.

There followed in the fifties a bank enthusiasm with the chartering of large new institutions, for banking was essential in our staple crop and direct European trade program and in the great railroad building of the decade which served this program. New business resulting from the banking collapse of the early fifties in Florida, Mississippi, and Alabama vastly increased banking profits for South Carolina institutions, fortified with a nation-wide repute. But the Bank of the State prudently preferred to serve its own constituency, where borrowers were paying unusually high rates because of the diversion of capital to the South and West.

Calhoun's Presidential Candidacy, 1843-44.—South Carolina's resentment at the tariff of 1842 is indicated by the refusal of F. W. Pickens to accept the ministry to England or any other office under the Federal government while that law existed. The attempt to prevent these feelings from wrecking Calhoun's candidacy for the presidency and his policy of educating the South to unite in defense of Southern interests filled these years with confusion. A pitiful blindness prevailed—with many, perhaps, a willful blindness—to the fact that the tariff was only a minor injury to South Carolina, with her butchered soil and unscientific agriculture, compared with the competition of the fertile black lands of the Southwest. "The fiscal action of the General Government is the root of all the evil, and here the South must strike," wrote Rawlins Lowndes in 1837. McDuffie in 1844 declared "on my responsibility before God . . . that man never before invented such a system of grinding oppression as this tariff." In this "mad belief of his distempered mind," said the *Courier,* October 1, 1844, Langdon Cheves was not far behind him. At the same time that they nominated Calhoun for the presidency the South Carolina legislature of 1842 denounced the tariff of that year as a breach of the faith plighted in 1833, which would be endured only until the Democratic party had time to redeem its pledge to correct it. "But in the event that their reasonable expectations are disappointed, they feel themselves bound to declare, that they must, in accordance with their principles and recorded pledges, adopt such measures to redress their wrongs and restore the Constitution, as in their opinion may be due to themselves and their property."

But the *Courier* thought that South Carolina's sufferings had been due chiefly to deranged currency, extravagance, speculation, commercial revulsions, worn-out lands, persistent dependence on a single staple, absenteeism, and luxurious living.

Calhoun, having resigned his senatorship on March 3, 1843, turned his thoughts to his presidential candidacy.[2] Seeing no chance of defeating Van Buren for the nomination unless delegates from each congressional district were elected and voted independently, he threw over his whole tradition of State solidarity, etc., and proclaimed the presidency the direct possession of the people. There could hardly be a more striking illustration of the influence of political expediency on the views of a man who would not even consent to allowing the people of his State to choose presidential electors or their own Governor. Stamped indelibly as the sectional candidate of the weaker section and as an independent eclectic Democrat, Calhoun never had the ghost of a chance. Long before the convention Van Buren's shrewd organization had virtually secured a majority. In February, 1844, in a five-thousand-word letter, Calhoun, professing to have been passively in the hands of his friends, withdrew in such a way as to leave them disorganized and confused. His impulse to run as an independent was checked by advice to save himself for 1848.

Now a veritable special Providence seemed to intervene for Calhoun's salvation, i.e., Van Buren's letter opposing the annexation of Texas and therefore making his nomination impossible. On Texas Calhoun was all that the Democratic party held sound (unless his unwillingness for war, when that issue arose, is considered); but so thoroughly were his forces disorganized that the rallying cries of special friends hardly drew attention, and South Carolina only sent Elmore and Pickens to the convention as "observers." Polk, sound on Texas and no fanatic on the tariff, rode into the nomination and the election, while the greater man, hoping for 1848, pledged his support to the party.

To Calhoun's intense, pure, and introspective nature this third[3] and decisive defeat of his great ambition was a terrible blow. Before 1848 events had forever barred reasonable hope. From 1843 there settled upon him a bitterness which the events following the Mexican War deepened into the gloom of a patriot despairing of the future of his country.

[2] In 1843 there appeared an anonymous campaign *Life of John C. Calhoun,* later supposed to have been written by R. M. T. Hunter of Virginia. Robert Barnwell Rhett wrote, on October 25, 1854, that Calhoun wrote the *Life* and asked him to father it, and that when he declined this Calhoun secured R. M. T. Hunter, who, says Rhett, added about a page and a half. Mr. C. M. Wiltse in his *John C. Calhoun, Nationalist* (1944), pp. 401-2, heavily discounts Rhett's statement and emphasizes Calhoun's, saying, "Mr. Hunter has rewritten most of [it]; so much so as fairly to be entitled to the authorship." Mr. Wiltse's verdict is "that the *Life* is an 'official' biography, prepared under Calhoun's eye and perhaps in part by his hand; but it is not in any legitimate sense of the word an autobiography."

[3] 1824, 1836, and 1844.

There was an active Clay Club in Charleston in 1844, and neither there nor in the up country did the party lack talent, as is attested by such names as Dr. F. Y. Porcher, Richard Yeadon, editor of the *Courier,* W. C. Preston, Thomas Butler King, Dr. S. H. Dickson, Dr. William Read, Jas. L. Petigru, Henry Grimké, Dr. J. P. Jervey, James Adger, Dr. John Bellinger, H. D. Lesesne, P. J. Porcher, William Gregg, William Blanding, and B. F. Porter. Denounced as the party of tariffism and abolitionism, the South Carolina Whigs cast 6,000 votes to the Democrats' 52,000 and virtually ceased to exist as a party.

The Bluffton Movement.—South Carolina politics during 1844 had been exceptionally warm even within the Democratic ranks. R. B. Rhett, released from the restraint of caution by the wrecking of Calhoun's chances for the presidential nomination, determined to appeal to South Carolina, perhaps to the point of nullification or secession, against the tariff of 1842. The other South Carolina congressmen fell away at Calhoun's warning that Polk's election must not be jeopardized, but Rhett, even in defiance of Calhoun, made the appeal. On July 27, 1844, in an address to the people of the State, he launched what came to be known as the Bluffton movement, from the mass meeting there for its promotion. Said Rhett, "Let there be held a convention in the spring of 1845 to nullify the tariff or secede."

The *Mercury,* wavering between Rhett and Calhoun, soon threw its powerful influence to the latter, while Calhoun's critic, the *Courier,* now praised his wisdom. Rhett seems to have hoped to rouse such a movement as would force Calhoun to fall in line, but, apart from Calhoun's enormous power, South Carolina had no desire for a repetition of the all but civil war of 1832-34 within her own borders. Young men rallied to Rhett, proclaimed him "the sentinel on the watch tower of liberty," and exclaimed, Where are the leaders? The leaders had heard the quiet voice of Calhoun in conference and correspondence. The Bluffton movement subsided almost as suddenly as it had arisen.

It cannot be doubted that Calhoun to the last sincerely loved the Union, though he loved his own State and section more. He understood far better than most of his followers the terrible possibilities in dissolution; but it is equally clear that from 1832 the Union was to an increasing body of South Carolinians a matter of mere expediency. South Carolina knew her own mind and was determined, beyond the point of tolerating discussion, that any Federal action seriously threatening the ultimate abolition of slavery should be the signal for secession the moment it could be practically accomplished.

Along with the tariff went the question of acquiring Texas and Oregon and possibly California. From the raising of the question in

1836 Calhoun took strong ground for annexation, while Governor McDuffie in 1836 took the strongest ground against our meddling in Texas, though he came to support Calhoun when it became a vital issue in 1844. With F. W. Pickens, Rhett, and others in 1843 it was Texas for the South, in or out of the Union, while New England extremists threatened secession if Texas were annexed. Calhoun's acceptance of the office of secretary of state for the purpose of accomplishing annexation is too well known in American history to be repeated. Along with his determination to forestall the efforts of England to establish an independent Texas subservient to her commercial interests and (the South feared) as a nursery for abolitionism, went his determination to curb the Democratic cry for "54-40 or fight" and come to a reasonable compromise with England on the Oregon question. Though Tyler's and Calhoun's methods failed regarding Texas, they prepared the way for the accomplishment of both ends.

McDuffie's health was shattered, and Huger was unfitted by either experience or temperament for organizing Southern forces for the desperate combats being forced upon the country. From all over the country Calhoun was urged that his return to the Senate was imperative. Wearied with public labors and saddened by blighted ambition, he desired the repose of Fort Hill. He could be persuaded to return to public life, he wrote Pickens, only by "the utter incompetency of our two Senators" to prevent the great evils or accomplish the great good offered by the existing crisis. Judge Huger, magnanimous and disliking his senatorial duties, and aware of the state of opinion, continually urged that Calhoun take his place. He resigned, and Calhoun was elected on November 26, 1845.

A few days before his election Calhoun had shocked South Carolina strict constructionists by his concession to Western opinion on Federal improvement of the Mississippi. This opinion he expressed as a South Carolina representative to the Memphis convention of 583 delegates from Florida, Tennessee, Kentucky, Mississippi, Arkansas, Missouri, Alabama, Louisiana, North Carolina, South Carolina, Pennsylvania, Illinois, Ohio, Indiana, Iowa, Virginia, and Texas, which met to promote water and rail transportation for the Gulf, Atlantic, and Mississippi Valley States. Along his route to the convention Calhoun was hailed as the country's next president, and when as chairman he declared that the great river and those of its tributaries touching three states should be treated by the Federal government as "an inland sea" to be improved for navigation, he was accused of modifying his strict-construction principles to win the West to his candidacy. As senator he expounded his constitutional position in a long committee report on the convention memorial. R. B. Rhett, more downright, accepted it as political expediency necessary to unite the West and South; but in general, said Perry, "the legislative members appeared like Calhoun's slaves and refused to assert their opinions."

Calhoun opposed war with Mexico, as he did with England; for with a foresight beyond the habit or capacity of the hotheads uncalculatingly grasping at any immediate gain for the South, he realized the perils that must follow the division of the spoils. Southern opinion was generally pleased with the course of events, although South Carolina resented the talk that the act of 1846 had placed the tariff on a revenue basis; for, as a matter of fact, although large reductions were made on manufacturers' raw materials, the rates remained high on articles of large Southern consumption. Texas had vastly increased the South's sectional weight, and the end of a brilliant war, of which she boasted as peculiarly her own, promised her "peculiar institution" still greater expansion, prestige, and power. But how true had been Calhoun's sensing of danger one short year was to show.

CHAPTER XLIV

A MATURED SLAVERY ON THE DEFENSIVE, 1820-1860

Said the *Southern Episcopalian* of Charleston of slavery, in March, 1859: "The men of the Revolution and of the generation immediately succeeding, regarded it in the light of an evil, to be gradually remedied if possible by removal or emancipation. Experience and maturer reflection proved the impracticability of either course, and the assaults of abolitionism induced a more thorough examination into the grounds, moral and religious, on which it rested. The Southern mind became satisfied that the relation was not without a divine sanction, and that under existing circumstances it was the only one which could obtain between the two races brought together upon our own soil. Here was a sufficient vindication of the Southern system—a true and incontrovertible position upon which its defenders might take their stand against every assailant. For a time we were wisely content with it, and triumphantly maintained it. But latterly, perhaps in the wantonness of success—perhaps in the asperation of conflict—there has been manifested a disposition to break from our intrenchments and assume the offensive. Slavery has even been set forth as a necessary element towards the composition of a high and stable civilization—as a thing good in itself, without regard to the circumstances peculiar to Southern society—as in short the best mode in which labor and capital can stand associated. The sentiment of the South, and especially of South Carolina, seems verging toward the opposite extreme of a natural oscillation, passing from morbid sensitiveness into aggressive assertion."

This, the editor continued, was as unsound a position as the other, and he believed that such was the view of the soberer part of our people.

The editor was right. Though statesmen spun theories for constitutional defense, the attitude of the people was essentially practical, adopting any obvious means of meeting their overshadowing problem. F. W. Pickens's declaration, "The law of State sovereignty is with us the law of State existence," would have been changed into the statement that the law of national sovereignty was the law of existence if the slaveowner had faced dangerous local opposition to his interests against which only the Federal government could protect him. The constitutional arguments on either side were mere attorney's pleas claiming everything for his client. The Constitution was examined not for what it meant but for arguments to sustain what each side desired.

Professor Thomas R. Dew, teaching history, government, and economics in the College of William and Mary, in an elaborate condemnation in 1832 of the emancipationist movement in the Virginia legislature of 1831-32 taught the South to abandon its apologies and to regard slavery as best for both master and servant. Perhaps no one has ever stated the new position more strongly than Chancellor William Harper of South Carolina in his *Memoir on Slavery* in 1837. Both his and Professor Dew's utterances seem today to hark from an almost illimitable distance. Governor Robert Y. Hayne argued in 1833 that societies based on slavery were strong for war, and Governor McDuffie in 1835 held that no institution bore more expressly the marks of divine approval. Instead of being an evil, he held, it was a cornerstone of our republic; emancipation, however remote or with financial compensation, could not be considered; abolition agitators should be executed. And yet in 1835 Francis Lieber, the talented German member of the South Carolina College faculty, recorded the disgust with slavery expressed privately by William C. Preston, Professor Josiah Nott, and many others, and as late as 1846 strong expressions to the same effect from William DeSaussure and other prominent South Carolinians.[1]

R. B. Rhett also became one of the earliest and most extreme advocates of the Dew ideas, and Calhoun in 1837 was defending the same position; for his logical mind could not imagine success in defending an institution acknowledged to be an evil. South Carolina naturally felt extremely. She had in 1850 140 Negroes to every 100 whites; over 141 in 1860, while Louisiana and Mississippi, her nearest rivals, had 106 and 105 respectively. As nearly as can be determined, a little less than 49.96 per cent of her white population belonged to slaveowning families, though only 31.19 per cent to families owning ten or more slaves and only 18.78 per cent to families owning twenty or more.[2] Mississippi

[1] Frank Freidel, quoting from Lieber's letters and journals in *Jour. So. Hist.*, IX (February, 1943), 80 and note.

[2] I base my statement on the census figures for the size of families in each of the several States, which differ considerably from State to State; e.g., 3.77 for California to 5.98 for Minnesota. Even among the slave States the differences ranged from 5.04 for Louisiana to 5.89 for Missouri. Apparently the author of *Century of Population Growth* (quoted in *Am. Hist. Rev.*, XXI, 78, note) assumed that the average size of the family was the same for all the slave States, namely about 5.7, this being approximately the average as appearing in the summary, *Compendium of 11th Census, Population*, p. 856, and in *Compendium of Census of 1850*, p. 99. His percentages of persons directly interested in slavery and mine practically agree for States in which the size of the family did approximate 5.7 members. In my three-volume *History of South Carolina* (II, 496), I used his percentages without verification. Calculation on the basis of white population, the average size of the free family, and the total number of slaves in each State yields the following

stood next with 44.47 per cent of its white population belonging to slaveholding families. But it should be noted that the proportion of the whites directly interested as members of slaveholding families was smaller than indicated, for two reasons. First, there were some free Negroes owning slaves who are included in the census merely as slaveowners. Second, in numbers of families there might be found more than one person who was a slaveowner in his or her own right.

In South Carolina in 1850, 3,492 persons owned one slave; 6,164 owned from 2 to 4; 6,311 owned from 5 to 9; 4,955 owned from 10 to 19; 3,200 owned from 20 to 49; 990 owned from 50 to 99; 382 owned from 100 to 199; 69 owned from 200 to 299; 29 owned from 300 to 499; 2 owned 500 to 999; 2 owned 1,000 or more; total slaveowners, 25,596.

South Carolina was in tragic bonds, closing her mind to the inquiry, What is true? and pressing the supreme question, How can my position be defended? Freedom of thought on slavery had virtually disappeared by 1820. The brilliant sisters Sarah (1792-1873) and Angelina (1805-79) Grimké, daughters of Judge J. F. Grimké, having inherited from their Landgrave Smith as well as from their Grimké ancestors the uncompromising religious devotion to their ideals that enemies call fanaticism, and having imbibed anti-slavery convictions from South Carolina Quakers, moved North in 1835 and became avowed abolitionists and leaders for woman suffrage.

Judge Hoar Expelled from Charleston.—In the face of the results of West Indian emancipation, constantly played up, and the almost incredible bitterness and extravagance of abolition denunciations, Southerners reacted perfectly naturally. A woman at a New England summer hotel is said to have been requested by the proprietor to leave, on threat of losing his Southern patronage, because she declared there was not a virtuous woman in the South. She explained that slavery was immoral, and that everyone who practiced or endorsed it was immoral. The South Carolina legislature was deeply offended in 1824 when the legislature of Ohio transmitted to them their resolutions against slavery. For a half century, said Chancellor Harper in 1837, abolitionist literature as though carried by the birds had reached our slaves. Such literature or pictures came in packages of goods (the expectation being that Negro workmen would open them).

Under these irritations, South Carolina, warned by the Vesey plot of

---

results: Percentage of whites belonging to slaveowning families, South Carolina, 49.96 per cent (not 53.1); Louisiana, 40.77 (not 46.1); Mississippi, 44.47 (not 44.6); Florida, 39.44 (not 42.5); Georgia, 42.11 (not 42); Alabama, 39.9 (not 39.2); Virginia, 34.8 (not 35.1); Kentucky, 29.2; North Carolina, 28.14; Tennessee, 26.26; Arkansas, 21.14; Texas, 20.8.—*Compendium Census 1850*, pp. 45, 63, 82, 95, 99; *Compendium Census 1890*, Part I, Pop., p. 856.

1822, in December of that year enacted her Negro seamen's act by which any free Negro brought into a South Carolina port must be jailed during his stay and, if his expense was unpaid, must be sold as a slave. In 1823 Judge William Johnson of South Carolina in the Federal district court in Charleston declared the act unconstitutional, and was so offended by the consequent attacks upon him as to reply in the press.[3] A law eliminating enslavement as a penalty and other extreme features of the act of 1822 was at once substituted. So general was the fear of free Negro seamen from non-slaveholding States or countries that five Southern States in 1850 had laws imprisoning them while in their ports.[4] When England protested, United States Attorney General Wirt declared the South Carolina act contrary to the Anglo-American convention and Federal law, but Attorney General Berrien in 1831 advised the contrary.

In 1844 Massachusetts sent Judge Samuel Hoar to Charleston to prepare a test case involving some imprisoned Massachusetts free Negro seamen. The legislature resolved that Hoar "came here, not as a citizen of the United States, but as the emissary of a foreign government, hostile to our domestic institutions, and with the sole purpose of subverting our internal peace." They denied that Massachusetts could make a free Negro her citizen in the meaning of the Constitution, and requested the Governor to expel her emissary. Only Memminger in the House and Perry in the Senate voted against these resolutions, though Perry says many thought, but dared not act, with him. Popular action in Charleston deprived the Governor of the privilege of acting. Judge Hoar, faced by a great crowd, instead of forcing them to drag him out, walked to the carriage provided for him and was carried to the boat.

It is difficult to see how any person could, after this, expect the Union to endure, when, as Hoar complained, South Carolina prohibited, not only by her mobs, but by her legislature, a free white citizen of Massachusetts from residing within her borders or instituting a suit in the Federal Courts.

Governor Adams in 1855 doubted "that our safety requires a law of such unremitting and indiscriminate severity. . . . The remedy is worse than the disease that it seeks to cure," for free Negroes from abroad, confined with our lowest population, perhaps for long terms, without having committed any crime, would revengefully spread all the anti-slavery propaganda possible.

Revising the Negro Law.—The Negro seamen's act was part of a general tightening of the laws after the Vesey insurrection and the

[3] On the democratic nationalism of the independent-minded Judge Johnson and his influence as a Federal Supreme Court Justice, see D. G. Morgan's study in *Harvard Law Review,* LVII (January, 1944), 328-61.

[4] Miss Laura A. White in *Jour. So. Hist.,* I, 34.

growth of abolitionism, making the Negro law more humane on the one hand and more secure on the other. We must, however, remember the severity of the criminal code against whites at this time.

The Charleston grand jury charged in 1815-16 that murdering slaves was common. Until 1821 the murder of a slave by a white person could be punished only by fine or imprisonment, and not, like stealing a slave, by death. Chancellor Harper in 1837 thought the fine was better, as juries often acquitted rather than hang a white man for slave murder. But, as the public conscience improved, slave murder became less safe. Governor P. M. Butler in 1838 refused to save Nazareth Allen from hanging for slave murder, as he said law must be respected and our duties to our slaves maintained as imperatively as our rights. A white man was executed in Bennettsville for this crime in 1853. For the "Broxton Bridge horror" (killing a runaway slave with dogs) a young man, son of a wealthy father, and a poor white man were hanged in 1854, despite terrific social and political pressure and threats against Governor J. L. Manning for refusing a pardon, and rumors of rescue that caused militia to surround the scaffold.

Though many of the barbarous features of the Negro law remained they were in fact rarely used. They were instituted in an age of cruel laws everywhere for the control of newly arrived barbarians, throbbing with the instincts of freedom and resentment, and were no longer needed for the control of civilized slaves who had never known freedom, many of whom entertained deep affection for their masters. Governors Wilson in 1824 and R. I. Manning in 1826 urged the humane revision of the Negro law, and the latter urged the forbidding of execution by burning, as was still occasionally practiced in punishing particularly heinous crimes. Manning urged also trial of capital cases at the courthouse by jury, with various safeguards. Despite repetition of these recommendations, Governor Adams had to say in 1855: "The administration of our laws in relation to our colored population by our courts of magistrates and freeholders, as these courts are at present constituted, calls loudly for reform. Their decisions are rarely in conformity with justice or humanity. I have felt constrained in a majority of the cases brought to my notice either to modify the sentence, or set it aside entirely." His recommendations were of little effect. The life of the slave continued at the mercy of a court not of record, of two magistrates and three to five freeholders, convicting by majority vote. But by the law of 1833 the circuit judge was directed, "On application on behalf of the prisoner" (slave or free colored) in capital cases in which the judge considered the conviction unjust, to order a new trial in which no one who had sat in the first trial could participate. The same law abolished branding for black or white.

O'Neall's experience as a judge led him to condemn the law of 1820, forbidding emancipation, and that of 1841, forbidding even sending a slave abroad to make him free. He also considered unworthy the fear that forbade teaching slaves to read. The latter law was much disregarded.

Selling slave families apart was condemned by all decent owners. The "Negro splitter," even if rich and aristocratic, was despised in the best circles. And yet court records, advertisements, etc., show that much of this was done in the settlement of estates, levying for debt, etc.

Plantation Management.—The management of large agricultural properties offered opportunities for business ability and was utilized by active men to build great fortunes. Such were Henry Laurens of the colonial period, the Revolutionary Wade Hampton of the early nineteenth century, and Nathaniel Heyward (1766-1851) and James H. Hammond (1807-64) of the later period. Such men had many plantations, inhabited by from 50 to 400 slaves each, but more likely 100 to 150, each operated as a separate unit. Large wealth sometimes descended for generations among unindustrious owners, but the man who personally knew his property and kept an eye on all important operations reaped the usual rewards.

Nathaniel Heyward got a $50,000 estate by marriage (much larger than his own inheritance) and increased it to upward of $3,000,000 during his long life. He died in 1851 probably the richest ante-bellum South Carolinian. His personalty (including about 1,843 slaves on 16 plantations; he had besides given perhaps 500 to his children) was appraised at $2,018,000. The lands (then unappraised), about 4,400 acres of which were cultivated, probably equaled upward of $700,000. His bank stocks were often in small blocks, indicating the habit of putting away cash thriftily. His income in 1818 was $90,000 and in 1805, at the height of the Napoleonic Wars was $120,000. Until he was old, he knew almost every slave. Naturally he found little time for public life. Not a dollar did he leave to any public cause, though he generously helped many an impoverished gentleman. He was not a "typical" planter, but rather a modern businessman. Heyward's and a son's humane treatment of their workers is evidenced by the fact that among the 499 slaves of the son in 1865, 28 were between 70 and 80 years of age.[5]

[5] Dr. G. Manigault's "Heyward" (MS); Heyward plantation records; probate records, Charleston. Phillips, *American Negro Slavery,* p. 250, relying on the Manigault MS, omits the land value and numbers the slaves at 2,087. The probate records name 1,693 slaves and estimate 150 on one of the plantations. Dr. Phillips evidently includes the slaves given away by Nathaniel Heyward before his death.

George McDuffie's holdings rose from 300 acres in 1821 to 5,000 in 1848. That year he planted 750 acres in cotton, 325 in corn, 100 in wheat, 300 in oats, 10 in peas, potatoes, etc.

J. H. Hammond promoted in the 1840's the use of marl, the carbonate of lime, which, though beneficial, failed to fulfill expectations. On horseback at dawn, he supervised swamp reclamation and his entire operations. He provided hospitals, as did many large planters, recreations, and nurseries for the children of working mothers. Of brilliant, sardonic mind, despising democracy, this son of a New England teacher immigrant to South Carolina commanded respect throughout the Union as a political leader.

A few overseers were men of considerable intelligence and fair education, but in general they were inferior. Committing the actual management of plantations to them was a great bar to agricultural progress. Below the overseer was the "driver," a forceful Negro man, who, besides keeping the hands at work, was a sort of assistant overseer. Under the "task" system the stints could usually be finished by two or three o'clock, but such work as cotton-picking ran from sun to sun. The tendency was to easier tasks and better treatment from about 1800.

Intelligent masters desired moral and orderly conduct by their slaves, not to speak of the deep sense of moral responsibility felt by many. In his plantation manual of about 1835, James H. Hammond of Beach Island (Highland) directed that "Marriage is to be encouraged, as it adds to the comfort, happiness and health of those entering upon it, besides inducing a greater increase. No Negro man can have a wife, nor woman a husband, not belonging to the master. Where sufficient cause can be shown on either side, a marriage may be broken, but the offending party must be punished. Offenders can not marry again after such divorces for three years. . . . A third marriage shall not be allowed but in extreme cases. . . . No marriage shall take place without the master's expressed consent to it."

A five-dollar bounty for household goods was given for a first marriage, two dollars and fifty cents for a second, none for a third. Slaves having wives at other quarters had restricted visiting privileges. There were humane and intelligent provisions regarding pregnant women, and a regular plantation midwife, with an assistant in training, to attend births. Unweaned children and young weaned ones were cared for during the day at a separate apartment under a trusty nurse.

Large plantations often maintained their own hospitals with regular medical attendance. It was at such a hospital that Dr. J. Marion Sims made his discovery for relieving vesico-vaginal fistula. Smaller owners could sometimes send their slaves to hospitals kept by physicians at moderate rates. It was not only the systematic organization and administration of the plantation household on the basis of reasonable consideration, but the thousand little acts of human sympathy and spontaneous kindness of masters and servants living in habitual relations of interdependence that fostered the mutual affection in the great mass of owners and owned that rendered Lincoln's proclamation of emancipation a mere declaration of future policy, which produced no change in the daily conduct of Southern life.

Religious Work Among the Slaves.—To the religious work of Episcopalians and Presbyterians for their slaves in early colonial times was added in the late eighteenth century the more extensive work of the Baptists and Methodists, so much better situated for religious appeal to the Negro by their universal distribution throughout the State and by their stronger emotional appeal. The great revival in the Episcopal and Baptist churches in Beaufort in 1831-32 greatly stimulated the work of both among the slaves. In 1861, 2,979 of the Episcopal communicants in South Carolina were whites and 2,973 Negroes, according to the diocesan journal. The brilliant Baptist minister at Beaufort, Dr. Richard Fuller, or his assistant preached regularly every Sunday to a Negro membership of 2,000. The Baptists carried on their work with their Negro members on a remarkable basis of common Christian brotherhood with such success that today far more South Carolina Negroes adhere to that faith than to any other.

In 1848, under the direction of the Second Presbyterian Church of Charleston, Rev. James B. Adger took a step in advance of the custom of having the Negroes occupy the galleries. They were set off as a separate congregation, though still an integral part of the mother church. A $7,500 brick church for them was dedicated in 1850 and was replaced in 1859 by one costing $25,000. The opposition that had existed to the practice of having a separate congregation of Negroes, in memory of the Vesey plot of 1822 which was encouraged by a Negro congregation, now flared into such excitement that in 1859 the destruction by a mob of the rising walls of the Presbyterian building and of one being simultaneously erected by the Episcopalians was with difficulty prevented through the efforts of such citizens as James L. Petigru; but bitter opposition even in high political circles continued.[6]

It was in this, the largest church auditorium in the city, that Rev. John L. Girardeau worked as Presbyterian evangelist. White members, from whom alone the officials were chosen, were admitted in 1858 and soon constituted a sixth of the enormous congregation. The brilliant

[6] Howe, *Presbyterian Church in South Carolina,* II, 595, 608-9; *Journal of Cadet Tom Law,* 300, note.

Girardeau incurred the contempt of some "as a religious crank and bigoted fool, who was wasting his magnificent talents" on creatures little better than brutes. By stressing key words for the benefit of his ignorant hearers, as "Holy God," "sin hateful," he developed the faculty of sweeping along the Negroes while the thread of his thought fully satisfied his white hearers. When he had preached his last sermon at his former church at Willtown, the Negroes of his congregation had followed him down the road wailing, "O Lord, O my God, what mek our preacher lef us?"

The alarm roused by the opposition of the early Methodist ministers to slavery, which Wesley described as the sum of all villainies and Coke actively attacked, long excluded them from the plantations.[7] Gradually, however, their benefits to the character of the slaves led masters to desire their presence. Very notable was the work, systematized under the leadership of Rev. (later Bishop) William Capers in 1829, of missions to the great low-country plantations to which appointees of the conference gave their whole time. Yet as late as 1838 in Greenville and Abbeville districts fear was expressed that these Methodist missions and the teaching of the slaves to read would lead to abolition. The same year, Dr. (later Bishop) W. M. Wightman's public denunciation of cruelty to slaves (slaves being present in the congregation as usual) stirred sharp controversy; but the fact that slavery so thoroughly conquered the Southern branch that in 1845 it separated from the North on the issue so pleased Southern society that membership greatly increased, and planters of indifferent religious character built the Methodists houses of worship. In 1858 the twenty-four Methodist missions to the slaves comprised 12,101 of the conference's 46,740 colored members, while the white members equaled only 37,095.

The Free Negro—Race Mixture.—Free Negroes, though emerging early, did not become numerous until after the Revolution. In 1790 there were in South Carolina 1,801; in 1800, 3,185; in 1820, 6,826; in 1860, 9,914. Charleston district contained a disproportionate number (43 per cent of all in the State in 1850), the city a still larger proportion. City life offered them better opportunities. One kept a good hotel for whites. Many owned slaves. One was estimated to be worth $80,000. "The free Negroes, with the exception of those in Wilmington, Charleston, Savannah, Mobile, and New Orleans, were worse off in most other states than in Virginia."[8]

Despite the warning of several examples before and after the Revolution, South Carolina did not, before her "Black Code" of 1865, define

[7] Cf. Thos. L. Williams, "Methodist Missions to the Slaves," Yale Ph.D. thesis of 1943, MS.
[8] C. G. Woodson, in *Am. Hist. Rev.*, XLVIII (July, 1943), 812.

by statute the term Negro, or forbid intermarriage between the races. The prohibition of interracial marriage and the definition of a Negro as a person of one-eighth or more of African blood enacted in the "Black Code" of 1865 ended almost at once with the repeal of the code under Northern pressure. They were re-enacted in 1879, and were inserted in the Constitution of 1895.

The master's affection for his mulatto children, rewards for extraordinary fidelity, and a slave's purchase of his own or his wife's freedom mainly accounted for the free Negroes. Following the Revolution, a brief liberalism, and the mean desire to put off old slaves on the public during the comparative unprofitableness of slavery between the time that indigo was lost and cotton culture developed, operated perhaps in importance progressively in the order named. The law of 1800 made manumission difficult; that of 1820 forbade it; and that of 1841 forbade even sending the slaves abroad to be freed. Despite their general good behavior, the free Negroes were feared as an impeachment of some of the pro-slavery arguments. Clearly much of the denunciation of the class in 1840's and 1850's was a reaction against permitting any confirmation of the abolitionists' contention that Negroes were fit for freedom.

The tragedy and menace of the "brass ankles" (persons of slight Negro blood seeking to pass as whites), long widely known and occasionally mentioned in print, was in 1930 drawn into publicity in Mr. DuBose Heyward's drama *Brass Ankle,* and Mrs. Gertrude Shelby and Mr. Samuel G. Stoney's novel of the Hell Hole Swamp section, *Po' Buckra.* An occasional tolerance or semi-tolerance of Negroes in white society in the low country before and just after the Revolution, seeming now almost inconceivable, produced results for the elimination of which we must trust to Mendel's law and the strictest care instead of a squeamish conspiracy of silence. The loyalty of these mixed bloods as Confederate soldiers secured them a respect that made the problem still more difficult.[9]

Influence of Slavery on Southern Character.—The influence of slavery on Southern character was profound and contradictory. A recent South Carolina writer says that "The institution of slavery was largely responsible for the acute sensitiveness to criticism, restlessness under opposition or interference, and the promptness in meeting obligations which were marked traits in the planters of Edisto (Island) and the coast generally. As children playing with the young slaves, the foundation was laid.

[9] Professor F. A. Porcher, "Upper St. John's Berkeley. A Memoir," in *Transactions of the Huguenot Society of South Carolina,* November 13, 1906, p. 35, relates the case of a rich mulatto woman, educated and able, the wife of Dr. Hardcastle, widely accepted by those who accepted her hospitality (apparently about 1800-20) and futilely hoped to inherit her wealth.

They began 'bossing' those under them with an authority coexistent with their ability to stamp their little feet and shout their commands in half-articulated words. This domineering spirit increased with their years."[10]

Chancellor Harper in 1837 eulogized slavery as the buttress of morals. Our thieves and prostitutes, he held, were usually imported from the North. He traced the nobility of Southern manhood and the extraordinary chastity of Southern womanhood to the facts that men scorned every trait of the menial and that the women were protected by the welcome which slave women offered their masters. Edmund Burke's reference to certain influences of slavery on the character of the masters is to the same effect.

William Gilmore Simms acknowledged that there were great abuses in the easy gratification of white men's lust with black women—"illicit and foul conduct of many among us, who make their slaves the victims and the instruments alike of the most licentious passions."

The slave economy brought easy immediate profits, but was doomed to decline. Said General Johnson Hagood to the State Agricultural Society in 1870: "Cherishing his [the planter's] costly and highly prized labor, which was also, under the laws of the land, the largest part of his capital, his whole efforts were given to its increase, and the land bore the penalty of the favoritism—cut down, skimmed of its fertility, and thrown out to the recuperative efforts of nature, while the generous produce of its virgin soil was invested in additional laborers, and the planter and his gang passed on to other fields. There was prosperity under the system. . . . Yet was there not in all this as much of the prosperity of the Arab sheik passing . . . from oasis to oasis, as the prosperity of the agriculturist? But little improvement attached to the land. Few buildings were reared which were expected to last beyond the life of the tenant; . . . and seldom was any meliorating process vouchsafed to the soil. 'New grounds,' in plantation parlance, was the equivalent of productiveness, and 'old field' of sterility."

The reproach of Southern statesmanship is its failure, even its refusal, to attempt any solution of the slavery problem. Measureless energy was expended in proving what the South had a right to do instead of what she had better do. Few more barren fields of intellectual effort exist than the volumes of defense of the constitutional right to continue a system that the whole course of civilization had doomed. Yet solution of some kind there had to be, and it came at last, in the worst possible manner except servile insurrection, to a people who would not solve it for themselves.

[10] I. Jenkins Mikell, *Rumbling of the Chariot Wheels*, p. 204.

The mistake of the South was natural, and it was made the more so by the abolitionists. The South, in its belief that emancipation would Africanize the country and that the Negro was incapable of labor except under slavery, revealed an ignorance of the fundamental character of the Negro as great as that of the abolitionist, who thought the Negro merely a black white man.

But there was another problem, more difficult than that of slavery—the question of race. But for this, slavery would have vanished before economic and moral forces as did serfdom in Europe and indentured servitude in America. The problem of slavery was at last solved, but the problem of black and white remains.

CHAPTER XLV

AGRICULTURE, COMMERCE, AND MANUFACTURING, 1835-1860

THE ECONOMIC IDEAL of South Carolina up to 1860 remained the same as that adopted with the dominance of rice in the eighteenth century: a staple agricultural product raised in great quantities by slave gangs, a domestic transportation system to bring it to port, direct foreign trade in this commodity, with which the utilities of civilized existence were to be purchased from outside. The glorification of agriculture as morally superior to other industries discouraged the development of varied possibilities and contributed to the strength and weakness of an aristocratic planter-dominated society. Despite the great increase of population from 1790 to 1850, the average acreage of farms in South Carolina rose from 310 to 541. In many districts small farms were consolidated into plantations as the former owners moved west or degenerated. The State Agricultural Society in 1844 was interested in share-farming, a system which developed under economic compulsion after 1865.

"Summer absenteeism," a necessity in the rice region and a luxury enjoyed by many elsewhere, was an impediment to good farming. The planter's mistakes, said Colonel William J. Taylor in 1843, were leaving too much to overseers; neglect therefore to apply science to agriculture; debt, "an error of the first magnitude"; too much politics; and overemphasis on great cotton production to the neglect of stock and other crops and the preservation of fertility. Land butchery was constantly denounced, promoting, as it did, the drain of population to new Western lands, whose availability was a constant temptation to land butchery in the East. The difficulties of South Atlantic States agriculture from 1840 to 1860 were due to its own bad methods as well as to the competition of the West.

The movement of population into or out of a region is an infallible sign of its relative economic condition. The great tide of immigrants seeking opportunity in South Carolina during the twenty-five years preceding 1790 had more than trebled the population. The strong continuance of this tendency was marked by an increase of population by 40 per cent in the decade ending in 1800, but soon the effects of the causes noted above were forcing attention. The soil depletion which was already ruining some of the parishes in the early eighteenth century was now extensive and serious. The Pendleton Farmers' Society, organized in 1815, was constantly a leader for diversifying crops, checking soil erosion, and discouraging the abandonment of South Carolina for the West.[1] White population increased only 9 per cent in the decade ending with 1810, 11 per cent by 1820, 8⅔ per cent by 1830, less than .5 per cent by 1840, 6 per cent by 1850, and 6 per cent by 1860. After 1870 came the healthy increase of modern decades. Meanwhile the white majority of 31,283 in 1790 had disappeared before a Negro majority of 27,861 in 1820, which grew to 226,926 in 1890, from which it sank until in 1930 there appeared a white majority of 150,359. Fairfield County in 1930 had 19 per cent fewer white inhabitants than in 1820 and more than 200 per cent increase in Negroes. Newberry's white population of 1820 was not again equaled until 1900. In 1860, of the 470,257 white persons in the United States born in South Carolina, 193,389 had left the State—41 per cent of her most precious possessions given away largely to develop the West that was undermining her. As the superiority of opportunities elsewhere diminished, the proportion of her white children living elsewhere sunk to lower proportions: 1870, 35 per cent; 1880, 27 per cent; 1890, 21 per cent; 1900, 18 per cent; 1910, 17.1 per cent; 1920, 15.9 per cent; 1930, 18.7 per cent. Of our losses in 1860, 132,578 lived (in the order named) in Georgia, Alabama, Mississippi, Arkansas. In 1900 the State still was drawing only 38.5 per cent as many white immigrants as her white loss. *Who's Who in America* reveals the disagreeable fact that the loss of the successful has been even larger than of the average. Such must be the experience of States lacking great cities and vast natural resources.

John A. Wagener of Charleston was active in allaying the prejudice against immigrants, who were feared as possibly dangerous to slavery. In 1849 the land for the German settlement at Walhalla was bought, an economic and social benefit all too small for the State's needs. The Germans refuted the fears of their influence against slavery by proving in the War of Secession staunch defenders of their adopted State.

Progressive and Unprogressive Planters.—Thoughtful planters protested against unscientific tillage and the overemphasis on cotton. Absorption in politics or the pleasures of leisure diverted attention from such examples of skillful farming as presented by David R. Williams, George McDuffie, William Aiken, W. B. Seabrook, or James H. Hammond. Said Seabrook, pleading in the 1840's for diversification: "Maddened for a quarter of a century by the golden harvest which a delicate

[1] *Story of Soil Erosion in South Carolina Piedmont 1800 to 1860*, U. S. Dept. Ag., Mis. Publication No. 407 (1940).

shrub had spread before them, they have become men of one idea, and seemingly forever incapable to comprehend the plainest principles of domestic political economy. Still enveloped in a dark cloud of delusion, they practically persevere in the belief, that in cotton and their unaided powers, temporal bliss alone consists."

Interest in fertilization inspired the first two agricultural and geological surveys of the State. Lardner Vanuxem's hurried view of some northwestern districts accumulated some valuable general observations. The existence of marl in South Carolina and its agricultural use in Europe had long been known when widespread interest was roused by the movement for better agriculture generally about 1835 to '40. James H. Hammond, our largest experimenter with marl, in 1840 gave glowing accounts of its benefits. But the application of carbonate of lime through marling, though beneficial, failed to do all expected. Ground-up lime is now used as cheaper and better. The Virginian Edmund Ruffin's survey of South Carolina in 1843 was predominantly agricultural and economic, though he added valuable geological information. In 1844 the work was continued, but with a distinctly geological turn, by Michael Tuomey, whose final *Report on the Geology of South Carolina* in 1848 remains one of the two outstanding works on the subject. Oscar M. Lieber's work (like the others, at State expense), extending from 1856 to 1860, produced in four volumes the most valuable extant publication on our geology. As former surveys had been concerned chiefly with the low country and agriculture, he worked mainly among the crystalline rocks of the up country, for which his training in Germany especially fitted him, with the result that he greatly stimulated the mining enterprises then active. More gold is said to have been taken from the Haile Mine in Lancaster County than from any other opening east of the Mississippi. In the 1929-37 depression it was again worked, but was closed in the early 1940's by the return of prosperity and high costs of operation.

Eminent among leaders seeking from 1840 to 1860 and later to apply science, diversification, and the principle of self-support to our wasteful, declining agriculture were Dr. St. Julien Ravenel, H. W. Ravenel, and Professor Charles U. Shepard. As late as 1858, says Samuel DuBose, the plow was still little used in the parishes. The impoverishment of resources to which the Confederate soldier returned in 1865 had been bewailed as the forerunner of calamity for twenty years before the war.

Rice was a rich man's crop because of the large capital investment in dykes, etc. Olmsted in 1853-54 found that of planters each raising 20,000 pounds or over there were 446 in South Carolina, 88 in Georiga, and 25 in North Carolina. Already Louisiana was talking of her superior conditions. But in 1855 South Carolina rice took first prize in Paris, and in times of gloom we congratulated ourselves that of this crop at least we could forever almost retain a monopoly. William Gregg was shipping fine peaches in quantities to New York in the 1850's from his extensive orchard at his home at Kalmia near Aiken.

Commerce and Banking as Handmaids of Staple Agriculture.—Until a few years before the Revolutionary War the merchant was highly honored, but then, contrasted with a landed aristocracy growing rapidly richer, he declined in public esteem—a state of mind intensified after the Revolution because the merchants were generally Northerners or foreigners. The Scotch were conspicuous among the successful traders. "It is considered disreputable to attend to business of almost any kind," wrote E. S. Thomas of the years 1795 to 1816. Not a merchant but Mr. Stoney, he said, was a native, and not one was active in politics. Of our planters and professional men Blanding said in 1836 that "mercantile pursuits with them till lately have hardly been regarded reputable." Consequently, he continues, vast amounts of capital have been carried North or abroad where its retired owners may enjoy it. Charleston should "make it reputable for Carolinians to engage in trade" and should go for the Western trade. Merchandising, Governor McDuffie told the legislature in 1835, was as honorable as the professions or planting, and second only to agriculture for our prosperity. Friends of the merchants in 1839 boldly pointed out the business failings of the planters, and urged the training of their sons for trade. In 1884 William L. Trenholm, before the Charleston Chamber of Commerce, denounced this whole body of anti-commercial and anti-mechanical ideas of the ante-bellum planters.

Conditions were already changing when Henry Gourdin, son of a poor but well-born planter, at the age of twenty in 1824 took over the business of his retiring Northern employer and began one of the most honorable careers as a merchant in the history of the city. The soul of honor, the friend of Calhoun, and mainly instrumental in raising the $27,000 which relieved the embarrassed estate of the dead statesman, Gourdin was loved by all but the base, whose schemes he did not hesitate, at personal danger, to expose, and he fulfilled the highest ideals of the merchant and citizen. *DeBow's Review,* of intense Southern loyalty, like its Charleston editor, placed on its first issue, January, 1846, "Commerce is King," and kept it there, though slighting no aspect of Southern economic life.

Charleston needed all her native talent and patriotism. Said a committee of the City Council in 1828, when the exports of the city equaled about $7,000,000 annually; "Charleston . . . has for several years past retrograded with a rapidity unprecedented. Her landed estate has, within eight years, depreciated in value one-half. Industry and business talent driven by necessity, have sought employment elsewhere. Many of her houses are tenantless, and the grass grows uninterrupted in some of the chief business streets."

As Savannah and later Wilmington developed, Charleston's need of the interior far exceeded the interior's need of Charleston. Right bravely and intelligently did she combat natural disadvantages. Her three great needs were enlarged banking facilities, a railroad across the mountains, and a deeper harbor entrance to make possible direct steam lines to Europe. The Bank of Charleston was chartered in 1834 with a capital of $2,000,000 (larger than that of the Bank of the State), soon raised to $3,600,000. The Southwestern Railroad Bank, established in 1836 with authorized capital of $6,000,000, also soon gained a large business.

The Transportation Problem.—Hayne's heroic efforts a generation ahead of his times to create a railroad from Charleston to Cincinnati were doomed to failure. Hayne yearned for a bond of political as well as economic union between the sections, but the utterances of his associates and successors revealed rather the desire to band the South more firmly for the defense of her peculiar institutions. While the vast Charleston-to-Cincinnati scheme floundered amid interstate diplomacy and financial straits, Georgia shrewdly moved for the benefit of her own Savannah. The ghostly chance for a line from Charleston to the Ohio vanished with Hayne's death in 1839 and the withdrawal of Tennessee's co-operation a year later.

Charleston's third desideratum, direct steam lines to Europe, was mingled with a general Southern effort for this. She also sought steamship connection with the North. The little steamers tried in 1833 or earlier proved unsatisfactory. Success came with *The Southerner,* built for the New York-to-Charleston trade in 1846, followed by *The Northerner, The James Adger, The Marion,* and *The Nashville.*

The South's direct European trade movement was launched at a convention in Augusta on October 10, 1837, consisting of four delegates from Louisville in addition to those from South Carolina and Georgia. Such commercial conventions met in various Southern cities in many years until the one at Vicksburg in 1859, and became means of organizing sentiment on general Southern needs and grievances.

The ambitious railroad plans of the thirties were followed in South Carolina by a long period of inaction. After the completion of the South Carolina Railroad to Hamburg, 136 miles, on October 3, 1833, the next line finished was the 66 miles from Branchville to Columbia in 1842, followed by the Camden branch (37 miles) in 1848. The fifties saw great activity in South Carolina, as all over the country, and all but 239 of the 1,002 miles in the State in 1860 were built in eleven years. Charleston was the leader, in hopes of being enriched as the port for the trade of many States; but her politicians and capitalists, subscribing tiny amounts, sought to put the cost off on the city or the State.

The State aided the railroads liberally by buying stock or guaranteeing bonds. Before 1860 it had bought $2,279,000 of the stock of railroads in the State, besides a $100,000 loan on stock, and had guaranteed $2,225,000 of their bonds, besides $2,200,000 pledged to the unbuilt Louisville, Chicago and Ohio Railroad. The 1,002 miles in operation in 1860 had cost about $16,000,000. The only disastrous enterprise was the Blue Ridge, on which the State risked two millions, not to speak of millions after 1865. The thirteen miles in South Carolina of this ill-fated enterprise, a revival of Hayne's Cincinnati plans, this time by way of Rabun Gap in extreme northeastern Georgia, were built by 1860. Tunnels, cuts, and embankments in four States mark the unused route of the most calamitous railroad enterprise in South Carolina history. Every line of its connections led to a port—Charleston, Wilmington, or Savannah—revealing the rivalry of these ports for the commerce of the interior.

Professor Phillips thinks that railroads hurt the South by making it easier to export staples and import manufactures, thus intensifying the economic evils she suffered from and impeding the needed manufacturing and agricultural diversification. The world got its cotton cheaper and sold the South more goods at better prices.

Cotton Manufacturing.—Not until the South realized that slavery was in danger did she develop a systematic opposition to manufacturing. To the argument of economic and social protection was added a sentimentalizing of the nobility of agriculture as almost the only fit support for a gentleman. Faced in the 1820's with the alternative of staking all on slave-sustained agriculture or developing a varied agricultural and industrial life, she chose the former. In 1828 Elias Horry urged the weaving by our up-country streams of our needed cloth; but in 1831 an editor suffered a beating for charging a candidate with owning factory stocks.

Yet the Saluda Factory near Columbia was organized in 1832. Vaucluse (Aiken County), after having been burned, reopened under a charter of 1833. Unwisely organized and operated, Vaucluse's losses weaned McDuffie, an early stockholder and president, from his faith in Southern manufactures. The DeKalb Factory near Camden, organized in 1838, profitably made shoes and cloth. The Marlboro Factory closed shortly before 1845. The Pendleton Factory, now a part of the LaFrance Company, dates from 1838, with an extinct predecessor of about 1828 in the district. Bivingsville, chartered in 1837 and again in 1838, has become through reorganizations the D. E. Converse Company. Only Pendleton and Bivingsville of these early mills have operated continuously to the present. Vaucluse, burned in 1867, has again operated since 1877. David R. Williams' mill and Saluda (and Vaucluse for a while) used Negro labor, as did also Vaucluse in its early years. DeKalb used white labor. The fact that prospects were thus presented for further slave profits, and that the mills combated New England's monopoly, won the approval of editors and politicians of the late twenties and early thirties.

By 1841 we find a strengthening of sentiment in favor of manufacturing, though its advocacy had never ceased. Vigorous protest was registered in 1842 against the injustice to white artisans of teaching Negroes any mechanical occupation. The growth of this view alarmed Memminger, who wrote in 1849 that a mass of white craftsmen, sure to attempt to dominate capital, "is in truth the only party from which danger to our institution is to be apprehended amongst us. . . . [They] would soon raise here the cry against the Negro, and be hot abolitionists. And every one of these men would vote." Cheves, McDuffie, and Calhoun opposed all Southern manufacturing, as likely to create a pro-tariff element and destroy the unity without which slavery could not be protected. The best leaders of the movement for Southern manufacturing replied that, on the contrary, manufactures would not only benefit our poor whites but would draw them out of competition with slave labor, though a number of factories used slaves for operatives. In 1845 there were 15 cotton mills, employing 570 persons, and 3 small woolen mills in the State, and more were being urged, notably by William Gregg, as our salvation in the face of the competition of the Southwest's rich lands with our exhausted soil and the drain on our resources as buyers of finished products from the North.

The smallness of existing mills emphasizes the revolution wrought both in opinion and in production by the writings of William Gregg in 1844-45, and by his Graniteville factory, the first large-scale mill in the State and one of the first of that class in the South. Gregg, the chief founder of cotton manufacturing on a great scale in the South, whose policies strongly influenced the industry, was born in southwestern Pennsylvania* in 1800 and came to South Carolina in 1824 as a jewelry master workman. He quickly accumulated a fortune in Columbia, which

* A letter from Gregg's older sister, discovered a few years ago by Dr. Thomas P. Martin of the Library of Congress shows that Gregg was born in southwestern Pennsylvania. The previous statements that he was born in what is now West Virginia arose from the long dispute as to the boundary line.—*Jour. So. Hist.*, XI, 389-423 (August, 1945).

he increased in Charleston, and never took off his workman's apron until he was worth $50,000. In 1844 he published in the *Courier* a series of articles on "Domestic Industry." Southwestern fertility was taking the very bread from our mouths, wrote Gregg. Only by giving our poor whites factory employment could we save our profits and our people. We could never be prosperous while we imported hoe handles, stone, seed, vegetables, and dairy products from the North. "The manufacturer who adds more to the value of the cotton than the price the planter gets does a better service to the country than the men who continue to glut the market with cotton. Our enormous unused water powers offer us that profit." Slaves would make good factory hands, but, Gregg continued:

"Shall we pass unnoticed the thousands of poor, ignorant, degraded white people among us, who, in this land of plenty, live in comparative nakedness and starvation? Many a one is reared in proud South Carolina, from birth to manhood who never passed a month in which he has not some part of the time been stinted for meat. . . .

"That we are behind the age in agriculture, the mechanic arts, industry and enterprise, is apparent to all who pass through our State; our good city of Charleston speaks a language on this subject not to be mistaken; she has lost 1,000 of her population, according to the census of 1840, while her sister cities have doubled and quadrupled theirs. . . . Where is the city in this age of improvement, except Charleston, that a bookbinder or job printer is prohibited in the use of a small steam engine, to enable him to carry on his business with more facility, and to cheapen the price of those articles that we are purchasing from other cities, more liberal to their artisans? Where a carpenter is not allowed the use of the same, to turn a circular saw or drive a mortising chisel, to enable him to compete with others in supplying us with ready made doors, blinds, sashes, shutters, etc? This power is withheld lest the smoke of an engine should disturb the delicate nerves of an agriculturist; or the noise of the mechanic's hammer should break in upon the slumber of a real estate holder, or an importing merchant, while he is indulging in fanciful dreams of building on paper, the *Queen City of the South*—the *paragon* of the age."

Let our politicians, he concludes, who regard themselves as the representatives of a State the paragon of perfection capable of instructing the whole world in political economy, consider our prostrate agriculture, our vast white illiteracy, poverty, and the ready means of correcting these conditions. "Let us try to cultivate a good feeling among our people, for our northern brethren. . . . Let us offer inducements that shall bring their working men to our delightful climate. They will teach our children lessons of industry and economy . . . and above all, they will give some of our wise men practical lessons in Political Economy."

Thus, as it will seem to many a modern student, while Calhoun was expounding metaphysical doctrines of the Constitution to hold this State in a bondage that could only grow worse the better he succeeded, the industrial statesman was pointing out the means of really promoting the general and permanent interests of the State. Gregg stood where Calhoun had stood before he surrendered to the Southern conception of slave economy and, by becoming the faithful follower of his people, became their powerful and cherished leader. Gregg saw the South's economic problem as a whole, including the poor whites, created, neglected, and despised by the plantation system. He realized that the preservation of all the South's natural and human resources was the only basis for permanent prosperity.

There was still at that time even among the wealthy a widespread prejudice against corporations except for banking and transportation. The South Carolina limited liability partnership law of 1837 was denounced as a promoter of fraud. In 1845 the legislature chartered the Graniteville Manufacturing Company. The capital of $300,000 was quickly raised by thirty stockholders, a large proportion of them in Charleston. The launching of this large-scale factory, its eminent success, and its laying down of social and business lines since followed, constitute an era in Southern manufacturing and rank Gregg as one of the most important men in its history.

Gregg intended to organize a great Graniteville and then depend on hired experts, but he found this impossible. For eight years he gave his services free, and then accepted a moderate salary, and finally died from exposure in working waist-deep in water repairing the broken dam. The sacrifice was the more notable as he had retired from his jewelry business with an ample fortune; it marked him as an apostle of a new social and industrial era. The whole-souled companion of the village boys, he was just as much the benevolent despot. Regulations excluded low characters and held the moral standards at a level that meant high productivity as well as healthy home life. He enforced his prohibition of liquor by breaking jugs of violators, and followed this with the threat of his buggy whip. Compulsory attendance at the school maintained by the company was enforced by the whip on the children or fines on the parents—one of the first systems of compulsory education in the country. No child below the school age (twelve) could work in the mill.

Gregg's only wage dispute (1857) was easily settled, but not so the differences with his directors on the policy of dyeing and finishing goods and the policy of sales. A powerful director continued to enjoy a larger income as sales agent than the president ever got as manufacturer. Though originally holding that Southern coarse goods needed no tariff, by 1859 Gregg had fulfilled Calhoun's prophecy by becoming an open protectionist, and during the War of Secession, when Graniteville became a resource of the Confederacy second only to a munition plant, he bitterly complained of the government's unsympathetic attitude.

The lack of encouragement by the Confederacy toward manufactures (to glance forward) sprang from complex causes, among which was the belief that the war would be short, as well as from the traditional Southern politician's attitude. But Southern businessmen were ahead of the politicians. South Carolina indeed fell slightly backward in cotton manufacturing during the 1850's, but not so the South at large. The eleven States of the future Confederacy increased their manufactures 114.87 per cent during the decade ending with 1860 as against 85.5 per cent for the country as a whole.[2] Unheeded in South Carolina went Governor Seabrook's annual message in 1850 urging that the State remove all barriers to manufacturing so as to secure our independence of the North, with whom we would probably never be friendly.

The incorporation of Graniteville and Gregg's powerful public utterances led to the repeal in 1845 of Charleston's prohibition of steam engines, to a general incorporation law in South Carolina in 1847 for manufacturing, and to the building of several factories. But in 1848 Memminger defeated the effort of Charleston financial leaders to have the house institute a bureau of statistics and a standing committee on commerce, manufactures, and mechanical industry. It is incredible, said the committee favoring the request, that the very stones of the capitol gateposts were brought from New England, though the finest granite in the world is in sight of the building. "Our other natural resources remain in similar disuse," they continued. "Though agriculture is the basis of our fabric, it is but one remove from the hunter stage of civilization," and should be supplanted by mechanical arts characteristic of the highest civilization.

Iron Production.—As early as 1773 small quantities of iron were made in Catalan forges in the province along the Piedmont slope. William Hill, the grandfather of General D. H. Hill of the Confederate army, had his blast furnace on Allison's Creek in York County. Hill resumed operations in York County shortly after the Revolution. The Aera

[2] These figures, based on the federal censuses of 1840, 1850, and 1860, constitute a correction of the statement in my large *History of South Carolina,* III, 16, bottom of the page. Cf. also Avery Craven, *The Coming of the Civil War,* pp. 286-88.

Furnace, amid ore lying virtually on the surface, was erected two miles west of the Catawba River in 1787, and the Aetna near by in 1788.

A small blast furnace was erected on King's Creek near Blacksburg in 1822, and in 1824 Stroup began the erection of works on Broad River. These works were bought in 1824 by the King's Mountain Iron Company with a capital of $100,000. The company erected a blast furnace in 1827, which it replaced by a larger one in 1837. E. Graham erected a rolling mill in Union District in 1832.

In 1837 the Magnetic Iron Company with a capital of $250,000 built at Cherokee Ford on Broad River near Blacksburg four furnaces, a rolling mill, a nail factory, etc. About the same time a furnace was erected by the South Carolina Manufacturing Company near the old Cowpens battlefield. This company also built a rolling mill and a nail factory at Hurricane Shoals on the Pacolet, now the site of the Clifton Cotton Mill No. 1. These plants were operated to capacity during the War of Secession making bolts, shells, etc. They were bankrupted by the result of the war, not to speak of the scarcity of fuel and ore.

The Register of Mesne Conveyance records show there had been old ironworks on the east side of Tyger River near Hill's cotton factory before 1819. In 1825 a Spartanburg furnace was smelting gray ore, and one in that district and one in York were smelting brown ore. Mills's *Statistics of South Carolina* in 1826 noted that Benson's Iron Works were operating in Greenville, and that another near the Village had been burned. His *Atlas of South Carolina* shows ironworks in Greenville District on Enoree River just west of the Spartanburg line.

An enterprise that played its part in stirring the attack on the Bank of the State on account of its assistance to the private enterprises of its officers (though with no corruption) was the Nesbit Iron Manufacturing Company in the present Cherokee County, chartered in 1836 with authorized capital of $300,000. F. H. Elmore was not only president of the Bank of the State but also acting president of the Nesbit Company during its embarrassment.[3] The product of the Nesbit Company was of very high quality. The failure of the company was due to the financial stress of the panic of 1837 and the insufficiency of capital for large-scale operations. When the property was sold in about 1850 or a little earlier for $174,000, the proceeds were enough to save the Bank of the State all its loan except about two or three thousand dollars.

It would be wearisome to trace in detail the history of the several paper mills, sugar refineries, potteries, carriage factories, and shoe factories that either flourished or languished during the two decades before 1860. It is a typical story of the effort of a new section to build up diver-

[3] The Company was later reorganized as the Swedish Iron Manufacturing Company.

sified industry in the face of competition by established plants. The smallest difference in price caused merchants to buy in the North despite appeals to patronize Southern industries. Customers preferred Northern products because they were believed to be superior to those of South Carolina. At the second annual fair of the South Carolina Industrial Institute in Charleston in 1850, South Carolina manufactures on exhibit included textiles, a buggy made in Columbia, and iron from Spartanburg. The 1852 exhibit included a steam engine manufactured in Charleston, and, from various parts of the State, buckets, car wheels, fine coaches, harness, sewing machines, ironwork, agricultural machinery, shoes, brooms, rope, hats, etc. There were at about the same time in Charleston manufacturers of stained glass, silverware, a small schooner, freight cars (following the locomotive made there in 1834), paper, crockery, and furniture. About the 1830's and until driven out by the Connecticut clockmakers, Chester "made" handsome grandfather clocks, and Laurens, Hamburg, and Columbia smaller clocks; but Mr. A. S. Salley is doubtless correct in considering the craftsmen merely assemblers of works in cases made by themselves. The German Christopher Werner, the maker of the splendid metal palmetto tree in Columbia commemorating the Palmetto Regiment and the Simonton mansion sword gates in Charleston; Strohecker, the maker of the sword grating in the old Charleston police station; and I. W. Justi, the maker of the exquisite iron gates of St. Michael's churchyard, were among the craftsmen whose skill made Charleston ironwork before 1860 famous. Silversmithing was practiced by many craftsmen in Charleston and Columbia and some smaller places until localized in the Northeast.

Charleston, the Graniteville region, Greenville, and Spartanburg were the chief manufacturing centers. There were eight furnaces in 1856, the four in Spartanburg giving her the name of "the old iron district." Greenville's coach factory, employing 100 men and selling $80,000 worth of vehicles a year, was said to be the largest in the Southern country. Greenville and Spartanburg were already active in cotton manufacturing, though in small factories. The statistics of cotton mills in South Carolina for 1850 and 1860 respectively showed an actual loss in the decade; 18 mills to 17; 1,019 employees to 891; $857,000 capital invested to $801,825, with Graniteville alone representing $400,000 of the last figure. Virginia, North Carolina, and Alabama in 1860 each had more than 50 per cent more capital in cotton mills than did South Carolina; Louisiana and Tennessee almost a fifth more; and Georgia two and two-thirds as much. The total value of all manufactures in South Carolina in 1860 (omitting $1,100,000 put down in Georgetown as the total value of rice cleaned, and including everything from blacksmithing up) was $7,519,195, produced by a capital investment of $6,931,756.

The general Southern attitude had sunk back into the old view that manufacturing was not for the South. The eleven future Confederate States produced in the year ending June 30, 1860, 8.8 per cent of the total manufactures of the United States as against almost 13 per cent in 1930.[4] The South thus went into the War of Secession unprepared to win. An industrialized South could not have been conquered.

[4] United States Censuses of 1860 and 1930. The proportions stated in my three-volume *History of South Carolina* are incorrect.

CHAPTER XLVI

INTELLECTUAL LIFE AND INSTITUTIONS, 1783-1860

THE PUBLIC paid for the instruction of a few poor children in the so-called "free schools" of the province from 1710, but private enterprise long antedated public, and for a much longer time supplied a far superior service. "If ever a Carolinian has reason to blush for his country," wrote Chairman Richard Hutson of the Mount Zion board, "it must be, when he considers that it has advanced upwards of a century in age, before it has one academy of any reputation in it." The gentlemen who formed the Mount Zion Society in 1777 had conducted a flourishing school at Winnsboro until it was ruined by the Revolution, but had now, Hutson wrote in 1784, engaged as master a graduate of the College of New Jersey and were taking subscriptions. In 1785 the legislature chartered three colleges, one at Winnsboro on the Mount Zion foundation, one at Cambridge near the present Ninety Six, and one at Charleston. Considerable donations were divided among the three, all of which went into operation. That at Charleston began in 1790, though not until 1825-27 did it attain college rank. The present Winnsboro High School is the descendant without break of the Mount Zion College.

General Sumter and Dr. Richard Furman advertised on May 4, 1786, that the seminary of learning designed for Stateburg was now open, and that the gentleman who would preside brought remarkable testimonials from America and Europe. In 1795 Beaufort College was incorporated, and in 1797 the College of Alexandria near Pinckneyville, the now extinct court town for four counties, in the northeastern corner of Union County. The former opened in 1804 and became an important academy; the latter was apparently never organized. The "free school" existing in Columbia apparently from 1792 or earlier is evidently the same as the Academy incorporated in 1795. John De La Howe's legacy in 1796, at first primarily for illegitimate children (later broadened to serve poor children of any sort), originated the first manual labor school in the United States.

Dr. Waddel's Willington.—The most famous of the early academies was that of Dr. Moses Waddel (1770-1840). When his young brother-in-law Calhoun was put to his school, then in Georgia, the few schools within fifty miles of Calhoun's home imperfectly taught the three R's, says Calhoun's 1843 biography; but Abner Pyles's contemporary journal mentions schools in that region at that time taught by college graduates. Waddel as a teaching Presbyterian minister was typical of a class exceptionally important in educating the American people in the early nineteenth century. Such a number of its ministers left the pulpit for academies and college professorships as seriously to check the growth of the denomination. In 1826 Mills's *Statistics* stated the numerical strength of denominations in South Carolina in the following order: Methodists, Presbyterians, Baptists, Episcopalians, Roman Catholics, Jews, Unitarians, Universalists, Quakers.

In 1804 Waddel began his school at Willington, in the present McCormick County. Here in cheap log huts lived his 150 boys, ranging from the wealthy aristocrats of Charleston to the then poor and obscure McDuffie. Each small group of students were carried forward according to their ability. Calhoun went from here to the Junior class at Yale, and others to the same class elsewhere.

A famous school from 1820 to 1850 was that of the Englishman Christopher Coates of Charleston. Like the better academies generally, his had many boarding pupils from a distance. Academies dotted the State before 1860, besides many endowed, church-, or society-supported schools of lower grade.

South Carolinians liked military education, and from 1812 or earlier not only sustained several private military boarding schools, and from 1842 the publicly supported Arsenal in Columbia giving the first year and the Citadel in Charleston giving the last three years of a military course, but between 1820 and '40 (Colonel O. J. Bond tells me) sent about a hundred boys to Captain Partridge's famous military school in Vermont.[1]

The limited class patronizing the academies thus enjoyed excellent training.

Founding the South Carolina College.—A double motive led to the establishment in 1801 of the South Carolina College, which opened in 1804: the desire to avoid the necessity of sending boys away, and the need of obliterating the dangerous up-country-low-country sectionalism by educating the sons of the State together. Both aims were very considerably accomplished. Dean O. F. Crow of the South Carolina University School of Education shows that the statement of Chancellor DeSaussure in his old age that the up-country committee members op-

[1] Alden Partridge was a persistent pioneer advocate of military schools in this country. His school at Norwich, Vermont, and at times elsewhere, was crude but rigorous. See F. A. Porcher's "Memoirs," *South Carolina Historical and Genealogical Magazine,* XLV (July, 1944), 146 *et seq.*

posed is incorrect. Chancellor Harper's extreme statement in his eulogy on DeSaussure as to up-country opposition in general is probably derived from the same source. Again to quote Dean Crow, the college was established with hardly a record vote. The record votes that were demanded were overwhelmingly for the college. President Jonathan Maxcy and one professor instructed the twenty-nine students of the first session. Maxcy, of charitable breadth in religion, energetic, eloquent, and the successful ex-president of Rhode Island and Union colleges, was a learned Baptist minister. The college soon became the darling of the State, the most eminent public men prizing a trusteeship as an honor and jealously regarding every move that might raise up to it any rival.

The Free School System, 1811.—An aristocratic society in the most individualistic State in an individualistic age naturally neglected the education of the masses. In 1811 Governor Middleton, backed by petitions from numerous districts, recommended free schools. The chairman of the committee favoring the bill was Stephen Elliott of Charleston, leader of the intellectuals of the city, our most notable botanist, largely the founder, and first president, of the Bank of the State. The paucity of the appropriation of $37,200 made possible at most one elementary free school for each member of the lower house, that is 124 schools for all South Carolina. The preference ordered for the poor and orphans damned the system, thus predestined to become "pauper schools" instead of a public school system for all the people as the Elliott group had desired. This miserable makeshift, sometimes even in governors' messages called "pauper schools," defeated its own purpose, for the poor largely refused to accept a bounty that carried with it a stigma. Little improvement followed except doubling the appropriation in 1852, thus making the total $74,400 annually until after the War of Secession. In large towns there were free schools for the poor only, but generally the fund for the district (i.e., the later county) was used to pay the tuition of poor children applying at private schools. Thus in many districts there were no "free schools."

Seeking to Improve the Free Schools, 1825-52.—On December 20, 1825, the legislature requested the South Carolina College faculty to prepare a detailed system for the better regulation of "public schools" and other seminaries of learning. Said the report, November 28, 1826, the number of children taught at public expense in 746 schools is 9,061. Our "laborious citizens" revolt at alms. Even the poorest should be required to pay at least one dollar a quarter per child. To educate one's children is as obligatory as to feed them. The districts (counties) should be required to tax themselves as much as the State gives. Teachers should be certified by our faculty after examination and be paid at least $350 a year.

The result of the report was nil. The reactionary tone of a legislative committee report of 1833 reversed the generosity with which the low country had generally defended the educational interests of the up country against itself. The "lower division's" taxes (that is, the old districts of Georgetown, Charlestown, and Beaufort) in 1831 were $144,570 and its receipts for schools $14,172, said the committee, whereas the "upper division" paid $127,636 and received $22,005; this drain of $7,833 would ultimately impoverish the lower division. Thus the committee established the false principle of a paying section and a receiving section as does the tariff. Let each district, they said, receive the same proportion as it pays. The legislature rejected this excessive localism that denied a State-wide interest in the character of its population.

In 1820-21 the State government collected in taxes $254,651 and spent for the South Carolina College $55,900 and for free schools $40,466. The college took and held high rank in the country as did a number of the academies; but not so the teachers in the free schools. The distinction must always be maintained between the often splendid men and women of the church or fraternal order and society-owned or other private schools and the educational riffraff who taught the "pauper schools." Of the latter said Governor Henagan to the legislature in 1840: "The men who take charge of the public schools, and accept so miserable a pittance as a reward of their labors are they who cannot get employment on any other terms. . . . It is now in South Carolina a reproach to be a teacher in a free school, as it is regarded as prima facie evidence of a want of qualification."

But conditions were bad enough in many a private school. Said a writer in 1856: This low-country "old field school" was a log cabin of about 18 by 20 feet with cracks daubed with mud, and a window without glass. Opposite the door a log had been left out for the purpose of admitting light on the blackboard. "As we sat at the board with backs to the teacher, he would suddenly crack our knuckles so that the memory pains them. Our feet could not reach the floor from the hard benches." It was a peculiarity of the arithmetic that the master found that every hard example had the answer given wrong; and he refused to teach any Latin text except that of Clark, who printed the English translation in a parallel column, "which he advised us to keep covered while we studied." This school was in a rich neighborhood, and two of the trustees were worth a hundred Negroes apiece. The alternative in thinly settled regions, for those who were able, he continued, was a boarding school or a tutor, both highly objectionable, and this left the mass unprovided for.

The decade from 1840 to '50 was one of great educational activity in the United States and was marked at its beginning and its end by spasmodic but ineffective efforts in South Carolina. The legislature in 1838 ordered the School Commissioners of the forty-five "election districts" (that is, the low-country parishes and the up-country divisions now called counties) to report on the free schools with a view to their improvement. The reports of the twenty-six boards obeying were submitted to the Reverends J. H. Thornwell and Stephen Elliott, Jr., of the College and formed the basis of their report of 1839. The difficulties, said the professors, were physical and moral, that is, sparseness of population and the indifference of parents. The poor preferred a profit from their children or with foolish disdain refused to accept what they could not pay for. The system worked well only in Charleston. Free schools for the whole population, without sacrificing higher education and lowering school standards, were impossible except at an expense of $200,000 or $300,000 a year on a population "independent in their thinking and wedded to their notions and habits. Let us create a superintendent of free schools with a judge's salary. Let us dismiss the sectional prejudices of 1811 which forced the distribution of funds according to representation and put the funds where the poor children are. At present, the money goes, in the largest quantities where there are fewest people, and most wealth. Let the poor when placed in private schools be as nearly as possible on the same footing as the self-payers," so as to avoid neglect by the teacher or humiliation through dependence on the State. The Bible should be taught. The appropriation should be $50,000, and a training school for teachers should be maintained.

The recommendation for a State superintendent failed, as it was to fail again and again until 1868. The appropriation was doubled in 1852, and a normal school authorized in 1857, but the vicious system remained the same as it had been since it was founded in 1710 and refounded in 1811. Said Governor Seabrook in 1850, "Education has been provided by the legislature, but for one class of the citizens of the State, which is the wealthy class. For the middle and poorer classes of society, it has done nothing, since no organized system has been adopted for that purpose." Governor Seabrook even urged that the local authorities be allowed to assess a tax equal to the amount received from the State. "Many considerations press upon the State to rouse her from her lethargy, from her deathlike torpor," said a special committee of 1846.

In 1853 J. W. Tucker of Spartanburg appealed for a further and more varied reform than the doubling of the appropriation the year before. His bill provided for dividing the election districts into school districts, the creation of the office of State superintendent of common schools, the apportionment of the appropriation according to population instead of representation, and raising the amount to $100,00. Tucker spoke for the more democratic up country and took occasion to denounce the aristocratic theories of government widely held in the plantation section. Of a writer in the *Southern Quarterly Review* he said, "He has condescended to inform the freemen of the State that it is a matter of no consequence or interest to the humbler classes of the State whether they are educated or not; nor whether they possess the elective franchise or not; that the common education of the people is productive of as much evil as good; and finally, 'in spite of the falsehoods which constitutions proclaim to the contrary, the privileged few must govern.'" Tucker maintained the contrary. There is, he said, "no limitation to the progress and perfectibility of the people"; and if slavery itself is to be sustained against the united opinion of the world, it must be by elevating the entire white population in intelligence. "If you would build up Southern power, you must educate the Southern people, the people, the common people, and add tone, activity and energy to the Southern mind. Our danger is at home."

While it is true that the democratic ideals voiced by Tucker were more characteristic of the upper than of the lower part of the State, it is also true that liberal-minded low-country leaders, through their breadth of view and their public influence, were strongly influential in what progress was accomplished toward making the school system of service to the masses of the people. Governor Seabrook attempted in 1850 to organize the teachers of the State. The Teachers' Association then formed evaporated in eighteen months, but in 1870 it took form again for two years and was finally organized permanently as the State Teachers' Association in 1881.

In the fifties the uneasy consciousness was stirring that the accepted order of Southern society was unsatisfactory. Instead of the traditional order of an aristocratic class to lead and govern, a slave class to sustain them, and a sturdy poor white class to furnish the essential physical power to defend them, it began to be recognized that in order to avoid the antagonism observed in the rest of the world between the two white classes there must be emphasized their identity of interest. The poor white man must be made the owner of at least one slave, said the advocates of the reopening of the African slave trade. All white men must be given a common sense of unity and superiority, said the philosophical broad-minded Trescot and likewise the pro-slave-trade Governor Adams. Doubling the appropriation for schools was part of this program, but it failed to move the bulk of the ruling class from their ingrained ideas of an aristocratic republic.

Charleston Adopts a Modern School System.—The revolution in Charleston's schools in 1856, placing her on a par with the leading cities of the country, was possible (though such an advance was not then possible to the State at large) because she was a wealthy, concentrated community. C. G. Memminger and W. J. Bennett (son of the Governor who had adopted the orphan Memminger) visited New York and New England to study their systems. A. G. Magrath also was active. Successful common schools in Nashville and New Orleans proved that slave-holding communities could act for the common good.

The commissioners in 1856 launched the great experiment of transforming for Charleston the pauper free schools into what Stephen Elliott and his associates of 1811 had intended, genuine American common schools. The system was modeled on New York's. F. A. Sawyer of Boston and eventually nine Northern teachers familiar with modern methods were obtained. The commissioners prepared for three hundred pupils and were overwhelmed with six hundred, now that the stigma of "pauper school" had been removed. Textbooks were free. The legislature in December authorized a local tax of 15 per cent of the general tax. Before the year was out parents of all classes, converted by the character of the work, had sent in applications for 1,500 children. Enrollment in 1859-60 reached 2,786. The good manners and attainments of the children, said the commissioners, had cast to the winds the fears about mixing classes of society. A city normal school was established by 1860. Thus Charleston, by one of the most important educational advances in our history, was about to lead the State into a modern system when it was prevented by war.

The peculiar mingling of the publicly educated poor in the private schools, their partial segregation in their own free schools, and the bending of South Carolina terminology to that of the census make the census figures of 1860 unsatisfactory. The 757 schools classed under "public schools," teaching 20,716 pupils, clearly included schools being paid by the public for the tuition of pupils on the public funds; for (not to discuss other evidence) the income of these schools from endowments and tuition, neither of which the free schools possessed, far exceeded their income from "taxation" and "public funds," items which are reported in a way that cannot be understood. In addition, 226 "Academies and other schools" had 8,277 pupils, with an income per pupil of three and one-half times that of the "public schools." The total school enrollment was thus 28,993 out of an estimated school age population of 60,000. Persons over 20 years of age unable to read and write are stated at 14,792. This was a great improvement over the approximately 20,000 illiterates of 1840 and doubtless had its connection with the stimulated interest in education marked by the doubling of the free school appropriation in 1852 and the revolutionary advance of Charleston in 1856.

Seeking to Expel Dr. Cooper.—Returning to the South Carolina College: After the death of the Baptist minister Dr. Maxcy in 1820 the presidency passed in 1821 to Dr. Thomas Cooper, an aggressive materialist who denied immortality or Biblical inspiration. "Almost idolized for his genius and learning," he was an irrepressible propagandist for his ideas of truth and liberty. The backbone of the college consisted of the Presbyterians. Hateful to Cooper were the Presbyterian clergy, educated, able, the natural leaders of the evangelicals against Cooper's aggressive campaign against the Christian church. The composure with which the rationalistic Jefferson or the Unitarian Calhoun awaited the disintegration of Trinitarianism was impossible to Cooper, the propagandist incapable of tolerating unrebuked what he considered harmful error. In 1813 there were in the college 177 Presbyterian students, 31 Episcopalians, 20 Baptists, and a few Methodists.

So powerful were Cooper's prestige and his political support that only his persistent sneering at the clergy and his annual attack on the Bible in a lecture on the Pentateuch to each Senior class could rouse an irresistible opposition. In 1832 he was publicly tried before the trustees. He conducted his defense with great brilliancy from the point of view of one standing on his civil rights, but with little reference to the real question at issue, i.e., whether an open propagandist against revealed religion should use his position as president to assist his anti-Christian crusade. The students diminished in 4 years from 115 to 50 under a president whom the majority of the owners of the College abominated. South Carolina would soon have suppressed attacks half as ruthless on her system of government. Yet the culmination of ten years' attack upon Cooper resulted in 1832 in his acquittal. It was a complex verdict. Professor Malone, while considering it the essential defense of religious freedom by a State institution, thinks the controlling consideration was the determination of the Nullificationists, just then triumphant over bitter opposition, to stand by their champion. It doubtless also registered the widespread indifference to religion and the commonness of Jeffersonian deism that had been strong in South Carolina since before the Revolution. The next year, Dr. Cooper, now aged seventy-four, was offered the co-operation of distinguished lawyers in founding a law school, and resigned the college presidency. Thus ended the teaching career of one of the bravest, frankest, and ablest minds of American public life. His last years were spent not in teaching but in compiling the statute law of the province and State. The first five volumes of the *Statutes at Large of South Carolina* constitute a noble monument to his ability and industry.

In the reorganization of the faculty in 1835 another of the most brilliant minds in its history was enlisted, Francis Lieber. To placate evangelical opinion, the chair of Evidences of Christianity and Sacred Literature was created and offered to Dr. (later Bishop) William Capers of the Methodist Church, but his church, unwilling to lose him from its pulpit, objected. Rev. Stephen Elliott (later Episcopal Bishop of Georgia) accepted the chair, and the next year the eminent Presbyterian divine, Dr. James H. Thornwell, accepted another chair.

The turbulence of student life was at times astonishing. In 1814 Professor Blackburn's house was assailed, his daughter, appearing at a window of Mrs. Blackburn's sickroom to protest, was made a target for bricks, and she and her sister had to take shelter behind furniture in the sickroom. A tutor's windows were smashed. The militia were summoned and guarded one residence all night. Grave difficulty arose in 1823 when each student was asked whether he was the shameful defiler of the chapel pulpit. The police were at times severely beaten in true medieval town-and-gown fashion. In 1858, for tarring the benches when a holiday was refused, 102 of the students were suspended. At the same time there were disorders among the cadets at the Citadel, Yorkville, and the Arsenal, and soon the "urchins" of the Newberry Male Academy aspired to "college honors" by imitating the South Carolina College students and forced the closing of the Academy.

The College entered upon a prosperous era with the presidency of William C. Preston. Its faculty included men of intellectual distinction, and it educated a large proportion of the State's leaders. The political atmosphere descending from so long a tradition even in 1901 appears in the list entitled "Jewels of Carolina," including only alumni who had been generals, governors, congressmen, and senators—not a teacher, scientist, or industrial leader, unless he had also had one of the above titles, though these are elsewhere recognized. Of the 1,095 graduates from 1806 to 1844, by 1854, 244 had been in public life, 18 had become teachers, 152 physicians, 65 ministers.

City and Church Colleges.—The number of schools and colleges maintained by churches, etc., necessitates brevity of notice individually and the omission of many schools that perished. The College of Charleston, after granting a few college degrees, sank to a grammar school, and was closed for many years; after 1825 it was transformed into a real college by Rev. Jasper Adams, formerly of Brown University, in the face of much reactionism and mere stolidity. Financial difficulties led to its being taken over by the city government in 1837. Charleston loyalty to the South Carolina College and mere inertia prevented Adams from taking advantage of the Cooper trouble to create an institution of State-wide patronage. The faculty had enlisted an unusual number of intellectual leaders, particularly in science. Ephraim Baynard's $166,000 in 1865 remained until recently the largest gift to education in South Carolina. In 1927 Mr. A. B. Murray, whose varied Charleston philanthropies place him beyond all others in our history, added $100,000 to the endowment.

Cooper at the South Carolina College deepened the already existing aversion to unchristian teachers so evident in the statements of the founders of the early church academies. The denominational colleges began, therefore, as protective and conservative religious agencies. So jealous was the legislature for the State College that Erskine, founded by the Associate Reformed Presbyterians in 1839 on an earlier academy, was denied the privilege of a charter until 1850. Some legislators went so far as to maintain there should be no education at all unless given by the State.

Furman University, chartered in 1850, was opened in 1852 as successor to the Furman Academy and Theological Institution, which had existed at several locations since 1827. Its theological department developed into the Southern Baptist Theological Seminary at Louisville. After years of difficulty the institution attained a strong financial position through participation in the Southern Baptist $75,000,000 campaign of 1919 for education, missions, etc., and participation to the extent of 5 per cent in the $40,000,000 Duke Foundation of 1924.

The origin of Wofford College was a bequest of $100,000 by Benjamin Wofford, a local Methodist preacher of Spartanburg, whose business ability had increased his small beginnings to about $150,000. It was the largest educational donation up to that time (1850) in the history of the States.[2] The College was chartered in 1851 and opened in 1854.

Newberry College, preceded by the Lutheran Academy and Theological Institution established in Lexington in 1832, was chartered in 1856

[2] Dr. Ernest V. Hollis, Chief of Veterans' Educational Facilities Program, wrote Treasurer J. K. Davis of Wofford College April 30, 1948, that search in their rather extensive library found no other gift larger than Wofford's before that time. Professor Edgar Knight of the University of North Carolina makes a similar statement.

and opened as a college in 1859. It must be ranked with Erskine for its achievements in proportion to the numbers and resources of its denomination. Whatever may be the limitations upon higher education under church control, nothing but religious devotion and the discipline of character that goes with it could have carried these institutions through the difficulties that they have repeatedly mastered.

Colleges for Women.—The education of women was everywhere until the recent decades neglected as compared with that of men. Boarding schools for girls existed in the province. In 1828 Dr. Elias Marks, a converted Jewish Episcopalian, began his Barhamville Academy near Columbia which, until accidentally burned after the War of Secession, was under his and later other management one of the most famous girls' schools in our history. Dr. Marks secured cultured Europeans as instructors in languages, music, and art. The catalogue for 1849-50 announces this course for the Senior class of the collegiate department: intellectual philosophy, moral philosophy, logic reviewed, astronomy, arithmetic reviewed, university arithmetic, history, including lectures on nineteenth-century history, Kame's *Elements of Criticism,* Butler's *Analogy,* and bookkeeping. The usual arts were taught, and French, Italian, Spanish, and Latin.

Dr. Marks was followed at Barhamville by a truly romantic and heroic figure, Mme. Josef Stanislaus Sosnowski, née Sophie Wentz, daughter of the Court Physician of Baden. With her husband, a wounded refugee of the Polish rebellion of 1830-31, she came to America with $50,000, it is said, of which they recovered $7.50 from the failed St. Louis bank which they had trusted. After teaching in Northern and Southern cities, Madame Sosnowski, a widow soon after reaching America, took over Barhamville and surrounded herself with a gifted faculty. The Torrianis taught singing and instruments; the Russian Strawinski taught piano.

The almost frontier village of Spartanburg, at least as early as 1839, had a female as well as a male academy. The principal of the former was Miss Phoebe Paine of Pennsylvania, whose later fame as a teacher brought widespread notice throughout the country at her death. The high ideals and practical accomplishments of the best of such schools are expressed as follows by Eugenia C. Murrell Poston, who was born in Charleston in 1827 and died in San Francisco in 1907:

"From these preparatory schools [in Charleston] I passed to Spartanburg Seminary in the northern part of the State, and there completed my school education. The seminary was under the direction of a Board of Trustees, who engaged with Phoebe Paine of New York [?] as principal, giving her entire control of the course of study. I have never known a system better adapted to form character, to develop the crude girl into the efficient, loyal woman than that followed in this institution, of which I became a member in 1839, entering the Preparatory Department.

"The system adopted in our school in California was based upon Miss Paine's. . . . If you have derived any benefit from the Poston School, such benefit is largely due to Miss Paine—a teacher whom you never saw."

Mrs. Charles Spann advertised in the *Camden Journal,* September 14, 1842, that her girls' school there ran from the elementary branches through French, astronomy, botany, and natural philosophy; board and the English courses, $200; French, $40; music, $40; plain and fancy needlework, $20. The Johnson Female Seminary at Anderson in 1849, and at times conducted at Greenville or Edgefield, offered Latin, Greek, and German. Its Dr. W. B. Johnson, a D.D. from Brown in '33, was for three years President of the American Baptists and was a famous teacher and theologian. The Orangeburg Female College was founded by Rev. I. S. K. Legaré, the first Presbyterian minister of the town; the Cokesbury Female Seminary (1841), by the Masons. And so we might go over a large part of the State, but the details must be left to the monographist.

The churches enjoyed an unusual distinction in the early history of our women's academies and colleges. They early organized female academies as well as male, sometimes at the same places, as the Methodist Tabernacle Academies at Mt. Ariel, Abbeville District, in 1821, and the Presbyterian academies at Greenwood. Many schools not formally connected with churches were directly under religious influence, as, e.g., that of Dr. Thomas Curtis, a Baptist minister from England, and his son William. In 1845 they bought the Limestone Springs Hotel, built in 1835 at the present Gaffney, and conducted a girls' academy rivaling in fame Dr. Waddel's Willington for boys. After 1865 the property was given by Peter Cooper to the Spartanburg Baptist Association and is now the home of a woman's college of that denomination. "The schools for the education of women," wrote Colyer Meriwether as late as 1888, "are almost entirely the work of the denominations."

In 1854 the Methodists voted to establish two female colleges, one at Columbia and one at Spartanburg. In 1854 the Baptists took action leading to the establishment of the Greenville Woman's College. The Associate Reformed Presbyterians took similar action in 1860. Not until 1891 did the State enact the establishment of Winthrop Normal and

Industrial College for girls, to succeed the Winthrop Training School in Columbia which had been chartered in 1886.

It is significant of the relatively aristocratic and democratic aspects of Southern and Northern Society that in 1860 colleges in the South contained one in 312 of her white population and those in the North one in 651 of hers; Southern and Northern academies one in 54 and one in 61 respectively; and Southern and Northern public schools one in 8 and one in 4.8 respectively.

Medical Education.—The Medical Society of South Carolina, organized by Charleston physicians in 1789 and incorporated in 1794, promoted the scientific tendencies prominent almost throughout the city's history. From the society soon sprang the Humane Society, the medical dispensary, and in 1805 the Botanic Society with a scientifically kept garden. The number of physicians of South Carolina birth increased rapidly after the Revolution. Ramsay stated in 1808 that every operation possible in Paris or London could be equally well performed in Charleston. Shortly before 1808 an up-country medical society was meeting in Union. Not until 1817 did the law require examination and license for physicians and pharmacists (existing physicians being exempt). The law of 1828 required a medical diploma or a successful examination before the Medical College in Charleston.

In 1823 Drs. James Ramsay and S. H. Dickson lectured in Charleston publicly on surgery and medicine, but failed to persuade either the Charleston College or the legislature to assume any expense for establishing a medical school. Nevertheless in December, 1823, the Medical Society established "The Medical College of South Carolina" and elected the six professors, but declined to incur any expense. The faculty supplied valuable apparatus, etc., of their own; the city gave $15,000 and a lot, and the State by 1830 $17,000. In 1831, upon the question of filling the chair of a resigned professor, the faculty and the Medical Society each claimed control. Rivalry followed between a new college set up by the Society and that conducted by the old faculty under a charter of 1833 for "The Medical College of the State of South Carolina." The Medical Society's college ceased after a few years. The old faculty through their successors have continued to this day under their chartered name of 1833. In 1913 the college was made a State institution.

Hospitals in the colony were provided in Charleston for seamen, the indigent, and sufferers from contagious diseases, and resembled poorhouses and houses of correction rather than modern hospitals, the establishment of which came after the Revolution. Colonial provision for the insane was crude. Frequent mention of boarding out lunatics occurs. In 1745 provision was made for the parish to bear the expense of the lunatic slaves of the poor. The well-to-do were left to care for their own mentally as well as bodily sick. The Fellowship Society, organized in 1762 with the purpose among other charities of founding a hospital for the needy, had accumulated funds and was incorporated in 1769. Ramsay, whose memory should be reliable here, says that they planned for the insane, but his words incline us to believe that they confined their charities to education.[3] If they did indeed care for the insane, only the establishment of an insane ward in Pennsylvania Hospital antedates this. The first separate insane asylum in the United States, says Dr. Babcock, was at Williamsburg, Virginia, in 1733. In 1821 Samuel Farrow of Spartanburg, having for this express purpose left Congress after two terms, was mainly instrumental in securing an appropriation for an asylum in Columbia. He succeeded only by the aid of William Crafts of Charleston, who joined with it his plan for a school for the deaf. The plans for the latter were dropped, but Mills's fortress-like fireproof building for the insane was completed in 1828 and is still used.

Provision for the deaf began when the legislature in 1834 ordered as much of $2,500 annually as was needed to be used for educating our white sufferers at Hartford, Connecticut. In 1841 the blind were provided for at Boston out of the same fund. On January 22, 1849, Professor N. P. Walker opened at Cedar Springs near Spartanburg, with five pupils, his school for the deaf, where he, his son, his grandson, and his great-grandson have continued work (with the blind added in 1855) to the present. The State took over the school in 1856.[4]

Scientists.—The learned and able physicians who made Charleston a center for medical education were largely responsible for scientific pursuits in South Carolina. The *Gazette* announced in March and April, 1773, that the Charleston Library Society had appointed a committee to receive for their proposed museum specimens of every natural feature of the province—plants, marine and land life, soils, rocks, minerals. The collection we know existed in January, 1778, and is listed in a memorandum of 1798. The founding of the museum thus antedates by twelve years the next oldest in the United States, founded in Philadelphia in

[3] Stat. at L., VIII, 112; Ramsay, *South Carolina* II, 363. Drayton's saying that Gadsden should be lodged in a madhouse (a stock expression) does not prove the existence of an asylum in Charleston. W. G. Simms (*American Slavery,* pamphlet, pp. 36-37) speaks of the poorhouse and the madhouse in Charleston in 1780.

[4] Adams' Annual Message, 1855, says Walker began teaching the deaf in 1846; evidently the printer had turned the 9 upside down. Professor N. F. Walker appears to err in giving 1832 for 1834, and 1857 for 1856. My figures are from Statutes and Spartanburg Mesne Conveyance records, CC, 345, and HH, 79.

1785 by Charles Willson Peale, and its certified collection antedates the other's by at least eight years. In 1815 the library transferred its museum to the Philosophical and Literary Society, organized in 1813 on the suggestion of Dr. John Lewis E. W. Shecut, the electrical experimenter and botanist. By 1843 it had been transferred to the Medical College. As a result of Agassiz's suggestion at the 1850 Charleston meeting of the American Association for the Advancement of Science, the existing nucleus was greatly enlarged from the collections of Professor F. S. Holmes, Dr. John Bachman, and Agassiz. In fourteen months Holmes, having been appointed curator, "transform[ed] a cabinet of curiosities . . . into a scientific museum of the highest rank." After long residing in the College of Charleston, the museum in 1907 obtained its own home, the Thomson Auditorium, largely through the efforts of Professor Paul M. Rea. There has followed an era of activity in the museum already made famous by "Shecut, Elliott, Holbrook, Audubon, Bachman, and Agassiz, Ravenel, Dickson, Holmes, Gibbes, and [John] McCrady."

The absorption of talent in politics, the idealization of plantation society, the scarcity of mineral deposits, and the absence of great educational foundations and cities militated against scientific studies in South Carolina. Numbers of South Carolinians distinguished in science have therefore worked elsewhere. J. Lawrence Smith, M.D. (1818-83), the introducer of improved domestic animals into South Carolina, in his career in Turkey, Virginia, and Louisville, stood with the greatest American chemists. Josiah Clark Nott, M.D. (1804-73), after a brief practice in his native Columbia, took up practice in Mobile. His belief that yellow fever is transmitted by mosquitoes and that malaria is transmitted by insects and animalculae hardly belongs to South Carolina history.[5]

With W. G. Glidden of England, Nott published an anthropological work in 1854, incurring clerical condemnation. The voluminous works of the Belfast-born Charleston Presbyterian theologian Thomas Smyth (father of Augustine T. Smythe[6] and son-in-law of the eminent merchant James Adger) include a volume on the *Unity of the Human Races,* published in the United States in 1850 and in Edinburgh in 1851,

[5] Successive epidemics of yellow fever made it a subject of speculation by several Charleston physicians. Yellow fever deaths in the city were 272 in 1817, 235 in 1824, 351 in 1838, 672 in 1854, and 717 in 1858, not to detail the losses in others of the total of 20 outbreaks between 1817 and 1858 inclusive.—R. C. Aldredge in *Charleston Year Book* 1940, p. 245.

[6] Smyth and Smythe are both correct.

combatting Nott's multiple origin theory of 1849.[7] The most distinguished scientific physician South Carolina has given the world is J. Marion Sims (1813-83), one of the greatest gynecologists of all time; but, as with others, his achievements in Alabama, New York, and Europe hardly form a part of South Carolina history, except to enforce the mournful story of the loss of so many of our brilliant sons because of our lack of great cities.

Plants, animals, and fishes have naturally been the chief objects of scientific research in South Carolina. John Lawson of North Carolina attempted some slight classification of South Carolina plants in 1700. Mark Catesby's magnificent *Natural History of Carolina, Florida, and the Bahama Islands* records his stay here in 1722-24. Dr. Alexander Garden (1730-91; not the minister) was a distinguished naturalist, whose name is borne by the gardenia.

The English-born Thomas Walter (about 1740-89) lived on the Santee in the northwest part of St. Stephen's parish, where he kept a botanical garden. His 263-plus-viii-page *Flora Caroliniana,* entirely in Latin, *Auctore Thomas Walter, Agricola,* dated "Lon[d]ini; M. D C C, LXXXI, is a work of original observation. Governor John Drayton's MS "Carolinian Florist" (1807), though mainly a translation of Walter, with material also from Michaux of South Carolina and from Barton, contains some original matter including well-executed colored drawings.[8]

Dr. John Lewis E. W. Shecut (who enthusiastically named a son Linnaeus) published only Volume I of his *Flora Carolinaensis,* which is really a general botany of little original research on the Linnaean system (1806). His *Essays, Medical and Philosophical* (1819), displaying his electrical interests, are of more significance. His several novels are very dull.

Our three greatest contributors to botanical knowledge are Stephen Elliott (1771-1830), Henry W. Ravenel (1814-87), and Dr. Francis Peyre Porcher. Elliott's *Botany of South Carolina and Georgia* (2 vols., 1821-24, compiled 1800-08) added 180 genera and more than 1,000 species to those of Walter. H. W. Ravenel's *Fungi Caroliniani Exsiccati,* five volumes full of actual specimens, appeared in 1852-55 and won an international reputation. Dr. F. P. Porcher's *Resources of Southern Fields and Forests* served to inform the Confederacy of its possibilities (second edition greatly enlarged, 1869).

[7] An edition appeared also in England in 1855.

[8] In 1943 the South Caroliniana Library of the University issued under the editorship of Mrs. Margaret Babcock Meriwether a handsome printing of Drayton's "Carolinian Florist," made as completely representative of Drayton as possible by adding to the University's MS Drayton's botanical data from other sources.

The work of O. M. Lieber has been noted in connection with the geological survey of the State. Through two textbooks (one a translation) he was influential in introducing German methods in chemical assaying.

In 1857 Michael Tuomey, of the former geological survey of the State, and F. S. Holmes, of the faculty of the College of Charleston, published their handsome *Pleistocene Fossils of South Carolina,* with plates. In 1860 Holmes alone brought out a second volume, the *Post-pleistocene Fossils of South Carolina.* The acknowledgments by the author attest the extensive intellectual circle in Charleston, in which must be mentioned Dr. Gabriel Manigault. Professor Holmes was later prominent in connection with phosphates.

Noted throughout Europe and America are the works of Dr. John Edwards Holbrook (1794-1871), *North American Herpetology* (4 volumes with 147 colored plates from life; 1842), and *Ichthyology of South Carolina* (1855, revised 1860), with 27 colored plates. The former established his reputation as the foremost American zoologist. The State aided Holbrook's *Ichthyology* with a $3,000 appropriation, and also aided several other publications earlier and later.[9]

Rev. John Bachman (1790-1874) was not only one of the State's most eminent scientists, but a strikingly beautiful character, honored by the highest and beloved by the most humble. Coming from his native New York, he was for fifty-nine years the diligent pastor of St. John's Lutheran Church, Charleston, and was the founder of the Lutheran seminary antedating Newberry College. Yet he found time for accurate and extensive studies in natural history. A month's stay by Audubon in his home, the beginning of a lifelong attachment rendered stronger by the marriage of two of Audubon's sons to two of Bachman's daughters, led to his writing most and editing all of the text of Audubon's *Quadrupeds of North America* (1845-49). Evolution was to him a sore trial. In 1850 his *Unity of the Human Race* combatted Nott's book on the Biblical and scientific aspects of creation (1849). Thus two Charleston scholars, Smyth and Bachman, both active pastors, published books on the same subject in the same year.

It is clear, as Professor T. Cary Johnson holds, that the absorption of the ante-bellum Southern mind in politics and eighteenth-century literature and the classics has been overstated. North Carolina fostered a notable scientific group around her University, as South Carolina did

[9] The State aided Carroll's *Collections* with $2,000; Drayton's *Memoirs,* Landrum's *Upper South Carolina,* the South Carolina Historical Society, etc., with smaller sums, down to recent years.

around the Medical College in Charleston and to a lesser extent around the College in Columbia. Alabama, Georgia, and Virginia were marked by the same tendencies, as is attested by the fact, says Professor Johnson, that under the elective system at the University of Virginia more students chose chemistry than Latin.

Northern Contributions to Our Intellectual Life.—From colonial times until checked by the abolitionist movement South Carolina received a stream of teachers, preachers, etc., from Northern colleges, many of whom, or the sons of whom, contributed greatly to repair the damage the State sustained after 1815 or '20 because so many of her enterprising men sought their fortunes to the westward or northward. Whether Cooper and Lieber are catalogued as Northern or European, their residence in South Carolina strongly influenced the State. Perhaps South Carolina gave more than she received in talent as in numbers in the trying period 1815-60, for her brilliant sons were found from Massachusetts to the Pacific.

Besides its first New England President, the South Carolina College before 1860 numbered several gifted Northern men among its faculty. The New England Rev. Jasper Adams largely made the Charleston College, and Frederick A. Sawyer of Boston, with several Northern assistants, was secured to organize Charleston's public school system. Loring Andrews from Massachusetts founded the Charleston *Courier* in 1803. J. D. B. DeBow (1820-67), whose *Review,* in his native Charleston or in New Orleans, was of national importance, was the son of a New Jersey father. The father of J. H. Hammond, Governor and Senator, was a New England teacher, serving in Mt. Bethel Academy and in the South Carolina College. Governor James Hamilton's father was a Pennsylvanian. Holbrook, though born of a Massachusetts father in Beaufort, spent his childhood and youth in the North, and returned to South Carolina as a man educated in the North and in Europe. Josiah Clark Nott was born in Columbia of a Connecticut father, a Yale graduate of 1788, who became a South Carolina congressman and judge. B. F. Perry was the son of a Massachusetts father and a Virginia mother. Major-General David Rumph Jones's father was from Connecticut.

In religion, the Northeastern influence was long powerful, as attested by William Tennent, the leader of disestablishment; Oliver Hart and Richard Furman, the Baptist leaders; George Howe, the Massachusetts-born New Hampshire teacher, head of the Presbyterian Seminary in Columbia and the historian of his church. Woodrow Wilson's father, professor in the Presbyterian Seminary in Columbia, was from Ohio, a State to whose early intellectual and spiritual life South Carolina

Presbyterians made large contributions. The intellectual group among the Charleston Unitarians included Rev. Samuel Gilman and his wife Caroline, a very pleasing writer and the editor there of *The Rosebud,* the first child's paper in the country. Bishop Howe of the Episcopal Church came to South Carolina from the North after 1865. E. S. Thomas, active in the North before and afterward, was a power in early nineteenth-century Charleston journalism and politics. Robert Aldrich, father of the first Judge Aldrich, came to South Carolina as a young bookstorekeeper from Boston, the city that sent us the father of William Crafts. J. L. Hatch, the brilliant editor of the *Standard* and later of the *Courier,* though noted for his Southern views, was born in New England, and the publisher, A. S. Willington, was Northern-born. Abraham Blanding, a Brown University graduate who came to Columbia as a Yankee school teacher in 1797 or '98, became one of the State's leaders in public works and politics. Much less numerous doubtless were Northern mothers of South Carolina leaders (as, e.g., General M. C. Butler's mother, the sister of Commodores M. C. and O. H. Perry of Rhode Island).

The contribution of Northern artists to our culture was extensive. Malbone from Rhode Island, Morse from Massachusetts, G. W. Flagg of Connecticut (Washington Allston's nephew), and numerous other Northerners painted our portraits, and in return we gave Massachusetts Allston, the leading American artist of his generation.

The influence of Northern books and periodicals as sectionalism intensified constituted a grievance against which even Governors officially protested. Before 1800 about thirty-nine South Carolinians graduated at Princeton and about thirty other Princeton graduates settled in South Carolina. Later scores of South Carolinians were found in the leading Northern colleges, even though Northern institutions had not then acquired their later leadership over Southern through vast endowments. South Carolina, absorbed in a struggle over political and economic issues of the most desperate possibilities, cultivated the arts best suited to that circumstance and to a surprising extent imported her cultural agencies instead of producing them.

Northern contributions to industry were naturally large in a society whose circumstances turned its inclinations elsewhere. The Weavers and Hills, Clark, and Bates of the early cotton-milling in Spartanburg and Greenville, and Converse and Twichell shortly before the War of Secession, all New Englanders, and all skilled mechanics or superintendents imported by them and others, were a strain of great importance. The strength of the New England influence is attested by the New England Society of Charleston. But it is notable that, while South Carolina drew these rich streams of intellect and character from the North, she assimilated them to herself. Practically all of these Northerners except some coming shortly before 1860 became thorough South Carolinians, and many of them and of their sons gave their lives for the Confederacy.

Libraries.—The Revolution checked the attempt to replace the collection of the Charleston Library Society, which had been almost totally destroyed by the great fire of 1778. The books bought in 1792 form the basis of the present library, which in February, 1945, totaled 63,578 catalogued volumes and 5,685 catalogued pamphlets. The Apprentices' Library, founded in 1824, was threatening to eclipse the older institution when it was merged with it in 1874. The Library's eighteenth-century newspaper files and South Carolina history collection draw scholars from all over the country and from Europe.

Columbia had a Library Society in 1806. Beaufort College's unusual classical and general library was purchased in Europe by H. S. Legaré in the 1830's. The number of public libraries in country villages was considerable. The South Carolina College Library from the first was one of distinction. The census of 1860 gives South Carolina 193 public libraries with 366,517 volumes, and a total (including Sunday Schools, colleges, etc.) of 257 libraries with 471,542 volumes.

Art and Artists.—The patronage of art was generally confined to family portraits. St. Memin in his wanderings from New York to Savannah painted miniatures (and some larger pictures) of quite a number of South Carolinians of the Revolutionary and the succeeding generation. Edward G. Malbone (1777-1807) of Rhode Island, greatest of American miniaturists, is said to have painted more miniatures in Charleston than in any other city. Thomas Sully (1783-1872) spent most of his youth in Charleston, where are to be seen some of the earliest as well as some of the most beautiful mature works of his genius.

A brilliant visitant was the young S. F. B. Morse (1791-1872), who sought in Charleston in January, 1818, better opportunities than were afforded by New England country towns at $15 a portrait. In 1821 Morse was largely instrumental in establishing the short-lived South Carolina Academy of Fine Arts.

Washington Allston (1779-1843) is one of the great whom South Carolina follows with pride as of her blood and soil but can hardly claim for her culture, as he was educated from childhood in New England and lived there except for some years abroad, recognized as the greatest American artist of his day. Sending him to New England to break up his tendency to paint resulted in his becoming the pupil of Malbone.

His genius was fully awakened by the great artists of the Renaissance. Of deeply religious nature, his subjects are generally Biblical or of classic idealism.

Allston inspired South Carolina's greatest miniaturist, Charles Fraser (1782-1860), who, after accumulating a competence at the Charleston bar from 1807 to '18, devoted his life to art. A gifted speaker for civic and patriotic occasions, he was deeply respected as a man and citizen. In his *Reminiscences of Charleston* his "kindly tolerance . . . never leaves one in doubt as to his own views, but never mingles personal abuse with criticism." Fraser, possessing great strength, almost rivaling Malbone in delicacy, and certainly in trueness to life, ranks high in the history of American art. Except for a short time in Hartford, Connecticut, in 1831, he painted only in Charleston. The exhibit there in 1857 displayed 313 of his miniatures (of which over 150 more were said to be known) and 139 landscapes, large portraits, etc.[10]

The gifted James De Veaux (1812-44), alternating between depression at lack of recognition in his native Charleston and joy at kindness in Columbia, early manifested brilliant talent. He was sent North by Dr. R. W. Gibbes's father and Rev. Allston Gibbes for training. Colonel Wade Hampton sent him in 1836 to England, France, and the Low Countries, and later General and Colonel Wade Hampton, J. L. Manning, and J. S. Preston sent him to Italy to copy for them such masterpieces as he might select. Here his hypersensitive, morbid-enthusiastic mind flamed with inspiration until he died in Rome without knowing of the honor of having been elected to the New York National Academy of design.

To John Blake White of Charleston, dramatist and artist, we owe, Mr. A. S. Salley tells me, the likeness of General Marion, who would never sit for a portrait; but an unsuspected bundle of boyhood talent once sat on his knee, says the tradition, and years later produced the picture from which all others are taken. William H. Brown of Charleston (1808-83), the greatest of American silhouettists, possessed such

[10] Among the ten portraits were his "Henry Laurens" and "John Laurens," which, in my *Laurens,* not having then seen the catalogue perfectly identifying these, I called (following family tradition) replicas by Copley. A Copley "Henry Laurens" is said by Dr. G. E. Manigault to have been destroyed by fire in Charleston in 1861. The magnificent Henry Laurens of Copley now in the Mellon Collection in the National Gallery of Arts in Washington was brought here from Ireland in 1920 from the home of the historian Bagwell.—Letters from Mrs. Bagwell, the American owner, and Chief Curator John Walker of the National Gallery to D. D. Wallace. Fraser appears to have copied the face of his "John Laurens" from C. W. Peale's miniature. Fraser's "Henry Laurens" is clearly a copy from Valentine Green's mezzotint of the Copley, as the colors of costume differ from those of the existing Copley, though the shapes agree perfectly.

memory that he could cut a likeness from having seen a face years before. William Harrison Scarborough (1812-71), born in Dover, Tennessee, and of easy circumstances, painted in Tennessee, Alabama, and South Carolina. His portraits much excelled his subject pictures.

Transient portrait painters, often of admirable skill, and undistinguished artists whose portraits fill hundreds of homes from end to end of South Carolina, cannot be detailed. Of notable works of art produced elsewhere is Trumbull's Washington, painted for Charleston in Philadelphia in 1791, for which the city has refused fabulous sums. The famous portrait of Mr. and Mrs. Ralph Izard of the Revolutionary period was refused by the family for some reason when Copley painted it. In 1831 Mr. Charles J. Manigault bought it from Mrs. Copley.

Numbers of statues by masters, such as J. Q. A. Ward's heroic bronze of General Daniel Morgan in Spartanburg and his bust of William Gilmore Simms in Charleston, and the copy of Houdon's "Washington" in Columbia, attest the prevalence of general good taste. The Carolina Art Association dated from 1857, with its formal organization and first exhibition in 1858. After the destruction of its gallery with almost its entire contents in the 1861 fire, no loan exhibition occurred until 1880, when the extremely meager attendance and the almost total absence of young people revealed a distressing decline of cultural interest and inspired the organization of an art school. From its organization in 1882 dates a revival of art interest. The school extends, through many difficulties, to the art school in the Gibbes Art Gallery, an institution built in 1905 from the bequest of $100,000 by Mr. James S. Gibbes, a Charleston merchant who died in 1888. In 1885 there was opposition in the Charleston school board to allowing pupils to receive art instruction at public expense, a feature of public school teaching which has now long been general.

Not proposing an evaluation of contemporary artists, I may conclude with Albert Capers Guerry (1840-98), the uncle of Bishop Guerry and the surgeon Dr. Legrand Guerry. He left pictures of a large number of distinguished persons, including Preston, James H. Carlisle, Hampton, Toombs, Lee, President and Mrs. Cleveland, President and Mrs. McKinley, and at least two magnificent portraits of Calhoun.

Traits of Literature.—My desire to review literature must yield to the lack of both time and space. The number of persons who published trivial little volumes of verse is astonishing. Professor Snowden lists twenty-three South Carolina writers of textbooks before 1860, almost all of whose works were printed in Charleston between 1795 and 1858. Professor Wauchope's *Literary South Carolina,* briefly noticing the principal writers from 1700 to 1923, includes 160 pages.

The colonial beginnings of South Carolina literature were natural and free, whether in economics, religion, or the traditional eighteenth-century essays and vapid poems, or vigorous official and political papers. With the emergence of the slavery quarrel came the blight of the controversial. For a generation after 1865 literature, as Mr. Ludwig Lewisohn notes, quite generally shrank from the futility of public affairs into the futility of aloofness, revealing in its paleness nothing of the throbbing, tragic contemporary life. With the last three decades has come a vigor of realism some of whose aspects find their justification chiefly in their ruthless exposure of ugly truths festering under a conspiracy of silence. Ambrose Gonzales, DuBose Heyward, Mrs. Julia Peterkin, Mrs. Shelby, and Samuel Stoney are as truly descriptive sociologists as literary artists. Their deepest significance is that their pages, though shining with talent, are black with the great black problem of Southern life. Archibald Rutledge's poems and nature stories reveal a spirit of rare insight and beauty.

Periodical literature in the South has been largely political. The *Mercury* (1822-68), aggressive and able spokesman of the State rights extremists, and the *Courier* (1803 to the present; since 1868 the *News and Courier),* which has never lost the conservatism of its Federalist origin and its Unionism, led a newspaper press which in many country journals presented excellent writing. Thomas says that in his time (1795-1810) distinguished men flew to the aid of the editors, so that "the periodical press of South Carolina pours forth a torrent of intellect nowhere else to be met with." In the next generation the editorials of Richard Yeadon of the *Courier* and John Stuart of the *Mercury* were literature, but frequently so bitter that it is a wonder how in a duelling age they escaped violent death. Stuart was a good painter, a fair poet, like Yeadon a gifted public speaker, a constant student of the Bible, and so familiar with Shakespeare that, says his son, he could have played any role in the plays with only a few hours' notice. The *Mercury,* ably edited throughout its career (1822-68), was the leading organ both of nullification and of secession. Long owned and edited by the Rhett connection, it was the leader of the Southern State rights press and was read both for its brilliancy and its significance in editorial offices all over the country. The founding of the *News* by the English soldier of the Confederacy, F. W. Dawson, marked a new era in South Carolina journalism, for he made the paper a news agency to a degree never before known here, and continued the brilliancy of the editorial page.

The census of 1860 reports thirty-three political newspapers, and three religious and five literary periodicals in the State.

So numerous were magazines that Charleston has been called the graveyard of Southern periodicals; and so excellent was much of the material as to enforce the adage that the good die young. The *Weekly Museum,* founded in Charleston in 1797, is said to have been the first Southern magazine. The indifference of the Southern mind manifested toward mere literature did not extend to journals serving more specific needs, as is exemplified by the far longer life of *De Bow's Review* (1846 to 1880, with long suspensions in the sixties and seventies), and the *Southern Presbyterian Review,* at Columbia, from 1847 to '85.

Slavery and Statesmanship.—When F. H. Elmore, Calhoun's senatorial successor, died almost at once after his appointment, Cheves, Hammond, and Hamilton were all considered worthy of the position, but personal reasons prevented them from consenting. Robert W. Barnwell agreed to serve until an election should be held. The abundance and brilliancy of South Carolina leaders of the period, though not confined to politics, were disproportionately turned to them. Natural talent was greatly stimulated by circumstances. There was a class of wealthy men who were willing to give their own services or to uphold able men. There were issues, especially the ever-present, supreme issue of preserving or destroying the Union, on which what South Carolina might think was of the highest importance. Circumstances made her the anxiously observed keystone of the arch as, in a consolidated nation, a small State could never be. South Carolina not only realized her position in the Union, but she also realized how vital to her own existence were the national issues and expended her best talent upon them. Instead of the megalomania fostered by her ante-bellum situation, South Carolina of today faces a danger of the other extreme, an inferiority complex. There was a definiteness and decision in the conduct of South Carolina leaders before the War of Secession, even among men of ordinary endowments, for the reason that they knew what they wanted and were settled as to the means of attaining it.

Yet these men may almost be said to have been leaders only in the sense that a trumpeter is the leader of an army. Impelled by the circumstance of slavery, which had grown up by common consent without any leadership or even much thought beyond immediate profit, everybody was forced to think and feel alike. Leaders became merely those who could best state or defend the case. No contrary leadership would have been tolerated. The South Carolina mind thus became combative rather than constructive. Her thinkers became attorneys in a case, not seekers for essential truth in social and political relations, and expended vast resources in the defense of an impossible program in which success would have been the greatest calamity. The South Carolina mind, therefore, though a powerful one, was not a free mind.

Thus through slavery, and after emancipation through the race problem, South Carolina incurred the intellectual slavery of the one-party system. He who differed was worse than an enemy; he was a traitor. It was actually ruled in the Jim Tillman murder trial in 1903 that evidence might be offered that a witness was a Republican in order to injure his credibility—a ruling profoundly significant historically whether or not warrantable judicially. This insularity prevents South Carolinians from viewing their past critically; and yet only when so viewed can history confer its chief benefit.

CHAPTER XLVII

SOCIAL CLASSES AND CUSTOMS, 1830-1860

THOUGH the foibles, gifts, and graces of South Carolina society have constantly appeared in our narrative, we may here bring together more systematically some features of social life. The homes of the wealthy were often spacious, comfortable, and stately, with due ventilation for the climate, but were rarely ornate. Millford, the Clarendon County mansion[1] built by Governor John L. Manning in the 1850's at enormous cost, the finest country house in the State, was so exceptional as to earn the nickname "Manning's Folly." Designed with dignity, elegance, and propriety, it is almost as much palace as home. Its parlor and drawing room can be thrown into one by almost concealed sliding doors, and occupy an entire side of the ground floor, with walls consisting of the finest plate glass mirrors from Paris. The semicircular stair tower is divided from the great hallway by a wall of glass. As generally with great houses, grounds designed with skillful landscape gardening heighten the effect.

Of the pre-war Georgetown District, Richard Lathers wrote long afterward, "The entire property of the average planter at the time I started in business was hardly equal to the annual income of the Northern millionaire of today; but on this relatively modest sum he dispensed a liberal and refined hospitality which challenged the admiration of all visitors to the South." A rice plantation of 200 Negroes, worth $150,000 to $200,000, supported a family of five to ten persons in comparative luxury. "I knew very few planters," he continued, "whose annual expenditure exceeded $15,000; it was generally under $10,000." Spending a season in New York, Saratoga, or Newport was confined to the richer planters.

The Basis of the Ruling Class.—South Carolina pre-Revolutionary aristocracy was essentially the indigenous growth of natural talents pushing to the top. The emergence of contempt for trade shortly before the Revolution marked the hardening of the landed gentry into a superior class. The pre-Revolutionary distinguished families occupied the highest social level. The new men—Hamptons, Mannings, Kershaws, Richardsons, Pickenses, etc., whose character and force won distinction in the

[1] Now by a change of boundary in Sumter County.

Revolution, came next. Lastly were added men of talent and character who rose after the Revolution, as Calhoun, McDuffie, Cheves, Petigru, Hammond. For, though the aristocracy hardened with pride as its origin was forgotten, it remained open to talent accompanied by good manners and money to keep the pace. DeBow, in defending the South's openness to talent, pointed out in 1861 that the sons of non-slaveholders had always been among the ruling spirits of the South—as McDuffie, Cheves, Jackson, A. Clay, Rust, Hammond, Yancey, Orr, Memminger, Benjamin, Simms, Porter, Magrath, Aiken, Maunsel White, and a host of others.

The Pickenses well illustrate the emergence of talent. The backwoods community leader, shrewdly amassing good lands, became the General of the Revolution and passed fortune and ability to his son Andrew Pickens, who became Governor in 1816. The General's grandson Francis W. Pickens, Governor from 1860 to '62, brilliant, bold, imposing, father of the dashing beauty Douschka born while he was minister to Russia, was chosen to lead the State in the crisis of secession. When plain farmer Ben Tillman, who had hated the aristocracy, had become the dominator of South Carolina, his son married a Pickens. If Tillman's sons had carried on the tradition of his power, they, or at all events their sons, would have been hated by new popular leaders as "aristocrats."

E. S. Thomas, revisiting Charleston in 1838, noted the contempt for trade and the rise of new men. In 1795 the St. Cecilia, he said, was closed to all, or almost all, merchants. But, he said, in 1838, besides H. L. Pinckney, few of the distinguished men were of the old aristocracy. Aristocracy of family had yielded to aristocracy of mind, which had written its own patents of nobility represented by such men as Calhoun, McDuffie, Hayne, Hamilton, Petigru, Duncan (Dunkin), Cheves, Legaré, and Yeadon, forming an aggregate of talent not equaled, he thought, in any other State. Aristocracy, he continued, was carried to such an extent that it was hardly considered reputable to attend to business of any kind. "Even the learned professions were admitted into the *front* rank in society only to a limited extent." So much did J. H. Hammond, haughty son of a poor Massachusetts schoolmaster, enjoy his position as the husband of a wealthy South Carolina heiress that he wrote in 1848, "Planting in this country is the only independent and really honorable occupation. The planters here are essentially what the nobility are in other countries. They stand at the head of society and politics. Lawyers and professional politicians come next, then Doctors, Merchants, etc."

The abolition of primogeniture in 1791 was a blow to a continuous aristocracy. The division of estates in the low country, where physical conditions demanded large-scale operations, frequently ruined fine properties. Said Grayson, a dozen sons look forward to being planters on the small subdivisions of an estate that their father alone drew the income from. "They are to be planters. But the fragment of the estate fails to support the inheritor. It is too late when he discovers this to betake himself to any other pursuit and he sinks into a class who live on memories of the past and rest their claims to consideration on the virtues of a name. . . . They become component parts of the only aristocracy in America . . . the aristocracy described by General Foy as composed of men willing to live without working, to consume without producing, and to occupy all public offices without fitness for any of them." To this were often added the ruinous effects of excessive hospitality, expensive travel, and unbusinesslike management. Said I. Jenkins Mikell, "The Factor was the factotum of our business life, our commission merchant, our bookkeeper, our adviser, our collector and disburser, who honored our checks and paid our bills. Many of the planters did not really always know what money they possessed. One year's accounts would overlap another's and sometimes years would pass before the accounts were balanced and settlement made."

Notwithstanding the constant sinking into poverty among the old and the rise to distinction among the new, there remained a strong continuation of wealth or power among many families. Intellectual distinction and public service have marked several families from their early colonial arrival to the present. South Carolina prided herself on possessing a stabilized civilization. Europeans found satisfaction in the recognition by every class of its proper place. Above the poor white, it was a civilization dominated by ideals of personal dignity. Every man maintained his own position with a high self-respect, sustained by the pride of being in his own sphere a gentleman. But let us not be misled by the ideology which represents that there was no Southern middle class, but only aristocrats and "poor whites." It is hard to understand how even a propagandist for a new sociology can be blind to the existence in the old South of a vigorous class of small farmers and business and professional men.

Standards of Honor.—That a government by gentlemen would be characterized by personal honor was to be expected. Both State and local positions were served by the best element in the community to a much greater extent than today. In the departments of government determining policy, the slaveholding aristocracy held control, and they put their strongest men in office because they realized the necessity of protecting a vast body of wealth and a social system constantly under attack from the outside world and in danger of it at home.

But here again general statements must not be allowed to pass into idealization. The more carefully reality is examined the more obvious becomes the fact that before 1860 there was present quite an amount of inefficiency, confusion, and class selfishness. The glaring faults in the forty years following the Revolution have been rehearsed. In 1838 the South Carolina attorney-general and solicitors, by legislative order, reported on the whole system of local government. They noted in their report the universally admitted inefficiency of the free school system, highway administration, the condition of courthouses and jails, and the support of the poor. Multiplication of local boards, they said, crippled efforts for improvement, weakened responsibility, bred carelessness, indecision, inactivity. Each board seemed to work under the sense of enduring punishment instead of performing public service with willingness and pride. As a remedy they suggested a single board with additional authority and with taxing power. Delay and inefficiency of ordinaries (probate judges) were a grievance. Elaborate remedies were offered for the complaints against the inferior magistrates.

The bulk of special and local legislation had become so great by 1825 that a uniform act was passed in that year providing for many local duties. A number of acts of 1839 defined and tightened up the duties of some local officers; but the recommendation for co-ordinating or consolidating district (county) government was disregarded. Before 1860 the governor ordinarily did not live in Columbia except during the month that the legislature was in session. This was complained of but unremedied.

The complacency of Southern opinion is illustrated by Governor Pickens' contrast between Southern and Northern civilization in 1861: "This government of states was destroyed by the Northern people, who, without the conservative division of castes, which we have, endeavored to make the government a simple democracy of numbers. This ended, as all such governments must inevitably end, in corruption, usurpation, and revolution. As far as the Northern states are concerned, their government is hopelessly gone."

The virtues of Southern aristocracy were not due to slavery (except as slavery made an aristocracy possible) as slavery apologists maintained, for they were the common virtues of an enlightened landed aristocracy anywhere. Nor is it true that all the virtues claimed were distinctly aristocratic; for religion or plain manly honesty produced in thousands of men as immovable a courage and as incorruptible an integrity. Where religion and the gentleman's sense of honor (the only two bases of character) united, the result was a William Lowndes or a Robert E. Lee. Olmsted of New York in 1854 found that "there is less vulgar display, and more intrinsic elegance, and habitual mental refinement in the best society of South Carolina than in any distinct class anywhere among us." To the Viscountess Avonmore, "the South Carolinians seemed almost a different race. . . . There is more dignity—more polish—about him than the Northerner."

The unsurpassed virtue of Southern women cannot be disputed. Chancellor Harper in 1837 spoke of the one known instance of an unfaithful South Carolina wife of the upper class as almost unbelievable. Harriet Martineau in 1836 spoke of this exceptional purity, and Olmsted in 1854 found "the women of the South are unexcelled in the world for every quality which commands admiration, respect and love." The common explanation that men's easy access to slave women protected the white even from temptation is doubtless true so far as it goes; but it must be supplemented by the chivalric regard for women fostered by Southern society, and the consciousness that transgressions were at the risk of the man's life and the woman's social ostracism rather than divorce or damage suits. At least two first-class scandals in the highest South Carolina circles in the generation before 1860 might be cited; but the wives were Europeans. Cases could be cited of cruel attacks on female virtue and of infamous conduct toward wives by men of the highest social standing, apparently without loss of caste. That colored concubines were common among single men, and were occasionally kept under conditions of great depravity by married men, only calls attention to the fact that the most universal human passions know no class. On the other hand, it is true that in some plantation communities marriages were so early and marriage fidelity so constant that to this day mulattoes are rare. Standards of private and public conduct were higher in the generation before 1860 than earlier in South Carolina. The frank grossness of the eighteenth century and the cynical degradation of the Regency disappeared under the invigorating of all the churches following the Wesleyan revival and the toning up of religion and morals by the Evangelical and Oxford Movements, and others, in England and America.

Competition under post-bellum approximation toward equality of opportunity has proved the aristocratic stock to be composed of some first-class intellectual strains, but generally of an ability of no overwhelming superiority. The old regime rested on a moral rather than an intellectual foundation. Its basis was a state of mind as well as a state of property—the sense of personal, family, and social responsibility, and the confident aggressiveness of men in a favored position. Its removal from social and political leadership, where, like all class government, it served its own class interests with frequent disregard or sheer ignorance of the needs of the masses, has entailed a serious social loss as well as some gain. Its standards of personal and family honor and public service, powerfully permeating classes much wider than its own, are the priceless heritage of the old South, sadly neglected by the new. It and the type of government that it maintained are our most distinctive contribution to American history. Though their every shortcoming be magnified, the State must be proud of her ancient regime and the men and women under it who gave the world an exalted conception of the word South Carolina.

Human Failings under the Old Regime.—But lest we be considered as idealizing, let us acknowledge that an inspection of all sides of the record reveals the fact that human nature manifested itself in more nearly the same manner as now than is indicated by the conventionalized accounts that often pass current for descriptions of ante-bellum society and government. When he became a legislator, said William J. Grayson, he began to receive applications from candidates for his vote. When he was congressman he was flooded with applications for appointments and all sorts of favors. Rich men wanted their sons educated at public expense at West Point, and if the father had been educated there he seemed to think that an additional reason why his son should also have the privilege. When Grayson was collector of the Port of Charleston there was the same flood of applications for office, with imputations of unfairness from those whom he could not appoint.

The corruption of low-lying elements remained to the end. F. W. Pickens, in 1856, speaking of Calhoun's opposition to national nominating conventions, said, as an illustration his hearers would recognize, "And Mr. Calhoun's fertile genius could also, no doubt point out serious objections to the mode and manner of electing almost any deliberative assembly, if he chose to analyze it. Take for instance our own legislatures. He could easily prove that there has been corruption and even bribery at many of the election boxes—that there had been fraud and corrupt combinations in many of the Districts. And, even after the legislature was assembled, it could be proved that there was corrupt management and log-rolling, and unjust and unfair legislation."

This disagreeable subject may here be summarized for the whole period between 1800 and 1860. Charles Pinckney charged illegal voting in Charleston, about the beginning of the century, in which his own Democrats were doubtless as deeply involved as the Federalists. "Rusticus Scriblerus" protested against bribery and handing to illiterates in Camden tickets containing names they had not intended to vote. Edward Hooker, the Ninety Six schoolmaster, described the congressional electioneering at Pickensville in 1806, with Alston treating his proselytes in the barroom, while Earle presided over his own whiskey bench in the middle of the street. From 1816 to 1834, said Grayson, both sides bought votes at about equal prices in the bitter, meaningless Charleston city politics. Governor Henagan lamented to the legislature in 1840 that "it is not to be disguised that here, hundreds sell their votes for money and for whiskey." The "bull pen," which flourished in hot contests wherever a large low element existed, held venal voters in physical confinement and drunkenness until they were carried up to vote. So corrupt was the election in Richland in 1840 that the legislature ordered a new election. It was reported that General John S. Preston and General James H. Adams spent $35,000 and about $17,000 respectively in their famous Richland District race.

The decades immediately following the Revolution were disfigured with an unusual degree of intemperance, dishonesty, and violence. For years frauds or losses by tax collectors were common. Shortages of about a score of sheriffs and district tax collectors (treasurers) totaling $47,283, many of long standing, were reported in 1842 and repeated in 1845. Through 1812 impeachments of atrociously dishonest or criminally careless tax collectors and occasionally sheriffs or ordinaries (probate judges) were not uncommon. One of the worst cases was that of a former treasurer of Charleston, charged with misappropriating $10,000. He was unanimously convicted in 1807 and was disqualified for office for five years.

The most notable impeachment of the period was that of Attorney General Alexander Moultrie in 1792 and 1793. A fever of land speculation was sweeping the country. Capitalists from Boston to Savannah grasped for "Yazoo lands." Moultrie, like many men of prominence, was interested in Western land companies, four of which a little later, by bribery of the Georgia legislature, secured millions of acres for trifling prices and started one of the prime political scandals in American history. Moultrie, having collected £21,310 sterling due the State, lent it on what seemed good security to his land company associates. In his personal interest in the object thus aided, and not in lending the money, provided it had been done prudently, lay his offense, as, according to the customs of the time, such use of public funds was countenanced, though at the official's risk. The land speculators lost. Moultrie had also allowed large discounts to himself and others on debts due to the State. He was unanimously convicted and was sentenced to seven years' disqualification for office.

Drunkenness and Other Vices—The Temperance Movement.—Though many, like the singularly pure R. Barnwell Rhett, could sincerely say when tempted to bow to what he conceived the wicked social custom of dueling, "I fear God more than man," many more were stained by the traditional "vices of a gentleman." Gambling was common. A brave and gallant gentleman when accused of cheating at cards was reduced to this: "Col. —— admits that he is obnoxious to censure for playing too much with the young men about the town during the summer previous to his election as Governor, and he reproaches himself severely for it; he also says he was in the habit of taking liberties at the table . . . for the purpose of teasing. . . . Further than this, he avers in the most solemn manner that he is not guilty." When Major ——, son of two of our most ancient families and son-in-law of a third, was again served with a sheriff's levy, he asked the officer, "Is Mr. [rich father-in-law] dead?"

Dr. Ramsay said in 1808 that only a physician could know the ravages of drunkenness in good South Carolina society (which, we might add, was also the case elsewhere). Both gluttony and drunkenness were ordinary amusements in the generation following the Revolution, the former even among ladies. The commonness of intemperance even among judges to about 1840 has already been noticed. Said Grayson of the post-Revolutionary society of Beaufort:

"They were a jovial and somewhat rough race, liberal, social, warm-hearted, hospitable, addicted to deep drinking, hard swearing, and practical joking and not a little given to loose language and indelicate allusions. . . . They met monthly or oftener to hunt and dine. . . . At these festivals no man was permitted to go home sober."

Ministers of every denomination except the Methodists, whose young reforming zeal was at its height, drank at pleasure, and with a frequency far exceeding today. Numbers of brilliant clerical careers were totally wrecked. Said Professor R. Means Davis in a manuscript "History of Temperance in South Carolina," after picturing even the severe Associate Reform Presbyterian minister and his precentor taking their corn whiskey just before service, "Methodism swept over South Carolina with great power and introduced many new ideas about personal morality."

The motives for stringent regulations from colonial days to keep liquor from slaves are analagous to the fear of drunken Negroes which in recent decades has so strengthened prohibition sentiment in the South. But the colonial statute book abounds with attempts to regulate the abuse among whites also. The unorganized temperance movement was evidenced in 1784 by the publication of Dr. Rush's essay on the evils of alcoholic drinks and the recommendation of the Charleston Grand Jury that dram shops below a certain locality be suppressed. In 1836 Governor McDuffie urged that the legislature abolish liquor shops in

Columbia as nuisances corrupting the college students, our future rulers; but so little was he heeded that in 1857, says Judge O'Neall, there were in Columbia sixty-four grog shops and only sixty-two temperance men. Governor Gist (1858-60) was an ardent advocate of radical restrictions on liquor. The Prince William (Parish) Temperance Society in 1839 petitioned the legislature for prohibition. Grand Worthy Patriarch A. M. Kennedy, in 1852, at the State Convention of the South Carolina Sons of Temperance, urged State-wide prohibition, and his successor Henry Summer, in 1857, stressed that, though moral suasion must be the main reliance, prohibition by law must be the aim.

Judge O'Neall threw himself ardently into the movement and became head of the "Washingtonians" in South Carolina and of the later Sons of Temperance in Canada and the United States. R. B. and Albert Rhett, DeBow, T. S. Grimké, and prominent Charleston physicians also were active. The Tupper law of 1849, says Professor R. Means Davis, introduced a new era in South Carolina liquor regulation, restricting retailing to bona fide taverns furnishing food, lodgings, and stables. The act of 1874 legalized under licenses ordinary saloons in town and sellers of wine and beer anywhere. The local option law of 1856 kept Marlboro dry until liquor was forced upon her during Reconstruction. Still so strong was the liquor element among back-country Baptists that in 1859 the King's Mountain Baptist Association's refusal of fellowship to distillers, sellers, and drinkers caused a secession and the forming of "The Constitutional King's Mountain Baptist Association." In 1866 reunion came when the Association confined itself to moral suasion and left each church its rights.

Dueling and Its Social Background.—South Carolina, Georgia, Mississippi, Tennessee, and Kentucky were eminent as dueling States. The causes were complex—an ancient custom, a state of society, and a state of mind. The colonists brought dueling with them. They received a new stimulus to combat from the Revolution, after which dueling markedly increased. The Southern social system cultivated pride in personal honor and egotistic hauteur. The praise formerly common in South Carolina, he was "quick to resent an insult or forgive an injury," expressed an ideal distinctly emotional and uncontrolled.

So possessed was the South Carolina mind with the idea that no reflection must be permitted on one's honor, and so hypersensitive did the egotistical become in such an atmosphere, that lives were sacrificed on the merest trifles. About 1832 two young men of the highest standing in Beaufort died upon the field of honor because one remarked that the other was officious. When Roach and Adams, students at the South Carolina College, simultaneously took hold of a dish of food in the mess hall, both felt so insulted that a challenge passed. Roach, desperately wounded, drank himself to death in remorse at having killed Adams. The second of one and the adviser of the other were among the leading men of the State. Men who had hardly ever fired a pistol were at the mercy of practiced marksmen of natural calmness. The theory of a fair fight was in such cases ridiculous. John Lyde Wilson, an habitual duelist, is said by Perry to have bluffed off investigation of his "defalcation" of his contingent fund while Governor until Thomas S. Grimké, who on principle would not fight a duel, prepared to move his expulsion from the Senate, with the result that the money was accounted for. But, said Judge Huger, Grimké would stand upon a burning housetop longer than would Wilson if duty or manhood required. Petigru was saved, only by the pathetic circumstance of the death of his child, from a duel with a lawyer seeking by intimidation to deprive him of the leadership of the Charleston bar. Public indignation prevented Henry Gourdin from having to answer at the pistol point for warning the president against placing a totally unworthy applicant in an important position.

Unless they had already killed their man, few indeed could, as did Robert Barnwell Rhett, decline to fight without losing their standing. When denounced on the floor of the Senate by Clemens of Alabama as a traitor, coward, and liar (it is needless to say without the slightest warrant), he replied in words widely commended North and South: "But my second reason for not calling the Senator from Alabama into the field was of a still higher and more controlling nature. For twenty years I have been a member of the church of Christ. The Senator knows it—everybody knows it. I cannot, and will not, dishonor my religious profession." No station of usefulness or eminence (except clerical, judicial, and a few official positions) exempted a man from being called out by any person passing as a gentleman. Rev. Henry Purcell, rector of St. Michael's from 1784 to 1802, about 1795 challenged a fellow-clergyman for condemning his pamphlet against Bishop Seabury and was put under peace bond. W. C. Preston escaped a duel with Robert Cunningham[2] only by explaining that he meant no reflection on the Cuninghams of the Revolution by his denunciation of Tories. Calhoun in 1838 avoided meeting Waddy Thompson only by explaining that his contradiction of Thompson did not apply, in view of the latter's statement of what he had really said. Seconds were actually selected for a duel that friends prevented between Calhoun and Grosvenor of New York in 1814.

Dueling was part of a highly organized, responsible society whose legal organization, as J. H. Hammond remarked, bordered on anarchy (that is to say, anarchy in the philosophical sense of absence of restraint

[2] The post-Revolutionary Cunninghams added the second "n."

upon the individual). Its best excuse was, in the words of a condemner of it, that it protected a gentleman in a state of society in which another could insult him and still be considered a gentleman. Said Lathers, the duel, "while not justified by religious principles and out of harmony with modern civilization, yet had the redeeming quality of largely suppressing outbursts of passion, personal abuse, and outrage, and of prompting the good manners and strict regard for social amenities of which the South is justly proud."

The duel cultivated definiteness and decision of character. As an ideal it was an expression of the greater value of one's character and family than life; but in practice it frequently became inextricably mixed with fantastic self-esteem, desire to stifle criticism or opposition, or a fierce and implacable determination to kill an enemy. As a survival of paganism it highly emphasized truthfulness, integrity, and courage without condemning lewdness, pride, and hate. Based on the preposterous theory that absolute power of life and death can beneficially be left with every individual, it placed every man who abhorred murder at the mercy of every man without qualms at killing.

Opposition to Dueling.—Though for ages illegal, the duel was virtually a part of our legal system. The survivor, if tried, as rarely occurred, as a matter of course was acquitted if the fight had been fair. Opposition to dueling was long futile. Judge Pendleton in about 1784 so strongly urged a jury to observe their oath that they declared a duelist guilty of homicide, whereupon the gentleman drew from his pocket a pardon. The death of Hamilton stimulated General C. C. Pinckney to activity against the practice. The South Carolina American Revolutionary Society and the Cincinnati condemned it. Younger men merely scoffed that these elders had fought in their youth. John Blake White's drama, *Modern Honor,* performed in Charleston in 1812, was inspired by the death of two young men in particularly useless duels.

In 1807 Bishop Bowen preached in St. Michael's against the practice, on the occasion of a duel of shocking character. The sermon was printed in 1823, a year in which the Charleston Grand Jury called for action to prevent the loss of so many valuable lives every year. Such an entry shows how futile it would be to count, to say nothing of naming, the scores of duels I have noted. Scores were never mentioned in the press. It was a delicate personal matter, and gentlemen had a way of going, accompanied by a friend, to give a sound beating to editors not of their class who in any way became too personal.

Numerous challenges were sent in or near Charleston in 1812. Dr. P. A. Moser's law of December, 1812, prescribed, against principals and seconds, imprisoning, fining, and exclusion from law, medicine, or divinity, or any trade or profession or public office. This did not preclude punishment for homicide, also. The sentence in 1813, confirmed on appeal, of Walter Taylor in Edgefield to fine, imprisonment, and peace bond for challenging his son-in-law, A. Nesbit, was one of the few convictions, if indeed there were any others. To remedy the judges' having virtually interpreted away the Moser act, the law was amended, but without effect.

Wilson's Dueling Code.—Before John Lyde Wilson (1784-1849) published his *Code of Honor* in 1838, duels were conducted as the participants agreed. There is no reason to doubt Governor Wilson's statement that his motive was to prevent "unnecessary" duels and, if a fight was inevitable, to save lives by a regular routine. Duels were thenceforth usually conducted with punctilious decorum. The code was reprinted in 1858, and with slight changes in 1878, and may be summarized as follows: Never resent an insult (unless by blows or such like) in public. Never challenge until consulting your second. All communications must be in the language of gentlemen (thus preventing aggravation of the original difficulty). Everything must be left to the second, whose mind is more capable of a just judgment of every circumstance; and no second may serve without the assurance that the principal will wholly submit to his judgment. The second must compose the quarrel if honor permits. A night must intervene between an offense and a duel. The weapon must be that customary, in South Carolina the single-shot smooth-bore pistol, and the distance must be ten to twenty yards. If a principal fire too soon, his opponent's second may fire upon him, and must if his principal fall. Unless the insult has been gross, the seconds should propose shaking hands on "the middle ground" after one fire, but the second of the wronged man must insist on further shots for deep wrongs. The giving of the word is thus: "Gentlemen, are you ready? Fire; one, two, three, halt." Firing must be between the words "fire" and "halt." A man refusing to fight must be posted as a coward.

Some Notable Duels.—The height of the ridiculous was reached in the duel long before Wilson's code, between the middle-aged Henry Laurens and the youthful future Judge, J. F. Grimké. Grimké had the right to fire first, and his pistol snapped. Laurens, who condemned dueling, refused to take his turn. Some time was spent alternately abusing or urging each other to fire or to draw swords, until second Gervais removed Laurens as having amply met Grimké's challenge.

Very different was the duel fought because Edward P. Simons "damned" General Geddes and his son in a Charleston campaign in 1823. Their clothing was cut by the first four shots, and at the fifth young Geddes was shot through both thighs and Simons was killed.

McDuffie was challenged by William Cumming of Augusta in 1822 in a political quarrel. Cumming lodged a bullet against McDuffie's spinal cord which the physicians feared to remove. Their quarrel continued, and, after several attempted meetings at Cumming's demand, in a second duel McDuffie suffered a broken arm. The bullet in his spine is thought by some to have been the cause of his wrecked health, which ended in complete mental imbecility.[3]

After Perry had killed Bynum in a duel arising out of their activities as Unionist and Nullifier respectively, he could afford to refuse to fight William R. Taber, the famous *Mercury* editor, who challenged him because Perry criticized his oration.

William R. Taber of the *Mercury* figured in one of the most famous duels in our history, on September 29, 1856. Articles in the *Mercury* signed "Nullifier," by Edmund Rhett, Jr., attacking Judge A. G. Magrath, a candidate for Congress, said that his friends' cry of persecution was "that ready refuge from the pursuit of justice, of falling fortune, and of bankrupt character." An editorial note accompanying the first article was taken as endorsing them. Edward, the Judge's younger brother, challenged editors Taber and Heart, both of whom accepted, and since Magrath's challenge, they considered, contained insulting language, made their acceptance a cross challenge. The cross challenge introduced a complication rendering peaceful accommodation more difficult.

Taber maintained that he must defend the liberty of the press, which he denied abusing. It was agreed that Magrath should first fight Taber. After the second fire the seconds for almost an hour sought an accommodation. James Connor for Magrath demanded that Taber say that he "regrets the publication in the *Mercury* of whatever in those articles is personal." Taber's second, who had stated that they came to seek satisfaction as well as give it, would only consent to a simultaneous statement by Taber that he had not intended any reflection on Judge Magrath's private character, and by Magrath that he had not intended to insult Taber by the wording of the challenge. Less from Magrath or more from Taber, he held, would manifest a deliberate intention to accomplish Taber's humiliation. The principals being placed for the third fire, Cunningham (Taber's second) courteously requested Magrath to depress a little more the point of his pistol (held in the usual South Carolina position, arm straight downward). "Still more, Mr. Magrath," insisted Cunningham. At this point occurred a serious breach of the code by a relative of Taber's, who should have been excluded from the ground. This gentlemen had been walking around with a displayed pistol, taking

[3] E. L. Green, *McDuffie* (1936).

position "proximate to Mr. Magrath," and mandatorily exclaiming "Not enough yet, Sir." This diversion of Magrath's attention to a possible second antagonist was made with the intention of causing a general melee, as occasionally occurred in such affairs in other States. When it had passed, the third fire was given. Taber fell mortally wounded.

The duel between Magrath and Heart which was to follow if Taber did not render complete satisfaction of course did not occur. Rhett was at hand to demand the right to a duel should Judge Magrath intervene. The duel was notable for the parties concerned, the questions of personal and editorial responsibility involved, the irregularities permitted in defiance of the code when the circumstances demanded its strictest observance, and the bitter feelings all these circumstances stirred.

Homicide and "Low Crime."—Dueling and ordinary homicide flourished side by side and were the outcome of the same psychology of willful individualism. Carrying concealed weapons was not unlawful in South Carolina until January 1, 1881, but the act of 1859 severely penalized assaults made with such.

Nor was "low crime" (to recognize our common distinction) so uncommon as the idealizers of our past imagine. At a Charleston court in 1852 white men were convicted of pickpocketing, larceny, forgery, and obtaining goods under false pretenses. The sentences were whipping and imprisonment. There were frequent complaints of trading with slaves and keeping gambling houses for them. On February 1, 1850, a white man was hanged in Edgefield for wife murder. (He also murdered his slave, whom he had forced to kill his wife.) His female accomplice was not indicted; for, as one writer boasted, Southern chivalry refuses to hang a woman—the piratess and murderess Mrs. Fisher being (he says erroneously) the only woman ever executed in South Carolina.

The Classes and the Masses.—The duel was distinctly the habit of the aristocracy, though somewhat extended beyond its bounds. Pious middle-class persons eschewed it on principle, and the undisciplined lower element avenged themselves less formally. These differences of custom helped to accentuate the usual contrast of classes in South Carolina.

If there had not been a good share of arrogance along with the virtues of the aristocracy they would have been more than human. This was frequent among the Charleston upper class. Profusely praised both by themselves and by others, unjustly abused by Northern fanaticism and up-country ignorance or prejudice, their natural reaction was an arrogance often so complacent as to be unconscious. There was too much tendency to despise the masses and too little to permeate them sympathetically with higher ideals of culture and conduct; but it must be emphasized that the aristocracy of Charleston did very thoroughly perform this service for their own city, so that to this day persons entirely outside that class very generally bear the marks of this influence. Long after 1865 an aged Charleston gentleman remarked that he had for the first time observed a man to swagger on the streets. A writer in the *Constitutional Union* of Georgia, December 6, 1850, considered South Carolina the most aristocratic State in the Union, with less intercourse between rulers and ruled and less sympathy between rich and poor than in any other commonwealth; while another writer in the same journal found "an overweening pride of ancestry; a haughty defiance of all restraints not self-imposed; an innate hankering after power, and a self-opinionated assumption of supremacy." The aristocracy thus in a most serious respect failed of its proper and useful function, and bitterly has it paid for its faults. It is a serious question whether the reaction it met in Tillman's venomous assault was any worse violation of Christian charity and gentlemanly fairness.

When Washington Allston's mother who had married her first husband to please her family, married, to please herself, her second husband, Dr. H. C. Flagg, the son of a wealthy Rhode Island merchant and himself surgeon of the First South Carolina Continentals throughout the Revolution, her father, outraged at alliance with a "Yankee adventurer," threatened to cut off her inheritance. When, within the aristocracy itself, after 1865, the head of a family somewhat older in standing would let it be understood that he considered it a condescension for his daughter to marry the descendant of a Revolutionary patriot and aristocrat of exceptional distinction, the attitude toward the small up-country farmer may be imagined. A low-country friend to whom it was protested, "But So-and-So was a gentleman," replied, with the air of one making an admission more damaging to the other side than his own, "Oh, yes, an *up-country* gentleman." It was a Charleston gentleman who said that on the stagecoach he had conversed with a lady of decided culture and charm, "and she was from the up country." As a matter of fact, she was a lady whose beauty and culture graced the eminent position which her husband later held. The gentleman was more considerate than the Charleston lady who disdained to converse in the carriage with an up-country lady whose education and culture were doubtless not surpassed in the State.

Without bitterness these things may be smiled at, and the truth recognized that Charleston and some regions of the low country were before 1860 culturally far ahead of all but a few localities and a limited number of individuals in the up country. It is astonishing to note even today the large proportion of cultured persons in the up country whose families came from the low country or from Virginia. Low-country social ideals and social and intellectual leaders largely dominate Columbia, and did so even more fully before its recent commercial expansion.

Graduates of the South Carolina College by districts from 1807 to 1856 inclusive numbered: Abbeville, 73; Anderson, 11; Barnwell, 15; Beaufort, 77; Charleston (including the present Berkeley, Dorchester, and the Holly Hill section of Orangeburg), 280; Chester, 50; Chesterfield, 21; Clarendon (evidently generally included in Sumter), 1; Colleton, 21; Darlington, 57; Edgefield, 56; Fairfield, 79; Georgetown, 33; Greenville, 19; Kershaw, 49; Lancaster, 29; Laurens, 42; Lexington, 16; Marion, 9; Marlboro, 26; Newberry, 47; Orangeburg, 38; Pendleton, 28; Richland, 178; Spartanburg, 12; Sumter (evidently Sumter election district, including Clarendon judicial district), 76; Union, 29; Williamsburg, 15; York, 39.

There were, especially after 1825, scores of handsome mansions in the up country, the number increasing as agriculture and commerce grew. Waddy Thompson's estate on Paris Mountain, with its vistas in many directions, was a show place for travelers. The mansions built (it is said) by Governor Pickens for his two daughters in Newberry and Edgefield districts were very handsome, and in them, as in many another, educated men and cultured women dispensed thoroughly South Carolinian hospitality. The Rutherford mansion in the town of Newberry resembled a nobleman's seat.

Classes were much less separated in the up than in the low country, for the reasons that its upper class had so much more recently risen, and that there was no center in which it could collect as in a disdainful social fortress. And it must not be forgotten that there was always a broad-minded, liberal element in the ruling class in both sections that better understood the permanent interests of the masses and of the State as a whole than they were able to bring either their own class or the common people to see. The lack in our domestic politics was an educated lower class to appreciate, check, or support such leadership. When the masses were finally led to revolt in 1890 they repudiated the services of some of their best friends as well as of their supercilious superiors. The word "aristocrat" had come to mean to them a man who neglects and despises the people.

The Poor Whites.—This almost technical yet inexact phrase includes by no means all white men who were poor, but only the ignorant and shiftless lower stratum. By all contemporary testimony their condition was pitiful and, among appreciable elements, revolting. William Gregg in 1845 thought thousands never passed a month without hunger, and Governor Hammond estimated in 1850 that 50,000 out of a white population of 275,000 could not gain a decent living, and that stealing and dishonest trading on what slaves stole was common. Tillmanism and Bleaseism did not produce the ignorance and poverty that formed a conspicuous part of their following; they revealed them.

The origin of the poor white has been the subject of more speculation than investigation. My observations of the sources impress me that we produced, rather than imported, him. The poor immigrant of the eighteenth century degenerated under isolation, poor lands, and competition with the slave plantation. Hookworm, malaria, execrable diet, and the whiskey drinking that was, dieticians think, partly induced by it, promoted the downward course. Many when transferred to favorable environments have risen to prosperity and high public respect.

Our past has been so obscured and distorted by the idealizer, the apologist, and the propagandist as to recall the definition of history as "a tale that has been agreed upon." A Southern writer recently boasted of the old South as a country where white men did not work, whereas in reality a vast proportion of Confederates took arms with hands already hardened by toil, and the majority of them never owned a slave.

That the poor white was the real victim of slavery and the Negro its beneficiary (which is not saying he should have remained in school forever) is now a commonplace. The long class and sectional antagonism we have already traced from about 1765. The fear that it might prevent the up country from co-operation in secession was an ignorant exaggeration. The War of Secession and Reconstruction united classes as never before. The partial subordination of the Negro danger by 1890 at last tore away the mask and showed South Carolina as she really was, a divided, conflicting, and potentially class-wrecked society.

Rumblings of Class Conflict.—The movements of 1838 for the popular election and increased power of the governor, and of 1844 to 1858 for the popular choice of presidential electors, for a limited-term judiciary, and for new up-country districts, have already been noted. The early 1850's heard demands for a new Constitution to remedy the concentration of power in the hands of some 80,000 citizens in the blacker districts instead of the 190,000 in the whiter. A few up-country extremists favored an extra-legal convention to frame and enforce a new Constitution, and low-country extremists feared that if South Carolina seceded in 1852 the threats of the up country to leave Negro-owning planters to do their own fighting might be made good. The retiring Governor J. L. Manning and the incoming Governor Adams in 1854 both prayed that we be spared the spirit of innovation. The first step might be fatal, said Adams, as under the cry of reform may be "pulled down over your heads the best balanced system of government that the world has yet looked upon."

Professor F. A. Porcher recalled with pain that "The growing dissatisfaction" that only planters were being elected to the legislature in his parish was so great that in 1846 "the division between the two classes was attended with acrimony."[4]

J. H. Hammond in 1847 saw that it was essential to keep "the actual slave-holder not only predominant, but paramount within its [slavery's] circles," for it was "weakened by every accession of administration and executive power to the masses here." Trescot in 1859 was grieved both by the extravagances and violence of temper of the extremer defenders of the aristocratic regime founded on slavery, and by the proposals of those "who, wearied and disgusted with these extravagances, would rashly destroy those peculiarities of our State character and constitution, which are liable to such mischievous exaggeration; who would eradicate our old State pride; destroy the old conservative character of our State politics; strip us bare of all the glorious achievements of the past, and drive us, destitute and dishonored, into the fit companionship of a vagabond and demoralized democracy."

While sensing the dangers of democracy, South Carolina leaders ignored its cardinal virtue that it alone forces society for its own protection to elevate and do justice to the masses of men. Though liberal aristocrats in South Carolina as elsewhere strove for this, no aristocratic society has ever done so except under compulsion. Nor have the two South Carolinas, the one of the masses, the other of the classes, ever long held in unity except in the presence of the Negro peril or the emotional fusion of war. The two South Carolinas were moving toward their inevitable conflict when a far greater conflict postponed their trial of strength. When manhood suffrage, existing since 1810, would overthrow upper class control was merely a matter of time and circumstance.

[4] Porcher, "Memoirs," in *South Carolina Historical and Genealogical Magazine,* XLVII (April, 1946), 105.

CHAPTER XLVIII

THE MEXICAN WAR AND THE SECESSION MOVEMENT, 1847-1852

THE ANNEXATION of Texas in 1845 led directly to the war with Mexico; but the two issues were theoretically distinct and found many favoring one and opposing the other. Calhoun, for instance, ardently favored annexing Texas, for the sake of accomplishing which and in order to settle peaceably the Oregon question with England he accepted the Secretaryship of State; but he as earnestly opposed war with Mexico. Governor Aiken deprecated acquiring Mexican territory, and a long list of Southern leaders deprecated both war and acquisitions. Nowhere, said one of her Senators (whose opinion might be questioned) was the war immediately after its outbreak more detested than in South Carolina. On December 30, 1847, with the treaty almost made, the Charleston *Mercury* strongly opposed annexing Mexican territory. The war, whose possibilities as a fomenter of sectional strife Calhoun foresaw, dropped before him for the first time, he declared, a curtain obscuring the future. He feared that a war with Mexico would prove the prelude to a greater and more distressing war. This, with his conviction of the Africanization of the South as the inevitable result of emancipation, filled him with hopeless gloom. The war was most hated in New England. It was welcome in New York, but was most desired in the West and Southwest.

South Carolina's quota of volunteers was quickly raised and pledged "for the war." When the army disembarked at Vera Cruz, August 9, 1847, the Palmettos mustered 974. The South Carolina regiment, commonly known as "the Palmettos," says Mr. Justin H. Smith, "was made up of superior material. Men fit to be officers were in the ranks." Its Colonel, Pierce M. Butler (1798-1847) of Edgefield, a soldier by instinct, had served eleven years in the regular army. He was Governor from 1836 to 1838. He now returned to military life from a prominent business position. He held his men more by their fear of losing his respect than by fear of incurring punishment. Lieutenant-Colonel J. P. Dickinson of Kershaw had to be restrained, so dashing was his courage. Major A. H. Gladden of Richland, when called by the death of Butler and

Dickinson to command, manifested admirably both the fighting and the administrative qualities of an officer.

The South Carolinians soon won from General Scott the name "The Tigers," but it is forgotten in their old name. After taking part in the capture of Vera Cruz, the regiment at once began to pay its heavy toll of illness on the burning march down the sickly coast sixty miles and back in the Alvarado expedition. In all the battles of the valley of Mexico except Molino del Rey the Palmetto regiment participated. At Churubusco they lost 137, exceeding by over 30 any other regiment's losses. At Chapultepec and the City of Mexico their loss of 100 again exceeded all others'.

The Battles in the Valley of Mexico.—At Colonel Butler's earnest request for the Palmettos, General Quitman assigned the duty of his part in the attack on Churubusco, August 20, 1847, to the South Carolina and New York regiments. "Whatever may happen," said Butler in leaving, "we will maintain our honor." As Butler, already severely injured, stood beneath the flag he was mortally wounded. Lieutenant-Colonel Dickinson next fell mortally wounded. The whole force advanced, and the Mexicans fled toward the city, four miles away.

The army now moved upon the formidable fortified rock of Chapultepec, some 3,000 yards from the city of Mexico. Quitman on September 30 ordered the assault by the South Carolinians, New Yorkers, and Pennsylvanians. The New Yorkers claimed the honor of first planting the flag above Chapultepec.

Three thousand yards away lay the Gate of Belen guarding the southwestern entrance to the city. Quitman, thirsty for glory, carried his determination to take this only short of disobedience to General Scott. He selected the Palmettos and the regular Rifle Regiment for the assault. These entered the city simultaneously. Mounting the wall, Quitman, to signal to the rest of the army his victory, called for colors. Major Gladden rushed up with the Palmetto flag, which was thus the first to be planted on the walls of the city. The flag of the Rifles immediately followed.

The only remaining defense of the city was the citadel, some 300 yards ahead. In advancing against it Major Gladden was severely wounded and was succeeded in command by Captain Dunovant. During the night Santa Anna saved the city from sack by a midnight evacuation, and on the 14th the American army in an imposing ceremony occupied the grand plaza.

Of the 974 members of the Palmetto regiment who landed at Vera Cruz, 422 perished in Mexico and about 79 later died of wounds or exposure. On October 19, 1847, the State sent about 275 more men, but they arrived too late for anything but garrison duty at Vera Cruz. The South Carolinian Benjamin Huger of the regular army served as General Scott's chief of ordnance and for gallant conduct was successively brevetted major, lieutenant-colonel, and colonel.

The lack of a matured national patriotism permitted great freedom of expression in the 1840's. Calhoun in 1847 proclaimed it uncertain whether our army could reach Mexico City or dictate a peace, and after the city was captured Waddy Thompson maintained that we could not beat Mexico without ruining our finances. But Calhoun had finally to abandon urging merely holding a defensive line and acknowledge the necessity of large acquisitions. Webster's opposition to the war led him into remarks both "unpatriotic and unintelligent," and even during the war to suggest impeaching the President. A Boston journal declared it would be "a joy to hear that the hordes under Scott and Taylor were, every man of them, swept into the next world," and James Russell Lowell discouraged enlistments and urged that soldiers desert.

Questions of Slavery in the Mexican Cession.—The sectional conflict over the newly acquired territory quickly led straight to a far greater war. The Wilmot Proviso of 1846 that slavery should never exist in any of the acquired territory raised the specific issue which, broadened to all territory, became the platform of the Republican party soon to arise. Calhoun at once sought to rally the South to uncompromising opposition to this program; but, as usual, it took time to bring great masses of men to new views. South Carolina, as alert as Calhoun to the dangers threatening her peculiar institution, promptly adopted the dictum that the exclusion of slavery from the territories would mean the dissolution of the Union. This was her deliberate view, reasonable and proper if her premise was correct that emancipation would mean the Africanization of the South as it had meant of certain West Indian Islands.

Logic was supplemented by a passionate sense of injustice. The slave States had furnished 43,232 soldiers in the Mexican War and the free States, with their far greater population, 22,136. To see the North, which had largely opposed the war, seeking to deprive the South, whose soldiers had mainly conquered the new territory, of all share in it, roused indignant anger. But from the standpoint of the North, Calhoun's dictum that Congress could not exclude slavery from the territories, and that a territory on becoming a State could have it or not as it chose, was in effect a demand that no fighting should occur until his side had possessed itself of the citadel. To those condemning slavery, for a nation to allow its destiny to be thus cursed by merely allowing to grow up an ineradicable evil, was unreasonable in the last degree.

Calhoun's Senate resolutions asserting the absolute right to carry slaves into the newly acquired territory reached no vote, but they became the overwhelmingly approved South Carolina program. Admitting his premise that slavery was essential to civilization in the South, Calhoun's clear, bold, uncompromising position was a logical and moral necessity. "Instead of shunning, we ought to court the issue with the North on the slavery question," he wrote in 1847. "We are now stronger relatively than we shall be hereafter, politically and morally." But the Wilmot Proviso, he continued, was only one of the many aggressions on slavery that must be met. They must all be checked, if possible without dissolution of the Union, which should be the last resort. Northern commerce might be excluded from Southern harbors, etc. There should be a Southern convention, he concluded, to support such measures.

Virginia, on March 8, 1847, adopted resolutions similar to those of Calhoun in the Senate, expressing her determination to resist the Proviso "at all hazards and to the last extremity." The Charleston *Mercury* actively aided his work of creating a Southern party to force national acceptance of his constitutional views on the various aspects of the slavery question. At his death in 1850 Calhoun for the first time saw the South united behind his leadership.

James H. Hammond, perhaps the keenest mind in South Carolina next to Calhoun, showed at first a strange lack of appreciation of the crisis as he stood almost alone in opposing the creation of a Southern pro-slavery party, which he held would cause the formation of a Northern anti-slavery party. This was perhaps a reflection of his previously expressed less extreme view as to the existence of civilization in the South depending on the continuance of slavery. The South at large, far less prepared than South Carolina in thought and circumstances, while indignant at Northern aggressions, was by no means ready yet to follow South Carolina to the inevitable conclusion. Her uncompromising aggressiveness in 1850 to force the issue to disunion if need be, roused such resentment that her leaders found it necessary to remain in the rear until the movement grew sufficiently strong for other States to take some initiative. The Southern Whig press, while praising her heroism, denounced her rashness and folly in disturbing the country. Where will South Carolina find an ally in her crusade against the Union, asked the Richmond *Whig*; of all the States, she would lose most by the dissolution of the Union, whereas, if she were towed a thousand miles out to sea, the Union would not miss her. But the Democratic press generally praised South Carolina. The *Montgomery Advertiser* found her "unlike many of her sisters, 'unshaken, unseduced, unterrified.'"

The Wilmot Proviso, adopted by the House and rejected by the Senate, soon ended virtually all national party divisions in South Carolina except on the issue of whether the State should secede at once, alone, or should await co-operation with other States. Even B. F. Perry, lifelong Unionist in white-man Greenville, declared that the adoption of the Proviso would be "tantamount to a dissolution of the Union," and the Whig Waddy Thompson declared he was ready to dissolve the Union as the only alternative to "the conversion of the South into black provinces."

The crisis marks the beginning of a campaign to strengthen the slaveless white population in their support of slavery by representing it as the only means of preventing the Negroes from being forced upon them as equals in government and marriage. There soon followed the propaganda of 1855-58 to reopen the slave trade so as to make every white man the owner of at least one slave, and the plea on the part of men like Trescot in 1859 that the interests of a slaveholding society demanded the distinction of education for even the poorest white man. Everything tending to divide whites into hostile classes was recognized as dangerous, and the interests of the poor received a new consideration in the educational agitation of 1850 and 1853.

South Carolina Contemplates Secession, 1850.—W. B. Seabrook's election as governor in 1850 was a triumph for the immediate secessionists. Newspapers urged that no Southern youths, not even ministers, could be safely educated in the North. The *Courier* was denounced as "the organ of Northern plunder in Charleston." Maxcy Gregg wrote that the exclusion of slavery from California would justify the South in seceding, seizing California, and closing the Mississippi.

Opposed to Calhoun's policy of securing united Southern action was R. B. Rhett's demand for immediate secession by South Carolina alone. Every State would be forced to take sides for or against her, said Rhett, and he believed enough would rally to her aid to make Federal compulsion impossible. To Calhoun, who always sought to lead and not to drive the South, the proposal to force sister States was not only impractical, but was an insult to their sovereign right to act as each pleased. But irrespective of the action of other States, from the moment of the proposal to exclude slavery from the newly acquired territories South Carolina began to shape her policy in recognition that armed conflict with the Federal government might come at any time. The legislature in 1848 directed that muskets and rifles should be increased to 12,000.

Along with the Wilmot Proviso went other attacks on slavery. The abolitionists assumed an unprecedented activity in their program for preventing another slave State from ever entering the Union, abolishing slavery in the District of Columbia, and multiplying hindrances by mobs and State laws to the recovery of fugitive slaves. On May 14, 1849, the local committees of safety that had sprung up in South Carolina were welded into a State-wide organization with a Central Committee of Vigilance and Safety to correspond with persons and committees throughout the South. In September and October, 1850, Southern Rights Associations were springing up in many Southern States. Despite the desire of the extreme element in South Carolina to secede alone if need be, the whole movement was a manifestation of what is now called "Southern nationalism." Long before the term was used, there was the growing consciousness in the South that she constituted an entity within the Union, but different from it, which nature and interest and affection were impelling toward a Southern confederacy. Notwithstanding the emphasis on State sovereignty, the Southern States were tending toward an organic unity, the South.

The central committee of the South Carolina Southern Rights Association and Governor Seabrook officially corresponded with organizations in other States. Calhoun up to his death, March 31, 1850, with his clear, firm understanding, held the State to moderation, while he urged upon influential Mississippians that they take the initiative for a Southern convention. He secretly directed the movement, the leaders carefully concealing his hand, that led to a Mississippi convention which called a convention of the slave States for June, 1850, in Nashville, "to devise and adopt some mode of resistance" to Northern aggression. South Carolina leaders well understood that they were distrusted throughout the South as extremists, and in their private correspondence urged on each other the necessity of caution and of having their program openly presented by other States, and the impolicy of denouncing as "submissionists" the co-operationist faction in their own State.

The legislature bought $7,500 worth of arms and resolved that abolition of slavery in the District of Columbia or adopting the Wilmot Proviso would dissolve the Union. The people elected delegates to their congressional district conventions, each of which elected two delegates to the Nashville Convention in addition to the four chosen by the legislature. In accordance with Calhoun's plan, expressions were studiously moderate, thus avoiding alarm that South Carolina was going too fast. Calhoun even called it "the Mississippi movement."

Calhoun's Position and Death.—That Calhoun desired to preserve the Union if it could be done without abolishing slavery and thereby ruining the South cannot be disputed. But shortly before his death he despaired of the possibility of saving both slavery and the Union. Of the debate on Clay's measures he wrote Hammond on February 16, 1850, " I trust, it will be of a character to satisfy the South, that it cannot with safety remain in the Union, as things now stand and that there is little or no prospect of any change for the better. . . . The impression is now very general, and is on the increase, that disunion is the only alternative that is left us."

Hammond replied: "We must act *now,* and decisively.... Long before the North gets this vast accession of strength she will ride over us rough shod, proclaim freedom or something equivalent to it to our slaves and reduce us to the condition of Hayti. . . . If we do not act now, we deliberately consign, not our posterity, but *our children,* to the flames." Even those who did not vision such horrors felt existing violations of their rights intolerable.

Calhoun, fearing illness would prevent him from speaking in the great debate on Clay's compromise measures, wrote out his speech on the whole issue between North and South. On March 4, 1850, he sat in the Senate as, for two hours, Senator Mason read the speech. The occasion was solemnly impressive. The Union was trembling in the balance, even as was the life of the statesman whose genius and integrity commanded the nation's respect, who brought his dying message to warn and if possible to save. He said:

"I have, Senators, believed from the first that the agitation of the subject of slavery will, if not prevented by some timely and effective measure, end in disunion." The equilibrium of the government has been destroyed, and the South is at the mercy of the North, who controls all other branches of the government [that is, except the still evenly balanced Senate]. This has been caused by the exclusion of slavery from a large part of the territories, the greater appropriations of money for the North, and the growth of centralization. "How, then, can the Union be saved? . . . The North has only to will to accomplish it—to do justice by conceding to the South an equal right in the acquired territory, and to do her duty by causing the stipulations relative to fugitive slaves to be faithfully fulfilled—to cease the agitation of the slavery question, and to provide for the insertion of a provision in the Constitution, by an amendment, which will restore to the South, in substance, the power she possessed of protecting herself, before the equilibrium between the sections was destroyed by the action of this government. . . . If you, who represent the stronger portion, cannot agree to settle them on the broad principle of justice and duty, say so, and let the States we both represent agree to separate and part in peace. If you are unwilling we should part in peace, tell us so, and we shall know what to do, when you reduce the question to submission or resistance."

Thus passed the most powerful mind, the most impressive personality, the most talented, though by no means the wisest, leader in South Carolina history. No other man could have so immortalized himself while defending an impossible cause. So strongly identified is Calhoun with this that his great ability as an executive and his contribution to the solution of numerous public questions are forgotten. Despite his advocacy of a ruinous and impossible policy, he is an heroic figure in a great age. Calhoun possessed the power of personality which enforces one's ideas independently of their wisdom. It is this personality that still holds the imagination.

Calhoun's career is one of the saddest tragedies of American history —a great mind and character caught up in a mistaken cause without being great enough to perceive and conquer the error. It is incorrect to say that Calhoun led South Carolina to destruction. South Carolina was bent upon courses both in 1832 and from 1847 to 1860 which Calhoun did not originate, and to follow which she would have swept him aside as she swept aside other great leaders. He formulated and voiced her views and determination with unrivaled clearness and led the South toward acceptance of them, with an intellectual power and a skill of leadership of which no one else was capable; but so far as South Carolina was concerned he was the chosen leader of a predetermined course, in no sense a driver. He held back his State from the too precipitate action which would have shattered her cause far more quickly than was finally the case. But the question cannot be escaped: What of the statesmanship of a leader who plants himself on theories of society and industry the fallacy of which many of his South Carolina contemporaries exposed, and success in which would have been more disastrous than defeat? Slavery was at last abolished, and abolished by the North in the worst possible way short of servile insurrection, instead of by the South itself in the best way possible. The abolitionist has been proved by the outcome to have understood the essential nature of the Negro as a human being better than did the slaveholder himself, who could see in the slave only a brute labor force which, except under compulsion, would substitute the annihilation of civilization for productive industry.

Calhoun's prophecy of the downfall of civilization in the North with the probable massacre of the cultured and wealthy, unless she adopted the Southern view of the Constitution, his prediction of ruin from the protective system, which its strongest condemners must admit has not occurred, his seeking to prevent manufacturing in the South, are merely corollaries of his fundamental error of adopting slavery as the only possible basis of Southern society. In the support of these ideas he encouraged a worship of the letter of the Constitution, well illustrated by the South Carolina habit of carrying a copy of it in one's pocket and knowing it by heart, which as surely made constitutional bigots as the similar worship of the letter of Biblical text makes religious bigots of those who neglect the real interest which inspires both the Constitution and the Bible as a whole.

It is a stock assertion that the South under Calhoun's leadership has implanted in American public life the reverence for the rights of the States essential for the preservation of American liberty; but we must consider the fact that the insistence on taking this to the extreme led directly to the unexampled trampling on State rights in Reconstruction. Nor has the attitude of the South since Reconstruction manifested any superior regard for State rights, except where their right to control the Negro has been involved. It is a groundless assumption that Northern States have no jealousy of their local rights or are willing to see the Federal government become a centralized despotism.

R. B. Rhett's impetuosity made him appear more clear-sighted than Calhoun, for he much earlier accepted the impossibility of the continuance of slave and free labor in the same Union. But Rhett was hardly more acute. Calhoun saw the danger long before he felt it practicable to proclaim it as insurmountable; and he was restrained by a realization, shared by only a small minority in the South, of the desperate nature of the struggle that must follow secession and the difficulties and perils, both domestic and foreign, that would threaten a separate Southern confederacy.

A view more often held than uttered is that of Ben Robinson in his *Red Hills and Cotton* in 1942, speaking for the small white farmer of the up country: "He sold us out" [i.e., in favor of the large low-country planter]. We realize today that the dominant Southern leadership did this, but we may believe that in Calhoun's case it was not the expression of class selfishness. So convinced was he, like many others, that the small farmer and even the landless white man stood in peril of being reduced to an intolerable situation by emancipation that class interests among the whites seemed negligible. The abolition of slavery to a large degree emancipated the poor white men as well as the Negro; but few outside the non-slaveholding mountaineers recognized this before 1860. Yet there were mutterings even then voicing this discontent more commonly than is generally realized, as shown at pages 513-515.

However one may differ with Calhoun's views, it is impossible to come into contact with his mind and character without feeling profound admiration. The intellectual peer of Webster, and overtopping both him and Clay in character, this champion of a doomed cause occupies one of the most distinguished and honorable positions in American history. He died so deeply in debt from his losses as a cotton planter and his neglect of his own affairs for the public service that the gift of $27,000 by Charleston admirers saved his plantation for his wife besides supplying her with about $7,000,[1] though his splendid talents for the bar might have amassed a fortune.

The tribute of Senator Lodge of Massachusetts at the unveiling of the Calhoun statue in the national Capitol in 1910 is admirable. Calhoun, he says, understood the nature of the sectional conflict better than either Clay or Webster, or at least they did not let it be known if they did understand. But Senator Lodge seems mistaken in speaking of Calhoun as always sanguine and of invincible hopefulness, for he appears to have died with hope clouded by visions of war and perhaps of Southern ruin. Senator Lodge concludes:

"He was the greatest man South Carolina has given to the nation. That in itself is no slight praise, for from the days of the Laurenses, the Pinckneys, the Rutledges, from the time of Moultrie and Sumter, and Marion to the present day, South Carolina has always been conspicuous in peace and war for the force, the ability, and the character of the men who have served her and given to her name its high distinction in our history. But Calhoun was much more even than this. He was one of the most remarkable men, one of the greatest minds, that American public life can show. It matters not that before the last tribunal the verdict went against him, that the extreme doctrines to which his imperious logic carried him have been banned and barred. The man remains greatly placed in our history. The unyielding courage, the splendid intellect, the long devotion to the public service, the pure, unspotted private life are all there, are all here with us now, untouched and unimpaired for after ages to admire."

[1] There were also other large debts besides that on the plantation. Cf. Holmes and Sherrill, *T. G. Clemson,* p. 30, note.

CHAPTER XLIX

WAITING FOR THE SOUTH, 1852-1860

The Nashville Convention, 1850.—As the Nashville Convention (June 3-12, 1850) assembled South Carolina was divided into four factions: secessionists, favoring immediate action by South Carolina alone; the co-operationists, insisting that it was also essential to secure other States; conditional secessionists; and a much smaller group of uncompromising Unionists. Rhett was so precipitate for immediate secession by South Carolina alone that Hammond, long a convinced co-operationist, considered his indiscretion "criminal." The venerable Langdon Cheves, one of the State's greatest minds and characters, was of the same view as Hammond, as, of course, had been Calhoun. B. F. Perry, Unionist in 1832 and 1860, yet held now that the passage of the Wilmot Proviso would be "tantamount to a dissolution of the Union." Petigru and Poinsett regarded disunion as worse than any possible Northern aggression. Poinsett (1779-1851), who in 1832 was ready to fight for the Union against his own State, wrote, secession "will lead to immediate civil war and too probably terminate in defeat and humiliation. . . . If the revolution comes, for there can be no peaceable secession or dissolution of the Union, I am ready to take my part and stand among the sons of the South in the ranks or in organizing our defenses, but without hope."

How little the South was yet ready to follow South Carolina appeared when only nine States sent representatives to the Nashville Convention and only South Carolina sent a full delegation. Virginia's one representative was elected by the minority in one county after the majority had voted not to be represented. The convention repeated the old demand for equal rights in the territories and added the new one of the Federal protection of slave property there, though it said, as an extreme concession, the South would consent to a division of the territory by extending the Missouri Compromise line to the Pacific. It refused to recommend plans of resistance to measures not yet adopted (Clay's compromise measures being still under debate), but agreed to reassemble if Congress failed to meet its demands.

The moderate action of the Nashville Convention tended temporarily to quiet South Carolina secessionists, but not Rhett or Pickens. Rhett inaugurated an active campaign for immediate secession. The

North would not fight, he proclaimed. Abolition, he warned the non-slaveowner, would mean amalgamation or extermination. We would soon have the whole South with us and would take the whole of the territory ceded by Mexico and, when we pleased, as much of Mexico as we needed. E. B. Bryan concluded his huge pamphlet with the words, *"Give us* SLAVERY *or give us death."*

Clay's compromise measures of 1850 were adopted, admitting California as a free State; organizing the rest of the Mexican cession without settling the question whether the old Mexican abolition law still held and leaving the ultimate decision to the time for statehood; reducing the area of Texas (with compensation); forbidding the slave trade in the District of Columbia; and passing a stringent fugitive slave law. The South accepted, but South Carolina raged.

The extremer element of the Nashville Convention from seven States reassembled in November. Langdon Cheves, South Carolina co-operationist, declared in a three-hour speech that the North, by taking the territory that the South had won in the war with Mexico, had abolished the Constitution. "What is the remedy? I answer secession—united secession of the slave-holding States, or a large number of them. Nothing else will be wise—nothing else is practicable."

Shall South Carolina Secede Alone?—The failure of co-operation renewed the contest in South Carolina for separate action. Rhett, Pickens, Maxcy Gregg, J. H. Adams, disgusted with Southern conventions, combated Cheves, Memminger, Orr, J. S. Preston, A. G. Magrath, and Senators R. W. Barnwell and A. P. Butler, who were determined that South Carolina should not again be isolated as in 1832. Governor Seabrook, while professing the co-operation creed, came near to being practically for independent action. Southern Rights Associations covered the South with secession propaganda. Thompson and Perry, accepting the compromise, fought for Southern rights within the Union through Perry's new paper, the Greenville *Southern Patriot.* Grayson, Poinsett, Petigru, Perry, and O'Neall were for the Union unconditionally.

The legislature in December, 1850, prepared for secession and war. To that end provision was made for two conventions. One for slaveholding States, South Carolina suggested, should be held at Montgomery on January 2, 1852. For this she directed her people to elect delegates in October, 1851. The other convention was to be of South Carolina alone, to consider any recommendations which the general Southern convention might make, and to guard against dangers that might arise out of the State's relations with the Federal government. It was to be elected in February, 1851. The expectation was that the State convention would ordain the secession which it was hoped the Montgomery convention would recommend. A steamship company was promised aid if it would build ships capable of war service, the militia was improved, $300,000 was voted to the newly created Board of Ordnance, and a $50,000 military fund was voted to the governor in case of hostilities. Taxes were increased by 50 per cent, and the Governor was directed to secure from the Federal government the State's share of the public land money declined by South Carolina in 1841 on constitutional grounds. The Governor's recommendation to expel every free Negro not owning land or slaves was not adopted.

The South Carolina convention elected in February, 1851, was overwhelmingly for immediate independent secession. Only Greenville elected a delegation opposed to secession either independently or in co-operation. But South Carolina had again gone too far. Her call for a Southern convention fell flat. Even at home moderate men were offended by threats to punish Unionists as traitors, and by the obtruding of the State convention of the South Carolina Southern Rights Association in May, 1851, in an apparent attempt by a private organization to dictate the policy of the coming official convention of the people and arrogantly to force other States into secession against their will. Virginia begged South Carolina to desist. Alabama defeated the secession party in August by 6,000, Mississippi in September by 7,000, and Georgia in October by 19,000. The immediately following South Carolina election of delegates to the Montgomery convention, which it was now evident would never come into existence, was therefore a mere form, except as it revealed the reaction to the rebuff. Though the immediate secessionists had overwhelmingly carried the election for State convention delegates in February, the co-operationists now won by 25,045 to 17,710. The old alignment of 1832 reappeared. The black plantation districts were for the extremists, while Charleston and the white up country were moderate.

Class Cleavage on the Slavery Issue Threatened at Home.—A disconcerting feature of the October election was a slight stirring of the non-slaveholders against the slaveholders. In Chesterfield, thirty or forty men marched to the polls cheering their leader as he shouted "damn the Negroes and their masters." The analysis of the vote shows the opposition to the independent secessionists in the white districts. Said the *Black River Watchman* of Sumter, "They have succeeded in instilling into the minds of a portion of our population sentiments at war with our domestic institutions and dangerous to our future peace. The spirit of war upon slavery has been invoked to fill up their ranks. . . . We have among us idolizers of the Union,—men who think it treason to talk of resistance to the Federal government; . . . and last but not least, we have among us a class who look with envy and dislike upon all who are so fortunate as to own a slave and who will never under any circumstances lend their support for its maintenance."

This incipient opposition to slavery had appeared in 1849 when abolition literature came through the mails to persons whose names had apparently been furnished by local sympathizers. An abolitionist agent was arrested in Spartanburg, and others were suspected. This was a distinctly new movement, voicing the protests of the poor whites against their economic sacrifices on the altar of the planter, different from the humanitarian emancipation sentiment that had cropped out in the decades following the Declaration of Independence among the upper classes. The anti-slavery manifestation in the October, 1851, election proved that there were stirrings against the whole slavery economy among the class to whom in 1857 Hinton Rowan Helper, a North Carolinian who had risen from among the poorer whites, appealed in his *Impending Crisis of the South and How to Meet It.* Helper's insistence on excluding all slaveholders from office and thereby abolishing slavery as the enemy of the white masses, or even of seeking its overthrow through servile insurrection, stirred such excitement both North and South as to deserve to rank as one of the immediate means of bringing both sections to the fighting point. Professor J. G. deRoulhac Hamilton's remark that "the book had a significance not then realized as an expression of the growing feeling against slavery among non-slaveholders and small slaveholders in North Carolina" clearly might be extended to other States.

The attempt to swing the State into secession on the slavery issue was thus stimulating incipient opposition to slavery as a class interest. In 1851 "Brutus's" pamphlet appealed to "The Citizens of South Carolina" against the sectional advantage of the low-country slaveholding minority in the legislature and the secession movement designed to blast forever all hope of progress for "the masses of our population." Representing themselves as standard-bearers for the South, said "Brutus," they in reality despised the people and trampled underfoot the true sovereignty of the State. Not content with their despotism which had driven thousands of poor white men to the West to seek opportunity, they strove to close to them New Mexico and California by imposing there this "man-crushing power" of slavery. It was time for the nearly 200,000 virtually disfranchised citizens to teach the masters of "overgrown plantations" that the government of the State must be made in reality republican. Let the people elect a convention to prepare a constitution protecting the interests of free labor and establishing genuine republicanism. If the legislature refused to take steps for its adoption, Congress should be invoked to make good the guarantee of a republican form of government to every State. This failing, we might consider the next step. "Freemen of the Back Country!" wrote "Union" in the Greenville *Southern Patriot* May 9, 1851, "Your rulers are about to plunge you into the vortex of revolution.... Tell the barons of the low country that if they involve the State in war they may defend themselves as well as they can." Truly Professor Boucher remarks, such publications seemed to warrant James H. Hammond's opinion in 1847 that slavery's "only hope" was to keep "the actual slaveholders not only predominant, but paramount within its circles."

The response of the defenders of the existing regime was equally warm. "That hellish crew," newspapers called the authors of the 1849 letters and pamphlets, "who seek to break down the Constitution of our State, and destroy the barriers which protect the rights of the poor white man, and keep alive in him the spirit and independence of a freeman." The central committee of the Southern Rights Association, commenting on the October, 1851, convention election, charged that "throughout the State, with every appearance of systematic operation, alarms and falsehoods were covertly disseminated among the more ignorant class. They were told if they joined the Secession party, or attended meetings of that party, they would forthwith be drafted for military service. They were told that they would be taxed beyond their ability to pay. Non-slaveholders were told that they have no interest in the question of slavery—and that the horrible sufferings of war would be brought upon them, for the exclusive advantage of their richer neighbors. . . . A sufficient number of voters were thus controlled to reduce the party of action from a great majority . . . to a minority."

That class cleavage was feared is proved by the extraordinary efforts to convince the non-slaveholder that his interests and the slaveholder's were identical against emancipation, which would Africanize the country. The poor white man must be taught that he was the beneficiary of slavery, and so must be its defender. With all the exaggeration there was at least this truth—that the race issue was profounder and more lasting than the slavery issue.

The long deferred Convention of the People of South Carolina at last met in April, 1852, under very different circumstances from those anticipated. Its members realized the impossibility of independent secession, though the great majority had been elected in February, 1851, on that platform. The State was bitterly torn. Reasonable men must heal her factional wounds. The extremists Rhett and Maxcy Gregg were turned down by their own caucus. By 136 to 19 the convention adopted an ordinance that the State possessed the absolute right as a sovereign State to secede, and resolved that, in view of the encroachments of the Federal government, especially in relation to slavery, she would be amply justified in seceding, but that she forebore "from reasons of expediency only." Hammond denounced this as "too pitiful for comment," and Rhett resigned the United States senatorship as being an improper representative of a State adopting submission and waiting for co-operation. But Governor Means more truly sensed the situation in his satisfaction that divided factions were reunited, and that further Northern aggressions would bring our sister States to join us either to "force our rights to be respected in the Union, or take our place as a Southern Confederacy amongst the nations of the world."

Seeking Internal Harmony.—Turning from the futile effort at secession from 1847 to 1852, we may glance at conditions in South Carolina as she approached the end of an historic era. In matured culture, in dignified, graceful living, it was her golden age; but not so in the realm of creative statesmanship. Her scientists and men of letters were at their best; but in public life she was at a far remove below the level of her Revolutionary period, when her statesmen rose to great constructive achievements, or of the post-Revolutionary period down to about 1825, when her brilliant nationalistic era ended and she entered the blind alley bounded by slavery and sectionalism, ending in "the brothers' war."

Though deeply embittered, the defeated immediate secessionists recognized, as had the Nullifiers after 1832, that their next task was to restore harmony within the State. In December, 1852, John Laurence Manning, "a man too warm hearted, amiable and excellent to be a politician at all," said Grayson, was unanimously elected Governor after the withdrawal of all opponents. His earlier messages hardly alluded to the old controversy. The law of 1850 for the erection of a fireproof building for State records was enlarged to a plan for a handsome stone State House in place of the old wooden structure. Early bungling was ended by selecting John R. Niernsee, a Baltimore Austrian, as architect and starting over in 1855. The present building is Niernsee's design, except the dome, substituted for his square cathedral-like tower. The splendid building was the first deliberate luxury of a State government notable for its economy. The old capitol stood directly in the rear of the western wing of the new, on the west side of Main Street (which then ran uninterruptedly), facing east, until moved out of the way.

The Up-Country Rebels Against the Parishes.—The temporary calming of national quarrels permitted renewal of the old agitation of the up country against domination by the parishes with their small white population. The growing up country was in revolt against the Calhoun doctrine of the "concurrent majority," which, as a matter of fact, was no concurrent majority, but control of both houses by the section of the great slaveowners as the latter had spread up from the parishes toward Columbia. "Brutus" in 1851 complained that the lower section (in the enlarged sense) had four congressmen for its 115,470 white population, and the up country only three for its 143,614 whites, and refused to be comforted by the reflection that this was in imitation, without any constitutional basis, of the Federal assignment of representatives to States, as such, in proportion to their free population and three-fifths of their slaves. But this was not so extreme as the apportionment of 1822, by which the congressional district composed of Beaufort, Colleton, St. Andrew's, and St. John's Colleton contained one-fourth of the white population of the congressional district of Spartanburg, Union, York, and Chester.

So fundamental were the antagonisms roused by slavery that it was considered necessary to curb them even between South Carolina white men, then under a government marked by bitter rivalries which Calhoun described, for purposes of the Federal analogy which he desired, as one of ideal harmony between different interests. The words of George D. Tillman of Edgefield, speaking as a partisan of the up country in 1891, exaggerated though they are, serve to exhibit both the bitterness of ante-bellum feeling and its strength long after 1860. Said he: "The compromise of 1808 was sanctioned by the latter [the low country] only to avert civil war. The up country was actually preparing for a conflict of arms when Robert Goodloe Harper brought forward the compromise proposition, which the backwoodsmen adopted in a spirit of self-sacrifice—not because it was either a just or wise measure." When the low-country parishes finally consented to the creation of another judicial and election district from the old Pendleton district, he continued, they swore it should be the last outside the parish region. Every application for a new courthouse in the up country was treated with the utmost contempt. "Charleston's arrogant spirit of monopoly at home while eloquently advocating liberty and free trade abroad, would probably still be domineering the State as regards counties and many other things, but for the fact that" her power was reduced in 1865.

The internal sectional quarrel of the 1850's centered on two subjects: the division of Pendleton into two election districts (Anderson and Pickens), thus giving the up country an additional Senator, and the proposal for the people to choose presidential electors. Anderson and Pickens had been separate judicial districts since 1826. These movements, it was charged, almost amounted to a set war of the up country on the parishes; and yet Colleton and Charleston combined, with 26,795 white population in 1840, had thirteen times as many Senators and four and a half times as many representatives as Anderson and Pickens combined with 24,295. In 1854 the division of Pendleton election district was adopted by the two-thirds vote of both houses, and the Pendleton district was no more.

The undemocratic character of the Constitution, which gave such preponderance to the less populous low country, became more irritating to the up country as the latter grew in wealth as well as numbers. Taking the fall line of the rivers as the dividing line between the sections, United States Census figures for 1860 reveal the surprising fact that the wealth production of the two sections had come to be approximately equal:

Value of agricultural products, up country, $26,397,500; low country, $28,500,000;

Value of manufactured products, up country, $4,258,333; low country, 4,091,667.[1]

The movement for popular choice of presidential electors lasted much longer than that for popular election and greater powers for the governor. It was strong from 1844 to 1854 and finally subsided by 1858. Governor Adams warned the legislature in 1855 against the desire for constitutional change and rejoiced that South Carolina of all States had not fundamentally changed its Constitution, "in view of hideous phases which radicalism has elsewhere assumed." Cried the *Mercury:* "The principle that the numerical majority is the State and ought to govern, is the very essence of consolidation. It is the most subtle and deadly of all those fallacies which eat into and destroy free institutions. . . . Yet it is this same principle which is attempted to be introduced into the State. It is not enough that it desolates without. It must needs enter our homes and riot upon our very hearth stones."

The Struggle Over Kansas.—The uneasy peace of the 1850 compromise was broken by the Kansas-Nebraska act of 1854 repealing the Missouri Compromise and thus presenting the question of slavery or no slavery in the territories, in a more exciting form than ever. Provided territorial action against slavery was not to take place before statehood, the Kansas-Nebraska bill was the logical conclusion from Calhoun's position that Congress had no right to interfere with slavery in the territories; but neither Calhoun nor representative Southern leaders had ever demanded that existing compromises accepted in good faith should be abrogated. Their contentions were intended to guard the future.

The repeal of the law of 1820 was not sought by the South, but it was quite naturally accepted, though taking the bait was shortsighted.

[1] I compiled these figures in preparing my series of *Historical Maps of South Carolina* (Denoyer-Geppert Company, 1936). Fractional parts of thousands for the various counties are generally disregarded, thus preventing the figures from being exact.

If the South was to be free to carry slaves into the territory north of 36 degrees 30 minutes, the North would be free to seek to exclude them from the territories below that line; and there could remain no doubt as to who would win in such a race. The repeal of the Missouri Compromise produced the Republican party, pledged to the exclusion of slavery from all territories, and it vastly promoted the growth of abolitionism against slavery within the South.

Northern and Southern extremists immediately rushed into Kansas to win it for freedom or slavery by ballots or bullets. South Carolinians proposed to raise a hundred men in each of the six congressional districts. Thousands of dollars were contributed, and some 250 to 400 men, apparently, were dispatched from the State.

Out of the debate on Kansas came Preston S. Brooks's caning of Charles Sumner, May 22, 1856. Sumner ridiculed Senator Butler of South Carolina as the Don Quixote of slavery, his hideous mistress, in his eyes beautiful. He opened his mouth and out popped an error, etc. Sumner represented in aggravated form the fanatical, self-righteous, vituperative feature of anti-Southern feeling. He had no realization of the wounds his words inflicted, and his arrogance made his words doubly intolerable. Waiting until the Senate chamber was empty, Brooks, accompanied by L. M. Keitt, approached Sumner at his desk and gave him a beating with a gutta-percha cane that disabled him for months. This, Brooks had not intended, but merely a humiliation. Such a gross violation of law, and an apparent willingness even to murder if needful to prevent taking a beating if he failed to give one, were poor tactics from the side protesting for the most rigorous regard for the law.[2] Brooks's course disregarded the critical situation of the country, which called for the exercise of all available wisdom and statesmanship. He did not anticipate the political significance of his act, which implanted in millions of minds the idea that Southerners meant to dominate their congressional associates by the same methods that they used for slaves. The contempt with which Douglas met Sumner's grosser insults was much more useful to his side. Brooks intervened in a great public question as though it were a mere personal quarrel. Every blow administered reacted with an immeas-

[2] The statement that Brooks apparently went armed in order to kill Sumner if Sumner should overpower him is based on the following from Brooks's speech of July 14, 1856, in the House of Representatives in resigning his seat:

"I went to work very deliberately, as I am charged—and this is admitted—and speculated somewhat as to whether I should employ a horsewhip or a cowhide; but knowing that the Senator was my superior in strength, it occurred to me that he might wrest it from my hand, and then—for I never attempt anything I do not perform—I might have been compelled to do that which I would have regretted the balance of my natural life." (Appendix to *Congressional Globe,* 1st Session, 34th Congress, page 832, column 1, near bottom.)

urably broadened force on the whole South by adding the sanctity of martyrdom to one of the most dangerous mischief-makers in American history and helping him to gain the later leadership of the Senate, through which as a conscientious bigot, at last possessing through the passions of the time his opportunity, he inflicted upon his country deeper and more lasting wounds than those of war.

Resigning from the House after failure of a motion to expel him, Brooks was enthusiastically re-elected without opposition. Canes, cups, etc., rained upon him, and South Carolinians paid his $300 fine.[3]

Balancing of Moderates and Conservatives, 1857-58.—In the confusion precipitated by the Kansas-Nebraska act, three factions appeared in South Carolina, as in the whole South. There were those who still had faith in the Democratic party and believed that Southern safety depended on retaining control of its policy. Of these James L. Orr of Anderson, elected Speaker of the national House in 1857, was the leader in South Carolina. He was strongly seconded by Pickens. Others, having lost faith in the Northern Democracy, urged a Southern party to demand Southern rights on pain of secession. Rhett, L. M. Keitt, and Maxcy Gregg were among their leaders. They reproached the Orr faction as "Nationals." The third faction was the American party, or "Know-Nothings," with their professions of nationalism, Protestantism, and native Americanism. To them flocked the Whigs, no longer able to fraternize with their free-soilish Northern brethren and unwilling to join the Democrats.

South Carolina had her taste of Know-Nothingism chiefly in Charleston. Immigrants were feared as dangerous to slavery. The Irish Catholic laborers brought to work on the State House swelled from about 300 to 700 the membership of St. Peter's Church, which had been dedicated in 1824 as a result of importing Irish canal laborers in the 1820's. Their fellow-countrymen digging the Stumphouse Mountain tunnel for the Blue Ridge Railroad from 1856 to 1858 met strong prejudices.

The Orr faction, pleased with the repeal of the Missouri Compromise and the admission of slavery to all territories, preached the gospel of a South restored to her constitutional rights, Southern prosperity, industrial development, and national Democracy, against Rhett's wail of a tariff-ruined State that must secede, alone if necessary, to preserve slavery. Orr wished to end the State's isolation by participating in national conventions. When the State Democratic Convention met on May 5 and 6, 1856, to choose such delegates, representatives came from Georgetown and every district outside the older parishes except five,

[3] One blank vote is said by the *Carolinian* to have been cast by a friend of a relative of Sumner. Brooks had long been strong in his district.

but not a man from the other parishes except the city. It was Charleston and the back country, as so often, against the parish extremists. The convention elected delegates and endorsed the "Georgia platform" of acceptance of the 1850 compromise, but secession if it was violated.

The issue was thus clearly drawn between the fire-eaters, as they were called in the North, and sometimes even in South Carolina, seeking any means to precipitate secession, and the conservatives, determined to secede if Southern rights were disregarded, but hoping that through co-operation with the national Democratic party the Union might be preserved.

Amid these conflicting views occurred the election in 1857 of a successor to replace the deceased Senator A. P. Butler. Rhett, unpopular as a dogmatic extremist unsuited for responsibility, received but six votes. J. H. Hammond, who, on account of delicate personal involvements described in full by Miss Merritt in her life of Hammond, had been in retirement from public life since the conclusion of his governorship in December, 1846, now received a wonderful tribute to his ability. Uncommitted between conflicting factions, and, says his biographer, Miss Merritt, the second choice of all, he was elected on the third ballot, though having announced he would not serve. It was indeed a notable compliment to a mind second only to Calhoun's. Hammond was marked by a saturnine cynicism, voiced in cutting comments on his contemporaries, and by a belief in Unitarianism like Calhoun, but added to it spiritualism and a belief in a malign Providence thwarting his aims. He so esteemed his powers that he wrote in 1857 that, but for ill health, "I would throw every obstacle right & left as a lion shakes the dew drops from his mane, & rule this world." He shared without limit the South's faith in the power of cotton, deprived of which, he said in 1858, "England would topple headlong and carry the whole civilized world with her save the South. No, you dare not make war on cotton. . . . Cotton *is* King."

No less was his pride in Southern statesmanship: "We, the slaveholders of the South, took our country in her infancy, and after ruling her for sixty out of the seventy years of her existence, we surrender her to you without a stain on her honor, boundless in prosperity, incalculable in her strength, the wonder and the admiration of the world. Time will show what you will make of her, but no time can diminish our glory or your responsibility."[4]

The Supreme Court's endorsement, in the Dred Scott decision in 1857, of the Calhoun doctrine of Southern rights in the territories strengthened the Southern conservatives and weakened the secessionists per se. The attempt of Ruffin, Yancey, and Rhett in 1858 to organize a

[4] The monument over his grave at Beach Island bears this passage.

bold minority, analogous to the men who precipitated the Revolution, to carry the South out of the Union collapsed.

Hammond stated his position on October 29, 1858, against the Rhett-Gregg faction of immediate secession. No secession yet, he said; that alternative remains always at hand. "The Union of these states . . . is but a policy and not a principle. It is subordinate to rights and interests. But the Union of the slaveholders of the South is a principle involving all our rights and all our interests."

That Northerners hailed such a speech and mentioned Hammond for the presidency indicated recognition of how frail were the threads that held South Carolina to the Union.

Seeking to Reopen the Foreign Slave Trade.—The ugliest retaliatory excess into which South Carolina extremists were drawn, repelling a great portion of their own State and of the South, was the movement for reopening the African slave trade, an idea which a few had urged as early as 1839.[5] Taken up by L. W. Spratt of the *Charleston Standard* in 1853, it assumed importance when recommended by Governor Adams in 1856. Special committees of both houses, given a year to report, urged the Governor to bring it before every Southern State. J. Johnson Pettigrew filed a minority report which is one of the great documents on slavery. Pettigrew traced the process of transforming African barbarians into a docile, Christian race of servants, and showed how the introduction of hordes of new barbarians would imperil all this. His opponents met his practical argument with radical theorizing. Every white man, they urged, must be the owner of at least one slave. Even W. H. Trescot argued that slavery must either be abolished or made the thorough basis of our society by eliminating "free ideas of the relation of labor and capital," which even in a Southern confederacy, he said, would bring greater dangers than then faced slavery. Trescot thought three-fourths of the Southern slaveholders condemned "the Congo party." Wade Hampton publicly rebuked it.[6] The *Mercury,* which at first advocated the reopening of the slave trade as a ground for promoting secession, later dropped it as threatening to divide the South and denounced it as unspeakably cruel; but the idea was strongly held that the danger to slavery from free white labor must be eliminated by making practically every white man the owner of at least one slave. The agitation stimulated the illegal slave trade. There were few or no importations

[5] Thos. P. Martin, doctor's dissertation, Harvard, 1922, quoting the New York *Emancipator,* June 20, 1839, which quotes through the *New York Daily Express* from the *New Orleans Courier;* Martin, "Conflicting Cotton Interests," *Journal So. History,* May, 1941, p. 175.

[6] Lillian A. Kibler, "Union Sentiment in South Carolina in 1860," in *Journal So. History,* August, 1938.

between 1842 and 1858. The *Southern Episcopalian* stated that a slaver had not entered a South Carolina port for apparently fifty years. Certainly in 1858 and '59 there was activity. In May, 1858, papers were refused a Charleston firm evidently intending to import Africans. In August the *Echo,* loaded with Africans, was brought captive into Charleston harbor. With not a fact denied, the crew were acquitted. When the *Wanderer,* owned by C. A. L. Lamar of Savannah and others sold a cargo of Africans in Georgia and South Carolina, Federal Judge A. G. Magrath in Charleston threw the case out of court on the ground that, despite the Federal law so declaring, the foreign slave trade was not piracy. Such extraordinary verdicts and rulings were Southern protests against Northern violations of the fugitive slave law.

Senator Hammond condemned the entire program of the fire-eaters. He wrote, "The South has done nothing but stab herself since October. The *Echo,* the *Wanderer* case & all their incidents . . . ideal, impracticable and injurious . . . strip us of every supporter in the free States." The demand that Congress protect slavery in the territories and reopen the foreign slave trade he denounced as Southern suicide.

John Brown's Raid and the Election of Lincoln.—The hopes of the South Carolina conservatives were shattered by John Brown's raid. The South Carolina legislature voted $100,000 for military preparations and sent Memminger to express sympathy with Virginia, but more really to draw her co-operation for secession. But Virginia was unmoved. A few suspected strangers were beaten or tarred in South Carolina, and a lady in Aiken, whose private letter to a brother in the North had got into print, was given by a committee two days to leave. The gentry of St. Bartholomew Parish determined that no Yankee should come among them, and beat a poor Yankee woodchopper. J. L. Petigru took his case. Two lawyers labored to prove that the Yankee was tinged with abolitionism, but the jury awarded damages of $2,500. The parishes were hot for secession, but Charleston (her merchants denounced as putting money above principle) and the back country were unstampeded by the action of a few murderous fanatics at Harper's Ferry. Rhett and Yancey failed to unite the South in demanding that Congress carry the Dred Scott principle to the length of enacting a slave code for the territories, for moderate men saw the folly of inviting a Northern-dominated Congress to legislate at all on the institution which it was feared they would ultimately abolish. On December 11, 1856, Orr announced in Congress what Douglas offered two years later as the "Freeport Doctrine," to retain his Northern support, namely, that a hostile territorial legislature could kill slavery by refusing to protect it.

The peace that still held amounted to an armed truce. Hammond wrote Lieber on April 19, 1860: "So far as I *know,* and as I believe, every man in both Houses is armed with a revolver—some with two—and a bowie knife. It is, I fear, in the power of any Red or Black Republican to precipitate at any moment a collision in which the slaughter would be such as to shock the world and dissolve this government." In such an atmosphere four days later the Democratic National Convention met in Charleston. The platform committee agreed to the Southern demand for Jefferson Davis' Senate resolutions of February 2, 1860, i.e., that Congress enact laws to protect slavery in any territory which failed to give it adequate protection. But the convention, dominated by the North, rejected this, and adopted the Douglas principle of popular sovereignty, i.e., that Congress should permit each territory to act as it pleased, barring hostile legislation, which was unconstitutional according to the Dred Scott decision. Thereupon, in the order named, the Alabama, Mississippi, South Carolina, Louisiana, Florida, Texas, Arkansas, and Georgia delegations left the convention, which then adjourned to Baltimore.

The radical, or "anti-convention," South Carolina faction had refused to participate in the election of delegates to the State convention, which had accordingly sent a conservative delegation to Charleston. On the plea that all South Carolina should be represented in the slave States' Democratic Convention to be held in Richmond, a new State convention was elected. Every delegation that had withdrawn in Charleston stated that it had done so solely to reunite the party. The South Carolina radicals openly expressed the fear that unless they took control the Richmond convention would patch up some compromise with the Northern Democrats by which the South's secession from the Union would be prevented. They, therefore, through the disproportionate representation of the parishes, elected to Richmond a radical delegation headed by Rhett himself amid a storm of indignation on the part of the proscribed conservatives both in South Carolina and throughout the South.

The majority of the withdrawing delegates had acted merely for a daring party move; but events hurried them into what they had not desired. Being unable to obtain the hoped-for compromise at Baltimore, where the Northern Democrats nominated Douglas, they nominated Breckenridge. As the summer advanced, South Carolina became more and more determined upon secession if Lincoln should be elected. When the returns showed him designated as the next president, the event had occurred which liberated South Carolina from the restraint under which she had lived since 1847. She was agreed as to what she had, since 1847 or at least since 1850, desired to do, and at last was united as to the time and manner of doing it.

CHAPTER L

SECESSION AND ITS CAUSES

So OFTEN had South Carolina failed in her attempt to draw the South into secession that her leaders, now including many who had been for co-operation, were determined to force conclusions before indecision could dicker for new compromises. Aldrich wrote, "I do not believe the common people understand it. . . . We must make the move and force them to follow. That is the way of all revolutions and all great movements." Above all, there should be no Southern convention, anathema since the 1850 fiasco at Nashville, in which the border States might control. The way to secure co-operation, South Carolina held, was for her to lead off with an irrevocable act with or against which every other State would be obliged to act.

The legislature, having met to choose presidential electors, remained in session to await the national result. The grand jury in the Federal court in Charleston refused to function, as the North, "through the ballot box on yesterday, has swept away the last hope for the permanence, for the stability, of the Federal government of these sovereign States." Judge Magrath divested himself of his robe of office.

Magrath's act sent a thrill throughout the State and a feeling of discouragement to Washington as the official structure for the execution of Federal law crumbled. President Buchanan professed himself more disconcerted by this than by any other act except the occupation of Fort Sumter by Major Anderson. Magrath's course was the more influential as he had in 1850-52 opposed separate secession, and his dramatic stand is said to have brought the divided Charleston legislative delegation into unity for immediate action.

The legislature summoned the convention for December 17. At a militia and a mass meeting at Chesterfield on November 15, addressed by the legislators, on the proposal that those favoring immediate separate secession step forward four paces, every militiaman advanced. On the nineteenth a mass meeting at Chesterfield unanimously nominated a convention ticket pledged that "immediate separate secession was the only remedy . . . that could save the honor, and protect the rights and interests of the State." On November 22, on Magazine Hill (since called

Secession Hill) in Abbeville, 2,500 to 3,000 people listened to speakers mostly urging immediate secession.

Rhett felt keenly his winning only seventh place on the Charleston Convention delegation, and still more his being heavily defeated for governor by Pickens. "The father of secession," so powerful in propaganda, was never trusted with executive responsibility in either the State or the Confederacy. Francis W. Pickens, chosen for governor, was an effective orator, an extreme exponent of the Southern constitutional and economic views, though formerly a co-operationist, and a distinguished diplomat. Bold and clear in mind, he suited well the immediate responsibility.

The Secession Convention.—The solemnity of the occasion led to the choice for the convention of the best men the State possessed. When smallpox occurred, with rapidly increasing numbers of cases, one being just across the street, the convention adjourned from the First Baptist Church in Columbia to Charleston.[1] On December 20 the Ordinance of Secession was unanimously adopted in St. Andrew's Hall, and was signed in Institute Hall.

Commissioners were dispatched to the other slave States inviting them to meet for framing a Southern Confederacy on the basis of the Constitution of the United States, for the preservation of which they professed to act. A committee headed by C. G. Memminger prepared the Declaration of the Immediate Causes which Induce and Justify the Secession of South Carolina. This stated the compact theory, by which each State is the sole judge of violations of the compact between sovereigns (i.e., the Constitution). Violations had been acts of thirteen States annulling the fugitive slave law and less extreme impediments by others. Moreover, Northern States "have denounced as sinful the institution of slavery," and permitted abolition societies "designed to disturb the peace and eloign the property of the citizens of other States." They had aided thousands of slaves to escape and had incited servile insurrection. At last a sectional party had elected as president one hostile to slavery, who declared that this "government cannot endure permanently half slave, half free," and that the public mind must anticipate the ultimate extinction of slavery. "It has been announced that the South shall be excluded from the common territory; that the judicial tribunals shall be made sectional and that a war must be waged against slavery until it shall cease throughout the United States." The guarantees of the Constitution would then no longer exist; the equal rights of the States would be lost. The slaveholding States would no longer have the power of self-gov-

[1] Dr. C. E. Cauthen ("South Carolina Civil History 1861-65," MS) cites newspapers and legislative Journals reporting twenty-four cases Nov. 27-Dec. 16, 1860.

ernment or self-protection, and the Federal government would have become their enemy.

The causes of secession have been elaborately explained by modern writers, but they will probably never be more clearly or conclusively put than by the frank and able men who adopted this declaration. The tariff was a great and justly resented grievance, but it was a sectional grievance primarily on account of slavery. The diminishing grievance of inequitable expenditures on internal improvements arose largely because the South declined to seek appropriations on its strict-construction principles adopted to protect slavery. Southern nationalism arose from the peculiarities and dangers of Southern life flowing mainly from slavery. The selfish schemes of politicians, North and South, to benefit by a better chance of office and spoils, weighed too lightly as causes to merit emphasis. There were divergent Southern interests, some of which sharply clashed and, to South Carolina's mortification, long kept her isolated within the South; but as soon as the South as a whole recognized that slavery was actually in peril, the South Carolinians "naturally took the lead in the movement to destroy a nation which, it was plain, was making up its mind to destroy them." Their long-fostered conviction was that the Federal government was conducted with an unendurable discrimination for which there was no remedy but separation. The modern tendency to minimize slavery as the cause of secession is a natural reaction of writers weary of an oft-repeated disagreeable story. The secessionists knew why they seceded, and, in the various secession conventions, they crowned endless reiteration of the cause with the strongest statements, of the threat to slavery as the cause. It is hardly conceivable that secession would have occurred if slavery had not existed.

Innumerable expressions might be assembled like that of Governor A. G. Magrath to the United States government November 20, 1865: "Other considerations attached themselves to it [slavery]; they were merely incidents to it; of themselves they could never have produced the same result." In opposing those in the Secession Convention who preferred to play up the tariff instead of slavery to justify secession, as better calculated to win foreign approval, L. M. Keitt said that he and every other South Carolina congressman had voted for the tariff of 1857 and that every member of this convention would have done likewise had they been in Congress.[2]

It was the sincere belief of the mass of Southern people that abolition would mean Africanization. Secession was therefore to them a moral imperative. Thousands who scouted the constitutionality of seces-

[2] Cauthen, *op. cit.*, citing Magrath papers in the University of South Carolina Library and *Mercury*, December 22 and 25, 1860; Convention Journal, pp. 75-7.

sion obeyed this imperative on the right of revolution, and the others would have done so, no matter what the Constitution said; for constitutions are to serve, and not to destroy, civilization.

The Address of the Slaveholding States, written by Rhett, differed from the Declaration of the Causes of Secession in elaborating the secondary causes, emphasizing the development of two incompatible civilizations, and stressing what is now called Southern nationalism, in accordance with which, independently of the last grievance—the election of a president pledged to gird slavery about and cause it to die—the South should secede as a people of distinct civilization long wronged, for whom there was no hope of prosperity, justice, or safety under Northern domination. Thus, as Miss White points out, both factions in South Carolina found expression: the co-operationists, willing to avoid secession if possible, in the Declaration by Memminger of their faction, and the secessionists per se in the address by Rhett of their faction.

The Calhoun theory of the constitutional right of secession it is impossible conclusively to prove or disprove; but the McDuffie and Rhett declaration of a people's right to self-determination cannot be denied without denying the Declaration of Independence. The South's second claim to the right of secession could be overborne only by superior force, so far the ultimate arbiter in the conflicts of organized human masses.

South Carolina Unionists.—Secession ended in South Carolina the long strain of factional division as to method and substituted almost universal unity for a generally desired end. The South as a whole, believing her civilized existence at stake, was far more united than the North. Southern leaders, utterly mistaken as to the effects of emancipation, utterly miscalculated the economic and political forces in their favor in resorting to the most primitive of all courts of appeal, force. Wrote James H. Hammond on April 19, 1860, "I firmly believe that the slaveholding South is now the controlling *power* of the world. . . . Cotton, rice, tobacco, and naval stores command the world. . . . The North, without us, would be a motherless calf, bleating about, and die of mange and starvation." Governor Gist wrote on May 17, 1861: "Two battles will close the war and our independence will be acknowledged. Great Britain and France will offer their mediation and the Yankees will gladly accept it and make peace."

The Unionist William J. Grayson was deeply pessimistic. The war, he wrote, will be calamitous to the South either way. If we lose, our system of society is at once swept away and we will be ruled as conquered provinces. If we win, "anti-slavery interest will be born almost with the birth of the Southern Confederacy and will grow up speedily in the Southern States. The whole controversy substantially is one between the white man's labour and the black's." The prosperity which the South expected from independence would invite a horde of immigrants, and the conflict of white and black labor would be intensified and hastened. "Already in all the cities of the South the white man is displacing the negro in almost every department of labour." Other causes of conflict would develop, he continued. Already there had been little cordiality between adjacent Southern States or even parts of the same State. "We might fall into the disjointed condition of the Mexican provinces, always wrangling like ill-conditioned curs, the tools and prey of military rulers, wretches at home and contemptible abroad."

"Where's the fire?" asked James L. Petigru of young J. D. Pope, who answered, "Mr. Petigru, there is no fire. Those are the joybells ringing in honor of the passage of the Ordinance of Secession." "I tell you there is a fire," replied Petigru. "They have this day set a blazing torch to the temple of constitutional liberty, and, please God, we shall have no more peace forever." When a friend announced that Louisiana had seceded, this immovable Unionist's reply, embracing a whole volume of argument on States' resuming original sovereignty, was, "Good Lord, William, I thought we bought Louisiana." Judge O'Neall warned that the South would find "neither strength in her arm nor mercy in her woe," and B. F. Perry wrote that, as the State was determined to go to hell, he would go along with her.

Greenville, the up-country center of Unionist sentiment, had a few uncompromising opponents of secession. Such were B. F. Perry and the eminent Baptist clergyman, Dr. James P. Boyce. Mrs. Martha R. Roper, descended in ideas as in blood from Henry Laurens of the Revolution, had for years paid her skilled slave mechanics wages, as she did not feel warranted in accepting such services on other terms. When she was requested to lend the table on which the Declaration of Independence was signed (as was erroneously supposed) for the signing of the Ordinance of Secession, she replied that she would burn it to ashes before allowing it to be used for such a purpose.

Except in a few such outstanding cases it is difficult to determine, in the months preceding secession, the stand of men who had formerly expressed Union sentiments, for most of such men had already turned before 1860 or were engulfed in the emotional storm that swept the State toward the last.[3] Reluctant secessionists we may call them, but, though joining late, inflexible in their loyalty to their State: Wade Hampton, Professor Joseph LeConte, ex-Governor William Aiken, Samuel Mc-

[3] "The wild passions of that mad hour," said Dr. James H. Carlisle, who voted for secession as a member of the Convention, many years later to Dr. H. N. Snyder.

Aliley of Chester, and the Charlestonians George S. Bryan, Alfred Huger (had he become anti-Union after 1833?), Donald McKay, and Judge Frost.[4] William Gregg long discouraged anything tending to sectional hostility, but grew more and more resentful of abolitionist propaganda and was a member of the Secession Convention. Such were the outstanding representatives of the few Unionists in South Carolina, but none of these chose to leave the State. Perry even campaigned the mountain district to persuade its Unionist inhabitants to join the Southern army. Northern men thought they loved the Union more than they loved their State merely because the two loyalties had never come into conflict. If it had come to the necessity of choosing between the two, the vast majority of Northerners, as of Southerners, doubtless would have defended their own homes and firesides rather than join an army from a distance to slaughter their lifelong friends and the kindred of their own blood.

Negotiating for the Charleston Forts.—Obviously combat was likely to begin over the forts at Charleston. Three forts guarded the harbor: Castle Pinckney, an antiquated structure three-fourths of a mile from the city; Fort Sumter, three and a half miles from the city; and Fort Moultrie, built in 1811 near the Revolutionary fort, facing Sumter from Sullivan's Island a mile away. Sumter, begun in 1829, was still unfinished. The arsenal in the city had been restocked. Only Moultrie was garrisoned beyond a mere property guard. President Buchanan was at first determined to reinforce the forts, but, on being assured that mob violence was not probable if the status remained unchanged, he yielded to the dissuasion of his Southern cabinet members.

On December 8, South Carolina congressmen urged upon President Buchanan that sending reinforcements or changing the military status might precipitate violence, but that they were sure no attack would be made upon the forts until formal negotiations had failed, provided their status was not changed. The President, Congressmen Miles and Keitt reported, "said it was not his intention to send reinforcements, or make any change."

Assistant Secretary of State Trescot stated in February, 1861, in his narrative of his conversation with the President on receiving Pickens'

[4] I thank Dr. C. E. Cauthen for assistance on this list, and emphasize his observation on the difficulty of being sure in the shifting currents of opinion regarding the position of many men at particular moments before the final act of secession. Dr. H. T. Cook classes Waddy Thompson as a Unionist.

As highly as I value Miss Lillian Kibler's *Life of Benjamin F. Perry* (1946), I am obliged to think that she greatly overestimates the strength of Unionist sentiment in South Carolina in 1860, and for the decade of the 1850's. *Journal of Southern History,* IV (August, 1938), 346-66.

request of December 14 to be allowed to take over Fort Sumter: "He was pledged, he said, not to disturb the status in favour of the United States and the Governor ought not and could not justly ask him to disturb it in favour of the State."

On December 11 the Secretary of War ordered Anderson to refrain from anything that could appear hostile but to hold the forts to the last extremity. In case of an attack on any of the three forts he might put his command into any of them. He was authorized to take such a step "whenever you have tangible evidence of a design to proceed to a hostile act."

The closing words put an enormous responsibility upon Anderson. Popular excitement and official preparations led him to move his force to Fort Sumter after dusk on December 26 and destroy everything possible of military service that he could not carry.

On the twenty-seventh Governor Pickens took Castle Pinckney, in Charleston Harbor, from its guard, thus committing the first overt act of war, unless, as Pickens contended, Major Anderson's move from Moultrie to Sumter enjoys that distinction. The South Carolinians next occupied Moultrie and took the arsenal in the city, containing half a million dollars' worth of munitions.

The South Carolina commissioners, arriving in Washington on December 28, met the news that Anderson had entered Sumter. All discussion looking to a harmonious adjustment of relations between South Carolina and the United States must be suspended, they said, until a satisfactory explanation of Anderson's act was given. They urged the immediate withdrawal of Federal troops from Charleston harbor as a standing menace.

Buchanan replied that his alleged pledge was only a declaration of intention made to gentlemen unauthorized to make any agreement. South Carolina, he said, without waiting for any explanation, had seized two United States forts, the post office, the customs house, and the arsenal. He, therefore, could not and would not either order Anderson back to Moultrie or evacuate the harbor.

On January 9, 1861, the *Star of the West,* seeking to reinforce Sumter with about 200 men, etc., was forced by artillery fire to withdraw. On February 4 there assembled in Washington a peace convention, and in Montgomery the Confederate government was organized. Secessionists per se, of the Rhett type, feared lest "the dread spirit of reconstruction" should accomplish some compromise under which the South would remain in the Union; but President-elect Lincoln stiffened his wavering followers to refuse any compromise permitting slavery in any territory and thus dashed all hope of the only plan with any chance of success, the

"Crittenden Compromise" guaranteeing slavery south of 36 degrees 30 minutes.

The Confederate government took over the forces besieging Fort Sumter. President Lincoln pursued Buchanan's course until March 29, when he provisionally decided to reinforce Sumter. Seward's assurance, on March 21 and 22, to Judge Campbell, go-between for him and the Confederate commissioners, that Sumter would be evacuated, was thus negatived. Seward now, in his desperate hope that he could prevent the execution of Lincoln's purpose and so prevent war, began to deceive the commissioners by assuring them that the fort would be evacuated, and, when driven out of this pretense, substituted the statement that the fort would not be reinforced without notice. President Davis was not deceived, for he had no confidence in Seward's sincerity and merely used the negotiations to consume time until he was ready for action.

The Fall of Fort Sumter.—On April 4 Lincoln definitely decided to relieve the fort. On April 8, a day before the arrival of the first relief might be expected off Charleston, he informed Pickens of his intention to provision the fort but not reinforce it unless resisted. The expedition miscarried through a storm.

The Confederate government, whose position so far was morally very strong, now committed the blunder of attacking the fort.[5]

Beauregard's aides presented the final demand for surrender at three-fifteen A.M., April 12. Anderson replied that if he was not relieved or given controlling instructions by noon the 15th he would surrender. Without referring this reply to their superiors, the aides, in obedience to their instructions, went straight to Fort Johnson and ordered the bombardment to begin.[6]

After a bombardment of thirty-four hours from Morris, James, and Sullivan's Islands, while the belated Federal relief expedition of three gunboats and a troop ship looked on helplessly, with his ammunition

[5] In opposition to the generally accepted view that regards Lincoln's course as running true to the vein of indecision in his mental habits, Professor Charles W. Ramsdell in *Jour. of So. Hist.,* August, 1937, strongly presents the evidence that Lincoln by "consummate strategy" forced upon the Confederates the firing of the first shot.

[6] The romance of the error perpetuates the statement, arising from a misunderstanding, that Edmund Ruffin, the gray-haired Virginian who had come to help secession, and who killed himself upon the failure of the Confederacy rather than live in association with "the perfidious, malignant, and vile Yankee race," as he called them in his farewell letter, fired the first shot at Sumter. It seems, however, true that he fired the third shot, the first from the battery on Morris Island. The evidence seems conclusive that Lieutenant Henry S. Farley, of the east, or beach, battery, sighted and personally fired the first gun, obeying the order of Captain G. S. James, and that Lieutenant W. H. Gibbes fired from the west, or hill, battery the second shot. The eye-witness evidence is best given, and other evidence reviewed, in *South Carolina Historical Magazine,* July, 1911, pp. 141-45. See also Columbia *State,* July 5, 6, 13, August 10, 1903; Craven's *Ruffin,* pp. 217, 270, note 16.

and food almost exhausted, the quarters burned, and the magazines surrounded by flames, Major Anderson surrendered with about eighty soldiers and about half as many workmen. He was allowed the honors of war. The only lives lost on either side were those of a Federal soldier killed and another mortally wounded by the premature explosion of a gun saluting the flag after surrender.

South Carolina's Place in the Confederacy.—South Carolina was prosperous in 1860. Tax valuations for 1861 totaled $399,468,798, on which was levied a total tax of $1,997,343. Charleston's foreign exports had more than doubled since the Mexican War. The sharp check to general business by war had passed by November, 1861.

The Southern convention at Montgomery in February, 1861, elected a president, adopted a provisional constitution, put in force all United States laws not contrary to this, and declared itself the Congress of the Confederacy. The permanent constitution was that of the United States, of which the secessionists had always maintained they were the real defenders, with certain disputed points clarified and a few improvements of detail. Such were the right of Cabinet members to sit, but not vote, in Congress if Congress so ordered, and of the President to veto items of appropriation bills, and the requirement of a two-thirds vote for appropriations not asked for by the executive. A regularly elected Congress and President took office after a year.

South Carolina occupied a prominent place in these events, but in several important respects she was defeated. Her attempts failed to forbid appeals from a State Supreme Court to the Confederate Supreme Court; to require the choice of presidential electors by legislatures; to compel except during war, upon the demand of any State, the withdrawal of Confederate troops from its territory; to count all slaves (instead of three-fifths) in apportioning representation; to forbid Congress to pass general naturalization laws; to leave Congress free to re-open the African slave trade; and to refuse admission to any non-slaveholding State.[7] But on Rhett's motion the Confederate constitution limited the president to one six-year term, forbade bounties and protective tariffs, and modified the method of amendment. The lines of sectional controversy within the new Confederacy were already appearing. Naturally South Carolina ratified the constitution without enthusiasm and let it be known that when the crisis was past she would demand amendments of an extreme State sovereignty character. A peculiar situation developed in which South Carolina was less important than she had been in the Union. No longer a peril that must if possible be placated lest she

[7] Cauthen, *op. cit.*, p. 155, citing *Journals Confed. Cong.*, I, 861-2, 886, 873-4, 877, 880, 883-6, 893; White's *Rhett*, pp. 197 *et seq.*

destroy the Union, she sank into the position of merely a member of a Confederacy accepting her principles and therefore no longer needing her leadership. Her mission accomplished, she remained a reformer whose occupation was gone.

Rhett, always too extreme even for his own State, was disgusted to see her entire Montgomery delegation except himself and Keitt composed of co-operationists of 1852. His desire for the presidency failed to command the support of his own delegation. Not only his ambition but his extreme ideas were rejected, though several of his helpful suggestions were adopted. It appears unjust to explain his relentless attacks on President Davis throughout the war and after as due merely to his disappointment. The querulous and generally unjust denunciations of Davis for incapacity and bad policy that so distracted the South, in which Rhett was conspicuous, were the natural reaction from the unwarranted confidence with which a failing war had been begun. The malcontents sought to forestall Davis's foreign policy and force his military policy, and even to depose him, if necessary, by revolution. Rhett's desire to expel any State that abolished slavery contradicted too violently every Southern tradition of a State's sole right over slavery. The nationalism, prosperity, and happiness that he had pictured for a united independent South evaporated as he perceived that there was in fact less basis of economic unity among some parts of the Confederacy than between parts of it and of the neighboring Union States. He and his following so resented Davis's and Congress's "aggressions," as they called them, as to rouse fears that South Carolina would not remain five years in the Confederacy. And yet North Carolina and Georgia were to challenge Confederate authority more seriously than did South Carolina.

Rhett, essentially the agitator whose work was finished, was passed over. President Davis offered the secretaryship of state to R. W. Barnwell, who declined, as his delegation intended C. G. Memminger of Charleston for the treasury. Davis accepted the recommendation and substituted Toombs as secretary of state. Memminger resigned on June 15, 1864, after an administration fully identified with the disastrous financial policies of the Confederacy, and was succeeded three days later by George A. Trenholm, an able Charleston cotton exporter who, whatever might have been his course under earlier opportunities, could now do little but seek to check the effects of disordered finances. Davis's dislike (fully reciprocated) for Hammond and Trescot prevented him from using these able men. As usual, conservatives were relied upon to sustain the revolution without much regard for the radicals by whom it had been fomented.

CHAPTER LI

THE WAR THROUGH 1863

MISSISSIPPI, Florida, Alabama, Georgia, Louisiana, and Texas, in the order named, quickly followed South Carolina into secession. Upon President Lincoln's call for troops, Arkansas, Virginia, North Carolina, and Tennessee, in the order named, forced to choose between fighting for the Confederacy or against it, seceded. The story of the War of Secession forms a gigantic episode in American history, only the general course of which as directly involving South Carolina or her soldiers can be comprehended in this narrative.

South Carolina troops played an important part in the battle of Manassas, July 21, 1861. Colonel (later General) N. G. Evans, divining McDowell's attack at the Stone Bridge to be a feint, shifted his brigade to meet the real attack, thus affording time for the re-alignment of the Confederate forces and contributing essentially to the victory. The Hampton Legion stood beside Jackson in repulsing the enemy at the crisis of the battle.

The Fall of Port Royal—Negro Troops.—The loss of Fort Sumter ended the operations of the Federal government against South Carolina for almost seven months. The Federal government decided on Port Royal as best fitted as a base for military operations and headquarters for the blockade and accordingly, on November 7, 1861, with an overwhelming fleet seized that point.

The next day General R. E. Lee took command of the Department of South Carolina and Georgia. Unable to hold the numerous entrances and islands, Lee abandoned all except those essential to the defense of Charleston. The sea islands, especially near Beaufort, became the scene of missionary, educational, economic, and military experiments with the Negroes, in which exalted, impractical idealism, religious devotion, and rough military impatience of the various Northerners participating were strangely mingled with the stolidity of some of the most primitive and ignorant slaves in the State. But from among those isolated Negroes there came some striking personalities of the later Reconstruction era. Plantations and town property in and around Beaufort were seized as "abandoned lands" and either distributed at low prices to Negroes, soldiers, etc., or knocked down to the government.[1]

[1] See pages 558-59 below.

Here were mustered in November, 1862, the first slave, and except for some almost white "Negroes" of New Orleans, the first Negro troops in the Federal service. Thomas W. Higginson was colonel of this, the "First Regiment of South Carolina Volunteers." In 1863 followed the Second South Carolina Regiment of Negroes. There were ultimately about 180,000 Negroes in the Northern army, of whom South Carolina furnished 5,462. The Negroes, led by white commissioned officers, did some splendid fighting, with heavy losses, against fortified positions along the coast, equaled their white confreres in plundering the defenseless, and as postwar garrisons became a peril to communities and sometimes to their own officers.

The Rule of the Convention and the Council of Safety.—The collapse at Port Royal dismayed the State. The Secession Convention, which continued its life for a period supposed sufficient for ratifying a Confederate Constitution, was re-assembled to save the State. It virtually superseded the regular government by creating an executive council of extensive legislative and executive powers composed of Governor Pickens and four others, with the Governor allowed only one vote. It suspended parts of the Constitution and military laws and made the Council directly responsible to itself.

Against this system of dual government, with Governor and legislature playing a poor second fiddle, Pickens, a high-spirited, independent man, chafed strongly. The Council revamped the military organization, declared State conscription to supplement the Confederate conscription law, deprived troops of the right to elect their officers; and itself made appointments, declared martial law in places, provided for the manufacture of war supplies, built a gunboat, prohibited distilling as wasteful of grain and producing drunkenness, murders, brawls, and fatal accidents among troops, and impressed slaves for the erection of extensive fortifications.

The Council brought results, but it also roused a storm of protests from individualistic South Carolina. There ensued a repetition of the old argument of nullification times as to the nature of a convention. Was it, as some had always held, a body of delegates of the people with power to perform only the duty for which it was summoned or make proposals for the sovereign to adopt or reject; or was it, as Calhoun taught, itself "we the people of South Carolina in convention assembled"? Could such a body once elected go on indefinitely, fill its own vacancies, and rule forever as an oligarchy? Such in effect, Attorney-General Hayne informed the protesting Governor, was the accepted South Carolina doctrine, and such is still the accepted South Carolina practice, because of the presence of the Negro. When the Convention decreed its own dissolution for December 17, 1862, the legislature abolished the Council; annulled its existing orders (except contracts); almost unanimously condemned the Convention for having undertaken to govern without the separation of executive, legislative, and judicial powers, thus threatening despotism and anarchy, and declared that conventions should act only on the purpose for which called. As the disappointments of war accumulated, Governor Pickens suffered the same eclipse of popularity that overtook President Davis.[2]

The work of the executive council was vindicated so far as military results were concerned when, in the spring of 1862, the Federals began operations extending from Port Royal to James Island for the capture of Charleston and were repulsed from the extensive Confederate works with sharp losses.

The Virginia Campaigns of 1862.—In the period covered by these operations in South Carolina, her sons were engaged also in the operations of the spring of 1862 in Virginia. McClellan, having abandoned the original Federal plan of marching directly upon Richmond from the north, landed a great army at Fort Monroe and approached up the peninsula between the York and the James.

McClellan's attempt to turn the Confederate left precipitated the battle of Fair Oaks, June 1. General Hampton, leading the Hampton Legion, the only South Carolina troops in the action, repelled the attempt. Now followed the seven days' battles around Richmond, June 25 to July 1, smashing McClellan's campaign, though ending in Lee's rash and disastrous attack at Malvern Hill. At Mechanicsville General Ripley's artillery played an important role. At Gaines' Mill, June 27, were General Gregg's South Carolinians, Crenshaw's battery, McGowan's regiment, the Legion infantry under Colonel M. W. Gary, and General R. H. Anderson's brigade. At Savage Station, June 29, McClellan's retreat ("changing his base to the James") was unsuccessfully disturbed by Generals Kershaw's and Semmes's brigades and Kemper's battery. Continuing his retreat with a skill that matched Lee's pursuit, McClellan fought the hard-drawn battle at Frazier's Farm (Glendale) on the 30th. General Anderson directed Longstreet's front, and Colonel Jenkins began the battle. Gregg's brigade fought on the left. Colonels McGowan, Edwards, Hamilton, and Simpson won special mention. In Lee's overconfident attack, against odds of numbers and position that could not be overcome, at Malvern Hill on the James, July 1, Kershaw's, the only South Carolina brigade seriously engaged, suffered severely. Lincoln recalled McClellan's army and determined again to try the direct advance from Washington to Richmond.

[2] Cf. Cauthen, *op. cit.*, pp. 264-5.

While the main South Carolina forces were engaged in Virginia, the 10th South Carolina (Colonel A. M. Manigault) and the 19th (Colonel A. J. Lythgoe) were sent west to aid Beauregard, hard pressed after Shiloh. Brigaded with other troops under Manigault, the regiments participated in the terrible fighting in Mississippi, Kentucky, and Tennessee.

After winning the peninsular campaign, Lee watched McClellan on the James and Pope in Northern Virginia until, convinced that McClellan was embarking toward the north, he launched the brilliant second Manassas campaign against Pope. On August 20, 1862, on the Manassas field, Pope was sent in flight to the Potomac. With 54,000 men daringly divided to deceive his opponent and reunited after long detours, Lee had routed Pope's 80,000 and rendered McClellan's large force useless. Practically all the South Carolinians in Lee's forces were active in this battle or at Groveton the day before and suffered severely.

As Lee pushed into Maryland on his unsuccessful Sharpsburg (or Antietam) campaign, his army included South Carolinians under Evans, Kershaw, Jenkins, Drayton, Hampton, Bachman, Garden, Rhett, Boyce, Gregg, McIntosh, Hart, and Butler. Having been repulsed in Maryland, Lee took up a strong position at Fredericksburg, Virginia. Here, on December 13, 1862, he inflicted a fearful defeat on Burnside's army, which was almost double the size of his own. Northern morale was prostrated. Officers resigned, and desertions multiplied.

From November 27 through December General Hampton executed a number of brilliant cavalry successes, netting material gains and discouraging the enemy. Now ensued a rest in Virginia until the spring of 1863.

The Gettysburg and Vicksburg Campaigns, 1863.—In the spring of 1863 Grant's aggressive tactics in Mississippi had shut up Pemberton with an utterly dispirited army in Vicksburg. On May 2 the Confederate government ordered Beauregard at Charleston to send to his assistance 5,000 South Carolinians, Georgians, and Louisianians organized into States Rights Gist's and W. H. T. Walker's brigades. These reinforcements nobly assisted Johnston's hopeless attempt to save Pemberton, and continued in the western army. Gist was killed at Franklin.

After his brilliant victory May 1, 2, and 3, 1863, at Chancellorsville, Lee swept to the west and entered Maryland by the valley of the Shenandoah beyond the Blue Ridge. Meade, careful and determined, pursued him into Pennsylvania. An encounter of advanced columns at Gettysburg, on July 1, determined both commanders, seizing ideal positions for their purposes, to fight there. Lee, knowing that the fall of Vicksburg was inevitable, was striking a political more than a military blow; for victory in Pennsylvania might so confirm the widespread conviction in the North that the South could not be conquered that peace would follow. But so it was not to be. The fall of Vicksburg, July 4, coming the day after Lee's Gettysburg defeat July 1, 2, and 3, raised the North from a two years' despondency and sank into the heart of the South the conviction of her helplessness before the mighty resources against which she was bleeding herself to death.

South Carolina troops were active in the Chancellorsville-Gettysburg campaign and suffered heavily. On July 1 Perrin's brigade drove the Federals through Gettysburg, but lost very heavily, and continued hard fighting on the second and third. Kershaw's brigade, in desperate fighting in the peach orchard and the wheat field on the 2nd, lost very heavily. Major General R. H. Anderson of South Carolina was conspicuous for gallantry on the 2nd, as was the South Carolinian J. J. Pettigrew, leading North Carolinians in Pickett's charge on the 3rd.

The gloom of Gettysburg and Vicksburg was only partially relieved when Bragg, September 19 and 20, 1863, assaulted Rosecrans' position on Chickamauga Creek south of Chattanooga and won the South's last great victory. South Carolina troops were conspicuous and suffered terrible losses. Kershaw's, Manigault's, and Gist's brigades suffered heavily the 20th. The 24th South Carolina, starting from Rome, marched and fought for three days without sleep. Kershaw, commanding a division after Hood had been wounded, Manigault's and Gregg's old brigade, and Culpepper's battery with other troops wound up the battle by a furious hour and a half assault on Thomas, the Virginian Federal, "the rock of Chickamauga," on Snodgrass Hill. At sunset the assault had failed.

Fighting Around Charleston During 1863.—We may trace now the operations around Charleston harbor beginning a little before and extending a little beyond the Chancellorsville-Gettysburg campaign. In March, 1863, the Federals were preparing an elaborate attack on Charleston by a fleet co-operating with a land expedition to approach by the islands south of the Ashley. Of Beauregard's 22,648 men on April 7th guarding approaches from a little north of Charleston to the Savannah, 12,856 occupied the forts and islands immediately around the city. On March 28 the Federal General Hunter had occupied Cole's Island (at the southwest end of James Island) and Folly Island (southwest of Morris, between James and the sea). On April 7th Rear Admiral DuPont considerably damaged Fort Sumter but suffered grave damage to his five vessels and the loss of the monitor *Keokuk*.

On July 10 General Q. A. Gillmore (successor to Hunter), after thorough preparations on Folly Island, easily threw 3,000 men across Lighthouse Inlet to Morris Island and the next day attacked Battery

Wagner near the northern end of Morris Island. Battery Wagner was essentially an outpost of Fort Sumter to assist in the defense of that key position, whose activity rendered it impossible for the Federal fleets to enter the harbor. The plan of General Gillmore and Admiral Dalgren (successor to DuPont) was therefore to reduce Wagner by a combined land and naval attack, and then turn its guns on Sumter.

After a terrific bombardment by the Federal land and naval batteries, General Gillmore, on July 18, 1863, with 5,000 men, launched a desperate assault on Wagner and was repulsed with the loss of 1,515 as against the loss of 174 by the 1,000 Confederates.

General Gillmore was thus forced to institute regular siege approaches. For fifty days the fort was subjected to almost continuous bombardment, while the Federals crept closer in their parallels. The hardships of the garrison exceeded perhaps anything elsewhere and limited men's endurance to a few days. And yet they returned with undiminished spirit week after week.

On August 17, 1863, began the first of the three great, and eight minor, bombardments of Fort Sumter by the Federal fleet and their Morris Island batteries, which soon reduced it to a mass of water, mud, and wreckage. On August 22 the last cannon was fired from its walls. On September 1 it had not a gun to reply, and the dismounted or buried armament was being dug from the ruins and shipped to the inner harbor. So effective were the bombproofs that, during this fifty-eight-day bombardment, Fort Sumter lost only three killed and forty-nine wounded.

On August 22, 1863, Gillmore began to throw shells into Charleston from the "swamp angel" on Morris Island four miles from the city's southeastern point, but with surprisingly little damage.

Meanwhile, as part of the move to take Fort Sumter, the attack on Battery Wagner had also been in progress. The Federal sappers had pushed their trenches up to the very walls of the fortification. On the morning of September 7 would come the assault. During the preceding night the little garrison evacuated. At enormous sacrifice of life, during fifty-eight days of battle and siege, the Federals had secured possession of Morris Island, which failed, as the event proved, to serve their purpose of taking Sumter.

Discouragement, the Draft, Hardships, Desertions.—The loss of Battery Wagner deepened the gloom diffused over the Confederacy by Gettysburg and Vicksburg. Under the hardships of war people who had expected quick victory experienced before the end of 1862 bitter disillusionment. In Charleston leading secessionists were defeated for the legislature, while the moderates Trenholm, Yeadon, and O'Connor headed the ticket. Yeadon, Perry, and Orr, all anti-secessionists, though all loyally supporting the State when she had taken her stand, were legislative favorites. "There's one of the fellows got us into this trouble," Professor James H. Carlisle of the Secession Convention heard disagreeable-looking countrymen growl as he passed on the streets of Spartanburg. The draft was made bitter to the poor man by the exemption of owners of fifteen hands, and of one white man for every twenty slaves on a plantation or a group of plantations, and by the right to hire substitutes. An excessive number of men were excused for duties which disabled soldiers or men over 45, or even women, could perform. The sight of such men in bombproofs at home embittered the soldier. The enormous profits of the factories in the South, even after turning over a large proportion of their product to the government at or near cost, stirred such hatred as to elicit severe laws against extortion and even to rouse fear of mob violence. The manufacturers, conscious of being essential to Southern success, bitterly resented such opprobrium. One of them in South Carolina even sold his factory rather than endure it, while speculators in their products and blockade-runners grew rich undisturbed. Farmers charged fabulous prices for necessities while soldiers' families suffered cold and hunger. In neither North nor South was any system of taxation or trade regulation devised for preventing such inequities.

The first flush of enthusiasm over, North and South early resorted to conscription by both State and general laws. The Confederate act of February 17, 1864, conscripted seventeen-year-old boys and men over forty-five up to fifty for service in their own States and called into service men employing substitutes. The South Carolina law of December 6, 1864, subjected all between sixteen and fifty to service outside as well as inside the State at the Governor's orders, and those up to sixty within the State.

Superintendent of Registration Blake reported on January 25, 1864, that South Carolina had furnished 41,873 volunteers and 18,254 conscripts, totaling 60,127. In 1860 the approximate number of men in the State, aged eighteen to forty-five, was 60,000. Many South Carolinians enlisted in North Carolina because of her double bounty. Nobody knows the exact number of soldiers South Carolina furnished the Confederacy. The number of enlistments can be stated, but there is no knowledge how many were re-enlistments, or the same men counted in different regiments in which they served.

By autumn of 1862 war weariness had swelled the tide of desertions to alarming proportions. "Appalling in the Southern armies," says Miss Lonn, "it was even worse in Northern regiments." After Gettysburg, with hope fading, the evil increased. Greenville, Pickens, and Spartanburg districts were infested with deserters. Along a mountain frontier of 150 miles they were in armed organized bands, often preying upon the property of loyal Confederates. Angered at "the speculations and extortions so rampant throughout the land . . . they swear by all they hold sacred that they will die at home before they will ever be dragged forth again to do battle for such a cause." As defeat became inevitable to men frequently for days without food for a single fair meal, with their bare feet bleeding on rocky roads, the Confederate army, like any unfed, hopeless army, was melting away. Lee reported on February 25, 1865, "hundreds of men are deserting nightly." In March Superintendent of the Conscript Bureau John S. Preston reported over 100,000 deserters on the rolls. South Carolina had 3,579, two and a half times as good a record as the South as a whole. Many "deserters" were, as a matter of fact, absent on leave and unable to return.

Troops were necessary here and in other States to suppress resistance to the draft. Despite the fact that slavery was at stake, owners, in their objection to interference with plantation operations or to having their slaves abused, so frequently disobeyed the draft on slaves for military works (the owners being compensated), or evaded it by paying the small fine, as seriously to embarrass the government.[3] The murmur rose that it was "a rich man's war and a poor man's fight." A writer denounced "a round of balls" and other gaieties in Charleston, while in a single up-country village there were eight widows of gentle birth, the eldest not over twenty-eight, whose husbands had died for their country.

Even conservatives began to doubt President Davis's ability, and Rhett's Charleston *Mercury* and Pollard's *Richmond Examiner* were attacking him virtually as a public enemy. Holden was demanding in North Carolina a separate peace by that State. In response to such attacks Kershaw's brigade, assembled at the front, heard Colonel J. D. Nance of the Third South Carolina Regiment praise the President, and adopted unanimously resolutions repudiating the *Mercury*'s charge that Davis had lost the confidence of the army. Rhett, that "most offensive of beings," said the *Courier,* "the infallible, the impeccable," was beaten (for the first time in his home district) for Congress by young Ayer, who declared that to elect Rhett would be to make war upon the Confederacy. Original extreme secessionists were beaten in other States. The *Mercury* lamented, "Those who made this revolution do not direct it." Davis's visit to Charleston immediately afterward, and the fact that the legislature strongly expressed confidence in him and dropped its quarrel on conscription, left the Rhett faction crushed and discouraged.

[3] Cauthen, *op. cit.*, pp. 281-2, 332, 335, 339.

Women's Hospital Service, etc.—Despite Rhett's criticisms, and despite ugly acts of personal selfishness by the dissatisfied, which he was above, South Carolina was unexcelled by any State in its loyal support of the Confederacy. She was the first State to agree to endorse Confederate bonds, which failed because many States refused. The widespread disaffection, threatening most serious consequences, that appeared in several States had no place here.

There is no finer chapter in the history of war than the heroism of the Southern women, in which they evinced a devotion equal to the courage with which they inspired the men to fight. They greatly supplemented the government's inadequate hospital service. In Columbia, young women headed by Miss Sallie Hampton (Mrs. J. C. Haskell) and Miss Susan Hampton Preston (Mrs. H. W. Frost) founded late in 1861 the first wayside hospital, it is said, in the world. It was fully organized by March, 1862. It sheltered or fed about 75,000 soldiers. South Carolina organizations, some not confined to women, maintained at least nine hospitals in Virginia, one of forty rooms, and donated quantities of supplies. "Corn Associations," etc., supplied the poor, the embarrassed coast refugees, and needy soldiers' families. Salaries lagged far behind rising prices and left thousands in hardship, while blockade-runners, fortunate speculators, and contractors were in ease, and factories and railroads paid dividends enormous even when translated into the real value of Confederate money.

Mrs. Mary Amarintha Yates Snowden of Charleston (1819-93) was an outstanding woman leader. Before 1860 she raised a large sum for the Calhoun monument, finally erected in Charleston in 1887, for which the legislature presented her with one of the sets of Calhoun's *Works* reserved for persons of notable public service. She carried between $40,000 and $50,000 of securities sewed in her skirts during the burning of Columbia. She was honored by the Confederate government for her devotion and able work in hospitals. The Confederate Memorial Association founded by her in 1866 is believed to have been the first organized. She was the leader in bringing the bodies of South Carolina dead from Gettysburg to Magnolia Cemetery. In 1867 she founded the Home for the Mothers, Widows and Daughters of Confederate Soldiers and Sailors, for which she and her sister-in-law, Mrs. Isabella S. Snowden, her constant associate in war and postwar services, mortgaged their home, and continued until her death the president of the board of the institution after it had developed into the Confederate Home College. The legislature and the United Daughters of the Confederacy, in erecting in 1917 a memorial tablet in the State Capitol to one combining so notably the beauty and strength of Southern womanhood, honored through her thousands of Southern women, among whom she stands conspicuous for actualizing through her energy, enthusiasm, hope, and power of persuasion what was in their hearts.

In 1863 the legislature renewed the executive council's prohibition of distilling except for medical purposes, and fostered food-raising by forbidding more than three acres of cotton to the hand, an interference bitterly resented by apostles of individual liberty. The stay law of 1861, sheltering many able to pay, was said to undermine commercial integrity.

Mining and Manufacturing.—The State found its Spartanburg lead mine uneconomical, was glad to have the Confederate government take over its saltpeter plantation, and desired to get rid of its arms factory in Greenville, but had to be satisfied with moving it to Columbia. A few cannon were cast. By August, 1862, the State had received 220 double-barrel guns, 33,751 muskets, and 10,042 rifles. From January 1 to July 1, 1862, 332 flint and steel pistols were issued. Inferior paper-shelled cartridges were made in homes. About 1,000 pikes had been made in Greenville by October 1, 1863, and some in Columbia, as well as some shells and cannon balls. Sabers were made in Columbia and Charleston. A powder mill stood where the canal powerhouse now is, at the foot of Gervais Street, Columbia.

Manufacturing was greatly stimulated by the check of imports. Scores of articles were produced either in homes or in factories. The old coldness toward the manufacturing interest, the results of which were now strangling the South, was by no means fully removed. To meet the government demand for cloth (which was traded to farmers who would not take Confederate money for their supplies), Graniteville worked its hands fourteen hours a day, and would have run twenty-four hours but for shortage of help.

CHAPTER LII

EXHAUSTION AND DEFEAT, 1864-1865

After the first great bombardment from August 17 to September 1, 1863, Fort Sumter, with few cannon, remained from that time an infantry outpost for 200 to 300 men. Thrice abandonment of the fort seemed almost inevitable—September, 1863, December, 1863, and July to August, 1864; but each time the fortitude of the defenders took advantage of the weariness or ignorance of the enemy to prepare for further defense. The explosion of one of the magazines during profound quiet on December 11, 1863, killing eleven and wounding forty-one, was the worst single catastrophe of the four years except the killing of thirteen men, October 31, 1863, by a wall thrown upon them by a Union shell.

At 1:00 A.M., September 9, 1863, Fort Sumter was attacked by a landing party, who lost, in killed, wounded, and captured, 124. It was subsequently repeatedly reconnoitered for a landing, which never again occurred.

The eight or ten Federal bombarding monitors and several ironclads suffered severe losses. The three major attacks on Sumter lasted 117 days, the eight minor attacks forty days, and desultory firing 280 days. So effectively were the bombproofs maintained that from August, 1863, to February, 1865, only fifty-two men were killed and 267 wounded. The Federal fleet never ventured to run past the Sullivan's Island batteries or the entanglements and mines in the harbor.

On September 4, 1863, Colonel Alfred Rhett and the 1st South Carolina Artillery were replaced in Sumter by Major Stephen Elliott and the Charleston Battalion. Elliott was sent to Virginia in May, 1864, where as Brigadier-General he received the wound that ended his life in 1866. Captain J. C. Mitchel assumed command of Sumter on May 4, 1864, and on being mortally wounded on July 20 was succeeded by Captain T. A. Huguenin, who served until the evacuation, February 18, 1865. New troops had frequently relieved the old.

Blockade-Running.—Not only was Charleston harbor the scene of by far the heaviest and most prolonged naval operations by the Federals, but it was the chief center of the Confederate blockade-running. It was from Charleston that Mason and Slidell sailed, to be taken from a British mail steamer and bring war between England and the United

States within hailing distance. Available lists show twice as many blockade-runners from Charleston or Wilmington as from Galveston, and four times as many as from Savannah or Mobile. Without this means of securing arms and ammunition the military resistance of the Confederacy would have soon collapsed, and without the supplies of medicines, manufactures, etc., both civil and military life would have been strangled. The list of eighty-eight vessels known to have run in and out of Charleston, some making from six to eighteen voyages, is apparently incomplete. Two voyages were sufficient to pay for the craft and net a handsome profit.

Confederate Naval Achievements.—The Confederacy achieved wonders with its restricted naval equipment and added two new instruments to war, the submarine boat and the marine torpedo. In all areas, thirty-one Federal vessels were destroyed and nine injured by torpedoes. Around Charleston, the *New Ironsides* was seriously injured on October 5, 1863, and later two smaller vessels were slightly injured, and the *Housatonic* (February 17, 1864) and the *Patapsco* (January 15, 1864) were destroyed. Near Georgetown, March 1, 1864, the flagship *Harvest Moon* was destroyed.

Daring attacks were made with Captain F. D. Lee's "spar torpedo," attached to a thirty-foot pole and rammed against the enemy at the risk of the lives of the attackers.

Even more daring were the navigators of the submarine *Hundley.* Built in Mobile in 1863, designed to dive under her antagonist dragging a torpedo which would explode on striking the hull, she was brought to Charleston after having drowned one crew. She was propelled by eight men, and had fins (hence the name "the fish boat"), as well as tanks, for sinking or rising, but no extra air supply. In experiments around Charleston she drowned four crews, but there were volunteers when Lieutenant G. E. Dixon of Alabama asked permission to use her against the *Housatonic.* Beauregard consented on condition she use a spar instead of diving. She sank the *Housatonic,* and her own crew perished at the bottom, where she lay until after the war.

The War in Virginia and the West, 1864.—The year 1864 saw the North pressing more systematically than ever to crush the South simultaneously in East and West. Grant inaugurated the war of attrition in Virginia, destroying at fearful cost to his own larger forces, which could be constantly renewed, Lee's army, which could not be refilled.

On May 5 and 6 at "the Wilderness," McGowan's brigade alternately advanced and retired. Kershaw came up with Longstreet to save the line. McGowan's brigade was in the thickest of the fighting at "the bloody angle" at Spotsylvania. Kershaw's, Anderson's, Law's, and

Gregg's old troops were among those receiving and repulsing Grant's massive charges, reckless of his men's lives, all along the line at Cold Harbor, June 3. After Stuart fell at Yellow Tavern, May 11, 1864, the great cavalry campaign was continued by Hampton, who on August 11 was made commander of all the cavalry of Lee's army. At the same time, under Beauregard, Hagood's, Evans' and Elliott's infantry, Colonel Shingler's cavalry, and Kelly's battery, were guarding Richmond against B. F. Butler's army.

Five companies of the 22nd South Carolina and four of the 18th defending Petersburg were blown up with a loss of 332 (a fourth or more of them killed) at the Crater on July 30, 1864. Their survivors and the 23rd and 17th South Carolina were the first to meet the cannon-supported charge of the enemy. The South Carolinians held their ground in thirty yards of the Crater for five hours. There was nothing more heroic that day, says General Bushrod Johnson, "than the conduct of the 22nd and 23rd South Carolina regiments."

But the South was desperately near collapse. The South Carolina legislature elected a Governor (Magrath) unfriendly to Davis and prepared for its own defense. The Confederate Congress on March 13, 1865, adopted a measure destructive of the whole theory of slavery and perilous to slavery itself—the enlistment of Negro troops—though it left to each State the question of their freedom. The end came before these troops could be raised.

Relief came for the North when Sherman took Atlanta on September 3, 1864. In the campaign, which cost the Confederates more men than it cost Sherman's army of twice the size, were the South Carolina 16th and 24th regiments, Ferguson's battery of Gist's brigade, and the 10th and 19th regiments of Manigault's. No body of troops acted better than the whole South Carolina contingent that followed Hood to the virtual destruction of his army as an offensive organization by Thomas at Nashville, December 15 and 16, 1864.

The War in South Carolina, November, 1864–February, 1865.—Confederate resistance now amounted to mere futility. In a carnival of destruction Sherman marched from Atlanta to Savannah, making good his threat to "make Georgia howl." The Confederate armies felt the pinch of hunger as Sherman's men obeyed his order to "forage liberally" on the supplies that now could not go to Lee.

As Sherman neared Savannah the Federals left Hilton Head with 5,500 men, almost half of them Negroes, to cut the Charleston and Savannah Railroad near Grahamville. They were repulsed on November 30 at Honey Hill by a much smaller force having the advantage of the ground.

Sherman entered South Carolina with 60,079 men. Finding the Confederate government exhausted and its policy "unfortunate," Governor Magrath urged interstate co-operation upon Georgia, the Carolinas, and Alabama. His passionate pleas for aid (Charleston, as a port, was more important than Richmond, he urged) brought from General Lee the reply, Can his Excellency think that it would help the Confederacy to have Sherman and Grant both in South Carolina? Governor Brown agreed to help, though, he said, it would have been with better spirit if South Carolina had helped to save Atlanta. Such help, Magrath replied, the law did not then permit.

On February 2, 1865, the forces available to oppose Sherman were Hardee's regular infantry, 8,000; militia and reserves (the old and the very young), 3,000; light artillery, 2,000; Butler's cavalry, 1,500; Smith's and Brown's militia and reserves, 1,450; Wheeler's cavalry, 6,700. Many of those expected from the Army of Tennessee never arrived, and many joined the forces only in North Carolina.

Sherman moved his army into South Carolina in two wings, the right under Howard going by water to Beaufort and thence inland, and the left under Slocum crossing Savannah River thirty miles above the city of Savannah. Skillfully leading his opponents to believe he planned attacking Charleston or Augusta, he caused them to separate their forces widely. The Federals, wading the three-mile swamp of the Salkehatchie, took in flank on both its sides the Confederate brigade guarding Rivers' Bridge two miles south of Barnwell. The town of Barnwell was burned.

Kilpatrick, threatening Augusta, fought Wheeler at Blackville, Williston, and Aiken. The Confederates holding the bridge at Orangeburg were easily outflanked, and the town was partly burned. Flanking the Confederates out of their works below Columbia, Sherman sent his left wing on toward Alston and thence to Winnsboro, which was partly burned. The whole army except the cavalry reunited at Cheraw, and the cavalry rejoined at Fayetteville.

After throwing a few shells into Columbia at cavalry squads, the State House, and the South Carolina Railroad depot, where supplies he desired were being removed, Sherman crossed the Saluda at the factory (which he burned) and crossed the Broad at the Newberry road by pontoons.

Hatred for South Carolina as the leader in secession caused even more general burning and plundering than in Georgia. The railroads, workshops, cotton, and anything of military service were, of course, destroyed; but the same fate was inflicted on almost every residence along the march. Colonel Stone of Sherman's army wrote to the *Chicago*

Tribune, January 2, 1873, of having saved a mansion in South Carolina by being the last man to leave it; but that night some men, after having marched twenty-seven miles that day, added six more for the purpose of going back and burning it. "Their dreams would have been troubled had that building remained as a monument of their oversight or neglect." He continued, "This feeling of hatred was intensified as we approached Columbia."

Major G. W. Nichols of Sherman's staff told of stealing by officers as well as men. Besides the authorized foragers, thousands of soldiers looted and burned at will. The "bummers," men who left their regiments for weeks, were the worst. Of such said Captain Daniel Oakey of the 2nd Massachusetts Volunteers, "It was sad to see this wanton destruction of property, which, like the firing of the resin pits, was the work of 'bummers' who were marauding through the country committing every sort of outrage. . . . Our 'bummers,' who often fell to the tender mercies of Wheeler's cavalry, and were never heard of again, meeting a fate richly deserved."

Said Major Nichols of Sherman's Army (pp. 277-78): "Over a region forty miles in width, stretching from Savannah and Port Royal through South Carolina, to Goldsboro, in North Carolina, agriculture and commerce, even if peace come speedily, can not be fully revived in our day. . . . On every side, the head, center, and rear of our column might be traced by columns of smoke by day, and the glare of fires by night."

Sherman neglected the principle he proclaimed to his soldiers on March 13, 1862: "The laws of Congress make pillage and plunder punishable by death, but the disgrace which attends the practice attaches itself to the cause, and prevents the respect with which it should be our aim to impress our enemies now, who must become our friends before peace can be hoped for."[1]

On some roads hardly a dwelling except slave quarters was spared. Said Captain David P. Conyngham, press correspondent with Sherman's army, "I hazard nothing in saying that three-fifths (in value) of the personal property of the counties we passed through were taken by Sherman's army. . . . As for wholesale burnings, pillage and devastation committed in South Carolina, magnify all I have said of Georgia some fifty-fold, and then throw in an occasional murder, 'jist to bring an old hard-fisted cuss to his senses,' and you have a pretty good idea of the whole thing." When to this was added the foraging by Wheeler's cavalry, sweeping away eatables as ruthlessly as Sherman, the inhabitants often faced starvation.

Rape by the soldiers was almost unknown. Sherman swore to hear-

[1] *Reb. Rec.,* X, Pt. 2, 34.

ing of only two cases. General Hawley, April 1, 1865, reported three in the general confusion around Wilmington, with deserters and vagabonds from both sides uncontrolled. The facility of the Negro women doubtless protected the whites. Young wenches crowding around the camps were debauched until white inhabitants protested.

The Burning of Columbia.—Sherman had so misled as to his intended route that Columbia was crowded with refugees and treasure. By daylight, February 17, no troops remained but Hampton's and a small part of Wheeler's cavalry. The quartermaster and commissary stores were thrown open and distributed to the crowd, "whilst at the depot of the South Carolina Railroad, a reckless mob, composed of both sexes and colors, were plundering its contents in search of treasures of every description which had been accumulated there." Some kegs of powder, unknown to the crowd, had been stored among the goods. They were ignited, the property was destroyed, and about forty persons were killed. The fire, which did not spread, and which was a mile from the cotton on Main Street, caused some Federal officers to say they saw the city illuminated that morning by cotton fires.

Generals Hampton and M. C. Butler, Major A. J. Green (Post Commander), and Captain Rawlins Lowndes (Hampton's Assistant Adjutant General), several of whom remained until Sherman's troops were entering the city, state that not a bale was fired before the evacuation. Mayor Goodwyn, who drove through Main Street to meet the invader, says that there was no fire in the cotton then or when he returned. Only one gun was fired at the entering Federals, and that contrary to orders.

Mayor Goodwyn surrendered the city to Colonel Stone leading his troops toward the northern outskirts of the city early February 17. Between 11:00 A.M. and noon General Sherman entered and assured the Mayor, said that official, of the safety of the city.

Alderman Stork stated that he saw Federal soldiers occupying the middle of Main Street smoking and throwing matches along the cotton piled in the middle of that very broad thoroughfare. Rev. P. J. Shand of Trinity Episcopal Church, watching from the sidewalk, saw many soldiers smoking by the cotton. Rev. A. Toomer Porter, another Episcopal minister, said the soldiers were lighting pipes as they sat or lay on the cotton. Suddenly a bale blazed up, and the fire spread rapidly in the high northwestern wind. The fire department, aided by soldiers (though some of the latter cut the hose, etc.), so thoroughly extinguished and drenched the cotton that even in the conflagration that night it did not burn.

The army was widely permeated with the idea that the burning of the city would be agreeable to their leader. This is not surprising. On

December 18, 1864, General H. W. Halleck wrote General Sherman, "Should you capture Charleston, I hope that by *some* accident the place may be destroyed; and if a little salt should be sown upon the site, it may prevent the growth of future crops of nullification and secession." Sherman replied on December 24: "I will bear in mind your hint as to Charleston, but don't think 'salt' will be necessary. When I move, the 15th Corps will be on the right of the right wing, and their position will bring them naturally into Charleston first; and if you have watched the history of that corps, you will have remarked that they generally do their work up pretty well. The truth is the whole army is burning with an insatiable desire to wreak vengeance upon South Carolina. I almost tremble at her fate, but feel that she deserves all that is in store for her. . . . I look upon Columbia as quite as bad as Charleston."

Sherman swore as follows before the Mixed Commission, of 1873: "I could have had them [his soldiers] stay in the ranks, but I would not have done it, under any circumstances, to save Columbia." "Q. Although you knew they were likely to burn Columbia, you would not restrain them to their ranks, even to save it?" "A. No, sir; I would not have done such a harshness to my soldiers to save the whole town." Mrs. Anna W. Barclay, wife of the British Consul in New York, testified that at the house of Miss Telfair in Savannah she heard General Sherman say, "As for that hotbed of secession, Columbia, I shall lay it in ashes." The fact that Sherman later determined not to burn the city did not alter the understanding common in the army. Sherman swore before the Mixed Claims Commission that "The feeling [of vengeance against South Carolina] was universal, and pervaded all ranks. . . . We looked upon South Carolina as the cause of our woe [and thought] that she thoroughly deserved extirpation."

It would have been remarkable if Columbia had not been burned by its invaders. Why should the almost universal burning have continued up to the chiefly hated city and have skipped that, only immediately to begin again after it had been spared? What must have been the feeling of coarser Northerners as to what they would do if they could when Rev. Phillips Brooks wrote on February 20, 1865, after the burning, "Hurrah for Columbia! Isn't Sherman a gem?"

The Confederate civil and military authorities were severely to blame for having permitted large quantities of liquor to remain in Columbia. Negroes and citizens freely served whiskey to soldiers, not to speak of the latter's seizing what they pleased in the plundering of stores.

During the afternoon Hampton's, Wallace's,[2] Mrs. Stark's, and other houses in the country around Columbia were burned, says Dr. Treze-

[2] No relation to the author of this work.

vant. Colonel Stone of Sherman's army wrote in 1873, "I now had intimation that the Union officers released by us from the city prisons had formed a society, to which had been added many members from our soldiers and the Negroes, and the object of which society was to burn Columbia." Colonel D. J. Palmer, he continued, "commanding my regiment, the 75th Iowa, confirmed my opinion that a plot had been formed to burn the town by telling me several fires had been started in the part of the town he had been placed over" and said he could not hold out much longer.

The incendiaries evidently agreed to start the fires at the discharge of the regular signal rockets shortly after dark. So well was this understood that many citizens were warned by friendly soldiers, and some were told of the signal. To return to the Federal Colonel Stone's account: "All at once fifteen or twenty flames, from as many different places along the river, shot up, and in ten minutes the fate of Columbia was settled." Dr. Trezevant agrees with Colonel Stone in placing them southwest or north of the cotton, so that it would have been impossible for the cotton, even if it had been burning, to ignite them, as the wind was from the northwest. The incendiaries set the fires on the western side of the city for the obvious reason that the high wind which blew all day and a great part of the night from the northwest would thus spread them over the city.

When the fire started, Sherman was lying down at his headquarters on the opposite side of the city. At the glare on his chamber wall, he sent to inquire the cause, and found, he says in his *Memoirs,* "that the block of buildings directly opposite the burning cotton of the morning was on fire, and that it was spreading. . . .

"It was accidental, and in my judgment began with the cotton which General Hampton's men set fire to on leaving the city (whether by his orders or not is not material), which fire was partially subdued early in the day by our men; but, when night came, the high wind fanned it again into full blaze, carried it against the frame houses, which caught like tinder, and soon spread beyond our control. . . .

"In my official report of this conflagration, I distinctly charged it to General Wade Hampton, and confess I did so pointedly, to shake the faith of his people in him, for he was in my opinion a braggart, and professed to be the special champion of South Carolina."

This narrative omits the fact that the fire began on the side of the cotton from which the wind was coming, and therefore could not have caught from the cotton. Perhaps General Sherman had not been told this; for he had no personal knowledge of the fire's origin. Yet his loose statement, omitting essential circumstances and stating groundless surmises as facts, has been widely accepted in the North as though he were narrating what he had actually seen.

No human being has ever professed to have seen this cotton ignite a single house; and yet the cotton story spins out over the land, in the face of the testimony of men and women of the highest character that they saw Sherman's men setting the fires, and that the slight cotton fires of the morning had been at once thoroughly extinguished.

Strangely neglected have been General Sherman's *Memoirs* (II, 288), stating that his soldiers burned the city: "Having utterly ruined Columbia, the right wing began its march northward." Equally does he accept the responsibility for his army in writing in his *Memoirs* (II, 349) that in speaking to General J. E. Johnston, April 17, of the news of Lincoln's assassination, he expressed the fear that "some foolish woman or man in Raleigh [then occupied by Sherman's army] might say something or do something that would madden our men, and that a fate worse than that of Columbia would befall the place." It is to be regretted that the volume of General Sherman's *Home Letters,* published after his death, omits all letters during his South Carolina campaign.

General Sherman's official report of April 4, 1865, differs widely from his expressions to numbers of persons of the highest character in Columbia during the fire. Repeatedly, as he watched the flames after midnight, he bewailed the fact that the Confederates, by leaving stores of whiskey, had caused the drunkenness of his soldiers and made them incendiaries. He ordered the drunken troops removed, a process in which a number were killed for resistance, and, with the aid of the lull in the wind, he and his officers did help extinguish the flames. Especial credit is due the divisions of Generals Woods and Hazen, the latter of whom felt the deepest indignation at what had occurred.

Multiplication of testimony, by eyewitnesses of the highest character, to the burning and stealing by Sherman's soldiers would run into tedium. Conyngham, press correspondent with Sherman's army, wrote that he saw soldiers rushing from house to house, emptying them of valuables and then firing them, and that he saw officers and men reveling and drinking until the burning walls fell upon them. Eighty-four out of 124 city blocks were burned. The conduct of the soldiers on that terrible night differed as widely as their characters. Acts of chivalrous kindness, and even cases where guards risked their own lives in repelling marauders, are recorded by citizens. Many were warned beforehand to leave, as the city would certainly be burned. General Sherman protected individuals in his immediate vicinity and gave supplies to some old Charleston friends. On the 18th the public property, foundries, etc., were burned, and vast military and other supplies destroyed.

Evacuation of Charleston.—Sherman's position necessitated the Confederates' evacuation of Charleston. This was accomplished the night of February 17 and the early morning of the 18th. The Confederates fired the vast stores of cotton, and boys playing with powder near by caused an explosion that killed 100 to 150 persons. The Federals aided in extinguishing the flames, and on the 20th systematically stripped unoccupied houses of their contents and sequestered all cotton, all foreign goods in original packages, every horse and buggy, and liberal levies of fowls and rice.

The End.—General Edward E. Potter now gave the quivering body of wrecked and ruined South Carolina the last blow. Leaving Georgetown on April 5 with 2,700 white and Negro troops, he raided through Manning and Sumter to Camden with the purpose of destroying the locomotives and the cars loaded with supplies, mainly on the "Camden branch" of the railroad in the swamps above the Wateree River crossing. The constant skirmishing by little bands of the reserves of boys and old men, brave but untrained, was easily brushed aside. Some residences were burned, though where Potter was personally present he acted humanely. His incomplete report of destruction included 1,000,000 feet of lumber, 32 locomotives, 250 cars, vast stores, 100 cotton gins and presses, 5,000 bales of cotton, and much railroad trackage. On April 21 when he was halfway back to Georgetown, devastation was stopped by news of Johnston's surrender.

South Carolina Troops at the Surrender.—Meanwhile, in Virginia, Grant was closing around Lee's army, which, hopeless of success, was melting away. After Lee's surrender, Johnston warned Davis that the people considered the war over; that his army was deserting in large numbers and would melt away at the roads and paths leading to each man's home. The contest was indeed hopeless, even with Spartan heroism against odds constantly growing more overwhelming. On April 26, near Durham, North Carolina, Johnston surrendered to Sherman 39,042 men under his command, of whom about 20,000 were with him at Greensboro. Among these, as among the 26,675 surrendered by General Lee on April 9, were the greatly reduced organizations of many South Carolina brigades.[3]

The following Confederate Generals were appointed from South

[3] The names and distribution of the various South Carolina brigades and regiments about July, 1863, are given in my three-volume *History of South Carolina,* III, 181, and at the surrender in April, 1865, at III, 217-18.

Carolina (not including several South Carolinians appointed from other States) in the years and order indicated:[4]

Lieutenant-General: Wade Hampton, 1865.

Lieutenant-Generals with temporary rank: Richard H. Anderson, 1864; Stephen D. Lee, 1864.

Major-Generals: Benjamin Huger, 1861; J. B. Kershaw, 1864; M. C. Butler, 1864.

Brigadier-Generals: M. L. Bonham, 1861; B. E. Bee, 1861; T. F. Drayton, 1861; N. G. Evans, 1861; J. H. Trapier, 1861; Maxcy Gregg, 1861; J. B. Villepigue, 1862; S. R. Gist, 1862; Johnson Hagood, 1862; Micah Jenkins, 1862; Samuel McGowan, 1863; A. M. Manigault, 1863; C. H. Stevens, 1864; James Chestnut, Jr., 1864; Stephen Elliott, Jr., 1864; John Bratton, 1864; J. S. Preston, 1864; M. W. Gary, 1864; T. M. Logan, 1865; Ellison Capers, 1865.

Brigadier-Generals with temporary rank: John Dunovant, 1864; W. H. Wallace, 1864; J. D. Kennedy, 1865.

In addition to the above thirty-two generals appointed from this State, J. J. Pettigrew (1862) and James Connor (1864) were South Carolinians appointed Brigadier-Generals from North Carolina.

Several distinguished generals from other States were born in South Carolina, as Lieutenant-General Longstreet in Edgefield, and Major Generals D. H. Hill in York and David Rumph Jones in Orangeburg. Samuel Preston Moore, Surgeon-General of the Confederacy from June, 1861, to the end, was born in Charleston and graduated there in medicine.

So ended the lost cause, an impossible ideal fighting against overwhelming material odds and the world-wide tendencies of its age, but maintained, as says Woodrow Wilson, with a devotion hardly ever witnessed in a cause not religious. The South may accept the verdict of William H. Trescot, "History will vindicate our motives while she explains our errors."

[4] The exact dates of the President's nomination of the officer and of the Senate's confirmation are given in my three-volume *History of South Carolina,* III, 220-21.

CHAPTER LIII

PRESIDENTIAL RECONSTRUCTION, 1865-1867

The Prostrate State.—To the people of South Carolina in 1865, exhausted by war and stunned by the overthrow of their economic and social system, the overwhelming facts were confusion and hardship. To the glory of military prowess a conquered people now added the dignity of quiet courage and self-respecting endurance of privation and humiliation. Men of aristocratic antecedents or public distinction sought any honest employment. Lieutenant-General Richard H. Anderson worked as a railroad-yard worker and died a phosphate inspector. For years ex-Confederate officers in Charleston drove street cars, and when their Negro passengers were too disagreeable would shake their heads in warning to ladies not to get on.

"What is that *white woman* doing here?" asked a Northern visitor looking on the file of Negroes drawing rations from the Charleston City Council's charity provisions, which the Federal authorities had taken over. "My dear sir," replied Mr. George W. Williams, the alderman in charge, "that woman four years ago was worth half a million dollars and lived in a mansion on the Battery." The cashier of the Bank of Charleston, he continued, came every day for his rice or meal. Actual hunger was found as late as 1867, and many formerly wealthy were for years undernourished. "Here," wrote Sidney Andrews, "is enough of woe and want and ruin to satisfy the most insatiate heart. . . . One marks how few young men there are, and how generally the young women are dressed in black."

The city of Charleston itself was a mournful spectacle. The wharves were rotting, the water front resembled a tangled marsh, grass grew in the leading streets, and blackened walls and chimneys stood as monuments of the terrible fires of 1861 to 1865 over water-filled cellars yawning like graves.

On this scene of desolation there descended a rejoicing party of Northern philanthropists to celebrate the raising of the United States flag by Major Anderson over Fort Sumter. Henry Ward Beecher delivered an oration recognizing the military virtues of the South, while mercilessly chastising her political theories, and prophesying, in some respects truly, the future of a remade South. The whole expedition sought to exhibit everything in reverse, rubbing salt into open wounds. How far partisanship can blind philanthropists to low crime when committed by themselves is revealed by the glee of the committee report as "dozens of curiosity hunters were bending over them [documents and books in banks and homes] on hands and knees . . . and duly bestowing them in the voluminous depths of coat pockets. . . . Occasionally would be heard, 'Ah! here's a prize! Look! 1730, 1776,' etc. Enough of these valuable acquisitions were brought home to comfortably stock No. 25 Ann Street. . . . Simply to name the relics which were obtained at Charleston by our company, in their antiquarian researches, would require a volume." Mrs. Henry Ward Beecher appropriated a panel of the pulpit of St. Michael's Church, which she afterward restored.[1]

The committee enumerated two pages of especially rare specimens, giving the names of the philanthropists who had been so fortunate in spoiling the Philistines. Other Northern visitors were impressed with the buzzards that were perched about the ruined city.

The committee related with low venom a visit to Calhoun's tomb, and the choice information that the explosion of the Northeastern depot at the time of the surrender was the deliberate act of Major Pringle, who mined it and invited the poor, especially Negroes, to come for supplies so that he could blow them all up—an act, they continued, for which his brains were blown out by Negro troops.[2]

Citizens returning to Charleston found a large part of their property seized by the military as forfeited or "abandoned" and had to pay rent for their own houses, the income going to the Freedmen's Bureau or some government department. But it is true that in these days of desolation the Bureau and the military fed needy whites as well as blacks.

Confused Social and Economic Relations.—The attempt of Governor Magrath to continue the functions of civil government was promptly ended when General Q. A. Gillmore imprisoned him in Fort Pulaski, Savannah, where he remained for seven months. Military courts established throughout the State for the time administered government. The conduct of Federal army officers was usually such as to render their presence a welcome guarantee of order, and to the end of Reconstruction they played a role far superior to that of the Radical politicians. Though the Southern women were resentful, the men freely associated with uniformed gentlemen. There was not the slightest opposition to the Federal authority. The 7,408 troops in the State on January 1, 1866, or the 1,679 on September 30, 1867, were ample for police duty.

[1] Rev. Thomas Smyth, *Autobiographical Notes,* p. 367.

[2] The passage is used to illustrate the state of mind of the visitors. The charge against Major Pringle is absurd. Search of newspapers and family tradition fails to verify that he was killed.

Emancipation was orderly and good-natured where Federal troops had not appeared; but on the coast and wherever the Negro troops were garrisoned in the interior they were a source of profound demoralization. During the march of Potter, wrote the botanist Henry W. Ravenel, squads of Negro soldiers, at night, without white officers, would visit the plantations and take, besides other property, all arms and arm the Negroes with them. They "left those whom they had found a quiet, contented and happy people, dissatisfied, unruly, madmen intoxicated with the fumes of licentiousness, and ready for any act of outrage. In a week after, the Negroes of Pineville[3] were drilling with arms in the streets, overawing and threatening the whites. In less than a month followed as its consequence the massacre of Pineville, of these very deluded people by our scouts."

Mr. Ravenel wrote on July 4, 1865, of alarming conditions in Aiken due to the presence of Negro troops. "Where these savages . . . are quartered, the lives of the inhabitants are in danger. . . . At the instance of their own officers, the people must raise a home guard to protect themselves against their protectors, and to protect also their own officers, for these savages have been heard to threaten the life of their captain for locking them up in the guard house last Saturday night." After two captains had been intimidated, a stronger officer disarmed the mutinous blacks, who resented punishment for having threatened murder, and sent them to Augusta, where they were awed by white troops. Captain Parker asked armed white citizens in Aiken at the time of transportation to stand by for his assistance.

Land Seizures and the Freedmen's Bureau.—The Federals cultivated or distributed to Negroes the "abandoned" coast and islands seized by conquest in November, 1861. In March, 1863, 47 tracts (about a fourth of the "abandoned" plantations) were sold, Negroes buying six and Northerners the rest. This was the first attempt to put the Negroes in possession of the land. On January 15, 1865, General W. T. Sherman issued his famous Field Order No. 15, reserving for Negroes the sea islands from Charleston to and including the lands bordering the St. John's River, and the abandoned rice fields for thirty miles from the sea. The army was to protect them in the possession of not over forty acres per family until they could protect themselves or Congress should regulate their titles.

On August 5, 1861, Congress imposed a direct tax of $29,000,000, apportioning on South Carolina $363,570. An act of June 7, 1862, transformed this into an act of confiscation by enacting that, where collection had been obstructed by rebellion, 50 per cent penalty should be added

[3] In the present Berkeley County.

and the land should be sold, and if it did not bring the amount of the tax it should be knocked down to the United States government. Ignoring the fact that no rebellion existed on St. Helena Island, which had been in Federal possession since November, 1861, the commissioners proceeded to impose this forfeiture sale on the lands, at prices ranging from a few cents to a dollar an acre, and on town houses at depreciated values, which were bought by Negroes, soldiers, or other Northerners. By this means $222,690 was received by the Federal government. Long after the war Congress made inadequate compensation to the owners, thus dispossessed in defiance of all principles of equity, by refunding the tax and paying something for the lands that had irrevocably passed into the hands of purchasers.

Let us turn from these tax-forfeited lands to the larger quantity seized under military orders. The white owners returning after the war, visiting by military permission Edisto, Wadmalaw, John's, and James Islands, which had been reserved for Negroes, found their homes subjected to desecration and abuse, orchards cut down, mansions hacked up, and in one instance the family tomb used for a dog kennel. The Negroes so fiercely maintained possession that four men coming from Philadelphia to buy lands were in January, 1866, marched twelve miles by armed blacks under threat of their lives until they were rescued by the Commissary Department.

Into this tragedy of defeat and confusion there extended the hand of the Bureau of Refugees, Freedmen and Abandoned Lands, thus adding a second and sometimes conflicting authority. The bureau, established on March 3, 1865, was an attempt, among other things, to legalize the decrees of war regarding the confiscated lands. It contemplated assigning to each head of a Negro family forty acres. By the act of July 16, 1866, passed over President Johnson's veto, the powers of the bureau were enlarged and it was given jurisdiction over the civil rights and safety of citizens until regular courts should be re-established, and special power over land distribution in South Carolina. The admission of the State to Congress in 1868 ended bureau activities here except for the education of the freedmen and certain financial duties. The bureau was ended after two years of semi-suspended animation on June 30, 1872.

The Freedmen's Bureau did some good which South Carolinians forget in their resentment at its evil. Both it and the Federal army, in the distressing early days, fed starving blacks and whites. It not only protected the freedman against unjust contracts but did something to stabilize the social and economic situation, which it was at the same time doing much to disturb by its political agitation. It sometimes returned runaway laborers and regularly settled contract disputes, and was sometimes the only agency that could induce striking Negroes to return to crops threatened with ruin by desertion. It had centers in Greenville, Anderson, Edgefield, Columbia, Sumter, Darlington, Barnwell, Georgetown, Charleston, and Beaufort. The difficulty of securing good officials and the natural attraction of self-seekers early led to grave abuses. Soon its most conspicuous function was indoctrinating the freedmen, in preparation for the coming election, with hatred for the whites.

The history of the bureau is intertwined with the confiscation of lands along the coast and the disorders attending the postwar partial restoration to their owners. The difficult and complicated task of restoring the lands, the great bulk of which were in South Carolina, was begun by President Johnson's proclamation of May 29, 1865. General O. O. Howard, the best head the bureau ever had, experienced grave difficulty it inducing the Negroes to surrender the lands they held without authority and to make labor or rental contracts with the owners, for the Negroes feared that by signing any paper they might sign away their freedom. In the spring of 1866, army officers who had been made judges of the fairness of contracts evicted all Negroes who refused to contract and tore up their certificates for landholding before their faces. After having been three times promised lands and thus dispossessed, the coast Negroes distrusted all white men. Serious economic loss and a permanent embittering of race relations were the fruit of the land-confiscation policy.

On July 16, 1866, Congress enacted over the veto that sales by the tax commissioners were confirmed and that Negroes holding under Sherman's military order should have six years to buy their lands at $1.50 an acre. Lands not included under such tenures were restored to their dispossessed owners.

Heavy tribute on a ruined people was exacted by the seizure of cotton said to have belonged to the Confederate government. The United States Treasury agents, who were allowed 25 per cent on their seizures, were little interested in legal titles, and the owner was helpless. Abuses and corruption were enormous. A further tribute was the Federal tax of two or three cents a pound on cotton for three years—a burden whose inequity was at least equal to its technical constitutionality.

Emigration Movements.—In the general ruin of property and institutions many thought of abandoning the country for Mexico, Venezuela, or Brazil, all of which were extending liberal offers of land. A committee visited southern Brazil, but the movement from South Carolina was naturally far smaller than from the lower Mississippi Valley. M. F. Maury, as imperial commissioner for Maximilian, sought to draw Southerners by picturing the prosperity of prominent ex-Confederates already in Mexico. A considerable colony from the Alabama region settled in Honduras, where they were so shocked at the social racial intermingling that some returned to the United States. *De Bow's Review* discouraged migration. Most of the emigrants lost more than they gained by the change. "A few [South Carolinians] went to Mexico, and a slightly larger number, mostly from Edgefield and Chester, went to Brazil." The movement from South Carolina to other States cannot be blamed on the war, for it was the continuation, and in diminished proportion, of the steady drain of the State's population since 1820 or earlier, especially to the lower South and the Southwest.

New Adjustments in Agriculture, etc.—The turbulent conditions of a new regime led to vast shifting of fortunes. Some of the old aristocracy grasped new opportunities and became richer than before; others could never adjust themselves. Daniel Heyward, son of Miles Heyward of Beaufort, "was the only one of his name, and one of the very few of his circle, who [sic] the emancipation of his Negro slaves did not demoralize. Scarcely had peace been declared before Daniel Heyward was at work on his plantations, and by the time the next crop season opened, he had so mastered the new relations that he was found leasing for a term of years all the land within sight of his house, equaling three times as much as he owned or had ever planted with slave labor." General Hampton on the other hand, supposedly one of the richest of Southern planters, was already swamped with debt in 1860, went through bankruptcy in 1868, and was never able to regain prosperity.[4] Many a son of overseers of the better class rose in economic and social standing.

Restlessness among the Negroes, extending beyond their moving from plantation to plantation or into towns as an experience of freedom, led to an emigration movement. Thousands went to Florida or Alabama. During 1866 and '67 about 2,500 left the State for Liberia, where their experience was disastrous. In April, 1878, occurred a smaller migration to Liberia with similar unhappy results.

Cotton culture recovered rapidly after 1865 under prices holding generally above 28 cents through 1869; but rice interests were almost ruined. The State in 1866 raised 12,415 tierces as compared with ante-bellum crops of 70,000 to 85,000.

The revolution in South Carolina agriculture wrought by the war thus presents four major aspects: (1) Free labor which must be conciliated instead of slave labor that could be controlled. (2) Many great plantations were broken up into small farms, though successful men

[4] W. A. Sheppard, *Red Shirts Remembered*. The amazing mass and multiplicity of General Hampton's debts as recorded in the papers of the case in the Federal District Court in Jackson, Miss., total $1,041,991.

soon began the long-continued process of accumulating large holdings. (3) These farms were generally rented out on shares, first, because of the lack of ready money, and, second, in order to allow the landlord that direction of operation which was essential to secure steady work and the preservation of animals, tools, and natural fertility. (4) In the dearth of resources and banking credit, there developed the lien system, which preyed upon the farmer and undermined self-respect and character as the price of supporting him while he raised his crop. Out of these new economic and social relations, with minds still full of passion, ignorance, and misconceptions, the people of the South and of the nation had to evolve some sort of Reconstruction.

The Presidential Reconstruction Plan.—That Southern opinion was reconciled to reunion with the North, and that irregularities of recalcitrant elements could have been amply met by the normal processes of law, is now too obvious for argument. It is true that post-bellum feeling ranged all the way from the statesmanlike utterances of Trescot and Hampton to the bitterest refusal to be reconciled, but the calm and reasonable view represented the dominant sentiment of the State. South Carolina had lost her appeal to the court of her own choosing and was ready loyally to abide by the issue.

The Constitution contemplated no such event as Reconstruction, and hence, if any possible plan could be genuinely constitutional, it must be through a liberal interpretation of the implied powers; but at all events, no plan should have been adopted which violated the plain letter or the essential spirit of the Constitution. The plan finally applied, with glaring constitutional inconsistencies and the laceration of the public welfare, constitutes the outstanding failure of American statesmanship, fully deserving Professor Burgess' characterization as the blunder-crime of Reconstruction.

The termination of Congress on March 4, 1865, allowed the President a free hand until the following December. As preliminary to Reconstruction the President issued on May 29 a pardon to almost all those formerly in rebellion, with restoration of all property rights except in slaves and certain lands in adjudication, on condition that they swear allegiance to the Union and obedience to all laws and proclamations during the rebellion on the emancipation of slaves. Excepted were rebels now worth over $20,000, generals, and high officials. When 10 per cent of the number of voters in 1860 had sworn to observe the results of the war, they were to elect a convention for framing a Constitution. In thus adopting the plan which Lincoln had already instituted in Virginia, Louisiana, Tennessee, and Arkansas, President Johnson virtually announced war with the Radicals and greatly disturbed many moderate

Republicans. The former were bent on Negro suffrage, partly as a means of protecting the ex-slave but mainly as a partisan device for keeping their party in power, as the Republican Governor of South Carolina, Daniel H. Chamberlain, afterward averred. It is impossible to believe, he wrote in 1901, "that the reconstruction acts would have been passed if the Negro vote had been believed to be Democratic." That to Congress, and not to the President, rightly belonged the control of Reconstruction can hardly be doubted; for it was a grave problem of national policy, and not a war measure or an administrative duty; but unhappily wisdom and good will belonged to him who lacked the right to exercise them, while those possessing the right lacked those essentials.

In the carrying out of his policy President Johnson displayed not only statesmanlike realization of what the country needed but high executive ability. On June 30, 1865, he appointed Benjamin F. Perry provisional Governor of South Carolina and directed him to enroll, for the purpose of electing a constitutional convention, voters eligible under South Carolina law immediately before secession who had now taken the oath of allegiance. Governor Perry directed that each parish and district should elect a delegation equal to its members of the lower house. He thus refrained from an autocratic and violent break with the system of high representation of the parishes which he had always condemned, but modified it to the extent of allowing no representation for the senators.

The Constitution of 1865.—The Governor, on opening the convention, rather boldly traced the lines along which the new Constitution should be laid, and was almost uniformly followed; for the fact that Perry was known to stand well with the President gave prestige to reforms he proposed which had moreover been widely favored in the State before 1860.

The inevitable question of Negro suffrage haunted the minds even of those who did not speak of it. Governor Perry later expressed regret that he had yielded to advice to strike from his message the recommendation of qualified Negro suffrage, for, he said, its adoption might have prevented Congress's later extreme policy. He held that a moderate property qualification would disfranchise the Negro without committing the blunder of mentioning color. General Wade Hampton, Professor Joseph Le Conte, Rev. A. Toomer Porter, Judge Edward Frost, and a few others shared Perry's view, and it is important to note that President Johnson privately urged Mississippians to grant suffrage to Negroes who could read and write or owned $250 worth of property as a means of checking the Radical demand that all Negroes be given the vote.

The old rivalry of up and low country flared up in settling representation. The parishes as election districts were abolished by 97 to 9, and each judicial district (county, as called after 1868) was given one senator, except that the county of Charleston (consisting of ten old parishes) was given two. The lower house continued to be apportioned equally on white population and wealth, or taxes paid. The low country thus lost heavily in both houses: the parishes no longer had senators; their numerous Negroes were no longer property. By up-country development, the fixed classification of lands adopted in 1784 to correct the former injustice of taxing all lands at the same value had itself become an injustice to the low country. Hence it was enacted that all property should be assessed at its real value. The Governor was given the veto, and his election (for a four-year term) was given to the people, and the legislature was urged to provide popular choice of presidential electors. The Constitution was not submitted to the people.

This, then, was the kind of government under which the white citizens of South Carolina wished to live—a simple and compact Constitution which introduced some of the reforms the Constitution of 1868 is commonly credited with originating and under which, if the State had been left undisturbed, undoubtedly many other forward steps would have been taken by reason of the redistribution of power and the acceptance of new ideas.

Despite Hampton's insistence that he not be considered for governor, the vote of 1865 stood James L. Orr, 9,928; Hampton, 9,185. The legislature chosen at the same time contained an unusually large proportion of excellent men. It elected Benjamin F. Perry and John L. Manning United States senators. It also ratified the Thirteenth Amendment. The recognition, by all branches of the Federal government concerned, of the legislature's right to perform this highest function under the Constitution is still considered by Southern thinkers as endorsement of the State's restoration to legal equality in the Union. Such was the opinion of United States Supreme Court Justice Nelson of New York, and probably would have been the view of the Supreme Court. Said Justice Nelson in discharging a man convicted of murder in November, 1865, by a military commission in South Carolina, the trial was illegal, as "a new Constitution had been formed, a Governor and legislature had been elected under it, and the State was in the full enjoyment, or was entitled to the full enjoyment of all her constitutional rights and privileges."

On April 2, 1866, President Johnson declared the rebellion ended, the people loyal, and the civil authorities able to enforce the laws. Yet the garrisons and the autocratic authority of the Freedmen's Bureau were permitted to continue. General Sickles continued making military arrests, altering the laws of South Carolina, and nullifying the sentences of courts both State and Federal. Sentencing men to death by military commission for crimes triable legally only before the civil courts continued after the inaugurating of the Constitution of 1865, even though Federal judges from the Supreme Court down annulled several such convictions and the United States Supreme Court had in *ex parte* Milligan in January, 1866, declared trials by military commissioners where the courts were open unconstitutional.

To the first session of the new legislature the comptroller-general, on November 7, 1865, reported the liabilities of the State as follows: railroad bonds endorsed, $3,372,000; Blue Ridge Railroad bonds, $1,310,000; Charleston 1838 fire loan bonds, $802,603; State House bonds, $2,275,000; State stock, $38,836; war bonds, $3,241,840, making a total of $7,363,279 direct and $3,372,000 contingent liability. So desperate was the situation of private debtors that the legislature, December, 1865, enacted a stay law. When it was annulled by the court of errors, an act of September, 1866, suspended the court's sittings until the spring. When the court annulled this, Orr appealed to General Sickles, who, on April 15, 1867, among other relief for debtors, proclaimed two provisions of mercy that soon became a permanent part of our law. He abolished imprisonment for debt (which, however had been reduced in 1841 to restriction to the district, i.e., county); established a homestead exemption of a dwelling, twenty acres, and $500 personalty; suspended judgment in actions arising from December 19, 1860, to May 15, 1865, and all actions on debts for slaves; and stopped foreclosures for a year. Orr wrote Sickles that but for his order increased troops would have been necessary to protect records, sheriffs, and other officials from violence. But it should be noted that the South Carolina legislature had in 1851 established a debt-exempt homestead, outside municipalities, of a dwelling and adjacent buildings, fifty acres, a horse, and $25 worth of provisions, the whole not to exceed $500 in value.

Juries, apparently at the instigation of Governor Orr after he became a judge, found a means of scaling debts that courts of appeal could not annul. Said Judge Orr, on opening court in Greenville, a jury might justly render verdicts for one-third the amount of a war or pre-war debt the consideration for which had suffered such a decline. The jury took the hint, and this became common in upper South Carolina.

In the midst of this distress, the legislature in 1866 repealed the usury law in the attempt to increase loanable capital. The result was extortionate rates frequently reaching 30 per cent, until interest was limited to 7 per cent in 1877. Legal interest was fixed at 6 per cent in 1934, with permission to contract for 7 per cent, as previously for 8 per cent. (In 1777 interest had been reduced from 8 per cent to 7 per cent.)

The penitentiary was established in 1865 and during Orr's administration was put fully into operation with the inmates at useful labor.

The Black Code.—The outstanding legislation of 1865 was the "Black Code," an attempt to forestall economic and social disorder caused by the freedmen, who, it was believed, would neither work steadily nor behave safely without special restraint. All persons having one-eighth or more Negro blood were denominated persons of color. This is the origin of the one-eighth rule, for previously in South Carolina the proportion of African blood constituting one a Negro had been a jury question. For the first time in South Carolina history the "Black Code" declared null marriage between white and Negro.

All personal and property rights, except as therein modified, were extended to Negroes. Death was the sentence of any Negro for attempted rape. Attacking the employer, a member of his family, or agent, was an aggravated misdemeanor. A special court with jury in each district (county) was to hear cases civil and criminal concerning Negroes, with the right to appeal. All the crimes commonest among Negroes were guarded against with appropriate penalties of whipping, imprisonment, or fine, or, in case the fine could not be paid, leasing out by public outcry to the person who would pay the fine for the shortest term of service. No Negro could own weapons, except that a farm owner might possess hunting guns. All Negroes who had lived as husband and wife were declared legally married, and all existing colored children legitimate. Negroes contracting to continuous labor were "servants" and their employers (white or black) "masters," with their respective defined rights and duties under the protection of the district courts. Masters could chastise servants under eighteen years of age or apprentices. The servant could not leave the place except on Sunday without permission or bring persons upon it without permission. Work at night, in bad weather, or on Sunday was forbidden except under necessity. Vagrants were to be hired out by the courts. Distilling or vending liquor by Negroes was forbidden.

This code and that of Mississippi were the most drastic attempts to extend something of prewar control over the freedmen. These acts constituted one of the the two natural but fatal blunders by which the South fell into the hands of the Radicals. And yet the codes were sincere attempts of kindly paternalism to adjust appalling difficulties. Many Southerners, however, realized at the time their inexpediency.

On January 1, 1866, General Sickles declared the code void and forbade any laws discriminating in any way between races. Meanwhile, he said, he would enforce fair labor contracts. Congress, April 6, 1866, as its answer to the Black Codes, passed over the veto the Civil Rights

Act guaranteeing the Negro legal equality and soon incorporated this and more in the Fourteenth Amendment. The legislature responded by placing the Negro on identically the same legal footing as the white man, thus demonstrating how easy it was for the Federal government to secure to the ex-slave civil rights without giving him the ballot.

While condemning the Black Codes as unwise, we must recognize that their purpose was legitimate and did not contemplate re-enslavement. Professor Dunning of New York held in 1907 that "this legislation, far from embodying any spirit of defiance towards the North or any purpose to evade the conditions which the victors had imposed, was in the main a conscientious and straightforward attempt to bring some sort of order out of the social and economic chaos which a full acceptance of the results of the war and emancipation involved." John Wallace, a Florida Reconstruction Negro politician, wrote in 1885 that "any other people under like circumstances, would have passed the same character of laws"; and that some of the seemingly tyrannical clauses were in fact intended, as he had witnessed, for enforcement only on suspicious characters, and that the laws on contracts, though sometimes abused by whites, were generally observed to the letter.

Rejecting the Fourteenth Amendment.—After the blunder of the Black Codes, the Southern people were offered in June, 1866, a second opportunity to sacrifice themselves to the Radicals, and inconsiderately embraced it. The Johnson governments, said Congress, must agree to certain protection of the national safety and the rights of the Negro. These were embodied in the Fourteenth Amendment to the Constitution. Section One declared that "No State shall make or enforce any law which shall abridge the privileges or immunities of citizens of the United States; nor shall any State deprive any person of life, liberty or property, without due process of law; nor deny to any person within its jurisdiction the equal protection of the laws."

Section Two ordered the congressional representation of any State depriving its adult males of the right to vote except for "rebellion, or other crime," reduced in the proportion that those deprived were of the total adult males. The South was thus allowed freely to disfranchise Confederate soldiers, but was threatened with a heavy penalty for disfranchising illiterate ex-slaves, proposals at once insulting, injurious, and contrary to the whole history of the rights of the States over suffrage. In six Northern States Negroes were still disfranchised, and at this time four Northern States by large majorities reaffirmed their disfranchisement.

Section Three excluded from all office, until relieved by a two-thirds vote of Congress, every supporter of the Confederacy who had ever previously held a public office, including the thousands of petty officers, who (changed frequently to avoid overburdening men rendering unpaid or poorly paid services) constituted a large proportion of the substantial citizens of every neighborhood. It appeared a veritable conspiracy to make good government impossible.

Even though the position of the Southern States was logical in holding that the recognition by Congress of their ratification of the Thirteenth Amendment implied their complete statehood, and though President Johnson assured them that Congress could not force their acceptance of these conditions, the action of the Southern States (Tennessee excepted) in rejecting the Fourteenth Amendment was indefensible, as it was sufficiently clear that undefinable dangers lurked in inflaming the passions of a Congress already nearly in the control of radicals who were utterly contemptuous of constitutional limitations. The evils of accepting the amendment, it may be fairly contended, were in a degree definite and remediable; refusal was to plunge into a dark and stormy sea of limitless peril.

Governor Orr held "that if the amendment is adopted we not only have no guarantee that our representatives would be admitted to Congress, but there are unmistakable indications that they would still be excluded." That there were such indications cannot be denied. Sumner and Stevens scoffed at the idea of any obligation to readmit the Southern States upon their ratification of the Fourteenth Amendment, which they declared a mere step toward their ultimate goal. Sherman, Garfield, Chase, and other leaders held, on the other hand, that the conditions laid down in the Fourteenth Amendment constituted a virtual promise of admission on acceptance, and that if the States ratified the amendment they should and would be readmitted.

The South Carolina Senate unanimously and the House with one dissenting vote rejected the amendment. Every other ex-Confederate State but Tennessee took similar action. This second blunder of the South was natural, but it was fatal. Southern leaders soon realized how futile were such brave words by helpless men. Meeting in Washington, they proposed a substitute, yielding much that was demanded by the Fourteenth Amendment; but the Reconstruction bill, framed in anger upon the rejection of what Congress had set as their minimum, was already in process of passage, with the Radicals, at last in control, determined to construct governments in the South which would ratify the Fourteenth Amendment and more.

The first chapter in Reconstruction was ended, and a darker one was about to open.

CHAPTER LIV

EARLY YEARS OF CONGRESSIONAL RECONSTRUCTION, 1867-1870

THAT THE Negro needed Federal protection is amply proved by instances of peonage until recent years; but the fact that peonage was destroyed by the courts under the authority of the Thirteenth Amendment proved that enactment ample without the later measure granting Negro suffrage. Many sincere Northerners without animosity toward the South were convinced, by the rejection of the Fourteenth Amendment and by passionate misrepresentations, that unqualified Negro suflrage was a necessity. To this body of well-intentioned opinion there was added the force of the small group of fanatics who, as Professor Dunning remarks, are accepted as leaders only in times of abnormal excitement. Of these Senator Charles Sumner of Massachusetts was the most typical and one of the two most influential. Of a powerful mind and of an intolerance that dismissed as wicked or perverse difference with his fixed ideas, and of an unhappy personal experience with Brooks which could not incline him favorably toward anything Southern, Sumner passionately, eloquently, unceasingly overwhelmed the Senate with demands for the removal of every State law opposed to complete political and social equality. One of the most ignorant and undeveloped of races was to be placed by mere legislative fiat in absolute power over a large portion of a race notable for centuries for the highest success in self-government, to whom the independence and self-direction now to be destroyed were almost as dear as life.

A Vindictive North: A Resentful South.—Equally as influential as Sumner was Representative Thaddeus Stevens of Pennsylvania. Stevens represented both the philanthropic and the partisan element in Congress. Of strong mind and a dominating personal force that crushed weaker men by a sneer and ruled the House of Representatives as it had never before submitted to be ruled, Stevens defied social and political conventions. Having risen by bitter struggle from harsh conditions, he was such a sincere devotee of the equality of all men that he lived with a mulatto mistress and was buried in a cemetery which admitted Negroes. His feelings toward the South were not helped when the Confederate Army burned his ironworks. With an enormous capacity for hate, Stevens was the frankest of the enemies of the South, in his determination to have the blood of prominent leaders, to confiscate for the benefit of the ex-slaves all large rebel estates, and to place the foot of the Negro on white necks by means of unrestricted Negro suffrage.

The North began to demand not only that the South submit but that she repent—something that should not have been expected, for there was no moral wrong in defending rights which the noblest and purest men esteemed lawfully theirs and essential to their decent existence. In the pathos of crushing defeat, the South was driven to seek satisfaction in cherishing an idealized past and the honor and courage of the soldiers who had defended it. Thus was generated "the lost cause" state of mind, which healed hearts wounded by defeat with the passionate conviction that they were right. The long sojourn in the house of mourning exacted a heavy tribute from the energies needed for a new day.

Congressional Reconstruction, 1867.—When Congress assembled in December, 1866, the supreme issue was Negro suffrage. The November election had given control of the House to the Radicals, and the moderate Republicans surrendered to the will of a now thoroughly resentful North. The period of orderly government and reviving industry which existed in the South was thus described by Stevens in introducing the Reconstruction bill: "For two years the Southern States have been in a state of anarchy; for two years, the loyal people of those ten states have endured all the horrors of the worst anarchy of any country. Persecution, exile and murder have been the order of the day. . . . We have been deaf to the groans, the agony, the dying groans which have been borne to us by every southern breeze from dying and murdered victims." "Great criminals" with "unrepented crimes," "vagabonds and thieves," were the terms applied by him to the ex-Confederates.

On March 2, 1867, Congress passed over the veto the first Reconstruction act. "Whereas," it was enacted, "no legal State government or adequate protection for life or property now exists in the rebel States," they shall be divided into five military districts (North and South Carolina constituting No. 2), in each of which the President shall appoint a general with a sufficient military force, to try offenders of any kind by military commissions or to co-operate with the courts as he might see fit, and to enroll all adult males black and white except felons and persons disfranchised on account of rebellion for electing a Constitutional Convention. The Constitution adopted must enfranchise all who are hereby given the right to vote for Convention members, must be ratified by popular vote, and be approved by Congress. Moreover, the legislature must ratify the Fourteenth Amendment, and when enough other States shall ratify for its adoption, then the State shall be admitted.

"No law," said James Ford Rhodes of Massachusetts in 1912, "so unjust in its policy, so direful in its results, had passed the American Congress since the Kansas-Nebraska Act of 1854." "The occasional and widely scattered disturbances" in the South, wrote Professor Dunning, "were in fact a wholly insufficient basis for the sweeping generalization that was made as to conditions in the South. . . . The clauses of the act authorizing military commissions for the trial and punishment of crime were in direct and contemptuous disregard of the Supreme Court's opinion in the Milligan Case, rendered less than three months before, and were based upon the theory that a state of war still existed, though executive, judiciary, and Congress itself had concurred in regarding the war as long since ended."

President Johnson appointed to the district of the Carolinas Major-General Daniel E. Sickles. He served until superseded August 31 by Major-General E. R. S. Canby, who, though proving less offensive, continued the interference of the military with the courts.

Congress on July 19, forbade voting by any, even though pardoned, who had at any time held even the humblest office and had afterward aided the Confederacy. This excluded almost all of the classes accustomed to public service. Republicans, professing to believe that Democratic control would jeopardize the results of the war, openly justified giving the Negro control even of Southern States where he was a minority, as necessary to keep in control of the Federal government what they called "the party that saved the Union." The South was not to be readmitted, said Stevens, until the Constitution had been so amended "as to secure the perpetual ascendancy of the party of the Union." The judgment of Republican ex-Governor Chamberlain of South Carolina in 1901 on his former associates was even harsher:

"It may now be clear to all, as it was then clear to some, that underneath all the avowed motives and all the open arguments lay a deeper cause than all others,—the will and determination to secure party ascendancy and control at the South and in the nation through the Negro vote. If this is a hard saying, let anyone now ask himself, or ask the public, if it is possibly credible that the reconstruction acts would have passed if the Negro vote had been believed to be Democratic."

The leaders, continued Chamberlain, were profoundly ignorant of conditions in the South, and professed no desire to learn at first hand. He found it impossible with self-respect to continue his attempted conferences with Stevens, whose "mind was fixed, proof against facts or reason that suggested other views."

Negro control was thus forced on the South while six Northern States refused any Negro the right to vote, referendums in four were reaffirming the refusal, and the District of Columbia was refusing it by

7,369 to 36. So intolerable were the results after Congress forced it on the District as a noble example for the country, in the words of William Cullen Bryant, that all voting was abolished in 1874 and has never been restored.

Three attempts were made at once, and several later, to have the Supreme Court declare the Reconstruction acts unconstitutional. Professor Dunning of New York wrote in 1907: "Congress, in the reconstruction acts, established throughout the South the precise military tribunals which the [Supreme] Court had declared unconstitutional. The defiance was so patent that able lawyers hastened to bring before the court the new legislation, in sanguine expectation that it would be nullified. But technical objections promptly arose in bewildering confusion and insuperable magnitude. While in the Milligan case the court with glowing enthusiasm for the supremacy of the civil over the military order swept aside technicalities in the quest for substantial liberty and justice, it welcomed technicalities with obvious joy when they enabled it to evade jurisdiction over Congressional reconstruction."

And when at length, in *ex parte McCardle,* under a writ of habeas corpus the Supreme Court was obliged to face the issue, Congress hastened to take from it jurisdiction in such cases. When later there again appeared danger of the Court's pronouncing judgment on the constitutionality of Reconstruction, Radicals openly threatened any measures necessary to destroy such power or deter the court from a conflict. Congress, said Benjamin R. Curtis later, "with acquiescence of the country . . . subdued the Supreme Court" as well as "conquered the President." Thus, when the functions of the court were most needed to defend constitutional rights, representatives of the section which in 1832 had urged that South Carolina should submit her grievances to the court adopted the old nullification doctrine that the court could not be allowed to judge "a political question."

Congressional Reconstruction therefore proceeded unhindered. In South Carolina almost twice as many Negroes as whites were registered. The Union League swore the Negroes to vote Republican, and the Freedmen's Bureau, now degenerated into an unscrupulous political agency, drilled them to oppose anything favored by the whites, who, they were told, desired to re-establish slavery. The race issue, thus inflamed by the Radicals to the highest pitch, was relied upon by them as their only hope throughout Reconstruction. Negroes who voted with the Democrats were boycotted, denied marriage or marriage rights by many women, and sometimes severely beaten. The whites, on the other hand, could hope for victory only by insisting on eliminating race from politics; and this attempt they kept up until, its futility having been proved, their more aggressive leaders in 1876 at last made race the dominant issue to the overthrow of those who had introduced it.

The Constitution of 1868.—The constitutional convention elected November 19-20, 1867, consisted of forty-eight whites and seventy-six Negroes. All but four were Republicans. Twenty-three whites and fifty-nine Negroes paid no taxes, and all others, except one of each race, paid almost none. The convention met in Charleston from January 14, 1868, to March 18. It adopted a good constitution typical of the period, for the reason that the small group of superior members drew from contemporary Northern models.

The Constitution of 1868, one of the three that together have practically covered the State's life since 1776, marks the most violent break in our constitutional history. The large body of whites disfranchised by the proposed Fourteenth Amendment were forbidden to vote until Congress removed such disfranchisement. The way was left open for racial intermingling by omitting any prohibition of intermarriage and by requiring that all publicly supported schools and colleges should be open to all races. Practically no attempt was made to carry out racial mingling in the common schools, though it was enforced in the university. The original name "county" was restored to the areas dating from 1785 which since 1800 had been called districts. Prohibitions on legislative action, previously almost unknown in South Carolina, were multiplied, thus degrading the legislature under an idea of its untrustworthiness.

The new Constitution was a distinct advance in democracy, though it can hardly be doubted that this change as a part of an irresistible world movement would soon have come anyhow. On a groundless analogy to the Federal Constitution, each county was allowed to keep one senator,[1] an undemocratic custom now found in only two other States. Representation in the lower house was for the first time in our history based on population alone.

The most lamentable changes, except suffrage, were the impairing of the independence of the courts by substituting for tenure during good behavior terms of four and six years for the circuit and supreme court judges respectively, and by enacting that "Judges shall not charge juries in respect to matters of fact, but may state the testimony and declare the law." Divorces by the court of common pleas were authorized under legislative regulations. A good change, long unsuccessfully urged in South Carolina, was placing law and equity in the hands of the same judges, thus eliminating the separate chancery courts. The court of errors, consisting of all judges of the court of appeals and of the law

[1] With two from Charleston.

and equity circuits, summoned since 1859 whenever two of the three appeal court judges considered a constitutional question involved, was omitted. Solicitors were made elective by the people instead of by the legislature.

Imprisonment for debt, which had been reduced to mere confinement to the limits of the county in 1841, was abolished, and the principle of homestead exemption for debtors established by the act of 1851 was made permanent.

The governor was given a veto, to be overridden by a two-thirds vote, thus greatly increasing his power over that of the ante-bellum governor, who had no veto, or the 1865 governor, whose veto could be overridden by a majority. He was to be popularly elected for two years without limit as to re-eligibility. A two-thirds legislative majority was required to increase the State's bonded debt; but the corruption that soon flourished led to the amendment of 1873 requiring a two-thirds vote of the people also.

The provisions for education included establishing the office of superintendent of public instruction, an office for which South Carolina educational leaders had long unsuccessfully contended, and ordered the creation of a system of free common schools for all children without reference to wealth. Compulsory education, a six-months term, a reform school, a normal and an agricultural college, were councils of perfection that generally were realized long after the Constitution of 1868 was abrogated.

Married women were given full control over their own property acquired either before or after marriage, though their full right to contract regarding matters not connected with their property had to await the Constitution of 1895. Control over corporations was assured by the provision that their charters might be altered or repealed, and officers or directors of banks were forbidden to borrow directly or indirectly from their institutions.

The people of South Carolina allowed the Constitution of 1868 to endure for twenty-seven years, and would probably have continued it for a much longer period but for a crisis in the 1890's which seemed to require new means of eliminating the danger from the possible revival of the Negro vote.

So hopeless were the whites that fewer than half of those registered voted in the election for State officers, thus allowing the Republicans to win by three to one. The constitutional convention had gerrymandered the State into four congressional districts in order to overcome with low-country Negroes the white counties of the up country. Nevertheless Democrats carried two districts in the November election, but were unseated by Congress.

Governor Orr's administration had been allowed to continue with such assistance or interference as the military saw fit. After the election for officers under the new Constitution, General Canby ordered that on July 6, 1868, the newly elected Governor and legislature should take charge and Governor Orr should retire. The legislature having ratified the Fourteenth Amendment on July 9, General Canby remitted his authority to the civil government on July 24. Thus military rule, which had existed in varying degrees for more than three years, was ended, and Federal soldiers in future acted in South Carolina merely when requested by the civil government to uphold its authority.

The First Radical Legislature.—The first legislature under the new Constitution met in special session July 6, 1868. The white senators numbered 21 and the colored 10. The senators from Anderson, Horry, Lancaster, Oconee, Pickens, and Spartanburg were Democrats, as were also their representatives. The fact that Greenville sent a white Republican senator indicates a considerable number of white Republicans in that semi-mountainous county, traditionally of more than usual political independence. The House contained 46 whites and 78 Negroes, 14 being Democrats and 110 Republicans. Ninety-one of the Republicans were entirely innocent of taxes.

Thomas J. Robertson, the scalawag (i.e., a Southern white man joining the Republicans), and Frederick A. Sawyer were elected United States senators. Sawyer was one of the best of the outsiders and cannot be counted a carpetbagger. He had been brought to Charleston to superintend the new city school system of 1856, and was a man of ability and character. He opposed the tyrannical and corrupt practices in which his party in South Carolina was soon steeped, and was of course dropped at the end of his term, as, unlike Robertson, he had neither the inclination nor the money to buy a re-election.

The Radicals, as the Republicans were called, not yet in the exigencies of corruption, elected excellent judges; Franklin J. Moses, Sr., of a highly respected Jewish family, a lawyer of ability and character who had joined the Republicans, was elected chief justice. Associate Justice A. J. Willard was a New York lawyer of ability and experience. The third member of the court, S. L. Hoge, was an Ohio legal nonentity. The eight circuit judgeships were filled with lawyers of character and ability, excepting the feeble Mr. Platt from New York, all but two of them South Carolinians and several of them unassociated with the Republican party. Though several were later attacked by the Radical leaders for their fearless maintenance of justice, the bench suffered far less during the Radical regime than any other branch of government.

The Social Equality Functions.—The social mingling of the races began at this time at the receptions of Governor Scott, a carpetbagger from Ohio. Many prominent Radicals received Negroes into their homes and ostentatiously walked arm in arm with them upon the streets. Rev. B. F. Whittemore, a Methodist minister, was a carpetbagger from Massachusetts, magnificently bearded, unctuously handsome, with a stentorian bass voice gifted in song that charmed vast Negro audiences. Expelled from Congress for selling a cadetship and "vindicated" by immediate re-election, then excluded as "an infamous character" and revindicated by election to the State senate, contentedly steeped in the meanest forms of corruption, Whittemore exposed his family to extreme humiliation by the lengths to which he carried social equality in his Darlington home.

The social equality program under the second Radical governor, Franklin J. Moses, Jr., went farthest. "Moses, bloated and corrupt, prodigal in expenditures, and a master of entertaining, gave a series of notorious receptions at the Preston mansion, the finest house in Columbia. There he enveloped the colored belles and dandies in the garish splendors of an ostentatious age. A renegade Radical has described one of these occasions. 'The colored band was playing "Rally 'Round the Flag." . . . There was a mixture of white and black, male and female. Supper was announced, and you ought to have seen the scrambling for the table. Social equality was at its highest pitch. It was amusing to see Cuffy reaching across the table and swallowing grapes by the bunch, champagne by the bottle, and turkey, ham and pound cake by the bushel.' "[2]

Numbers of the Negro leaders were the moral superiors of the average carpetbagger or scalawag, and some were of high ability. Robert Brown Elliott, a black Massachusetts Negro educated at Eton, Speaker of the South Carolina House of Representatives, an incendiary agitator for racial equality, joined considerable legal ability with great moral depravity. Robert Smalls, a dark mulatto who as a slave had heroically run *The Planter* by Confederate batteries in Charleston Harbor, was a talented speaker. He was convicted of taking a bribe as a legislator. F. L. Cardozo, very light, free-born, reputed son of the Charleston Jewish economist J. N. Cardozo and a half-Negro, half-Indian mother, secretary of state for four years and treasurer for four years, was a graduate of Glasgow and a student of theology in London for two years. An imposing man of elegant manners, almost white, neither his virtues nor his vices have much racial significance. He was

[2] Simkins and Woody, *South Carolina during Reconstruction,* pp. 368-70.

convicted of fraud and, like Smalls, was pardoned by Governor Hampton. The Reverend R. H. Cain was, for the combination of ability and personal integrity, the most creditable of the Negro leaders with the possible exception of the upright Martin Delany. It is useless to enumerate the mere passing curiosities gifted with glib tongues and political shrewdness, and steeped in corruption, gross or petty, who briefly flourished in the prominence into which they had been thrown by the strangest of revolutions.

The situation was full of odd contradictions. Aside from these orgies, social and economic life went on much as usual. The mass of Negroes still felt strongly their reverence for the old master class and their old contempt for the poor whites. Gentlemen lamented that though the Negroes still consulted and trusted them in all their affairs except politics, on the latter they would listen to no advice. But outside those circles it was inevitable that there should be much friction. Negroes were frequently so boisterous on trains, etc., as to convince whites of intentional offensiveness. White women were at times obliged to leave the sidewalks by Negro women bent on proving more than their legal equality. The wives of Negro politicians from their carriages summoned clerks to exhibit to them goods which they were purchasing with the public's money. The Negro often carried as far as he dared an insolence which roused in the white man anger, to which was added the white workingman's hate and fear of an economic rival beating down his wages and threatening his livelihood.

The light-colored mulattoes, octoroons, etc., frequently free-born, became in Reconstruction natural leaders and in 1875 held fourteen times as many offices as the blacks and five times as many as the whites. They are today prominent in the professions. The expression of resentful pain sometimes seen on their refined and intellectual features bears silent witness to one of the most unhappy incidents of a two-race society.

Legislation and Corruption, 1869-70.—The session of 1869-70 saw the incorporation of Claflin University at Orangeburg under the patronage of the Northern Methodist Church, really for Negroes, but forbidding any racial discrimination. It continued under joint church and State aid until 1896, when the State organized its own Negro college.

The code of procedure adopted March 1, 1870, almost an exact copy of that of New York, was soon recognized as a legal masterpiece and remains the basis of practice. The same day was enacted over Governor Scott's veto the bill granting the Marine and River Mining and Manufacturing Company sponsored by leading Charleston businessmen the right to mine phosphate rock in the navigable waters of the State for twenty-one years, on the payment to the State of one dollar on each ton mined. A leading Negro, later speaker, swore that Attorney General Chamberlain paid him $250 or $275 for his vote for this. Tim Hurley, the carpetbagger from Connecticut, a prominent lobbyist for many measures, distributed through Speaker Moses $20,000 to $25,000 to pass the bill. It had early become the recognized necessity to pay for the passage of measures concerning large business interests. Governor Scott declared that if the Saviour were advocating the purest measure, he would be crucified again unless he bribed the legislature.

A conspicuous grab of the 1870's was the acquisition of control of the Greenville and Columbia Railroad by a ring of nine public officials and two of their favorites, all white except the all-but-white Secretary of State Cardozo, including those princes of corruption, future United States Senator Patterson, Treasurer Parker, Representative Joe Crews, and Financial Agent Kimpton. A member of the group was Attorney-General Chamberlain, holder of one twenty-fourth share in the agreement, and at that time hand in glove with the corruptionists. The conspirators bribed through the legislature an innocent-looking half-page act constituting Chamberlain, Neagle, and two others a sinking-fund commission authorized to sell all property of the State "not in actual public use," understood to refer to the damaged State House building material. On the day Governor Scott, one of the largest sharers in the ring, signed the act, Commissioners Chamberlain and Neagle sold to themselves and associates at $2.75 a share the railroad stock that cost the State $20 a share. To secure a clear majority of the stock the ring was said to have paid large fees to ex-Governor Orr, then a circuit judge, and Jacob P. Reed, later a Republican circuit judge, who were then directors of the road, to buy up the privately owned stock for unknown parties. This was done at $1.75 to $2 a share. Treasurer Parker later swore that the money for Scott, Neagle, Crews, Cardozo, Kimpton, Leslie, and (he believed) Chamberlain, the transaction totaling $288,000 (others said $240,000), was supplied by Kimpton from the amount for which, as financial agent, he sold State bonds above the price he reported. The road failed to prosper, and the ring, by arguments "metallic, not oral," put through the legislature a bill prepared by Attorney-General Chamberlain in his capacity as ring member depriving the State of its prior lien as guarantor of $1,500,000 of the road's bonds, and thereupon attempted the issue of a similar amount secured by a first mortgage. Kimpton, regretting that "the whole seems to be known here, as I feared," reported the bonds selling at 55. In 1872 the road was bought under foreclosure by the South Carolina Railroad.

Attorney-General Chamberlain thus comes early to the front, hand-in-glove with the corruptionists. Daniel H. Chamberlain, of Massachusetts, a graduate of Yale and a student of law at Harvard, cool, keen, broadly cultured, positive in character though suave in manner, was the most brilliant of the Northern adventurers shunted by events into Southern governments. He had entered the army as lieutenant of Negro cavalry in 1864, and in 1866 came to South Carolina to settle the estate of a friend. Despite circumstantial evidence and the direct testimony of his criminal associates heavily against him from 1868 to 1872 while he was attorney-general, many still doubt his personal corruption; and in 1874 to 1876 as a reforming carpetbagger he so won the gratitude of a large conservative element that it dislikes even yet to recall his earlier associations. Without previous experience of courtroom practice, he was soon as attorney-general holding his own amid the able bar of South Carolina.

An act of the special session was one for enriching, at the expense of all other creditors, the speculators who had bought up (at ten cents per dollar, it was said) the notes of the Bank of the State. The assets of the Bank were ordered turned over to the Governor, who was to issue to the holders of the notes the State's twenty-year 6 per cent bonds. Attorney-General Chamberlain's opinion upheld the act; but the State Supreme Court annulled it as violating the State's contract with other creditors of the bank.

The first Radical legislature thus fully established its anticipated character. In eighteen months the debt of the State had swelled from $5,407,306 to (says Reynolds) $14,833,349, and in another year to $18,575,033.[8] Taxes had greatly increased, and the schools were receiving a little more than had been given for the education of the poor alone before the war. The land commission was squandering money under the pretense of providing lands for the landless, and dividing public money among themselves. The legislature was soon running a free barroom in the capitol for themselves and friends. These stealings were surpassed by those connected with the bonded debt, treatment of which may conveniently be postponed to 1871.

The Campaign of 1870.—As the campaign of 1870 approached, opinions of the whites, overborne, disheartened, unorganized, were divided as to a proper course toward the infamous parody on government. A straight fight was obviously hopeless. Abstention from politics until the Negroes should react toward intelligent and upright leadership appeared futile if not unmanning. A convention representing all but eight counties, summoned by a conference of Democratic editors, assembled in Columbia June 15, 1870, including along with many of the best white

[8] Reynolds, *Reconstruction,* p. 134, gives these figures; but the deceptions practiced by officials and at times their sheer ignorance and carelessness make knowledge of the true amount very difficult.

men in the State a large proportion of Negroes as a bid for an element without which victory was impossible. The convention, adopting the name Union Reform Party, declared their purpose to be to organize the people, irrespective of party, against "the present incompetent, extravagant, prejudiced and corrupt administration." Generals M. C. Butler and Joseph B. Kershaw declared that "black and white are a common people" who should be united in all their purposes—a statement which gave offense among whites throughout the State. The Republican Circuit Judge R. B. Carpenter of Charleston, an ex-Kentuckian of ability, force, and character, was named for governor, and General M. C. Butler for lieutenant-governor. Negroes were included in the legislative and county tickets.

The Republicans renominated Governor Scott and bid for the Negro vote by making the Negro A. J. Ransier his running mate. Governor Scott declined an invitation to joint debates, but made active use of the Negro militia and of his State police, reinforced for the occasion by New York toughs. After declaring in Washington that the white people of South Carolina were fit only to be ruled by Winchester rifles, he proceeded to arm the above forces with those weapons.

It was in this campaign that the Kuklux Klan became active in South Carolina. A few "bushwhackers" in 1865 had terrorized disorderly Negroes, and there had been fruitless attempts at control by refusing to employ or rent to Republican Negroes. The Klan originated in Tennessee in 1866 and is said to have existed in South Carolina from 1868; but its connection, if any, with the slight disturbances of that year in some upper counties is unproved. It was charged that some men who tried to crowd Negroes away from the ballot box at Rock Hill in 1868 were Kuklux.[4]

The arming of the Negroes under the form of militia stimulated the whites to measures of defense, and, in a number of counties, to joining the Klan. The organization was extremely loose and entirely beyond the control of even county heads, if indeed such existed outside York and Spartanburg. Operations were most active in York, Spartanburg, and Union, but occurred slightly in Chester, Newberry, Fairfield, Chesterfield, and very slightly in Sumter, Orangeburg, and Clarendon. The greatest activity was generally where the Negro militia were most active.

The black militia paraded on numerous occasions, and frequently in

[4] "Kuklux" (Greek *Kuklos,* a circle) as popularly used covers in fact many organizations ranging from neighborhood protective groups to South-wide elaborate orders, although the rituals, etc., and even the central officers, were poorly observed, and often not even recognized. "Kuklux" as a pungent name spread in popular parlance to all sorts of groups, such as the Knights of the White Camellia, the Constitutional Union Guards, the Pale Faces, the White Brotherhood, the '76 Association. Its spelling varies.

such formation as to force everyone else from the road, and divided into squads moving in every direction firing their guns—not the 1876 white "shotgun policy," but the 1870 Negro Winchester rifle policy, the purpose in both instances being not to kill but to terrorize their opponents. They attended the campaign meetings in array, usually stacking their arms near the stand. At Chester, with fixed bayonets, they prevented Judge Carpenter from speaking.

During the 1870 campaign Judge Orr, the ex-governor, announced his support of Scott and Ransier. The Union Reform movement, he held, was impracatical in the face of a 25,000 Negro majority which rendered reform possible only through white leadership within the Republican party. Judge Orr co-operated, entirely ineffectively, with the small reform element of the Republicans for the brief remainder of his life.

The returns showed 85,071 for Scott and 51,537 for Carpenter. Apparently the Negroes had voted almost solidly for Scott, and about 10,000 whites had not voted. General Butler testified that many of the managers, all of whom were Republicans, were ex-convicts, and expressed the conviction that the three days allowed for counting the votes and the counting of them in secret served the purpose which the framers of such a law intended. Republicans were elected in the four congressional districts, gerrymandered in stretches joining masses of coast and middle-county Negroes to piedmont and mountain counties, seeking to put a Republican majority into every district. The Union Reform movement, like all the attempts to draw the blacks away from those who had given them their privileges to those who now acknowledged them only through compulsion, proved futile.

Climax and Decline of the Kuklux, 1870-71.—After the great 1870 victory the Negro militia became more threatening, and in reply the Kuklux soon reached their greatest activity. In several counties occurred riots accompanied by loss of life. The town of Chester was threatened by Negroes with burning. The Negro militia frequently treated the legal arrest of a fellow member as an act of war to be avenged by the whole company called out for that purpose. The most shocking collision occurred in Union County, where in January, 1871, Negro militiamen murdered a white man because of his refusal to give them the whiskey he was hauling. On January 4 hooded Klansmen took from the jail and killed two of the militiamen. An order arriving on February 10 for the removal of the remaining prisoners to Columbia was generally taken as an attempt to prevent their punishment. On the night of February 12 five or six hundred Klansmen so disguised that "the mothers that suckled them could not have known them" rode into the town in military formation, picketed houses and gave orders in military terms to men designated by numbers, and took from the jail and shot, in the exact style of military executions, eight more of the militiamen. A written message declared, "The benignant efficacies of concealment speak for themselves. Once again we have been forced by force to use Force. Justice was lame, and she had to lean upon us. . . . We want and will have Justice, and this cannot be till a bleeding fight for freedom is fought. Until then the Moloch of Iniquity will have his victims, even if the Michael of Justice must have his martyrs. K. K. K."

House burnings and other misconduct were sharply checked; but this lawless method of redressing wrongs quickly led to mob violence in no way connected with politics. Negroes and scalawags began to conceal their own crimes under the cover of Klan disguise, and Kuklux garb concealed vengeance for private grudges. Public meetings in York, Union, and Spartanburg, in alarm at threatened anarchy, begged people to rely on the law for the redress of grievances. Governor Scott promised co-operation, did finally disband the Negro militia in the disturbed counties, substituted worthy white men for some incompetent officials, and appeared willing to check his liberal grants of pardons. After about May 15, 1871, there was no further complaint of Kuklux. Afterward, says Reynolds, the Federal government used the power of the bayonet to "suppress" a "conspiracy" that no longer existed, by means hardly less subversive of civil government than the worst acts of the Kuklux. Under the act of April 20, 1871, President Grant, October 17, 1871, suspended the writ of habeas corpus in nine South Carolina counties for suppressing the "rebellion." Federal soldiers crowded jails with suspects. Eighty-two were sentenced to imprisonment, but President Grant's pardons ultimately prevented any man from serving more than a year. The Klan organization was thus destroyed.

But it can hardly be denied that the Klan as a revolutionary agency against a corrupt and tyrannical government served to protect society against widespread and menacing evils. Even Attorney-General Chamberlain told the congressional committee that the movement "has been greatly aggravated by the misconduct of the Republican party." The plain truth is that the Klansmen struck for the preservation of the civilization enjoyed by many too refined or timid to do the things then essential for their own protection.

Increased Corruption after the 1870 Election.—Assured by their victory of the absence of all danger of being called to account, the second Republican legislature launched more freely into corruption. When United States Senator Thomas J. Robertson's short term expired, he bought re-election for the sum (a Republican editor asserted) of $40,000, which accords with his total vote at the reputed price for ordinary fellows at $500. As in 1868 excellent judges were honestly elected, for the judiciary was the last branch of the government attacked by the corruptionists.

One of the hugest swindles of Reconstruction was the public printing. In 1870 Governor Scott, Attorney-General Chamberlain, Comptroller Neagle, Treasurer Parker, the forger and thief L. Cass Carpenter, and two Republican editors formed the Carolina Printing Company, under whose management the printing bill at once rose from $45,000 to $173,000 a year. How little these men realized their opportunities was shown when the clerks of the two houses the next year awarded to themselves, as the Republican Printing Company, the public printing for $450,000. These then vast sums from the State's own treasury were the source for bribing legislators. Many of the most extensive bribing jobs were done with money stolen from the State, and not, as by the wealthy Senator Robertson, with his own money. It is impossible to realize how regular was the use of bribery unless one reads the diary of Josephus Woodruff, clerk of the senate, in which he records the men bought and the sums paid as the ordinary routine of the day.

The Public Debt.—The Radicals assumed control with a State debt of $5,407,306. The story of extravagance and fraud by which the debt was, under Scott, enormously swelled may be condensed as affording no instruction except as a warning in either finance or morals.

Debt management was committed to the Financial Board, consisting of the Governor (Scott), the Attorney-General (Chamberlain), and the Treasurer (Niles G. Parker), under very lax laws. These officials appointed as their New York financial agent H. H. Kimpton, who was almost as bare of banking experience as of integrity. Parker testified that this was done on the recommendation of Chamberlain, who secured from Kimpton an agreement to divide his commissions with the three members of the board, and that Chamberlain admitted to him receiving part of this from Kimpton. Comptroller-General Neagle represented that only Chamberlain could at times persuade Scott (who had some conscience) to put his name to bonds for some of Kimpton's irregularities. It is difficult to decide whether Chamberlain, later the foe of all corruption, was at this time merely the complacent witness of the corruption of the bond thieves or whether he was, as the thieves charged, sharing their loot.

The custom was early adapted of having Kimpton contract short-time loans on the hypothecation of the large quantities of bonds committed practically without security to him, instead of issuing the bonds at the low prices obtainable. In this way quantities of bonds, sinking in value, got on the market by being sold by the creditor for his protection. The carelessness of the Financial Board and their ignorance of the bonds sold or the amounts realized are almost incredible even in dishonest men. The bill of February, 1872, enabling the ring to cover up these transactions, was bribed through with money stolen from the State by Kimpton.

The First Taxpayers' Convention, 1871.—The act of March 7, 1871, for issuing £1,200,000 sterling refunding bonds opened possibilities that caused widespread alarm. The Charleston Chamber of Commerce called a Taxpayers' Convention in Columbia for May 9. Thirty of the thirty-two counties were represented. The membership included many of the State's ablest men. Attorney-General Chamberlain, flirting now with reform, and a few other Republicans, several of them Negroes, were members.

Attorney-General Chamberlain, say Parker and Neagle, prepared the Financial Board's statement of the debt to be submitted to the Convention, deliberately falsifying its amount. Thus, while Chamberlain spoke for honesty and economy in the convention, Governor Scott lustily did the lying for the board to the convention committee. The convention, misguided by the false statements submitted by Governor Scott and other officials, concluded that the State's direct debt was $10,665,908 and its liability for endorsing railroad bonds $8,695,608.[5] This debt the convention declared valid, but warned that future debt created by the government as then constituted would be held null, and its payment resisted.[6]

The convention condemned the legislature for having in March, 1871, sacrificed the State's interest in the Blue Ridge Railroad. In 1868 the State had guaranteed the bonds of the road to the extent of $4,000,000 on condition of retaining a statutory lien upon the entire property in the Carolinas and Georgia and Tennessee. But in 1871, President Harrison had bribed through the legislature over Governor Scott's veto an act renewing the State's guarantee, but giving Henry Clews, Henry Gourdin, and George S. Cameron a first mortgage upon the road. The Convention condemned "this fraud upon the property holders of the State" as a breach of trust "unauthorized and void."

To conclude this unsavory story, the road, which has never been laid

[5] Last page of *Proceedings,* in which as reprinted in *Affairs of Late Insurrectionary States Committee Report, South Carolina,* I, 515, at page 520, there is an error of a million. Governor Scott six months later reported the direct debt as approximately $12,000.000.

[6] The constitutional amendment of 1873 requiring endorsement of new debts by a two-thirds endorsement by the voters prevented any further increase of the bonded debt until recent years.

beyond Walhalla, though large sums were wasted in grading in several States, soon fell into the hands of the arch-corruptionist John J. Patterson. On February 3, 1872, the legislature was bribed to repeal its guarantee of the $4,000,000 of bonds and to order that they be taken up in exchange for $1,800,000 of "revenue bond scrip," the latter to be retired by a three-mill tax on the people for four years. The State Supreme Court in 1873 and the Federal Supreme Court in 1904 annulled the scrip, and the whole incident passed out of current history after leaving for decades the very words "Blue Ridge bonds" hateful.

Although the Taxpayers' Convention caused the corruptionists little anxiety, it was one of the essential forerunners of a vigorous assertion of their rights by the responsible element of the population. It probably had some effect in reforms and pretended reforms.[7]

C. C. Bowen moved to impeach Governor Scott and Treasurer Parker for unlawfully issuing bonds and falsifying reports. J. J. Patterson played on Scott's fears while he egged on the impeachers, with the result that the Governor bought off his pursuers with $48,645 drawn from the military fund. Speaker Moses got $15,000, and the Negro R. B. Elliott $10,500. Patterson was finding it true, as he said when a com-

[7] An incident connected with the 1871 Taxpayers' Convention later embarrassed Generals M. C. Butler and M. W. Gary. Shortly before the convention they signed a contract with a group of New York and Columbia bankers "desirous to take action to reinstate the value of the bonded debt of the State" that the bankers should "pay to M. C. Butler and M. W. Gary 10 per cent of the net gains that may arise from the purchase and sale of at least $500,000 of said State bonds, the increase to be measured by the advance due to an endorsement of the public meeting to be held on or about the third day of May next, at Columbia, approving the payment in full of all of the present bonded debt of the State, and agree to use their best efforts to that effect."

The speculation failed, and the contract was published in a suit that occurred in New York among the speculators. Republican newspapers published the contract with severe comments on Butler's and Gary's accepting membership in the Taxpayers' Convention when under contract to influence the subject under consideration for a fee as attorneys. (See *New York Sun,* February 1, 1878, etc., and court records in New York, *Lysander D. Childs et al.* against *W. E. Everett et al.,* February, 1878.) Gary's MS copy of the contract has the word "valid" before the word "bonded," but the copy in the court records does not. Both are copies of the original, which at present would be difficult or impossible to find.

Gary replied that he and Butler were retained to select the classes of bonds and to render professional services in and out of court. (Gary's speech in the South Carolina Senate is printed in full in the *Abbeville Press and Banner* of February 13, 1878.) The fact that Gary wrote on April 17 to Colonel McClure of Chester a letter published in a Charleston newspaper against the coming convention's repudiating any existing bonds, that Chamberlain wrote Kimpton on April 23, *"I will coöperate* with Butler and Gary *in any possible way,"* and other circumstances indicate that political as well as legal services were understood to be involved. The convention was so easily deceived by the replies of State officials to their queries into endorsing the entire existing debt that there is no evidence that Butler as a member of the bond committee or Gary did anything in the convention to bring about the result.

panion feared that it was necessary to reform, that still "there are five years good stealing in South Carolina."

Governor Scott reported "about 67,098 pupils" in the schools and upward of $300,000 "appropriated" at this session for their maintenance; but a year later teachers had not received a dollar and were selling their pay certificates at 50 per cent or in some counties finding them valueless. The asylum, penniless for six months, was saved from closing by personal endorsements by Superintendent Ensor, Governor Scott, and Attorney-General Chamberlain, and generous credits by merchants. Governor Scott deserves praise for his constant protection of the asylum from the spoilsmen. Forced to a compromise, he assented to the removal of the efficient superintendent but saved the institution by securing the substitution of a competent ex-army surgeon instead of the unfit candidate of the corruptionists.

The incident is characteristic of Scott. A weak and not a malicious man, whose feeble instincts of decency dissolved amid circumambient corruption, his character offered facility to every form of social and public degradation. The elements of ignorance and wickedness, which developed from the outset of his administration, by its end so enveloped his party that they selected as his successor a character notorious for private debauchery and public corruption. For the four years that were to come, to this man who was a complex of ignorance and iniquity, who could not of himself have obtained or retained power and whose hideous story had become a national scandal, Congress gave its unfailing support and the President any necessary number of soldiers. Conquered peoples have frequently been subjected to severer tyranny; but never in history has a conqueror, in professed attachment to the most lofty moral ideals, placed upon a people acknowledged, with the single exception of owning slaves, to be of unusual honor and capacity, a government so steeped in incompetence and corruption.

CHAPTER LV

CLOSING YEARS OF RECONSTRUCTION, 1871-1876

THE CONFUSION and iniquity of the Reconstruction government so overshadow the period that the economic and social forces for ultimate recovery may be overlooked. Barring the small minority whose hands were folded in despair, the white population, impelled by the necessities of existence and the pride of family, community, and race, at once set to making the best of a bad situation. The double object of developing resources and overcoming the black majority was present in the law of December, 1866, appropriating $10,000 for promoting immigration from Europe. Immigration societies in a number of counties and individual agencies helped to bring in some hundreds, mainly Germans. General M. W. Gary planned to bring in immigrants and also to force Negroes from the State by reducing cotton acreage. It is clear why the Negroes bitterly opposed the movement and abolished the office of commissioner in 1868. The poor whites also feared immigrant competition, and most farmers preferred the black labor.

Agricultural Revival and Hardships.—By 1870 the State (barring those large planters unable to readjust) had gone far toward economic recovery. The South's 1870 cotton crop was the largest since 1861. The crop of 1879 was the largest ever grown. Many prominent men resolved to eschew politics until corruption wore itself out and to devote themselves to building their own fortunes. South Carolina phosphates, discovered in 1867, made some rich and many prosperous and greatly increased the value of lands which without it were hardly worth cultivating. D. H. Jacques, D. Wyatt Aiken, J. L. Coker, Johnson Hagood, William M. Shannon, Thomas G. Clemson, and the men who revived the "State Fair" of the South Carolina Agricultural and Mechanical Society in 1869 inspired better agricultural methods.

The Grange, as the Patrons of Husbandry were popularly called, entered South Carolina in 1871 and during the nine years of its prominence stimulated legal and social movements for the benefit of the farmer, got him a discount in trade, cultivated his mind, and virtually laid the foundation on which more aggressive men in the eighties built the "Farmers' Movement" and engineered the Farmers' Alliance and

Tillmanism. The Grange flourished in the up country and appealed to and for the mass of small farmers.

There was indeed need of elevating the small farmer. The lien system fed him on credit while he made his premortgaged crop, and held him in debt-slavery. The advance of lien "time prices" over cash prices amounted frequently to charging interest at 100 to 200 per cent per annum. In bad years thousands of farmers belonged economically to the merchant, to whom alone they could look for necessities, and who, on account of cotton's high character as security, helped to keep the farmer a "cottontot" by insisting on this crop for his lien.

The Discovery of Phosphates, 1867.—Several scientists, dating from 1837, collected specimens which later investigation proved to be phosphates. Edmund Ruffin, Charles U. Shepard, Sr., and J. Lawrence Smith discovered phosphate of lime in South Carolina without realizing its importance, though Shepard in 1859 seems to have partially glimpsed the possibilities. In 1867 Dr. St. Julien Ravenel, having discovered 15 per cent of phosphate of lime in such rocks, revealed the fact to Dr. N. A. Pratt of Georgia, who on telling Professor F. S. Holmes, received specimens from his large but imperfectly understood collection in which Pratt found a proportion of almost 60 per cent of the precious constituent. Holmes's wide acquaintance with the field revealed to Pratt specimens up to 67 per cent and enabled them to secure control of extensive beds of unrivaled richness. When all but a few Charleston capitalists refused to be convinced, Holmes and Pratt easily secured ample capital in Philadelphia and organized the $1,000,000 South Carolina Mining and Manufacturing Company with Holmes as president and Pratt as chemist and superintendent. Dr. Ravenel organized the Wando Company with inadequate local capital, and soon the new industry was crowded.

There were eight principal phosphate rock beds in the State, including both river and land deposits. Those bordering the Ashley were the best on land; those under the Coosaw the best subaqueous. The strata lay on the surface and down to twenty feet below and were usually eight or nine inches thick, though ranging from three to thirty-six inches. Nothing contributed more to the revival of the ruined fortunes of the State than the discovery made by these scientists.

Developing Manufactures.—It was evident that the great break with the ante-bellum past imposed as one of its revolutionary changes in the life of the State the necessity of manufactures. The white legislature in 1865 enacted that only the lots and buildings of factories and railroads should be taxed, and the Radical legislature in 1870 exempted for four years from State and local taxes cotton and woolen manufactories, and in 1873 exempted for ten years from all taxes, except the two-mills school tax, capital invested since January 1, 1872, in varied manufacturing. Existing cotton mills made tempting profits. Henry P. Hammett, after three years of effort, opened the modern Piedmont in 1876 with 10,000 spindles. This thoroughly modern mill marked a new era which developed rapidly under the more favorable conditions of the eighties. The State's total manufacturing capital in 1870 was only $5,400,418 as compared with $6,931,756 in 1860; but so rapid was progress by 1880 that capital then equaled $11,205,984.

Education.—The Constitution-makers of 1868 ordained a public school system which, despite the fact that it remained largely an unorganized and ill-served mechanism until the white man's government after 1876 pushed it forward, deserves the compliment of Hugh S. Thompson, the first Democratic State superintendent, in 1877, that "with all its defects and too often deplorable infirmities ... [it] was a great and good departure for the public." J. K. Jillson, a Northern white man, during Reconstruction the State superintendent, honest and earnest, was permitted little power. The schools at times had to close, and Jillson feared the collapse of the system for lack of money, despite the large nominal, but often unpaid, appropriations.

In the year 1875-76 there were reported in the public schools 52,283 white and 70,802 Negro children. Oconee paid its men teachers $7.55 for their one-month term, and Charleston its men $121.66 a month for their ten-months schools. The city of Charleston's system of 1856 had made her a leader throughout the Southeast. Seventeen of the 2,084 (2,094?) schoolhouses were brick; 1,116 were log.

The State contained in 1860 eleven colleges for men and five for women. Every male college was closed when its students entered the war, except that two professors kept at Wofford a classical high school. Negro education until 1872 was assisted by the Freedmen's Bureau and, during the whole period and until today, by Northern church and other agencies.

There were, in 1870, 17 private academies attended by 650 boys. There were numerous girls' seminaries and three colleges (all supported by churches) for young women. The State in 1874 supported no high school.

Traditions of South Carolina were broken by the law of 1872, moderate and well guarded, permitting divorce for adultery or for desertion for two years. It was repealed in 1878 after a few divorces had been granted. The colonial Commons' voting to allow a man to bring in a bill for his divorce is the only tolerance South Carolina white lawmakers had ever shown the custom.

Not until 1879 did the white legislature renew the prohibition first enacted in 1865 against racial intermarriage. The law of 1879 excluded also the Indian from white marriages.

The University Becomes a Negro Institution.—The contempt of the corruptionists for the upright element in their own party and for the whites who were held in subjugation by Federal garrisons was expressed when the Republicans in 1872 nominated for governor the lowest of their party, Franklin J. Moses, Jr. At the summons of Judge Orr the Republican minority withdrew and nominated Reuben Tomlinson. The whites generally abstained from voting. Moses was elected by 69,838 to 35,533. The legislature, over two-thirds black, contained 130 Republicans to 27 Democrats.

"Honest John" J. Patterson bought the United States senatorship at $50 to $2,500 a vote. Printing jumped to its highest figure, $450,000, for Moses' first session, an appropriation for the signing of which he swore he received the $15,000 with which he made the first payment on the Preston mansion. Ohio, with nearly four times the population and nine times the wealth of South Carolina, was paying $63,000 for its printing, which included $27,000 worth of work not required in South Carolina. The legislature adjourned with its usual plea for the continued presence of Federal trocps for the maintenance of "law and order."

The establishment in February, 1873, of a normal school for common use of both races in the University buildings was the prelude to the virtually complete turning over of that institution to the Negroes. The trustees tartly accepted the resignations of the faculty and installed strangers (with two exceptions), one being a well-educated Negro. Chamberlain joined with Moses and the Negro trustees in commending this equality of opportunity. Several of the new faculty were of excellent preparation and ability. The Negro students, a number of whom had been attending Northern institutions, deserve credit not only for improving the opportunities offered but for the record of numbers of them in after life. Tuition was abolished, and 124 scholarships worth $200 each were established. The enrollment, which had been pitifully low, rose to 231 in 1875, nine-tenths colored. The preparatory department registered 102, law 20, medicine 2, academic 107.

The contemporaneous requirement of absolute social equality at meals and in dormitories at the Cedar Springs School for the deaf and blind at once closed that institution until after Reconstruction. This was the most deliberate attempt to enforce social equality by law. It was the declared policy of the aggressive element among the blacks to educate the children of the two races together, but other prominent Negroes professed to disdain to force themselves where they were not wanted.

The credit of the State now reached its lowest. Payment of interest on the State debt practically ceased in 1873, and bonds sold at fifteen cents on the dollar. Since the State Supreme Court had ordered the comptroller-general to levy a tax sufficient to meet the claims of certain bondholders, Governor Moses called the legislature for October 21. The bonded debt ($15,027,503), defaulted interest ($2,342,293), and miscellaneous floating debt ($2,964,104) totaled $20,333,900. The emergency was met with great simplicity. Of the recent "conversion bonds" $5,965,000 was annulled as illegally issued, and the holders of all other bonds and defaulted coupons were forced to accept 6 per cent "consolidation bonds" (the origin of our "consols") to half the old amount. An influential group of Negroes advocated complete repudiation.

The only subsequent funded debt created by Radicals arose out of frauds in the refunding and exchanging of these bonds. The constitutional amendment of 1873 requiring a two-thirds popular vote for bonds put it in the power of the white minority to block new issues. The immense floating debt was gradually reduced under Chamberlain.

Second Taxpayers' Convention.—On February 17, 1874, there met on the call of the executive committee of the first Taxpayers' Convention the second Taxpayers' Convention, representing all but two counties and containing a somewhat enlarged membership including about a half dozen Negroes and Republicans. The convention petitioned Congress for relief, but that body, which had signalized itself by unlimited contempt for State rights, now found that that principle forbade their interference to correct abuses which they had themselves created.[1]

The Republican State organization sent to Congress an ably written reply to the taxpayers, for the party was never without a circle with brains and training to defend its sins. This paper was sent to Washington by a large committee, a majority of whom were corruptionists, and the expenses of whose trip to prove Republican honesty were stolen from the treasury on a fraudulent pay certificate in a fictitious name.

The reception of the taxpayers' committee by President Grant was one of the queerest incidents of that queer administration. Immediately before their arrival Grant had been filled by "Honest John" Patterson with a distorted report of General M. W. Gary's attack on the President in the Taxpayers' Convention. Grant was so angry that he repeatedly interrupted the committee chairman. When Richard Lathers detailed the misdoings of the Freedmen's Bureau, the president exclaimed he did not believe it. Lathers replied that he was reading verbatim the report to President Johnson on conditions in South Carolina by Lieutenant-General Grant. The President dismissed the committee with the

[1] My statement in my larger *History of South Carolina,* III, 326, that the second Taxpayers' Convention endorsed the State debt as adjusted in 1873 is erroneous. The statement regarding the action of the first Taxpayers' Convention on the debt is correct.

statement that South Carolina must help herself. The advice was remembered.

The End of Moses.—Governor Moses was indicted along with a county treasurer for stealing. He prevented his own arrest by surrounding himself with Negro militia and evaded trial by securing a decision that he could not be tried while governor. His name was not offered for renomination. Says Allen, the biographer of Governor Chamberlain, from whom he must have derived his statement, "Probably no form of the misrule of the State under Scott and Moses was more degrading and intolerable than the system of the wholesale pardons for political, personal, or pecuniary considerations. The sale of pardons was open and notorious under Moses." Chamberlain wrote Senator O. P. Morton, January 13, 1876, that Governor Moses, possessing the sole appointment of commissioners of election, in 1874 sold them to the Democrats and the independent Republicans for $30,000, half actually paid in cash and the other half contingent upon the election of Chamberlain's opponents.

Soon after leaving office, Moses, ruined by his extravagance, confessed bankruptcy. He went to the North, underwent imprisonment in Detroit, Massachusetts, and New York for stealings, some pitifully small, and was found asphyxiated in 1906 in a Massachusetts boarding house.

Governor Chamberlain Defies the Corruptionists.—On September 8, 1874, the Republicans nominated for Governor Daniel H. Chamberlain, who for the two years since his term as attorney-general had taken no part in politics. The Negro corruptionist Gleaves was all but unanimously renominated for lieutenant-governor over the upright and able Negro Martin R. Delany.

Chamberlain was still regarded almost universally as a corruptionist despite his irreproachable private life, or at best as the complaisant friend of the corruptionists. He was the deliberate choice of the corruptionists in the convention; for they knew that during his four years as attorney-general he had been in intimate association with some of the most notorious thieves without protesting against their conduct, except for such devoirs to virtue as speeches in the Taxpayers' Convention. He was known as a member of the ring of public officers who sold to themselves by an unworthy trick, if not by actual corruption, the State's Greenville and Columbia Railroad stock. Accordingly the reform element bolted, organized as Independent Republicans, and nominated Judge John T. Green and Major M. R. Delany, unimpeachable white native Republican and upright Northern Negro. The Independents invited the support of the whites, which was given so largely that the vote exceeded any ever previously cast, and Chamberlain won by a margin of only 11,585. The "Conservatives" (as the Democrats called themselves until 1876) elected thirty-three members of the House and three senators, giving them seven in the Senate. For the first time under Reconstruction the joint vote showed a majority of whites, though by only three.[2]

Reviewing in his inaugural "the gross abuses" and "startling grievances" of former Republican administrations, Chamberlain warned that the whole policy of Reconstruction was in question: "The evils which surround us . . . are deplorable, but they will be transitory. The great permanent influences which rule in civilized society are constantly at work and will slowly lift us into a better life. . . . Through us or through others freedom and justice will bear sway in South Carolina."

The inaugural was heard with alarm by the element which elected Chamberlain, and with such gratification by his opponents as to draw the hearty commendation of almost the whole Democratic press. The Governor's words were soon confirmed by his acts. Against the deprecations of his friends, he determined to attend the caucus of the Republicans as the only means of defeating the intention to place on the circuit bench the corrupt Negro W. J. Whipper, whose selection was assumed as a foregone conclusion. Chamberlain rose to speak amid interruptions and sneers. He described Whipper as unfit in either ability or character. The latter replied furiously, and, with other prominent Negro leaders, insisted that the color line must be held tight. In a near riot the caucus broke up without nominating. The legislature chose Chamberlain's candidate, Jacob P. Reed, a capable Anderson white man recently turned Republican. A few days later F. J. Moses' candidacy for a judgeship was defeated, as Whipper's had been, by the combination of Democrats and reform Republicans. The action of Chamberlain against Whipper confirmed the hopes of the better element and made him the leader of a large proportion of the white population, whose little legislative minority gave him their constant support.

Governor Chamberlain enforced economy and checked frauds by a series of nineteen vetoes, every one of which was sustained. The lawmakers were urged to end their fostering of illegal voting by providing registration of voters as ordered by the Constitution, and to end the abuses in the appointment of trial justices. These requests were disregarded, as were also many of his nominations. Fifteen per cent of all State taxes since 1868, he told the legislature, remained unaccounted for by county treasurers in 1875, and the financial condition of many, if not most, of the counties was deplorable.

Sound as were Governor Chamberlain's financial principles, his racial policy, if nothing else, would have doomed him to failure. It was a public reproach, he said in January, 1875, that the school for the deaf

[2] Reynolds gives the "Conservatives" by name. Allen's *Chamberlain* in saying forty-two Democratic representatives and eleven Democratic senators perhaps includes the Independent Republicans.

and blind had been closed since 1873, when he knew that the only reason for its closing was his own superintendent of education's requiring that the white and Negro children must eat, sleep, and recite together. He also gave his approval to the mixing of the races in the University. It was not because of anything distinctly political that the white people of the State finally refused to accept Chamberlain as their leader, but because they considered that his theory of the equality of the races, whatever its result might be where Negroes were so few as to be negligible, would in South Carolina result in subjecting the whites to the blacks or in eventually transforming both into mulattoes. In later life Chamberlain himself fully adopted the traditional Southern view on the race question.

The most suspicious act of Chamberlain as governor was his gross favoritism to Hardy Solomon's rotten bank. Chamberlain and the comptroller-general stand in a poor light as having required Treasurer Cardozo, who had withdrawn most State moneys, to redeposit $200,000; for Solomon's character, the protest of Cardozo, and the weak and suspicious items in the bank's condition, which he clearly pointed out, were all known to them. Chamberlain's excuse (that others had proved wiser than he) was, in the mouth of an able lawyer and reformer, an insult to a child's intelligence, and left many doubting his integrity.

The Question of Chamberlain's Integrity or Corruption.—The question of Chamberlain's guilt or innocence in the crimes that disgraced the four years while he was attorney-general under Scott must be decided by weighing against each other, on the one hand, the sworn statements of some of the corruptionists that he was their partner and the condemnatory circumstance of his having been their intimate associate without having disturbed their doings (which it was his especial duty as attorney-general to prosecute); and, on the other, his unflinching opposition to corruption during his two years as governor.

Even if the Solomon bank incident were dismissed as merely an extraordinary blunder, there are two questions that remain: the sale of the stock owned by the State in the Greenville and Columbia Railroad, and the stupendous stealings of "the bond ring," i.e., the Financial Board consisting of Governor Scott, Attorney-General Chamberlain, Treasurer Niles G. Parker, and their Financial Agent Kimpton. Parker was a convicted and confessed thief. He swore before the investigating committee, on January 11, 1878, to specific extensive acts of corruption by Chamberlain in that most prolific and daring of all the frauds, the division of part of the proceeds of bond sales among the board and Kimpton. He also charged Chamberlain with preparing for Scott, in Parker's office, the false statement of the public debt for deceiving the first Taxpayers' Convention. On January 18, 1878, James O. Ladd, formerly Parker's chief clerk, repeated his statement that $50,000 of stolen coupons were put aside for Chamberlain. Ex-Comptroller Neagle's testimony was also damaging to Chamberlain.

To these charges during the campaign of 1874, Chamberlain replied, August 19, in the Columbia *Union Herald* with a long detailed denial. His denial in the same communication of having been a party to any fraud in connection with the sale of the State's Greenville and Columbia Railroad stock is less satisfactory. He asserted that "there was no fraudulent sale of that stock, so far as my knowledge or belief extends. The sale was made at a price fully equal to the value of the stock at that time." This ignores the fact that the sale was made by trust officers to themselves by deceptive means, in secret conclave. His statement that the charge that he was one of the purchasers of the stock from himself as a public officer "is wholly false and utterly incapable of being sustained by any evidence," was met a year later by the publication in the New York *Sun* of his letter of January 5, 1870, to Kimpton, which bears every mark of genuineness and which his admiring biographer Allen does not question. If the letter is genuine (and if Chamberlain ever denied it, I have missed it), it proves that the Attorney-General was guilty of a gross abuse of his position, even if not of outright corruption.

An indictment was found in 1878 against Chamberlain (then a resident of New York) and others for conspiracy to defraud the State in some land commission misconduct. He manifested the greatest willingness for trial. The case was nol-prossed in 1881.

The evidence of Josephus Woodruff shows that Chamberlain in his private practice while attorney-general accepted fees from the Republican Printing Company, which were larger on account of his political influence than was warranted by his services as a lawyer, and that as a Republican partisan he was willing to overlook a good deal of corruption in the early years of the great experiment of equal political rights for the Negro. But his bold, sincere, unflinching support of honesty as governor, and his fearless battling with the corruptionists, who would have been glad to drive him into hiding by any revelations at their command, throw doubt on the charges of corruption in connection with the bond and land commission rings. Whatever may have been his former failings, Chamberlain was convinced by 1874 that reform was essential to the life of the Republican party and the civilization of the State, and his better nature rose to the occasion.[3]

[3] Enemies of F. W. Dawson, the brilliant editor of the *Charleston News* and of the merged *News and Courier*, charged him with improper relations with the corrupt Reconstruction government. The following seems to be the truth of the matter. Dawson denied charging the government more for printing than he charged private patrons, but he allowed Treasurer Parker 20 per cent graft for prompt payment.—*S. C. Reports and Resolutions 1877-78* ("Fraud Reports"), pp. 1283, 1294-5.

That Dawson's editorial policy could be influenced by favors is indicated by his writ-

"Civilization . . . Is in Peril."—The enthusiasm for a bold opponent of corruption led to Governor Chamberlain's being invited to deliver addresses at Yale, Erskine, Wofford, and Furman, and at the centennials of the battles of Lexington and Fort Moultrie. At the 1875-76 legislative session he originated the requirement that no money should be paid from the treasury, except on the public debt and legislative salaries, without the warrant of the comptroller-general, with vouchers preserved by him. This nine-line statute, which is still the law, erected one of the most effective barriers against the stealing which Radical laws had deliberately encouraged.

This same session brought an event which jeopardized Chamberlain's administration and contributed more than any other one incident to wreck his hopes. The corruptionists whom he had kept off the bench in 1874 took advantage of his absence for a day, December 16, 1875, to elect as judges Whipper and F. J. Moses, Jr. Chamberlain admitted that even if he had been present he could not have prevented the election, for "the color line, the party line, and the line against my administration, all were sharply drawn.... *This calamity is greater, in my judgment, than any which has yet fallen on this State, or I might add, upon any part of the South.*"

Chamberlain refused to commission the two corruptionists on the ground that the judges whom they were to displace were entitled to full terms, though elected to fill places vacated in the midst of terms. Impeachment of the Governor, says Allen, was prevented only by the storm of public indignation at the proposal. To an invitation to attend the annual banquet of the New England Society in Charleston Governor Chamberlain replied: "I cannot attend your annual supper tonight, but if there ever was an hour when the spirit of the Puritans, the spirit of undying, unconquerable enmity and defiance to wrong ought to animate their sons, it is this hour, here, in South Carolina. The civilization of the Puritan and the Cavalier, of the Roundhead and the Huguenot, is in peril."

Whipper's threats to seize the courthouse by force were so violent that the Governor issued his proclamation calling on officers and citizens to resist and enlisted special constables. The Supreme Court sustained the Governor's action in refusing the commissions.

---

ing on November 24, 1868, to his Columbia reporter, Woodruff, who later became a prime Republican corruptionist, "We want to make all we can, and will go as far as we can to support Scott and the government if we are treated well. We cannot be blind advocates. . . . We must be independent, but we will always be more than just to our friends." Dawson's partner Riordan wrote Woodruff on March 18, 1871, "My *silence* is often more valuable than any action. For instance, if I had telegraphed the strong points of Perry's letter . . . it would have given the [bond] market a terrible black eye."—*Ibid.*, pp. 1293, 1297. For Dawson's testimony, see *ibid.*, pp. 1335-40.

Dawson became a severe critic of Scott and of Woodruff's corrupt printing affairs.

CHAPTER LVI

THE OVERTHROW OF RECONSTRUCTION, 1876

Governor Chamberlain's grief at the election of Whipper and Moses was both patriotic and partisan. It means, he said, the organization of the Democrats as never since 1865. That dispirited party had thus far maintained a feeble existence, seeking partial escape from intolerable conditions by fusing with reform Republicans or hopelessly doing nothing, and under the designation of "Conservatives" even disowning its own name. All was now changed by the suicidal act of the Republicans. If, under the best Governor that Southern Republicans could ever be expected to elect, only a handful of his party could be rallied to oppose the pollution of the bench, what hope was there of decent government except by the restoration of white control?

Probably a majority at this time expected a great Democratic rally to support Chamberlain for re-election, for Republicans both here and in the North were raging against him as a traitor. When the Governor, to assert his leadership, announced his candidacy as national delegate at large before the April convention of the South Carolina Republicans, Senator Morton of Indiana, to whom he had elaborately explained that his loyalty to the party was as unimpeachable as his opposition to corruption, delegated his colleague, "Honest John" Patterson, to destroy him. The Governor's chances seemed hopeless when he was defeated 40 to 8 for temporary chairman. Nominated for delegate at large amid derisive laughter, he was attacked with all the bitterness of a disappointed party deprived of its expected plunder and enraged at his praise of the civilization of the Puritan and the Cavalier. Rising in the all-night session at four A.M., Chamberlain for an hour and a half held the convention spellbound by a defense which the metropolitan reporters classed with the greatest orations of the generation. The men who an hour before were ready to destroy him elected him by an almost two-thirds majority.

Meanwhile the Democrats were divided into two warmly contending factions: the Co-operationists, or Fusionists, who believed that success was possible only by combining with Chamberlain; and the Straightouts, who stood for a direct fight "from Governor to Coroner." With a 20,000 or more Negro majority, said the *News and Courier,* a Straightout victory is impossible without armed force, which "would end in disaster and ruin."

The Race Issue in the Campaign.—The race issue was now more strongly forced to the front. The Negro leaders had constantly insisted on it. It now flamed out in a series of outrages both by and against Negroes, until the question of whether the united white race or the solid phalanx of blacks should hold the other in subjection overshadowed mere questions of stealing public money or maladministering government. It was this consciousness of race, which M. W. Gary, as early as 1874, stressed as essential, that put into the whites a determination without which success would have been impossible.

In May and August, 1876, occurred alarming strikes of Negro farm hands in Colleton and Beaufort. On May 23, in Edgefield County, six Negroes were shot for the murder of Mr. and Mrs. J. L. Harmon. This was the culmination of a series of troubles. In January, 1875, Ned Tennant, Negro militia captain, had summoned his soldiers to resist his being arrested for having General Butler's house burned. Governor Chamberlain sent the Republican Judge T. J. Mackey to investigate, who found that the Edgefield sheriff's "whole intelligence and sense of duty seem to have lapsed into a strong instinct of self-preservation"; that every treasurer of the county under Reconstruction had defaulted heavily; that the activities of the officials constituted "a vast system of larceny"; that "the government is wholly composed of Negroes elected on the race issue, asserted even against white Republicans," and "that, in my deliberate judgment, no such iniquity as the county government of Edgefield has been inflicted upon any portion of the English-speaking race since the Anglo-Saxon wore the iron collar of the Norman. In that case, however, the harsh domination was that of a superior civilization which elevated while it chastened. In this it is the reverse." The Governor immediately disbanded the entire Edgefield County militia, and ordered the disbanding of all extra-legal military organizations, i.e., the "rifle clubs" of the whites.

On July 8, 1876, occurred the riot in Hamburg. The place had long been disliked by the whites as harboring disorderly Negroes. An altercation, July 4, between two young white men impeded by Negro militia in the street led to a warrant against the captain for obstructing the highway. When the Negroes were reported to be threatening to lynch the young men at the hearing before the Negro trial justice, who was a major-general of militia, a body of whites came prepared to protect the two young men and determined "to make a row" that would teach the Negroes a lesson. The Negro captain did not appear, and the proposed trial ended in the demand by General M. C. Butler, the attorney employed to prosecute, that the militia's guns be surrendered for shipment to the Governor. This being refused, firing began (by which side is disputed). McKie Meriwether, a young white man, fell dead. The Negroes fled from their armory. The whites killed one in fighting and that night three, or perhaps five, more as they were told to run. This was stopped by General Butler's threat to shoot the next man who killed a captive.

Straightout Fight and No Fusion.—Governor Chamberlain's assumption of what was taken as a strong pro-Negro attitude on the Hamburg affair assured the victory of the Straightouts. In the May convention they had been overwhelmingly defeated, and even after Hamburg they carried the convention by only a small majority. Under the leadership of M. W. Gary, the outstanding Straightout leader, Hampton was nominated for governor.

Though united for a straightout fight, the Democrats were divided both as to the fundamental issue and as to the proper campaign program. Was the issue merely that of good government, in which the Negro should fully participate, as the platform stated and Hampton maintained, or was it what Gary insisted—the bald, unescapable issue of race against race? Blink the fact as some might, and conceal it for policy as did others, the campaign and later events made it clear that dominating all else was the question of which race as a race should rule the other. The Republicans also worked the race issue to the full.

Campaign Methods.—On August 12 Chamberlain was to address a monster Republican meeting in Edgefield. The town, says Chamberlain, was full of heavily armed white riders uttering the "rebel yell" as they dashed through the streets. Their cavalcade swept up to the stand on which he was to speak, upon which Butler and Gary stepped at the same moment as Chamberlain. Butler took charge and made the first speech. Gary, "the bald Eagle of Edgefield," followed amid deafening shouts, abusing Chamberlain, said the latter, with threats and bitterness and violence he had never known paralleled. His purpose, said Gary later, was to impress upon the dull mind of the Negro his leader's helplessness.

Chamberlain was at last allowed to speak amid a torrent of insults and interruptions from which General Butler at last protected him. His speech was followed by another denunciation by Gary. After three hours and a half, in which only two of the six Republicans had been allowed to speak and the stand had collapsed under the crowding intruders, Chamberlain left amid yells of derision. He was similarly treated at four other Republican meetings captured by the Democrats, and this ended the joint debates; for those to which the Democratic Executive Committee invited the Republican State nominees never occurred. The

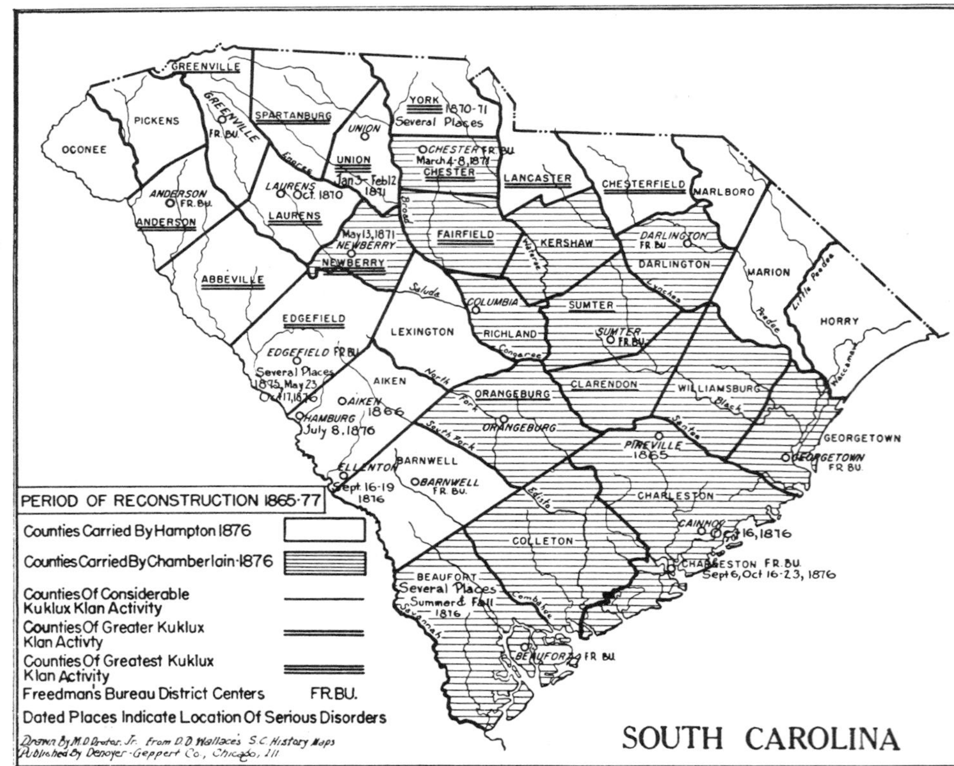
PERIOD OF RECONSTRUCTION 1865-77
Counties Carried By Hampton 1876
Counties Carried By Chamberlain 1876
Counties Of Considerable Kuklux Klan Activity
Counties Of Greater Kuklux Klan Activty
Counties Of Greatest Kuklux Klan Activity
Freedman's Bureau District Centers FR.BU.
Dated Places Indicate Location Of Serious Disorders
Drawn By M.D. Dreter, Jr. From D.D. Wallace's S.C. History Maps
Published By Denoyer-Geppert Co., Chicago, Ill
SOUTH CAROLINA
OCONEE
PICKENS
GREENVILLE
SPARTANBURG
UNION
YORK 1870-71 Several Places
CHESTER FR.BU. March 4-8, 1871
CHESTER
LANCASTER
CHESTERFIELD
MARLBORO
ANDERSON FR.BU.
ANDERSON
LAURENS Oct. 1870
LAURENS
UNION Jan 3 - Feb 12 1871
May 13, 1871 NEWBERRY
NEWBERRY
FAIRFIELD
KERSHAW
DARLINGTON FR.BU.
DARLINGTON
MARION
HORRY
ABBEVILLE
EDGEFIELD
EDGEFIELD FR.BU.
Several Places 1875, May 23 Oct 17, 1876
LEXINGTON
COLUMBIA
RICHLAND
SUMTER
SUMTER FR.BU.
AIKEN
AIKEN 1866
HAMBURG July 8, 1876
ORANGEBURG
ORANGEBURG
CLARENDON
WILLIAMSBURG
GEORGETOWN
GEORGETOWN FR.BU.
PINEVILLE 1865
BARNWELL
BARNWELL FR.BU.
ELLENTON Sept. 16-19 1876
CHARLESTON
CAINHOY Oct 16, 1876
COLLETON
CHARLESTON FR.BU. Sept 6, Oct 16-23, 1876
BEAUFORT
Several Places Summer & Fall 1876
BEAUFORT FR.BU.
Saluda
Broad
Enoree
Wateree
Congaree
North Fork
South Fork
Edisto
Combahee
Savannah
Santee
Black
Lynches
Peedee
Little Peedee
Waccamaw

Governor refrained from attending any more meetings for fear of precipitating violence.

The fundamental race issue cropped out on September 6 in the attack of Charleston city Negroes on white men guarding Negroes who had addressed a Negro Democratic club. Two Democrats were killed, and Negro turbulence throughout the city was suppressed with difficulty. Conditions in the city were so alarming that a citizens' meeting sought protection from Washington, and for three months mounted men patrolled the city all night.

Growing out of the attempt of Negroes to release a burglar, there occurred September 16 to 19 the Ellenton riot, in which one or two whites and perhaps forty or fifty Negroes were killed. The whites explained the affair as self-protection against Negro crime and riot. Republican journals in well-policed North cities, ignorant of the exigencies of rural life in the presence of a preponderantly Negro population with its armed militia, heralded it as merely a part of the Democratic plan of campaign.

The Democratic campaign meetings, one for each county, began at Anderson on September 2 before an audience estimated at 6,000. The red shirt, not covered by a coat, became the distinctive uniform of the Democrats, and gave a cavalcade of mounted men a peculiarly menacing aspect.

At Abbeville Hampton was met by 3,000 mounted men, including 700 uniformed Negro Democrats. "A bowed figure draped in robes of dense black and wrapped with chains" represented South Carolina. As Hampton approached the stand, she cast aside her chains and robes of mourning, and "a young woman in pure white stood tall and stately, head uplifted and eyes shining like stars." Crowds cheered, while the booming of cannon roused the appropriate opposite emotions in the hearts of Democrats and Republicans. Scalawags rushed into print with renunciations of Republicanism. Varied devices, some of them appearing ludicrous afterwards, were adopted to intimidate or persuade the Negro; but the commands of leaders were positive against acts of violence as certain to bring Federal intervention. Indeed it is probable that much more actual violence was inflicted on Negro Democrats than on Negro Republicans, for large numbers of the former were beaten, sometimes by mobs of women. Hampton claimed to have won 17,000 Negroes by his mild and fair policy. If so, they alone were far more than sufficient to turn the tide.

On October 7 Governor Chamberlain ordered dispersed the rifle clubs, a well-drilled extra-legal white militia, of whom there were more than 290 companies. This was considered by the whites as intended to leave them at the mercy of the armed blacks. On October 16, at a joint local meeting near Cainhoy, Charleston County, the Negroes, having secretly violated the agreement to come unarmed, killed five white men and wounded sixteen. Governor Chamberlain at the request of the whites sent a company of Federal troops for their protection.

In the city of Charleston Democratic Negroes on parade were seriously injured. On October 23 Mount Pleasant was terrorized by an armed and firing Negro mob threatening to massacre the white population. Hampton's meeting at Beaufort was broken up by a Negro mob. Whites were ambushed and one was killed returning from the Edgefield meeting, October 17. The same day, directing his proclamation solely at the rifle clubs, President Grant answered Governor Chamberlain's request by placing at his service all available troops in the Atlantic division with the promise of the entire army and militia of the United States if needed.

The two white Republican Supreme Court justices (the third justice was a Negro) and a number of the circuit judges agreed that the conditions asserted as justifying the President's intervention did not exist. Two of the Republican circuit judges (Mackey and Cooke) took the stump for Hampton, as did Martin R. Delany, the best type of Negro carpetbagger. Mackey and Cooke proposed to the Democratic State Executive Committee withdrawing the Democratic candidates for presidential electors and thus securing Republican aid for electing Hampton. So desperate was the situation that Hampton's view was sought. The charge later made that Hampton favored the plan was, when brought into the open, proved groundless.[1]

There was much intimidation and fraud on both sides at the election, but no bloodshed. In St. Andrew's parish, bands of Negroes armed with spiked maces, rifles, and bayoneted muskets inspected every Negro voter's ticket under threat of death or serious bodily harm if he dared to vote Democratic. The white terror in Edgefield and Laurens could not exceed the black terror in Beaufort and Charleston counties.

The Edgefield plan, as the Mississippi tactics of intimidation of the year before may be called for South Carolina purposes, was organized principally by General M. W. Gary and was followed in Abbeville, Laurens, Newberry, Edgefield, Aiken, Barnwell, and Colleton. In all of these except Colleton and Newberry and in no other largely black counties Hampton won majorities, in some cases very large. In the bickering soon begun among the victors the advocates of the Hampton plan resented the claim that the Edgefield plan had won the election, and maintained that they had accomplished just as much by methods

[1] See pages 610-611 below.

better suited to their own situation. At the demand of the Democrats, Governor Chamberlain appointed in each county one Democrat and two Republicans as commissioners of election, and Democrats were given representation also as polling place managers. That tricks, intimidation, and fraud were abundant on both sides is freely admitted, although fraud by the whites has been far more emphasized, and, being conducted with more intelligence and daring, was doubtless more extensive. The fact that many conservative men of the highest probity considered that fraud and intimidation were the only possible means of circumventing a large Negro majority and an overwhelming body of soldiers sent in by virtually a foreign enemy (for the government of the United States under President Grant was in effect nothing less), is worthy of the most respectful consideration. Governor Chamberlain's own mature view of 1901 is of interest:

"If there is any interest still attaching to the writer's own view, he is quite ready now to say that he feels sure there was no permanent possibility of securing good government in South Carolina through Republican influences. If the canvass of 1876 had resulted in the success of the Republican party, that party could not, for the want of materials, even when aided by the Democratic minority, have given pure or competent administration. The vast preponderance of ignorance and incapacity in that party, aside from downright dishonesty, made it impossible.... The real truth is, hard as it may be to accept it, that the elements put in combination by the reconstruction scheme of Stevens and Morton were irretrievably bad, and could never have resulted except temporarily or in desperate moments, in government fit to be endured."

The vote totaled 183,388. On the face of the returns, Hampton was elected by 1,134 and the Republican presidential electors by an average of 816. The Democrats elected 65 and the Republicans 59 to the new House, while the Senate (half being holdovers) counted fifteen Democrats and eighteen Republicans.

Contesting the Election.—There now began a dispute over counting the vote that all but precipitated civil war. The State Board of Canvassers consisted of five State officers (three of whom were candidates for re-election) and a legislator. The Republican candidates contested before this board the election of the Democratic House members from Barnwell, Edgefield, and Laurens, though they possessed large majorities, on the ground of fraud and intimidation. The Democrats contended that the board possessed merely ministerial powers, and must certify to the Secretary of State the persons reported by the county canvassers as having the largest vote, without attempting to forestall the constitutional order that "each house shall judge of the election returns and qualifications of its own members." On this hung the whole issue of the election; for if the Board of Canvassers excluded the Democrats in question, the majority would be shifted to the Republicans, who by throwing out the vote from the contested counties would give the governorship to Chamberlain and his entire State ticket. The Supreme Court (composed of three Republicans) upheld the Democratic contention, and ordered the State canvassers to certify to the Secretary of State as elected the senators and representatives for whom the highest votes were reported. On the last day of their legal existence the Board of Canvassers certified the election of legislators for every county except Edgefield and Laurens, thus annulling the election in those counties and reporting the new House as consisting of fifty-seven Democrats and fifty-nine Republicans. There thus remained eight vacancies, corresponding to the five representatives from Edgefield and the three from Laurens.

Governor Chamberlain, at midnight before the legislature assembled on November 28, placed Federal troops in the State House under orders to obey his agent. Fifty-nine Republicans (five of them white) assembled in their hall and elected E. W. M. Mackey speaker. The sixty-five Democrats approached the door, headed by the five Edgefield claimants followed by the three from Laurens. These eight bore the Supreme Court's certified copy of the returns showing them to have received the majority, and the others the certificate of the Secretary of State. Governor Chamberlain's agent, flanked by soldiers, refused the claimants from Edgefield and Laurens admission. The Democratic members of the house, leaving W. H. Wallace, elected from Union, to observe the Mackey House, marched to Carolina Hall, organized as the only House of Representatives possessing a legal quorum, and elected Wallace speaker.

Dual Government.—We have here the crux of the dispute which for four months kept in existence two bodies, each claiming to be the lawful House of Representatives and two Governors each claiming to be the legal executive. The Democrats maintained that a quorum consisted of a majority of a full House of 124. This quorum they claimed to possess in the sixty-five members of the Wallace House.

The Republicans maintained that a quorum consisted of a majority of all the members elected, and that, as the State Board of Canvassers (possessing, according to them, judicial powers) had declared that no election had occurred in Edgefield and Laurens, their 59 members constituted a majority of the 116 members elected.

The Republicans were at once embarrassed by their own theory, for five of the Mackey body joined the Wallace House, thus giving it a quorum on the Republican theory without its disputed members. The depleted Republican (or Mackey) House, though now possessing no quorum on any possible theory, resurrected itself by "unseating" the Democrats certified by the State Board of Canvassers as elected from Abbeville, Aiken, and Barnwell and seating their Republican opponents, thus making their number sixty-eight.

On November 30 the Wallace House marched into the legislative chamber before the Republican doorkeeper realized what was happening. The Mackey House, entering a few moments later, were astonished to see Speaker Wallace installed. The two speakers continued side by side. General Ruger refused to use his soldiers to evict the Edgefield and Laurens representatives.

Governor Chamberlain thereupon commissioned as special officers about a hundred Negroes notorious for violence in Charleston as members of the "Hunkidori Club." The Democrats telegraphed for support which promptly arrived in the form of three to five thousand men.

The contending bodies continued four days and nights in the hall, eating and sleeping there. Speaker Wallace now manifested the same prudence which characterized General Hampton during these days when one false step would have precipitated bloody and incalculable consequences. He announced that he was officially informed that upward of a hundred armed men were to enter the hall to eject certain members, and that, if resistance were offered, General Ruger's soldiers would assist Governor Chamberlain's agents, not in order to decide who were members of the House, but to sustain the executive authority as ordered by his superiors. Speaker Wallace, therefore, to prevent bloodshed, recommended that his supporters, constituting the quorum of the House, withdraw to another hall. This was done, and the most serious threat of physical violence was past.

The Wallace House withdrew to Carolina Hall. Two days later, December 6, the Supreme Court declared that "William H. Wallace is the legal Speaker of the lawfully constituted House of Representatives." The ruling was based on a South Carolina Supreme Court decision in a time of calm that a quorum must possess a majority of all the 124 constitutionally prescribed members. The Mackey House on December 5, without any form of contest or investigation, threw out the total vote of Edgefield and Laurens, declared Chamberlain elected by a majority of 3,145, and inaugurated him on December 7. One week later, the Wallace House, with 71 persons (63 of whom, a clear majority of 124, bore certificates of the canvassing board), inaugurated Hampton.

It was on the night of Chamberlain's inauguration that Hampton, in response to calls from an excited crowd, made his famous speech counseling the strictest observance of order and declaring, "The people have elected me Governor, and, by the Eternal God, I will be Governor or we shall have a military Governor." Here, as during the campaign, Hampton manifested his clear, direct intelligence, but still more his eminence fundamentally of character rather than intellect, resting on a balance, moderation, magnanimity, and coolness that no danger could excite and no complications confuse.

The Senate during these events with its majority of five Republicans co-operated with the Mackey house. The Wallace House was therefore unable to secure the passage of any bill. The courts (with the exception of one circuit judge) recognized Hampton's government and enjoined the Republican treasurer against paying out money.

To feed the State's prisoners and meet other immediate necessities Governor Hampton called for 10 per cent of the taxes last paid by each citizen, practically the whole of which was promptly contributed. Chamberlain's government meanwhile collected less than one thousand dollars. President Hayes invited both Hampton and Chamberlain to conferences, the result of which was his removal of the troops on April 10, 1877. The next day the governor's office in the State House was transferred to Hampton.

There thus passed from the history of South Carolina one of her most distressful epochs and one of her most remarkable governors. Made attorney-general before he had conducted a case in court, Chamberlain's ability made him an antagonist putting the ablest opponents upon their mettle. Leaving the attorney-generalship under almost universal suspicion of corruption, he became two years later a bold and persistent foe of corruption and a leader for economy and enlightened legislation. He adorned public office with an intellectual culture, eloquence, and personal dignity worthy of the best traditions. In all except his inexcusable assembling of Negro roughs to drag legislators from their places, he conducted his failing cause with a courage and skill which even enemies must respect. On being overthrown he at once entered upon a lucrative law practice in New York, from which he retired to scholarly leisure in his native Massachusetts. He died in 1907 after having fully adopted Southern political and social views concerning the Negro.

CHAPTER LVII

READJUSTMENT UNDER HAMPTON, 1877-1886

Some Results of Reconstruction.—With the close of the incredible decade of 1867 to 1876 there began the real reconstruction, which was largely the undoing of "Reconstruction." Many of the miscreants fled, and a few were prosecuted as examples. Some of the fugitives approached South Carolina congressmen in Washington with suggestions of compromise. Large numbers of South Carolina Democrats were under prosecution under the election laws. The President and the Governor agreed, and "the exchange of prisoners" was consummated by the mutual abandonment of prosecutions and the pardon of those already convicted. The results of the war and Reconstruction, which for the South were parts of one whole, exercise to this day a profound influence in every department of Southern life. Apologists point to certain social legislation enacted during Radical rule as a justification for Reconstruction; but it is clear that this legislation would soon have come if a Negro had never voted. The State as a whole would soon have done what Charleston had done in 1856 in creating a thoroughly modern common school system. Nor can Reconstruction justly be praised or blamed for the democratizing of South Carolina politics. There had been a strong current of democratic protest in South Carolina until the exigencies of approaching war compelled concentration on external defense. The long step toward modern democracy which was taken in the white-man Constitution of 1865 would, but for Reconstruction, have been followed by others in the path of world-wide democracy long before 1890. Reconstruction, by forcing concentration on the maintenance of white supremacy, thereby withdrawing attention from social and economic problems, in effect postponed democratic reform. The democratic legislation of Reconstruction South Carolina retained, because it effected what South Carolina was already largely ready to do of herself.

One effect of Reconstruction was the political solidarity of the whites. The remembrance of what Negro rule meant, and what even the possession of the balance of power in the hands of an educated Negro minority would mean, has stiffened South Carolina politics into an intolerance of political action outside the organized white party which is unintelligible to persons unaware of South Carolina's history and situation. Fraud was adopted by the whites in 1876 as a necessary means of overcoming the Negro; but, as the *News and Courier* later said, "it demoralized public sentiment, and in course of time was used by white men against white men."

This reaction against intolerable Negro rule involved also intensifying race prejudice. As never before, the white man has set himself, in the law and even in unlawful relations, against racial intermixture, and the Negro woman has slowly changed from the attitude of welcoming a mulatto child as assuring her kinder treatment from her master to a racial pride that tends to resent immoral relations with a white man merely as white. This feebly stirring racial pride affords a barrier against miscegenation and some compensation for the cruelty of race prejudice.

The war and Reconstruction broke up the natural alliance between the agricultural South and West and threw the latter, intensely national and anti-slavery, into the arms of the financial and manufacturing East, which long fattened on the voluntary subjection of its ally. The South, thus conquered, humiliated, impoverished, rifled, was compelled not only to rebuild its own fortunes and to bear the expenses of its side of the war and to pension its own veterans, but also had to pay enormous reparations not yet ended in the form of pensions and war debt incurred in its subjugation. Out of this calamity and helplessness there emerged a psychology of inferiority as injurious as ante-bellum delusions of grandeur. The heart took refuge in idealizing "The Lost Cause." The essential reconstruction of Southern ideas and aims and methods was thus hampered by a devotion to a cherished, blood-sanctified past that long made the words "the New South" almost moral treason. The reconstruction of ideas was harder than the reconstruction of industry and institutions. The tragedy is that we have lost the nobler part of past ideals faster than we have acquired the best part of the new.

With the Negro the case was very different. Democratic pledges to regard his political rights were quickly forgotten. The thought of the periodic repetition of 1876 was intolerable. Finally the privilege of Negroes who voted for Hampton to participate in the Democratic primaries was destroyed by unsurmountable restrictions. The Negro has profited and suffered by the opportunities and perils of freedom. Immorality and disease have made inroads that would never have been permitted under slavery; but as a race he has made wonderful progress and deserves respect for it in the circumstances inimical to health and virtue in which large masses of the race live. When all is said, he remains the one insoluble problem of American life.

Adjusting the Public Debt, etc.—Upon the retirement of Chamberlain, Governor Hampton summoned the legislature in special session.

The Republican majority of three in the Senate was converted by resignations into a Democratic majority. Wright, the corrupt Negro member of the Supreme Bench, resigned under charges, and the Supreme Court unseated all the circuit judges elected by the Republicans on the flimsy technicality that they had been elected viva voce (as the Constitution stated that they must be elected), instead of by "joint ballot" (i.e., written paper tickets) of the two houses.[1] Judge Mackey's adhesion to the Democrats in 1876 was rewarded by re-election. Judge Willard's great services in Supreme Court decisions affirming the Democratic victory in 1876 were, on Hampton's insistence and at the cost of bitter Democratic dissent, rewarded by his election as chief justice to fill the unexpired term of the deceased F. J. Moses, Sr. The contest over the debt was complicated, prolonged, and bitter. At one extreme stood the pledge of the Democratic Executive Committee in 1876 to abide by the settlement of 1873, scaling the debt to half.[2] At the other were those who demanded a somewhat drastic reduction based on the report of the legislative committee that certain fraudulent bonds had been included in the settlement of 1873. Governor Hampton, always conservative, while urging careful scrutiny for frauds, leaned to moderation. Senator Gary ardently supported the report of the committee. Unhappily, in the contest the old antagonism between Charleston and her up-country critics was revived because many bondholders resided in the city. In 1877 "conservative" Democrats united with the Republican minority to defeat the bond committee report. As a compromise, a court of claims of three circuit judges was created, on whose findings, ratified by the Supreme Court, new bonds were issued for all debts found to be legal. The Commissioner for carrying out the decision reported, November 26, 1880, that $1,126,763 of the consolidated bonds and stocks of 1873 were invalid, leaving valid consolidated bonds and stocks of $4,479,048. Of the securities issued from 1794 to 1867 ($3,983,543), holders of only $2,155,542 had accepted the 50 per cent scaling of 1873. All were now compelled to accept that act of partial repudiation, as the legislature endorsed the refunding act of 1873 and enforced it upon the holders of ante-bellum and Orr government securities who had held out in hopes of ultimate justice. The Democratic legislature thus denied payment of the sum of $1,991,771 borrowed by our own people, besides about $250,000 accrued interest, to which should be added $212,675 (i.e., half the amounts borrowed by the Radicals in 1868 to pay the notes of the Bank of the State, some accounts, and accrued interest on the old debt). Whether a two-thirds popular vote for placing again upon the people this honest

[1] State *vs.* Shaw, 9 S. C., 94-147; January 22, 1878.

[2] The statement in my three volume *History of South Carolina,* III, 326, that the Taxpayers' Convention also endorsed this settlement is erroneous.

debt from which the Radicals had freed them could have been obtained is a mere guess. When the refunding was virtually complete, October 31, 1882, including floating debts, accrued interest, etc., the public debt stood at $6,571,825.

In 1877 the State still had in addition a contingent liability (from which it suffered no loss) on railroad bonds guaranteed before 1861 of $4,705,608, and owned railroad stocks valued at $980,700. The bonded debt remained about the same until the enormous issues under the $65,000,000 highway loan act of 1929.

Rich Versus Poor—Fence Law.—The factional quarrels among the Democrats that have since only intermittently ceased broke out even before the withdrawal of Chamberlain. They flamed up hotly in the bond contest and the question of making Willard chief justice, and in the longer-lived quarrel over the "stock law," or "fence law." How near the frontier was South Carolina is seen from the fact that livestock had always been permitted to forage at large, thus necessitating the fencing of crops. The contest, extremely bitter in low-country counties having great areas suitable for grazing, continued for a generation over this communistic privilege of raising cattle, hogs, etc., on other men's land. The introduction of better stock, better agricultural methods, and the necessity of controlling cattle tick and Texas fever, resulted in 1921 in the last two coast counties having to fence in their cattle in the portions of them still excepted. The constant emphasis on the fence law as the rich man's oppression of the poor played its part in preparing for the class conflict of 1890.

The Hampton-Gary Feud.—So bitter were the personal and factional feuds reaching back into the half-suppressed conflict of democratic and aristocratic elements before 1860 that, following the election of 1876, they broke into renewed activity before it was even certain that white South Carolina would be allowed to install its officers. The election to the Senate on December 20, 1876 of Butler instead of Gary was followed by expressions of discontent among the Gary faction. An anonymous correspondent charged in the *Augusta Chronicle and Sentinel* of January 10, 1877, that Hampton favored the withdrawal of the South Carolina Democratic candidates for presidential electors in return for Republican support, as proposed by two leading Republicans in September, 1876. Gary, generally credited with the article, denied that he wrote it but did not deny that he inspired it. Gary now sought to keep his way to the Senate open either by representing the continuance of Hampton as governor as essential to the safety of South Carolina or by dangling before him the nomination for the vice-presidency. Hampton's election to the Senate, December 10, 1878, blasted Gary's hopes. Resentment at being denied adequate reward for his services in 1876 now drove Gary, whose nature was so tortured by ambition as to obscure his judgment, into an attack on Hampton in the hope of swelling the scattered discontent with some of Hampton's policies into an opposition that would end his dictatorship of party policies. In an interview with the *New York Herald* correspondent on December 5, 1879, he repeated the charge that Hampton in 1876 desired to withdraw the Democratic candidates for presidential electors in return for Republican support for the Democratic State ticket, as proposed by two leading Republicans. Hampton absolutely denied the charge, and the other members of the conference to which the proposal was submitted wrote in response to Gary's inquiries completely exonerating Hampton—letters which Gary did not reveal, though continuing in interviews to reiterate his charge.[3] More or less openly, Hampton's having dined at the same table with two Negroes was circulated, but with studious refraining from direct statements in the press lest the unworthy trick by which Hampton and Superintendent of Education Thompson had been thrown into this situation should be explained.

The sweeping claim of Gary's friends that, as the pre-eminent Straightout, he was chiefly responsible for the victory of 1876 offended the friends of other leaders. So calamitous was Gary's attack on Hampton that his campaign for governor as "the people's man," "the poor man's friend," netted him only a handful of delegates in the 1880 convention, which nominated unanimously Hampton's candidate, Comptroller-General Johnson Hagood. There were stirrings of Republicanism and independentism in a few counties, in the groundless hope that Gary might become their leader. The old fighter was looking to renewing the campaign within the party when he died in 1881, leaving devoted disciples whose long-cherished determination for revenge swelled the uprising of 1890 and supplied many of its leaders.

Intimidation and fraud in 1880 in Edgefield and Aiken, rivaling 1876, gave George D. Tillman a majority for Congress in this black district, but the Negro Smalls was awarded the position by Congress. Conservative men realized the necessity for better means of defense than the agencies which threatened to debase the entire electoral system. Edward McCrady (the later historian) devised the "eight box law" and a stringent

[3] The letters were given publicity by the present writer in an address before the Southern Historical Association, November 7, 1940. Seeing announcement of the forthcoming address, Mr. W. A. Sheppard, who in his *Red Shirts Remembered* (1940) had revived the charge against Hampton but had not referred to the letters exonerating him, though familiar with them, printed a pamphlet dated November 2, 1940, giving the letters. Publication of my address in the *Journal of Southern History* of August, 1942, led to other letters and papers to the same effect being sent me, photostats of which I have.

registration of voters. A complete revision, February, 1882, of the loose election laws inherited from the Radicals included both these provisions. Shifting the plainly labeled boxes (one for each office) imposed a simple educational qualification, for no vote was counted if deposited in the wrong box.

The Cash-Shannon Duel.—This period saw the era of formal dueling ended through the shock to public opinion of the Cash-Shannon duel. About 1874 Robert G. Ellerbe in a drunken orgy assaulted Conrad Weinges. On December 9, 1878, Weinges sued for damages. Ellerbe, on January 7, 1879, by arrangement with Colonel E. B. C. Cash, confessed judgment of debt to Ellerbe's sister, Mrs. Cash, in the sum of $15,000. In September, 1879, Weinges was awarded damages of $2,000 for the assault by Ellerbe.

In the attempt of Weinges' attorneys, Captain W. L. DePass and Colonel W. M. Shannon, to prevent the transfer of Ellerbe's property, Colonel Cash conceived that his wife had been insulted by the inference that she had been party to a fraud in the settlement with her brother. Shannon declined a challenge from Ellerbe as no gentleman.

The Cashes, father and son (since they could not challenge Shannon after he had submitted to being posted by Ellerbe as a coward), then began scurrilous attacks upon Shannon, with the outcome that a challenge by one of Shannon's sons, or perhaps a bloody feud between the families, seemed inevitable. Apparently to prevent this, Colonel Shannon himself challenged Colonel Cash. Shannon was killed at the first fire, July 5, 1880. The first trial of Cash resulted, to the outrage of the ancient duelist element, in a mistrial, and the second in an acquittal. A letter two days after the duel from Associate (later Chief) Justice McIver of the State Supreme Court assuring Cash that he could understand "how impossible it was for you to permit even the semblance of an imputation to rest upon the memory of a devoted wife" was typical of many, whose writers doubtless assumed that, as usual, no trial would occur, or, if any, a mere formality. But General M. C. Butler publicly denounced Cash's abusive hounding, contrary to the accustomed dignity of affairs of honor, of an attorney in the performance of his duty to his client.[4]

There were several duels after this in South Carolina or between South Carolinians who went outside the State to fight, but none of them was fatal. The law of 1881 disqualifying for office any person acting as principal or second in a duel, or even carrying a challenge, from that date ended formal dueling. The unreadiness of public opinion

[4] Cash MSS, University of South Carolina Library. I stated erroneously in my three-volume *History of South Carolina* that the later Chief Justice Watts was Cash's second. Watts was Ellerbe's second in the latter's challenge to Shannon, which Shannon declined as not from a gentleman. Willie Saunders was Cash's second.

for accepting the abolition of personal combat as a means of settling grievances was long demonstrated by the mounting number of homicides, in which the safeguards of deliberation and fairness imposed by the code play no part.

Governors Hagood and Thompson.—Brigadier-General Hagood, elected governor in 1880, well represented the ante-bellum class who had so long ruled the State. An incisive thinker and excellent administrator, an advocate of scientific agriculture, he probably enjoyed more his presidency of the State Agricultural Society than the governorship, to which he positively declined re-election.

A bitter contest between Generals John Bratton and John D. Kennedy in the convention of 1882 was prevented by the nomination of Hugh S. Thompson as a "dark horse." Whatever may have been the faults of the convention system, its virtues were here illustrated. Thompson was completing six years of notable work as superintendent of education. He made an eminently successful governor. He resigned July 10, 1886, to become second assistant secretary of the United States Treasury. Later, as civil service commissioner and as comptroller of the New York Life Insurance Company, he commanded nation-wide respect as an executive.

The Charleston Earthquake, 1886.—A dozen shocks in South Carolina from 1698 to 1876 are recorded before the disaster of 1886. The great earthquake of August 31, 1886, was preceded by a light tremor in June in Charleston and two slight tremors separated by several hours at Summerville, August 27, and one on August 28. The great shock came on August 31 at 9:51 at night. It was accompanied by a loud roaring noise. Four shocks followed in rapid succession. Slight shocks continued with great frequency for many months. The total in the years 1886-1913 in the Charleston-Summerville region was 351.

The severity of the Charleston earthquake was greatly limited because the crystalline rocks in which the faulting occurred a half mile below the surface were covered with a very soft, water-soaked soil. The seriousness of the faulting is indicated by the enormous area disturbed, 2,800,000 square miles, the largest on record. The Charleston quake had two centers, one halfway between Charleston and Summerville and the other about thirteen miles due west of Charleston. There were ninety-two persons killed in the Charleston quake, all of whom were either in the streets or rushing out of houses. Property damage exceeded $5,000,000. Relief funds were contributed to the extent of $792,733, of which $180,559 came from New York State, $99,846 from Massachusetts, and $18,208 from South Carolina.

Slight shocks occurred in Union County in 1912 and 1913, and a slight one was felt in many parts of the State on July 26, 1945.

CHAPTER LVIII

AGRARIANISM AND DEMOCRATIC REVOLUTION, 1886-1894

John C. Sheppard of Edgefield, who filled out the last five months of Thompson's second term, was defeated for the 1886 nomination by John P. Richardson of Clarendon. Governor Richardson, of the Manning-Richardson group of six governors, was the son of one Governor, the nephew by marriage of another, the grandnephew of another, and the first cousin of another. It was his misfortune to assume office just when the regime which he represented was to encounter in a peculiarly violent form its share of an almost nation-wide agrarian and democratic upheaval which neither his aristocratic antecedents nor his moderate talents fitted him to meet.

Following the laws of 1882 eliminating the Negro vote, men were freer to vent their grievances. Primary elections were held in 1876 in Fairfield, Pickens, and Abbeville and were recommended by the State executive committee in 1878 for all county officers. This was in effect a revival of our ante-bellum custom, explained the Winnsboro *News and Herald,* for, as South Carolina had been a one-party State, every voter had had in the general election his full and free share in choosing officers. Only the necessity of organizing in conventions during Reconstruction had deprived the voter of this right, which was now to be rescued from convention rule and caucuses. Every county had the primary before 1890 for local officers and legislators. When the low country in 1882 rejected the "Greenville idea" of representation in the State convention on the basis of Democratic voters instead of the total population of each county, the tendency toward a State-wide primary was greatly strengthened. This disproportionate power of the white minority in the low country in the legislature and party conventions still exists on account of its large silent Negro population.

Tillman Organizes the Farmers' Movement.—The economic distress of the eighties made agitation easy. Tillmanism was the South Carolina aspect of a movement sweeping the South and West for righting the farmer's and the poor man's wrongs. It was propelled by the hopes and indignation of men who had been taught by the Grange that government could relieve their ills, the brooding resentments of the devotees of Gary, the ambitions of a younger generation of shrewd politicians, and the passionate belief of many in the enthronement of the common man. Benjamin Ryan Tillman (1847-1918), the leader of the new movement, though not of the aristocracy, whose air of superiority his family resented, was of the strong, intelligent, well-to-do sort, inferior to the highest only in polite culture. There was in his stock a desperate strain that flowered in numerous homicides in peace and distinguished gallantry in war. As a forerunner of Benjamin, his brother George, twenty years older, was denouncing, before the war and in 1865, the parish system that gave a few hundred low-country planters the same representation as thousands of up-country farmers.

In 1881 B. R. Tillman was a successful farmer running thirty plows. Four years of crop failures and falling prices turned the successful, happy farmer into a thinker and agitator on the misfortunes of himself and his class. In an address before the South Carolina Agricultural and Mechanical Society and the Grange in 1885 he shocked the assembled planters[1] and gentlemen farmers by his ruthless exposure of the agricultural evils and of some "disreputable politicians" in the Agricultural Society. Half the landowners, he said, were "hewers of wood and drawers of water. . . . The yoke of the credit system that used to gall no longer frets. The decay of that sturdy independence of character, which once was so marked in our people, is rapid, and the lazy 'descent into hell' is facilitated by the State government, which has encouraged this reliance on others. . . . The people are being hoodwinked by demagogues and by lawyers in the pay of finance."

This address created a State-wide sensation and publicly launched the "Farmers' Movement," soon to be merged into the Tillman movement, which was to make him the political dictator of the State. With the pen of a rural Junius and an unrivaled gift of stump oratory, whose quality challenged the scholar's admiration and roused the unlettered masses, he presented ideas of agricultural reform which rallied to him many of the leading farmers of the State. The South Carolina College at once sought to make its agricultural annex more practical. But his uncompromising demand was for a separate agricultural college, experimental stations, and farmers' institutes. He organized the Farmers' Movement, in whose annual convention he preached that though the farmers were three-fourths of the population they did not govern the State. The State government, he charged, had degenerated from antebellum purity to "political leprosy."

It was hard to co-operate with a man who said such things, and the

[1] The large low-country farmers, particularly near the coast, are commonly called planters. The term is not used in the up country.

men who were slandered did not feel inclined to try. Personal and class hostility thus became an outstanding feature of South Carolina politics for a generation, embittering a business by nature bitter enough and hindering all co-operative helpfulness. The slanderous, raucous Tillman and the stiff, contemptuous element of the upper crust at whom he sneered as "broken down politicians and superannuated Bourbon aristocrats, who are thoroughly incompetent, but are ready to put in their claims for every position of honor and profit," must both share the blame. That thousands of men of good birth embraced the popular movement does not alter the fact that the Tillman movement was mainly along class lines. There had been many leaders who had risen from the ranks, but they had assumed the attitude and manner of the class to which their success secured them entrance. Now, as Professor Simkins says, for the first time the farmers of the State were led by a man who saw life from their angle and spoke their ideas.

The Farmers' Movement, which in 1886 and 1888 had barely missed controlling the State Democratic Convention and would doubtless have won if a direct appeal to the electorate had been possible, was now a definite political organization. In 1888 the demand for a State primary was a second time refused, but the demand that in 1890 State candidates must be invited by every county chairman to speak in their respective counties was granted.

The Founding of Clemson College.—The Farmers' Movement's winning control of the House in 1888 derived immense significance from the circumstance that in April of that year Thomas G. Clemson died leaving property worth about $90,000 (the bulk of his estate) to the State for founding an agricultural and mechanical college.[2] Tillman was thus afforded a favorable setting to fight for his leading demand.

Clemson, born in Philadelphia in 1807, became a friend of Calhoun, whose daughter Anna Maria he married. For some years as a farmer, first in South Carolina and later in Maryland, educated in science, he put his ideas into practice. Concealing his fortune in the North, he served the Confederacy in supervising mines and metal works, and from the surrender lived at Pendleton or at Fort Hill (the later Clemson College) until his death. Clemson sought from 1866 to establish a scientific institution in upper South Carolina. After buying at public sale for his wife and daughter the John C. Calhoun homestead, Fort

[2] His granddaughter, for whom he made equitable provision, unsuccessfully attacked the will. Prejudices against Clemson as a Yankee, as a rationalist, and as a six-foot-six-inch recluse considered peculiar, and the antipathy of certain enemies filled the State with slanderous and absurd stories, and later sought to eliminate from the college the name of a man notable in America for a type of education the State so much needed. He had saved the Calhoun property with his own money.

Hill, his mind turned to this as a proper location. This great educational advance was jealously regarded by many friends of the existing State and denominational colleges, not to speak of mere reactionaries. In 1889 the House readily and the Senate barely accepted the conditions. The college opened in 1893 with 446 students, at that time much the largest number in any institution in the State. Despite some bungling in early years and atrocious public meddling in the then somewhat frequent student disorders, the institution has accomplished in considerable degree what should have been done in South Carolina generations ago.

Mutually Unappreciative Aristocracy and Democracy.—Tillman was criticized for not subsiding, for he had said he would not seek office, now that his aim of agricultural education had been attained. That Tillman was a selfish office-seeker as well as an agrarian prophet is not to be denied; but indignation at his self-seeking ignored the fact that it was not peculiar to him or his followers, who now rushed to the public crib with a greediness shocking to their predecessors, who had concealed hunger under better manners.

Irrespective of Tillman, the democratic upheaval which had been so long held back by circumstances was overdue. It assumed its lamentable form partly because of Tillman's personality and partly because of the selfishness and narrow class outlook of the ruling element who, despite their admirable virtues, were blind to the fact that they lived in a new day with new needs. The undercurrent of democracy so strongly manifested in the 1760's, in the years following the Revolution, and intermittently later when it was not submerged in the vortex of external dangers, was sure soon to sweep South Carolina as it had swept western Europe and the North. The old South Carolina, with its contrasted low-country and up-country civilization, with the marked individuality of the coastal border and of such up-country regions as Edgefield, Abbeville, York, and Camden, before standardized universal education, good roads, and the automobile had smoothed them down to a monotonous similarity, was about to crumble.

The earlier South Carolinians had lived in a spacious isolation fostering individuality, self-reliance, and self-assertion, all of which had been accentuated by the long-continued attitude toward the Union as a possible enemy. At this aristocratic civilization the war struck a crippling blow. To this was added after 1876 the conflict of agrarianism and industrialism. The old ruling class was kept in power for a brief period after the overthrow of the Negro by the fear of his return and by patriotic memories. The picturesque, characteristic South Carolina was passing into the twilight of the gods, for its leaders knew not how to bend their stiff pride to hold their leadership under new conditions, as they might have done for the inestimable benefit of a people sorely needing the services which the best of them could have afforded. But there was a fatal lack of touch, particularly below Columbia, between the masses and these often impoverished gentlemen sneered at by new men as "broken down aristocracy." They were no longer popular leaders in defense of Southern civilization, but often pathetic clingers to office as a means of livelihood. South Carolina was about to have one form of class government roughly superseded by another which, though supplying some of the former's deficiencies, lacked some of its virtues.

Though the end of the old regime was at hand, its representatives could look back with pride on their record of capable, though rather unprogressive, but above all upright, government. It was government by gentlemen, which, despite the narrow outlook of all class government, has distinct advantages no other class government possesses. Tillman, who to gain power did not scruple to slander them, as a United States senator in 1897 paid the highest tribute to their integrity. It is the tragedy of South Carolina's politics since 1890 and of her life in general that in repudiating her ancient aristocracy and their shortcomings she has also in sad measure forgotten their virtues, which are the most precious heritage of the Old South.

The March Convention, 1890.—It is true that with 1889 a large part of the formal program of the Farmers' Movement had been achieved; but that is no adequate ground for those who criticize Tillman's emergence as a candidate for governor in 1890. In addition to the demand for specific measures, there was the desire of the masses to wrest political control from a class notoriously out of touch with the common man. In mere numbers they had always been able to control; but circumstances and the power of tradition had prevented. They had been drained of their natural leadership by its absorption in the upper class. But now new conditions enabled a unique leader to precipitate, with startling suddenness, elements long held in suspense. On January 13, 1890, appeared the "Shell Manifesto" (written, we now know, by Tillman) calling a convention of Farmers' Movement supporters for March 27, to nominate State officers and plan for controlling, within the Democratic party, the coming election. It was time, it proclaimed, "for the common people, who redeemed South Carolina from radical rule, to take charge of it. Can we afford to leave it longer in the hands of those who, wedded to ante-bellum ideas, but with little of the ante-bellum patriotism and honor, are running it for the benefit of a few families and for the benefit of a ring of selfish politicians?"

The motion to "suggest" candidates (the word "nominate" being withdrawn by Shell) failed by one vote. John L. M. Irby, Tillman's most brilliant, desperate, and accomplished lieutenant, turned defeat into victory by inducing a few to change while the chairman withheld his announcement.[3]

The ticket headed by Tillman commanded respect for ability and character and proved how much wider than merely the farmers were the group that demanded a new deal in politics; for, apart from some who desperately needed the offices, there were men above such necessity who would have been a credit to any administration. The complete absence from the ticket of men representing the tenant farmer or the then comparatively new factory operative class suggests how far the pandering to them later in our history was absent from the movement of 1885 to '90. It was distinctly a land-owning farmers' movement, co-operated in by their sympathizers. Unfortunately, from the moment of the manifestation of its power, it gathered politicians who preyed upon it—"Tillman's coat tail swingers."

The Campaign of 1890.—Under widespread pressure the State Democratic Executive Committee granted Tillman's demand for a joint debate in each county between the candidates for State offices.[4] This provided Tillman with the best possible stage for his unrivalled powers of popular appeal. Near the end of a bitter campaign, in which long-pent-up passions repeatedly threatened violence, the State convention met in August to frame the party rules. The Conservatives, as Tillman's opponents called themselves, demanded that the nominating convention to meet September 15 should be elected by a primary. The Tillman faction, knowing that their control of the county conventions would give their faction a large representation and assure the election of their entire State ticket, refused. A new party constitution, little changed since, except that beginning in 1896 State officers and United States senators have been nominated by direct primary, replaced that of 1876.[5]

[3] Irby said in 1897 that he originated the idea of the March convention a year beforehand, and that, at the crisis, "I cheated the question of nomination in," which he justified on the ground that some were voting who had no right to be present.

After Tillman's opposition to him for re-election to the Senate, where Irby's fast living had put him into disrepute, Irby in a newspaper interview virtually warned Tillman to be prepared for one to kill the other when they met. Irby was a desperate man of intellectual ability and aggressive and attractive personality. In his trial for the murder of Kilgore his acquittal turned on the uncertainty as to whether his was the fatal bullet. Though posing as the special friend of the poor man, he on one occasion horsewhipped, or even worse, made a Negro horsewhip, a poor white man who had offended him. He was of good Revolutionary ancestry on his father's and of distinguished family on his mother's side. He was an example of what disturbed conditions, heavy drinking, and a passionate disposition not infrequently produced in the South Carolina of his youth.

[4] The resolution of the convention of 1888 only ordered the county chairman to invite the candidates to speak, but did not require the State Executive Committee to order and arrange a county-to-county campaign.

[5] Simkins, *Pitchfork Ben Tillman*, pp. 149, 162.

To return to the campaign: The Conservatives, without organization, were represented by Joseph H. Earle and General John Bratton, both suited by character and ability, and Earle by legal training, for the governorship. How little Tillman's quality was understood was revealed by the attempt to cow him at the Columbia meeting in retaliation for the howling down at other meetings of the Conservative candidates, which resulted, through his boldness and brilliant repartee, in a triumph's being handed him by his enemies. In revenge for Columbia, General Hampton was howled down at Aiken. The era of hoodlumism that for several decades was intermittently to reign was fully under way. The county-to-county campaign, with both sides on the same stand, has proved itself a means of eliciting the maximum of passion and the minimum of reason, and should have been at once abandoned as a demonstrated blunder. It was a war measure suited only to such purposes as it had served so well in 1876. Its continuance has been one of the chief agencies for debasing public life.

Colonel A. C. Haskell, declaring the regular party convention in September which nominated Tillman, "illegal and void," summoned a convention to make opposition nominations for the general election, because of the slanderous, disloyal, and illegal course of the "Reformers" since the Shell Manifesto. He would appeal to the Negro, he said, for election, but would allow the Negro no offices. The Haskell convention, October 9, contained some outstanding men and many of sterling character. So blind were these gentlemen as to believe that they could save the State by making the Negro the arbiter of its politics, thus affording another illustration that those whose eminence elevates them above possible economic competition with Negroes and gives them an easy control over them as employees are less reliable guardians against Negro political activity than are men whose daily lives bring them much nearer to racial and economic realities.

The passions of the period are today almost incredible. Said the Haskell convention, "We further solemnly allege that B. R. Tillman . . . has done more harm and brought greater sorrow on the State than the sword or the hand of man in any other shape has effected." The tragic blunder, the secret comfort of every possible unprincipled seeker for power through the Negro, was endorsed by the Republican executive committee, but the Negro paid no heed. His attempt to vote would, in the state of feeling, have precipitated bloodshed. Tillman received 59,159 votes to Haskell's 14,828. Haskell's Straightouts carried only Beaufort and Berkeley, and were strong elsewhere only in Charleston, Colleton, Florence, Georgetown, Horry, Fairfield, Marion, Richland, Sumter, Union, and Williamsburg counties. With a few exceptions these were counties in which vast Negro populations rendered white unity peculiarly essential, and which in 1876 generally showed themselves unable or uninclined to protect themselves by the vigorous methods used in some counties.[6]

The Social Aspects of Tillmanism.—There is a tendency among anti-Tillmanites to minimize the importance of Tillman's achievements and to deny the reality of the rising of the masses to overthrow the aristocracy. The assertion or denial that Tillmanism overthrew aristocratic rule rests on the definition of aristocratic. In 1890, to large masses it meant all who were distinctively above them in worldly goods and culture. In higher circles it meant only those whose distinction was of several generations, and perhaps might not include newer men freely admitted to aristocratic associations because of talent, wealth, and gentlemanly character. And so on, with all degrees of snobbery or envy, to the fine old families of a distinction antedating the Revolution.

The South Carolina democracy is utterly unsubmissive. Suspicion of disdain or memory of it even to a grandfather is a potent force. Of such disdain by the "aristocrats," sometimes exhibited very offensively, there was enough in itself to raise a revolution. The truth is that a large part of the ruling element, in this crisis of the State's history, lacked the insight to realize that Tillman was anything but a ranting country cracker; they opposed to him an attitude in which selfishness and narrowness of view counted for as much as outraged class and State pride. The way in which they met the crisis sustained Tillman's charge that they were not fitted to give South Carolina what she needed.

On the other side was abundance of mere envy of culture and success, as well as of just resentment and of foolish faith that "Moses" Tillman (or "Jesus" Tillman, one man called him) could raise the price of cotton and make it easier to pay the lien merchant. Its strongest motive was mere democratic self-assertion. Says Tillmanite Thomas J. Kirkland, "At bottom the people seem to have been chiefly animated by a craze for equality, one of the profound passions of the human heart," and not to have cared a fig for economy or anything else, for they soon

[6] Reports and Res. 1890, I, 604; *News and Courier,* November 22, 1890. Colonel Haskell told the writer in 1909 that he had urged on old leaders that some change must be made in managing the politics of the State to avoid an upheaval, and that looking back on 1890, he realized that an upheaval was inevitable.—D. D. W.'s memorandum of November 1, 1910.

Mr. Joseph W. Barnwell, the Haskell candidate for Attorney General, told the writer on November 30, 1929, that the move was the utmost folly, but that "we felt we could not let Haskell stand alone"; that some tickets were sent out from Columbia to be distributed to Negroes, but that no move was made to organize them. Other sources prove that what slight thought there was of that plan on the part of a few men in the low country was confused and impracticable.

allowed the expenses of government to increase. As to Tillman's overthrowing the aristocracy, we may say that he overthrew the rule of the aristocracy and the upper class by the help of a goodly fraction of the upper middle class as leaders of the masses. As Tillmanism degenerated, mere prejudice became worse, and class antagonism remained the strongest force in South Carolina politics.

How could such events occur? South Carolina farms in 1890 were burdened with mortgages; in many cases South Carolina crops were picked only to be delivered to the lien merchant for goods already consumed. Cotton was selling at nearly its lowest price in history. South Carolina had allowed entirely too many of her adult whites to grow to maturity absolutely illiterate, and at least as large a percentage in addition, practically illiterate. As when clouds charged with opposite electricities are roused in storm, there occurred a terrific lightning flash. After all, the most important facts of history are states of mind.

Tillman in Power.—The clearness and force of Tillman's inaugural address commanded the respect of his enemies. No radical, but a rough type of the conservative Southern landowner, he denied the equality of men, white or black. He asked for authority to remove sheriffs who failed to protect their prisoners from mobs. His demand for a three-dollar poll tax was not the tactics of a demagogue. Reading the message's recommendation of educational advance and reform in taxation and institutional administration compelled an opponent to pronounce it "perhaps the strongest state paper we have ever read." The important legislation of his term was in answer to his demands. The "University," consisting of the South Carolina College, Claflin, and the Citadel, was dissolved into its three parts. Though he took no steps to crush the college, whose students had "soured" him by following him to his hotel with insulting songs in March, 1890, or the Citadel "dude factory," which he considered useless, his active support was given to two new institutions emphasizing the practical—Clemson and Winthrop.

No corruption under the regime he overthrew was discovered. For carelessness in the Asylum, the board was reorganized and the superintendent displaced. Representation of 1876, ten years out of date, in defiance of the Constitution, was re-apportioned, Charleston losing over a third of its members, other low-country counties one each, and the up country correspondingly gaining.

Some readjustment of tax assessments was made to throw more of the burden on banks and railroads. The Governor enforced his desires, where possible, against judicial orders by threatening auditors with removal, and, when checked by judges, demanded that they be not re-elected. His repeated blows at the courts, unseating judges eminent for independence and ability, and finally assisting in writing into the Constitution provisions weakening both the Circuit and the Supreme Court, have inflicted incalculable damage to the most precious public interests. He seldom or never stooped to persuasion, but crushed opposition. He imparted an efficiency to government which, under our American system of deadlock and hindrances called "checks and balances," can be obtained only by such extra-legal autocracy.

Tillman's phosphate policy, seeking to correct the sacrifice both of the natural resources and of the interests of the State government perpetrated by the Radical charters then expiring, calls for slight notice, as the industry was facing death from outside competition when he forced through new corporate relations and doubled the royalty rate to the State. His system, roughly imposed in ignorance and anger on a sick industry, hastened its collapse, though the system might have been an improvement if Floridian, Tennesseean, and Algerian competition had allowed South Carolina phosphates to survive. In 1894 the royalty was reduced to fifty cents a ton, but by 1904 every river mining company had failed or suspended.

Naturally the Governor of the "Reformers" (as Tillman called his faction) was unable to reduce expenditures in the face of his enlarged educational program. Hampton's administration, coming into office in protest against Republican extravagance, had cut expenses almost in half, and this extreme economy had been continued under his successors. As everywhere, the enlarged social functions of government that democracy always brings soon began the swelling of South Carolina taxes and expenditures, which did not cease until it was temporarily checked under the compulsion of the great depression beginning in 1929.

The ugliest feature of Tillman's first administration was refusing General Wade Hampton re-election to the Senate. Irby, Tillman's political manager, had to be rewarded, though he was unworthy of such promotion. No single act of the greedy victors was more injurious in its immediate results on interclass relations than turning out the leader of 1876.

The greed for office of Reformers exceeded that of the "Bourbon aristocrats" whom they had denounced for this sin. The natural concentration of offices in families interested in politics appeared among those who had denounced it as undemocratic. Four members of the family of Mart Gary, for instance, were given high places.

Tillman entered the 1892 campaign with the demand that the "driftwood legislature" be dismissed (because it had had the independence in some matters to resist him), and one be chosen to do his will. The request was met by the election of 102 Tillmanite representatives almost universally subservient, 22 Conservatives, and a Senate of 28 Tillmanites to 8 Conservatives. The campaign was more violent than that of 1890, barely missing, at several places, combat between candidates or general riot. The Haskellites were readmitted to communion on the oath to support the nominees of the party.

The Conservatives in 1892 nominated in a convention J. C. Sheppard for governor and James L. Orr for lieutenant-governor, thus imitating the 1890 precedent of the Reformers, which, unhappily, has not been continued as a practice within the Democratic party, for each faction to put forward its best men. They were defeated by about 54,500 to 32,500 in the county primaries for delegates to the State Convention, the Reformers, as practical politicians, again refusing to sacrifice their power of gaining a larger representation by swinging entire county delegations.

A feature of the election of 1892 was the defeat of George D. Tillman for Congress by Jasper W. Talbert because of his refusal to swallow the Farmers' Alliance Program, which the Tillmanites had adopted. George Tillman was never a member of his brother's faction. Professor F. B. Simkins in his *Pitchfork Ben Tillman,*[7] concludes that the rumors are groundless that B. R. Tillman betrayed George in 1892 or that he sacrificed him to Irby in the 1890 senatorial election because he considered that his brother's presence in the Senate would hinder his own election in 1894. Nevertheless, this was the beginning of George's hatred of his younger brother which later blazed into public conflict.

Creation of the Dispensary.—Tillman's second administration was almost an unbroken success. Measures now practically universally endorsed were passed over Conservative opposition, neither faction being able to see good in anything identified with the other. Railroad regulation was made more effective; labor in textile mills was limited to sixty-six hours a week. Confederate pensions were increased, salaries cut 10 per cent, taxation reduced a half mill, and the State debt refunded at 4.5 instead of 6 per cent. In addition, Tillman forced upon an unwilling legislature and people a revolutionary liquor law, and enforced it against armed uprising with an ability that elicited admiration from out-of-State opinion for his maintenance of law. Not even at the height of Calhoun's dominance had there been a more startling exhibition of control by a powerful personality.

Tillman's legislation on the liquor problem holds an important place among his acts and in the history of American state socialism. Its substitution for prohibition, though prohibition had been demanded by popular referendum and the legislature had already decided upon it,

[7] Pp. 207-8.

was an astonishing exercise of his dictatorship. Tillman was neither a teetotaler nor a reformer of other men's conduct. He drank "only when he wanted it," and supposed he had consumed less than a gallon for each of his fifty-nine years. He was an extreme individualist, a disbeliever in the enforceability of prohibition, and a thorough utilitarian. The prohibition bill had passed the House and was about to pass the Senate when Tillman demanded instead a State monopoly. Astonished South Carolina found herself, on December 24, 1892, by the casting vote of Lieutenant-Governor Gary, saddled with a momentous change in public policy of which she had hardly heard and which she did not desire.

The Dispensary State Board of Control consisted originally of the governor, the comptroller-general, and the attorney-general. The governor appointed the commissioner to operate the system. The State Board of Control appointed county boards of control, which appointed one dispenser for each county to do business at the county seat, except that there might be three for Columbia and ten for Charleston. Towns other than the county seat might have dispensaries if the County Board of Control approved; but in any case a majority of the freeholder voters must petition for it. No users of liquor might be officials, and no dispenser might sell to any minor, addict, or intoxicated person. The purchaser must sign an application, to remain on public file, for his package from a half pint to five gallons, which could not be opened on the premises. Stringent regulations forbade private manufacture or sale of intoxicants, but persons might make wine for their own use. Profits of the State Dispensary went into the State Treasury, and those of local dispensaries to the municipality and county equally. Counties or towns already under prohibition were not affected until later.

Hatred of Tillman was so intense after his decreeing the defeat of Hampton as frequently to cause the enforcement of the new liquor law to verge on riot. Darlington, bitterly opposed to Tillman and flagrant in violation of the law, was so wrought up by false reports that constables were to search homes without warrants that a secret association was formed to resist this by force. To meet the encouragement to "blind tiger" liquor-sellers Governor Tillman sent to Darlington twenty-two constables. The constables, March 30, 1894, after searching the yard of a Negro suspect without results, were awaiting the train to depart. Two citizens had had a fisticuff, and one, accompanied by five companions, pointed out Constable McLendon as having held him while his antagonist beat him. "You are a liar, you" vile and-so-forth, said the constable. "Yes, and you're another damned" vile ditto, chipped in a citizen spectator. "I won't take that," said Constable McLendon, and shot the man dead.

When the general firing which this precipitated on both sides was over, another citizen and one constable lay dead, and a number of men were painfully wounded.

Captain Henry T. Thompson, gathering a handful of his militia, protected the wounded constable. The mob, composed of eminently respectable citizens, wrecked the dispensary, fired on the train bearing some constables away because it would not stop, and scoured the country unsuccessfully for those secreted, with threats of lynching.

The Columbia *State,* which habitually denounced mob violence toward even the vilest criminals, declared the dead citizens "martyrs of Liberty" whose "lifeblood stains yet glorifies the bosom of their mother State," and gloried in the offer of Columbians to help Darlington.

Governor Tillman declared Darlington and Florence counties in rebellion. Many militia companies refused to obey and were dishonorably dismissed as "bandbox soldiers." The Governor then organized a militia from the rural districts and assumed control of all municipal police, the railroads, and the telegraph, the latter in order to stop the inflammatory appeals that were threatening riot in Columbia, which in the existing excitement and class hatred might have assumed serious proportions. One of the leading citizens of Columbia was deterred from his efforts to persuade the troops to desert by their commander's threat to fire.

Before the troops reached Darlington the better sense of the community had re-established peace. In England and the North the same class as those in South Carolina whose sympathies were with the mob complimented the Governor for his promptness and efficiency. Tillman, doubtless with exaggeration, always held that his "fearless assumption of responsibility had nipped the bud of revolt before the deadly flower could unfold its poisonous petals." It was one of the ugliest manifestations of defiance to authority in South Carolina history, and left in a poor light our two leading journals, habitual denouncers of lynchers of rapists, now loosing their own passions against the officers of the law in sympathy with a property-destroying mob of man-hunters.

Almost immediately after "the Darlington war" the two anti-Tillman Supreme Court judges, overruling their Tillmanite associate, annulled the dispensary as an unconstitutional monopoly. Justice McGowan, whom Tillman had had defeated, soon left the bench, and Tillman's new judge, E. B. Gary, had the satisfaction of writing the opinion sustaining the revised dispensary act identical in principle.

The 1894 gubernatorial campaign was a contest among Reform

leaders for Tillman's support, as the Conservatives abandoned all effort at organization after 1892. Tillman declined to choose between farmer Ellerbe, "a bashful backwoodsman," and the impeccably dressed and accomplished combative lawyer of distinguished ancestry, John Gary Evans, who had served him so well as legislative leader, and whose ability and determination were needed particularly for defending the dispensary.[8] Evans was nominated in a Reform convention elected in a Reform primary, denounced by the unsuccessful as "ring rule." Tillman refused to allow a Democratic primary, as the Conservative vote would have caused the election of the more moderate Ellerbe, and Evans as a matter of course was nominated by the regular Democratic State Convention. Evans' temporary success by "the Colleton plan" and his placing the metropolitan police in Charleston to enforce the dispensary law account for his three defeats for United States senator.

Tillman's Influence, Good and Bad.—The race for the senatorship in 1894 brought Tillman for the first time intimately in touch with national issues. He heartily accepted the demands for the free coinage of silver at 16 to 1, the increase of money, by the use of paper if necessary, up to $50 per capita, and the abolition of national banks—points which the bulk of the Reformers and probably a good portion of the Conservatives favored; but he refused to accept the government ownership of railroads, telegraphs, and telephones, and the scheme for the government to lend money directly to the people demanded by the Farmers' Alliance.

After a campaign of such acrimony as to threaten physical combat with his opponent, Tillman defeated General M. C. Butler for re-election before the legislature by 131 to 21. A fiercely dominant man whom his lieutenants more feared than loved, the unexampled idol of the masses, he passed into the Senate with a national reputation based mainly on the uglier aspects of his character.

The good and evil of his influence, deeply incised in the history of the State, it is yet too early confidently to apportion. The admirer of brilliant fighting qualities will cherish his career as a stirring drama. At worst, Tillman was only one factor in the inevitable opening of the floodgates to world-wide democracy. He uncovered as well as created faults, for South Carolina as he found her had been left by her former rulers singularly unfitted to meet the strain of democracy. Who is more to blame, Tillman or his predecessors? His accepting free railroad passes and telegraph franks after having denounced such as corrupt in his predecessors was a cheapness unworthy of a mind capable of the appre-

[8] Professor F. B. Simkins in his *Pitchfork Ben Tillman*, p. 275, holds that the commonly held belief that Tillman favored Evans and deferred Ellerbe is erroneous.

ciation of the virtues of South Carolina's past, as was manifested in his able and eloquent oration at the unveiling of the tomb of Marion. His forcing his clerks, paid entirely by the Federal government, to work on his farm without any other pay[9] was a cheap coarseness little better than graft.

In the dispensary Tillman imposed upon South Carolina the most profound, insidious, and widespread agency of corruption in her history; but in this he was dealing with a business which has vexed civilized man for ages and under all forms has generated crime and corruption. Altogether lamentable were Tillman's attacks upon the judiciary. He punished judges for their opinions, and in the Constitution of 1895 allowed, if he did not encourage, the diminution of their legitimate authority as effective agents of justice.

Passing to more favorable aspects of Tillman's influence (and let us remember there will be much to commend in his career as senator), his influence on the Constitution of 1895 is, except for the judiciary, admirable. Tillman and the conservative leaders co-operated in devising the safeguards against Negro suffrage. To Tillman's continued insistence is chiefly due the undertaking of the calling of a convention for that purpose.

Tillman's influence was powerful in securing liberal support for Clemson and Winthrop colleges until this became an established habit. Though he urged better schools for the masses, he did nothing notable for them, and his intense individualism, his instinct against political inexpediency, and his fear of forcing the Negro into school left him cold to proposals for compulsory education.

With labor, either rural or urban, he had no special sympathy. He was less a creative reformer than the attacker of obnoxious delinquencies. The State's industrial development, which went forward rapidly in the 1880's and 1890's, came mainly after his social and economic ideas had taken permanent shape; but there appears little ground for the charge that he drove away outside capital. A fair chance for the land-owning farmers largely summed up his social program. Modern social legislation had no place with this intensely individualistic, highly conservative landed proprietor. Tillman, less philosophical than his better-educated brother George, if he had been widely and thoroughly educated might, with his power, his practical, utilitarian, common-sense mind, have produced remarkable results and have added more materially to his achievements as a statesman rather than an agitator.

[9] Simkins, *Pitchfork Ben Tillman,* p. 475. Professor Simkins says nothing about room and board.

A calm and detached view of the circumstances forces the conclusion that there was much in South Carolina government before 1890 that needed change; that those in control, with few exceptions, stubbornly resisted change; and that those who forced change did so with an entirely useless, damaging, and frequently unscrupulous violence. In the years of bitterness that followed, prejudice was so rampant on both sides as to make a humiliating story. Measures were lauded or condemned for no better reason than that they were associated with adored or detested leaders.

CHAPTER LIX

THE END OF THE REFORM PARTY, 1895-1902

FEAR OF RENEWED participation of the Negro in politics had long troubled the lower South, as is evidenced by a number of new State constitutions since 1890. Tillman's demand since 1885 for a new constitution succeeded in securing a referendum in the general election of 1894. Conservatives opposed, for fear of Tillmanism's being grafted into the fundamental law; and many Tillmanites, for fear that illiterate whites would be disfranchised. A change of 940 votes would have turned the referendum against a convention. Guarding the suffrage was rendered more urgent by Haskell's appealing in 1890 to the Negro, supported by a goodly proportion of the upper class, on the theory of preventing the evils feared from the supremacy of the roughly led white masses by substituting control through Negro votes under the frail safeguard of decent white leadership. Another appeal based on belief in the possibility of good government without a good electorate was the call by Dr. Sampson Pope, the Independent candidate for governor in 1894, for a convention of Republicans of all colors to meet on April 14, 1896. The danger thus threatened from both sides; for Dr. Pope had been an active Tillmanite and a champion of the dispensary. Some white Republicans and a few Democratic converts feebly joined in the suggestion for that classic futility, "a respectable Republican party" in South Carolina.

The constitutional convention of 1895 brought the first co-operation between factions and mollified the bitterness that had culminated in Tillman's second administration. The brewings within his own faction, and also the possibility of the Negroes' along with Conservatives' defeating his constitution if the latter were not treated fairly, led Tillman to an agreement for complete white co-operation. Senator Tillman and Governor Evans agreed with two leading Conservatives (J. C. Hemphill, editor of the *News and Courier,* and Joseph W. Barnwell) for a joint ticket in each county equally representing both factions. When extremists on both sides scouted the plan, Tillman repudiated it, with the result that the convention contained 40 Conservatives and 114 Tillmanites, or, as they called themselves, Reformers. The Republicans captured the entire Beaufort delegation (five Negroes) and one (a Negro) of the Georgetown delegation.[1]

[1] The *News and Courier* named 43 as Conservatives, but on August 26 agreed with

Eliminating the Negro Vote.—Senator Tillman was the outstanding leader in the convention. Governor Evans' opening address as president made many suggestions that were adopted, including penalizing a county for lynchings, and others that might well have been adopted in the interest of executive and legislative efficiency. The work of constitution-making derived valuable aid from the legal and legislative abilities of the Conservatives J. P. K. Bryan and Theodore G. Barker of Charleston, J. C. Sheppard and George D. Tillman of Edgefield, George Johnstone of Newberry, and D. S. Henderson of Aiken. Julian Mitchell of Charleston contributed prominently to the educational clauses.

The suffrage clause is said by Joseph W. Barnwell to be indebted principally to J. P. K. Bryan for the skill with which it excluded Negro voters without running afoul of Federal law. It was opposed in able, eloquent speeches by the Negro Thomas E. Miller, for some years president of the State Negro College at Orangeburg, and by the notorious Negro corruptionists of Reconstruction days, Whipper and Smalls. Whipper's and Smalls' references to the past brought upon them Sheppard's cold narrative of the evidence of their and their associates' crimes as it had passed before him as a member of the investigating committee of 1877. A heated argument was waged between Irby, the champion of the freedom of white illiterates to vote, and Tillman, who contended that any man coming of age after 1898 who failed to learn to read and write did not deserve to vote. Tillman had his way in the convention, but Irby's desire has been fulfilled by officials' registering whites with no questions asked as to their property or literacy. Suffrage was conferred on all men able to read and write the Constitution or, failing that, paying taxes on $300 worth of property, which under the custom of under-assessment amounts to much more. All taxes due must have been paid and the registrant must never have been convicted of any of a long list of crimes. To care for existing white illiterates (particular sympathy being felt with Confederate veterans who had missed schooling), until January 1, 1898, all who could interpret the Constitution when it was read to them were to be registered for life All not on this list must register every ten years. The payment of the poll tax as a qualification for voting was abolished by constitutional amendment in 1951.

As late as 1897 educational and property qualifications were defended on the stump by John Gary Evans as justly disfranchising white men who would not qualify themselves by learning to read and write. But

The (Columbia) *State* that they numbered 40. Professor Simkins' figures for factions (*Tillman Movement*, pp 208-9) total the impossible figure of 162 instead of 160. He repeats the error in his *Pitchfork Ben Tillman*, p. 284.

in a few years this whole attitude was abandoned, with the consequent encouragement of illiteracy and the undermining of morals. Slackness in the Democratic primary, the real election in South Carolina, sacrificed decency still further by allowing the vote to paupers, idiots, and criminals of all classes. On the other hand, though swearing the voter to support the nominees of the party, the rules did not require a registration certificate that would make it possible for him to perform his oath. The determination to exclude the Negro or whites who might sympathize with his political activity was further manifested by appointing only Democrats as general election officers and by exposing at the ballot box plainly identifiable party tickets on separate slips. Proposals for fairer methods met practically no response until 1950.

The discouragement to Negro registration resulting from the new Constitution and from the strengthened determination to maintain white supremacy growing out of the discussion is evidenced by the decline in the Negro vote. Far larger numbers could qualify; but, in view of the hopelessness of Republican victory, what is the use? The Republican vote in the State for the years indicated was as follows: 1884, 21,733; 1888, 13,736; 1892, 13,345; 1896, 9,313. It has since sunk ordinarily to two or three thousand. Under the unusual conditions of 1944 it was 7,799. South Carolina thus escaped the distressing experience of North Carolina from 1896 to 1900, when that State suffered the repetition of many of the features of Congressional Reconstruction because the divided factions of the whites appealed to the Negro vote. There was at least this compensation for the South Carolina Democratic party's so largely adopting Populism instead of waging a stiff fight against it as in North Carolina: it prevented any appeal to the Negro to decide the great question of which of two white parties should be allowed to share with him the rule.

Racial Questions, Divorce, etc.—The Constitution of 1895 erased all features of that of 1868 looking toward social equality. Such provisions had been allowed so long to stand either to avoid irritating a Republican national administration still seeking excuses for intervention, or because they were dead letters. The new Constitution accordingly forbade marriage of a white person with one of one-eighth or more of Negro blood. This gave constitutional sanction to the statutory provision of 1865 and 1879. The mingling of the races in schools was forbidden. Counties were made liable in $2,000 to the heirs of any person lynched. It has never been thought worth while to sue for damages except in a few cases in which the person lynched was clearly innocent or was guilty of merely a minor crime.

The rest of the Constitution merely perpetuates the usual American system of a split-up executive department, with a governor denied adequate power to execute the laws he is sworn to uphold;[1a] a legislature encumbered with local legislation and so shackled with limitations that it is frequently straining its morals to circumvent the restrictions it has sworn to observe; and a judiciary hamstrung in its functioning against crime and legal delays, all of which is largely a heritage of such influences as George III's convincing the American people that government is the enemy of liberty. Of the enlightened statesmanship which in a number of States has to some extent remedied these chronic evils of American State government, South Carolina has given slight manifestation. Until something of that lesson is learned another constitutional convention is useless.

A Difficult Inheritance.—Tillman ruled our politics as absolutely as did Calhoun, but with this difference: Calhoun retained his dictatorship until the end, but Tillman gradually lost his authority after his election in 1894 to the United States Senate, for in his time South Carolina's interest was so largely confined to State politics. The economic distress of the 1890's continued through Governor Evans' administration (1894-97) and that of his successor. As one of the youngest members of the legislature, Mr. Evans had been prominently identified with a mass of social, educational, and administrative legislation which now meets with almost universal approval. He was the first governor to sense the needs of the factory operatives, already of rapidly growing importance. Governor Evans inherited the task of enforcing the dispensary law against a large recalcitrant element, to which there was added the difficulty of the corruption so early becoming manifest. Purity would have been difficult under any circumstances in a business traditionally corrupt, and partisanship made it worse. Says Dr. W. W. Ball, "The eager predictions and wish of the Conservatives that the system fail, fail disgracefully and disgrace Tillmanism with it, smoothed the path of rascals to gain control of it and feather their nests." Corruption was facilitated too by the large admixture of men who floated into office as Tillman's "coat tail swingers," devoid of fitness save as being of "the common people." By 1895 county officials of this class had begun a series of defalcations, plain stealing, and shortages from incompetency such as the State had never experienced except under Reconstruction, and which long continued, sometimes in huge sums. State administration, however, apart from the dispensary, has been only rarely and slightly smirched.

The Degenerating Dispensary.—Rebates were early offered for dis-

[1a] By constitutional amendment of 1949 the Governor was deprived of the pardoning power further than to commute death sentence to life imprisonment. Pardons rest with the Board of Pardons.

pensary officials' private pockets, and were at first refused. In 1896 the members of the Dispensary State Board of Control were changed from the Governor and other State officials to directors elected by the legislature, and this soon brought out grafters eagerly seeking the $400-a-year directorships on which many grew prosperous. The capital swarmed with liquor drummers lobbying the legislature or the board and distributing substantial favors. The plan to check drinking soon gave way to the desire for profits. Judge Earle, in 1896, told the Greenville grand jury that he was informed that persons high in the councils of the State had instructed constables and dispensers to disregard the provisions of the law. "Beer privileges" and "hotel permits" directly violating the constitutional prohibition of drinking on the premises, established saloons in which the customer bought on one side of a screen and drank on the other.

Charleston Under Metropolitan Police.—The city of Charleston eschewed the dispensary law, first, because it was "Tillman's baby," and second, because of her ancient opposition to any stringent regulation of liquor. Her insolent defiance of the law of the State stimulated resentment toward the city, already widely disliked for its sense of superiority. Governor Evans, after repeated warnings to the city council, finally said that if the new administration under Mayor J. Adger Smyth did not retain Chief of Police J. Elmore Martin he would put the metropolitan police law in force; early in February, 1896, he appointed three excellent Charleston citizens commissioners of police. The commissioners appointed Chief Martin the same day the council rejected him.

The Governor removed the State constables and left the law enforcement to the Charleston police thus controlled. The result was a great improvement in the enforcement of the liquor law. After a year twenty-three ministers of every Protestant denomination in Charleston, including those of the most conservative Episcopal and Presbyterian congregations, issued a statement strongly endorsing the administration of Chief Marshal Martin. So narrow was the partisanship of the period that the *News and Courier* refused to publish the ministers' statement. The hysterical cries that Charleston had been deprived of local self-government were as excessive as most of the partisanship of the time. The council continued to govern the city as usual, except that, as in London or Paris, for instance, the officers for arresting violators of State law (as well as mere ordinances) were under State control.

After some misunderstanding and acrimonious exchange, Governor Ellerbe, without conditions, ended the metropolitan police administration on September 30, 1897. The Mayor and a large majority of the council had promised to enforce the liquor law. The whole State, though generally condemning Charleston's defiance of law, was relieved at the ending of an irritating situation.

"Original Packages" and the State's Police Power.—In 1896 Federal Circuit Judge Simonton declared null that portion of the dispensary law prohibiting the importation of liquor for personal use, and was upheld by the Supreme Court. On May 31, 1897, Judge Simonton annulled the portion of the law forbidding private dealing in liquor. So long as the State recognizes the liquor business as legitimate by engaging in it, especially for profit, he ruled, she cannot forbid private persons' selling imported liquors under the same regulations. This decision was in spite of the fact that Congress had in 1890 enacted the Wilson Law for the express purpose of stopping the practice that Judge Simonton now authorized.

At this denial of the State's right to regulate her internal affairs, leading opponents of Tillman, time out of mind champions of extreme doctrines of State rights, loudly rejoiced. Editors who had never "lain down" and who habitually had gloried that South Carolina never "lay down," adjured their sovereign State to stop fighting and take lying down a humiliation that should have stung the cheeks of every citizen, irrespective of his views on any transient man or measure. Eminent South Carolinians in Washington, whose very names were eloquent of defense of State rights to the point of blood and life, sought to prevent the passage of Senator Tillman's bill to enable the court to maintain the right of the State to regulate the liquor traffic as it saw fit. When the Senate unanimously passed his bill, they gloated over "Czar Reed's" refusal to allow a vote in the House. Never had South Carolinians so pitifully exhibited "the opportunism of contemporary prejudice." Men who had denounced Tillman for shocking South Carolina traditions blindly left him the honor of maintaining her most sacred traditions.

But their immoderate joy at seeing the sovereignty of their own mother trampled under the feet of a horde of "original package" dealers representing outside liquor houses was soon cut short. The United States Supreme Court, on May 9, 1898, after a series of inconsistent interstate commerce decisions since 1827 generally favoring the outside liquor dealers, definitely turned to the defense of a State's right to regulate the liquor traffic as it pleased. The court sustained Judge Simonton's defense of the right of any resident in South Carolina to order liquor for his own use, but annihilated the "original package" stores with which his ruling had covered the State.

Under this decision the Wilson law gave a certain protection to the States, but a very imperfect one, because the court had held that "arrival" meant arrival not within bounds of the State but into the hands of the consignee. To end this defiance by outsiders of a State's management of its own internal affairs, "Congress passed the Webb-Kenyon Act of 1913, penalizing the shipment or transportation of liquor intended to be received or sold either in original package or otherwise in violation of State laws."

Tillman's Senatorial Debut.—Turning back to the course of politics in 1896, Tillman's entering the Senate drew to him many Conservatives in addition to those who had responded to his co-operation in the constitutional convention. A powerful senator controls favors for individuals, cities, and classes too valuable to be ignored. Moreover, Tillman's national policies generally were approved by the larger portion of the Conservatives. On January 29, 1896, before packed floor and galleries, "Pitchfork Ben" defended free silver and abused President Cleveland (into whom he had promised to jab his pitchfork) as a besotted tyrant who had abused his appointing power and violated his oath. Already alarmed at the general unrest, which they were more bent on repressing than understanding, the *News and Courier* called him a "black-guard and buffoon," and the New York *Herald* "the champion of the anarchists." When he predicted armed revolt unless the people's rights were restored, the Philadelphia *Public Record* warned that blood might be spilled in consequence of his doctrines, and contrasted him with Calhoun and McDuffie, in strange oversight of the oceans of blood that had been shed as a consequence of theirs. The New York *Tribune,* more philosophical, recognized in the man who had by a single speech placed himself in the forefront of national attention a new force in the Senate that must be reckoned with.[2]

Tillman was prominent in the fight of 1897 for fixing prices of armor plate at $300 instead of $400 a ton. In 1901, by swearing in language forceful and picturesque that he would otherwise block every pension bill, he compelled the restoration to the pension roll of South Carolina Mexican War veterans who had been cut off because of being Confederates. He did good service in steering the Inter-State Commerce Act of 1906 through the Senate and as chairman of the Naval Affairs Committee was an effective leader for stronger sea power.

Divisions on the Money Issue.—Tillman dominated the State convention of 1896 which by 253 to 67 killed Irby's proposed declaration of

[2] Tillman's "irreversible cow" inspired two good cartoons. The United States, he said, was like a cow with her head to the West and South, where she ate up the produce of the farmers, while her udder, from which the rich bankers drew all the milk, hung over Wall Street. The farmers sought to turn the cow around and let her eat in Wall Street and give her milk in the South and West. But when they did this by means of the income tax law, the United States Supreme Court, as represented in the second cartoon drawn from this suggestion, took her by the throat and put a stop to her eating the income taxes of the wealthy.

South Carolina's duty to acquiesce in any action of the coming national convention. If that convention betrays Democratic principle by opposing the free coinage of silver, said Tillman, let us reassemble the State Convention for new instructions. Extremes met when, in reply to J. W. Barnwell's defense of the right to bolt, as he had bolted the regular State ticket headed by Tillman in 1890, Tillman, though he opposed bolting from the Democratic party now, apologized for any words that seemed to reflect on Mr. Barnwell. They were strong men who, despite their differing antecedents and opinions, respected each other. Each chafed under the political slavery imposed by the perpetual threat of the Negro. The convention almost unanimously nominated Tillman for the presidency, which was neither more nor less ridiculous than many "favorite son" moves. His violent sectional speech in the National Convention was displeasing to Bryan, the nominee. But by 1900 he was a power there. When the platform was finally beaten into shape by the committee, Tillman grabbed it and read it with such dramatic effect that he was selected to read it to the Convention.

William H. Ellerbe was elected governor in 1896. The race for the United States Senate by Governor Evans and Judge Joseph H. Earle witnessed a new low level, under the inevitable degradation of political manners with opponents speaking for weeks from the same platform. Money and whiskey were said to have been used in State and county contests to an unprecedented extent. The "bond scandal" and the dispensary scandal urged by John T. Duncan (who also ran) left Governor Evans guilty of nothing but legitimate services as attorney, while a legislator, for a broker, in the refunding of the State debt. Evans' language to Earle was so insulting that public opinion justified even a judge for striking him. Evans, favored by Tillman, failed of a majority by only about 314 votes in the first primary, defeated in effect by John T. Duncan, an habitual candidate who always polled a tiny vote. Despite Tillman's active intervention, Evans lost in the second primary by about 3,348. The Conservatives, unorganized and dispirited, hopeless of beating Evans in the first primary, turned out and beat him in the second.

The result revealed the disintegration of the Reform party. Its very name had become a ghastly joke when, as Reformer J. Y. Jones said, there was more rottenness in the Reform movement to the square inch than there ever was in South Carolina to the square yard from 1876 to 1890. Larry Gantt's *Piedmont Headlight* lamented (as he, extreme Reformer, had held for two years) that Reform had failed in all its promises: the same men had been in the State house since 1890; taxes were higher; and only the well-to-do could send a boy to the agricultural college for which every tenant farmer paid a tax with every bag of fertilizer he bought.

Gantt's position was typical of that of many Reformers. Deluded men were learning the futility of expecting the State government to be a kind father to help them out of trouble, instead of an honest and efficient servant to administer common interests. "Reform" had accomplished something, but at a fearful cost in vulgarizing and coarsening public life among even honest men and in introducing strong, shrewd corruptionists and petty thieves soon to multiply and exhibit the arrogant cynicism of men fearing no punishment. High men to a large degree were driven from public life, with the consequence of progressive degradation of political calibre, manners, and conduct. Tillman angrily warned that Evans' defeat would be the beginning of the end of his party, and protested against the injustice of expecting Evans to defend his character by proving a negative. Tillman was getting a taste of his own medicine. When he was slandering honorable men in 1890 his axiom was, "It is my part to make the charges; it is your part to disprove them." His virtual confession in 1897 of the falseness of his charges was a poor amend.

But at all events the big, strong man stood personally triumphant, and as his party disintegrated he drew more and more of his old enemies. Said W. W. Ball[3] in the New York *Evening Post* in 1897, the Conservative party in South Carolina is dead. Those who desire office must fall in with the triumphant Tillmanism as well as they can. "The political atmosphere is saturated with compromise and conciliation. . . . B. R. Tillman is at the moment about the only man left in the State who represents a positive and aggressive idea in politics, bad as that is. All the other politicians, Conservatives and Tillmanites, are a race of tallow dips." Even *The State,* the last to make its Pickett's charge against "Reform," as it said, got tired of being bushwhacked and fired into from behind and adopted the policy of wiping out factionalism and supporting men or measures that were good in themselves, as "politics in South Carolina today is individualistic, not aggregational."

Senator Earle, whose death in 1897 deprived the State almost immediately of a valuable official, had run independent of faction. He had long been in sympathy with the Farmers' Movement, but repudiated Tillman when he sought office through abusing good men. Elevated to the bench by a legislature dominated by his political opponents, he had helped to heal the asperity of factions without losing the respect of either.

In 1896 in national, as in 1890 in State, politics it was the anti-Till-

[3] Dr. Ball, though condemning Tillman, voted for him in 1890 as the regular Democratic nominee, and not for Haskell, as I stated in my three-volume *History of South Carolina.*

manites who did the bolting. An electoral ticket of non-politicians of the highest character announced itself as Palmer and Buckner gold Democrats, and its head, Colonel F. W. McMaster, said that gold Democrats should vote for McKinley if necessary to prevent debased money. Hundreds of Democrats, especially in Charleston, which was overwhelmingly for gold, did vote for McKinley, besides the 824 in the State who voted for Palmer and Buckner. Columbia was practically solid for silver. Feeble approaches by Republicans were repelled by South Carolina Palmer and Buckner Democrats.

The Spanish-American War.—Factionalism by no means died with the inauguration of the mild and moderate Ellerbe (1897), but he deserves credit for helping as better economic conditions, disillusionment, and mere weariness of strife lulled it temporarily. The young Governor of thirty-five had served creditably as a very young comptroller-general, which is remarkable, for, though well intentioned, he was neither strong nor brilliant. He dismissed a private from the militia for participating in a riot with Carolina College students, but declined to follow the Court of Enquiry's recommendation to reprimand Adjutant-General Watts for lawlessly precipitating the trouble, on the ground that Watts was a constitutional officer.

Governor Ellerbe also met creditably responsibilities in the Spanish-American War. As the war allayed American sectionalism, so it contributed to mollifying factionalism within South Carolina. The volunteers were accepted after strict examination. An alarmingly large proportion were rejected as physically unfit.[4] The poor support and small numbers of South Carolina's militia accounted for her failing to fill her quota promptly and for the fact that only about 30 per cent of the men were militiamen. The Second Regiment was the only South Carolina organization to reach Cuba, where it arrived too late for combat.

M. C. Butler, ex-major-general of Confederate Cavalry, was made major-general. Major (ex-Governor) John Gary Evans was put in charge of the civil government of Havana. N. G. Gonzales, son of the distinguished General Ambrosio José Gonzales, an exiled Cuban patriot and later a gallant Confederate colonel, left his editorship of the *State* to serve in the Cuban forces. Major Micah Jenkins of the "Rough Riders," Captain G. H. McMaster of the Regular Army, Lieutenant Victor Blue of the Navy, and Lieutenants W. S. Guignard and W. H. Simons of the Army were among South Carolinians rendering distinguished service.

[4] *News and Courier* report, as condensed in *Newberry Observer* of May 11, 1898, says: Abbeville Volunteers, accepted 72, rejected 26; Richland Volunteers, accepted 52, rejected 30; Lee Light Infantry, Chester, accepted 53, rejected 36; Catawba Rifles, Rock Hill, accepted 71, rejected 23; Newberry Rifles, accepted 53, rejected 43; Butler Guards, Greenville, accepted 53, rejected 44. Some rejections were on account of age.

McLaurin's Commercial Democracy.—John L. McLaurin, appointed to the deceased Senator Earle's position pending an election, sought to secure tariff protection for Southern products, as protection was the settled national policy. His inclination to Republican policies was perhaps aided by his residence (though born in South Carolina) in New Jersey most of his life until he was twenty-one. He was overwhelmingly elected in 1897 over Evans and Irby.

McLaurin was soon defending the gold standard, the ship subsidy, a larger army, and the annexation of the Philippines. "Commercial Democracy" he pictured as promising the South the wealth of varied industries enjoyed by the North. Under the Democratic tariff, South Carolina rice had almost perished, but under the Dingley law the South was raising more rice than in 1861, he said. The prosperity of Southern lumber was due to the same law's exclusion of Canadian pine. It was time to abandon mawkish sentimentality for more business and less politics. President McKinley realized, "as I believe President Roosevelt will," he said, that "property and intelligence must control in the South as elsewhere, that business men must fill the offices and administer affairs of government in the South as in the East, the North, and the West."

The new gospel stirred strong amens in hearts impatient of Democracy's stolid policy of opposition and of invoking dead saints instead of heeding living facts, while politicians derived through office the only benefits.

McLaurin was soon obtaining favors for his State which Tillman could not get; but when his association with the Republican President became so close that he controlled important South Carolina patronage, the suspicion strengthened that he was lending himself to building a respectable Republican party in the South. The Democratic caucus dropped his name from its roll. On the invitation of a group of Greenville financiers, manufacturers, etc., McLaurin, on May 22, 1901, defended there his "progressive" or "commercial Democracy." An engagement two days later at Gaffney was rudely broken in upon by 250 stand-patters who invited Tillman to speak also, with the evident purpose of crushing McLaurin before he had time, pending a regular election, to educate the people. The debate, though bitter, was conducted by both men with great ability, and by its vast intellectual superiority to the conventional clap-trap of mummified one-party oratory gave South Carolinians a taste of the combat of ideas which genuine two-party politics affords. It was a debate, indeed, which many South Carolina voters, accustomed to settling political issues by howling down opposition candidates in the county-to-county "one-ring circus," could not comprehend. There were in fact, writes Mr. George R. Koester, armed men present ready to turn the argument into one the rudest could join in. Tillman had all the advantage—his unrivaled power of popular appeal, a generally sympathetic audience, perfection of physical condition—while McLaurin was in frail health and faced a crowd most of whom suspected or opposed him.

The suspicion that McLaurin was lending himself to Republican aims in the South was too well grounded. He wrote John D. Archbold of the Standard Oil Company asking to be "generously supported" against Tillman. He again wrote that a little aid would defeat Tillman, and in 1904 revealed to Mr. Archbold a remark of Theodore Roosevelt, "as it will show anyway that I am not unmindful of your various kind actions toward me."

The affair ended in a humiliating farce. Tillman charged in the Senate, February 22, 1902, that McLaurin's vote for the Spanish peace treaty shortly after having denounced the annexation of the Philippines was secured by giving him the South Carolina patronage. McLaurin again explained that the Filipinos' firing on the flag justified his change, and said that Tillman's statement "is a willful, malicious and deliberate lie." Tillman struck McLaurin's forehead and had blood drawn from his own face before the men were pulled apart.[5]

The circumstances of his vote discredited McLaurin throughout the country. A great opportunity—perhaps an opportunity overtaxing the power of any man—was gone. McLaurin lacked the ability and the weight of character to lead South Carolina white men to tolerate differences of view on national questions provided they would loyally

[5] President Roosevelt requested Senator Tillman to withdraw his acceptance of an invitation to dine with Prince Henry of Prussia, as his being under sentence of contempt of the Senate rendered an official meeting with the Prince improper. Tillman refused, and Roosevelt withdrew the invitation. Tillman considered that Roosevelt's feelings in this matter were the cause of the President's seeking to discredit him in the Oregon land matter in 1908. Efforts were being made in 1908 to force the sale of certain valuable timber lands in Oregon granted in 1868 to a road company on condition that they sell alternate 160-acre quarter sections at $2.50 an acre. October 19 and 20 1907, Tillman wrote to the real estate firm seeking to bring the lands on the market that Tillman's agent was authorized to pay for nine quarter sections (1,440 acres) for Tillman and family when the lands had been located. January 31, 1908, Tillman introduced a bill to compel the sale of the lands. In February he came upon a circular of Dorr, salesman for the real estate firm, stating that Senator Tillman was so sure of the lands' being made available that he had paid the fees for eleven (sic) quarter sections. February 19, in the Senate, Tillman denounced Dorr as a swindler and denied having bought or attempted to buy any land in the West, and had the post office stop delivering mail to Dorr. In the investigation which Dorr demanded the inspectors checked upon Tillman's communications. President Roosevelt submitted photographs of these to the Senate. Tillman defended his right to buy the land (which was undoubted, whatever might be thought of the propriety), and maintained that he had not lied in denying that he had attempted to buy any. (Cong. Rec., Vol. 43, pt. 1, pp. 718-41, 887-8, 892.)

accept the decisions reached in their Democratic primary and stand unitedly for white supremacy in the general election. He declined the appointment to the court of claims, which President Roosevelt said his public service deserved, apparently to save himself from the charge of being bought. Tillman, carrying the momentum of 250 years of social and economic compulsion, was the nominal victor over the normal freedom of self-governing men; but behind Tillman in the shadow was the Negro, who had imposed on Carolina thinkers, from Calhoun down, as binding a slavery of the mind as they had imposed upon him of the body. The most notable attempt to make the Democratic primary the free means of all white men's settling their differences, with freedom of opinion on everything except white supremacy, had utterly broken down, and South Carolina politics had experienced another spasm of rigidity. When the question again arose in 1928 it was hardly allowed the dignity of discussion. South Carolina Democrats have steadily become more and more determined to refuse freedom of political thought and action except through the virtually impossible means of becoming Republican. This situation was hardly altered when the State Democratic Convention of 1938 eliminated the primary voter's oath to support the Democratic presidential candidate, in revulsion at the national convention's pandering to the Northern Negro vote in 1936.

The McKinley-Roosevelt move, for which McLaurin had been used, for a reformed Southern Republican party exploiting the nationalism roused by the Spanish-American War, succeeded nowhere. The few respectable white Republicans continued a small contingent, respect for whom was impaired by the fact that even they were frequently rewarded with office. The "lily white" movement soon roused the resentment of Northern Negroes, feared in closely balanced states, and met President Roosevelt's determination to divide Southern (though not Northern) offices with the Negro. Southern Republicanism was soon running its usual course of black and white fraternizing in machines maintained for getting Federal appointments.

The Degeneration of Politics.—But let us not suppose that all South Carolina white Democrats are good. The buying of low-lying elements that had existed before 1860 continued. Before the existence of primaries, candidates for mayor were known to "bull-pen" Negroes in Greenville (and doubtless elsewhere), feeding and swilling them until they were marched to the polls. In the local option elections in Spartanburg in the 1880's, buying Negroes with whiskey and money was extensive. The Tillman movement inevitably increased corruption, as, amid the overthrow of old standards along with old leaders and customs, new men, frequently of lower grade, battled with intensified ambition before masses who had been taught their power. The dispensary added unprecedented resources for corruption. Vote-buying in the 1904 primary led to corrective legislation, but the use of money for legitimate purposes continued to grow. Mr. George E. Prince's bill to require the same qualifications for primary as for general election voting failed; for political ideals had steadily declined since it was thought in 1895 that the qualifications would really be enforced on whites as well as blacks.

Charleston politics, said the Charleston *Post* in 1898, had sunk to the level of selling the soul for the pettiest office. The democratic movement breaking out intermittently in the city since the pre-Revolutionary agitation was greatly augmented by the Tillman movement. In John P. Grace the democratic and Catholic elements found an able leader defiantly contemptuous of upper-class pretentions. In defending a Grace partisan, who was being tried for voting corruptly under instigation thereto by an alderman, Grace sneered in court, as he had done two years before, at the hypocrisy of men far higher than himself, who, like himself, had corrupted the ballot, and were now striking at him by persecuting poor devils without money. A series of mistrials was the natural outcome of this skirmish in the bitter class conflict that long intermittently kept Charleston politics at white heat.

The county-to-county campaign, with candidates facing each other for weeks, degenerated to such intellectual inanity or hoodlumism that Senator Tillman expressed the fear in 1902 that the farce would lead to the abandonment of even the primary.

Dissatisfaction with the Dispensary.—Before the dispensary was five years old it had fallen into serious disrepute. There were corrupt dealings with it by near relatives of the management, soon to swell into gross habitual scandals. Dispensaries were being forced upon unwilling communities by means of the transformation of penniless Negroes into tiny freeholders so as to secure the requisite number of signatures to petitions for the institution. Sales were pressed in violation of legal limitations. Drinking was being transferred from the bar to homes and "clubs." Larry Gantt, the dispensary's foster father, complained that instead of being run as intended it was increasing drinking.

After five years of disappointment the prohibitionists in 1898 put out a strong ticket headed by C. C. Featherstone and applied to the State Democratic Executive Committee to be allowed to run their convention ticket in the primary. Refusal destroyed another attempt to create normal party freedom and organization for all white men, subject to the decision of the primary, as public displeasure had nipped it when practiced by the Reformers in the 1894 "Colleton plan."

So strong was Featherstone, running merely as an individual, that Governor Ellerbe, fearing defeat, entered a secret agreement with N. G. Gonzales (editor of the Columbia *State*) between the two primaries to abandon his insistence on the dispensary in favor of county option among high license (which Gonzales favored), dispensary, or prohibition. If the *State* turned 2,600 votes it elected Ellerbe. Ellerbe, evidently intimidated by Tillman, soon began to evade his promise. When Ellerbe broke his promise Gonzales published the affair in detail. It passed as merely another ugly feature in the history of an ugly institution.

Whatever spark of the Reform party still flickered, amid the mere scramble for office, weariness, and disillusionment, quietly expired by 1900. Tillman himself was too powerful to be opposed, though 18,213 voters, mainly in the prohibition counties, scratched his name from the ticket. How fully he had gained his old enemy Charleston, which owed him much as a senator, was proved when only eighty-nine in that county refused him their vote. Tillmanism had gone dead in ten years or less, as Hamptonism in fourteen. Certain inevitable changes had been accomplished, but with a wholly unnecessary mixture of evil, for which Tillman, though mainly, was not wholly, responsible.

CHAPTER LX

A NEW ERA TRIES TO DAWN, 1880-1910

HARDSHIP for the farmer continued until the late nineties. When such conditions were driving thousands from the farms, the rapidly expanding cotton mills of the 1880's and 1890's were a godsend. Hard necessity forced better farming. Owners assumed a stricter supervision, amounting to complete control, over the share tenant, who was thus reduced to a laborer on a profit-sharing basis. But still thousands unfit to farm continued to butcher the land and glut markets with cotton representing loss to themselves and depression of prices for those fit to farm. The burden of the Negro was shown, as it had been under slavery, by the superior productivity throughout the South of counties of small Negro population. The needs were education, diversification, and a better credit system. By 1903 decided progress had been made in all these respects.

Agricultural Hardships and Achievements.—In 1904 E. McIver Williamson, a college-bred scientific farmer, the son of an educated planter, and one of the long succession from David R. Williams to David R. Coker who have made Darlington agriculturally eminent, perfected a system of culture securing from poor lands a larger yield of corn than was common even on good soil. David R. Coker, following lines laid down by his father Major James L. Coker, rendered inestimable services to American agriculture as a scientific breeder of more productive and disease-resisting seeds of cotton and grain.[1] This is carrying on a great South Carolina tradition; for as early as 1857 Superintendent J. W. Parker of the Asylum established a world's record by raising 359 bushels of shelled corn on two acres in Richland, the best acre yielding 200 bushels and 12 quarts. A new world record was established in 1889 when Captain Z. J. Drake of Marlboro raised 255 bushels on an acre. In 1906 A. J. Tindall of Clarendon won the world prize by raising 182 bushels. A school boy, Jerry Moore of Florence County, in 1910 won the world prize by raising 228¾ bushels, which in a sense excelled Drake, for Moore made a profit of $130.70, whereas Captain Drake spent more on his crop than its commercial value except at curiosity prices.

[1] Major Coker, in addition to his constructive leadership in agriculture and business was the founder of Coker College for women.

The prize offered by the Southern Railway for the ten best ears of corn raised by any boy in eight Southern States was won in 1925 by William Patton Boland of Pomaria, Newberry County, South Carolina, and in 1927 by Daniel Bickley, of Irmo, Lexington County, South Carolina.

Rice and sea island cotton were seeking protection in 1896. The fatal enemies of South Carolina rice were Louisiana, Arkansas, and Texas, as the Southwest had been, and is, of our cotton. The 1898 coast storms, a danger from which Western rice culture is free, cut the Beaufort region's anticipated 250,000 bushels to 12,000 or 15,000. In 1908 Georgetown was planting only five to seven thousand acres. Governor Heyward was probably the last large rice planter to give up the hopeless fight against the Southwest. There could hardly be a more depressing scene of ruin than today meets the eye in the jungles that once supported a wealthy and cultured society, housed in splendid mansions, in the South Carolina rice belt.

About 1890 or earlier Mr. F. M. Rogers, of Florence by his writings and practical success, was pioneering a movement for tobacco culture. About 1890 the *News and Courier* began active propaganda for reviving South Carolina's long extinct tobacco industry as a correction to the "cotton-tot." It distributed seed when few had faith. In 1895 the crop, principally from Florence and Darlington, but also from Sumter, Clarendon, and Williamsburg, was approximately 10,000,000 pounds and sold for about $1,000,000.

Peonage.—The presence of ignorant Negroes on the farm and Italians in the phosphate diggings led to abuses. From 1885 to 1900 abuses had existed in the latter. Italian immigrants, brought from New York on the promise of high wages, found low wages which were consumed in their board, while they worked under armed Italian padrones.

Negro peonage had been common for years and had developed an ugliness, not originally intended, when the Philadelphia *North American* ventilated it in 1901. A landlord to collect debts would induce a Negro to sign a contract to labor the next year, although he might not intend to work the Negro. Another white man, hiring the Negro, would pay the debt. Petty offenders agreed to work for men who paid their fines. The statute for the protection of farmers against shiftless Negroes' abandoning crops declared that obtaining wage advances and later leaving before the termination of the contract (which was usually for the year) was *prima facie* evidence of obtaining property fraudulently, a punishable offense. In 1907 Federal Judge W. H. Brawley of Charleston declared the statute null under the Thirteenth Amendment. The widespread fears of the results of this decision have proved groundless, largely, we must believe, on account of the improved character of the Negro.

Negro Crime—Lynching.—The release of the Negro from the discipline of slavery led to a great increase of immorality and crime. To explain Negro immorality as the product of slavery, as is sometimes attempted, overlooks the fact that masters restrained immorality as destructive of the value of their property. A Negro wrote discouragingly of moral conditions in Sumter in 1872, as he might have found them anywhere. But there was a Negro element of which his jeremiad was untrue, and that element has steadily grown larger under the influence of education, a sounder religion, and self-discipline, and deserves respect.

Yet the Negro continues a baffling problem and, where in large numbers, is felt to be a potential menace of which the whites, however friendly, cannot be unconscious. For some twenty years after about 1885 acute consciousness of the economic, political, and social dangers of the race problem kept opinion in a state of nervous irritability. Doubtless the Negro on his part thinks the white problem quite troublesome.

Two instances of the Negro mass violence, which rarely occurs, will suffice. In 1896 a Negro mob threatened to burn Fort Motte in Calhoun County and lynch a white man for shooting a Negro. They refused to disperse until forced by militia. Later their chief leader attempted to kill the deputy sheriff and was himself shot dead, after which the others surrendered.

The Phoenix, Greenwood County, riot of November, 1898, the most serious race conflict since Reconstruction, was caused by the Tolberts' stirring Negroes to vote. John R. Tolbert, a Confederate soldier of great physical and moral courage, had been hated and feared since becoming an active Republican in 1868. For many years at a later period he or his son Joe, as official head of the Republican party in South Carolina, distributed patronage in the manner that sank their party into contempt. As Thomas P. Tolbert was having Negroes deposit blanks at the poll saying they had been unlawfully denied registration and voting, an election manager from another precinct who objected was murdered by a shot from a Negro behind him. Firing by armed bodies was followed by the whites killing seven Negroes with the purpose of cowing the race. Several Tolberts fled to Columbia, where they were protected in the penitentiary from possible lynching by Spanish-American war soldiers from their section encamped near by. In August of the next year low whites began whipping Negroes with the purpose of renting lands cheap after driving off black competing tenants.

Rape of white women by Negroes, very rare before emancipation, became alarmingly frequent in the 1880's and '90's, after which it declined. With inadequate or no police protection men, necessarily leaving their wives and daughters with no help at hand, felt that the

Negro must be made to understand that certain death would follow this hideous crime, more maddening than murder itself. Lynching spread to other crimes, partly from the feeling in communities of large Negro majorities that the race must be held in terror. The almost complete abatement of the original provocation has been followed by the almost complete disappearance of the lawless punishment.[2]

President Theodore Roosevelt nominated the Negro Dr. Crum as Collector of the Port of Charleston on January 5, 1903, at the same time that a Negro postmistress was forced on a Mississippi town. The question of ability was secondary in both cases. Roosevelt appointed Crum merely because he was a Negro, and the South objected for the same reason. Even Northern Republican journals condemned a mortification that would not have been forced upon a Northern community, but the President doubtless understood the exigencies of the Negro vote in close Northern States.

Before leaving this subject, recognition should be given Sheriffs Jno. M. Nicholls, a notably brave Confederate veteran, and W. J. White, both of Spartanburg, in preventing lynching by fidelity and personal courage, in 1891 and 1913 respectively, and to Sheriff Adam Hood of Fairfield, who gave up his life in protecting a prisoner successfully from relatives of the woman whom the Negro had assaulted, who intended their shots not for the sheriff but for the criminal. Sheriff Hood, mortally wounded, dragged the Negro into the courthouse on whose steps he had been shot, and said, "Judge, here is your prisoner." Nicholls armed his prisoner (the white murderer Turner, whom he ultimately legally hanged) as well as his deputies. White, not depending solely upon his well-built jail, stood at the gate, warning, "Gentlemen, I'd hate to do it, but I'll kill the first man who comes in that gate."[3]

In 1896 a Negro legislator sought to stop whites from teaching in colored common schools, as they did in the city of Charleston. White legislators later were deterred from pressing legislation upon the subject when the Charleston City School authorities agreed to take white teachers out of the Negro schools, which they did during 1919 to 1921. But of recent years, in at least one large South Carolina hospital, white women nurses render the same service to Negro men and women that they do to patients in the white wards. Separate coaches or compartments on trains have been required for the races since 1898. Politicians years afterward lived or died by their votes on this; for demagogues found cultivating an increasing sensitiveness on anything touching the

[2] See my *History of South Carolina,* III, 400 ff., for a more extended treatment of this subject.

[3] In my long *History of South Carolina,* Nicholls is erroneously spelled with one "l," and White's initials are reversed.

Negro profitable among the white masses. Governor Ansel was attacked in 1908 for having appointed a Negro notary, although every governor from Hampton down had done so for the accommodation of Negroes in law or business.

In May, 1947, there occurred in Greenville, South Carolina, a trial unprecedented in this State, that of twenty-eight white men, nearly all cab drivers, accused of lynching a Negro who had murdered and robbed a white cab driver who was taking him to a distant point in another county. The case attracted nation-wide interest. Despite the written confessions of several of the prisoners and the earnest efforts of the prosecution, all were acquitted.

Contrasted with these darker phases of the Negro problem is the attitude of the churches, constituting an interesting and important story of helpfulness despite baffling difficulties which, to the author's regret, space requires to be omitted.

Homicide.—Homicide, since the Revolution a characteristic offense by dueling or less-ordered combat, became from about 1880 to 1910 more common than ever. The *News and Courier* declared (March 3, 1880), in discussing the increase of serious crimes, that "whiskey is a worse foe than radicalism, and brings worse ills in its train." Those were the days, says A. B. Williams of 1876, when a reporter too drunk to articulate or a city editor (and much the same was sometimes true of their superiors, he might have added) sprawling helpless in the office were passing incidents. The same journal declared a few years later, and again on February 16, 1903, that about eight-tenths of South Carolina homicides were due more or less to whiskey.

The Attorney-General's reports showed a long mounting murder rate; but more significant was the standing of men killing each other. "Too often," said Judge C. A. Woods, "public sentiment has allowed the slayer to escape on incredible pleas of self-defense." Since (say) the early 1930's homicides have become less common, especially among the middle and upper classes.

Criticism of the Courts.—Jurors, legislators, and to some extent judges, and behind them public sentiment, are responsible. Said Judge Robert Aldrich to the Aiken grand jury in 1908, the jury commissioners are in politics and seek the favor of the better class by omitting them from the jury lists. "They also know that the lawless class of society, or those who sympathize with lawlessness, to whom the little pay of a juror is a consideration, and who enjoy the distinction, and to whom it is an honor to serve on a jury, will be pleased if they are put there, and the consequence is that those who ought to be on the jury are left off, and those who ought not to be are left on, and the result is a failure to perform duty properly." "Outlooker" (a South Carolina circuit judge), voicing the storm of condemnation at the acquittal of dispensary corruptionists in 1909 (a period of great degeneration of juries), criticized the abuse of the law for selecting jurymen, the excusing of about forty classes of citizens, the requirement of unanimous verdict, and the permitting of ten peremptory challenges in trials for the seven most serious crimes, making the rejection of good jurors "almost automatic." "Public opinion," he continued, "is not arraigned on the side of the law, and juries, like men, follow public opinion." That such indictments as those just quoted from judges pass with a shrug is merely another indication of tolerance of murder. In 1921, for example, 83 per cent of all prisoners were convicted, but only 55 per cent of homicides. To this is to be added the abuse of the pardoning power by many governors.

But South Carolina is no worse than many other States in making the administration of criminal justice, as Chief Justice Taft said, a national disgrace. Said Dean W. H. Vance of George Washington University Law School in 1909: "Our inefficient procedure in civil actions is a reproach to the nation and a disgrace to the bar, while our procedure in criminal cases, with its enormous expenses, its incredible delays and its frequent and gross miscarriage of justice, is a stench in the nostrils of the nations."

Our judges, being drawn from the bar and elected for short terms by a political body, many of whose most influential members practice before them, are subjected to political influence from which the bench should be protected. Electioneering for judicial office has grown worse during the past thirty years. When a judge fines a Negro $150 (or six months' imprisonment) for cursing a constable, and fines another constable $10 for trying to shoot a man for calling him a dirty dog, and compliments him as thus being worthy of his father, it is obvious that not jurors alone substitute folk standards for sworn upholding of the law.

Judges have at times congratulated our citizenship that its white men rarely commit crimes of moral turpitude, as though numerous murders of defenseless victims have no such savor; but that is no longer possible. In 1927, 1,386 whites and 1,256 Negroes were convicted in the circuit courts, the white majority being due to liquor violators. But all the embezzlers except one were white, as were 147 of the 341 housebreakers, and 70 of the 221 convicted of larceny, and 35 of the 49 forgers.

More humiliating than the evils complained of is the inability to remedy them. Exposure of conditions does not even stir public interest. The exclusion of unworthy characters from the bar was recognized by the South Carolina Bar Association Committee in 1885 as merely a pious wish, since the Supreme Court is virtually obliged to admit any applicant who can meet the intellectual test. Governor Blackwood's specific designation in his inaugural address in 1931 of legal abuses crying for remedy roused no response in the legislature, and the Governor did not press the subject during his four years in office.

The Murder of Gonzales.—Though old factional lines had weakened, the campaign of 1902 developed intense personal hates. N. G. Gonzales of *"The State,"* with constant reiteration during the campaign, exposed James H. Tillman (son of George), candidate for governor, as a "proven liar, defaulter, gambler and drunkard." Gonzales had written nothing about Tillman since August 26 when on January 15, 1903, while still lieutenant-governor, Tillman, walking from the Senate chamber to the corner facing the State House, met and shot the unarmed Gonzales by an apparently deliberate plan. The murder sent a thrill of indignation throughout the country, but thousands in South Carolina considered it "persecution" to expose an infamous character and the killing of the persecutor justifiable. A Lexington jury (to whom a change of venue gave the case), after hearing both the farcical plea of self-defense and the open declaration by an attorney of the right of revenge, found Tillman blameless. The murder of Gonzales removed one of the half dozen outstanding editors in the history of South Carolina. He had defended impartially the rights of the laborer, the capitalist, and the farmer, and fearlessly opposed what he considered unwarranted in each. The finest courage of two courageous races united in his veins. With the ideal of unflinching public service, he repeatedly risked his life. In controversy he was often overbearing, and relentlessly pursued an antagonist, rubbing salt in the wounds that his shafts had opened. His faults were virtues carried to excess. His strength lay in his dauntless courage and sun-clear integrity.

It is to be noted that the above references to crimes of violence and criticisms of the courts refer particularly to the early years of the twentieth century. I think I am warranted in saying that such conditions were worse than either before or since in the period from 1890 to 1915, when political excitement, whiskey dispensary corruption, factional hatred, and race prejudice were putting an unusual strain upon the morals and sanity of South Carolinians.

Reaction Against Factionalism.—Two governors formerly anti-Tillmanites served from 1903 to 1911. Said a leading "Reform" editor in 1901, he was sick of twelve years of wrangling that had embittered the people of the State, with no result but easy jobs for a few politicians. Weary of professional politicians, the public welcomed the candidacy in 1902 of a high-toned gentleman of exceptional personal charm, appealing for support to no faction. Duncan Clinch Heyward was a Colleton rice planter of distinguished family, with all the associations which had excluded men from office since 1890. Neither sacrificing his dignity nor parading it, he administered the governorship in touch with progressive modern ideas in the best traditions of the old South Carolina.

Charleston's Commerce—The Exposition.—The years immediately before and after 1900 saw the city of Charleston seeking to regain among her younger rivals her former importance as a port. The refusal of any system to bid for the South Carolina Railroad running from Charleston to Augusta and Columbia when it was sold for $1,000,000, terminating its 1889 to 1894 bankruptcy, was a pathetic revelation of Charleston's unimportance. Belated efforts of her business men were redoubled, and a new day dawned with the lease of the road by the Southern Railway, penetrating the most valuable non-coast regions between the Ohio and the Gulf. Hayne's dream, which, if it could have been accomplished in his day, might have changed the commercial map of the Southeast, became a belated reality.

The new spirit found expression in the South Carolina Interstate and West Indian Exposition, December 1, 1901, to May 31, 1902, intended to advertise the city's commercial advantages. The exposition stimulated Charleston's energies and awakened the State to Charleston, whose pluck and cordiality did much to remove ignorance and prejudice concerning the city.

Freight rates favoring other coast cities continued to hamper Charleston. Her ocean trade declined from $100,619,562 in 1910 to $46,800,741 in 1914 and gradually rose to $154,454,542 in 1921. In 1937 it was $130,268,519. In 1903 Senator Tillman, who had earlier been mercilessly ridiculed, was lionized as the city's guest after he blocked the Crum appointment and secured liberal grants for the exposition and the navy yard. Exploiting her advantages as a winter resort offering unique architectural, historical, and social charm, the city substituted modern sewerage for outmoded cesspools near cisterns of drinking water under houses, thereby vastly improving health; relieved buzzards of their duties as market scavengers; cleaned her streets as never before; extended the magnificent drives and walks along her waterfront; and soon saw handsome modern hotels filled with winter tourists.

Expressive of the spirit of industrial expansion and the desire for a white majority was the movement for securing North European immigrants. Under the leadership of Governor Heyward and Commissioner of Agriculture, Commerce, and Immigration E. J. Watson, by January, 1908, about 2,500 immigrants had been brought in. But the *Wittekind,* finding return cargoes disappointing, discontinued its trips, and the fear of competition felt by white workers and the possibility of bringing in bad immigrants turned State aid to the difficult task of turning immigration from industrial centers and the new West, a task rendered harder by the exaggerated fame of Southern peonage and fourteen homicides in South Carolina in one week in the fall of 1907.

In 1903 Senator Tillman brought the United States to pay South Carolina $202,230 for unreimbursed expenditures in the War of 1812, with interest. Against this the United States required payment in full of $125,000 State House bonds of 1856 with interest, on which it had refused to accept the 50 per cent repudiation of 1873 by the Radicals, which white South Carolina ratified and enforced, even against her ante-bellum creditors. The State therefore received $89,137.86 in cash. Payment has not yet been secured of the Revolutionary War claims of $316,947, and of Florida and Mexican War claims of $75,000 still due the State, as established by the Black Report of 1858.

Corruption in the Dispensary.—The dispensary continued under Governor Heyward, as before, the most vexing public question. On gross sales of $2,917,998 in 1903 there were profits of $638,482, of which $126,266 went to the schools and the balance equally to towns and counties. The Brice act of 1904 permitted any county to vote out the dispensary. Violations of the liquor laws were common throughout the State. "Social clubs" flourished as drinking places with liquor imported by members under interstate commerce protection. In Charleston grand and petty juries dismissed the obligation of oaths as violators smiled at the farce. The "king of the blind tigers," an imposing man of Italian extraction, who while a violator was present on the jury list and again a city councilman, actually sought to have one governor stop the troublesome raids on condition that he confine his selling to a restaurant system. Charleston in 1903 developed the practice of fining the blind tigers $25 every three months, or six times as high if they hindered the public revenues by purchasing their supplies elsewhere than at the dispensary. On these terms the tiger and the law lay down together, barring occasional spats, with a virtual license income to the city of about $7,500 a year. By 1912 these rates were doubled. Not until about 1915 did a modified public sentiment support for a brief period the efforts of governor or circuit courts.

A legislative investigating committee of 1905 under the leadership of Senator Niels Christensen and Representative J. Fraser Lyon, two young men of twenty-nine and thirty-four, respectively, serving their first terms, uncovered a State-wide system of graft. An ex-commissioner swore that one house offered him a bribe of $30,000, and the same house was shown to have employed as its attorney a senator whose name, by the closest possible vote, the committee declined to ask. Legislators were complimented with fine liquors, and an editor hurled the lie at all who said he was bought for $400 because he published for that sum as ordinary communications a series of letters defending the dispensary. Lyon's life was threatened on the street by one director, and an editor who sarcastically contrasted the former poverty and present prosperity of another (a man of gigantic strength who was supposed to be ready to carry out his threat to kill if certain questions were asked) was given a terrible beating.

Since reform of the State dispensary was deemed impossible, that institution was abolished in 1907 and every county was left free to operate its own dispensary or to adopt prohibition. County after county voted out the institution, until in 1909 twenty counties were dry and twenty-one wet. Corruption proved less virulent under the county dispensaries than it had been under the State institution; but enough remained to stimulate strongly the growing sentiment for absolute prohibition. In 1909 the legislature enacted general prohibition, but allowed the twenty-one counties still having dispensaries to vote upon whether they would retain them. A State-wide referendum abolished by 35,000 to 15,000 votes the few remaining county dispensaries in 1915 in favor of State-wide prohibition.

To return to the general course of politics: In 1906 Martin F. Ansel, the leading advocate of local option, who personally favored prohibition, was chosen as governor. The fact that Governor Ansel, the son of a German immigrant, was our first executive of that ancestry illustrates the comparative political inactivity of that large and valuable element of our population.

Although the administrations of Heyward and Ansel were paralleled by a sort of second government dominated from the lower political regions and threatening to defy all other government, the period was already marked by the humane, educational, and progressive movement that reached larger development during and after World War I. In 1906 was founded, mainly through the efforts of women's clubs led by Mrs. Martha Orr Patterson, the Industrial School for white boys. In 1908 Ellison DuRant Smith was elected by an overwhelming majority to the United States Senate, to which he was re-elected for his sixth term in 1938, so peculiarly the representative of agriculture as to have earned the title of "Cotton Ed Smith." Defeated in 1944 by Governor Olin D. Johnston, he died a few days later (November 17) after the longest continuous service in the history of the Senate. But events were about to prove that along with abundance of energy, there was still, amid conflicting class prejudices and social forces, a highly unstable political equilibrium.

CHAPTER LXI

A NEW FACTIONALISM, 1910-1914

The Nature of Tillmanism and Bleaseism.—The administrations of Governors Heyward and Ansel were an interlude in a movement which took definite shape in the 1880's and continued at least to 1936. Its early leader was Tillman; its leading later representative, Coleman L. Blease. Particular leaders merely rode the waves of the nation-wide democratic movement as it surged through South Carolina with a frothy fury determined by our somewhat rigid social structure. Tillmanism and Bleaseism are misleading terms unless understood merely as indicating the noisy bubbles on the current as it dashed against those angular personalities. South Carolina has never had a leader combining unselfish heart, intellectual stature, and effective personality to give adequate expression to the aspirations of modern democracy. Tillman and Blease possessed the externals of political leadership. Richard I. Manning, who best expressed the ideals of modern democracy without its crudities, was handicapped by origin, surroundings, and personality, which made him seem a benevolent upper-class patron rather than one who could become the darling of the people.

Tillman's office-seeking and abusive speech alienated many friends of the original Farmers' Movement.[1] Blease's platform and some of his measures looked fair enough; but his conduct and associations rendered his attempt to revive the name "Reform party" a mockery. Tillman overwhelmingly controlled the State, ruled the legislature, and was never defeated for office. Blease was repeatedly defeated, never won high office except by small majorities, and never commanded a majority in the legislature. His forceful personality, oratorical talent, and ability to make and hold personal friends and inspire the devotion of the tenant farmers and factory operatives gave him a personal prominence far beyond his influence on legislation. The poor and ignorant felt profound disappointment at the outcome of Tillmanism and waited for a new agitator. But so undeveloped and so unorganized were their ideas that they pressed few demands. The strength of Blease's appeal was not any platform of measures, but his personality and viewpoint. He not only offered no program of benefits to labor, a program which long remained repug-

[1] For a summary of Tillman's aims and accomplishments, see pp. 627-28.

nant to South Carolina individualism, but won favor by railing against measures which labor, where organized and informed, demands. He associated with the masses intimately and gave them what they valued more than measures—recognition and equality. They did not want legislation, but did want to be treated with respect, and they felt that Blease was making them a force in the State. Men paying no taxes shouted when he denounced high taxes. In the semi-socialistic program of social reform that makes the taxpayer sweat for the benefit of the proletariat neither he nor his followers had any part. Without rendering them any benefits, he held large masses through their ignorance, individualism, and personal devotion. With all his violence of speech, his pardons, and his tolerance of lawlessness, Blease was a conservative in legislative policy.

Of this fact some cool men of big business were well aware, and occasionally supported him in revenge against anti-Blease leaders who expressed sympathy for strikers, etc. Blease's opposition to the American Federation of Labor for textile operatives, and his proposal for local unions instead, were welcome to cotton mill executives. His cousin B. L. Abney, the able attorney for the Southern Railway, lived in the executive mansion, and numbers of officials of the system were understood to be for Blease.[2] Self-interest of another sort brought him the support of a large group of experienced and able politicians; for, aside from State politics, where his stamp was always of doubtful value, in many counties the Blease vote was essential to success.

Tillman, in condemning Bleaseism in 1914, was right in attributing its strength to class antagonism. The social scorn toward the cotton mill operative by the revived Bourbonism, which thinks itself alone fit to rule, said Tillman, drives them to Blease for revenge.[3] "You can tell a crowd of Bleaseites as far as you can see them," was a common gibe. Said an illiterate citizen of Berkeley in 1912, who knew little of either candidate, "I know I ain't goin' to vote for no aristocrat"; and a candidate in Dorchester County in about 1900, turning to some of that hated class, shouted, "You think we were laid by a buzzard in a hollow stump and hatched by the sun." They were determined to assert themselves as being as good as anybody. It was a passionate defiance of the whole class that they conceived to have looked down upon them.

[2] Governor Blease stated, message No. 4, 1913, that nearly all the Southern Railway attorneys and high officials were against him. The *State* said editorially, August 1, 1912, that high officials of the Southern Railway were so active for Blease in the 1910 campaign as to excite comment.

[3] Farewell Address. The instinctive treatment of mill operatives as a *tertium quid* was illustrated when Dr. S. Pope, himself a Reformer, announced after the December, 1897, smallpox outbreak that he would at one hour vaccinate white people, at another hour Negroes, and at a third hour factory people.

Blease as Governor.—Blease, elected governor in 1910 and 1912, in pandering to this feeling represented himself as more common than he really was. Born in 1868, of good middle-class English descent on both sides, he had the advantage of a collegiate education. Intensely ambitious, he terminated his career at the South Carolina University by plagiarizing an essay for a prize. He soon entered the legislature, where his parliamentary ability made him a conspicuous leader. As a member of the committee investigating the dispensary, he had been regarded as the friend of the men under charges of corruption. The hate he had inspired was expressed in the cartoon in the *State* of September 8, 1910, representing him as a buzzard with wings marked "Dispensary grafters, ignorance, race prejudice, lawlessness, blind tigers, injustice, class prejudice, demagogy," while South Carolina stood guard armed with a sword, "the ballot." The gross cartoon doubtless swelled Blease's vote; for his unexampled organization and his opposition to prohibition operated strongly for him. Charleston, set against prohibition (represented by C. C. Featherstone), gave Blease 3,565 to Featherstone's 820—a large proportion of his majority of 5,645, the largest he ever received.

Blease was largely made by the newspapers, for his style of saying and doing things made "news." His enemies made the tactical blunder of circulating incredible falsehoods, often easily proved untrue, instead of confining themselves to criticism founded on fact. He was said to have engaged in a drunken orgy the night before his inauguration; whereas actually he was carried to Columbia ill upon a cot and spent the night with his family physician at his side. The exposure of such a slander nullified a hundred legitimate criticisms.

Governor Blease's inaugural opposed compulsory education, the use of white taxes for Negro schools, and any further laws regulating child or adult labor, and urged marriage certificates or registration, the separation of the races among convicts, the privilege of a county to choose high license as well as dispensary or prohibition, and liberal though not extravagant grants for education, etc., on the ideal of "a poor government and a rich people, in place of a rich government and a poor people."

The new Governor's autocratic spirit at once found expression in his refusal to appoint as special judges the persons nominated by the Supreme Court, as directed by law. He then demanded that the legislature give him power to appoint special judges independently of the court, lest there be conflict. He also defied the law by appointing as township commissioners in Beaufort persons of his own choice instead of those nominated by the county delegation—action which was unanimously condemned by the Supreme Court. When his Negro chauffeur was twice fined $3.75 for speeding, he pardoned him. The city authorities disregarded the pardon and imposed $15.75 for a third offense on the ground that, although the question had never been decided here, the courts of other States denied that the pardoning power extended to persons punished by city courts. The Governor retaliated by placing extra liquor constables on the city payroll and promising another for every time his chauffeur was "persecuted" on account of his employer's politics. But the chauffeur of a prominent Columbian was a few days later fined more severely.

"The statute outlawing race track gambling," remarked the Charleston *Post,* "went into effect July 1, 1912." But the manager of the races, to prevent the running of which the law was enacted, remarked to the Cincinnati *Enquirer* that the racing would proceed despite the law, as Charleston was peculiar in taking its own way with laws it did not like. The racing interests, said the Anderson *Daily Mail,* would feel safe after Attorney-General Lyon's retirement, January 14, 1913. Governor Blease said in his second inaugural (January, 1913), "They are yelling, 'What is the Governor going to do about the Charleston races?' Do they expect me to dress up like a preacher and beg them not to race?" Said Bishop Guerry in a powerful sermon in St. Philips's Episcopal Church, Charleston, on March 2, 1913, representative citizens declined his request to take part in protests against race track gambling and blind tigers because they belonged to clubs that were legally blind tigers. "The situation is indeed serious when our most respectable citizens are aiding and abetting the spirit of lawlessness in our midst which threatens to overturn the very foundations of our civilization, and is making our fair city a byword and a reproach to the whole county. How can you blame the professional gambler, or those who make their living by unlawful practices, when the most respectable element in the life of the city tells you 'their hands are tied' through their own failure to keep the law?" The *News and Courier* said editorially that this powerful sermon should be pondered in view of "the lethargy that exists in Charleston today in the face of moral conditions which have made this city a byword and a reproach from one end of the land to the other."

For these disgraceful conditions the city and county government, and the portion of the public profiting by the presence of visitors good and bad, must share the responsibility. The racing stopped after four annual meets of about two months each as a matter of course, immediately before the inauguration of Governor Manning in 1915.[4]

[4] The last races at the old Washington Race Course were in the 1880's. The contrast between modern race track gambling and the gambling of ante-bellum gentlemen on the sport is supposed to have contributed to its abandonment. The revived racing was held January-February, 1912-1913, 1914, and December-January, 1914-15 (the date being changed to avoid Governor Manning's accession) on the opposite, or Cooper, side of

Governor Blease's relations with the legislature were tempestuous. His numerous vetoes were generally overridden. He denounced two of the legislative leaders as North Carolinians born and another as of Northern parentage. Factionalism was so strong that anti-Bleaseites revolted at supporting even his recommendations which they approved, and were in danger of being proclaimed Bleaseites if they did. Physical combat between the Governor and various opponents actually within the legislative chamber or capitol was repeatedly imminent. Several messages were devoted to charges that the father of one of his senatorial enemies had commanded Negro troops, that the senator was trustee of a Negro school, and that a Negro was a school trustee in Beaufort. "I have no fear of Negro contacts," said the Governor, "neither for me nor any of my family—for each of them, I am proud to say, is physically able to pull a trigger whenever it should become necessary. But I am pleading for the white girls and white women of my State."[5]

We must go back almost two hundred years to Governor Nicholson for such hostility as Governor Blease's to the press. In vetoing a bill to modify the severe libel law, he used the word "lie" thirty-three times, "liar" eight times, strewed along "cowardly," "slime," "scurrilous blackguard," "low down," attacked newspapers by name, branded the newspaper fraternity as a dirty set of liars, and glorified Jim Tillman's murder of Editor Gonzales. The House expunged all but the essential parts of the message, as self-respect forbade such language in its records. The Senate refused to record the accompanying exhibits, and the *News and Courier* felt restrained by court decisions from printing some of the passages.

Never before in the State's history had there been an individual who so fully made his own personality and interests the center of politics. Amid the welter of personalities and passion Governor Blease made

Charleston Neck from the old Washington track. The Washington course was just east of the present Citadel, near the Ashley. See J. C. Hemphill, *New York Times,* January 26, 1913.

The 1912-15 track was outside the city limits.

[5] Senator Christensen, a native South Carolinian, stated that his father, a Federal officer (whom the Confederate veterans of Beaufort highly honored), did not command Negroes in the War of Secession, as, when assigned to that duty, he secured a transfer to other duty. The Senator was one of the four white men composing the board of a Negro agricultural school. Governor Blease, he remarked, was ex-officio trustee of a Negro school, and had formerly been a candidate for specific election as such a trustee in 1902. The Negro school trustee in Beaufort supervised the Negro schools and took no part in anything touching white pupils or teachers.—Senate Journal, 1914, pp. 283, 345, 485-91, 496, 1159.

The incident was merely an illustration of the use to which Governor Blease often put the Negro bugaboo. The charge regarding the Negro troops was first made in 1906 by a dispensary official under investigation by Mr. Christensen, the official who declared he would shoot dead anyone who asked certain questions regarding his private affairs.

little systematic effort to press any consistent program, although the statement of a writer sympathetic with his professed aims that he left not an act for the benefit of the masses might be considered extreme. He did promote some measures for the unfortunates, such as the separation of the races on chain gangs, the abolition of the penitentiary hosiery mill as unhealthy, the establishment of the State tuberculosis sanitarium, and the adoption of the Medical College in Charleston as a State institution. He insisted on better provision for common schools, a special tax on hydroelectric companies, and the assertion of the State's rights in the Columbia Canal. On the other hand, he was the strongest dependence of the liquor element and opposed factory inspection, compulsory education, and the medical examination of school children. The latter he represented to credulous ignorance as endangering female modesty and threatening to blast reputations because doctors would tattle that girls were not pure. He would telegraph a pardon, he declared, to any man who killed a doctor violating his daughter's modesty.

The Governor's opposition to factory inspection incurred the displeasure of organized labor (which, however, then included few cotton mill operatives), who could not understand why tens of thousands of free operatives should not have as good protection against unsanitary conditions as the Governor insisted upon for a few score convicts working under constant government supervision in the penitentiary. But Governor Blease was an extreme individualist, and he knew that the individualism of the unorganized operative was stronger than his realization of the need of modern social protection. He would veto any law, he declared, for improving the conditions of adults, who were free to work where they pleased; he knew more about factory workers than organized labor did, and persons mistreated must see him in person. When the Columbia Federation of Trades condemned him, he promised to have liquor constables inspect factories. Equally strong was his condemnation of compulsory school attendance, which he denounced as but "another form of Republicanism" in vetoing a bill for that purpose for Spartanburg County (passed, however, over his veto): "I consider this bill an outrage on the decent white fathers and mothers of this State, and if I were guilty of signing it I would feel that I would deserve the contempt of every child and every parent who would come under its provisions, as I feel those who vote for it will deserve."[6]

Charges and Counter-Charges Over Dispensary.—The dispensary added greatly to the bitterness of this unhappy era. As Governor Blease was the firm friend of the dispensary and its accused officials, a member of the commission created by the legislature to wind up the abolished

[6] Message No. 48 to Senate, February 28, 1914.

State dispensary remarked that the commission had discussed the new Governor's possible attitude. Governor Blease said that if they had done no wrong, they had nothing to fear, and called for a legislative investigation—a demand which the commission seconded. The legislature enacted the requisite act, which the Governor vetoed after adjournment, to see it passed over his veto unanimously in the House and thirty-six to three in the Senate at the next session. The Governor declined the invitation to supply the grounds of his criticizing the commission. Meanwhile his own appointees had sought to jail the chairman of the winding-up commission, Dr. W. J. Murray, one of the purest representatives of the State's highest citizenship, for refusing to surrender, until his legal discharge, the vouchers connected with the half million dollars collected for the State. Dr. Murray was saved from the humiliation of imprisonment by the prompt decision of the Supreme Court, which fully sustained his action.

During this time there raged a bitter and scurrilous controversy between Governor Blease and T. B. Felder, the Atlanta attorney whose extraordinary ability as lawyer and sleuth had so largely contributed to unearthing the proof of dispensary corruption. Felder charged Governor Blease with a series of crimes and challenged him to sue for damages, for paying which he said he possessed a quarter of a million. Governor Blease retaliated by unsuccessfully seeking indictments against Felder and demanding nevertheless his extradition. The disgusting exhibition dragged through the campaign of 1912 and culminated in the failure of a legislative committee of Governor Blease's enemies, aided by Felder and by Burns detectives, to fasten any crime upon the Governor. Incidentally, the dispensary and constables in Charleston were shown to be reeking with corruption.

A Second Term of Passion and Conflict.—The resignation of Chief Justice Ira B. Jones to oppose Blease in 1912 was a boon to the latter, for Jones on the stump was a failure. Senator Tillman's condemnation of Blease was far more serious; but a new generation had arisen that knew not Benjamin. Mayor Grace, charging that Blease had not only broken his promise not to put constables on Charleston but had installed the most corrupt grafters in the history of the dispensary, in speech and press rivaled Felder in abuse, while both, and also Governor Blease, sank to unexampled levels of mutual abuse. Grace and Felder so overreached themselves with obvious slanders as to cast doubt on their other charges.

The irregularities in the 1912 primary election proved that the corrupt voting which had long characterized low-lying elements in Charleston and Richland was spreading, under the stress of ambition and passion, among both the tenant farmers and the Piedmont industrial and urban centers. This led to widespread demand for tightening up the extremely loose primary, a system which had grown up under semi-rural conditions. Bleaseites opposed the move as directed against them. Tillman, alarmed for the existence of the primary, suggested that "no man should participate in the primary who is not willing and able to stand the test of registration to participate in the general election"; but he retreated from this admirable position the next year. This reasonable suggestion was too much for South Carolina political courage, and the revised rules left criminals, lunatics, paupers, and illiterates eligible for the only elections[7] that count.

The new rules adopted by the Democratic Convention in May, 1914, were enacted as State law in February, 1915. Enrolling by one's own hand (a rule since relaxed), with age and occupation given, provisions against corruption or carelessness, American citizenship, two years' residence in South Carolina, six months in the county, and sixty days in the precinct, were required. Party membership was not defined by the statute, thus seeking to leave the Democrats, as a non-governmental organization, free to exclude the Negro without violating the Fifteenth Amendment. Governor Blease's charge that the qualifications were planned to disfranchise his poor or ignorant supporters was met by the party's forbidding any property or educational qualification. In 1944, fearing that the Federal Supreme Court might annul the South Carolina Democratic Party's practice of denying membership to Negroes, as it had annulled a Texas statute to that effect, the legislature repealed all laws relating to primary elections so as to leave them purely private affairs. In 1914, records from thirty-two of the forty-three counties of the State revealed 19.8 per cent of the voters enrolling for the Democratic primary unable to sign their names. Some of the richest counties were among the worst, a fact which illustrates the sharp contrast of classes: Marlboro, 27.5 per cent; Spartanburg, 25 per cent; Cherokee, 29.3 per cent; Pickens, 26.4 per cent. Well-to-do South Carolina, intent on its own class interests, had allowed the seeds of ignorance and poverty planted in the past to rest undisturbed, and now cried out in surprise at their fruit. In 1918 the law prescribed the Australian ballot system for primaries except in small precincts, but not for general elections.

The Campaign of 1914 and Pardon Abuses.—The campaign of 1914 exhibited a repetition of the coarse personalities of 1912. Governor Blease opposed E. D. Smith for re-election to the United States Senate. Lang D. Jennings and W. P. Pollock, running for the same office, overwhelmed the Governor, the one with invective, the other with ridicule.

[7] Except in commission-governed cities, and in them also now.

He was passionately denounced for having, on baseless tittle-tattle, written that if decent women employees in the State hospital knew of conditions, they would leave, and for having subjected to humiliating questioning, the pure and noble young woman physician referred to, with her father and counsel excluded, so that she went weeping from the room.[8]

Governor Blease's abuse of the pardoning power was his fault most generally condemned. Pardons, paroles, commutations exceeded, it is said, 1,700 during his four years, including pardons for rapists, murderers of women, or of men defending women. But, bad as is the record, it should be remembered, first, that he pardoned many who had already served longer than law or judicial discretion would then decree; and, second, that though far the worst abuser of clemency that the State has ever seen, he was carrying to greater lengths a common abuse of American governors. It was commonly supposed that any personal friend or dispensary corruptionist was safe from punishment so long as Blease remained Governor. A lucrative practice in obtaining pardons was carried on by lawyer friends of the Governor, but elaborate efforts to prove the Governor shared their fees completely failed.[9]

How serious was the situation was illustrated in connection with the pardon of a man who defiled a child relative in his home, a pardon for which Governor Blease was reproached during the 1914 campaign. Dr. James H. McIntosh, whose name was attached to the typed letter stating that the convict's health demanded release, declared the letter a forgery, for his letter was hand written and had stated the opposite. The Doctor was shot down (though not killed) after midnight on the day he was to confront the Governor at the Columbia meeting by a man who shouted as he fled, "Coley won't be bothered with you tomorrow."

Senator Tillman attacked Blease heavily on August 14, 1914. He blamed resurgent Bourbonism and social injustice for Blease's vogue, and regretted that twenty-four (*sic*) years of the primary had so far failed to educate that "audacity, aptitude at repartee, coupled with a striking personality, have made the people an easy prey . . . to the wiles

[8] March 4, 1914, Governor Blease appeared in the House to deliver a message in person on the incident. He denied he had reflected on the lady, denounced as liars any who said he had, and challenged his critics to fistic combat, which was barely prevented on the spot.—Governor Blease's message January 20, 1914; Senate Journal, 1914, 941; Rept. Legislature Investigating Committee; Stenographic report of Governor Blease's secretary of asylum meeting of December 12, 1912, in *Columbia Record,* reprint in *Newberry Observer* of February 20, 1914; *State,* February 18, 20, March 14, 1941; *News and Courier,* March 5, 1914.

[9] Governor Manning placed Governor Blease's clemencies at 1,708; Governor Blease's secretary in a biographical sketch at over 1,500. I have examined them extensively but have not counted them.

and tricks of demagogues." The primary of 1914 returned E. D. Smith to the Senate by 72,266 against Blease's 56,913, Jennings' 2,258, and Pollock's 1,364. Blease fell the victim of political suicide, for, furious as were the attacks of enemies, his own acts compelled his defeat. The response of many old opponents to his conservative campaign for the United States Senate in 1924 in which he was elected, even after he deeply offended patriotic sentiment during World War I, argues that in the long run he lost more than he gained by his large contribution to coarsening public life.

The gubernatorial contest, sufficiently interesting with "Bleaseism" being combated by Richard I. Manning and compulsory education being championed by Professor John G. Clinkscales, for the first time by anyone in a State campaign, derived a dramatic suspense from the danger that the large number of anti-Blease candidates would so divide their vote that their faction would be under the necessity of choosing between two Bleaseites in the second primary. The outbreak of World War I aided the efforts to concentrate on Manning as the practical man of affairs. The second primary showed 73,739 for Manning and 45,091 for the Bleaseite John G. Richards. Every Bleaseite congressional candidate was defeated.

The Cotton Panic, 1914.—Governor Blease's conduct in the cotton panic early in World War I, with Southern farmers already depressing the price by an enormous crop, was creditable. It is true that he signed the act restricting acreage to one-third of the total planted in all crops in 1914; but the act was repealed before the season for the next planting. By holding the $24,000,000 cotton bond bill (which he never signed) until election day, he made impossible a popular vote for the bonds. This was cool and statesmanlike conduct while thousands of conservative men had utterly lost their heads. He was a combination of clear, cool thinking when employing his reasoning faculties only, and of impulsive, violent action in the realm of his emotions. The latter was illustrated, in a quarrel with the Federal government, by his disbanding the entire militia about a week before the expiration of his term. Having sent the legislature several of the longest messages in American history recounting his political career, he resigned, without reason assigned, five days before the natural end of his term. Charles A. Smith then became governor for five days. Thus Governor Blease was not succeeded by his hated rival, Governor Manning.

CHAPTER LXII

PROGRESSIVE CONSERVATISM AND THE FIRST WORLD WAR, 1915-1918

Richard Irvine Manning (1859-1931), elected governor in 1914 and '16, was a large Sumter farmer and banker of wide business connections and success and legal education, though he never practiced. He was active in the Episcopal Church and deeply interested in social and economic reforms. Since the first American Manning married the daughter of his fellow-Revolutionary officer General Richardson, three Richardsons and three Mannings have been governors. R. I. Manning (1824-26) was the grandfather and J. L. Manning (1852-54) the uncle of the governor of 1915 to 1919.

Governor Manning's business experience had been supplemented by service in the State Senate, etc. His ideas were always more popular than himself; for, although easy and courteous, he lacked both the instinct and the arts of popular appeal.

It is hard to realize the feeling of relief and triumph with which the conservative classes saw the administration assumed by Manning after fourteen years of dispensary corruption and wrangle and four years of Blease's defiance of so many traditions associated with the governorship. Governor Manning considered himself a crusader against lawlessness. He revoked Governor Blease's order disbanding the militia. The race track gamblers departed as a matter of course.

Governor Manning had been an advocate of a purified dispensary as the best solution of the liquor question. After prolonged efforts to stir Mayor Grace to action, Governor Manning sent constables to Charleston and a warning to the sheriff. After the Governor's insistence on better jurors, the Charleston grand jury found forty-eight true bills for violation of the liquor law, petty juries convicted four persons, and thirty-nine pleaded guilty. Sixty-nine were said soon after to have surrendered their licenses from the Federal government, which still licensed men to violate the police regulations of a State. Judge M. L. Smith imposed fines with imprisonment suspended, since for twenty years violators had been taught by the city authorities that they could operate under a virtual license system. It thus remained for the quiet churchman of 1915 to carry out Governor Tillman's threat in the 1890's "to raise hell on Chicco Street."[1]

Economic and Social Legislation, 1915-1917.—No South Carolina governor ever secured better co-operation with the legislature or saw more of his recommendations adopted. While many were measures naturally to be expected from a progressive legislature, the extent and consistency of the program enacted during his administrations owed much to the earnestness with which Governor Manning urged a matured and harmonious policy. Tillman, while governor, drove through measures by sheer force of a popular dictator. Governor Manning had neither the temperament nor the mass support for dictatorship, but possessed unusual talent for presenting convincingly the defects or merits of a policy. Humane accomplishments were the establishment of the Board of Charities and Corrections and the modernizing of the State Hospital for the Insane, which through failure of legislation to meet growing needs had reached a deplorable condition of physical depreciation and faulty organization. Governor Manning secured a nationally known expert, on the basis of whose report he pointed the way to practical solutions. From his private funds the Governor liberally supplemented the granted salary to employ a superintendent of unusual medical and administrative skill, Dr. C. Fred Williams, and secured from the legislature enormous appropriations which created, in all but external walls, a new institution on modern standards, ending, as he said, "needless misery heaped on hopeless tragedy."

Governor Manning had long been active in seeking to prohibit child labor. The age limit was now raised from twelve to fourteen years for workers in mines and factories, releasing about 2,400 children. Operatives were protected against excessive docking. Prolonged textile strikes in Anderson led to armed defiance of law, even threatening the murder of persons attempting to enter the plants. The Sheriff's refusal to co-operate necessitated the Governor's sending troops to protect magistrates' constables and preserve peace. The Governor's refusal to act more drastically lost him the support of some prominent mill officials. Textile strikes accompanied by violence occurred later in Anderson and Greenville.

Tillman's old argument that compulsory education would endanger white supremacy had grown rather stale in the face of 131,577 Negroes to 124,339 whites in the common schools in 1918. State appropriations for education more than doubled from 1915 to 1918, and a mild compulsory law, soon largely neglected, was enacted in 1919. The most important fiscal legislation for years was the creation of the State Tax Com-

[1] Alderman Chicco was known as "the king of the blind tigers."

mission, appointive by the Governor. The Commission became the chief tax advisory and superintending agency of the government, and began equalization of property valuations. The income tax, very much a farce since its enactment in 1897, was made eventually one of the chief sources of revenue, and the corporation, gasoline, soft drink, and other taxes necessitated by expanding social services were administered with a success for which some such agency, separated so far as possible from politics, was essential. The creation of the Tax Commission, the re-creation of the asylum, and his service in his second administration as one of the great war governors constitute Governor Manning's chief title to statesmanship.

The Bitter Campaign of 1916.—Against Governor Manning appealing for re-election, ex-Governor Blease became a candidate for a third term. Manning had done more for the masses through legislation than any former governor, illustrating in this the frequency with which such leadership in all countries comes from the upper classes; but so superior was Blease in popular appeal that a change of 2,343 votes would have given him the election. Charleston showed its resentment to Manning's anti-race-track and liquor-law enforcement by giving Blease a heavy majority. The class antagonism which had for decades constituted the chief force in South Carolina politics was intensified by Governor Manning's congratulating the State upon the triumph of law and order and by his partisans' joy that "South Carolina is redeemed." Senator Tillman was doubtless substantially right in saying, on September 14, that "all the tin horn gamblers, all the blind tigers, all the red light habitues, all the criminals and near criminals—those who have been pardoned and those not yet caught and convicted—were for Blease." But he held that 45,000 of Blease's supporters were good men misled. How little the masses who believed Blease their friend were moved by Tillman's powerful presentation of Governor Blease's pardons of a particularly infamous rapist, a wife murderer, and the slayer of an old man defending his daughter's virtue, was proved when the counties to which these criminals were returned gave Blease majorities. The simple truth is, a large part of the electorate have a feeble abhorrence of crime.

The destruction of the confidence of each side in the common honesty of the other amounted to a civic tragedy. On October 4, 1916, Blease addressed by invitation the faculty and students of Allen University, a Negro college in Columbia. The Negro Bishop Chappelle introduced him as "the strongest white man in the State of South Carolina," whose casting vote on the canvassing board had given the Negro Murray the election to Congress against a white man, and the sting of whose harsh words had been removed by the pardon of so many Negroes.

If the Democratic Executive Committee had been as honest as he was in voting to seat the Negro congressman, said Mr. Blease, he would have been declared governor in 1916. He had always, he said, advocated Negro taxes going to Negro schools, but the school boards chiseled the Negro out of them.[2] He urged Christian citizenship, though himself seldom a church attendant, he said, because of the hypocrites, and he thought sometimes that all prisons and courthouses might be abolished; why them and churches too? (Great applause.) Hitch your wagon to a star. "You're coming to higher things. They can't hold you back, despite what I or another man may say."

Manning's second administration continued the program of economic and social betterment—the State Highway Commission, the school for the feeble-minded, the Industrial School for delinquent girls, the separation of the Negro boys' reformatory from penitentiary control, and the collection, after the Board of Charities and Corrections' investigations, of tuition at State institutions of about twice the total expense of the board. Taxable values, largely through the Tax Commission, rose from $279,755,349 in 1910 and $307,178,882 in 1914 to $376,178,581 in 1918. The insurance companies which had left the State under the anti-rate-agreement law of 1916, giving the insurance commissioner large power in rate revision, returned under the compromise acts of 1917. The State had obtained some improvements, but had failed to secure free competition in rate-making.

The Industrial School (or reformatory) for Negro girls was established in 1949.

Blease Condemns America's Entering War.—During the uneasy period of disturbed relations with Mexico, two South Carolina regiments and a troop of cavalry spent several months guarding the border near El Paso. On the outbreak of World War I, August, 1914, South Carolina's considerable German-descended element and the much smaller Irish contingent largely sympathized with the Teutonic powers. As America's entrance into the war impended, about 200 Lexington people, many of the best standing, protested, April 2, 1917, against our entering a war precipitated by the privileged, from which only that class in the United States could profit. But a larger Lexington meeting, on April

[2] More accurately, he had opposed white men's taxes being used to help support Negro schools. In fact Mr. Blease's was no more the "casting vote" in making Murray Congressman than that of any other member of the board. This act, honest and courageous, in later campaigns cost him dear when he was paid for it in his own coin of appeals to race prejudice.

In summarizing the speech before the Negro college, the report in the *State* is followed virtually in all particulars, as being moderate and detailed, as might be expected from the character and experience of the reporter, Mr. Irby Koon, rather than that of the Negro paper, the *Samaritan Herald,* of October 12.

19, applauded Governor Manning when he declared a patriotic government could have kept us out no longer. Every South Carolina congressman but one, Mr. F. G. Dominick, voted for war. The die cast, German descendants rallied practically unanimously to the government and supplied notable patriotic leaders.

On May 14 about 300 Blease leaders met in Columbia to protest against alleged mistreatment of their faction. John P. Grace denounced Congress for declaring war. Blease strongly endorsed him and declared that winning "the political war of 1918" was almost as important as defeating Germany. On July 27 Blease attacked the national administration and its entering the war, before an audience largely of German descent at Pomaria. In York County in August he declared that the President and every congressman who voted for war would be removed if he were able, and that "Dick Manning is the worst Governor the State ever had, worse than Scott, Chamberlain, or Moses, because they only stole money, but he is trying to steal the souls and bodies of your boys." "They talk about a free America. I don't care what kind of America it is when I am dead and gone. Neither does your boy."[3]

Almost all the Blease leaders vigorously supported the war; but such was the cohesion of the faction that it supported its chief's 1918 race for the Senate with an unrivaled organization. Governor Blease's old bodyguard, Beard, turned editor, was imprisoned in 1917 for seeking to stir mutiny and obstruct recruiting. A writer on the Charleston *American* was convicted for helping sink a ship, and the paper was excluded from the mail as long as Grace remained its editor.

On the American declaration of war, April 6, 1917, Governor Manning appointed a Commission on Civic Preparedness for War (David R. Coker, chairman), which accomplished remarkable results. The Negro population co-operated loyally in all aspects of the war. Strong and upright men whose very characters, temperaments, and achievements constituted a bar to public participation in our amorphous, passion-ridden one-party personal politics gave themselves to the public service. Said the Secretary of War, "The South Carolina Council of National Defense is ranked . . . as among the very first in the entire Union, because of the variety and value of its activities, the closeness of its co-operation with the National Council and the thoroughness of its local organization." The women contributed their full share in this unexampled national co-operation, which presented a manifestation of organized power that is still awe-inspiring to contemplate.

South Carolina's mild winter climate caused the establishment here

[3] *Charleston American* and *Yorkville Inquirer* (Blease Papers); reprint in *News and Courier*, June 21, 1918; also the *State*, August 3, 1917, August 20, 1918.

of Camp Jackson at Columbia, Camp Sevier at Greenville, Camp Wadsworth at Spartanburg, the Marines' recruiting depot at Parris Island, and the Marine Corps Supply Service at Charleston. The fear of disorderly and immoral conditions from assembling 40,000 to 60,000 soldiers in one locality proved groundless as a result of the police and moral regulations employed by the government authorities.

The Heated Political Campaign of 1918.—While the South Carolina soldiers in France were nearing their greatest achievement, the bitter primary campaign of 1918 was in progress at home on the issue of united support of the President. N. B. Dial, a successful businessman, moderate, of strong common sense, and a firm supporter of President Wilson, announced for the Senate. Ex-Governor Blease launched his campaign in a "Reform party" convention, April 20. He urged hearty support of the war and related his offer of a rifle range free and his heavy purchase of liberty bonds, and denounced his enemies for seeking to use patriotism for political selfishness.

Senator Tillman, standing for re-election, was highly esteemed in Washington, where, as a member and later chairman of the Naval Affairs Committee, he had contributed to strengthen our "first line of defense." His winning of many old opponents brought the loss of old friends. Though he had been enfeebled by a paralytic stroke, he was supported by many South Carolinians as essential for defeating Blease. But the anxiety of Governor Manning to be assured of a senator who would fully support the war caused him to warn Senator Tillman of the perilous situation created by his health, and, when this produced no result, to seek to have the administration act for Tillman's withdrawal in favor of A. F. Lever. But President Wilson, confident that Blease could not succeed, insisted on Lever's remaining chairman of the House Agricultural Committee, on which he had rendered notable service. Tillman was angered on discovering the plan to displace him; but in less than a month he was dead. Though his term has since been exceeded by E. D. Smith, he had served longer in the Senate than any other South Carolinian, and longer than all but three living Senators. From being the butt of metropolitan ridicule, he had come, by personal force, intelligence, and integrity, to command nationwide respect. But for his unsystematic education and impatient mind, his abilities might have raised him to high rank as a statesman.

The death of Tillman left Dial, sensible and safe, but unimpressive, as the antagonist of Blease. Running at the same time for the short term were W. P. Pollock and Christie Benet, whose merciless attacks were directed at Blease rather than at each other. Blease, refusing to accompany the campaign party, appeared however at some meetings. At

York, June 20, refusing to be bound by the thirty-minute rule, he spoke long to an adjourned meeting, saying there should be free discussion of the war, which he would debate with any representative sent from Washington; that 90 per cent of the people were against the war, and 75 per cent of the South Carolina soldiers were "Reformers"; that men who said he had uttered a disloyal word were liars, and, if they would not fight for that, he would "call them a name which no decent man would take." At Florence, July 16, Dial faced him with a charge of being "disloyal from the crown of his head to the sole of his foot," and Blease declined to speak. Tillman denounced Blease as a characterless traitor to God and country, and Blease described his old chief as having betrayed the Reform party as Judas did his Master.

Two weeks before the election there was published President Wilson's reply to an inquirer as to whether the Charleston *American's* claim that Blease would be as acceptable to him as Dial was correct: "Let me say that I have perfect confidence that the people of South Carolina will judge rightly in the senatorial contest, and I have not the least fear that they will believe that Mr. Blease is or can be a friend of the administration. The record of his opinion is already written and it is a little late to expunge it."[4]

The campaign of 1918 was another proof that the custom of dividing time, introduced into South Carolina by force against the Republicans in 1876, was unsuited for any but semi-war purposes. Dial was elected senator by 65,064 to Blease's 40,456, while Robert A. Cooper's vote about doubled that of John G. Richards, the Blease candidate for governor.

Mr. Blease vastly mistook the temper of the people and reaped the natural reward of attacking the President and the war. He was accustomed to being very violent when not able to have his own way, and might, if able to rouse popular response, have caused serious consequences. The vote he received was far more an expression of devotion to an individual and, in the minds of many, to a democratic ideal, than of discontent with the war.

South Carolina Soldiers in France.—The vastness of the operations

[4] At the Richland County Democratic Convention, 1918, Blease seconded the resolutions endorsing Wilson's administration, saying it was now a time for unanimity. John T. Duncan commented that it was gratifying to see such unanimity, especially when some had talked of soldiers' shooting officers in the back. (Account of A. S. Salley, who was present.)

The allusion was to Blease's being reported to have said at Pomaria, in sneering at Manning's sons "in their pretty uniforms," that their men would shoot them in the back. A man shouted that he had a boy good to do it. The papers refused to publish this. A hearer present at the Pomaria incident related it to the writer's father.

Six of Governor Manning's sons (all the sons but one surviving from his thirteen children, all of one mother) entered the war. One was too young for service. One, Major W. S. Manning, was killed in action, November 5, 1918. Mr. Blease was childless.

and the distribution of the men through many organizations render specific account of the part played by South Carolina soldiers impossible except for a few localities. The old territorial organization of the army was abandoned and the appeal to local pride in regiments' State names sacrificed, as modern war involves the danger otherwise of almost annihilating the young manhood of particular communities. National feeling was disseminated by uniting men from all sections in the same units. Nevertheless, South Carolina troops formed important parts of certain divisions.

The 42d (or Rainbow) Division was one of the first completed of the new army. It consisted of selected National Guard units from twenty-six States and the District of Columbia. South Carolina supplied a battalion of the 117th Engineers and the regimental colonel and lieutenant-colonel. It occupied positions from Château-Thierry on the west to Baccarat, southeast of Lunéville. As part of the Third Corps, First American Army, it participated in reducing the Marne and St. Mihiel salients, operations protecting Verdun, which were completed September 12, 1918. It participated in the great Meuse-Argonne offensive which was driving the Germans when the armistice came.

Many South Carolina Negroes served well in the 371st Regiment of the 92d Division (Negroes), which fought severely as part of the First American Army around Verdun and in the drive toward Metz.

The 321st infantry, composed largely of South Carolinians, was helping to smash a section of the Hindenburg Line at Ville-en-Woevre, south of Verdun, when the armistice was signed.

South Carolina is most strongly connected with the 30th, called the Old Hickory, Division, because of President Jackson's connection with North Carolina, South Carolina, and Tennessee, whose National Guards formed its basis. Men from these States formed its majority after thousands of drafted men were added from them and from Indiana, Illinois, Iowa, Minnesota, and North Dakota. More than 95 per cent of its men were born of American parents. It was trained at Camp Sevier, Greenville. Predominantly South Carolinian were the 118th Infantry Regiment, formed on the old First South Carolina Regiment; the 105th Ammunition Train, formed on the Second South Carolina Regiment; a field hospital; and the Headquarters Troop, formed on Troop A, South Carolina Cavalry (the Charleston Light Dragoons).

The 30th Division landed at Calais on May 24, 1918. After training and fighting in Belgium, it, along with the 27th Division, made up of New Yorkers trained at Camp Wadsworth at Spartanburg, forming together the Second Corps, was attached to the British Fourth Army.

The 30th and the 27th Divisions took over from Australians and British respectively the attack at Bellicourt on the Hindenburg Line, which here lay before 6,500 yards of tunnel through which ran a canal. The 30th Division was to attack the southern 3,500 yards and some distance to the southward, and the 27th, the 3,000 yards beyond on their left. Attacking shortly before 6:00 A.M., September 29, the 30th Division that day took the entire trench system, the tunnel behind it, and the troops it sheltered, defeated two divisions, and captured 1,481 men. The 27th Division, whose way had not been so effectively prepared, completed the capture of its part of the line after severe fighting covering September 29 and 30, and October 1. The relationship of the South Carolina and the New York troops in the taking of Chapultepec before the City of Mexico was thus duplicated in France.[5]

On October 1 and 2 the 30th was relieved by Australian troops, but resumed its old sector the night of October 4-5, and advanced October 9 to 11, taking 1,934 prisoners. Relieved by the 27th, the 30th returned on October 17, 18, and 19 and advanced 9,000 yards, taking 418 prisoners. The Armistice came during the next rest period, and the 30th and 27th were detached from the British, with whom the 30th had been since arrival. The 30th now joined the American army in the LeMans area.

South Carolina's contribution in money, including bond purchases and donations, approached $100,000,000, which ranks the State, by capacity, among the highest in the Union. The official roster of her soldiers, sailors, and marines contains 64,739 names (including a few women in war office service), of whom 2,085 died in service, 460 in battle or of battle injuries.

South Carolina soldiers won a remarkable proportion of distinctions for bravery. The highest American award was the Congressional Medal of Honor, given for conspicuous gallantry at the risk of life in actual conflict with an enemy above and beyond the call of duty. Of the 78 awarded among the 1,200,000 Americans in battle, 6 went to South Carolinians, all of whom were of the 118th Infantry, Thirtieth Division. Only New York with ten, Illinois with eight, and New Jersey with seven received more, and only California, Missouri, and Tennessee received as many as South Carolina. The 30th Division, with twelve Congressional Medals, exceeded any other division by three.

The Distinguished Service Cross was won by eighty-eight South Carolina soldiers, and the Distinguished Service Medal (awarded for services of great responsibility, not in combat) was awarded to five officers from South Carolina. South Carolina soldiers carried into the World War a great tradition and sustained it. The view that sees glory

[5] Pershing, *My Experiences in the World War*, II, 304-5.

only in the distant past and only degeneration for the future disregards this heroism and devotion of every class.

Governor Manning was fortunate in that his administration fell at a time when currents of social reform were running strongly and a titanic struggle was evoking patriotic activity. He subordinated himself to his duty, met great opportunities greatly, and left one of the administrations of our history notable for both civic and military achievements. He gave six sons to the army and was rejoicing in American victory when news arrived that one had been killed in action six days before the armistice. To the exigencies of politics pushing for the appointment of men for any reason but their fitness, he yielded remarkably little. Large as were his achievements in administration and legislation, his greatest service was practicing high ideals of citizenship, public duty, and regard for law, in which he was sustained by those strongest motives of worthy living, never paraded but always present —religion and honor.

CHAPTER LXIII

POLITICAL AND RACIAL PROBLEMS, 1919-1948

THE BITTER factionalism since 1910, partly submerged during World War I, was followed in the 1920's by a period of comparative calm soon settling into political stagnation. Meanwhile, in the world of business, a period of inflated prosperity was followed by years of disillusionment, emotional exhaustion, and economic collapse.

Racial Unrest Following World War I.—The World War disturbed the traditional relations of the races, as was inevitable. A convention of South Carolina Negroes, January 4, 1919, resolved that the lethargy of the Republican party in South Carolina should be ended by every eligible Negro's registering. They demanded representation on every school board controlling Negro schools, better schools, and better Negro teachers' salaries, and protested, not against the "jim crow" car law, but against the unequal accommodation offered for Negroes, and the freedom allowed whites of coming into the Negro car to drink liquor. Bishop Chappelle said that what he desired was for the Negro to be the balance of power between white factions. He would be willing, he said, to follow the devil himself as the leader of a split in the Democratic party.

Serious race riots had just occurred in Washington. Rumors of an impending Negro uprising in Columbia led hundreds of men to arm and plan for assembling women and children in designated places. A committee of prominent citizens published a statement that they had investigated every rumor and found no "organized attack" being plotted by Negroes, but deprecated personal clashes and warned the Negroes against "allowing violent and incendiary speakers, especially those from a distance."

Two widely different organizations emerged to meet a danger which was serious over a large part of the United States—the Inter-Racial Conference and the Kuklux Klan. The one worked through conciliation and the other through inspiring fear. The secretly organized and excited Klansmen for some years not only held the Negroes in awe, mortified the Jews, and inflamed the Catholics by their loud propaganda of Anglo-Saxon Protestantism, but inspired dread of their political power among non-member whites. The movement subsided with the conditions by which it was fostered, but flickered up again in 1938 to '40. During 1940-41 Klansmen were convicted for whipping Negroes or other unlawful activities. New Klan activity occurred in 1950.

Another political reaction was a new attempt, feebly reminiscent of President Theodore Roosevelt's, to organize a Southern white Republican party. The "lily white" movements of the 1920's amounted in South Carolina only to maneuvers of one set of Republican patronage seekers to dispossess the set fortified by black support.

Free Spending and Reaction.—Robert A. Cooper, elected governor in 1918, proposed to carry on the progressive program of the past several years. His program of reform, which a few years before would have constituted a politician's funeral song, resulted in his re-election without opposition, as wartime enthusiasm had not yet been deflated by depression; but South Carolina conservatism spoke in the House's rejection in 1920 of the woman suffrage Federal amendment by 94 to 20. Ex-Governor Blease, contending again in 1922 for a third term, demanded the abolition of the Tax Commission and the Board of Public Welfare. It was Blease's tenth State-wide race, and he suffered by the election of Thomas G. McLeod, 100,114 to 85,834, his eighth State-wide defeat. Although Charleston, remembering Blease's leniency on liquor, gave him a majority, the *News and Courier* hailed McLeod's election as a victory for good government.

Governor McLeod suffered the misfortune of having his two terms fall in the midst of the prolonged depression which fell upon agriculture in 1921. He possessed neither the opportunity nor the aggressive personality for striding across the barriers to the good administration and executive leadership which the organization of our State presents in extreme American form, and his leadership was largely limited to continuing liberal support to education and recommending two ends which have so far baffled legislatures and Governors—reorganizing State administration and equalizing the general property tax.

Senatorial and Presidential Campaigns.—In 1924 ex-Governor Blease defeated for re-election to the Senate N. B. Dial, who had defeated him in 1918. Dial, a conservative, working senator, had offended veterans by opposing liberal pensions. The Democrats, he said in the Senate on January 3, 1925, incurred national defeat by abandoning principle for the opportunities of socialism and bolshevism. President Coolidge he considered a better Democrat than many claiming the name.

The ex-Governor had conducted his campaign of 1924 with such moderation and dignity as to be spoken of as "a new Blease." Many of his positions in the Senate voiced his sound sense, as, e.g., his votes against reducing the Federal income taxes and against the McNary-

Haugen agricultural bonus bill. His thus opposing almost all his Democratic colleagues was characteristic, as was his refusal to be bound by the caucus. His energy and determination secured the enactment of the King's Mountain battlefield bill when it was considered dead for the session. On January 3, 1929, he defended Joe Tolbert, long the Republican boss of South Carolina, then in disfavor with President Hoover, against charges of selling postmasterships. But shortly before the general election of 1928 Senator Blease said in his Gaffney speech, in effect, that every postmaster in South Carolina paid Tolbert for his job. Blease was defeated for re-election by James F. Byrnes in 1930, and lost by 114,840 to 150,468 when seeking to defeat for re-election Senator E. D. Smith in 1932.

Byrnes was elected twice to the Senate, and after a distinguished career in that body, in the later years of which he became one of the most influential members, was in 1941 appointed to the Federal Supreme Court. Resigning from the bench in October, 1942, to render war service as Director of Economic Stabilization, he served in that position until May, 1943, when he became Director of War Mobilization with such extensive powers as to be called colloquially "assistant president." He would, it is believed, have been the Democratic nominee for vice-president in 1944 (and consequently ultimately president) but for his being unacceptable to the Catholics, who considered him a deserter from the church of his father, to the Northern Negroes, and to organized labor. He was secretary of state from July, 1945, until January 20, 1947, when he retired from public service and became a member of a leading Washington law firm, though retaining his residence in Spartanburg, South Carolina. His patriotic sense of duty in resigning from one of the most attractive lifetime positions in the world to take up war service, and the discretion and firmness marking him as one of the wisest heads in the national councils, entitle him to an honorable place in the history of his State and country. Mr. Byrnes, who came up the hard way, as his father died shortly before the son's birth, has dedicated the income from his book, *Speaking Frankly,* to giving orphans or half orphans four years in college by donating $2,000 to each recipient. The total fund, by June, 1949, amounted to $100,000, besides $5,000 given for crippled children. In 1950 he was overwhelmingly elected governor over several opponents.

John Rutledge, associate justice 1789-91, chief justice *ad interim,* 1795, but unconfirmed, and William Johnson, associate justice, 1804-34, have been the only other Supreme Court justices from South Carolina, though C. C. Pinckney and Edward Rutledge declined appointment. No other South Carolinians except Hugh S. Legaré (1843) and John C. Calhoun

(1844-5) have been secretary of state, though C. C. Pinckney declined the position.

The national election of 1928 stirred deep feeling in South Carolina because of the nomination by the Democrats of Alfred E. Smith for president. South Carolina felt strongly the anti-Catholic prejudice and was determined to defend national prohibition, which Smith opposed. Efforts failed to eliminate from the oath required at the State Democratic primary the pledge to support national as well as State nominees (the famous Rule 32), although presidential electors are not voted for in the primary. It was said that in no other State was there such an iron-clad requirement of 100 per cent party regularity. Some thousands gave up their right to vote in the only election that counts in South Carolina, thus being totally disfranchised by an iron-clad party requirement, and a few Democrats voted for Hoover. So keenly do almost all South Carolinians realize the peril of any move that looks toward dividing the whites that they submitted to this otherwise intolerable party tyranny. The Democratic National Convention of 1936, pandering to the Northern Negro vote, led to South Carolina's repealing in 1938 the presidential part of the voter's pledge, as presidential electors are not voted for in the primary. United States Senator E. D. Smith walked out of the 1936 convention and in 1938 played up the re-invigorated Negro issue strongly, and in spite of President Roosevelt's opposition to him as not a good "New Dealer," and John L. Lewis's opposition as not a friend of organized labor, he was re-elected by a large majority over Governor Olin D. Johnston, who boasted of having been a cotton mill operative as a youth and of endorsement by President Franklin D. Roosevelt.

The Negro and the Democratic Primary.—The legislature in 1943 and 1944, dreading Federal interference with the exclusion of the Negroes from membership in the Democratic party and therefore from voting in its primaries, repealed all laws for punishing frauds or otherwise regulating primary elections, with the intent of leaving them legally as purely private arrangements as a social club. On July 12, 1947, the Federal district court invalidated the rule restricting party membership to whites as depriving other persons of their political rights on account of race. The Supreme Court refused, on April 19, 1948, to review the ruling of the circuit court of appeals upholding this decision. The principle applies, of course, to all party positions and activities. In 1950 the State law made the qualification for primaries the same as for the general election, and made a thorough Australian ballot system compulsory for both. The secret ballot, with all candidates on one ticket, had always been used in the primary, though individual booths for voters were of only recent use.

The Negroes' revived interest in politics dates back several years, but as yet is not general. In 1944 they organized in the State the Progressive Democratic party, upholding F. D. Roosevelt, but not State Democratic candidates, and cast perhaps 3,500 of the 90,601 votes in the State for Roosevelt. In 1948 their convention elected delegates for the National Democratic Convention in hope of having them seated instead of those of the regular Democrats, who had been instructed by a convention under covert threats of bolting in case of President Truman's being nominated as the party candidate. The Democrats in 1936, representing, whether sincerely or merely shrewdly, in the enthusiasm for F. D. Roosevelt, that sectional issues within the party were dead, repealed the rule requiring a two-thirds majority for nominations—a rule which had secured the nomination of Woodrow Wilson in 1912 instead of Champ Clark. Only Alabama, Georgia, Mississippi, South Carolina, Tennessee, Texas, Virginia, and six non-Southern States opposed, and so the South was deprived of its protective power of veto over unfriendly candidates.[1] In 1948 the lower South in their opposition to candidate Truman's pro-Negro policies repeated their tactics of 1860 by nominating a Southern candidate for the presidency in opposition to the regular Democrats, thus threatening (as it proved ineffectively) the defeat of the only party from which they could expect any special consideration. Governor J. Strom Thurmond of South Carolina, nominated by the State Rights Democratic party for president, carried his own state by 102,607 to Truman's 34,423, Dewey's 5,386, and Henry Wallace's 154. Judging from the straight Democratic versus Republican race for senator, about 5,000 Negroes voted. Alabama, Louisiana, and Mississippi also voted for Thurmond.[2]

State Politics, 1926-30.—To return from national to State affairs: The campaign of 1926 illustrated the vacuity to which politics had been reduced. A candidate for the United States Senate who almost unseated E. D. Smith asserted (on the strength, when he was called down, of somebody's having told him) that three judges of the World Court were Negroes; and huge excitement raged against the one-cent tax on soft drinks—a device raising a large revenue, an appreciable amount being from persons who escape almost all other contribution to the State which protects them.

John G. Richards, a Bleaseite, elected in 1926, was the first governor under the amendment fixing the term of State officers at four years and making the governor ineligible for immediate re-election. Throughout

[1] The two-thirds rule was adopted in 1832 at Jackson's demand in order to render impossible the re-nomination of Calhoun for the vice-presidency.

[2] Thurmond was defeated for the U. S. Senate in 1950 by the incumbent, Senator Johnston.

his administration he sought the abolition of the Tax Commission and the Board of Public Welfare and condemned proposals to value property for taxation at 100 per cent as required by law, instead of the professed but very poorly carried out custom of valuation at 42 per cent. He incurred ridicule by excessive efforts to suppress Sunday golf and gasoline sales, while freight trains thundered along on the Sabbath and serious crime was alarming. His warning against atheists in the schools was seconded by a bill forbidding the teaching of evolution in State-supported schools or colleges. This died in committee, as there was no organized movement behind it. Governor Richards' refusal to re-appoint the highly valuable lawyer member of the State Tax Commission, J. Fraser Lyon, and the Senate's refusal to confirm anyone else, was settled by confirming the new appointee and making Lyon the salaried counsel of the commission, for which as a member he had just won an enormous railroad tax suit.

Popular votes for biennial instead of annual sessions of the legislature in 1924, 1930, and 1940 failed of legislative ratification, as did also the popular vote for State-wide prohibition in 1940.

The $65,000,000 Road Bond Act.—Governor Richards won the support of the strong element sponsoring the rapid development of good roads by falling in with their plan for a $65,000,000 bond issue without a vote by the people. The perennial talk of good roads had been given an effective turn by the automobile. Improved earth and gravel construction was followed by concrete in the wealthier counties. By 1910 scientific road engineering was fairly under way. The State Highway Department was created in 1917 to study the best methods and advise and assist the counties. The department was soon given the duty of building and maintenance, and gradually thousands of miles of through roads were placed under its control.

The movement for a huge State bond issue was launched at a good roads convention in January, 1923. In 1924 came the "pay-as-you-go" act, under which, with gasoline tax, gradually mounting to six cents a gallon, and heavy license-plate fees, construction went rapidly forward. By June 30, 1940, there had been constructed 6,308 miles of hard-surface roads.

In 1929, without having been discussed in the recent campaign, the plan for a $65,000,000 bond issue was launched upon the legislature without the popular vote which the Constitution requires, as it was thought that a two-thirds popular vote for increasing the public debt could never be obtained. The Supreme Court found itself divided three to two against the constitutionality of the measure. The Constitution requires the Court when not unanimous on a constitutional question to call in the circuit judges. The *enbanc Court* overwhelmingly overruled the Supreme Court justices and declared the bond issue legal without popular vote on the ground that the dedication of revenues from taxes connected with the use of the roads put the bonds outside the constitutional prohibition of increasing the State's debt without popular vote.

Public condemnation of making waste paper of the Constitution was widespread. Even men of moderate views agreed that the decision cost the courts a serious loss of popular respect. The great public benefit of good roads was thus attained with the highest rapidity not only by that sacrifice but by tying up for a generation the State's easiest and richest source of revenue, forming a large proportion of all public income, irrespective of future financial difficulties or needs. Several judges during these years lamented in the strongest terms the common disregard of law and the ineffectiveness of the courts. Governor Blackwood's inaugural in 1931 urged a number of sorely needed court reforms, but the legislature was not interested, and the Governor dropped the subject. The prestige of the courts was further damaged when those circuit judges whose terms were still unexpired allowed their compensation to be increased during their terms, contrary to the words of the Constitution for shielding them from either intimidation or reward, by the addition of large "expense money" without any corresponding increase in their expenses. It was thus sought to place these on an equality with the one elected and the four re-elected in 1929. The economy budgets of 1932, '33, and '34, with the disregard of the Constitution which has become so common, reduced the salaries of the judges and other officers whose salaries are guaranteed against reduction during their terms. The Supreme Court, consisting of a bench of lawyers having no interest involved, appointed for the case, in December, 1934, unanimously ordered the full salaries paid.

Governor Johnston Attacks the Highway Department.—Governor Johnston's opposition to what he, like many others, denounced as "the Highway ring" was inflamed by his personal antipathy to Benjamin M. Sawyer, the executive head of the department. Failing to persuade the legislature to oust the commission of fourteen members appointed by previous Governors for staggered terms, Governor Johnston declared several commissioners removed and, on October 28, 1935, proclaimed the commission in rebellion, insurrection, and insurgency, declared martial law over the department, and occupied it with troops. The Supreme Court ruled that only the Governor could decide when "rebellion" or "insurrection" existed, but declared illegal his removal of the commissioners, forbade the persons to whom he had handed over the department to exercise any function, and took possession of all funds of the department until the lawful commissioners should be in unhindered control. Governor Johnston defended his coup, and his order that automobile plates should be sold for $3.00 instead of the legally prescribed rates, as sanctioned by the people in voting for him on his promise to conquer the commission and oust Sawyer; he ignored the fact that thousands voted for him only to avoid a third term for his opponent and erstwhile chieftain Blease. To a special session of the legislature he complained that he had been opposed by the "aristocrats" who sneered at his "having lint in his hair" as once "a cotton mill boy." The House voted 108 to 3 and the Senate 39 to 3 for the restoration of constitutional civil authority. It was finally agreed that the Governor would withdraw the troops and sign an act placing the department for sixty days under control of two expert employees of the old commission and an advisory committee of three State officials. The Governor's two months' possession of the records of the department failed to discover the slightest irregularity.

The original commission, reinstated by the Supreme Court, functioned until May, 1936, when the General Assembly revamped the department over the Governor's veto by giving to the legislature instead of the Governor the selection of the commission, and temporarily transferred from the Governor to the State Treasurer the duty of signing road bonds. The new commission consisted of nine of the old members and five new men. The conflict was ended by the Governor's failure by a narrow majority in 1937 to have his nominee elected speaker of the new house. Sawyer continued as chief commissioner until his death, December 22, 1940, after having, as the executive agent for fourteen years, with an economy and efficiency perhaps unsurpassed in the country, constructed the State's modern roads. Far more ominous for the future than the failure of a governor to realize the significance of his unlawful violence was the fact that such a large proportion of the voters approved a course which, if unchecked, would substitute personal dictatorship for constitutional government.

Governor Johnston's unprecedented blundering in the highway department matter revealed him as of stronger impulses than judgment in contrast with Sawyer, who conducted himself with a prudence and moderation beyond criticism; but it should also be remembered that Governor Johnston actively co-operated in a great deal of humane and progressive legislation.[3]

Taxation, Public Debts, and Finance.—The period since the first

[3] Mr. Johnston was in 1941 defeated in the primary election for United States senator by Governor Burnet R. Maybank by 92,100 to 70,687. Mr. Johnston was again elected governor in 1942, and in 1944 won the senatorship from E. D. Smith.

World War has seen improvement in financial methods but greatly increased expenditures, and of late years financial difficulties. The Sinking Fund Commission insures State and local public property. The budget, by the law of 1919, is prepared by the Governor and the finance committee chairmen, but is merely suggestive and exercises less influence than it deserves.

In the booming years before 1929 the people assumed bonded debts (mainly for school buildings, streets, and roads) whose irreducible charges constituted in depression a serious burden. In addition were the greatly increased appropriations for current costs of education. Education and roads consumed the vast bulk of the taxes. Another heavy item was for the insane. Appropriations rose from about $900,000 in 1900, with a 5-mill levy on property raising practically the entire revenue, to $6,091,241 in 1920, with a number of new special taxes, and to the highest figure until then of about $10,950,000 in 1930. New services such as social security legislation (which incurred large deficits), Federal aid, etc., have since vastly expanded State finances. On June 30, 1940, 25,033 persons (a great majority on account of old age) were receiving aid through the Department of Public Welfare, and in 1947 over 48,000. Receipts for the year ending June 30, 1940, totaled $66,197,575, which included about $18,000,000 raised by fees and taxes for general purposes, $13,117,313 gasoline taxes for roads, about $4,008,000 from the Federal government, and large sums borrowed to pay maturing notes or bonds. Total receipts for 1947 were $136,602,434. The total State debt, nearly all for highways, on June 30, 1947, was $48,213,097.

Efforts for a more equitable form of taxation have been fairly successful so far as State taxes are concerned, but almost futile as touching the far heavier burden of local taxes. The Tax Commission continued to explain unavailingly the impossibility of equitable assessments without means for requiring the original local assessors to act equitably. The ablest presentation of the whole problem is that of the legislative joint committee in 1921, known from its chairman as the (J. H.) Marion report. It drew largely on the reform of 1919 in North Carolina. Its recommendations of various State taxes to relieve property have been largely adopted, soon reducing the State general property levy from 13 to 5½ mills; but its plea for complete reorganization of the general property tax and its assessment has been neglected. As the State general property tax has been entirely superseded by other taxes, equalization is not so eagerly sought. The State income tax enacted in 1897 remained a farce until 1906, since which time it has grown to be one of the largest sources of revenue. County and municipal governments still suffer the injustice of having practically all their enormously swelled revenues drawn from the general property tax, apportioned among their citizens with gross inequity. The easier, more exciting, and publicity-enjoying career of State politics leaves the unattractive and difficult problems of county government neglected by all but a few unheeded thinkers. There is far more talk about State taxes, while there is far more real grievance in local taxes.

As the general distress of 1929 to 1933 was added to the depression under which agriculture had suffered since 1921, tax collections fell into arrears, and thousands of school teachers were left unpaid for months. The State was driven to borrow from Federal agencies. Moderate reductions of appropriations were made in 1931 and 1932, with a drastic cut in 1933. Regardless of constitutional prohibition of such action, the legislature voted appropriations beyond the taxes they were willing to levy. The deficit amounted to $2,169,022 on December 31, 1926, the bulk of it created in that year. It steadily mounted to $4,989,400 in 1931, when it was converted into a short-time bonded debt. Discontinuing the five-mill general property tax in 1938 again created a deficit. Governor Burnet R. Maybank (elected in 1938 by a small majority over Wyndham Manning) urged diverting part of the gasoline tax from roads to general purposes, a State police system (as had his predecessor Governor Johnston), and a convention to modernize the State Constitution, especially as to taxation.

Protracted efforts at reorganizing the State government for more efficient service at last came to fruition in the adoption in 1948 of Governor Thurmond's plan, the details of which are still to be worked out.

CHAPTER LXIV

SOCIAL AND ECONOMIC PROGRESS, 1900-1948

Hospitals and Health.—A feature of the general humane and scientific spirit of the past generation has been the multiplication of hospitals and health services. Charleston early developed an active health department. The State Board of Health was created in 1878. The increase in hospitals during the past twenty years has been rapid, but still left South Carolina in 1940 with only 1.8 beds for 1,000 of population, as against 3.5 for the entire country. December 31, 1940, there were forty-nine general hospitals in South Carolina (several special hospitals and Federal institutions not included).[1]

The pure food laws of 1898 and 1907 were badly needed. For years spoiled meat had been regularly sold in South Carolina to certain classes. The outbreak of smallpox in December, 1897, caused a panic; but its complete eradication was long delayed by very partial enforcement of vaccination, which is rigidly observed only in the best-regulated schools.

Medical inspection from 1910 to 1913 revealed the frightful degree of infection from hookworm in the Southern States. Of 415,000 school children examined in 413 Southern counties, 43 per cent were found to be infected. South Carolina was one of the worst sufferers. Rarely has an organized medical campaign resulted in more prompt and widespread conquest of a curse than has been the case with this debilitating disease, which has been largely responsible for the tradition of Southern laziness.

The course of pellagra has followed the rise and fall of prosperity, as it is entirely dependent upon the diet. The decrease of deaths from this cause from 729 in 1916 to 306 in 1920, a rise to 811 in 1930, and a decline to 163 in 1940, reflect not only the spread of knowledge but also the fluctuations of dietary conditions among the poor, accompanying the course of agricultural and business depression. A pathetic tribute we pay for ignorance and poverty is our high infant and maternity death rate. State instruction is now given to midwives, who deliver the vast majority of babies. The typhoid death rate has been reduced from 36

[1] Forty-two hospitals in South Carolina received from the Duke Foundation during 1940, at the rate of $1.00 for each day of free bed service, $373,706. (Free bed days were 39.9 per cent of the total.) Orphanages, colleges, universities, and churches received a much larger total.

per 100,000 of population in 1915 to 4.7 in 1940, which is high as compared with the rate in States having the best sanitation. Malaria is still one of our greatest sources of sickness, but the death rate has been reduced from 16 to 8.2 in the decade 1930-40. Scientific methods have reduced the death rate for lobar pneumonia in that decade from 76.4 to 34.8, for tuberculosis from 14.9 to 4.7, and maternity deaths from 10.5 to 6.2 per 1,000 live births. The cancer death rate rose during the decade 1931-40 from 44.9 to 58.6 per 100,000 population. Medical examination of the first million recruits for the first World War found only Virginia, Alabama, and Florida with a higher percentage of venereal infection than South Carolina. In 1940 the State Board of Health reported that of recent draftees 23.01 per cent of colored and 3.17 per cent of white men showed venereal infection. Clinics throughout the State show that between 25 and 30 per cent of the many thousands of Negro women tested are syphilitic. Data do not exist for estimating infection among South Carolina white women, as a very small fraction of them visit clinics.[2] The deplorable conditions among Negroes which affect so adversely all of our sociological statistics thus again manifest themselves. For treating venereal diseases there are in the State 170 clinics. Of the 85,850 cases of communicable diseases reported in the year ending June 30, 1940, 9,041 were syphilis, being exceeded only by malaria with 11,095 and influenza with 37,125. Gonorrhea added 6,947 to this catalogue of misery and shame. The legislature has repeatedly refused to require premarital medical examination.

When South Carolina came under the national prohibition law of 1919, she had already been under State-wide prohibition since 1915. In 1933 (the year of the repeal of national prohibition) she legalized the sale of beer and wine, while leaving stronger liquors still forbidden under the law of 1915. The referendum in the Democratic primary of August, 1934, went against prohibition by about 25,000 out of 235,000, and the law of 1935 authorized liquor stores selling in unbroken packages in the daytime with no drinking on the place. The Democratic primary referendum of 1940 by about 50,000 majority out of 265,000 favored the re-enactment of prohibition; but the legislature, doubting the earnestness of the movement and reluctant to increase either the existing deficit or the taxes by surrendering liquor revenues, declined to act.

[2] The Annual Report of the South Carolina Board of Health for 1939-40, page 66, in stating that South Carolina's "known incidence [of syphilitic infection] in pregnant women approximates 25 per cent," without explaining that the number of Negro women tested was eleven times the number of white women, is as misleading as are Southern sociological statistics in general which do not state figures by races. Nevertheless the danger of communication of disease from black to white, whether directly or through a corrupt white husband, makes Negro health a vital concern to white as well as black. The decimals above are as corrected by a letter from a Board official to D. D. Wallace which also gives the eleven to one proportion.

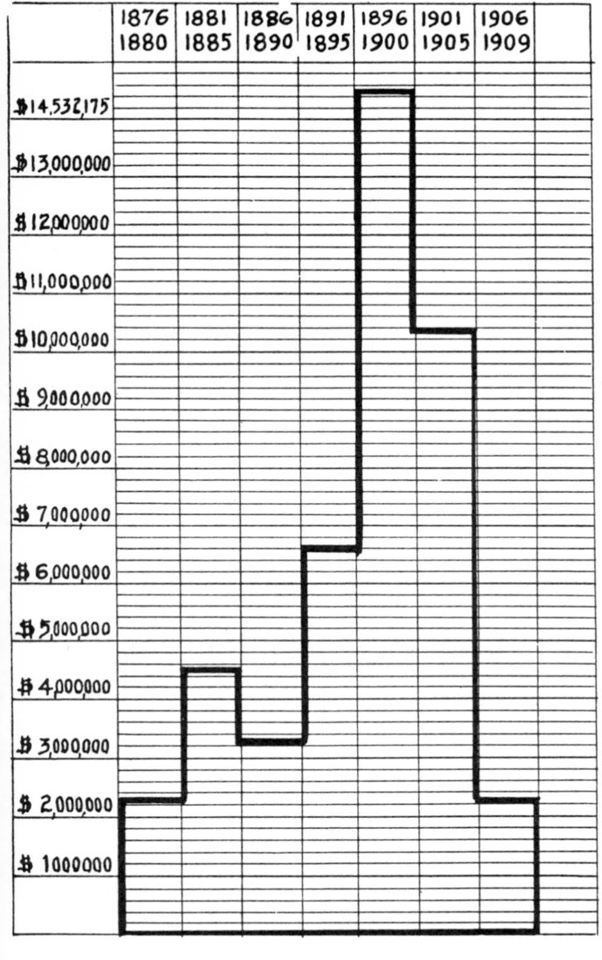

Capital Invested in Cotton Mills in South Carolina, organized in the indicated years, 1876-1909. From South Carolina Reports and Resolutions, 1910, Vol. II, Table No. 21, following page 790. (Several of these Mills were organized earlier than the table on which this is based states. This distortion is not serious)

The legislature in 1947 passed an amendment to the State Constitution providing for divorce for adultery, desertion, physical cruelty, or habitual drunkenness. The vote of the people in the general election of 1948 endorsed it. The legislature elected at that same time gave it final ratification in 1949.

Agriculture.—Agriculture is still our leading industry in the sense that it employs the largest proportion of substantial, dependable, characteristic South Carolinians, but no longer in the sense of the value of its product. The value of the State's manufactures in 1940 of $446,000,000 was over three and a half times that of its crops. Much of our land is naturally too poor for profitable agriculture, and much good land has been butchered. The fact that South Carolina buys more fertilizer in proportion to area than any other State in the Union, and more in gross amount than any except Georgia, is expressive of soil exhaustion as well as good farming. Soil erosion remedies, begun by progressive farmers before 1860, have under the "New Deal" policies of the 1930's made unprecedented progress.

The long agricultural depression beginning in 1921, following a period in which farmers and thousands whose prosperity was dependent on theirs had contracted debts based upon inflated values of land and produce, inevitably led to widespread distress. Between January 1, 1921, and February 28, 1933, 34 National and 283 State banks in South Carolina closed their doors. There had been, in 1919, 78 national banks and, in 1920, 387 State banks. More than 95 per cent of the State's cotton farmers voted in 1939, 1940, and 1941 for the continuance of government-controlled crop quotas.

Manufactures.—Even under the unfavorable influences of slavery, cotton manufacturing was struggling toward its natural place. In 1820 South Carolina had 588 spindles; in 1840, 16,355; in 1859-60, 30,890 in 17 mills; in 1869-70, 34,940 in 12 mills; in 1874-75, 70,282 in 18 mills; in 1879-80, 82,424 in 14 mills. Then came the 300 per cent expansion of the next ten years, and the 400 per cent increase in the decade ending 1900, not sustaining very well the charge that Tillman drove capital from the State. Steady growth brought the number of spindles in 1931 to 5,689,642, the mills to 239, the employees to 73,559 (9,488 fewer than the year before), the estimated mill village population to 187,305 (6,967 fewer than the year before), and the invested capital to $210,714,900. The mills were a God-send to the suffering small farmers of the 1890's and later. The State's total manufactures equaled, for the year ending June 30, 1948, $1,797,461,287; and employees 179,859. A State so small and so much of whose soil is barren, either by nature or butchery, cannot regain even approximately its old relative position in the nation except by extensive development of varied manufactures.

This social and economic revolution since about 1885 came so suddenly as still to present a raw and unstable social situation. For years the churches failed to realize their opportunity and duty, and legislation was silent as an essentially paternalistic relationship, generally kindly and contented, developed between the management and the unorganized operatives. The sudden organization of the operatives in 1933 and '34 under the labor policies of President Franklin D. Roosevelt opened a new era in South Carolina industrial and social relations, in which violence and murder flamed up ominously. The nation-wide textile strike of 1934 involved almost all South Carolina mills, where resentment against the "stretch-out" (increasing the looms per weaver) was strong. Two men were killed in the Buffalo Mill strike in the spring of 1935. Following the removal of troops from Pelzer, a battle between strikers and workers who had declined to strike resulted in the death of one worker and many wounds by firearms, September 2, 1935.

For years the stupid clack prevailed that it was better for children to be in the mills than on the streets; but, with unequal pace, age limits and pitifully ineffective compulsory education laws have improved conditions. The law of 1903 took all under ten years from the mills. This age limit was raised by 1917 to fourteen years, and in 1938 to 16, with prohibition of night work by children in mills or mines.

Many mills have instituted admirable welfare work, embracing equipment and skilled services equal to the best in our cities, partly from humane feeling and partly to stave off the troublesome era of organized self-assertion. The operatives and other citizens tend, though somewhat decreasingly, to remain sharply isolated, mutually suspicious classes. Numbers of operatives own farms or lend thousands of dollars, and a few attain prominence as politicians, etc.; but their general contribution to the talent of the State is far below their numerical proportion. The educational system is now seeking, and quite often through management initiative, to afford them opportunities for developing mechanical and scientific talents.

In the 1880's and '90's textile dividends were often enormous, and again in the years following 1917; but generally earnings have been moderate and often precarious. The huge profits after the first World War led to the purchase of South Carolina mills by Northern capitalists in addition to the large holdings of stock, often constituting control, by wealthy Northern selling agents. It formed a part of the persistent movement of cotton mill capital from New England to the raw material and the then unorganized Southern labor, and exhibited in pathetic degree the relative poverty of the South in its position of colonial dependence.[3]

Hydroelectric investments in South Carolina were estimated as of 1931 at about $160,000,000 by the companies, and at about half that figure by the State's special power-rate investigating committee after discarding investments not directly contributing to power purposes and scaling down others. The great dam of the Lexington Water Power Company at Dreher Shoals on the Saluda River ten miles west of Columbia was completed in December, 1930, at a cost of over $20,000,000. The dam, 208 feet high and a mile and half in length, is the largest high earth

[3] Kendrick, "The Colonial Status of the South," in *Journal of Southern History*, vol. 8, pp. 4-22.

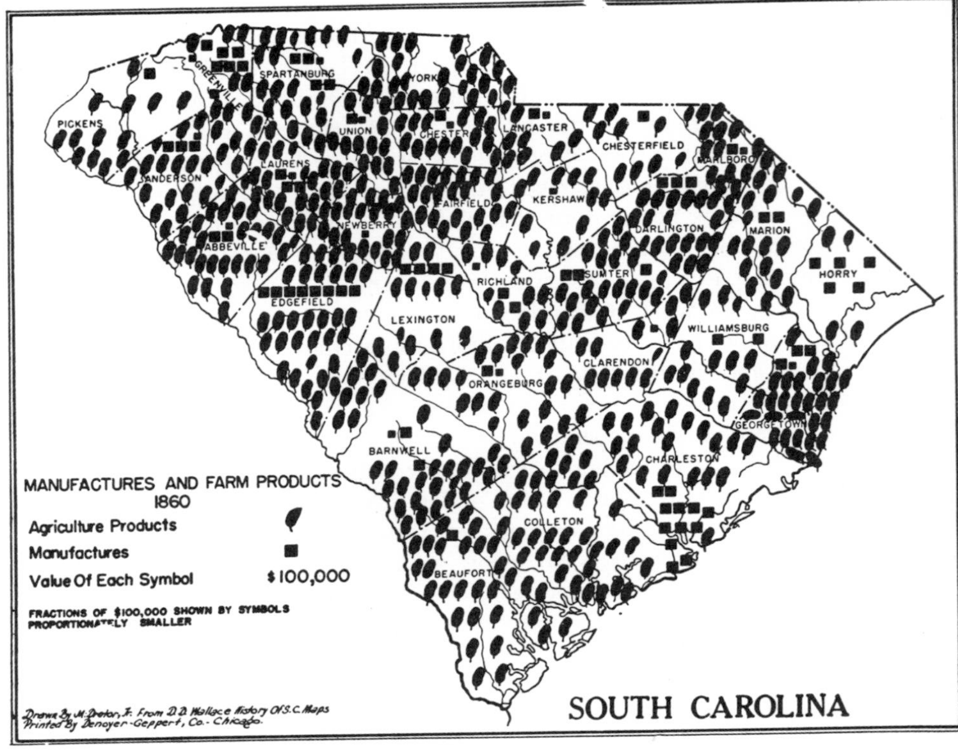

dam in the world, and was, when built, exceeded in cubic contents only by the Gatun Dam at Panama. Lake Murray, which is thus impounded, is forty-five miles in length and was then the largest power reservoir in the United States. Its ultimate horsepower is 222,600.

In 1934 the legislature established the South Carolina Public Service Authority for developing navigation and hydroelectric power by dams across the Santee and Cooper rivers where the head of the latter closely approaches the Santee about fifty miles from the sea. The State assumed no financial responsibility, the $59,479,535 cost to June 30, 1944, having been met by a Federal loan of $26,524,000, a Federal grant of $21,701,000, W.P.A. service in $20,970,000, and loans of $26,055,000 from Federal agencies. Operation began in February, 1942. Water records promise a constant service of 430,000,000 kilowatt hours a year at all times and at the rate of 270,000,000 additional available 75 per cent of the time. The five turbines have a combined horsepower of 173,300.

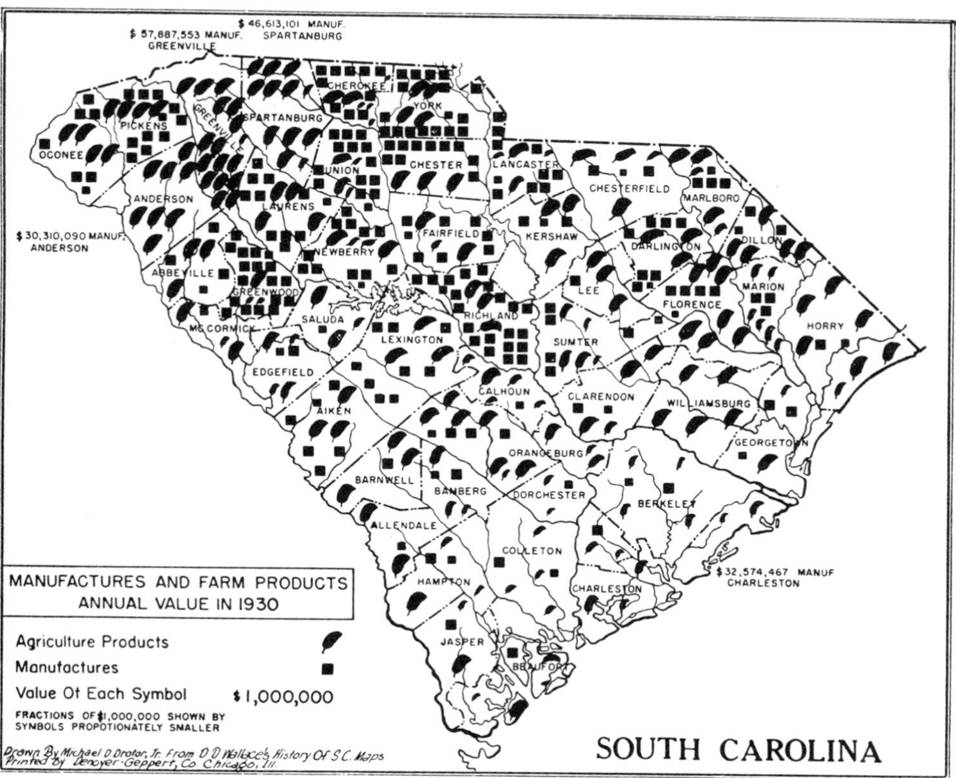

Education.—The Constitution of 1868 and the general school act of 1871 gave South Carolina machinery for popular education beyond the hopes of her educational leaders before 1860. The ante-bellum principle of support directly by the State was continued, but greatly enlarged. The old appropriation of $74,400 a year for the poor was increased to $300,000 for everybody. The law of 1871 also gave the voters of any district the right to tax themselves in addition up to $3.00 for every child of six to sixteen in the district.

The school policy of the legislature for a generation after 1876 was narrow and reactionary. The State appropriation was cut in 1877 to $100,000, and the right of each school district to vote an extra tax upon itself was repealed, except that the city of Charleston's school trustees retained this power granted in 1856. After the ratification of the 2-mill constitutional tax amendment in 1878, the proceeds to be retained by each county, State aid ceased.

Winnsboro at once rebelled at this reactionary policy and in 1878 secured a law permitting her taxpayers to assess themselves 1½ mills. Such special acts multiplied, until the law of 1896 gave all districts the right to levy 4 mills (raised in 1910 to 8). But educational leadership had freer scope through the fact that many special districts were outside these limitations. The right of each taxpayer (now rarely exercised) to direct his special taxes built up the white schools. Extreme decentralization impaired progress and almost made the term "State school system" a misnomer until about 1910.

The Constitution of 1895 raised the constitutional tax to 3 mills (abolished in 1939), and ordered the legislature to aid poor counties enough to bring their school income to $3.00 per enrolled child and further to supply necessary funds to run their schools the full term fixed by legislature.

The common school problem is the poor district. In 1923-24 special taxes were maintained in all but forty-five of the 1,975 districts; but in 1910 in some districts 2 mills would raise only $25. In 1921-22 the 3-mill constitutional tax raised $1,108,404; special local levies, $4,327,010; State aid, $1,350,064; and the total common school income (including $864,880 from bond sales) reached $10,652,761.

The "6-0-1" law of 1924 was our longest single step in popular education. It fixed minimum standards and standard salaries, imposed a new 4-mill county tax, and pledged the State to give enough in addition to run the schools six months, provided the country or district contributed enough to run them a seventh month. Existing conditions in advance of this in progressive districts were not distributed. The consolidation of weak schools, the multiplication of high schools, the transportation of children, the vast improvement in the character of buildings and equipment, and the advanced standards required of teachers, in twenty years revolutionized the common schools. In 1910 State support was 3.9 per cent; in 1930, 25.5 per cent; and in 1940, 50 per cent of the total spent for schools. Increasing State aid has diminished the great differences in length of term and qualities of teaching in different counties and has multiplied the types of service so as to fit the child through vocational training, etc., for modern industrial and social life. As late as 1902 a few counties had terms barely above one-third of those of the most advanced counties. By 1940 the State guaranteed an eight-month term and better salaries, both of which local authorities in progressive communities increase. The State now guarantees support for 180 days, but does not prescribe any length of term, which in some backward communities is shorter. In 1939-40 the white public schools enrolled 265,845 and the Negro 215,905, 77 and 65 per cent respectively of the school-age population; in 1947-48, 251,363 and 207,457.[4]

Illiteracy is a curse inherited from the ante-bellum period. Out of a white population of 259,000 in 1840, 20,000 adults were illiterate, and 70,000 between five and twenty years of age were in no school. Requiring every man to sign his name to the Democratic Club rolls in 1914 showed how untrustworthy pride and carelessness render the census report that 10.8 per cent of our white adult males were illiterate; for 19.2 per cent of the voters made their marks, and in 1916, 18.2 per cent.

Despite (and because of) such conditions South Carolina long rejected compulsory education. In 1915 any district or group of districts was permitted to vote compulsory education for eighty days for eight- to fourteen-year-old children. The law of 1921 made such attendance compulsory everywhere; but hard times soon left no attendance officers. Every county is now supposed to have at least one; but the "attendance teachers" are too few for effective enforcement. The ages are now seven to sixteen.

In 1911 Rev. D. E. Camak, a Methodist minister deeply interested in mill operatives, borrowed $100 to found the Textile Industrial Institute. He taught one group while their companions worked in the mill. Partners relieved each other alternately as learners and breadwinners. In a few years the Institute (now turned over to the Methodist Church, but also aided by members of other denominations and renamed the Spartanburg Junior College) held almost a half-million-dollar property, including its own elaborate mill. Depression wrecked its commercial enterprise and forced a return to the original plan of having its students work in near-by mills, stores, etc., with gratifying success.

The sharp opposition of the 1880's and '90's by church institutions to State colleges has subsided, though there is some opposition to the State's giving free tuition to all who swear inability to pay. In 1914-15 four-fifths of the students in State colleges paid no tuition, and the State gave food and clothes through scholarships to 17.5 per cent of their entire body of students. Inspection of such applications, beginning in 1915, increased tuition payers at Clemson College from 15.5 per cent to 63 per cent, at the University from 31.5 per cent to 56.9 per cent, and at Winthrop from 12.2 per cent to 51.6 per cent, but this attempt to require those able to pay to do so was soon abandoned.

The decade of the forties saw decided progress in common school education. Colleges were also crowded, the men's colleges indeed overcrowded. The public schools in the year 1946-47 enrolled 457,955 pupils, of whom 249,897 were white and 207,058 colored. It is significant that,

[4] Smaller numbers for later dates may be due to more systematic rules for enrollment.

though Negro children of ages involved were 20,000 fewer than white children of corresponding ages, the enrollment of the Negro children in the schools below the high school in 1946-47 was 678 greater than that of the whites—quite a commentary on the prating of some politicians that compulsory attendance is dangerous as putting the Negro into school. Equality of salaries of white and colored teachers of similar preparation and experience was established as a result of Federal court decisions requiring equality of treatment. Salaries of teachers were considerably increased as a necessary means of retaining the better class of teachers and continuing to attract suitable material to the teaching profession. The amount spent on white schools in 1946-47 was 88.75 per cent greater than in 1930-31, and on the Negro schools 339.88 per cent greater. Moreover some of the joint expenses, especially for administration, are included in the figures for white schools, thus making the increase for white schools slightly less and for colored schools slightly more than stated.

The population of South Carolina in 1940 was 1,889,804, of which 1,084,308 were white, 814,164 Negro, and 1,332 other races. In 1930 the white population exceeded the black for the first time since 1810.

In 1947 the Federal district court denied the petition of a Negro to be admitted to the law school of the University of South Carolina, but ruled that he must be admitted if the State had not by the opening of the next session provided a law school at the State College for Negroes. The result was the establishment of such a school. The State continues if requested to pay the tuition of Negro medical students desiring to attend institutions outside the State, and is co-operating with other Southern States for providing through the Meharry Medical School at Nashville, Tennessee, high-grade medical education for Negroes from the supporting States. The more extreme Negro leaders reject this solution and demand admission without discrimination to the existing professional schools in the different States.

World War II.—Reference has already been made to the service of South Carolina's statesmanship in the Second World War. The State bore her full share of the terrible losses of life and treasure in that frightful conflict for the very preservation of freedom. From November 1, 1940, to June 30, 1945, accessions of South Carolinians to the United States Army personnel totaled 119,000 men and 1,886 women. South Carolinians enlisted in the Navy from December 1, 1941, through June 30, 1947, totaled 51,924 men and 732 women. Again the State stood true to her motto, *Animis Opibusque Parati*—"Ready with Minds and Fortunes!"

CHAPTER LXV

PAST AND PRESENT, 1670-1948

South Carolina's Place in the Empire and the Nation.—Only because the strength of Spain was overtaxed with other enterprises did South Carolina become English. Spain's brief settlement in 1526 far exceeded the trivial touch by France in 1562, and Spain's occupation at Port Royal from 1566 to 1586 might easily have become permanent. South Carolina, whose English settlers seized a strategic location on the American coast and extended their trade to the Mississippi, by holding the southern frontier against the Spanish and the French, exercised an influence on British and later American destiny that is only now coming to be understood. The prompt action often necessary for maintaining this position was made possible largely through the dominance of the province by Charles Town. Nowhere was there a more perfect example of the harmony between a town and the surrounding planters. The agriculture of the latter and the trade of the former were the basis of the wealth and power on which were founded a notable culture and political leadership.

The broad divisions of our history have been the British province, the aristocratic republic, and the modern democracy. The provincial period is the most vitally creative, for then were planted the seeds of all our later problems. If we could remake those irretrievable beginnings we could remake our destiny. The middle period is the most characteristic and brilliant, for during this time South Carolina occupied a position of national leadership far beyond her resources of population or wealth and carried to the highest development the noblest qualities of her earlier history. Calhoun, with his eyes blind, as were his contemporaries' generally, to important facts, expressed the ideal in the statement that we could never achieve any greatness except in citizenship. What South Carolina thought on public questions in that period became a matter of highest national moment and was noted throughout the world. South Carolina was the leader of the South, partly because of her brilliant statesmen, but largely also because she had gone furthest in exploiting the benefits and incurring the perils of slavery. She considered that to hold down the Negro was her salvation and thought that slavery alone would avail for that end. That South Carolina's power was so great before 1860 was because the unstable and undeveloped character of

American nationalism made it possible for a small State holding positive ideas appealing to a wide circle to threaten the upset of national life.

The middle period was separated from the other two by great wars, each ending one era and inaugurating another. The first elevated South Carolina to eminence and power, the other devastated her institutions and so overwhelmed her with adjusting herself under economic, racial, and social difficulties to modern democracy as to leave her nationally insignificant. The intellectual experience has been tragic, plunging her into an inferiority complex as lamentable as the delusions of grandeur from which she fell. She saw the whole fabric of her constitutional, economic, and social ideas shattered. Even the second generation could with difficulty recover from such a desolation of ideas. But new ideas we must develop. The evils of the outside world we cannot exclude save by filling minds with other ideals; its elements of strength we must adopt. Loyalty to our ancestors must not be allowed to harden into loyalty to their mistakes. South Carolina's future is not in the past.

Throughout her development South Carolina has been dominated by conditions of climate and soil which invited the African as an easy means of immediate wealth to a ruling class and of permanent calamity to the State. With these natural conditions and the then existing opinions, African slavery was inevitable. With all its nobility, a large part of our history has been a huge mistake in economics, sociology, and politics, enslaving the master to his slaves in a bondage from which there is no emancipation. The intellectual and moral energy expended in defense of an impossible institution was sufficient, if differently directed, to have built an empire. Here lies the outstanding fact of Southern life. The white man in enslaving the Negro fatally limited his own freedom in thought, industry, and politics. With one insoluble problem depressing Southern thought, how could mind flower into literature, science, and art? Talent was demanded for a sterner purpose. The central theme of Southern history, says Professor Ulrich B. Phillips, is the necessity of keeping this a white man's country. Therefore the poorest slaveless white and the aristocratic owner of a thousand bondmen both fought for a fundamental purpose which both understood to be far more important than maintaining property rights.

The Democratic Trend.—Almost from the day of settlement, the dominant political fact in our colonial history was the encroachment of the popular upon the prerogative element in the government. The Revolution could have been avoided only by Engand's consenting, as bitter experience later taught her to do, to be the mother of a sisterhood of nations.

The demand of the back country, populous before the coast was aware, for self-government and equality, strongly voiced from the 1760's, was expressive of the same spirit, in which the older section for a while played somewhat the same role that the still older government in England had played against it. This internal conflict, interrupted by the Revolution, found no settlement until economic and social forces had prepared the way for the compromise between the sections in 1808.

The class conflict involved in this struggle was another phase of the great trend of popular self-government, brought in its native English vigor by the first settlers and unfolded in modern democracy. Charlestown mechanics and up-country backwoodsmen, demanding in the decade before the Revolution to share power with the planters and merchants, were part of the same movement. The exigencies of defense against abolitionist aggression brought subsidence of contest and delay of realization.

Individualism.—Individualism has strongly marked South Carolinians; but the political dominance of leaders of powerful personality has been misunderstood. Even Calhoun dominated because he so perfectly voiced the wishes of the great body of his constituents, who would have retired him had he adopted undesired policies. South Carolina has had strong leaders but no master, however politicians have sought favor by cringing to the accepted chief.

The isolation of the province in the face of Indian, Spanish, and French enemies fostered a remarkable self-reliance. So did the presence of "a domestic enemy" regarding whom no internal faltering or outside interference could be tolerated. Individualism was fostered by a landed aristocracy selling in world markets, free from haggling with local tradesmen. The poorer white man felt the same influence and was stimulated rather than spirit-broken by the upper class. Individualism, impatient of interference with personal liberty by State law, when extended to Federal relations and inflamed by abolitionism, naturally saw in the Union only a partnership for mutual protection and not a sovereign with right to dominate. The same causes, reinforced by ignorance and resentment at possible interference with our race problem, fostered a prejudice against outsiders. South Carolina's abundant dueling and the atrocious murder record of classes otherwise respectable are indexes of an individualism approaching philosophical anarchism which has made us troublesome in peace and formidable in war.

Racial Influences.—Explanations of peculiarities of "the Hotspur State" by race elements are imaginative, especially the romantic magnification of the fiery Gascon blood thundering through our veins, of which South Carolina has in fact a small infiltration among her very small French element, an element which has been much more notable for sane and orderly conduct than for the qualities it is lugged in to explain, as, for example, Manigault, Laurens, Marion, Huger, and Petigru. Other States assimilated essentially the same race elements without such results. Such evoking of emotional plumed knights battling on fields of France for religious liberty, or of tartaned Scots hurling defiance from the crags, fastens on circumstances not peculiar to South Carolina and overlooks others both characteristic and powerful that have affected this more critically than any other State. It is of course not meant to deny the profound significance of race. Our excellent national elements—English, Irish, Scotch-Irish (that is, Scotsmen from Ireland), German, and French—have all made earth resound with their heroism for liberty and right; but the extremes and peculiarities manifested here would have been produced in the essentially similar population of many other American States before 1850 by the same causes—territorial isolation, and a staple agriculture based on a mass of African slaves dangerously outnumbering freemen. There is nothing peculiar about ante-bellum South Carolinians except what is due to their peculiar situation.

Changed Ideals.—The old ruling class tended to assume that the world was made for them. It has been a hard discipline to adjust themselves to the stupendous changes beating in upon them the lesson that this is everybody's world. Two generations have hardly sufficed for the reorientation forced by the destruction of much that they stood for before 1865. In addition to war, the superiority of the Southwest for rice and cotton has robbed us of the one and almost ruined the other. But for the growth of manufacturing our condition would have been desperate; but far more must we convert unfit cotton lands to forestry or grazing, cultivate fit lands with greater skill, and multiply the number and variety of our factories. The resources of mechanical and scientific talent wasting for want of opportunity are unrealized fortunes in wealth and culture. Too long have the unheeded voices of Henry Laurens, Stephen Elliott, William Lowndes, David R. Williams, and William Gregg pleaded against social and economic blunders by a ruling planter class satisfied with its own interests. The complacent conceit that agriculture (removed but one stage from the hunter state, the civilization of barbarians, as R. F. Reynolds remarked in South Carolina in 1849) is alone fit for gentlemen, and is peculiarly blessed of God, led the ante-bellum Carolinian to despise mechanics, who are characteristic of an advanced civilization, and to view applied science patronizingly, and still hampers our progress into a more intellectual and fruitful civilization. To this is added the intellectual rigidity fostered by our one-party system.

Up-Country Democracy and Power.—Population and wealth have steadily drifted for a hundred and fifty years toward the northwest of the

State. Anderson, Greenville, and Spartanburg counties contained in 1940 18.58 per cent of the population and produced 36.8 per cent of the manufactured products of the State. These newer regions are of necessity democratic and their civilization immature. It is striking what a large proportion of culture in the up country has been brought in by low-country men and Virginians.

Ideals of Public Life.—The ideal in South Carolina before 1860 was that the class having the preponderant economic interest should carry on government, in harmony with the interests of that class, with honesty and simplicity, and that the best citizens should administer local affairs, while the ablest men of the State defended her peculiar institution in Washington. The ideal from 1865 to 1890 was much the same, except that the sectional conflict, which had called out our best talents before 1865, no longer vitalized politics. The ideal since 1890 is that every man has an equal claim to consideration for office, and that persons who assume the contrary are to be retired to private life. Delayed and thwarted democracy, brooding with suppressed desires for a generation, tends to narrow extremes. Raging at the upper class that had held in check his fathers and would, he believes, hold him down if it could, the modern democrat seems sometimes to despise honor and pride in spotless integrity because he associates them with a hated class, and thus public life has suffered inestimable loss. Fortunately this aspect of our crude democracy shows signs of late years of improvement in this regard. Passionate attachment to personal leaders, with questions of policy given little thought, evokes the emotions rather than the intelligence. Lacking the necessary moderation and that consideration of the other side of public questions which is cultivated by two-party contests, interest centers in the element of combat. Politics are the South Carolina bull ring, an exciting and (erroneously supposed) inexpensive sport. But recent decades, we have ground for believing, showed definite signs of betterment.

From democracy there is no retreat. The only possible course for reasonable men is to make the best of democracy by making the people the best they can be made. The essential virtue of democracy is that it is the only form of government in which the safety of society depends on those who possess talent, wealth, and power using them to elevate instead of depress the masses, and to satisfy instead of suppress legitimate popular aspirations. With the narrow selfishness of men of all classes, so feebly moved by altruistic motives, nothing but compulsive fear of the masses will cause the minority of wealth and talent to serve the common good.

Ante-bellum South Carolina had the most definitely integrated and delicately though firmly organized society in the United States. The democracy which roughly shoved aside its shattered remains in 1890 is still so young in its triumph and so crude in its ideals as to have required some decades to extend very definitely beyond simple self-assertion. We have reaped an abundant crop from the ignorance and prejudice blandly permitted beside the road which the old ruling class traveled so pleasantly. While problems have been becoming more numerous and complex, the character of our public officials has been suffering a serious depletion through the exclusion of the "aristocrat," a term extended in the more heated period of our factionalism to include men of eminent success and exacting standards, even though of plain parentage. But there is an abundance of character and talent which democracy, as it becomes more sure of itself, is beginning to show that it will utilize. Old State rights ideas have little hold on the present electorate. A Spartanburg labor paper, the *News Review,* editorialized on January 19, 1936, concerning the opponents of the "new deal": "These reactionaries are clamoring for 'states's rights.' That's exactly the issue the reactionaries of 1860 raised when they were terrified by the prospect that Lincoln and the new-born Republican party might free the slaves. ... Now the American people are facing an issue infinitely more important than slavery. The producers of this country—the farmers and the industrial workers—are demanding economic freedom. It is as clear as the sun at noonday that they can only attain their goal through national action."

The reminders of ignorance and poverty define for South Carolina her duty of broadening her education and increasing her wealth, while cherishing the richest heritage of her past, the ideals of personal honor and patriotic public service. Powerful as are the natural forces that still influence our history, and complex as are the social and economic problems that demand solution, we can pursue policies that tend to elevate and strengthen instead of to impoverish and ruin. South Carolina should be ready for the self-criticism enabling her to profit by her past and so to make the future more fully what it should be.

APPENDICES
BIBLIOGRAPHY
INDEX

APPENDIX I

GOVERNORS OF SOUTH CAROLINA

Dates indicate actual administration unless otherwise specified.[1]

1. William Sayle, July 26, 1669—March 4, 1671.
2. Joseph West, March 4, 1671—April 19, 1672.
3. Sir John Yeamans, April 19, 1672—August, 1674.
4. Joseph West, August, 1674—October, 1682.
5. Joseph Morton, October, 1682—August, 1684.
6. Sir Richard Kyrle, August, 1684.
7. Joseph West, August or September, 1684—about July, 1685.
8. Robert Quary, about July, 1685—October, 1685.
9. Joseph Morton, October, 1685—November, 1686.
10. James Colleton, November, 1686—1690.
11. Seth Sothell, 1690—about April, 1692.
12. Phillip Ludwell, about April, 1692—May, 1693.
13. Thomas Smith, May, 1693—November 16, 1694.
14. Joseph Blake, November, 1694—August, 1695.
15. John Archdale, August, 1695—October, 1696.
16. Joseph Blake, October, 1696—September 7, 1700.
17. James Moore, September 11, 1700—March, 1703.
18. Sir Nathaniel Johnson, March, 1703—November 26, 1709.
19. Edward Tynte, November 26, 1709—June 26, 1710.
20. Robert Gibbes, June, 1710—about March 19, 1712.
21. Charles Craven, about March 19, 1712—April 23, 1716.
22. Robert Daniel. Proclaimed his commission, April 25, 1716. Term ended between June 29 and October 29, 1717.
23. Robert Johnson, between June 29 and October 29, 1717. Deposed December 21, 1719.
24. James Moore, December 21, 1719—May 30, 1721.
25. Francis Nicholson. Served May 30 (wrongly stated as May 29 in Council Journal), 1721—May 7, 1725.
26. Arthur Middleton as President of the Council. Assumed authority May 7, 1725—December, 1730.
27. Robert Johnson arrived December 15, 1730. Died May 3, 1735. (SCHM, XII, 115.)

[1] Dates of commissions in the colonial period often long antedate the beginning of the administration and administrations often extended for months before notice of a new appointment arrived.

28. Lieutenant Governor Thomas Broughton, May, 1735. Died November 22, 1737. (PR, XVIII, 312.)
29. Lieutenant Governor William Bull, November 22, 1737—December 17, 1743.
30. James Glen, December 17, 1743—June 1, 1756.
31. William Henry Lyttelton, June 1, 1756—April 5, 1760.
32. Lieutenant Governor William Bull, April 5, 1760—December 22, 1761. (Son of the former Lieutenant Governor.)
33. Thomas Boone, December 22, 1761—May 14, 1764.
34. Lieutenant Governor William Bull, May, 1764—June, 1766.
35. Lord Charles Greville Montagu, June 12, 1766—May 20 or 23, 1768.
36. Lieutenant Governor William Bull, May 20 or 23, 1768—October 30, 1768.
37. Lord Charles Greville Montagu, October 30, 1768—July 31, 1769.
38. Lieutenant Governor William Bull, July 31, 1769—September 15, 1771.
39. Lord Charles Greville Montagu, September 15, 1771—March 6, 1773.
40. Lieutenant Governor William Bull, March 6, 1773—June 18, 1775.
41. Lord William Campbell, June 18, 1775—September 15, 1775.
42. John Rutledge, of Charleston, elected President, March 26, 1776. Resigned March 5, 1778.
43. Rawlins Lowndes, of Charleston, President, March 7, 1778—January, 1779.
44. John Rutledge, of Charleston, Governor, January 9, 1779—January 31, 1782.
45. John Mathews, of Charleston, January 31, 1782—February, 1783.
46. Benjamin Guerard, of Charleston, February 4, 1783—February, 1785.
47. William Moultrie, of Charleston, February, 1785—February, 1787.
48. Thomas Pinckney, of Charleston, February, 1787—January, 1789.
49. Charles Pinckney, of Charleston, January, 1789—February, 1791.
50. Charles Pinckney, of Charleston, February, 1791—December, 1792.
51. William Moultrie, of Charleston, December, 1792—December, 1794.
52. Arnoldus Vander Horst, of Charleston, December, 1794—December, 1796.
53. Charles Pinckney, of Charleston, December, 1796—December, 1798.
54. Edward Rutledge, of Charleston, December, 1798—December, 1800.
55. John Drayton, of Charleston. Succeeded on death of governor, January 23, 1800, and served out term to December, 1800.
56. John Drayton, of Charleston, December, 1800—December, 1802.
57. James Burchell Richardson, of Clarendon, December, 1802—December, 1804.
58. Paul Hamilton, of Charleston, December, 1804—December, 1806.
59. Charles Pinckney, of Charleston, December, 1806—December, 1808.
60. John Drayton, of Charleston, December, 1808—December, 1810.
61. Henry Middleton, of Charleston, December, 1810—December, 1812.
62. Joseph Alston, of Georgetown, December, 1812—December, 1814.
63. David R. Williams, of Darlington, December, 1814—December, 1816.

64. Andrew Pickens, of Edgefield, December, 1816—December, 1818.
65. John Geddes, of Charleston, December, 1818—December, 1820.
66. Thomas Bennett, of Charleston, December, 1820—December, 1822.
67. John L. Wilson, of Georgetown, December, 1822—December, 1824.
68. Richard I. Manning, of Clarendon, December, 1824—December, 1826.
69. John Taylor, of Richland, December, 1826—December, 1828.
70. Stephen D. Miller, of Sumter, December, 1828—December, 1830.
71. James Hamilton, Jr., of Charleston, December, 1830—December, 1832.
72. Robert Y. Hayne, of Charleston, December, 1832—December, 1834.
73. George McDuffie, of Edgefield, December, 1834—December, 1836.
74. Pierce M. Butler, of Edgefield, December, 1836—December, 1838.
75. Patrick Noble, of Abbeville, December, 1838, to his death April 7, 1840.
76. B. K. Henagan, of Marlboro, April 17, 1840—December 10, 1840.
77. J. P. Richardson, of Clarendon, December, 1840—December, 1842.
78. J. H. Hammond, of Barnwell, December, 1842—December, 1844.
79. William Aiken, of Charleston, December, 1844—December, 1846.
80. David Johnson, of Union, December, 1846—December, 1848.
81. Whitemarsh B. Seabrook, of Edisto Island, Charleston District, December, 1848—December, 1850.
82. John H. Means, of Fairfield, December, 1850—December, 1852.
83. John L. Manning, of Clarendon, December, 1852—December, 1854.
84. James H. Adams, of Richland, December, 1854—December, 1856.
85. R. F. W. Allston, of Georgetown, December, 1856—December, 1858.
86. William H. Gist, of Union, December, 1858—December, 1860.
87. Francis W. Pickens, of Edgefield, December, 1860—December, 1862.
88. Milledge L. Bonham, of Edgefield, December, 1862—December, 1864.
89. A. G. Magrath, of Charleston, December, 1864—May 25, 1865.
90. Benjamin F. Perry, of Greenville, Provisional Governor. Appointed by the President of the United States, June 30, 1865. Served to November 29, 1865.
91. James L. Orr, of Anderson. Inaugurated November 29, 1865. First Governor to be elected by the people. Removed by General Canby, July 6, 1868.
92. Robert K. Scott, carpetbagger from Ohio, July 6, 1868—1870. Elected from Charleston.
93. Robert K. Scott, carpetbagger from Ohio, 1870—1872. (Charleston.)
94. Franklin J. Moses, Jr., of Sumter, December, 1872—December, 1874.
95. Daniel H. Chamberlain, carpetbagger from Massachusetts, December, 1874—December, 1876. Elected from Richland.
96. Wade Hampton, of Richland, December, 1876—December, 1878.
97. Wade Hampton, of Richland, December, 1878—February, 1879.
98. W. D. Simpson, of Laurens, succeeding when Hampton became United States senator, February 26, 1879—September 1, 1880.
99. Thomas B. Jeter, of Union, succeeding as President *pro tempore* of the senate when Simpson became Chief Justice, September 1—November 30, 1880.
100. Johnson Hagood, of Barnwell, November 30, 1880—December, 1882.

101. Hugh S. Thompson, of Columbia, Richland County, December, 1882—December, 1884.
102. Hugh S. Thompson, of Columbia, Richland County. Inaugurated December 4, 1884. Governor Thompson was appointed Assistant Secretary of the Treasury by President Cleveland July 10, 1886; he resigned the governorship. Lieutenant Governor Sheppard succeeded him the same day.
103. John C. Sheppard, of Edgefield, July 10, 1886—November 30, 1886.
104. John Peter Richardson, of Clarendon, November 30, 1886—December, 1888.
105. John Peter Richardson, of Clarendon, December, 1888—December, 1890.
106. Benjamin Ryan Tillman, of Edgefield, December, 1890—November, 1892.
107. Benjamin Ryan Tillman, of Edgefield, November 30, 1892—December, 1894.
108. John Gary Evans, of Aiken, December 4, 1894—January 18, 1897.[1]
109. W. H. Ellerbe, of Marion, January 18, 1897—January 18, 1899.
110. W. H. Ellerbe, of Marion, January 18, 1899. Died June 2, 1899.
111. Miles B. McSweeney, of Hampton, June 2, 1899—January, 1901.
112. Miles B. McSweeney, of Hampton, 1901—1903.
113. Duncan Clinch Heyward, of Colleton, 1903—1905.
114. Duncan Clinch Heyward, of Colleton, 1905—1907.
115. Martin F. Ansel, of Greenville, 1907—1909.
116. Martin F. Ansel, of Greenville, 1909—1911.
117. Coleman Livingston Blease, of Newberry, 1911—1913.
118. Coleman Livingston Blease, of Newberry, 1913—1915.
119. Charles A. Smith, Governor for five days, Governor Blease having resigned, 1915.
120. Richard I. Manning, of Sumter, 1915—1917.
121. Richard I. Manning, of Sumter, 1917—1919.
122. Robert A. Cooper, of Laurens, 1919—1921.
123. Robert A. Cooper, of Laurens, January, 1921—May 20, 1922.
124. Wilson G. Harvey, of Charleston. Succeeded R. A. Cooper, May 20, 1922, Cooper having been appointed to Federal Land Bank Board in Washington, D. C. Served until inauguration of Thomas G. McLeod, January, 1923.
125. Thomas Gordon McLeod, of Lee County, 1923—1925.
126. Thomas Gordon McLeod, of Lee County, 1925—1927.
127. John Gardiner Richards, of Kershaw County, 1927—1931. First governor under the four-year term.
128. Ibra C. Blackwood, of Spartanburg County, 1931—1935.
129. Olin D. Johnston, of Spartanburg, 1935—1939.
130. Burnet R. Maybank, of Charleston, 1939—1941. Governor Maybank, having been elected United States senator, resigned the governorship November, 1941.

[1] From 1897 Governors, unless succeeding to unexpired terms, have taken office in January.

131. J. E. Harley, of Barnwell, succeeded from Lieutenant Governorship November 4, 1941. Died February 27, 1942.
132. R. M. Jefferies, of Colleton, succeeded from presidency of the senate on the death of Governor Harley. Inaugurated March 2, 1942.
133. Olin D. Johnston, of Spartanburg, January 19, 1943, to his resignation January 2, 1945, as United States senator-elect.
134. Ransome J. Williams succeeded from Lieutenant Governorship January 2, 1945—1947.
135. James Strom Thurmond, of Edgefield, 1947—1951.
136. James F. Byrnes, of Spartanburg, 1951—.

APPENDIX II

(From Edward Ingle's *Southern Sidelights,* p. 362)

Owners of Slaves According to Number Owned—1850, 1860

STATES	1850									1860
	1	*Under 5*	*Under 10*	*Under 20*	*Under 50*	*Under 100*	*Under 200*	*More than 200*	*Aggregate*	*Aggregate*
Alabama	5,204	7,737	6,572	5,067	3,524	957	216	18	29,295	33,730
Arkansas	1,383	1,951	1,365	788	382	109	19	2	5,999	1,149
District of Columbia	760	539	136	39	2	1	...	...	1,477	1,118
Delaware	320	352	117	20	...	...	...	...	809	587
Florida	699	991	759	588	349	104	29	1	3,520	5,152
Georgia	6,554	11,716	7,701	6,490	5,056	764	147	28	38,456	41,084
Kentucky	9,244	13,284	9,579	5,022	1,198	53	5	...	38,385	38,645
Louisiana	4,797	6,072	4,327	2,652	1,774	728	274	46	20,670	22,033
Maryland	4,825	5,331	3,327	1,822	655	72	7	1	16,040	13,783
Mississippi	3,640	6,228	5,143	4,015	2,964	910	189	27	23,116	30,943
Missouri	5,762	6,878	4,370	1,810	345	19	...	1	19,185	24,320
North Carolina	1,204	9,668	8,129	5,898	2,828	485	76	15	28,303	34,658
South Carolina	3,492	6,164	6,311	4,955	3,200	990	382	102	25,596	26,701
Tennessee	7,616	10,582	8,314	4,852	2,202	276	19	3	33,864	36,844
Texas	1,935	2,640	1,585	1,121	374	82	9	1	7,747	21,878
Virginia	11,385	15,550	13,030	9,456	4,880	646	107	9	55,063	52,128
Total	68,820	105,683	80,765	54,595	29,733	6,196	1,479	254	347,525	384,753

APPENDIX III

Population of South Carolina—1670-1950

The figures for whites are mere estimates from 1700 through 1775. The figures for Negroes are more reliable, for they are often taken from the tax books. Estimates of white population were sometimes swelled or pinched to serve a purpose.

The figures from 1790 are from the United States Census.

Data whose dates are in parentheses are from McCrady's *South Carolina under the Royal Government*, p. 807.

	Whites	*Negroes*	*Total*	
1670	About 148	5 are known		See text of this history.
1700	......	......	About 5,500	Edward Randolph's estimate.
1715	6,000	......	......	Pub. Rec., VI, 147, saying 1,400 fighting men. Colonial estimates frequently estimate population at four or five times fighting men.
1715	6,700	......	......	Pub. Rec., VII, 114, saying 1,500 fighting men. See above.
1719	5,000	7,000	12,000	Pub. Rec., VII, 221, stating "house keepers" at 1,000.
(1719)....	6,400	......	......	Gov. R. Johnson, *Col. Hist. Soc. S. Car.*, II, 239.
1720	6,800	......	......	Francis Yonge says upward of 1,700 families. (Carroll, II, 142.)
1720	6,525	11,828	18,353	Tax returns. (D. D. W. estimates 5 to white family.)
(1721)....	9,000	12,000	21,000	Rep. Board of Trade, Col. Records N. Car., II, 418.
(1721)....	14,000	......	......	Drayton's *View of S. Car.*, 193
1722	12,000	......	......	Commons Com., Nov. 23, 1722, multiplying 2,400 fighting men by 5.
(1723)....	14,000	18,000	32,000	*Ibid.*
(1724)....	14,000	32,000	46,000	Gov. Glen, *Carroll's Coll.*, II, 261; Hewatt's *Hist. of S. Car.*, II, 266.
1730	15,000	......	......	Pub. Rec., XIV, 143. (3,000 families.)
(1734)....	7,333*	22,000	29,333	Drayton's *View of S. Car.*, p. 193.
(1735)....	......	40,000	......	Ramsay's *Hist. of S. Car.*, I, 110.
1736	"Near 15,000"	......	......	Commons Journal, July 17, 1736
(1739)....	......	40,000	......	Hewatt's *Hist. of S. Car.*, II, 71.
(1749)....	25,000	39,000	64,000	Gov. Glen, *Carroll's Coll.*, II, 218.
1753	30,000	......	......	Mills, *Statistics*, p. 177.
1757	25,000 or 30,000	......	......	Estimate based on over 6,000 militia.
(1760)....	31,000 or 32,000	52,000	84,000	Bull, Pub. Rec., XXVIII, 348-55.
1761	30,000	57,253	87,253	Bull in PR, XIX, 83-92.
(1763)....	35,000	70,000	105,000	Bull in PR.
(1765)....	40,000	90,000	130,000	Hewatt's *Hist. of S. Car.*, II, 292; Drayton's *View of S. Car.* p. 193.
(1769)....	45,000*	80,000	125,000	Lieut. Gov. Bull to Board of Trade, Dec. 6, 1769.
(1773)....	65,000	110,000	175,000	Report Hist. Com., Charleston Library, 1835, apparently on authority of Wells's Register for 1774.
(1775)....	60,000*	80,000	140,000	Henry Laurens to French Minister.
(1775)....	70,000	104,000	174,000	Dr. Milligan's *Revue*, chapter on "Colonial History of Carolinas," p. 67.
1775	93,000	......	......	Continental Congress estimate for requisitions.
1790	140,178	108,895	249,073	United States Census from 1790.
1800	196,255	149,336	345,591	
1810	214,196	200,919	415,115	
1820	237,440	265,301	502,741	
1830	257,863	323,322	581,185	
1840	259,084	335,314	594,398	
1850	274,563	393,944	668,507	

	Whites	*Negroes*	*Others*	*Total*
1860	291,300	412,320	88	703,708
1870	289,667	415,814	125	705,606
1880	391,105	604,332	140	995,577
1890	462,008	688,934	207	1,151,149
1900	557,807	782,321	188	1,340,316
1910	679,161	835,843	396	1,515,400
1920	818,538	864,719	467	1,683,724
1930	944,040	793,681	1,044	1,738,765
1940	1,084,308	814,164	1,332	1,889,804
1950	....	......	......	2,117,027

*Probably underestimate of whites.

APPENDIX IV

White, Negro and Total Population of South Carolina by Counties, and Total for State—1790-1860

	1790			1820			1840			1860		
	White	Negro	Total	White	Negro	Total	White	Negro	Total	White	Negro	Total
Abbeville	7,505	1,692	9,197	13,488	9,679	23,167	13,880	15,471	29,351	11,516	20,869	32,385
Aiken	......	......	......	......	......	......	......	......	......	......	......	......
Allendale	......	......	......	......	......	......	......	......	......	......	......	......
Anderson	......	......	......	......	......	......	12,747	5,746	18,493	14,286	8,587	22,873
Bamberg	......	......	......	......	......	......	......	......	......	......	......	......
Barnwell	......	......	......	8,162	6,588	14,750	10,533	10,938	21,471	12,702	18,041	30,743
Beaufort	4,364	14,389	18,753	4,679	27,520	32,199	5,650	30,144	35,794	6,714	33,339	40,053
Berkeley	......	......	......	......	......	......	......	......	......	......	......	......
Calhoun	......	......	......	......	......	......	......	......	......	......	......	......
Charleston	11,801	34,846	46,647	19,376	60,836	80,212	20,921	61,740	82,661	29,136	40,912	70,100
Cherokee	......	......	......	......	......	......	......	......	......	......	......	......
Chester	5,881	985	6,866	9,611	4,578	14,189	9,889	7,858	17,747	7,096	11,024	18,122
Chesterfield	? 2,077	? 921	? 2,988	4,412	2,233	6,645	5,537	3,037	8,574	7,354	4,480	11,834
Clarendon	......	......	......	......	......	......	......	......	......	4,378	8,717	13,095
Colleton	3,601	16,737	20,338	4,341	22,063	26,404	5,874	19,674	25,548	9,255	32,661	41,916
Darlington	? 3,041	? 1,348	? 4,389	6,407	4,542	10,949	7,169	7,653	14,822	8,421	11,929	20,361
Dillon	......	......	......	......	......	......	......	......	......	......	......	......
Dorchester	......	......	......	......	......	......	......	......	......	......	......	......
Edgefield	9,605	3,684	13,289	12,864	12,255	25,119	15,020	17,832	32,852	15,653	24,233	39,887
Fairfield	6,138	1,485	7,623	9,378	7,796	17,174	7,587	12,578	20,165	6,373	15,738	22,111
Florence	......	......	......	......	......	......	......	......	......	......	......	......
Georgetown	......	......	......	1,830	15,773	17,603	2,093	16,181	18,274	3,013	18,292	21,305
Greenville	5,888	615	6,503	11,017	3,513	14,530	12,491	5,348	17,839	14,631	7,261	21,892
Greenwood	......	......	......	......	......	......	......	......	......	......	......	......
Hampton	......	......	......	......	......	......	......	......	......	......	......	......
Horry	......	......	......	3,568	1,457	5,025	4,154	1,601	5,755	5,564	2,398	7,962
Jasper	......	......	......	......	......	......	......	......	......	......	......	......
Kershaw	......	......	......	5,628	6,804	12,432	3,988	8,293	12,281	5,026	8,038	13,086
Lancaster	4,864	1,438	6,302	5,848	2,868	8,716	5,565	4,342	9,907	6,054	5,743	11,797
Laurens	8,210	1,127	9,337	12,755	4,927	17,682	12,572	9,012	21,584	10,529	13,329	23,858
Lee	......	......	......	......	......	......	......	......	......	......	......	......
Lexington	......	......	......	5,267	2,816	8,083	7,401	4,710	12,111	9,333	6,246	15,579
McCormick	......	......	......	......	......	......	......	......	......	......	......	......
Marion	? 5,118	? 2,269	? 7,387	6,652	3,549	10,201	8,593	5,339	13,932	11,007	10,183	21,190
Marlboro	? 2,300	? 1,019	? 3,319	3,250	3,175	6,425	4,188	4,220	8,408	5,373	7,061	12,434
Newberry	8,186	1,156	9,342	10,177	5,927	16,104	8,208	10,142	18,350	7,000	13,879	20,879
Oconee	......	......	......	......	......	......	......	......	......	......	......	......
Orangeburg	12,412	6,101	18,513	6,760	8,893	15,653	6,321	12,198	18,519	8,108	16,788	24,896
Pendleton	8,731	837	9,568	22,140	4,882	27,022	......	......	......	......	......	......
Pickens	......	......	......	......	......	......	11,548	2,808	14,356	15,335	4,304	19,639
Richland	2,479	1,451	3,930	4,499	7,822	12,321	5,326	11,071	16,397	6,863	11,444	18,307
Saluda	......	......	......	......	......	......	......	......	......	......	......	......
Spartanburg	7,907	893	8,800	13,655	3,334	16,989	17,924	5,745	23,669	18,537	8,382	26,919
Sumter	4,228	2,712	6,940	8,844	16,525	25,369	8,644	19,248	27,892	6,857	17,002	23,859
Union	6,430	1,263	7,693	9,786	4,340	14,126	10,485	8,451	18,936	8,670	10,965	19,635
Williamsburg	......	......	......	2,795	5,921	8,716	3,327	7,000	10,327	5,187	10,302	15,489
York	5,652	952	6,604	10,251	4,685	14,936	11,449	6,934	18,383	11,329	10,173	21,502
Total*	140,178	108,895	249,073	237,440	265,301	502,741	259,084	335,314	594,398	291,300	412,320	703,620
Others	......	......	......	......	......	......	......	......	......	......	......	‡88
Grand Total			249,073			502,741			594,398			703,708
Free Negroes†	......	1,801	......	......	6,826	......	......	8,276	......	......	9,914	......

*Totals are correct for State, though occasionally figures for a county are lacking. Figures are for areas of dates indicated. New districts or counties diminished the size of some old ones.

†These totals of free Negroes for the State are included in figures for each county. Charleston contained over a third of the free Negroes.

‡Occasionally the total for a county exceeds the sum of whites and Negroes on account of including other races.

Appendix IV (continued)

White, Negro and Total Population of South Carolina by Counties, and Total for State—1880-1930

	1880			1900			1920			1930		
	White	Negro	Total	White	Negro	Total	White	Negro	Total	White	Negro	Total
Abbeville	13,172	27,637	40,815	11,331	22,069	33,400	11,702	15,436	27,139	12,258	11,055	23,323
Aiken	12,936	15,170	28,112	17,388	21,640	39,032	21,582	23,988	45,574	25,872	21,530	47,403
Allendale	......	......	......	......	......	......	3,601	12,497	16,098	3,533	9,761	13,294
Anderson	18,747	14,865	33,612	32,232	23,496	55,728	50,028	26,312	76,349	58,355	22,594	80,949
Bamberg	......	......	......	5,658	11,638	17,296	6,605	14,355	20,962	6,935	12,475	19,410
Barnwell	13,853	26,003	39,857	10,088	25,416	35,504	7,496	15,583	23,081	7,756	13,465	21,221
Beaufort	2,442	27,732	30,176	3,349	32,137	35,495	4,801	17,454	22,269	6,243	15,571	21,815
Berkeley	......	......	......	6,481	23,973	30,454	6,199	16,349	22,558	7,182	15,051	22,236
Calhoun	......	......	......	......	......	......	5,780	12,604	18,384	4,299	12,408	16,707
Charleston	30,922	71,868	102,800	27,647	60,312	88,006	44,127	64,236	108,450	46,198	54,812	101,050
Cherokee	......	......	......	13,952	7,396	21,359	18,975	8,595	27,570	23,729	8,472	32,201
Chester	7,635	16,517	24,153	9,243	19,372	28,616	14,050	19,338	33,389	15,345	16,457	31,803
Chesterfield	9,498	6,847	16,345	12,256	8,145	20,401	19,336	12,633	31,969	21,583	12,751	34,334
Clarendon	6,282	12,908	19,190	8,033	20,151	28,184	9,771	25,106	34,878	8,473	21,563	30,036
Colleton	12,184	24,181	36,386	11,187	22,265	33,452	12,529	17,366	29,897	11,755	14,063	25,821
Darlington	12,929	21,556	34,485	13,083	19,304	32,388	16,921	22,196	39,126	19,815	21,611	41,427
Dillon	......	......	......	......	......	......	12,223	12,936	25,278	13,299	12,067	25,733
Dorchester	......	......	......	6,202	10,089	16,294	8,018	11,439	19,459	7,788	11,166	18,956
Edgefield	16,018	29,826	45,844	7,347	18,131	25,478	7,286	16,642	23,928	7,055	12,271	19,326
Fairfield	6,885	20,880	27,765	7,050	22,375	29,425	6,487	20,672	27,159	7,597	15,690	23,287
Florence	......	......	......	11,819	16,654	28,474	25,480	24,924	50,406	33,452	27,573	61,027
Georgetown	3,466	16,146	19,613	5,336	17,507	22,846	7,254	14,461	21,716	7,733	14,005	21,738
Greenville	22,983	14,511	37,496	33,999	19,488	53,490	65,034	23,461	88,498	89,139	27,855	117,009
Greenwood	......	......	......	9,437	18,906	28,343	16,878	18,912	35,791	20,470	15,608	36,078
Hampton	6,286	12,453	18,741	8,236	15,502	23,738	7,702	11,847	19,550	7,422	9,821	17,243
Horry	10,632	4,942	15,574	17,042	6,320	23,364	24,373	7,698	32,077	29,765	9,610	39,376
Jasper	......	......	......	......	......	......	2,756	7,112	9,868	3,203	6,785	9,988
Kershaw	7,892	13,646	21,538	10,002	14,693	24,696	12,333	17,065	29,398	14,425	17,644	32,070
Lancaster	7,935	8,957	16,893	12,201	12,110	24,311	15,534	13,063	28,628	16,970	11,001	27,980
Laurens	11,756	17,688	29,444	15,205	22,177	37,382	20,454	22,105	42,560	24,383	17,709	42,094
Lee	......	......	......	......	......	......	8,777	18,050	26,827	7,849	16,246	24,096
Lexington	11,096	7,467	18,564	16,961	10,303	27,264	23,947	11,728	35,676	25,496	10,998	36,494
McCormick	......	......	......	......	......	......	5,176	11,268	16,444	3,773	7,696	11,471
Marion	15,881	18,226	34,107	16,992	18,160	35,181	10,563	13,147	23,721	12,301	14,911	27,221
Marlboro	8,026	12,571	20,598	11,226	16,413	27,639	13,517	19,661	33,180	13,379	18,008	31,634
Newberry	8,236	18,261	26,497	10,351	19,831	30,182	14,910	20,641	35,552	18,527	16,154	34,681
Oconee	11,955	4,301	16,256	17,530	6,104	23,634	23,719	6,398	30,117	27,367	5,999	33,368
Orangeburg	12,942	28,453	41,395	18,220	41,442	59,663	22,163	42,718	64,907	23,087	40,640	63,864
Pendleton	......	......	......	......	......	......	......	......	......	......	......	......
Pickens	10,673	3,716	14,389	14,574	4,801	19,375	23,398	4,931	28,329	28,812	4,897	33,709
Richland	9,185	19,388	28,573	17,513	28,070	45,589	41,619	36,499	78,122	49,520	38,127	87,667
Saluda	......	......	......	8,819	10,147	18,966	10,453	11,635	22,088	9,325	8,823	18,148
Spartanburg	26,372	14,035	40,409	44,391	21,167	65,560	66,871	27,392	94,265	86,207	30,111	116,323
Sumter	9,979	27,058	37,037	12,881	38,353	51,237	12,521	30,508	43,040	14,927	30,974	45,902
Union	10,516	13,551	24,080	10,943	14,558	25,501	16,287	14,076	30,372	18,540	12,380	30,920
Williamsburg	7,758	16,352	24,110	11,818	19,867	31,685	13,084	25,452	38,539	11,572	23,341	34,914
York	14,033	16,620	30,713	19,784	21,839	41,684	26,218	24,230	50,536	31,326	21,932	53,418
Total*	391,105	604,332	995,437	557,807	782,321	1,340,128	818,538	864,719	1,683,257	944,040	793,681	1,737,721
Others	......	......	140	......	......	188	......	......	467	......	......	1,044
Grand Total			995,577			1,340,316			1,683,724			1,738,765

*Totals are correct for State, though occasionally figures for a county are lacking. Figures are for areas of dates indicated. New districts or counties diminished the size of some old ones.

(Continued)

Appendix IV (continued)

White, Negro, and Total Population of South Carolina by Counties, and Total for State—1940

	White	Negro	Other races	Total
Abbeville	13,190	9,741	..	22,931
Aiken	28,995	20,921	..	49,916
Allendale	3,630	9,409	1	13,040
Anderson	65,323	23,379	10	88,712
Bamberg	7,339	11,304	..	18,643
Barnwell	7,519	12,618	1	20,138
Beaufort	7,255	14,781	1	22,037
Berkeley	9,548	17,555	25	27,128
Calhoun	4,351	11,867	11	16,229
Charleston	61,487	59,573	45	121,105
Cherokee	25,495	7,795	..	33,290
Chester	16,948	15,631	..	32,579
Chesterfield	22,262	13,701	..	35,963
Clarendon	8,923	22,576	1	31,500
Colleton	12,249	14,019	..	26,268
Darlington	22,627	22,571	..	45,198
Dillon	14,910	14,111	604	29,625
Dorchester	8,484	11,439	5	19,928
Edgefield	6,594	11,300	..	17,894
Fairfield	9,214	14,970	3	24,187
Florence	38,627	31,953	2	70,582
Georgetown	10,976	15,375	1	26,352
Greenville	106,142	30,432	6	136,580
Greenwood	25,230	14,852	1	40,083
Hampton	7,370	10,095	..	17,465
Horry	37,879	14,037	35	51,951
Jasper	3,955	7,056	..	11,011
Kershaw	15,311	17,584	18	32,913
Lancaster	22,147	11,395	..	33,542
Laurens	27,843	16,342	..	44,185
Lee	8,590	16,315	3	24,908
Lexington	27,067	8,921	6	35,994
McCormick	3,330	7,036	1	10,367
Marion	13,287	16,810	10	30,107
Marlboro	15,052	17,924	305	33,281
Newberry	19,335	14,242	..	33,577
Oconee	30,743	5,764	5	36 512
Orangeburg	23,791	39,908	8	63,707
Pickens	32,220	4,891	..	37,111
Richland	62,472	42,359	12	104,843
Saluda	9,548	7,644	..	17,192
Spartanburg	97,260	30,473	..	127,733
Sumter	18,692	33,771	..	52,463
Union	20,112	11,248	..	31,360
Williamsburg	13,739	27,269	3	41,011
York	37,247	21,207	209	58,663
Total	1,084,308	814,164	1,332	1,899,804

APPENDIX V

The following list of the existing South Carolina counties in 1951, with the dates of their creation, is from D. D. Wallace's *Civil Government of South Carolina and the United States,* with a few changes. The facts are taken from the statutes. The varying functions of these areas, either under the name of county or that of district, are traced in the body of this history:

The counties now number forty-six. They were formed at the following dates:

Abbeville, Barnwell, Beaufort, Charleston, Chester, Chesterfield, Clarendon, Darlington, Edgefield, Fairfield, Lancaster, Laurens, Lexington, Marlboro, Newberry, Orangeburg, Richland, Spartanburg, Sumter, Union and York, in 1785.

Saxe-Gotha continued the name of the election district until discarded for Lexington in 1852.

Lexington formed a part of Orangeburg circuit court district from 1800 through 1804, when Lexington became such a district.

Liberty County was created in 1785; but in 1798 the name Marion was given to the judicial district, though Liberty continued the name of the election district until 1859.

Greenville, 1786; Kershaw, 1791; Colleton and Georgetown, 1798. (Georgetown had been used since 1769 to indicate as a judicial district the territory included in the present Georgetown, Horry, Williamsburg, and Marion, and the portion of Florence which would lie east of the Marion-Marlboro line extended southwestward. See map of South Carolina in 1785. The name Georgetown was in 1798 given to a judicial district including the present Georgetown, Horry, and Williamsburg. Subsequently reduced to its present limits, it became an election district on the abolition of the parishes as election districts in 1865.)

The name Horry was substituted in 1801 for Kingston as designating the territory which had been cut off as a county in 1785, and had been made an election district in 1790.

Williamsburg, a county and court district 1785-1798, and an election district since 1790, was re-erected into a judicial district in 1804.

Anderson and Pickens were created in 1826, out of old Pendleton, which had been created in 1789; but not until 1854 were Anderson and Pickens made election districts. The constitutional convention in 1868 cut off Oconee from Pickens.

Aiken was created in 1871; Hampton, 1878; Berkeley, 1882 (thus reviving an old county name borne fiom 1785 to 1798 by a territory differing slightly in boundary from the present Dorchester); Florence in 1888.

Saluda was created by the constitutional convention of 1895 after a fierce struggle between the brothers, George and Benjamin Tillman, as to whether it should be called Saluda or Butler, George Tillman favoring the latter name.

There then followed an era of new county making. Bamberg, Cherokee, Dorchester, and Greenwood were created in 1897, and Lee County, after vexatious delays, in 1902, including along with other territory part of old Salem County of 1792. Calhoun County was created from Orangeburg and a small corner of Lexington in 1908, with almost the same boundaries as the old Lewisburg of 1785. Dillon was created from Marion in 1910. Jasper County was created in 1912, McCormick County in 1916, and Allendale in 1919.

The boundaries of Sumter County have a very complicated and interesting history. Claremont, as set off as a county and judicial district in 1785, comprised all the territory (except a small strip in the southeastern corner, next to Lynch's River) bounded by Clarendon County, Lynch's and Wateree rivers, and a line drawn between these streams midway of the later Kershaw County. In 1800 Clarendon ceased to be a district for the holding of courts, and Sumter judicial district was made to include all that territory between the rivers down to Williamsburg. The name Sumter was not employed until

1800, and then only for the judicial district. Clarendon elected representatives to the legislature as an election district, and the remainder of Sumter judicial district elected representatives as the election district of Claremont—a name which originated in 1785. Clarendon was made a judicial district in 1855; but not until 1859 was the name Claremont superseded by that of Sumter as the name of the election district now known as Sumter. At the same time the name Liberty was displaced by the name Marion. Before 1859 the senator from Sumter was officially the senator from Claremont, and the senator from Marion, the senator from Liberty.

SELECTED BIBLIOGRAPHY

(Full documentation of this book, including all primary sources, may be found in the author's three-volume *History of South Carolina.* The following bibliography, which the author's death prevented his checking, is a selected list of books referred to in the text, placed here for convenient reference. Other references will be found in the footnotes.)

Adair, James. *History of the American Indians.* London, 1775.

Aikman, Mrs. Louisa Susannah (Wells). *The Journal of a Voyage from Charlestown, South Carolina, to London, . . .* (The John Divine Jones Fund Series of Histories and Memoirs, Vol. II.) New York, 1906.

Allen, Walter. *Governor Chamberlain's Administration in South Carolina.* New York, 1888.

Anderson, Charles Carter. *Fighting by Southern Federals. . . .* New York, 1912.

Bailey, James Davis. *Some Heroes of the American Revolution.* Spartanburg, S. C., 1924.

Ball, William Watts. *The State That Forgot. . . .* Indianapolis, 1932.

Bancroft, Frederic. *The Life of William H. Seward.* 2 vols. New York, 1900.

Barry, Richard. *Mr. Rutledge of South Carolina.* New York, 1942.

Benton, T. H. *Thirty Years' View.* 2 vols. New York, 1854, 1856.

Bolton, Herbert E. (ed.). *Arredondo's Historical Proof of Spain's Title to Georgia.* Berkeley, Calif., 1925.

——— and Ross, Mary. *The Debatable Land: A Sketch of the Anglo-Spanish Contest for the Georgia Country.* Berkeley, Calif., 1925.

Boucher, Chauncey Samuel. "The Ante-Bellum Attitude of South Carolina towards Manufacturing and Agriculture," *Washington University Studies,* Vol. III, Part 2 (1916), (Humanistic Series, No. 2).

———. *"In Re* That Aggressive Slaveocracy," *Mississippi Valley Historical Review,* Vol. VIII, Nos. 1 and 2 (June-September, 1921).

———. "The Secession and Co-operation Movements in South Carolina, 1848 to 1852," *Washington University Studies,* Vol. V, Part 2 (Humanistic Series, No. 2).

———. "Sectionalism, Representation, and the Electoral Question in Ante-Bellum South Carolina," *Washington University Studies,* Vol. IV, Part 2 (1916), (Humanistic Series, No. 2).

———. "South Carolina and the South on the Eve of Secession, 1852 to 1860," *Washington University Studies,* Vol. VI (1919), (Humanistic Series).

Bryce, Mrs. Campbell. *The Personal Experiences of Mrs. Campbell Bryce during the Burning of Columbia. . . .* Philadelphia, 1899.

Calhoun, John C. *The Works of John C. Calhoun,* ed. Richard K. Crallé. 6 vols. New York, 1851-56.

Capers, Ellison. South Carolina. (*Confederate Military History,* ed. General Clement A. Evans, Vol. V.) Atlanta, 1899.

Capers, Henry D. *The Life and Times of C. G. Memminger.* Richmond, 1893.

Cardozo, Jacob Newton. *Reminiscences of Charleston.* Charleston, 1866.

Carroll, Bartholomew Rivers. (ed. and comp.). *Historical Collections of South Carolina.* 2 vols. New York, 1836.

Carson, James Petigru. *Life, Letters, and Speeches of James Louis Petigru,* . . . . Washington, 1920.

Chicken, George. ["Journal of the March of the Carolinians into the Cherokee Mountains, 1715-1716"], *Year Book of the City of Charleston,* ed. Langdon Cheves. Charleston, 1894.

Conyngham, Captain David P. *Sherman's March Through the South* . . . . New York, 1865.

The Cotton Plant. (Publications of the United States Department of Agriculture.) Washington, 1896.

Crane, Verner W. *The Southern Frontier.* Durham, 1928.

Craven, Avery. *The Coming of the Civil War.* New York, 1942.

Crawford, Samuel W. *The Genesis of the Civil War.* . . . New York, 1887.

Davis, Jefferson. *The Rise and Fall of the Confederate Government.* 2 vols. New York, 1881.

Derrick, Samuel M. *Centennial History of South Carolina Railroad.* Columbia, 1930.

DeSaussure, Mrs. Nancy B. *Old Plantation Days.* . . . New York, 1909.

Dickert, D. Augustus. *History of Kershaw's Brigade.* Newberry, S. C., 1899.

Doubleday, Abner. *Reminiscences of Forts Sumter and Moultrie in 1860-'61.* 1876.

Drayton, John. *Memoirs of the American Revolution,* . . . . 2 vols. Charleston, 1821.

———. *A View of South Carolina, as Respects Her Natural and Civil Concerns.* Charleston, 1802.

Dunlap, William. *History of the Rise and Progress of the Arts of Design in the United States.* New York, 1834.

Dunning, William A. *Reconstruction, Political and Economic, 1865-1877.* (*The American Nation: A History,* ed. A. B. Hart, Vol. XXII.) New York, 1907.

Easterby, James Harold. "The Granger Movement in South Carolina," *Proceedings of the South Carolina Historical Association.* 1931.

Ellet, Elizabeth Fries. *Women of the American Revolution.* 3 vols. New York, 1848-50.

Elzas, Barnett A. *The Jews of South Carolina from the Earliest Times to the Present Day.* Philadelphia, 1905.

Fiske, John. *The American Revolution.* 2 vols. New York, 1891.

Flagg, Jared B. *Life and Letters of Washington Allston.* New York, 1892.

Fleming, Walter L. *A Documentary History of Reconstruction.* 2 vols. Cleveland, 1906-1907.

Fraser, Charles. *Reminiscences of Charleston.* Charleston, 1854.

Garden, Alexander. *Anecdotes of the American Revolution.* Charleston, 1828.

Gibbes, Robert Wilson. *Documentary History of the American Revolution,* . . . . 3 vols. Columbia, 1853.

Gillmore, Quincy A. *Engineer and Artillery Operations Against the Defenses of Charleston Harbor in 1863* . . . . New York, 1865.

Grayson, William J. *James Louis Petigru. A Biographical Sketch.* 1866.

Gregg, Alexander. *History of the Old Cheraws.* New York, 1867.

Gregorie, Anne King. *Thomas Sumter.* Columbia, 1931.

Grimké, John F. "Journal of the Campaign to the Southward, May 9-July 14, 1778," *South Carolina Historical and Genealogical Magazine,* XII (1911).

Grimké, Thomas S. *An Oration . . . Delivered . . . Before the South Carolina Bar Association* . . . . Charleston, 1827.

Hamer, P. M. "John Stuart's Indian Policy," *Mississippi Valley Historical Review,* XVII (December, 1930).

———. *The Secession Movement in South Carolina, 1847-1852.* Allentown, Pa., 1912.

Hammond, M. B. *The Cotton Industry.* (American Economic Association Publications, New Series, No. 1.) Ithaca, 1897.

Hewat, Alexander. *An Historical Account of the Rise and Progress of the Colonies of South Carolina and Georgia.* 2 vols. London, 1779.

Heyward, Dubose. *Mamba's Daughters.* Garden City, 1929.

Heyward, James Barnwell. *The Colonial History of the Heyward Family of South Carolina.* . . . Nashville, 1907.

Hirsch, Arthur H. *Huguenots of South Carolina.* Durham, 1928.

Hodge, F. W. (ed.). *Handbook of American Indians North of Mexico.* 2 vols. Bulletin 30, Bureau of American Ethnology. Washington, 1907-10.

Holmes, Francis C. *Phosphate Rocks of South Carolina and the Great Carolina Marl Bed.* Charleston, 1870.

Howe, George. *History of the Presbyterian Church in South Carolina* 2 vols. Columbia, 1870-83.

Hudson, Joshua H. *Sketches and Reminiscences.* Columbia, 1903.

Hughson, Shirley Carter. *The Carolina Pirates and Colonial Commerce, 1670-1740.* (Johns Hopkins University Studies in Historical and Political Science, Vol. V-VII, Ser. 12) Baltimore, 1894.

Hunt, Gaillard. *John C. Calhoun.* Philadelphia, 1908.

Hunter, George. *Map of the Cherokee Country and the Path Thereto in 1730,* ed. Alexander S. Salley, Jr. (Bulletins of the Historical Commission of South Carolina, No. 4.) Columbia, 1917.

Izard, Ralph. *Correspondence of Mr. Ralph Izard of South Carolina,* ed. Anne Izard Deas. New York, 1844.

James, Marquis. *Andrew Jackson, the Border Captain.* Indianapolis, 1933.

James, W. D. *Life of Francis Marion.* Charleston, 1821.

Jervey, T. D. "Charleston During the Civil War," *American Historical Association Annual Report for 1913.*

Johnson, Charles. *A General History of the Pyrates. . . .* London, 1724.

Johnson, John. *The Defense of Charleston Harbor. . . .* Charleston, 1890.

Johnson, Joseph. *Traditions and Reminiscences, Chiefly of the American Revolution in the South.* Charleston, 1851.

Johnson, William. *Sketches of the Life and Correspondence of Nathanael Greene.* 2 vols. Charleston, 1822.

Kibler, Lillian. *Life of Benjamin F. Perry.* Durham, 1946.

Kohn, August. *The Cotton Mills of South Carolina.* Charleston, 1907.

———. *The Water Powers of South Carolina.* Columbia, 1910.

Landers, Colonel H. L. *King's Mountain and Cowpens.* Army War College, 1928.

Landrum, J. B. O. *Colonial and Revolutionary History of Upper South Carolina.* Greenville, 1897.

———. *Spartanburg County, South Carolina.* Atlanta, 1900.

Lawson, John. *A New Voyage to Carolina.* London, 1709.

Lee, Henry. *Memoirs of the War in the Southern Department of the United States.* 2 vols. Philadelphia, 1812.

Legaré, Hugh Swinton. *Writings of Hugh Swinton Legaré,* ed. Mary S. L. Bullen. 2 vols. Charleston, 1845-46.

Lowery, Woodbury. *Spanish Settlements within the Present Limits of the United States, 1513-1561.* New York, 1901.

———. *Spanish Settlements within the Present Limits of the United States: Florida, 1562-1574.* New York, 1905.

McCrady, Edward. *South Carolina under the Proprietary Government* (Vol. I); *South Carolina under Royal Government* (Vol. II); *South Carolina in the Revolution, 1775-80* (Vol. III); *South Carolina in the Revolution, 1780-83* (Vol. IV). New York, 1897-1902.

McGee, W. J. *The Siouan Indians.* 15th Annual Report, Bureau of American Ethnology. Washington, 1897.

Malone, Dumas. *The Public Life of Thomas Cooper, 1783-1839.* New Haven, 1926.

Martineau, Harriet. *Society in America.* 3 vols. London, 1837.

Meigs, William M. *The Life of John Caldwell Calhoun.* 2 vols. New York, 1917.

Meriwether, R. L. *The Expansion of South Carolina.* Kingsport, Tenn., 1940.

Mills, Robert. *Statistics of South Carolina.* Charleston, 1826.

Mitchell, Broadus. *William Gregg, Factory Master of the Old South.* Chapel Hill, 1928.

Mooney, James. *Myths of the Cherokee.* 19th Annual Report, Bureau of American Ethnology. Washington, 1900.

———. *Siouan Tribes of the East.* Bulletin 22, Bureau of American Ethnology. Washington, 1894.

Moore, H. J. *Scott's Campaign in Mexico.* Charleston, 1849.

Morse, Jedediah. *The American Universal Geography.* Boston, 1796

Moultrie, William. *Memoirs of the American Revolution.* 2 vols. New York, 1802.

Nichols, G. W. *The Story of a Great March.* New York, 1865.

Oberholtzer, Ellis P. *A History of the United States since the Civil War.* 5 vols. New York, 1917-37.

O'Connell, Jeremiah Joseph. *Catholicity in the Carolinas and Georgia.* New York, 1879.

Oldmixon, John. *The British Empire in America.* 2 vols. London, 1708. Chapters relating to Carolina in Salley, ed., *Narratives of Early Carolina.*

Olmsted, Frederick Law. *A Journey in the Seaboard Slave States.* New York, 1856.

O'Neall, John Belton. *Biographical Sketches of the Bench and Bar of South Carolina.* 2 vols. Charleston, 1859.

———. *The Negro Law of South Carolina.* Columbia, 1848.

Parkman, Francis. *A Half-Century of Conflict.* 2 vols. Boston, 1897.

———. *Pioneers of France in the New World.* Boston, 1865.

Perry, Benjamin Franklin. *Reminiscences of Public Men.* Philadelphia, 1883.

Phillips, Ulrich B. *American Negro Slavery.* New York, 1918.

———. *Life and Labor in the Old South.* Boston, 1929.

———. *Transportation in the Eastern Cotton Belt to 1860.* New York, 1908.

Pickens, Andrew L. *Skyagunsta, the Border Wizard Owl, Major-General Andrew Pickens. . . .* Greenville, 1934.

Ramsay, David. *History of the Revolution in South Carolina.* 2 vols. Trenton, N. J., 1785.

Ramsey, James G. McG. *The Annals of Tennessee to the End of the Eighteenth Century.* Charleston, 1853.

Ravenel, Harriott Harry Rutledge. *Eliza Pinckney.* New York, 1896.

———. *The Life and Times of William Lowndes of South Carolina, 1782-1822.* Boston, 1901.

Reynolds, John S. *Reconstruction in South Carolina.* Columbia, 1905.

Rivers, William James. *A Chapter in the Early History of South Carolina.* Charleston, 1874.

———. "Printing in South Carolina," *Russell's Magazine* (September, 1858).

Roman, Alfred. *Military Operations of General Beauregard.* 2 vols. New York, 1884.

Royce, Charles C. *The Cherokee Nation of Indians. . . .* 5th Annual Report, Bureau of American Ethnology. Washington, 1887.

———. *Indian Land Cessions in the United States.* 18th Annual Report, Bureau of American Ethnology. Washington, 1899.

Sabine, Lorenzo. *Biographical Sketches of Loyalists of the American Revolution.* 2 vols. Boston, 1864.

Salley, Alexander S., Jr., (ed.). *Colonel William Hill's Memoirs of the Revolution.* Columbia, 1921.

———. *The Introduction of Rice Culture into South Carolina.* (Bulletins of the Historical Commission of South Carolina, No. 6.) Columbia, 1919.

———. (ed.). *Narratives of Early Carolina.* New York, 1911.

———. *The Origin of Carolina.* (Bulletins of the Historical Commission of South Carolina, No. 8) Columbia, 1926.

———. *President Washington's Tour Through South Carolina in 1791.* (Bulletins of the Historical Commission of South Carolina, No. 12.) Columbia, 1932.

———. (ed.). *Warrants for Lands in South Carolina, 1672-1711.* Columbia, 1910-1915.

Schaper, W. A. *Sectionalism and Representation in South Carolina.* American Historical Association Report for 1900.

Scharf, John Thomas. *History of the Confederate States Navy.* New York, 1887.

Schwab, John Christopher. *The Confederate States of America, 1861-1865: A Financial and Industrial History of the South during the Civil War.* (Yale Bicentennial Publications.) New York, 1901.

Sellers, Leila. *Charleston Business on the Eve of the American Revolution.* Chapel Hill, 1934.

Simkins, Francis Butler, and Woody, Robert Hilliard. *South Carolina during Reconstruction.* Chapel Hill, 1932.

Simkins, Francis Butler. *The Tillman Movement in South Carolina.* Durham, 1926.

———. *Pitchfork Ben Tillman.* Baton Rouge, La., 1944.

Simms, William Gilmore. *Geography of South Carolina.* Charleston, 1843.

———. *History of South Carolina.* Charleston, 1840.

Singer, C. G. *South Carolina in the Confederation.* Philadelphia, 1941.

Sloan, Earle. *A Catalogue of Mineral Localities of South Carolina.* (South Carolina Geological Survey, Ser. 4, No. 2.) Columbia, 1908.

Smith, Alice R. Huger, and Smith, D. E. Huger. *Charles Fraser.* New York, 1924.

Smith, Justin H. *The War with Mexico.* 2 vols. New York, 1919.

Smith, William R. *South Carolina as a Royal Province, 1719-1776.* New York, 1903.

Sonneck, Oscar George Theodore. *Early Concert-Life in America.* Leipzig, 1907.

———. *Early Opera in America.* Boston, 1915.

Stevens, Benjamin F. (comp. and ed.). *The Campaign in Virginia, 1781. An Exact Reprint of Six Rare Pamphlets on the Clinton-Cornwallis Controversy. . . .* 2 vols. London, 1888.

Stephenson, N. W. *Texas and the Mexican War.* (*The Chronicles of America,* Vol. XXIV.) New Haven, 1921.

Swanton, John R. *Early History of the Creek Indians and Their Neighbors.* Bulletin 73, Bureau of American Ethnology. Washington, 1922.

Tarleton, Sir Banastre. *History of the Campaigns of 1780 and 1781 in the Southern Province of North America.* Dublin, 1787.

Thomas, E. S. *Reminiscenses of the Last Sixty-five Years, Commencing with the Battle of Lexington.* 2 vols. Hartford, 1840.

Thomas, John Peyre. *History of the South Carolina Military Academy.* Charleston, 1893.

Thompson, Henry T. *Ousting the Carpetbagger from South Carolina.* Columbia, 1926.

Thornwell, Dr. James H. *The State of the Country.* Columbia, 1861.

Townsend, Leah. *South Carolina Baptists, 1670-1805.* Florence, S. C., 1935.

Trent, William P. *William Gilmore Simms.* (American Men of Letters Series.) Boston, 1892.

Tuomey, M. *Report on the Geology of South Carolina.* Columbia, 1848.

Turner, Frederick J. *Rise of the New West, 1819-1829.* (*The American Nation: A History,* ed. A. B. Hart, Vol. XIV.) New York, 1906.

Uhlendorf, B. A. (trans., ed.) *Siege of Charleston.* Ann Arbor, 1938.

Underwood, John L. *The Women of the Confederacy. . . .* New York, 1906.

Walker, Cornelius Irvine. *History of the Agricultural Society of South Carolina. . . .* [Charleston, 1919].

———. *The Life of Lieutenant-General Richard Heron Anderson of the Confederate States Army.* Charleston, 1917.

Wallace, David D. *The Life of Henry Laurens.* New York, 1915.

Wauchope, George Armstrong. *The Writers of South Carolina.* Columbia, 1910.

Weeks, Stephen B. *Southern Quakers and Slavery.* (Johns Hopkins Univ. Studies), Baltimore, 1896.

Wharton, Francis. (ed.). *Revolutionary Diplomatic Correspondence of the United States.* 6 vols. Washington, 1889.

White, Horace. *Money and Banking. . . .* Boston, 1895.

White, Laura A. *Robert Barnwell Rhett, Father of Secession.* New York, 1931.

Williams, George Croft. *Social Problems of South Carolina.* Columbia, 1928.

Willis, Eola. *Charleston Stage in XVIII Century.* Columbia, 1924.

Winsor, Justin. *Narrative and Critical History of America.* 8 vols. Boston, 1884-89.

INDEX